Factory Lives

Nineteenth-Century British Autobiographies
series editors: Janice Carlisle and Linda H. Peterson
textual editor: Elizabeth Reed

Factory Lives:
Four Nineteenth-Century
Working-Class Autobiographies

Edited by James R. Simmons, Jr.

Introduction by Janice Carlisle

Nineteenth-Century British Autobiographies

Library and Archives Canada Cataloguing in Publication

Factory lives : four nineteenth-century working-class autobiographies / edited by James R. Simmons ; introduction by Janice Carlisle.

(Nineteenth-century British autobiographies)
Includes bibliographical references.
ISBN 978-1-55111-272-5

1. Working class--Great Britain--Biography--Textbooks. 2. Working class writings, English--Textbooks. 3. Great Britain--Social conditions--19th century--Textbooks.
I. Simmons, James R. II. Series.

HD8393.A1F32 2007   305.5'62092241   C2007-900015-0

Broadview Editions

The Broadview Editions series represents the ever-changing canon of literature in English by bringing together texts long regarded as classics with valuable lesser-known works.

Advisory editor for this volume: Michel Pharand

Broadview Press is an independent, international publishing house, incorporated in 1985. Broadview believes in shared ownership, both with its employees and with the general public; since the year 2000 Broadview shares have traded publicly on the Toronto Venture Exchange under the symbol BDP.

We welcome comments and suggestions regarding any aspect of our publications—please feel free to contact us at the addresses below or at broadview@broadviewpress.com.

North America
Post Office Box 1243, Peterborough, Ontario, Canada K9J 7H5
3576 California Road, Post Office Box 1015, Orchard Park, NY, USA 14127
Tel: (705) 743-8990; Fax: (705) 743-8353;
email: customerservice@broadviewpress.com

UK, Ireland, and continental Europe
NBN International, Estover Road, Plymouth PL6 7PY UK
Tel: 44 (0) 1752 202300   Fax: 44 (0) 1752 202330
email: enquiries@nbninternational.com

Australia and New Zealand
UNIREPS, University of New South Wales
Sydney, NSW, 2052 Australia
Tel: 61 2 9664 0999; Fax: 61 2 9664 5420
email: info.press@unsw.edu.au

www.broadviewpress.com

Typesetting and assembly: True to Type Inc., Mississauga, Canada.

PRINTED IN CANADA

MIX
Paper from responsible sources
FSC
www.fsc.org
FSC® C103567

Contents

Acknowledgements

This volume has an interesting history. I first became intrigued by working-class autobiography when I read *A Memoir of Robert Blincoe* in a Victorian nonfiction prose class taught by Dr. William B. Thesing at the University of South Carolina. The *Memoir* piqued my interest, and as I started to research and read other working-class autobiographies, I discovered two things. First, I learned that hundreds of working-class autobiographies had been written by Victorians from all walks of life, including chimney sweeps, beggars, ratcatchers, butlers, and workers of almost every other occupation imaginable. Secondly, I learned that very little scholarship had been produced about these texts and that the scholarship that did exist had been written primarily by historians. Taking these factors into consideration, along with my genuine interest in these texts and the light that they shed on works of nineteenth-century literature *about* chimney sweeps, beggars, ratcatchers, and butlers, I decided to write my dissertation using the Victorian working-class autobiography as its focus. The first and longest chapter examined working-class autobiographies by Victorian factory workers and included an examination of the four texts in this volume.

As I was working on that project, I was fortunate enough to be introduced to Linda Peterson at a conference. Linda was (and is) considered one of the preeminent experts in Victorian autobiography, and eventually I asked Linda to serve as an outside reader when I finished my research, and she graciously agreed to do so. I little knew how significant having Linda read my dissertation would be.

A year after I received my doctorate, as I settled into my role as an assistant professor, I decided that for one of my first major projects I would submit a proposal to Broadview for a new edition of Harriet Martineau's *Autobiography*. What I did not know was that Linda and Janice Carlisle had agreed to edit a series of Victorian autobiographies for Broadview, and before long I was contacted by Linda with an interesting proposal: instead of working on Martineau's *Autobiography*, she asked, would I be interested in doing an edition of a working-class autobiography instead? I proposed seven texts that I would be most interested in doing, including *A Memoir of Robert Blincoe, A Narrative of the Experience and Sufferings of William Dodd*, and the

"Autobiography of Ellen Johnston, 'The Factory Girl.'" Though the original idea was to do just one autobiography, Janice suggested that I do a volume containing not only the three titles listed above, but also James Myles's *Chapters in the Life of a Dundee Factory Boy*. The end result was this edition, to which Janice contributed the title *Factory Lives*.

Even though I had worked with these four texts previously, this project turned out to be much more involved than any of us had anticipated. What initially started out as a relatively simple project became more and more complex as we decided to reproduce early editions of each work. The magnitude of textual variants necessitated involving a fourth person, Elizabeth Reed, without whom this book could not have been completed. She is certainly the unsung heroine of this volume.

The end result is a text that has changed considerably over its five-year gestation period. As with any other complex project written over an extended period of time, there were a number of people who contributed in ways that were extremely important. I am grateful for the help of the following people for the assistance they gave, whether in research, preparation, inspiration, or moral support: Lynell Buckley, Laura Ogden, and Peggy Schenk at the Louisiana Tech University Library; Ruth Lamb and Warren Ober at the University of Waterloo Library; Margaret Lowden at the Dundee Library; Paula Morehouse at the Manchester Central Library; Jackie Fay at the Kendal Library; Hilary Attfield, Marjie Bloy, Florence Boos, Gaye Dewitt, Paula Feldman, Jessica Flowers, Ina Rae Hark, Ed Jacobs, Jason Pierce, Maaja Stewart, and Bill Thesing. Again, thanks to Linda Peterson, Janice Carlisle and Elizabeth Reed. Finally, thanks to my late mother, who did not live to see this volume in print, and to my father, sister, and, above all, Sue, Courtenay, and Cord.

—James R. Simmons, Jr.

* * *

Work on this volume has been more than usually collaborative, with all three editors—James R. Simmons, Jr., Elizabeth Reed, and Janice Carlisle—participating in every stage of its production from choosing the texts included to introducing and annotating them. First, we would like to thank Rick Simmons for his patience as we completed our parts of this project. Professor William M. Murphy generously reviewed our list of unidentified references. Ellen Kline of Colophon Books located valuable material through out-of-print searches. Deirdre Sweeney and Eileen Moran of the Local Studies department of the Central Library in Dundee were particularly helpful in providing the information that identifies Myles's *Chapters in the Life of a Dundee Factory Boy* as a work of fiction. We are deeply indebted to Elizabeth Sudduth of the G. Ross Roy Collection of Scottish Literature, Rare Books and Special Collections, Thomas Cooper Library, at the University of South Carolina, for her invaluable assistance in establishing the copy-text of the *Dundee Factory Boy*. Also responsive to inquiries was Pam York of Derbyshire Local Studies. The staff members of numerous libraries—at Columbia, Cornell, Harvard, Tulane, and Yale, as well as the New York Public Library—aided us in locating information for the Note on the Text, the annotations, and the headnotes to the appendices. Verifying the place names in Brown's *A Memoir of Robert Blincoe*, which demonstrate the accuracy of Blincoe's recall some twenty years after the events in his story, would not have been possible without the resources of the Map Collection at Yale's Sterling Memorial Library and the Rare Books and Manuscripts Collection at the Yale Center for British Art. Special thanks go to Rebecca Boggs for her painstaking proofreading of the appendices against the original texts and to Linda Peterson for providing her perspectives on this project. Janice Carlisle would like particularly to acknowledge two debts: first, to Andy Nicholson, Nottingham local historian, for kindly answering many e-mail inquiries and locating a photograph of the factory in which Robert Blincoe first worked; secondly, to her daughter Catherine Roach, for her assistance during a memorable research trip to Dundee and for obtaining a copy of one of the title pages reproduced here. Finally, we are grateful to Julia Gaunce and Judith Earnshaw at Broadview Press for their understanding throughout a process that turned out to be more complex and lengthy than either of us could have imagined at the outset.

—Janice Carlisle and Elizabeth Reed

Introduction

Janice Carlisle

The confrontation in the House of Commons on the evening of March 15, 1844 could scarcely have been more divisive. On one side was Anthony Ashley-Cooper—son and heir of the Earl of Shaftesbury, member of Parliament representing Dorsetshire as his father had before him, and ardent proponent of legislative protection for the women and children who worked in Britain's textile factories. Opposing him was John Bright—son and partner of a Rochdale cotton-mill owner, recently elected member of Parliament for the city of Durham, and fierce critic of legislative restraints on the freedom of trade and commerce. Since 1832 Lord Ashley had led the parliamentary campaign to limit the hours of young textile workers, and now he was proposing that the House of Commons amend a government bill so that it would mandate a ten-hour day for adolescent and female laborers (Thomas 202). Before the debate Ashley had confided to his diary that he anticipated "a most violent attack" from Bright.[1] Ashley's prediction proved accurate. The verbal contest that ensued was sharp and, at times, almost nasty. According to the *Times*, which printed a full transcript of the debate, Bright's accusations raised a "storm" of "vociferous exclamations and discordant noises" from the members who heard them that night ("Committee" 5). At issue between the two speakers were concerns about the welfare of factory workers and the fate of Britain's industrial supremacy, but the exchange became decid-

---

1   Hodder 2: 22. This encounter unfairly casts Bright as the enemy of factory workers since it obscures his sympathies for their causes, particularly his often lonely championship of the franchise reform that would extend the vote to working-class men. On the process that granted Lord Ashley (later Shaftesbury) virtual sanctification for his part in the history of child-welfare reform, see Cunningham, ch. 2. The allegiances that separated the two men were many and various: Ashley, the Tory Evangelical, as opposed to Bright, the Liberal Quaker, represented, respectively, agriculture versus industry, south versus north, country versus city, aristocracy versus the middle classes. On the self-consciousness of the two figures as representative men, see Hodder 1: 48-49; Briggs 204. See Gallagher on Ashley's speech (123-25).

edly more personal when Bright began to question the credibility of a particular working-man's autobiography, *A Narrative of the Experience and Sufferings of William Dodd, a Factory Cripple. Written by Himself* (1841).

The confrontation between Bright and Ashley was an extraordinary and probably unprecedented event in the history of parliamentary debate: two members of Parliament—both, presumably, gentlemen—were arguing over the reliability of a life story written about and by a former factory worker. Bright attacked Ashley for the gullibility that he displayed by believing Dodd's account, which repeatedly attributes his physical deformities to the labor he had done as a child working in a woolen mill. After listening to Bright's evidence against him, Ashley offered his colleagues in the House of Commons a description of the marks that factory labor had left on Dodd's body: "Certainly," Ashley testified, "I never saw a more wretched object. He had lost his hand, and I may say had almost lost his shape. He hardly looked indeed like a human being."[1] Ashley's words, therefore, brought before his listeners the kind of proof that Bright was trying to discredit—the image of a worker scarcely recognizable as human, so twisted and diminished by his childhood labors as to have almost no shape at all.

During this debate William Dodd, for a number of reasons, could not have appeared on the floor of the House of Commons to represent himself. After the passage of the so-called great Reform Act of 1832, which enfranchised a large number of middle-class men, workers did not qualify to vote, and they lacked the financial resources that would have allowed them to serve there even if they could have been elected since members of Parliament were not paid. During the first half of the nineteenth century, however, when factory legislation was being debated in the House, workers did find a number of ways to bring their own experiences and views to bear on the issues being considered. In the first several decades of the century, they expressed their discontent through strikes and sabotage in the form of machine-breaking. As Parliament seemed to become more willing to protect children and, later on, women from the most extreme conditions of industrial labor, factory workers organized

---

1 *Hansard's Parliamentary Debates*, 3rd series, 73 (1844): 1154-55. See Appendix B.1 for the full text of this interchange. All references here to the four main autobiographical texts in this edition are to its page numbers.

their forces and developed more effective ways of communicating their views: they formed what were called "short-time committees," which publicized the need to limit the hours worked in factories; they sent working-class delegates, whose expenses they paid, to lobby members of Parliament; they drafted and submitted petitions with thousands of signatures, initiated prosecutions against manufacturers who failed to uphold the laws that were enacted, and gathered in huge demonstrations, marching in processions through and between the cities of the manufacturing districts in the north of England.

Equally committed to the goal of achieving legislative reform of factory conditions were working-class writers, who used an increasing number and range of opportunities to publish inexpensive pamphlets and local newspapers in which they encouraged working-class protest by exposing the problems requiring amelioration. Along with poetry and reportage, autobiography was one of the chief forms that such writing took. The central decades of the nineteenth century, when the discipline of statistics was emerging as a dominant way to configure human experience as a mass or in the aggregate, were also, in the words of the social critic Thomas Carlyle, "these Autobiographical times of ours" (*Sartor* 73): the evidence offered by a single individual was gaining new respect and significance. Individual testimony, like the evidence provided by computed numbers, often addressed matters of public interest. As the example of William Dodd's 1841 *Narrative* suggests, autobiographies written by workers in the first half of the century found a major impetus in their necessarily preeminent concern with the political life from which they were formally—but only formally—excluded.

I. Factory Lives

The four major texts reprinted in this volume—John Brown's *A Memoir of Robert Blincoe* (1832); the *Narrative* by William Dodd; James Myles's *Chapters in the Life of a Dundee Factory Boy* (1850), the story of the fictitious Frank Forrest; and Ellen Johnston's "Autobiography" (1867, 1869)—describe factory labor from the end of the eighteenth century to the third quarter of the nineteenth, and they represent a variety of British textile industries—cotton, woolen, flax, and jute, respectively—in a variety of manufacturing districts. The historical and industrial range of these texts is matched by the diversity of their autobiographical forms—fact and fiction, memoir and first-person recollection.

The value of bringing such quite different works together is both historical and literary. Because they participated in industrialization by recording the conditions of factory labor, they contribute to our understanding of what was arguably the single most important transformation in the material and cultural conditions of nineteenth-century British life. Because they illustrate not only the changes that conceptions of autobiography have undergone since the nineteenth century but also some of the shortcomings inherent in current definitions of the genre, these texts both confirm and challenge critical thinking on the subject. Although these two transformations—one economic and industrial, the other literary—occurred on vastly different scales and had incomparable impacts on the cultures in which they took place, the two phenomena were often linked. Written not only to address but also to alter the course of historical events, working-class autobiographies in the nineteenth century provided effective ways of engaging in public debate, both inside and outside Parliament. This collection therefore offers an opportunity to understand the political potential of autobiography, a literary form that we still often take to be primarily private and personal.

When Thomas Carlyle examined what he famously called "the condition of England" in the early 1840s, he highlighted one of the central issues raised by the texts reprinted here, the ability and authority of workers to speak for themselves. In *Past and Present* (1843), Carlyle defined Britain as a land of plenty suffering from want, both material and spiritual, and he pointed to a bewilderingly complex and even frightening array of social problems: the role of government in the relief of poverty, which had become a highly contentious issue with the passing of the Poor Law Amendment Act of 1834; the political status of unenfranchised workers, many of whom supported the adoption of the democratic Charter, among whose six points were calls for universal manhood suffrage, annual parliaments, and pay for M.P.s; the fate of the Corn Laws, which protected domestic agriculture from foreign competition, keeping high the price of bread; and crises in health and sanitation caused by Britain's population growth and its startlingly rapid urbanization. But the "imperatively pressing Problem of the Present," according to Carlyle, was that raised by the approximately 80 per cent of the British population constituting the working classes: "How to deal with the Actual Labouring Millions of England" (255). Significantly, Carlyle conveys the extent of the threat posed by workers by speculating about what they would say if he thought them capable of speaking for themselves. His imagined workers address the readers of *Past and Present*: "They put their huge inarticulate question, 'What do you mean to do with us?... Behold us here, so many thousands, millions, and increasing at the rate of fifty every hour.... We ask, ... What is it you expect of us? What is it you mean to do with us?'" (22-23). In Carlyle's commentary, the workers' voice, the collective "we" of these questions, is a rhetorical fiction. That voice wants to know what "you," presumably Carlyle's middle- and upper-class readers, will do "with us," a formulation that grants all power and agency to "you," all need and subjection to "us." Carlyle makes clear in *Past and Present* his sympathy for working-class suffering, but workers might rightly have taken exception to his presumption in speaking for them, in defining them as "inarticulate."

Related in the nineteenth century to the question of authority raised by Carlyle in *Past and Present*—who had the right to speak for workers?—were two other uses of the word *authority* as it pertained to factory legislation: did the government have the right, the authority, even the duty to regulate the conditions of industrial production? If so, on whose testimony, on whose authority or claim to be believed, should such decisions have been made? These two questions came together when workers tried to convey the lessons of their experience of factory labor and to demand change on the basis of that experience. The contest between Bright and Ashley over William Dodd's veracity reveals the increasingly prominent role that workers were playing in the development of factory legislation. The texts in this volume—the four factory lives and many of the appendices that offer perspectives on those lives—prove that working-class writers were fully able to present authoritative accounts of their experiences as ways of understanding and, they hoped, remedying "the condition of England."

Stories and Their Contexts

This introduction offers two different arguments, one literary and one historical. In both instances I make the case for the value of studying these works by telling stories: first, an account of the changing definitions of autobiography as it has become a subject of academic inquiry from the mid-twentieth century to the present; secondly, a narrative of factory legislation in the nineteenth century. I do not, however, in either case recount the most dramatic episodes from the lives of Blincoe, Dodd, Forrest, and

Johnston; that I leave for them to do in their own words. Like all stories, mine are partial and selective; and like most traditional Western narratives, they attempt to shape events into coherent forms for the purposes at hand. Yet both these histories differ from other treatments of similar material because they are told in response to the evidence offered by the working-class accounts reprinted here.[1] Until relatively recently such texts have been used mainly as sources of historical information, as repositories of more-or-less reliable facts about working-class life, particularly in relation to questions of literacy and education.[2] These four very different accounts of factory life, however, also reveal working-class perspectives that change the shape of previously told histories of both autobiography and industrialization.

Gauging the significance of these texts depends, at least in part, on understanding the economic and industrial conditions from which they issued and to which they responded. Factory labor was one of the chief features of what is still called the industrial revolution, although the extent and speed of the changes that it involved have been widely debated (Berg, ch. 1). Propelled by inventions that applied mechanical power to previously hand-driven processes and fueled by the expanding markets of Britain's world-wide empire, industrial developments from the 1770s and into the first decades of the nineteenth century were genuinely transformative. Their effects were initially evident in the cotton industry located largely in Lancashire, where the processes of first spinning and then weaving came to be dominated by more and more powerful machinery, a development that extended later to the woolen and worsted industries in the West Riding of York-shire (Mathias, ch. 5). Inventions like the spinning jenny, the self-acting mule, and, most important, the steam-driven engine dramatically increased productivity in such textile industries. According to contemporary statistics, the value of cotton exports in 1830 was over forty times greater than it had been in any of the years of the 1780s (Henriques 68), and cotton constituted 45 per cent of Britain's exports between 1831 and 1850 (Hoppen 285). One commentator fancifully concluded that Britain produced so much cotton thread in one year that it would cover the

---

1 Like both Gray (pt. 1) and Cunningham (ch. 9) in their separate accounts of factory legislation, I focus here on different kinds of voices telling different stories.

2 See Altick, ch. 11; Vincent, *Bread*, pt. 3; Murphy 13-21. For more diverse historical uses of such material, see Vincent, *Literacy*; J. Rose.

distance from the earth to the sun fifty-one times (Baines 431-32). As larger and more efficient machinery was used in the manufacture of textiles, an expanding workforce, of whose numbers only about a quarter were men (Nardinelli 106), was concentrated in unprecedentedly large workplaces. By 1851 there were approximately 1.2 million people working in Britain's textile industries, with about half a million manufacturing cotton. Such "operatives," as factory workers were called, therefore constituted a sizable proportion of the population of almost sixteen million people above the age of nine (Mathias 242, 239).

The mechanization of labor in the nineteenth century was not, however, a consistent, steady development that affected all regions of Britain equally. Even by mid-century most Victorian workers were artisans, farmhands, or servants; they labored in small workshops or fields or private homes, not in factories.[1] Yet contemporary observers and participants were convinced that a revolutionary change had taken place, not only in the processes of manufacture, but also in an entire way of life. Textiles, primarily woolen and worsted, had been in the eighteenth century the products of domestic or "cottage" industry: adult, male weavers, supported by the efforts of their wives and children, who prepared the wool for manufacture on hand looms, worked in relative autonomy, typically also depending on small-scale gardening that broke up the long hours spent at the loom. When set against the new practices of the factory, the image of the hand-loom weaver as a free and independent worker was often idealized, especially since those who remained in this trade became increasingly destitute,[2] and the force of this nostalgic image explains why so many of the factory reformers were shocked by the contrast between past and present. During the early stages of industrialization, mills were powered by water available only in relatively remote locations, and a large proportion of the workforce in them was constituted by poor and often orphaned children. After the introduction of steam power, which allowed the build-

---

1 See Joyce; Hoppen 59; cf. Mathias, ch. 9. On the regionalization of industrial development, see Berg, ch. 5; Hamilton, ch. 6.

2 E.P. Thompson 269-95. In 1851 there were 50,000 hand looms in operation, and the workers using them were producing only specialized weaves (Mathias 242-43). Even Engels, who thought the political awareness of hand-loom weavers was more like that of animals than of human beings, wrote in the 1840s a glowing description of the relative comforts of the way of life that they enjoyed (50-52). See also Baines 337-39.

ing of factories in more highly populated towns and cities, however, factory work was often termed *"family labour,"* as one cotton master explained in 1832, since children in many of the early steam-powered textile mills worked for and with their parents.[1] Yet the pressures of technological change and legislation soon broke up the family unit so that its members more often worked separately in the same or neighboring factories (Mathias 182). Under such arrangements, as one observer explained in 1833, children were "let out ... upon the same principle as a postmaster [of a coaching station] lets out post horses" (qtd. Cruickshank 19).

From the late-eighteenth century on, the work that these operatives did became increasingly intensified, regimented, and commodified. By the early decades of the nineteenth century, contemporaries often noted that industrial production had come to constitute a "factory system," a complicated organization of interrelated parts that was, like a machine, self-propelled and self-governing. Depending on one's perspective, this system seemed either in need of control or beyond it, but its establishment as a fact of economic life seemed indisputable.[2] Factory labor compared unfavorably not only to that of earlier hand-loom weavers but also to the current conditions of skilled artisans, who served customary apprenticeships so that they could become "free" men able to compete in a presumably fair labor market (see Dodd 207). To many early Victorians, factory life, in contrast, constituted a regime under which no workers, young or old, male or female, were "free agents." As one writer put it in 1832, "While the engine runs, the people must work—men, women and children are yoked together with iron and steam ... chained fast to the iron machine, which knows no suffering and no weariness" (qtd. Ward 65). Factory life was often called "white slavery," as if its horrors could be conveyed only by comparing it

---

1 Qtd. Ward 414. The extent to which that was the case is now widely debated: see Horn 37-39, Tuttle 132-36.

2 Recent historical scholarship has suggested that "the all-encompassing system of industrial manufacture" in the early and middle decades of the nineteenth century "probably did not exist" as fully as contemporary observers assumed (qtd. Freedgood 4, n5). To most early Victorians, however, it seemed completely developed and "perfectly organized" (Ure 15; cf. Kay 46). On the damage done to that system by the immorality of the poorest workers, see Kay 49. On the factory system as an integrated and even organic system, see Bizup 30-37; for an account of the rhetoric typical of accounts supporting it, see Bizup, ch. 1 and 3.

unfavorably to the forced labor of black slaves in the British colonies.[1]

Because of its novelty, size, and visibility, the cotton factory soon became the central image of the factory system.[2] "It is in a cotton mill," as one of the staunchest proponents of mechanization proclaimed, "that the perfection of automatic industry is to be seen" (Ure 2), and children working there contributed to its success for a number of reasons: their labor was relatively cheap, their fingers delicate enough to work with thread, and their bodies small enough to fit between and under the low-built machines that needed to be cleaned. In the process of turning raw cotton into thread and then into cloth, children were particularly useful during the spinning stage as "piecers" or "pieceners," who worked for adult spinners by tying together the ends of any yarn that had broken. Determining the numbers and ages of the children employed in such work remains difficult.[3] According to one estimate, 114,000 people worked in the cotton industry in 1815, "most of them women and children" (Hunt 26; cf. Hamilton 135). In 1835 the number of women and children alone had reached perhaps over 160,000 (Kovačević 81), and another account of workers in the 1830s estimates that a third of them were children, of whom half were younger than fourteen (Baines 380). By 1867, of the approximately one half million employed in producing cotton, over 70 per cent were women and children, with about 40 per cent labeled "boys" and "girls" (Baxter 45). Since female workers of thirteen years and older were counted as adults, the figure of 40 per cent is most likely, by our standards, a significant underestimate. Not surprisingly,

---

1 For typical instances of such rhetoric, see Oastler, reprinted here in Appendix G.1; Engels 114-15; Fielden 14-15; qtd. Marx 353-54; cf. Marx 378-79. For discussions, see Gallagher, ch. 1; Gray, ch. 1.

2 Gray, ch. 5; Joyce 2: 131; Marx 408. Mathias explains that even by the mid-nineteenth century "cotton manufacture was the *only* branch of the textile industry where the large plant was dominant" (243). Berg qualifies this emphasis on large mills (ch. 10).

3 One historian argues that the economic importance to the cotton industry of very young children was negligible since fewer than 1 per cent of workers in cotton mills in 1833, for instance, were under ten years of age (Nardinelli 105), but a more recent study concludes that much-needed child labor "may well have played a crucial strategic part" in Britain's unprecedented industrial development (Horrell and Humphries 99). For commentaries on this debate, see Kirby 74-76; Tuttle 10-14.

then, children's labor has been central to both past and present conceptions of the industrial revolution. As E.P. Thompson explained, young workers were part of a "dramatic visual image—the barrack-like buildings, the great mill chimneys, the factory children ..." (192). Inescapably associated with that image were the conditions and practices that led to the worst abuses of child labor: long hours in overheated and unventilated rooms, intense and continuous attention to the running of machines, physical postures and repeated motions that deformed growing bodies, rigid discipline enforced by clocks and overseers.

Whether such a description is accurate, however, was an issue intensely debated throughout much of the first half of the nineteenth century, particularly in the 1830s and 1840s. Like the question of William Dodd's credibility—to which I return in a later section of this introduction—the nature of child labor in Britain's textile industries evoked passionate responses from both sides of the ideological divide that it epitomized. Lists of the ill effects that factory life had on children became an expected convention in debates over factory labor, which often included accounts of such problems as: high mortality rates; deformity and maiming; stunted development, both mental and physical; extreme fatigue; debility and pallor; as well as, more specifically, "pain in the back, hips, and legs, swollen joints, varicose veins, and large, persistent ulcers in the thighs and calves" (Engels 174); along with a host of fevers and "a variety of chronic diseases" exacerbated by long hours, poor nutrition, and unhealthy housing (Gaskell 162-63). Much of the evidence for such diagnoses came from doctors and physicians, many of whom had worked for years in manufacturing districts and offered eyewitness accounts of their encounters with young workers (Wing lxviii). One of the most eloquent responses came from a physician who, having traveled to Manchester, reported what he saw on its streets: "I stood in Oxford Road, Manchester, and observed the stream of operatives as they left the mills at twelve o'clock. The children were almost universally ill-looking, small, sickly, barefoot, and ill-clad. Many *appeared* to be no older than seven. The men, generally from sixteen to twenty-four, and none aged, were almost as pallid and thin as the children.... It was a mournful spectacle" (qtd. Baines 462). As this passage makes clear, the factory child set the standard for visible destitution and debility, a standard that adult workers came close to meeting.

Yet numerous commentators, defending free trade and championing industrial progress, were ready to sing the praises of the employment of young children in Britain's textile industries. According to one observer, "juvenile labour ... is in fact a national blessing" (Cooke Taylor 21). To others, it was a blessing not only to the nation but also to the children so employed. Working in spacious, clean, airy, and uncrowded spaces, such children, according to numerous accounts, did virtually no work because machines did it all for them. The respected political economist Nassau Senior referred in general to the "extraordinary lightness of [factory] labour, if labour it can be called" (11), and *light* and *lightness* were the terms typically used to describe "juvenile" work.[1] Children attending machines, as these arguments proposed, had only to watch for the few moments during which their "light" efforts were required. Such workers "seemed to be always cheerful and alert, taking pleasure in the light play of their muscles" (Ure 301). Piecers, in particular, had almost nothing to do. Three quarters of their time as factory workers were spent in leisure: because the spinning machine worked for three quarters of a minute as the piecer looked on, the child was "idle," and "consequently ... if a child remain[ed at work] during twelve hours a day, *for nine hours he perform[ed] no actual labour*" (qtd. Baines 459; cf. Ure 312). Earlier in the century, when the working day was even longer, children who put in eighty-four hours in a six-day week at a mill in Backborough, Lancashire, were said to have jobs "far from laborious" ("Previous Workhouses"). A second, more widespread argument in support of the ease of children's factory work involved comparing it to the other sorts of childhood employments typical in the early nineteenth century. Piecers were better paid, and they did less demanding work than those engaged in "sewing, pin-making, or coalmining" (Ure 288), in the last of which industries half-naked children were chained to carts of coal that they hauled on hands and knees to a mine's surface. The young factory worker was also judged to be better off than the "juvenile mendicant" or "juvenile vagrant" or "juvenile delinquent" that he or she might become if not working in a mill. Even the enforced idleness of boys and girls at boarding schools was said to create more suffering and physical deformity than factory labor did (Cooke Taylor 23, 66). Any problems that arose from employing children in textile manufacture were often blamed on either parents too eager to profit from

---

1   Baines 456, 481; Gaskell 157. See Fielden's response to this claim (Appendix G.3).

the work of their sons and daughters or on overseers, the workers responsible for keeping their young assistants at their tasks. Although ardent supporters of the benefits of child labor sometimes conceded that the earliest mills, like those in which Robert Blincoe had worked, were sites of exploitation and abuse, they also claimed that they now saw no physical evidence of what their opponents called the "evils" or the "curse of the factory system."[1]

As one twentieth-century history noted without exaggeration, the "controversy ... round the factory system" was one that "raged" on (Pinchbeck 314), making more intractable the responses to conditions of child labor, which the opponents in this debate continued to depict in very different ways. To the mix of theory, speculation, statistics, expert testimony, and reportage that constituted the contentious discourses dealing with child labor, working-class autobiographers added the perspectives authorized by their personal experiences not only as observers but also as participants. By recounting events typical of childhood years spent within the confines of a wide range of factories, the texts in this volume, therefore, provide grounds for evaluating the so-called "light" labors of their authors or their subjects.

II. Autobiography and Working-Class Testimony

During the deliberations of one of the most prominent of the British government's formal inquiries into the conditions of factory labor in the nineteenth century, the royal commission of 1833, a worker named Charles Aberdeen concluded his testimony with this succinct claim: "If I was in solitary confinement I could write a history of my life, and I could show up the factory system then."[2] Implying that he lacked the material conditions necessary to the writing of one's life, Aberdeen could not imagine having the peace, quiet, and time to compose an autobiography unless he were imprisoned alone in a jail cell. Yet he had no

---

1 These terms come from the titles of books by Wing and Fielden, respectively. Cooke Taylor (64-66) and Baines (475) quote evidence that factory labor no longer causes deformity. For even-handed accounts of this debate, see Pinchbeck 194-96, Rule 143-50, Horn 29-40, Cruickshank 48-53. Nardinelli argues vigorously that, "given the circumstances of the time, children benefited" from factory labor (156; cf. ch. 2 and ch. 4). For the opposite point of view, see E. P. Thompson (331-49).

2 *Parliamentary Papers* 20 (1833): D.2: 1 [751].

doubts that his life story could become a political weapon and that its telling would necessarily "show up the factory system" by exposing the conditions that required reform.

The actual circumstances in which Aberdeen made this statement are almost as significant as the statement itself. He had been called as a witness by the 1833 commission because he had already offered testimony before the parliamentary committee of 1832, an investigative body headed by the Tory M.P. Michael Thomas Sadler, who had introduced a bill to set the minimum age for factory labor at nine and to limit to ten hours a day or fifty-eight hours a week the work of those under eighteen (Thomas 38). Of the eighty-seven witnesses interviewed by Sadler's committee, sixty were workers (Driver 170). Some of them were exposed to "fairly sharp exchanges" with their examiners, but the "adult male working-class witnesses," according to Robert Gray, "insisted on the validity of their own experience and observation." The royal commission appointed in 1833 was charged with reviewing the work of the 1832 committee; and its examiners were presumably chosen so that they could discredit the findings of Sadler's investigations, which had offered shocking accounts of the abuses suffered by those engaged in industrial labor. Some of the operatives interviewed by Sadler were recalled in 1833, and their evidence was subjected to "a quasi-juridical" process of interrogation (Gray 67, 69). Facing a skeptical middle-class examiner in 1833, then, Aberdeen stoutly confirmed the spoken history of his life that he had previously provided. His story had become a written record in the *Parliamentary Papers* of 1831-32 (see Appendix E.1), as did his testimony in 1833, and there they occasioned further debate on the "factory question."[1] Unlike the factory owners whose views were surveyed by the 1833 commission, working-class witnesses, who had to appear before its investigators in person, were required to take an oath (Gray 69). Aberdeen boldly refused to be sworn in, therefore

---

1 Aberdeen, 1832 testimony, *Parliamentary Papers* 15 (1831-32): 439-48 (see Appendix E.1); 1833 testimony, *Parliamentary Papers* 20 (1833): D.2: 1 [751]. In an apparently highly edited rendition of the evidence gathered by E.C. Tufnell for the 1833 royal commission, Aberdeen's testimony appeared first, and it was criticized by W.R. Greg in his 1834 *Analysis of the Evidence Taken before the Factory Commission*. Gray examines these documents (69-70) and uses Aberdeen's comment on being able to "show up the factory system" as an epigraph to his book. Aberdeen's responses were widely cited in the 1830s: see Ure 291-92; Greg 65-66; Wing li.

implicitly establishing that he, not God, was the authority for his evidence.

In one sense, then, Aberdeen had already used this authority to tell his story, to do what he said he could do only if imprisoned, during his appearance before the 1832 committee. In response to the questions asked him, he had offered a full outline of his life and detailed accounts of some of its more significant episodes. The tale that Aberdeen told was becoming familiar by the early 1830s. Sent as a parish apprentice to work in a textile factory in northern Wales in approximately 1796, he had recently been fired from his position in a Manchester mill because he supported a ten-hours bill. Aberdeen's lengthy description of this episode is complete with dialogue, settings, an array of conventional characters, and depictions of gestures and psychological motivations. His account becomes more terse and even more effective, however, when, after having answered almost ninety questions, he is asked to explain why he thinks that factory labor shortens the life of a factory child: "I have seen many instances ...; I have seen men and women that have worked in a factory all their lives, like myself, and that get married; and I have seen the race become diminutive and small; I have myself had seven children, not one of which survived six weeks; my wife is an emaciated person, like myself, [she is] a little woman, and she worked during her childhood, younger than myself, in a factory" (Appendix E.1, 396). Having given a new meaning to the term *factory child*—here it means the doomed offspring of the "race" of factory workers rather than a young operative—Aberdeen epitomizes his factory life in the spare details of domestic tragedy. His 1832 testimony was, in effect, his autobiography.

In the middle of the nineteenth century, identifying Aberdeen's oral testimony as an example of autobiography would have seemed an unremarkable, even casual categorization. At that time the term *autobiography* embraced a number of particularly fluid definitions because it had not yet become, as it is now, the label for a canonical genre of literary art.[1] When Henry Mayhew, for instance, published in 1862 the fourth volume of *London Labour and the London Poor*, including in it interviews with the unemployed and criminal poor, the advertisement for the volume claimed that it contains "very many deeply interesting autobi-

---

1 For accounts of the origins and nineteenth-century understandings of autobiography, see Vincent, *Bread*, ch. 2; Olney, "Autobiography"; Marcus, ch. 1; Peterson, *Traditions*, ch. 1.

ographies, faithfully transcribed from their own lips," and the terms *narrative* and *autobiographies* appear interchangeably in the table of contents to indicate interviews included in Mayhew's text (4: [v], viii-ix). Moreover, nineteenth-century readers seem to have viewed parliamentary testimony in particular as a narrative expression of a witness's experiences. In an early history of factory legislation, Samuel Kydd announces that he is presenting the parliamentary testimony included in his account, not in the question-and-answer form of the *Parliamentary Papers*, but "condensed ... into [a] narrative form" that carefully "preserve[s], as far as convenient, the words in the questions asked, and the answers given" (1: 275). Interestingly enough, however, when Kydd recounts these tales, he does so using the witness's answers while eliminating the questioner's words so that each account becomes an encapsulated life history told in the first person. By treating testimony in this fashion, Kydd was following the practice of many of the reports on the interviews gathered by parliamentary committees and royal commissions, which often abstracted their results by citing the name of the source and then adding to it a long series of predicates that constitute a portion of a life story. (For an example of this effect, see the parliamentary testimony reprinted in Appendix E.2.)

Even more telling in establishing the autobiographical effect of such testimony is the use to which it is put in James Myles's fictional *Chapters in the Life of a Dundee Factory Boy*. When its autobiographical narrator includes in his own story testimony about another worker drawn from the evidence of an 1833 "committee," he speaks to the narrative impact of the recorded answers: "The witness, in a few words, gives the elements of a melancholy story." So moved is Myles's narrator by this tale of a girl tempted into sin and crime by the conditions of factory labor that he repeats it until it finally forms a complete life story coming alive before his eyes in clear and distinct visual detail: "Alas! poor girl, in imagination I see thee an innocent child.... I see thee consigned ... to a country mill master.... I see thee forced to fly, covered with blood.... Lastly, I see thee entrapped in the nets of the wicked, ... [a] pure and guileless child ... become a criminal ..." (264-67). Here the narrator of the *Dundee Factory Boy*, taking on the role of a reader of parliamentary testimony, offers a model of how such testimony is to be construed: like, I believe, most Victorian readers, he almost inevitably creates a full and connected story from the questions and answers that he encounters in the parliamentary record.

Identifying such testimony as autobiography, however, would have been extremely unlikely, if not unthinkable, in the context of the literary-critical values that predominated in the middle decades of the twentieth century. During that time, when autobiography was being established as a subject worthy of academic attention, it was understood in a relatively straightforward way as a writer's first-person, historically verifiable account of his or her—but much more often *his*—past experience; its classic examples were taken to be works by St. Augustine, Rousseau, and Franklin.[1] By the 1980s, when the study of autobiography, like other critical practices, was expected to have a theoretical grounding, the genre was often defined by examining the implications of the three Greek roots that constitute its name, but inquiry into the nature of self-life-writing, as it was often called, still involved a number of powerful and often unspoken assumptions. Each of its components, moreover, was understood in culturally specific ways.[2] The self implicit in the prefix *auto-* of autobiography was presumed to be a generally successful embodiment of the Western, humanistic ideal of the unique individual, the source of whose interest for the reader was his introspective access to an interior world of thoughts and emotions. The primary goal of such works was self-directed: "self-explanation ... self-scrutiny ... self-expression ... self-invention."[3] The life or *-bio-* that an autobiography recorded was expected to be a

---

1   For examples of the early humanistic criticism of autobiography, see Gusdorf; Pascal; Weintraub; Olney, *Metaphors*. Numerous critics have recounted the story of the changes in definitions of autobiography over the last five decades; among them are: Olney, "Autobiography"; Friedman; Folkenflik, "Introduction"; Marcus, ch. 5, 6, and 7; Corbett 3-10; Smith and Watson 4-16. My use of the model of testimony to define autobiography distinguishes this account from theirs. Critics who have noticed the pertinence of such a model include: Gilmore, who bases her arguments about autobiography on the disciplinary model of confession ("Policing Truth") and testimony (*Limits* 3-7); and Bruner, who calls autobiography a "discourse of [both] witness" and "interpretation" (45). Kestner also notes that the *Parliamentary Papers* contain "revealing miniatures, encapsulated case histories of individuals" (12). See also Sommer's work on Latin American women's *testimonios*, though she ultimately draws a line between such public forms of testimony and autobiography (130).

2   For commentary, see Olney, "Autobiography" 6-7; Watson 58; Wong 5-6.

3   Spengemann, xvi. See also Peterson, *Victorian*, ch. 1; Marcus 3-4.

coherent whole, given meaning by narrative, a form linking events together as cause and effect. Like the *Bildungsroman* or novel of development, with which autobiography was seen to have much in common, it was often conceived of as a success story, charting the ways in which an individual grows to maturity to find his rightful place in the world. The writing implicit in the suffix -*graphy* was equally specific in its implications. The autobiographies most worthy of notice, according to critics of the middle decades of the twentieth century, were those demonstrating a well-educated author's ability to use language as a sophisticated means of self-expression. That an autobiography came naturally from the pen or typewriter of an author who had often established himself as a writer in other genres or for other professional ends, that autobiographies were works written for publication—both of these assumptions were so central to mid-twentieth-century definitions of the genre as not to require mention.

For a number of obvious reasons, members of the nineteenth-century working classes were unlikely to have produced works that could be categorized as examples of what Regenia Gagnier has called "the classic realist autobiography" (43). Despite advances in education and the cheapening of forms of publication, particularly in the years of the Victorian mid-century, writing was a medium of self-representation unavailable to most workers. Literacy may have been relatively high in the first half of the nineteenth century: some estimates are as high as 75 per cent of the population, although the figures of 60 per cent for men and 40 per cent for women are generally accepted as accurate up into the 1830s. Yet the rudimentary abilities demonstrated by signing a marriage register do not necessarily prove the signer's capacity to read a complex text, much less write one.[1] Even literate workers lacked the kind of formal, advanced education that would have allowed them to conceive of their lives as narratives drawing on traditions of high art and classical learning. More important perhaps, the material conditions of working-class lives did not easily accommodate the ideals of success and stability

---

1 Murphy 7-13; Vincent, *Literacy* 53. Altick cites an 1867 survey of a working-class area in Manchester in which "barely more than half of the adults could read" (170). One particularly optimistic sample from the manufacturing districts, which put literacy in the 1830s at 86 per cent, estimates the number of people able to write as only half those able to read (Greg 35). On the difficulties and advantages of using marriage registers to determine literacy rates, see Vincent, *Literacy*, "Introduction."

that determine the form and endings of so many middle-class autobiographies, even of those whose authors cannot attest to having realized such goals. Because manual labor—more obviously than the so-called mental labor of managers, business people, and professionals—depended on the health of workers' bodies and of the economies to which they contributed, it was by definition insecure and often temporary. Such conditions, as Charles Aberdeen's testimony confirms, were not conducive to the act of writing one's life history—which, as David Vincent points out, is not an everyday activity for members of any class.[1] In the early years of the study of autobiography, then, it might have seemed simply natural and inevitable that workers would be neither motivated nor able to write autobiographies—although, in fact, hundreds of nineteenth-century texts have now come to be recognized as working-class examples of the genre.[2]

The triumphant individualism characteristic of the "classic realist" definition of autobiography even more effectively established it as a club from which working-class writings might be automatically excluded. In the context of the several decades after World War II, an individualistic conception of autobiography made cultural sense. After all, two nations founded on self-proclaimed values of individualism—Britain and the United States—had saved civilization from the threats of German totalitarianism, and they were continuing to fight the Cold War against the collectivist forces of Soviet Communism. As one of the earliest and most insightful theorists of the genre noted without irony in 1956, autobiography expresses a concern "peculiar to Western man," a "man [who] knows himself to be a responsible agent: gatherer of men, of lands, of power, maker of kingdoms or of empires" (Gusdorf 29, 31). Nineteenth-century workers, however, as they themselves repeatedly pointed out, often found the most compelling sources of their identities, not in middle-class conceptions of unique individuality, but in their sense of

---

1   *Bread*, 6-7. See Vincent's accounts of the material conditions of working-class lives (*Bread* 68-70, 154, 199).

2   In her study of self-representation, Gagnier explains that she has read all or part of approximately three-quarters of the nearly eight-hundred texts listed in *The Autobiography of the Working Class*, the bibliography by Burnett, Vincent, and Mayall (5), and Vincent in his earlier work on the subject, *Bread, Knowledge, and Freedom*, consulted 142 (3). On the failure of such working-class texts to conform to traditional conceptions of autobiography, see Vincent, *Testaments* 4, 16; Hackett 16.

community with other workers, their sense of being part of a group defined in some cases by class affiliations and in others by their loyalties to the particular trades or industries in which they worked and to the regions in which they lived. Such communal conceptions of identity were thought to be unsuited to the literary form of self-life-writing, and workers, therefore, unlikely to have the kind of authority—in this case, an authority based on the conviction of their uniqueness—to justify their adoption of such a genre.

Expanding Conceptions of Autobiography

Not surprisingly, however, in the changing contexts of the Civil Rights movement of the 1960s, the feminism of the 1970s, and the multiculturalism of the 1980s, the exclusionary model of autobiography was put into question. The first challenge it faced—a challenge that prepared the way for the inclusion of working-class lives within a revised definition of the genre—came from the study of African-American texts, particularly of fugitive slave narratives. As stories sometimes solicited from illiterate speakers and recorded and published by abolitionists, such narratives had had the obvious and overriding political goal of exposing the evils of slavery, and they had often been dismissed as simple propaganda. When scholars of African-American literature and culture argued for the historical accuracy and complex artistry of works such as the *Narrative of the Life of Frederick Douglass, an American Slave* (1845) and Harriet Jacobs's *Incidents in the Life of a Slave Girl* (1861), they also expanded the definition of autobiography.[1] Further revaluations came in response to interest in works by women and by such ethnic minorities as Native Americans. If such texts were to be categorized as autobiographies, then the three constituent parts of self-life-writing would have to encompass a new range of meanings and values, different forms and sources of identity, enlarged conceptions of what constitutes a life, and varied modes of communication.

---

1 Baker 31-56; Gates, ch. 4. For accounts of this development, see Mostern 11-12, 50-53; Kawash 26-33. Andrews's *To Tell a Free Story* contains many perspectives on slave narratives that are relevant to working-class autobiography, particularly to Blincoe's *Memoir*, which was published through the efforts of what Andrews calls an "amanuensis-editor" (33). Cf. Hackett on the similarities between slave narratives and working-class autobiographies (11, 38).

Pertinent to such instances of self-presentation was the point made in the 1980s by feminist critics when they explained that the conventional model of autobiography serves a narrow and rigid conception of identity. It is not only class- but gender-specific, excluding, along with former slaves and workers, all those middle-class, white women who do not see their lives from the isolating and masculinist perspectives of Western individualism. Women's experience, according to such critics, is "relational," defined in terms of those around them, and a woman's life story, as in the case of a memoir, may provide accounts of family members and friends as fully adequate and appropriate ways of presenting her own experience.[1] Similarly, the speaker of a slave narrative defines as valuable the life being recounted, not primarily because it is unique, but because it is representative. By the third sentence of his *Narrative*, Douglass, an extraordinary individual by any measure, is speaking of the conditions he endured as typical of those experienced by all slaves. If middle-class women use a number of different written forms to convey the meaning of their experience, Native-American life histories may be told in a number of different media—spoken and written and drawn—and they often emerge from collaborative attempts to record communally defined lives.[2]

This reorientation in the understanding of self-life-writing has come, at the beginning of the twenty-first century, to define autobiography as a form—or, rather, as a range of diverse forms—particularly suited to the representation of shared, culturally defined identities. As Leigh Gilmore points out, "identity-based movements have shaped recent developments" in both the production and the study of autobiographies and memoirs (*Limits* 16). Since the 1990s it has become commonplace to think of a particular text as an example of, say, Asian-American or lesbian autobiography, just as autobiographical works by writers with disabilities or from a particular nation or region are seen as constituting distinct categories within the larger classification. Autobiography is now also understood to be, as Laura Marcus cogently argues, a

---

1 See Friedman for an early and particularly insightful statement of this view. See also Corbett 15-16; Marcus 219-23; Peterson, *Traditions*, 22-27; Smith and Watson 16-18.

2 On the relation between representative and unique qualities in autobiography, see Gilmore, *Limits* 8, 19-24. For an account of Native American forms of self-presentation in relation to Euro-American conceptions of autobiography, see Wong, ch. 1.

particularly hybrid literary genre (7), often combining in one text many different strategies of self-presentation, and the proliferating range of identities that it is currently seen to represent has only increased the diversity of the forms it is routinely recognized to take, which includes diaries, letters, stories, and performance pieces.

According to this culturally and formally pluralistic definition, the stories of Blincoe, Dodd, Forrest, and Johnston are all easily recognized examples of autobiography. Even Ellen Johnston, the writer who claims a greater degree of uniqueness than the others, declares herself "The Factory Girl," defining her identity in terms of the groups to which she belongs by pointing both to her class position as a laborer and to her gender. The example of Blincoe's story is equally instructive. Since it is represented as being told sometimes in his own words, but more often in those of John Brown, the working-class journalist who recorded Blincoe's life story, the traditional distinction between written and spoken accounts of one's life breaks down. Like a Native-American life told to an amateur white enthusiast or to an academic investigator, like a slave narrative transcribed for its illiterate subject, Blincoe's account has sources too interwoven with each other to allow one to establish its authority on the basis of locating its supposedly pure origin in a single consciousness, but that fact can no longer be used to deny its status as an autobiography. Moreover, if the political motives arising from "identity-based movements" can generate valuable forms of self-representation, the doubts cast by John Bright on the reliability of Dodd's story simply make it a more, not a less, revealing example of autobiography. Finally, the four major texts in this volume demonstrate their hybridity even more obviously than do "classic realist" examples of the genre. At times Dodd's *Narrative* reads as if it were a technical handbook, but it also includes letters, a table of wages, a transcript of an election speech, a medical explanation of factory injuries, an essay in economic theory, and a poem by Robert Burns. Myles's *Dundee Factory Boy* is equally inclusive, combining moral essays on the evils of drink and the theater with a short history of factory labor, character sketches, a dialogue with a fictitious reader, quotations from parliamentary testimony, as well as brief, historically verifiable biographies of Myles's fellow artisans. According to traditional definitions of autobiography, none of this material would be relevant to the telling of a psychologically rich, introspective account of unique individuality. According to more recent understandings of that definition, however, all these different discursive forms contribute appropriately to the expression of the diverse values and material realities represented by them.

The emphasis on the hybridity of autobiographical forms has been confirmed by poststructuralist literary theory, which has also been responsible for a further widening of the definition of self-life-writing, one that blurs the distinction between fact and fiction. Much of the most revealing work on autobiography in the 1990s was done by critics who recognized that every life story, no matter how tied to the historicity of a particular person's experience, is a narrative construction that draws upon the traditions and conventions of different discourses to present what Jonathan Loesberg calls a "fiction of consciousness." As retrospective accounts of past experience, autobiographies therefore attempt less to establish their factual reliability than to create meaningful pasts that will serve the needs of the autobiographers' present selves.[1] In the early years of the twenty-first century, studies of both queer autobiography and of autobiographical representations of trauma demonstrated the creatively productive uncertainty with which such works distinguish—or fail to distinguish—between fact and fiction, just as they ratified encompassing conceptions of what kinds of works are considered autobiographical by analyzing diaries and letters, memoirs and novels.[2] In his most recent commentary, Paul John Eakin, one of the foremost theorists of autobiography, blends traditional and revised conceptions of both its status as self-expression and its fictionality when he asserts, "for the autobiographers who interest me the most, ... the allegiance to truth that is the central, defining characteristic of memoir is less an allegiance to a factual record that biographers and historians could check than an allegiance to remembered consciousness and its unending succession of identity states, an allegiance to the history of one's self" ("What" 125). According to such a definition, conventional distributions of truth and falsehood, as well as any attempts to ferret out the difference between them, become irrelevant.

The "classic," mid-twentieth-century conception of autobiography tended, however, to draw a firmer line between fact and

---

1 See also Eakin, *Fictions*; Olney, "Autobiography." For the effect of poststructuralist theory on autobiography, see Eakin, *Touching*, "Introduction" and ch. 3; Marcus, ch. 5.

2 For examples of such criticism, see the two special issues of *a/b* called "Autobiographical Que(e)ries," ed. Spear; Gilmore, *Limits*; and Stewart.

fiction, one that might have included by this standard alone the lives written by Dodd and Johnston and perhaps even that written for Blincoe because they are verifiable accounts of historical persons, though it would have decisively excluded James Myles's life of Frank Forrest. *Chapters in the Life of a Dundee Factory Boy* might then have been considered "autobiographical" on the basis of its form as a first-person narrative, but its contents would not have allowed it to be labeled as "autobiography." Although Frank Forrest tells his own tale and, as its narrator, insists throughout on its authenticity as a "story of real life" (293), it is largely a fiction written by James Myles. He publicly announced himself as its "author," and he retold a readily recognizable version of its story in his *Rambles in Forfarshire* (see Appendix C.1), which he published in 1850 shortly after the appearance of the *Dundee Factory Boy*.[1] Yet if autobiography by definition mingles fact and fiction beyond the possibility of their differentiation—if the distinction is itself suspect—then even Myles's tale of a presumably fictitious factory boy merits reprinting here as a text that meets the standards set for the conception of autobiography authorized by poststructuralist theory.

From this perspective *Chapters in the Life of a Dundee Factory Boy* has more in common with the most easily verified of the historical accounts here, Ellen Johnston's "sketch" of her life, than with the stories of Blincoe and Dodd because Myles's and Johnston's narratives are both thoroughly dependent on the interpenetration of fact and fiction. If Myles plays fast and loose with the "real life" that he is creating, Johnston cannot even begin to imagine her own experience, either in the living or the telling of it, unless she uses the terms offered her by the romantic novels of Elizabeth Helme and Sir Walter Scott (cf. Gagnier 53; Swindells 146, 150). As Johnston says in a telling formulation, hers is a "romance of real life, sufficient to fill three ... volumes" (313), the publication mode characteristic of Victorian fiction. In the case of Myles's *Dundee Factory Boy*, fiction also gives form to fact. Although the narrator's childhood seems to reflect Myles's experience in a small village outside of

---

1 The Dundee Central Library has in its local-studies collection a catalogue that Myles printed of the books published and/or sold by him; there "Chapters in the Life of a Factory Boy" [*sic*] in "a new and cheap edition, complete, only 6d.," appears as one of the "BOOKS BY JAMES MYLES," along with *Rambles in Forfarshire*, which carries his name on its title page.

Dundee, the "model" for Frank Forrest was more likely to have been a man named John Deans (Whatley 72, 75). There is no proof that Myles himself ever worked in a textile factory; rather, he was trained as a stone mason before becoming a writer and publisher (see Appendix C.2). Like Tom Braine, a particularly intelligent character in the *Dundee Factory Boy*, Frank Forrest is an allegorically named, exemplary figure. Yet the "episode" of the "transcript from real life" offered in Chapter 9 (293) seems actually to have taken place. Robert Nicoll and William Jackson, two of the young men involved in the event, were both well known in Dundee as aspirants to literary and scientific eminence, men whose great promise was cut short by their early deaths. By 1850 Myles, as Forrest says of himself, was the sole survivor of the group.[1] Fact and fiction could not be more inextricably linked, and both contribute to what Myles calls an account of "real life."

Realigning the Boundaries of Autobiography

So far I have told the story of the criticism of autobiography as if it were a version of the plot that Victorians of all classes liked best—a tale of development, improvement, and progress. Yet such stories, even their Victorian versions, often require qualification, their outcomes having negative, unintended consequences. While it has been productive to reformulate the boundaries demarcating autobiography from other literary forms, thus expanding its territory, there have been disadvantages associated with this change. This point is exemplified by the factory lives collected in this volume. Most obvious among the limitations of even an expanded conception of autobiography is the one that it shares with all definitions: it has tended to become prescriptive. Having granted the importance that many women or workers or Native Americans place on their relationships to others, critics too often assume that the only so-called genuine autobiographies that such people can compose are those based on a model of relational identity. Yet there is no reason why working-class writers cannot

---

1   In addition, the event that Forrest locates at Campbell Hotel in 1836 (289), a commemoration of the tricentenary of the Reformation, in fact took place in 1835 at the Crown Hotel, and Robert Nicholl's hymn to the occasion was prominently featured at the celebration (see Appendix C.2).

adopt for their own purposes the forms and assumptions of "classic realist" autobiography.[1]

The four texts collected here do just that. Although all the persons depicted in these stories stress their identities as representative members of particular groups, they also make claims for the unusual or unique qualities of their experiences. Blincoe's story presents him as an early example of a factory child subjected to unusually harsh treatment. Dodd sees himself as crippled to an exceptional degree by the factory system. Forrest uses the first paragraph of his story to assert that he has as much "individuality" as the writer of an "autobiographic" account of fashionable life (229). Ellen Johnston is a self-declared genius, set apart from her fellow factory workers by her poetic gifts; as Florence Boos puts the point, Johnston is well aware that "her publications [are] remarkable simply by virtue of their existence" (60). In addition, these stories both respond to the factory system and provide evidence of the quality that John Brown attributes to Robert Blincoe, "susceptibility of heart" (95), and they demonstrate the relation between those two functions. Only by establishing the psychological impact of factory labor on persons who are capable of being affected by it can these indictments of the factory system be effective. Ellen Johnston even attributes to herself multiple "highly susceptible and sympathetic natures— physical, intellectual, and moral," all of which have been influenced by "the TIME and COUNTRY of my BIRTH" and all the "varied conditions of [her] life" (303). As Dodd specifies, he wants to "show the *effects* of the [factory] system upon my mind, person, and condition" (186). Introspection, then, is necessary to his story, as it is to those of Blincoe and Forrest and Johnston.

Nor is the supposedly middle-class success story a model that these writers avoid. Rather, James Myles gives to the *Dundee Factory Boy* the kind of coherent aesthetic shape typical of classic autobiographies. Like the plot of Frank Forrest's first published

---

1 Although Gagnier explains that "middle-class autobiography [is not] constitutive of autobiography as such" (151), she identifies "narrative and psychological disintegration" as the fate of working-class writers who attempt to convey their experience by using middle-class literary forms (48, cf. 45). Swindells discusses the possibility that the identities portrayed in working-class autobiography can be both subjective and representational (205). For objections to the prescriptive use of a relational model of autobiography, see: Friedman 44; Neuman 219-22; Peterson, *Traditions*, ch. 1; Mostern 44-45. Cf. Maidment on dialect writing (355).

story, which he composed out of the elements of his own experience, the *Dundee Factory Boy* tells a success story, "the truthful history of a poor boy, who has ... triumphed over many difficulties" (230). Brown, in telling the story of Blincoe's life, includes a prophecy on the outcome of its subject's endeavors that was offered to him by a local fortune teller; by doing so, Brown can point to the fulfillment of her prophecy, thus providing a satisfying example of virtue rewarded and cruelty punished. Even Ellen Johnston's sad, short account of her sad, short life ends triumphantly as she glories in the "sympathy, friendship, and love" of her readers (314). To suggest that workers should not find appropriate to their experience the forms of self-life-writing identified with middle-class literary traditions is to make even more rigid and limiting the class distinctions that were inescapable features of nineteenth-century British culture.

Autobiography as it is practiced by and for these workers also helps to restrain the most extreme tendencies of postmodern theory. If self-life-writing can come in a variety of forms, if it can freely mingle fact and fiction, however those terms are understood, then what does one exclude from the genre? Is all first-person narration not simply autobiographical but autobiography? Where does one draw the line? Part of the answer to such questions is provided by the goals and assumptions that are inscribed within the texts of these working-class lives. They all insist on a quality of autobiography that is too often overlooked or even denied in the postmodern emphasis on the primacy of language and discourse: claims to authority based on the relation of a text to a real world. A number of twentieth-century theorists of autobiography have also insisted on the importance of this quality, its referentiality; and they do so by pointing to the historical actuality of the person whose name appears on the title page of an autobiography and in its pages (Lejeune 29) or by charting the dependence of autobiographies on historical and biographical fact. Working-class texts, not surprisingly, define the reality to which they refer in both more general and more specific ways, confirming, as one critic puts it, that "autobiography is nothing if not a referential art" (Eakin, *Touching* 28; cf. Sommer 119-22).

Instead of being concerned with the status of the speaker's relation to the text or with the actuality of the events in a person's life, Blincoe and Dodd and Forrest and Johnston all make claims for the reality of the conditions, material and moral, to which they are responding. In their original historical contexts these stories were narrative arguments for change: they sought better working conditions, more respect and consideration, greater governmental protection. Such openly practical goals could be attained only if their readers saw as factual the depictions of the circumstances of their subjects' experiences. As one recent theorist has suggested, autobiography is a "discourse of witness" comparable to trial testimony, and it depends on "signs of evidentiary probity" (Bruner 45, 46). Such signs constitute a particularly prominent feature of these factory lives. Implicit or explicit in these narratives is the assumption that their tellers are the best— the most accurate, the most insightful, the most trustworthy— authorities on the experiences to which they are testifying. Even Myles has his narrator attest frequently to the veracity of his account, offering at one point to bring forth a witness to prove it "true to the very letter" (251). These writers often stress the difference between themselves and less reliable sources: Dodd dismisses as irrelevant the commentaries on the factory system written by those "who can know nothing of the factories by experience" (186; cf. Brown 98). Significantly, like Charles Aberdeen testifying before the M.P. Michael Sadler, all four narratives establish their credibility by scrupulously pointing out what their writers cannot affirm on the basis of their personal experience.

As if speaking for the other autobiographers represented here, Forrest even includes in his tale a commentary on the "metaphysics" of his day, the idealism that casts doubt on an individual's unmediated experience of "material bodies" and the realities of space and time. When a university student from St. Andrews pontificates on this doctrine, a worker tartly responds, "My troth, if you had to trench in a muir [dig a ditch on a moor] ten hours every day, you would ken whether there's time or no. I doubt you would conclude, friend, that the practice was mair a reality than an idea" (281). Blincoe and Dodd, the "factory cripples"; Myles, the former stone mason; and Johnston, the "factory girl"—all would have agreed, and as autobiographers they present their "practice" as "mair a reality than an idea." Such an assertion of the factuality of their narratives is, of course, an invitation to belief that any particular reader may accept or decline. Yet these texts are all careful to offer this invitation; and readers, including those who have taken the *Chapters in the Life of a Dundee Factory Boy* as a statement of historical fact, have often accepted that invitation.[1] Such a reality-effect, dependent on literary and aesthetic qualities that obscure their own status as such, continues to define not only the particular appeal of autobiography, but also its political usefulness.

Finally, these texts display an attitude toward autobiographical authority that is perhaps their most important quality. As early in the development of the theory of this genre as 1980, James Olney, rephrasing the work of another critic, questioned a writer's "ability to say 'I' in a written text and to have any authority for that assertion" ("Autobiography" 22-23). Yet, like fugitive slaves, workers depicted in their factory lives practice what William Andrews defines as "self-authorization": they establish their authority by the "act of having claimed it" (103). As Laura Marcus says of women's autobiography, such a practice is performative, creating the condition that it enunciates: for workers as for women, "'speaking out' [is] a way of authorising identity" (287). Although it is important not to accept naive reassurances that such enunciations are unproblematically liberating (Neuman 221; Kawash 31-33), their power should not be dismissed. Like working-class witnesses before parliamentary committees and royal commissions, these workers offer testimony, but the oath they take is based, not on allegiance to a divinity, but on their continually demonstrated sense of their own integrity. Like the insistence of these texts on their referentiality, the emphasis that they place on acts of individual testimony recaptures as it redefines some of the qualities of "classic realist" autobiography.

As Carlyle's rhetorical strategies in *Past and Present* suggest, middle- and upper-class writers and professionals were not at all hesitant about presenting their versions of working-class experience and creating imaginary working-class characters to speak of that experience. In this volume are included passages from works

---

1 Vincent treats the *Dundee Factory Boy* as one of the "genuine" autobiographies he studies in *Bread, Knowledge, and Freedom* (2), citing it in particular as an authority on the material conditions of working-class life (69-70); and the definitive bibliography of working-class autobiographies lists it as "edited by J. Myles," although the entry also speculates that "it is likely that the volume was written by Myles, basing it on material told to him by a factory worker, possibly Frank Forrest" (Burnett, Vincent, and Mayall 64-65). Kiernan treats Myles's work as simple fact (Engels, "Introduction" 20). For the use of the *Dundee Factory Boy* as historical evidence, see also Whatley 70-72. Eakin comments on the problems involved in making readers' responses the test of autobiography (*Touching*, 29-30).

that demonstrate how frequently writers such as Harriet Martineau, Charlotte Elizabeth Tonna, Michael Sadler, and Elizabeth Barrett Browning felt justified in presenting "A Voice from the Factories," as Caroline Norton called a poem also reprinted here (see Appendices F and G).[1] Such acts of imaginative sympathy with working-class suffering were and remain powerfully effective. The former child-laborer Charles Shaw, for instance, looked back on Barrett Browning's "The Cry of the Children" as "a sort of poetic autobiography" that he and "many other children" had uttered "in heart-piercing accents" and "bitter tears" (15). Yet the four factory lives reprinted here demonstrate that workers could tell their own stories, not in cries and tears, but in words; and as they did so, they revealed that there was neither a single, essential nineteenth-century worker's voice to be heard nor a single way in which workers should be expected to speak. Significantly, even Ellen Johnston's brief autobiography, which seems in some of its goals to differ markedly from the stories of Blincoe and Dodd and Forrest, makes this point. She recounts having given sworn testimony in a court of law on the specific facts of one episode in her life as a factory girl. Like the workers who had come before her, including Charles Aberdeen addressing the 1833 commission, Johnston demonstrated her authority as an expert on the conditions of her labor. As the writer of her own life story, she encourages her readers, as if they were observers in a courtroom, to take her word for its validity; and specifically in the case of the abuses that she suffered earlier as a child, she, like Blincoe and Dodd, asks directly for such credence.

III. Working-Class Testimony and Factory Legislation

In 1833 when a procession of children, all young factory workers, paraded the streets of Manchester with banners calling for "Manufactures without child-slaying" (Kydd 2: 42), they were making manifest the concern about child labor that initiated the factory movement in the early decades of the nineteenth century. A prominent reformer angrily noted, also in 1833, that Britain's industrial prowess seemed to depend on the work done by "30,000 little girls in Lancashire" (qtd. Ward 106). Providing embodied evidence of the effects of long hours of labor, therefore, became a central form of working-class protest against the

---

1   For further examples of such largely middle-class Victorian commentary, see Bradshaw and Ozment.

factory system. On one occasion "some 3,000 ragged and grimy children" marched to a Leeds hotel in which members of the 1833 royal commission on factory labor were staying and treated them to choruses of the "Song of the Factory Children":

> We will have the Ten Hours Bill,
>   That we will, that we will;
> Or the land shall ne'er be still,
>   Ne'er be still, ne'er be still;
> Parliament say what they will,
>   WE WILL HAVE THE TEN HOURS BILL.
>
> (qtd. Driver 229-30)

The parade of Manchester children who used their banners to call for an end to industrial murders also presented a written memorial to the commissioners, challenging them to use their eyes to see the evidence inscribed on the marchers' bodies: "Indeed, we tell you no lies, when, we say that our bodies are wasted, and our strength sinking, under our daily tasks.... Look at us, and say if it is possible that we can be disbelieved!" "Factory-made cripples" offered "ocular corroboration" of spoken and written claims about the evils of the factory system (Kydd 2: 43). At issue then, as it was later when Ashley described Dodd's deformed body to the members of the House of Commons in 1844, was the testimony offered by physical bodies on the harsh physical conditions of factory labor; and during the decades when the advantages and disadvantages of factory legislation were being contested, working-class autobiographies often presented themselves as verbal equivalents of such bodily evidence.

As the concept of a "factory system" suggests, no single issue in the debate over its future could be divorced from the others raised by it. Opponents of legislative reform repeatedly argued that one part of the system could not be regulated without disastrously affecting another. As a doctor writing in the early 1830s explained, "every part of the system appears necessary to the preservation of the whole" (Kay 59). According to such reasoning, the hours that children worked could not be limited without decreasing the hours of adults since younger workers were required to assist adults and to clean machinery. "The child was actually part of [the] machine," said one factory owner (qtd. Ward 171). Workers' wages would fall if their hours were cut. The time-honored status of the adult, male Briton as a "free agent" would be endangered by the passage of factory legislation. British manufacturers would then face unfair competition from unregulated foreign producers. Similarly, proponents of reform stressed the interlinked advantages of factory legislation. Humane masters, limited in their ability to alter conditions in their mills by fear of competition from less scrupulous owners, would finally be free to improve the lot of their workers. The reduction of women's and children's hours, resulting from a humanitarian concern for their welfare, would yield a healthier, more efficient workforce. Moral benefits would result from allowing factory operatives time for education and domestic life. Limiting hours for all workers—a goal that could be achieved only by legislating the number of hours during which factory engines were allowed to be kept running—would reduce unemployment by spreading the work more evenly, actually increasing wages by increasing productivity. An adult, male worker might then be able to earn what was called a "breadwinner's wage," a weekly income large enough to support the needs of an entire family. These issues were, in turn, related to the other questions that Carlyle defined as central to the "condition of England"—democracy, poverty, free trade, sanitation, urbanization. Linked together as they were, all these factors created complicated alliances and loyalties (Henriques 73-74; Hunt 212-13; cf. Gray 7-8): radical workers aligned themselves with ultra-conservative Tories; Benthamite progressives, with industrial magnates.

The story of factory reform is, therefore, long and complicated. In telling it to introduce the texts reprinted in this volume, I highlight only the major acts passed from the beginning of the century through the 1860s and describe only their major provisions. Moreover, since the questions related to hours and inspection—how long should the standard working day be? how can government oversee the conditions of factory labor?—predominate in these texts, I do not focus on other problems such as the need to educate factory children and the dangers posed by unenclosed machinery. Even within these limits, however, it is possible to present a remarkably comprehensive survey of factory legislation by paying attention to the polemical purposes served by the accounts of Blincoe, Dodd, Forrest, and Johnston—a goal that could not be achieved if one were dealing with the now better-known genre of Victorian industrial novels, which includes such works as Elizabeth Gaskell's *Mary Barton* (1848) and Charles Dickens's *Hard Times* (1854). The story of legislative reform that emerges from these four factory lives is, in some ways, unlike that told in many conventional histories, which continue to emphasize the role of middle-class and aristocratic reformers.[1] Also in contrast to most stories of nineteenth-century industrialization, the account offered here does not view the passage of factory legislation as a necessarily progressive development that ended triumphantly before the Victorian mid-century. Most important, it places workers at the center of the story, not on its peripheries.

To follow this story one must understand at the outset that the long-sought-after and often limited achievements of factory legislation were not the product of a fully developed modern state with efficient methods of inspection and control. A bill's having become law did not mean that its provisions would be honored. The need to regulate the factory system was, rather, one of the major reasons why state bureaucracies developed over the course of the nineteenth century. Gauging the import of the issues central to the factory movement also requires a certain amount of historical imagination. The question in the mid-1830s, for instance, was whether twelve-year-olds were adults capable of working a sixty-nine-hour week (Driver 321). When workers organized their short-time committees, the "short" day for which they were agitating was one ten-hours long, a day to be worked from Monday through Friday and to be followed by an eight-hour day on Saturday, which was called a "half-holiday." Conditions that we would consider simply beyond the physical endurance of young children were exactly those that the reform-

---

1 On the ideological uses that such histories serve, see Cunningham, ch. 2. For typical narratives of the efforts of great men, see Kydd's early history and the two accounts of early legislation offered by Thomas and Ward. Correctives to such a view include: Driver; Gray; Kirby and Musson (ch. 1 and 10); Cunningham 11-12. One of the most effective, brief accounts of the legislation up to 1864 is offered by Marx in the chapter "The Working Day" in the first volume of *Capital* (389-411). Marx sees such legislation as epitomizing "the spirit of capital" and the limitation of workers' hours as simply a way of keeping the capitalist economy in good working order (390, 348). Cf. Engels in the 1892 preface to the English edition of *The Condition of the Working Class in England* (36). Interestingly, the texts in this volume do not generally touch upon the other major historical developments to which factory legislation was linked, the New Poor Law and the Corn Laws and Chartism; for those connections, see Driver, ch. 22 and 29; Ward, ch. 7, 8, and 12. Yet, as Haywood claims of popular accounts of needlewomen (6), these stories are earlier and often more comprehensive accounts than those offered by middle-class commentators.

ers were trying to have mandated for them. As narratives responding to and often proposing to influence the passage of such legislation, the stories of the four factory workers in this volume mark the chief milestones on the way to only relatively effective control of the conditions of factory life, a journey that was far from completed by the 1860s.

Robert Blincoe and the Early Factory Acts

The first narrative in this volume, the story of Robert Blincoe's life as recorded by the working-class journalist John Brown, was published twice in 1828 and reprinted in 1832 (see Note on the Text). As one of many works testifying during those years to the sufferings of the individuals, particularly the children, who worked in factories, *A Memoir of Robert Blincoe* responded more directly than most of these writings to the shortcomings of early attempts to improve the conditions of factory children, and it called explicitly for more effective legislation in the future. According to the account that Brown drafted in 1822 and confirmed and expanded in 1824, Blincoe began working in a mill near Nottingham in 1799 when he was about seven years old. An orphan who had been raised in the St. Pancras workhouse near London, Blincoe, along with as many as eighty other children, had been shipped north to work as an apprentice in a cotton factory called Lowdham Mill.

The practice of sending orphaned or poor children to work in such a remote location developed as a response to the severe shortages of labor in the first large, water-powered cotton mills built during the last decades of the eighteenth century in isolated rural settings in the north of England. Parish officials in the more populous sections of the country, who were responsible for the care of destitute children, readily agreed when factory owners proposed to use such children as a source of extremely cheap labor, and the story of a particular parish that bargained to send "one *idiot*" for "every *twenty sound* children" was often recounted as a way of conveying the cynicism that motivated this practice (Fielden 12). In calling these typically very young workers "apprentices," both parish officials and mill owners were claiming to participate in the time-honored system of apprenticeship, which for centuries had customarily required that an apprentice's family pay a master craftsman a fee, often amounting to hundreds of pounds in the richer trades, for the youth's training in skills that would lead to a livelihood. In this new form of industrial apprenticeship, however, parish officials paid small fees, often as little as £1.1s for the "disposal" of children to manufacturers who had no intention of teaching them a trade (Chapman 172; Brown 103). Sometimes, according to an early history of the factory system, the exchange of money was actually reversed, and factory masters became the "buyers of pauper children" through the middlemen who had transported them north (Kydd 1: 17). In place of the usual term of seven years, Blincoe was indentured to serve a fourteen-year apprenticeship without any of the traditional safeguards against a master's irresponsibility or abuse.

Even as one of these so-called apprentices, however, Blincoe should have found some form of protection early in his time at Lowdham Mill because Parliament in 1802 passed the first bill to regulate labor in factories, the Health and Morals of Apprentices Act. This measure was largely the work of the elder Sir Robert Peel, who was horrified by the conditions of the almost one thousand apprenticed children working in his mills (Thomas 9). Although its provisions for health pertained to all those working in textile mills employing twenty or more operatives, its clauses regulating the hours of labor affected only apprentices, limiting their days to twelve hours and prohibiting by 1804 any work at night, defined as the time between 9 p.m. and 6 a.m. (Thomas 10, n29; Ward 19). The act did nothing to exclude very young children from factory labor, but Blincoe's account of his days at Lowdham Mill suggests why even this measure might have seemed progressive. In his first years there the children typically worked fourteen hours a day, six days a week, and sometimes as long as fifteen or sixteen hours when they were needed to clean the machinery or when they were required to make up for "lost time" if the supply of water power had been interrupted (117). Brown offers a contradictory account of the effect of the passage of this act on the conditions at Lowdham Mill. Yet he is certain that one of the primary measures of the act, the one requiring that a copy of it be posted where workers could see it, had been evaded: Brown explains that Blincoe did not learn about the enactment of the bill until eleven or twelve years after the event (125). The Act of 1802 was, as Brown says twice, "all but a dead-letter!" (131, 135), unenforced and unenforceable—a point amply proved by the account of Blincoe's work at the next factory in which he was employed.

By the time Blincoe was telling his story to Brown in the 1820s, a second factory bill had passed, and it, like the first, had quickly become "a dead-letter!" The Regulation of Cotton Mills and Factories Act of 1819 improved over the earlier act by applying its measures to all children between the ages of nine and fifteen working in cotton mills—paupers and "free children" alike—and by prohibiting the employment of anyone younger than nine, though it essentially repeated the limitations of the 1802 Act by allowing a seventy-two hour week with a twelve-hour day between 5 a.m. and 9 p.m. (Thomas 22, 25-26; Ward 27). In one respect at least, this act was even weaker than the previous one since it contained no provisions at all for the independent inspection of factories. Brown attributes the shortcomings of this act to the biases of those who were asked to testify before the parliamentary committee charged with exploring the need for its passage. At the end of the first chapter of the *Memoir*, Brown refers to "the testimony given by the owners of cotton-factories, or by professional men on their behalf" (98), one of whom was a physician who "could not be drawn to admit that 23 hours' labour would necessarily be harmful" to a child operative (Ward 25). Brown contrasts the misrepresentations that he finds characteristic of such testimony to the "evidence wholly incontrovertible" offered by Blincoe's narrative.[1] Brown argues that Blincoe should have been a witness before the committee of 1819, where he would have been "the most impressive pleader in behalf of destitute and deserted children" (99). Such an appearance would have been both unlikely and risky. The 1816 committee had heard from no workers at all (Thomas 20); the one in 1819, from very few, and those who did appear were apparently fired and blacklisted by their masters (Ward 27). For Brown and presumably for Blincoe, the worker's role as representative of his own interests and experiences was very much the central issue, and the *Memoir* offered the kind of direct testimony that the members of Parliament had failed to consider in 1816.

That situation, however, was changing. As if in direct answer to Brown's dissatisfaction with previous investigations, Blincoe was among the former child laborers who were called, like Charles Aberdeen, to testify before the royal commission of 1833.

---

1   Brown 98. The reliability and relevance of Blincoe's account have been debated by twentieth-century historians: for overviews and positions on this controversy, see Chapman 199-209; Musson; Rule 147-49. The extreme cruelties that Blincoe describes might cast doubt on his claims, yet the propensity of those who abuse or oppress others to treat their victims as if they were not human beings capable of feeling pain could be used to argue for the plausibility of Blincoe's account.

Now described as "a small Manufacturer," Blincoe provided sworn testimony that appeared in the text of the commission report published in the *Parliamentary Papers* of 1833 (see Appendix A.3).[1] The record of Blincoe's responses proves not only a worker's ability to witness to what he has experienced, as I argue above, but also the power of his body to provide evidence of his sufferings. He was one of what Friedrich Engels memorably characterized as the "crowd of cripples" interviewed by agents of the commission (173). When the physician in charge of the questioning asked Blincoe why he had stopped working in cotton mills after almost twenty years there, he pointed to his limbs: "I got deformed there [in the mills]; my knees began to bend in when I was fifteen; you see how they are (*showing them*)." Like the children of Manchester and Leeds parading before the 1833 commissioners, Blincoe displayed his childhood injuries as visible proof of his testimony.

During the campaigns for factory legislation in 1832 and 1833, Blincoe's body continued to serve as frequent witness for the need for reform. When John Doherty, the Chartist publisher and union organizer, republished Blincoe's memoir in 1832 shortly after Sadler introduced his ten-hours bill, Doherty prepared the way for it by printing in his new journal, *The Poor Man's Advocate*, a drawing of Blincoe's deformed body (see Note on the Text). That image gained further visibility later in the year. When Sadler and Richard Oastler, the Tory-Radical reformer who worked closely with the short-time committees composed of workers, prepared to visit the industrial north to garner support for Sadler's measure, Doherty encouraged his Manchester colleagues to turn out in force to receive them. Depictions of Blincoe's body participated in the ensuing demonstration: Sadler and Oastler were "escorted by a large procession, carrying banners on which Blincoe was pictured, to a meeting on Camp Field, attended by crowds estimated at between eight and twenty thousand" (Kirby and Musson 376-77). Like the deformed workers who displayed themselves by mounting the platforms at meetings of those calling for reform, images of Blincoe's body offered physical evidence of the claims of his *Memoir*.

The *Memoir* itself seems to have had even wider and longer-lasting currency than such visual depictions. In the response to the next-to-the-last question put to him during his testimony

---

1 *Parliamentary Papers* 21 (1833): D.3: 17-18 [145-46]. See also Musson 198.

before the commission of 1833, Blincoe described the cruelties to which he and his fellow apprentices were subjected, adding, "I have a book written about these things, describing my own life and sufferings. I will send it to you." As the footnote to this statement reveals, a copy of the *Memoir* was duly included by the commission's examiner in his report and was therefore made available "for the inspection of [the three members of] the Central Board" (Appendix A.3). In other venues Brown's *Memoir* was judged to be an effective weapon in the battle for factory reform. In 1836 Fielden cited it prominently at the beginning of *The Curse of the Factory System* (see Appendix G.3). Oastler added a copy of Blincoe's story to his carefully gathered library of materials on factory life; and it may have been among the "pamphlets and scrapbooks" that Oastler loaned Frances Trollope as she was collecting evidence for her novel dealing with factory labor, *Michael Armstrong* (see Appendices F.4 and G.5).[1] In the 1850s the *Memoir* was still the focus of attention, serving as the account of apprenticed factory labor that Geraldine Jewsbury contradicted in the first three chapters of *Marian Withers* (1851; Kestner 152) and appearing as a "well-attested" story of factory sufferings in Kydd's *The History of the Factory Movement* of 1857 (1: 22).

The legislation that was passed at least in part as a result of working-class testimony such as Blincoe's—the 1833 Act to Regulate the Labour of Children and Young Persons in the Mills and Factories of the United Kingdom—was not the ten-hours measure for all workers under eighteen that both Sadler and the operatives had hoped it would be. Influenced by the Benthamite members of the royal commission, the act did, however, include several important advances over previous measures. It appointed for the first time four factory inspectors, gave them powers equivalent to those of local magistrates, and required the inspectors to report twice a year on their efforts to enforce the law. Factories producing wool, linen, worsted, flax, tow, silk, and hemp, as well as cotton, were now encompassed by the legislation. Within thirty months of enactment, it would limit the time worked by children between the ages of nine and twelve, except those in silk factories, to nine hours a day or forty-eight hours a week; no one

---

1 Driver 568, 140-41, 404. Trollope also met and dined with John Doherty, who, as the second publisher of Brown's *Memoir*, might have provided her with it (Chaloner, "Mrs. Trollope" 161, 164). On the relation between Blincoe's life and Trollope's novel, see also Kovačević 99-100; Kestner 52-54.

under eighteen would work at night from 8:30 p.m. to 5:30 a.m. or longer than twelve hours a day, sixty-nine hours a week (Thomas 65-70; Ward 110). The act also required certificates proving the ages and therefore the eligibility of children employed in factory labor. Because most factories were now powered by steam engines and could therefore be located in more populous areas of the industrial north—near the end of the decade, 80 per cent of the mills were steam-driven (Mathias 121)—it might also have seemed that control over them, unlike the water-powered factories in which Blincoe had first worked, could be more easily achieved.

Despite such changed circumstances and the provisions for inspection, however, the Act of 1833 proved to be as unenforceable as earlier measures had been. Faced with the choice of limiting the work of adults to the shorter hours now mandated for children under thirteen years of age, factory owners decided either to fire the youngest children working for them or to use them in "relays" spread over the fifteen-hour day—half the children starting early in the day, the other half working late into the night. The relay system was so complicated that it was impossible for the inspectors to gauge whether children so employed were being overworked. At one point the inspectors themselves advised that the law ought to be amended and the minimum age lowered to eight (Thomas 86). Moreover, magistrates refused to convict factory owners charged with breaking the law. The inspector employed to oversee the largest district, which included Yorkshire and Lancashire, had no more than two staff members to help him investigate the working conditions of over 250,000 operatives in approximately 2,700 mills (Thomas 98). The measure for whose passage Blincoe's sufferings had witnessed met the same fate as the Acts of 1802 and 1819: it was, in most of its provisions, a "dead-letter."

William Dodd and the Ten-Hours Movement

Like Blincoe's, Dodd's *Narrative* was written to detail and therefore to expose the effects of factory work on young children employed in the textile industry in the early years of the nineteenth century. Like John Brown speaking of Blincoe, Dodd, who had worked in a woolen mill since the age of six, used the term *sufferings* as the most cogent summary of his long experience of factory life. Whether Dodd knew Blincoe's *Memoir* in 1841 when he published his *Narrative* is unclear. By 1847, however, when he published *The Laboring Classes of England* in the United States, Dodd was recounting Blincoe's story as that of a worker whom "we will call CHARLES SMITH," a story that the author claimed to have learned about from a "parcel of documents" that "Smith" had given him (65). At one point in the *Narrative*, Dodd comments directly on the workings of the 1833 Act with which Blincoe's *Memoir* had become associated. As a timekeeper in a mill in 1834, when the age requirements of the act were being implemented, Dodd had as his unpleasant duty the task of bringing children to be certified as eligible to work: he had "great difficulty in convincing the doctor" that the "little stunted figures" of the children, "some of whom had been working in the factories for years," were at that time old enough to do so (204). (Before 1837 births were not required to be registered; only in the 1840s, therefore, were there available official records to prove that a child had reached the age of eligibility for work in textile factories.)

Like Brown, Dodd refers to the improvements gained by earlier laws as a way of arguing for further regulation. He invokes a theme characteristic of much Victorian social criticism—the contrast between past and present—but unlike writers such as Thomas Carlyle, Dodd uses it to praise the reformed conditions of the present in contrast to the evils of the past. He explains that children "now, owing to the introduction of some wise laws for the regulation of factories," cannot begin work before the age of nine. He elaborates, "They now enjoy many privileges that we had not, such as attending schools, limited hours of labour, &c.; but still it [the factory] is far from being a desirable place for a child" (192). Here Dodd suggests that child labor be, not limited, but prohibited. Before such a utopian regulation could be attained, however, if it could ever be attained, limiting the hours when factories operated and therefore the hours that all workers were required to labor was the first priority, and it was as a contribution to the struggle for a ten-hour day that Dodd's *Narrative* received prominence in the 1844 debate between Ashley and Bright.

By dedicating the *Narrative* to Lord Ashley and addressing it to him as a "means of assisting the strenuous exertions your Lordship is making on behalf of that oppressed class of workpeople to which I belong" (185), Dodd was directly identifying his story as testimony to be considered in support of the ten-hours movement, with which by the 1840s Lord Ashley's name had become synonymous. Early in this decade he employed

Dodd to gather information on conditions in the industrial north; and Dodd had published first his *Narrative*, which was dedicated to Ashley, followed by reports addressed to his noble patron, which appeared as *The Factory System Illustrated; in a Series of Letters to the Right Hon. Lord Ashley, M. P., Etc. Etc.* (1842). In *The Laboring Classes of England*, Dodd states that he received a weekly wage from Ashley as well as letters of praise from him for work done in 1841 and 1842 (see Appendix B.2); and Dodd seems as well to have had financial support from John Fielden, a prominent factory-owner and member of Parliament who supported the ten-hours movement and later led it when Ashley was not in the House of Commons (Ward 221). Dodd also collaborated with other leaders of the movement, whose goal was a shortened day for all workers, male and female, young and old,[1] and he was a "regular" visitor of Richard Oastler when that reformer was imprisoned for debt (Ward 219). Not surprisingly, then, Ashley frequently used Dodd's work to publicize the ten-hours cause. In the fall of 1841, Ashley sent a copy of the *Narrative* to a "new ally in the Factory cause." In December 1841, Ashley was referring to Dodd as his "jewel": "Every day brings fresh stories of suffering and oppression from the factory districts. My poor cripple Dodd is a jewel, his talent and skill are unequalled; he sends me invaluable evidence" (Hodder 1: 362-63, 384).

At the beginning of the debate on March 15, 1844, when Bright and Ashley crossed swords over the credibility of Dodd's writings, Ashley had moved his potentially historic ten-hours amendment. He had spoken for over two hours, delivering a speech of great passion and eloquence. Championing the rights of children and women not to be abused by a system that required of them extraordinarily long hours in often miserable working conditions, he had concluded with words that would become famous in the history of factory legislation: "We ask but a slight relaxation of toil, a time to live, and a time to die; a time for those comforts that sweeten life, and a time for those duties that adorn it; and, therefore, with a fervent prayer to Almighty God that it may please him to turn the hearts of all who hear me to thoughts of justice and of mercy, I now finally commit the issue to the judgment and humanity of Parliament" (Appendix

---

1   Driver 83, 249; Hunt 214; Ward 101, 396-97; Cunningham 10; Gray 8, 37. Such leaders were often accused of using the cause of the more vulnerable workers, children in particular, to achieve shorter hours for adult, male operatives. For a rebuttal of this argument, see E.P. Thompson 339.

B.1, 339). Adapting the well-known passage from *Ecclesiastes* delineating the timeliness of various human activities—"To every thing there is a season ... a time to be born, and a time to die" (3: 1-2)—Ashley asked simply that workers be given time, time to rest from their labors.

Dodd's *Narrative* supports this cause, not only in its dedication to Lord Ashley, but also in the lessons to be drawn from the story it tells. When Dodd refers to the shorter hours "now" worked by children, he continues, "Formerly, it was nothing but work till we could work no longer" (192). His narrative is even more impressive than Blincoe's story in the evocation of the concrete, material reality of factory life—the physical pain of swollen, chapped hands; the stink of the animal fats used to lubricate machines—but overriding all such details is the question of hours. Dodd thanks at length the master who voluntarily shortened his day by one hour so that the young, ambitious worker could spend that time studying during "every evening for a whole winter" (198). This instance of charity on his master's part argues for legislating a shorter day so that children serving less kindly masters could do the same.[1] When Dodd looks to the question of his wages, he does so by evaluating them in terms of the hours that they cost him: "When we were busy, I have worked as many as 18 hours per day; and yet all I have received, whether as wages, over-time, perquisites, &c., does not [in over twenty-five years of work] amount ... to more than 550*l.*; and for this paltry sum I have sacrificed my health, strength, constitution, nay, almost life itself" (207). The chart that he provides to reveal the insufficiency of his wages covers not just his young years, but his working life up to the age of thirty-two (206). The "sacrifice" that he made for his earnings was one, therefore, that he continued to offer up to the factory system when he was an adult, and it was a sacrifice, according to Dodd, that no child or adult ought to be forced to make. Like Brown introducing Blincoe's story (93), Dodd concludes that it would have been better for him to have suffered infanticide than to have been the victim of the factory system (221).

As telling as Dodd's commentary on his own experience may

---

1   Interestingly, in *The Laboring Classes of England* Dodd is less convinced than he is in the *Narrative* that a ten-hour day is the solution to workers' problems (139-43), and he therefore tells this story differently in the later text, claiming that his kind master gave him a weekly stipend for the purchase of books (18). This account appears in Letter II, "Incidents in the Life of the Author," which casts Dodd's story in the third person under the self-confessed pseudonym of James Graham.

be, however, Ashley's earlier confidence in Dodd seems to have wavered by the night in March of 1844 when Bright questioned the worker's credibility. During his contest with Ashley, Bright produced his most damaging evidence against Dodd by reading to members of the House from letters in which Dodd seemed to be offering to sell his services to a manufacturer, claiming that he had supplied Ashley with information only because he had been paid by Ashley to do so. In one of the letters Dodd confessed that he was "almost ashamed of" his "book," though he did not specify which one he was ready to disavow, the *Narrative* or *The Factory System Illustrated*. Similarly, Lord Ashley was moved to admit to his parliamentary audience that he now found Dodd "unworthy my kindness," though he did so in a voice so "very subdued" that the *Times* could not report with certainty what he had said ("Committee" 5). Who won the contest over William Dodd's credibility— whether it was "the hon. Member for Durham" or "the noble Lord, the Member for Dorset"— remains a matter of debate.[1] (To

1 Bright declared himself the winner, "I got the better of [Ashley] by universal admission of the House" (qtd. Trevelyan 157). Bright's biographer, G.M. Trevelyan, concludes, "The incident, in fact, reflected discredit on neither party" (157). For a full account of the episode from the manufacturers' point of view, see Boyson 178-83. Ashley's loss of faith in Dodd is reflected in a diary entry of March 16, 1844, in which his former employer calls Dodd "a fiend in the form of [a] man" (qtd. Boyson 181). Hodder, Ashley's official biographer, not surprisingly, awards victory to Ashley, even including a retraction by Bright—"I readily withdraw any offensive expressions" (2: 28)—that does not appear in *Hansard's Parliamentary Debates* (1154), although it is also recorded by a working-class writer (Grant 79; cf. Ward 287) and by the *Times* ("Committee" 5). In the two leaders or editorials in the *Times* devoted to Ashley's speech, there is no reference to Dodd except indirectly in the account of the "good deal of agitation" with which Ashley "rebutted" the "personalities against himself" that Bright had raised in his speech (March 16, 1844: 6) and in the unspecified rejection of Dodd through the assertion that Ashley had "been conscientiously and nervously careful not to be misled by partial or hasty informants" (March 19, 1844: 5). Later in 1844, Cooke Taylor used Dodd's story as it emerged from this parliamentary debate to discredit the "unfair arts" used by those opposed to the factory system (71-72; cf. Chaloner, "Introduction," xii-xiii). Dodd still seems to provide himself as a ready object of polemical use. In an edition of Dodd's *The Factory System Illustrated* and his *Narrative*, Chaloner misrepresents Dodd's presentation of himself as a worker in the woolen industry in an attempt to discredit him (v) and reprints without commentary much of Ashley and Bright's parliamentary debate.

examine the materials involved in this question, see Appendix B.1, which reprints the parliamentary exchange between Ashley and Bright, including the footnotes that transcribe Dodd's letters.) For a tantalizingly brief moment, however, it seemed that Ashley had achieved the long-sought-after goal of the ten-hours movement: three days after the contest with Bright, Ashley's amendment was approved, only to be reversed by a vote taken four days later (Ward 287-91).

Whether the example of Dodd's sufferings or the image of his deformed body as it was conjured up by Ashley during the debate actually helped or hindered the ten-hours cause is also unclear. That the two men shared the same goal is, however, beyond dispute. From that perspective it is possible to read the concluding words of Dodd's *Narrative* as more than a conventional statement of early-Victorian religious piety. When Dodd addresses his "fellow sufferers," he asks them to look to the Scriptures for the "only source of happiness that is left us," acceptance of their lot and admiration for God's power: "Let us look abroad and examine the works of our Creator, and we shall soon learn to admire his wisdom, and tremble at his power. We shall learn to despise the riches and pageantry of this perishing scene of things, and fix our hopes on those which are perma[n]ent and worth our care—to tread with patience the rugged paths of virtue, which will at length conduct us to the happy mansions of eternal repose" (222). Such a fervent hope in the peace of the afterlife might be read, in Karl Marx's terms, as an example of religion providing the masses with a powerful opiate. From the perspective of the ten-hours movement, however, and in light of Ashley's plea for "time" for the worker—time for comfort, time for duty, "a slight relaxation of toil"—Dodd's image of heavenly "mansions of eternal repose," in contrast to earthly factories of unceasing labor, might seem quite poignant.

Dodd and the Dundee Factory Boy: Gender and the "Normal Day"

The Act of 1844, the Act to Amend the Laws Relating to Labour in Factories, resulted from the parliamentary debates that included the contest between Ashley and Bright. Although it did not mandate a ten-hour day for factory workers, it was historic as the first attempt to deal with an issue about which Dodd is passionate: the effect of factory labor on women, young and old. When Dodd looked around him for a wife, he noted that the idea of wedding a female operative was out of the question:

... to have married a factory girl, would only have involved both myself and her in greater troubles, I being a cripple; and it would have been something remarkable, if I could have met with one able to make a shirt. How could it be expected from those who had been so wretchedly treated?—who were sent into this world to be the comfort and solace of man, and who, had their faculties been allowed to develope under a more genial sun, might have been the pride and ornament of the age in which they lived. But how different is the sad reality! They have been kept as slaves at one toilsome task, till every fine feeling of their nature is blunted. Ignorant of everything calculated to elevate and raise them to that high station originally intended for them by their Creator, is it to be wondered at, if we find them sunk, degraded, and almost lost to every sense of shame? (201)

Contrasting a woman's providentially ordained role as a man's helpmate to the reality of the moral degradation of factory girls had been a favored tactic of factory reformers since the 1820s and '30s (Kirby and Musson 399), and the focus on women's factory labor had intensified in the early 1840s.[1] Parliamentary testimony and journalistic accounts during that decade repeatedly describe, for instance, the factory women who were forced to drug their infants with the opiate called Godfrey's Cordial so that parents and older siblings could go off to work (Engels 134-35, 166). If young male workers like Dodd needed time to learn to read and write—or so the argument went—young female workers needed time to learn how to sew shirts and cook, while older female workers, especially married women, needed time to provide cleanly and inviting households for their men.

Central to concern over women's conflicting duties as factory workers and housekeepers was the related problem of the "breadwinner's wage," an issue that involved increasingly rigid definitions of gender roles (Clark, ch. 11, 266-68). In 1844 an Anglican priest memorably declared, "The business of woman, is to make home comfortable and happy for man, after he has earned sufficient for the support of his family" (qtd. Kydd 2: 214). Each of the two parts of this equation depends on the other: men need

---

1 For contemporary responses, see Cooke Taylor, ch. 5; Kay 11, 42-43; Engels 169-70; Gaskell, ch. 4. For commentaries on this issue, see Cruickshank 58-61, 66-67, 82; Gray 35-37; Ward 235; Gallagher, ch. 5 and 6; Clark; S. Rose.

the domestic comfort that women can offer, but women can provide it only if their men can provide for them. Particularly galling to both workers and reformers were stories of unemployed men living off the wages of their wives and children, men who were able to contribute to the family's survival only by carrying their exhausted children to and from the mills. Commenting on the story of a male worker who had wept when he was discovered mending his wife's stockings while she was working in the mill, Engels asked, "Can anyone imagine a more insane state of things" than "this condition, which unsexes the man and takes from the woman all womanliness?" (168). Ashley's speech in support of his ten-hours amendment in 1844 deplored the gender reversals characteristic of industrial labor. He described in detail the ways in which factory girls "perform the labour [and] occupy the places of men"; such women actually behaved as if they were men by joining clubs "to drink, sing, and smoke" (1096; see Appendix B.1). Ashley was so impassioned on this point that one of his opponents rightly accused him of wanting to exclude all women from all factory work.

As Ashley's failed ten-hours amendment of 1844 had proposed, the 1844 Act did for the first time define women as a group of "protected persons," though it protected them far less effectively than Ashley had hoped it would. Like "young persons" between the ages of thirteen and seventeen, female workers were to put in twelve hours a day, a sixty-nine hour week. The act also contained important measures dealing with children—those from eight to thirteen (a lowering of the earlier age requirement) would work six and a half or seven hours a day for the entire week or ten hours three days a week; and the system of age certification was improved (Thomas 209-13; Ward 300)—but the major innovation involved adult female labor. Whether this measure actually improved the lot of women working in the textile industries is a genuine question. The loss of wages that shorter hours might involve could have been outweighed by other gains, increases in comfort and economy that would be obvious to all members of the families in which women were responsible for work both inside and outside the home. Yet the impetus to limit women's hours had also resulted from the openly stated goals of securing the breadwinner's wage for men and of preventing women from taking over the kinds of relatively well-paid work that men customarily did in the mills. The long-term effect of defining women's status as the same as that of young persons, therefore, may not have been entirely beneficial. According to

Robert Gray, women were "rendered ... all but invisible" in sub-sequent legislation (217), and the economic dependency of working-class women may actually have been increased by the passage of such apparently well-intentioned measures.[1]

Three years later the Act to Limit the Hours of Labour of Young Persons and Females in Factories of 1847 confirmed the definition of women as "protected persons." More important, it also, at first, seemed to provide a triumphant conclusion to the long struggle to decrease the length of the working day. Immediately in 1847, young persons and women were to be limited to eleven hours a day in a sixty-three hour week; in 1848 that limitation would finally be reduced to ten hours a day in a fifty-eight-hour week (Thomas 295-96; Ward 346). Because it was impossible to keep the engines of factories running for more hours than women and young persons could work, so dependent were male workers on their assistance, the ten-hour day seemed to be within everyone's grasp. Workers had organized mass gatherings, speeches, and processions to encourage the passage of such a bill (Gray 23; Ward, ch. 13). Now they celebrated in earnest, participating in what one historian called a "frenzy of rejoicing; festivities were held on an unheard-of scale; Ashley and Fielden [sponsor of the 1847 bill during Ashley's absence from Parliament] were fêted wherever they went. Broadsheets, elaborately and expensively printed in black and gold, setting out the terms of the new Act and commemorating the leaders of the struggle, were widely distributed" (Thomas 297). Workers repeatedly praised the Lord, along with Ashley and Oastler and Fielden, for their delivery from servitude. Ashley wrote the short-time committees, "giv[ing] most humble and hearty thanks to Almighty God for the unexpected and wonderful success that has attended our efforts" (Hodder 2: 195). His use of the pronoun *our* may have been as inclusive as it was justified: in the long campaign, Ashley and reformers like Oastler and Fielden had cooperated with and depended upon the efforts of the factory operatives whom such legal restrictions had been meant to aid.

In the same spirit of celebration, James Myles dedicated to Richard Oastler his fictional *Chapters in the Life of a Dundee Factory Boy*. It was probably in a similar spirit that Oastler gave a copy of this book in May of 1850 to Samuel Kydd, the working-class writer who would go on to publish a history of the factory

---

1 Davidoff 2: 97. An earlier account, however, praises the 1844 act precisely because it recognized women as workers (Pinchbeck 201).

movement in 1857.[1] The second of Myles's *Chapters*, titled in part "The Long Hour System contrasted with the Short Hour System," concludes with praise for "the beneficent reign of the Ten Hours' Bill" (242), and it treats the contrast between past and present in terms of the related issues of hours and wages. Although opponents of the legislation frequently warned that a shorter day would involve disastrous consequences for workers because they would necessarily be paid less than they had been when they had put in longer hours, the narrator claims that boys' "wages are as good under the Ten Hours' Act as they were under the Twelve Hours' Act" (240). The wages that had fallen, those of female spinners, had done so, not because of their shorter hours, but because of the increased number of available workers "greatly aggravated by the immense influx of Irish women during the last twenty years" (241)—an opinion about the ill effects of Irish immigration that he apparently shared with many English and Scottish workers (Hunt 167-69; Kay 52). The narrator, who views the unreformed mills as "huge instruments of demoralization" (238) and who sees previously "unprotected" children working in them as "victims of monotonous slavery" (239), openly rejoices in the improvements that have been made since he had served his time there.

Yet as soon as the 1847 bill was enacted, there were fears that it would be repealed, and the conclusion to *Chapters in the Life of a Dundee Factory Boy* speaks directly to that issue. Forrest reiterates the goal of his story: "My purpose has been, to develope, as far as I could, the evils of the long hours' system, and the necessity there was for Legislative interference in the factory branch of industry. The old system, with all its horrors, is, I hope, forever blasted with the detestation of the wise and good, and its cruel reign will surely never be imposed on the young females and helpless children of our country. God grant that my anticipations may be fully realised" (300). As the doubt implicit in this prayer suggests, the triumph of the ten-hours movement was not at all secure when Myles was writing the *Dundee Factory Boy*. Because a measure to limit the hours during which factory engines could be run had not been part of the Act of 1847, factory owners real-

---

1   This copy of the *Dundee Factory Boy* is inscribed, "Presented to his friend and fell[ow labourer?] S.M. Kydd—by Richard Oastler May 3.rd 1850" (Sterling Memorial Library, Yale University). Kydd, Oastler's secretary in 1851, was "an Arbroath shoemaker who became a Chartist lecturer, journalist and barrister" (Ward 391; 473, n47).

ized that they could conform to the letter of the new law and still keep their mills going for fifteen hours a day: by working children, young persons, and women in complicated series of interrupted shifts (starting at 5:30 a.m., working for two hours, idle for two, and so on), their masters could keep adult men continuously at their machines for fourteen or more hours a day. The magistrates, who might have put a stop to such evasions when factory inspectors initiated prosecutions against factory owners, including John Bright and Co. of Rochdale, ruled over and over again in favor of the owners (Thomas 299-308). A furious response to this development came from Richard Oastler, writing in *The Champion*: "In this very Lancashire, magistrates, not a few, have ruled their own will to be higher than the law, saying in effect that they would work their mills as they thought fit, in spite of queen, lords, commons, bishops or anybody else" (qtd. Thomas 302). After the Court of the Exchequer upheld the manufacturers' liberal interpretation of the law (Ward 371-72), the *Times* concluded, "The Factory Act is practically a nullity" (qtd. Thomas 313).

Most twentieth-century accounts of factory reform in the nineteenth century end with the passing of the 1847 Act, as if its goal had been achieved, and that was that. The prayer voiced at the conclusion of the *Dundee Factory Boy* suggests otherwise. The battle had not been won, nor would it be in the next several decades. In the summer of 1850, just months after Myles's narrative was first published, Parliament passed the Act to Amend the Acts Relating to Labour in Factories, and finally legislated what was called a "normal day." That term derives from the custom, established early in the eighteenth century, that limited the hours of craftsmen in most trades to those that could be worked, with breaks for meals, between 6 a.m. and 6 p.m.—their "normal day" (Henriques 67). The 1850 Act required that young persons and women put in their allotted hours only between those customary times (starting and ending one hour later during the winter), with an hour and a half for meals, and only until 2 p.m. on Saturdays. According to such a schedule, they would work ten and one half hours per day, five days a week, with a "half-holiday" of eight hours on Saturday (Thomas 324-25; Ward 389).[1] Despite the fact

---

1 Driver offers a useful summary of the provisions of the legislation to date:

Thus, after 20 years of struggle, the regulation of factory labor resulting from the four piecemeal Acts of 1833, 1844, 1847, and 1850 amounted principally to this:

that textile operatives were now working a shorter week than most other manual laborers (Hunt 215), the anger of factory workers and their supporters over this betrayal of the ten-hours principle was intense. One reformer in the House of Commons noted bitterly that the Act of 1850 was "in reality a compromise of nothing but the rights of the people and of the honour of Parliament" (qtd. Driver 505).

Not even this unhappy outcome was the end of the story. Due to a bureaucratic oversight or a conscious attempt to sabotage the act—it is hard to tell which—the category of children was not mentioned in the 1850 amending act, and the youngest laborers therefore could still be worked in relays every night until 8:30 p.m., thereby keeping adult males at work for as long as fourteen and a half hours a day. In response to yet more disappointment over ineffective factory legislation, committees of reformers continued their efforts into the 1850s (Driver 513-17; Ward 397-403). Only in 1853 did Parliament pass an act that specified that the hours when children could work were those of a "normal" or ten-and-a-half hour day. This measure therefore limited the running of textile factories to twelve hours each day, including an hour and a half set aside for meals (Thomas 327). Even after 1853 factory owners renewed their attempts to repeal previous legislation; and some attempted to evade the law by employing workers who did not meet the mandated age requirements, as an 1859 advertisement suggests: "Wanted from twelve to twenty boys, not younger than will pass for thirteen years of age" (qtd. Cruickshank 85). Workers continued to press for shorter hours, and the earlier gains that they had made were not eroded more than they had

---

(1) Three "protected" classes of workers had been established, namely children (between the ages of 8 and 13), young persons (between the ages of 13 [i.e., 14] and 18 [17]), and women. Adult males [18 and older] were unregulated.

(2) Children could not enter the factories until they were 8 years old, and their work was restricted to 6½ hours a day. But that spell might be taken any time between 5:30 A.M. and 8:30 P.M., and nothing prevented their being used in relays throughout that period.

(3) Women and young persons were classed together. Their labour was now restricted to 10½ hours daily (exclusive of meal times) taken between 6 A.M. and 6 P.M. on five days a week; but

(4) On Saturdays their work ended at 2 P.M., half an hour being allowed off for breakfast. This made a total working week of 60 hours.

(5) All this was supervised by regional Inspectors and their assistants who made quarterly reports to the Home Office. (505-6)

been by the compromise of 1850. The "old system," as Frank Forrest called it in the *Dundee Factory Boy*, was not quite "forever blasted," but the likelihood of the return of the full twelve-hour day or the sixty-nine-hour week had been diminished.

The problem that most concerns Forrest, the evils attendant upon women's employment in textile mills, however, had not been solved. *Chapters in the Life of a Dundee Factory Boy* is typical in its concern over this issue, though the passion with which Forrest addresses it is remarkable in its intensity. Twice in his narrative, he engages in diatribes against the effects of the factory system on female workers. Good girls enter the mills, Forrest suggests, only and inevitably to become prostitutes who then spend "one week in a brothel, working the next in a mill." While employed in factories, such "abandoned females" lead others into drink and degradation (244). Although he concedes that the current short-hours system has at least partially alleviated such ills, he seems to agree with "the opinion of some men that the inevitable tendency of the mill system is to injure female character, however well it may be conducted" (264). The uncertain reference for the pronoun *it* in this sentence is telling: presumably Forrest is saying that the factory, no matter how well it is conducted, has a bad effect on "female character," but he is also saying, as factory reformers repeatedly did, that "female character," no matter how well it is conducted, is so weak that it cannot withstand the demoralizing temptations of the workplace. By defining women as inherently weak, workers like Forrest were arguing that women ought to be excluded from factory labor. Such a measure would protect women, but it would also and, perhaps more importantly, protect men from the competition they faced because women, now able to run increasingly powerful machinery, customarily received lower wages than men did.

Twice Forrest tells stories of young girls led into sin by the temptations typical of factory labor. One is a beautiful Irish Protestant whom he has personally known; the other's story, he says, is taken from the parliamentary records of 1833. The first became the mistress of a young mill-owner; the second, a prostitute and transported thief (246, 266). These melodramatic tales, complete with scenes in which the mother of each of these formerly innocent girls is imagined either as mourning the loss of her child or daydreaming over her cradle, are typical of working-class fiction that focuses on the ways in which the privileged characteristically prey on the poor. In these cases, however, the factory system itself is cast as the primary villain. Many of the passages in the *Dundee Factory Boy* are also typical of working-class temperance literature—workers will never thrive, so the lesson goes, until they spend less money on drink and less time in taverns—but here as well, the point is related to the evils of employing women in factories: such women spend much of their earnings to appease their male overseers by keeping them well supplied with drink (263).[1] The strength of Forrest's feelings on this subject are made clear not only by the excesses of the language in which he tells these tales, but also by the fact that he tells the second story three times, in each instance repeating its main facts and elaborating on its most pathetic implications. Ending with an address to the transported factory girl, Forrest exclaims, "When we realise such a history as thine, like Ebenezer Elliot we exclaim 'Lord help the poor!'" (268). Words of the working-class poet associated with the earlier anti-Corn-Law cause are made in this instance to apply to the concerns of the 1850s. Despite the gains made by half a century of factory legislation, the system—according to Forrest and, presumably, according to his creator, James Myles—was still committing many crimes for which it had to answer.

Ellen Johnston and Reformed Factory Labor

As prefaces to the two editions of her poems (see Note on the Text), Ellen Johnston offered brief accounts of her life as a "factory girl," and the story that emerges from them exhibits both the differences between her experiences and those of the other lives represented here and its continuity with them. Some of those differences simply reflect facts of chronology: coming to factory labor some fifty years after Blincoe, fifty years in which significant if not always effective legislation had been passed, she did encounter, even as a child, relatively improved working conditions. Unlike the three earlier narratives, her account does not focus insistently on questions of long hours, hard labor, or the material disadvantages of daily life in textile mills. When she refers to factory life, she tends to dwell on her personal relations with other young, female operatives. (The importance of the

---

1 Whatley's analysis of the *Dundee Factory Boy* rightly emphasizes its qualities as a didactic novel and temperance tract, concluding that this text "should not be read therefore as a critique of industrial capitalism" (73–76), but the narrator's outrage over the abuse of women resulting from the factory system does constitute such a critique.

support that such "girls" typically offered each other is demonstrated in Appendix F.6.) Johnston is also deeply concerned by, even obsessed with, both her relationship with an unidentified lover and the unidentified "torment" to which she was subjected by her stepfather. Moreover, Johnston had some advantages that earlier operatives lacked: as a worker, she had rights, and she knew what they were. Unlike Blincoe, who simply walked away from a particular mill when it became clear that he was not going to be paid his wages and who was fired from another when he politely requested a modest raise (164, 168), Johnston had legal recourse when she felt she was being victimized.

Yet Johnston does include enough information, in the words of Charles Aberdeen, to "show up" the factory system. She mentions hearing at 5:30 a.m. the "morning factory bells" that signalled the long day ahead (308). Although Johnston was not crippled by early factory work, as Blincoe and Dodd had been, she seems to take for granted the fact that her work has twice caused her to become seriously ill. She remarks, in a completely matter-of-fact manner, "my health began to fail, so that I could not work any longer in a factory" (311). The connection between factory labor and illness becomes explicit soon after when she notes that continued factory work would have been for her "certain death" (311). Johnston's account of her domestic miseries can also be read as an indictment of the factory system. From the perspective offered by James Myles in the *Dundee Factory Boy*, her relationships with her stepfather and her lover are simply two more instances of the immorality caused by putting female children and adolescents to work in factories. Johnston herself confirms such a reading when she dates the beginning of her stepfather's "torment" of her, not from his marriage to her mother, but from her own entry into factory work under his supervision when she was approximately eleven. Much more than the factory boys Blincoe or Dodd, Johnston lived within a fantasy world of her own creation, and her distinctively energetic imaginative life may have been her way of escaping conditions that differed from theirs more because she was a woman than because she participated in a relatively reformed factory system.

Even the rights that Johnston asserted reveal the similarity of her story to those recounted in the earlier texts. When she was employed in the recently developed jute industry at Verdant Works, she was fired without proper notice and for no apparent reason: "Smarting under this treatment, I summoned the foreman into Court for payment of a week's wages for not receiving notice, and I gained the case" (313). Turning to the law to vindicate not only her "own rights, but ... the rights of such as might be similarly discharged" (314), she became a representative of her class. Although she won her case, Johnston was still subject to the apparently arbitrary actions of her overseer. Moreover, the week's wages that Johnston gained could not have compensated her for the long period of unemployment that she endured when she lost her position, becoming for a "period of four months ... a famished and persecuted factory exile" (313). According to Blincoe and Dodd, factory work was a sentence of "slavery" to be served in English "Bastiles" (Brown 171). For Ellen Johnston, to be "a factory exile" is a greater punishment. Yet for Johnston, as for Blincoe and Dodd and Forrest, survival depends on such labor—without it, she is "famished."

While Johnston was composing the first edition of her volume of narrative and verse, Parliament considered proposals for the protection of industrial workers and did so with much less fanfare than had been typical of the debates of previous decades. In the workplaces that manufactured such products as lace, matches, pottery, and percussion caps, the labor of very young children was as important in the 1860s as it had been in the cotton mills of the first decades of the century. Girls as young as two were employed in lace-making, as they had been in the 1840s (Hunt 13); in 1862 it was typical for six- and seven-year-old lace-makers to work up to sixteen hours a day (Hutchins and Harrison 147). By the time that Ellen Johnston published her volume of poems in 1867, Parliament was passing both the Factory Acts Extension Act and the Workshops Regulation Act, which applied to a wide range of such workplaces, including small workshops and private homes (Hutchins and Harrison 168-72; Gray 230-33). Although there were numerous exceptions to the stipulations about hours in the acts of the 1860s—there was to be, for instance, no "normal day" for women and young persons employed in printing and bookbinding (Hutchins and Harrison 169)—the principle of protective legislation for industrial workers had been established.

To most Victorians of the 1860s, as Robert Gray concludes, "a regulated factory system formed part of the image of orderly progress" (209), just as the image of ruthlessly exploited children slaving away in cotton mills had symbolized the evils of an unregulated factory system. The substantial growth of British manufacture, the "Great Victorian boom" (Hoppen 278-83), seemed to promise enduring prosperity. The good effects of earlier legislation—evident in healthier and better-educated working-class children—were, as Marx tartly noted in the first volume of *Capital*, "visible to the weakest eyes" (408). By 1867 *Punch* could joke about "the consumption of children" by the factory system because it was no longer perceived as a troubling reality ("A Few Friends"). The widespread laments over the impending end of Britain's industrial glory, which had attended every legislative advance since 1802, were finally muted. As one reformer explained with some exaggeration in 1861, "There is now scarcely a manufacturer to be found who does not thank God for the factory regulation laws."[1] Also by 1867, workers, at least a large number of male workers, had gained the franchise through the passage of the Second Reform Act, though it was not until 1874 that the first workers, two in number, were elected to Parliament (Hunt 269). Such a long-delayed and slight improvement in the opportunities for working-class representatives to speak for themselves suggests that workers would have to depend on time-honored methods of participation—writing, petitioning, gathering, and marching—if they wanted to exert any authority over the course of legislation in the House of Commons.

The story of factory legislation did not conclude, therefore, with the 1867 Acts. Prompted by pressure from larger, more effective, and now legally protected trades unions (Hunt 264-69, 255), Britain's legislators continued to deal with the problems of unregulated industrial labor, congratulating themselves, as they did so, on the great progress that they had already achieved, often assuming that the problem of child labor had somehow disappeared.[2] That, unsurprisingly, was not the case. In a series of articles published in 1899 as *The Effects of the Factory System*, the working-class journalist Allen Clarke exposed the damage still being done to young children who at eleven could begin work as "half-timers" laboring six hours a day in Britain's workshops and factories: their bodies stunted, injured, and sickened, if not deformed; their minds uneducated and enslaved by toil more

---

1 Qtd. Ward 403. See also Burnett, "Labouring" 39; Cunningham 11-12.
2 Cunningham, 12, ch. 7 and 9. Late nineteenth-century legislation did give some order to the mass of sometimes conflicting, always confusing laws enacted earlier by consolidating and extending them in acts passed in 1878 and 1901, the latter of which prohibited the employment of children under twelve and finally legislated a fifty-five and a half hour week (Hutchins and Harrison 171; Burnett, "Labouring" 37).

"ceaseless" than it had been when its pace was determined by the smaller, slower machines in use earlier in the century (section VI; 49). Echoing the arguments of the 1830s and '40s, Clarke concluded that, if "the factory system is not so hard upon the children now" as it once had been, "it is not good; it never will be good" (95-96). Similarly, Hutchins and Harrison wrote their history of factory legislation in 1903 to protest the fact that "there are hundreds of trades [in which] the majority of workshops may be said to be in very much the same position that cotton factories were in the early part of the nineteenth century, when the law ... remained almost a dead letter" (249-50). Using the phrase with which Brown had described the Act of 1802 and that Marx applied to all the legislation before 1833 (390), the authors of the 1903 study, like Blincoe and Dodd and Forrest before them, pointed to the gains achieved by previous factory legislation so that they could emphasize how much had yet to be done. The last words of Johnston's autobiographical sketch provide further evidence for a less-than-triumphant view of the history of factory legislation. In one of her poems, she laments that "my life is one dark history of toil-worn heart-sick woe" (1867: 170), but in her autobiography she concludes more simply by referring to "the incessant toils of a factory life" (315).[1] Like Johnston's earlier accounts of her illnesses, this phrase defines the labors of a "factory girl," even under the relatively improved conditions of the mid-century, as something other than "light."

★ ★ ★

Traces of the industrial culture to which Johnston contributed both her labor and her poems are still discernible in everyday life. Nineteenth-century purpose-built factories are now turned into luxury condos or fancy office spaces. More specifically, the mill in which Blincoe reputedly began his working life was transformed into a luxury residence in 1980. Verdant Works, where Johnston was once employed, has become a highly successful tourist attraction. Complete with a gift shop, it sells note cards with watercolor images of the factory under snow, rather as if one

---

1   In the 1867 version of the "Autobiography," that phrase seems to suggest that her poems will provide her readers with relief from such labor, but the emendations in the 1869 edition announce the goal of Johnston's poems to be to "relieve me from the incessant toil of a factory life" (324). See Note on the Text.

of the sites of her "incessant toils" had become a sentimental scene out of Dickens's *A Christmas Carol*. Oddest, perhaps, of the various residual evidences of factory life is the icon used by Motorola on its cell phones, on the screens of which work numbers are identified by tiny factory buildings, each with two smoke stacks. Such modest and simple architectural forms have not been typical of mechanized industry since the early nineteenth century, but they now serve not only to evoke the origins of the current commercial economy, with its emphasis on consumption rather than production, but also to express a naive nostalgia for that past. How thoroughly the industrial predominance once enjoyed by Britain and, later on, by the United States has been eroded, how decisively it has been relegated to former times, is beyond dispute. The last jute mill in Dundee shut down in 1999; and as Michael Moore has insisted in every one of his documentaries from *Roger and Me* to *Fahrenheit 9/11*, a town like Flint, Michigan, continues to be devastated by the closing of its General Motors plants in the 1980s.

Yet even as the post-industrialism of so-called developed countries has transferred manufacturing, with its physical demands on workers' bodies, to developing countries, factory life has not entirely disappeared from its former sites. When the U.S. Department of Labor issued new guidelines in 1999 to deal with repetitive-stress injuries in the workplace, the ensuing debate, with employers predicting their financial ruin and employees witnessing to their physical injuries, might have been taking place in the mid-nineteenth century. One worker from a poultry factory served as a witness and said, "We all have damaged bodies." His injuries were the result of nine years of doing a job that consisted of hanging chickens on hooks—twenty-six chickens a minute, eight hours a day.[1] Like Robert Blincoe before him, this worker pointed to his own body as proof that the conditions of industrial labor demand regulation. When my daughter and I

---

1 National Public Radio, 22 November 1999. The difficulty of legislating effective protections for workers was demonstrated in January of 2002 when the Supreme Court ruled that workers, even those injured by the jobs they have been doing, cannot be considered disabled if their physical limitations restrict only their capacities to work, but not other "major life activities" such as brushing one's teeth and gardening; this judgment was based on the reasoning that "the manual tasks unique to any particular job are not necessarily important parts of most people's lives" (United States Supreme Court, *Toyota Motor Manufacturing, Kentucky, Inc., Petitioner v. Ella Williams*).

visited the museum at Verdant Works in 1998, a retired worker, now a volunteer demonstrating the processes involved in producing jute, paused at one point and extended his right hand for us to see. Several of its fingers deformed, patches of his flesh turned white and rigid by a lack of circulation, his hand displayed the symptoms of Raynaud's disease, the result of repetitive motion and continuous contact with vibrating machinery. This former worker in an industry that no longer existed at the end of the twentieth century was still dealing with the effects of the occupational hazards and the specific disease that had cost William Dodd his right forearm more than one hundred and fifty years earlier.

Nor has child labor become a thing of the past in developed nations, much as we, like the late Victorians, would like to think that it has. Children working in violation of labor laws in the United States may number over three-hundred thousand. Approximately half the adolescents in Britain between the ages of thirteen and fifteen are illegally working part-time, many of them doing strenuous adult jobs for pay as little as 10p an hour. In one particularly telling anecdote of current British industrial practices that is recounted in the publications of the United Nations' International Labour Organization, a factory owner in 1996 was employing ten-year-old girls for six-hour shifts and then paying them with money or chocolates, depending on his fancy on any given day.[1]

Such stories of abuse, however, do not begin to suggest the magnitude of the problem of child labor in other parts of the globe, where vastly greater numbers typically work at harder jobs for longer hours. In country after country, employing young workers is a fact of life—and often the only way to make life better. Counting only those who are doing dangerous and harmful work or jobs that interfere with their schooling, the ILO estimates the number of children younger than fifteen who work worldwide at two hundred and forty-six million, seventy-three million under the age of ten. Most are engaged in agriculture or hunting and fishing, yet almost twenty million are employed in industrial occupations, such as those in Southeast Asia who work to manufacture brass, matches, leather, and glass. Whether they labor in mills, workshops, or homes, such children often

---

1   *Child* 32, 35; Leonard 181-83; *Child* 36. Leonard cites a 1998 study that
    puts the injuries of working children in the previous year at 44 per cent
    (186).

endure conditions that equal or exceed the worst horrors of Britain's nineteenth-century factory system. Approximately twenty-two thousand are killed each year by the work that they do. Debates over such labor, particularly in "transition economies," repeat now centuries-old arguments: its status as slavery in the form of debt bondage; its importance to economic development; its effect on pliable, compliant, and unprotected young bodies; and the impossibility of effective regulation and inspection. Similarly, those who claim that the alternatives to such work are worse than the work itself have a point, as did their Victorian predecessors.[1]

In this context the legacy of the autobiographical texts collected in this volume once again seems relevant, calling, as it implicitly does, for testimony that might, in Charles Aberdeen's words, "show up" the material conditions of industrial labor. As Allen Clarke said of British half-timers in the 1890s: "If the children could only hold a congress and speak, what shameful revelations would be made!" (106). Clarke, like the Carlyle of *Past and Present*, asked his readers to imagine what such witnesses would say; but, unlike Carlyle, Clarke doubted neither the authority of their perspectives nor the ability of even young workers to offer articulate accounts of the conditions to which they were subjected. Indirectly offering evidence of the ongoing significance of the testimony of operatives like Robert Blincoe and William Dodd, the ILO includes in its list of ways to support its initiatives the interviewing of child workers and the publicizing of their experiences, though it concedes the difficulties and even dangers involved in gathering evidence from exhausted children engaged in illegal occupations.[2] Despite the national and international legislative measures that have been enacted, then, the stories that factory workers tell still deserve a hearing, and

---

1   "Facts"; *Child* 16, 29. For two defenses of child labor in developing nations, see Porter and Kristof, the latter of whom notes that children protected from such employment by well-intentioned international efforts may "end ... up in worse jobs, like prostitution." Others argue that keeping children from work simply imposes on them Western, middle-class conceptions of childhood as a "time of freedom, education and protected growth," an imposition from which they are mistakenly thought, according to Lavalette, to be in need of liberation so that they can work (12; cf. ch. 1).

2   *Child* 177–79. Other advocates for limiting child labor, however, warn against accepting uncritically the statements of children who often say that they "want" to work (Lavalette 27–28).

Ellen Johnston's last words continue to resonate: "incessant toils," as she testified, and the marks that they make on human bodies, young and old, remain defining features of "factory life."

Works Cited

Altick, Richard D. *The English Common Reader: A Social History of the Mass Reading Public 1800-1900*. Chicago: U Chicago P, 1957.

Andrews, William L. *To Tell a Free Story: The First Century of Afro-American Autobiography, 1760-1865*. Urbana: U of Illinois P, 1988.

Baines, Edward. *History of the Cotton Manufacture in Great Britain*. 1835. Intro. W.H. Chaloner. Rpt. London: Frank Cass, 1966.

Baker, Houston A. *Blues, Ideology, and Afro-American Literature: A Vernacular Theory*. Chicago: U Chicago P, 1984.

Baxter, R. Dudley. *National Income: The United Kingdom*. London: Macmillan, 1868.

Berg, Maxine. *The Age of Manufactures: Industry, Innovation and Work in Britain, 1700-1820*. Oxford: Blackwell, 1986.

Bizup, Joseph. *Manufacturing Culture: Vindications of Early Victorian Industry*. Charlottesville: U of Virginia P, 2003.

Boos, Florence S. "Cauld Engle-Cheek: Working-Class Women Poets in Victorian Scotland." *Victorian Poetry* 33 (1995): 53-73.

Boyson, Rhodes. *The Ashworth Cotton Enterprise: The Rise and Fall of a Family Firm 1818-1880*. Oxford: Clarendon, 1970.

Bradshaw, David J., and Suzanne Ozment, eds. *The Voice of Toil: Nineteenth-Century British Writings about Work*. Athens: Ohio UP, 2000.

Briggs, Asa. "John Bright and the Creed of Reform." *Victorian People: A Reassessment of Persons and Themes 1851-67*. 1955. New York: Harper, 1963. 197-231.

Bruner, Jerome. "The Autobiographical Process." In Folkenflik, ed., *The Culture of Autobiography*. 38-56.

Burnett, John. "The Labouring Classes." *Useful Toil: Autobiographies of Working People from the 1820s to the 1920s*. Ed. John Burnett. London: Allen Lane, 1974. 23-54.

——, David Vincent, and David Mayall, eds. *The Autobiography of the Working Class: An Annotated, Critical Bibliography*. Vol. 1: 1790-1900. Brighton: Harvester, 1984.

Carlyle, Thomas. *Past and Present*. 1843. Ed. Richard D. Altick. Boston: Houghton Mifflin, 1965.

——. *Sartor Resartus: The Life and Opinions of Herr Teufelsdröckh*. 1833-34. Ed. Rodger L. Tarr and Mark Engel. Berkeley: U of California P, 2000.

Chaloner, W.H. "Introduction." William Dodd. *The Factory System Illustrated* [and] *A Narrative of the Experience and Sufferings of William Dodd*. 1842, 1841. Rpt. New York: Augustus M. Kelley, 1968.

——. "Mrs. Trollope and the Early Factory System." *Victorian Studies* 4 (1960): 159-66.

Chapman, Stanley D. *The Early Factory Masters: The Transition to the Factory System in the Midlands Textile Industry*. Newton Abbot (Devon): David and Charles, 1967.

Child Labour: A Textbook for University Students. Geneva: International Labour Organization, 2004. January 18, 2005. <http://www.ilo.org/public/english/standards/ipec/publ/download/ pol_textbook_2004.pdf>.

Clark, Anna. *The Struggle for the Breeches: Gender and the Making of the British Working Class*. Berkeley: U of California P, 1995.

Clarke, Allen. *The Effects of the Factory System*. London: Grant Richards, 1899.

"Committee on the Factories Bill." *Times* (March 16, 1844): 3-5.

Cruickshank, Marjorie. *Children and Industry: Child Health and Welfare in North-west Textile Towns during the Nineteenth-Century*. Manchester: Manchester UP, 1981.

Cooke Taylor, W. *Factories and the Factory System; From Parliamentary Documents and Personal Examination*. London: Jeremiah How, 1844.

Corbett, Mary Jean. *Representing Femininity: Middle-Class Subjectivity in Victorian and Edwardian Women's Autobiographies*. New York: Oxford UP, 1992.

Cunningham, Hugh. *The Children of the Poor: Representations of Childhood since the Seventeenth Century*. Oxford: Blackwell, 1991.

Davidoff, Leonore. "The Family in Britain." In F.M.L. Thompson, *Cambridge Social History* 2: 71-129.

[Dodd, William.] *The Laboring Classes of England, Especially Those Concerned in Agriculture and Manufactures; in a Series of Letters. By an Englishman*. Boston: John Putnam, 1847.

Driver, Cecil. *Tory Radical: The Life of Richard Oastler*. New York: Oxford UP, 1946.

Eakin, Paul John. *Fictions in Autobiography: Studies in the Art of Self-Invention*. Princeton: Princeton UP, 1985.

——. *Touching the World: Reference in Autobiography*. Princeton: Princeton UP, 1992.

——. "What Are We Reading When We Read Autobiography?" *Narrative* 12 (2004): 121-32.

Engels, Friedrich. *The Condition of the Working Class in England*. 1845. Ed. Victor Kiernan. London: Penguin, 1987.

"Facts on Child Labour." June 2004. January 18, 2005. International Labour Organization. <http://www.ilo.org/public/english/bureau/inf/download/child/childday04.pdf>.

"A Few Friends. (From My Photograph Book)." *Punch* 53 (September 28, 1867): 123.

Fielden, John. *The Curse of the Factory System*. 1836. Intro. J.T. Ward. Rpt. New York: Augustus M. Kelley, 1969.

Folkenflik, Robert. "Introduction: The Institution of Autobiography." *The Culture of Autobiography: Constructions of Self-Representation*. Ed. Robert Folkenflik. Stanford: Stanford UP, 1993. 1-20.

Freedgood, Elaine, ed. *Factory Production in Nineteenth-Century Britain*. New York: Oxford UP, 2003.

Friedman, Susan Stanford. "Women's Autobiographical Selves: Theory and Practice." In Benstock, Shari, ed. *The Private Self: Theory and Practice of Women's Autobiographical Writings*. Chapel Hill: U of North Carolina P, 1988. 34-62.

Gagnier, Regenia. *Subjectivities: A History of Self-Representation in Britain, 1832-1920*. Oxford: Oxford UP, 1991.

Gallagher, Catherine. *The Industrial Reformation of English Fiction: Social Discourse and Narrative Form 1832-1867*. Chicago: U Chicago P, 1985.

Gaskell, P. *Artisans and Machinery: The Moral and Physical Condition of the Manufacturing Population*. 1836. Rpt. New York: Augustus M. Kelley, 1968.

Gates, Henry Louis, Jr. *The Signifying Monkey: A Theory of Afro-American Literary Criticism*. New York: Oxford UP, 1988.

Gilmore, Leigh. *The Limits of Autobiography: Trauma and Testimony*. Ithaca: Cornell UP, 2001.

——. "Policing Truth: Confession, Gender, and Autobiographical Authority." Kathleen Ashley, Leigh Gilmore, and Gerald Peters, eds. *Autobiography and Postmodernism*. Amherst: U of Massachusetts P, 1994. 54-78.

Grant, Philip. *The Ten Hours' Bill: The History of Factory Legislation*. Manchester: John Heywood, 1866.

Gray, Robert. *The Factory Question and Industrial England, 1830-1860.* Cambridge: Cambridge UP, 1996.

Greg, Robert Hyde. *The Factory Question and the "Ten Hours Bill."* London: James Ridgway, 1837.

Gusdorf, Georges. "Conditions and Limits of Autobiography." 1956. Trans. James Olney. In Olney, ed. *Autobiography: Essays Theoretical and Critical.* 28-48.

Hackett, Nan. *XIX Century British Working-Class Autobiographies: An Annotated Bibliography.* New York: AMS, 1985.

Hamilton, Henry. *The Industrial Revolution in Scotland.* Oxford: Clarendon, 1932.

Hansard's Parliamentary Debates. 3rd series. 73 (1844): cols. 1095-1158.

Haywood, Ian. "'Graphic Narratives and Discoveries of Horror': The Feminization of Labour in Nineteenth-Century Radical Fiction." *British Industrial Fictions.* Ed. H. Gustav Klaus and Stephen Knight. Cardiff: U of Wales P, 2000. 5-23.

Henriques, Ursula R.Q. *Before the Welfare State: Social Administration in Early Industrial Britain.* London: Longman, 1979.

Hodder, Edwin. *The Life and Work of the Seventh Earl of Shaftesbury.* 1886. 3 vols. Rpt. Shannon: Irish UP, 1971.

Hoppen, K. Theodore. *The Mid-Victorian Generation 1846-1886.* Oxford: Clarendon, 1998.

Horn, Pamela. *Children's Work and Welfare, 1780-1880s.* London: Macmillan, 1994.

Horrell, Sara, and Jane Humphries. "Child Labour and British Industrialization." In *A Thing of the Past?* Ed. Lavalette. 76-100.

Hunt, E.H. *British Labour History 1815-1914.* Atlantic Highlands, NJ: Humanities P, 1981.

Hutchins, B L. and A. Harrison. *A History of Factory Legislation.* London: P.S. King, 1903.

Johnston, Ellen. *Autobiography, Poems and Songs of Ellen Johnston, The "Factory Girl."* Glasgow: William Love, 1867.

——. *Autobiography, Poems and Songs of Ellen Johnston, The "Factory Girl."* 2nd ed. Glasgow: William Love, 1869.

Joyce, Patrick. "Work." In F.M.L. Thompson, *Cambridge Social History* 2: 131-94.

Kawash, Samira. *Dislocating the Color Line: Identity, Hybridity, and Singularity in African-American Literature.* Stanford: Stanford UP, 1997.

Kay, James Phillips. *The Moral and Physical Condition of the*

Working Classes Employed in the Cotton Manufacture in Manchester. London: James Ridgway, 1832.

Kestner, Joseph. *Protest and Reform: The British Social Narrative by Women 1827-1867.* Madison: U Wisconsin P, 1985.

Kirby, Peter. *Child Labour in Britain, 1750-1870.* Houndmills: Palgrave Macmillan, 2003.

Kirby, R.G., and A.E. Musson. *The Voice of the People: John Doherty, 1798-1854, Trade Unionist, Radical and Factory Reformer.* Manchester: Manchester UP, 1975.

Kovačević, Ivanka. *Fact into Fiction: English Literature and the Industrial Scene 1750-1850.* Leicester: Leicester UP, 1975.

Kristof, Nicholas D. "Put Your Money Where Their Mouths Are." *New York Times* April 3, 2004: A15.

[Kydd, Samuel.] "Alfred." *The History of the Factory Movement from the Year 1802, to the Enactment of the Ten Hours' Bill in 1847.* 2 vols. London: Simpkin, Marshall. 1857.

Lavalette, Michael. "The 'New Sociology of Childhood' and Child Labour: Childhood, Children's Rights and 'Children's Voice.'" In *A Thing of the Past? Child Labour in Britain in the Nineteenth and Twentieth Centuries.* Ed. Michael Lavalette. New York: St. Martin's, 1999. 15-43.

Lejeune, Philippe. *On Autobiography.* Ed. Paul John Eakin. Trans. Katherine Leary. Minneapolis: U of Minnesota P, 1989.

Leonard, Madeleine. "Child Work in the UK, 1970-1998." In *A Thing of the Past?* Ed. Lavalette. 177-92.

Loesberg, Jonathan. *Fictions of Consciousness: Mill, Newman, and the Reading of Victorian Prose.* New Brunswick: Rutgers UP, 1986.

Maidment, Brian, ed. *The Poorhouse Fugitives: Self-Taught Poets and Poetry in Victorian Britain.* Manchester: Carcanet, 1987.

Marcus, Laura. *Auto/biographical Discourses: Theory, Criticism, Practice.* Manchester: Manchester UP, 1994.

Marx, Karl. *Capital: A Critique of Political Economy.* Vol. 1. 1867. Intro. Ernest Mandel. Trans. Ben Fowkes. London: Penguin, 1976.

Mathias, Peter. *The First Industrial Nation: An Economic History of Britain 1700-1914.* 2nd ed. London: Routledge, 1983.

Mayhew, Henry. *London Labour and the London Poor.* 1861-62. 4 vols. Rpt. New York: Dover, 1968.

Mostern, Kenneth. *Autobiography and Black Identity Politics: Racialization in Twentieth-Century America.* Cambridge: Cambridge UP, 1999.

Murphy, Paul Thomas. *Toward a Working-Class Canon: Literary Criticism in British Working-Class Periodicals, 1816-1858.* Columbus: Ohio State UP, 1994.

Musson, A.E. "Robert Blincoe and the Early Factory System." *Trade Union and Social History.* London: Frank Cass, 1974. 195-206.

Nardinelli, Clark. *Child Labor and the Industrial Revolution.* Bloomington: Indiana UP, 1990.

Neuman, Shirley. "Autobiography: From Different Poetics to a Poetics of Differences." In *Essays on Life Writing: From Genre to Critical Practice.* Ed. Marlene Kadar. Toronto: U of Toronto P, 1992. 213-30.

Olney, James. "Autobiography and the Cultural Moment: A Thematic, Historical, and Bibliographical Introduction." *Autobiography: Essays Theoretical and Critical.* Princeton: Princeton UP, 1980. 3-27.

——. *Metaphors of Self: The Meaning of Autobiography.* Princeton: Princeton UP, 1972.

Parliamentary Papers. 15 (1831-32); 20 and 21 (1833).

Pascal, Roy. *Design and Truth in Autobiography.* Cambridge: Harvard UP, 1960.

Peterson, Linda H. *Traditions of Victorian Women's Autobiography: The Poetics and Politics of Life Writing.* Charlottesville: UP of Virginia, 1999.

——. *Victorian Autobiography: The Tradition of Self-Interpretation.* New Haven: Yale UP, 1986.

Pinchbeck, Ivy. *Women Workers and the Industrial Revolution, 1750-1850.* 1930. Rpt. New York: Augustus M. Kelley, 1969.

Porter, Karen A. "An Anthropological Defense of Child Labor." *Chronicle of Higher Education.* November 19, 1999. B11.

"Previous Workhouses." *My Brighton and Hove.* February 2005. March 4, 2005. <http://mybrightonandhove.org.uk/brighton_general_hospital_history5.htm>.

Rose, Jonathan. *The Intellectual Life of the British Working Classes.* New Haven: Yale UP, 2001.

Rose, Sonya O. "Protective Labor Legislation in Nineteenth-Century Britain: Gender, Class, and the Liberal State." Laura L. Frader and Sonya O. Rose, eds. *Gender and Class in Modern Europe.* Ithaca: Cornell UP, 1996. 193-210.

Rule, John. *The Labouring Classes in Early Industrial England, 1750-1850.* London: Longman, 1986.

Senior, Nassau W. *Letters on the Factory Act, As It Affects the Cotton Manufacture*. London: B. Fellowes, 1837.

Shaw, Charles. *When I Was a Child*. 1903. Rpt. Firle, Sussex: Caliban, 1977.

Smith, Sidonie, and Julia Watson, eds. *Women, Autobiography, Theory: A Reader*. U Wisconsin P, 1998.

Sommer, Doris. "'Not Just a Personal Story': Women's *Testimonios* and the Plural Self." In *Life/Lines: Theorizing Women's Autobiography*. Ed. Bella Brodzki and Celeste Schenck. Ithaca: Cornell UP, 1988. 107-30.

Spear, Thomas C., ed. "Autobiographical Que(e)ries." Special issues, *a/b: Auto/Biography Studies* 15. 1, 2 (Summer, Winter 2000).

Spengemann, William C. *The Forms of Autobiography: Episodes in the History of a Literary Genre*. New Haven: Yale UP, 1980.

Stewart, Victoria. *Women's Autobiography: War and Trauma*. Houndmills: Palgrave Macmillan, 2003.

Swindells, Julia. *Victorian Writing and Working Women: The Other Side of Silence*. Minneapolis: U of Minnesota P, 1985.

Thomas, Maurice Walton. *The Early Factory Legislation: A Study in Legislative and Administrative Evolution*. Leigh-on-Sea, Essex: Thames Bank Publishing, 1948.

Thompson, E.P. *The Making of the English Working Class*. 1963. New York: Vintage, 1966.

Thompson, F.M.L., ed. *The Cambridge Social History of Britain 1750-1950*. 3 vols. Cambridge: Cambridge UP, 1990.

Trevelyan, George Macaulay. *The Life of John Bright*. Boston: Houghton Mifflin, 1914.

Tuttle, Carolyn. *Hard at Work in Factories and Mines: The Economics of Child Labor during the British Industrial Revolution*. Boulder: Westview, 1999.

United States Supreme Court. *Toyota Motor Manufacturing, Kentucky, Inc., Petitioner v. Ella Williams*. January 8, 2002. January 24, 2005. <http://supct.law.cornell.edu/supct/html/00-1089.ZO.html>.

Ure, Andrew. *The Philosophy of Manufactures: or, An Exposition of the Scientific, Moral, and Commercial Economy of the Factory System of Great Britain*. London: Charles Knight, 1835.

Vincent, David. *Bread, Knowledge and Freedom: A Study of Nineteenth-Century Working Class Autobiography*. London: Europa, 1981.

——. *Literacy and Popular Culture: England 1750-1914*. Cambridge: Cambridge UP, 1989.

———, ed. *Testaments of Radicalism: Memoirs of Working Class Politicians 1790-1885*. London: Europa, 1977.

Ward, J.T. *The Factory Movement 1830-1855*. London: Macmillan, 1962.

Watson, Julia. "Toward an Anti-Metaphysics of Autobiography." In Folkenflik, ed. *The Culture of Autobiography*. 57-79.

Weintraub, Karl J. *The Value of the Individual: Self and Circumstance in Autobiography*. Chicago: U of Chicago P, 1978.

Whatley, Christopher A. "Altering Images of the Industrial City: The Case of James Myles, the 'Factory Boy,' and Mid-Victorian Dundee." In *Victorian Dundee: Image and Realities*. Ed. Louise Miskell, Christopher A. Whatley, and Bob Harris. East Linton, East Lothian: Tuckwell, 2000. 70-95.

Wing, Charles. *Evils of the Factory System Demonstrated by Parliamentary Evidence*. 1837. Rpt. New York: Augustus M. Kelley, 1967.

Wong, Hertha Dawn. *Sending My Heart Back Across the Years: Tradition and Innovation in Native American Autobiography*. New York: Oxford UP, 1992.

Significant Nineteenth-Century Factory Legislation and Factory Literature: A Brief Chronology

1802	An Act for the Preservation of the Health and Morals of Apprentices (Sir Robert Peel's Act).
1805	William Godwin's *Fleetwood: or, the New Man of Feeling*.
1819	An Act to Make Further Provisions for the Regulation of Cotton Mills and Factories.
1825	An Act to Make Further Provisions for the Regulation of Cotton Mills and Factories (Sir John Hobhouse's Act).
1828	John Brown's *A Memoir of Robert Blincoe*.
1832	John Doherty's edition of *A Memoir of Robert Blincoe*.
1832	John Walker's *The Factory Lad: A Domestic Drama in Two Acts*.
1832	Harriet Martineau's *A Manchester Strike*.
1833	An Act to Regulate the Labour of Children and Young Persons in the Mills and Factories of the United Kingdom.
1833	Caroline Bowles's *Tales of the Factories*.
1836	Caroline Norton's *A Voice From the Factories*.
1839	Frederic Montagu's *Mary Ashley, The Factory Girl*.
1839-40	Frances Trollope's *The Life and Adventures of Michael Armstrong, the Factory Boy*.
1839-41	Charlotte Elizabeth Tonna's *Helen Fleetwood*.
1841	*A Narrative of the Experiences and Sufferings of William Dodd, A Factory Cripple*.
1842	Elizabeth Stone's *William Langshawe, The Cotton Lord*.
1843	Elizabeth Barrett Browning's "The Cry of the Children."
1844	An Act to Amend the Laws Relating to Labour in Factories.
1847	An Act to Limit the Hours of Labour of Young Persons and Females in Factories.
1848	Elizabeth Gaskell's *Mary Barton: A Tale of Manchester Life*.
1849	Charlotte Brontë's *Shirley*.
1850	James Myles's *Chapters in the Life of a Dundee Factory Boy*.

1850	An Act to Amend the Acts Relating to Labour in Factories.
1853	An Act Further to Regulate the Employment of Children in Factories.
1854	Charles Dickens's *Hard Times.*
1855	Elizabeth Gaskell's *North and South.*
1862	Herbert Glyn's *The Cotton Lord.*
1863	Mary Elizabeth Braddon's *The Factory Girl.*
1864	The Factory Acts Extension Act.
1867	The Factory Acts Extension Act.
1867	The Workshops Regulation Act.
1867	"Autobiography of Ellen Johnston, 'The Factory Girl'" in *Autobiography, Poems and Songs of Ellen Johnston, The "Factory Girl."*
1871	The Factory and Workshops Regulation Act.
1874	An Act to Make Better Provision for Improving the Health of Women, Young Persons and Children Employed in Manufactures.
1878	An Act to Consolidate and Amend the Law Relating to Factories and Workshops.
1891	An Act to Amend the Law Relating to Factories and Workshops.
1893	Charles Shaw's *When I Was a Child.*
1895	An Act to Amend and Extend the Law Relating to Factories and Workshops.
1899	Allan Clarke's *The Effects of the Factory System.*
1901	Factory and Workshop Consolidation Act.

A Note on the Text

Elizabeth Reed

All the texts in this volume have been edited to achieve both accessibility and scholarly accuracy. Unlike other modern editions of working-class writings, this one reproduces as exactly as possible both the substantives (the words) and the accidentals (the spelling, punctuation, and typography) as they appeared when originally published. Readers should be aware that obvious errors in this volume (for instance, "a certain rank, oily, smell" [111] or "unpaired turnips" [134]) have been retained from the original texts to give a sense of the way in which they were first printed. Most reproduced nineteenth-century texts, even those by canonical authors such as Dickens, now appear in a more polished and consistent form than that in which they were initially printed because their spelling and punctuation have been modernized. (Interestingly, there are often as many obvious errors in the works in the appendices by middle-class writers like Trollope and Tonna as there are in the principal working-class texts, and these too have been left uncorrected.) Retaining the relatively heavy punctuation in a work like John Brown's *A Memoir of Robert Blincoe*, composed from interviews, has the advantage of giving readers a sense of the rhythms of speech suggested by that punctuation: in the description of children who "wore, what, in London, are called, pinafores" (112) instead of "wore what in London are called pinafores," the constantly qualifying movements of the prose are rendered through Brown's or his printer's use of commas.

Textual Guidelines

1. Spelling is reproduced exactly as it appeared in any text selected for accidentals. Nineteenth-century spelling was not always standardized, so alternate spellings remain in these texts ("Lowdam" and "Lowhdam" [105 and 110], for instance).
2. Any accidental errors that affect the reader's understanding have been emended in square brackets [ ] or indicated by the use of [*sic*]. Corrections have been made most often in cases when the original punctuation would begin and end sentences incorrectly. Inconsistent uses of apostrophes to form possessives have not been noted. Nothing has been emended silently, with the sole exception of galley numbers, which have been deleted. Some

technical apparatus, such as a list of line-end hyphens, have not been included.

3. The original typography of these texts has been maintained, except in the following instances: quotation marks down the left-hand margins in the original texts have been deleted; the Gothic script used for the titles of Ellen Johnston's poems in her two editions of her works has not been reproduced; and in accordance with Broadview house style indented quotations are not printed in a smaller type than that of the main text, periods marking ellipses have not been spaced, and the first lines of chapters, of excerpts, and of the first paragraphs of texts have not been indented.

4. The first three of the four main autobiographies in this edition were originally printed as separate volumes, so they have been reproduced here from their title pages to their conclusions.

5. The amount of information available to describe material such as periodical appearances and even authorship necessarily depends on the extant records about works that were often published under difficult circumstances. As the following bibliographical entries reveal, the material for different texts varies considerably in quantity and certainty.

A Memoir of Robert Blincoe, An Orphan Boy; Sent from the Work-house of St. Pancras, London, at Seven Years of Age, to Endure the Horrors of a Cotton-Mill, through His Infancy and Youth. With a Minute Detail of His Sufferings, Being the First Memoir of the Kind Published. By John Brown. Manchester: Printed for and Published by J. Doherty, 37, Withy-Grove. 1832.

Blincoe's life story first appeared as the "Memoir of Robert Blincoe, an Orphan Boy, *Who, with others, was sent from the Work-house of Saint Pancras, London, to one of the horrible cotton-mills and cotton-masters in Nottinghamshire,*" which ran in weekly installments in *The Lion,* the periodical published in London by Richard Carlile, reformer and advocate for legislation to protect the rights of factory children. Labeled there "Original Biography," its installments appeared from January 25 through February 22, 1828. The author of the "Memoir" was listed as J. Brown, for the journalist John Brown (d. 1825?). Brown, along with William Smith, a leader in the factory movement, had planned to publish the "Memoir" in 1822 and 1823 in a new paper that they hoped to inaugurate in Manchester during those years (Kirby and Musson 349), but apparently the "Memoir" was not printed until it reached Carlile in London. Later in 1828 Carlile republished the *Memoir,* this time with an expanded title and as a separate pamphlet; and the last pages of the February 15, 1828 issue of *The Lion* (224) bore the following announcement: "We have also published, price One Shilling, the *Memoir of Robert Blincoe*, in a pamphlet extracted and distinct from the numbers of 'THE LION.'" The *Memoir* appeared again four years later. In 1832, John Doherty (1798?-1854), an Irishman, former child laborer, working-class leader in Manchester, as well as book seller and printer, began publishing *The Poor Man's Advocate*. He put on the title page of the issue for June 9, 1832, a drawing of Robert Blincoe's crippled form, with a notice on the following page that a printing of the *Memoir* "with considerable additions" would shortly appear "in about three or four twopenny numbers" so that it could "give the most extensive publicity to the horrors of this infernal factory system," which "forms one black catalogue of cruelty and crime." Blincoe knew Doherty well enough to stand as one of the two guarantors of his bail when Doherty was imprisoned after being sued for libel; and the connection between the two men was so significant that one of Doherty's sons honored his father by naming a road that he built "Blincoe" (Kirby and Musson 376, 437, 5).

In the history of this particular text, we have the most complicated of the four autobiographical works that comprise *Factory Lives* and an excellent illustration of what Jerome McGann calls "the textual condition," the collaborations involving writer, editor, and publisher that determine the contents and forms of printed books (33, 60). The collaborative ventures that led to the multiple publications of *A Memoir of Robert Blincoe* justify the choice, as the end-product of such relationships, of a text composed of the following:

1. For substantive authority, the 1832 Doherty volume has been chosen because Blincoe appears to have participated in its publication by offering additional information on his life. Its citation of more accurate place names than those found in the Carlile editions is particularly striking.

2. For accidental authority, the Carlile pamphlet has been used because it was proofread more carefully than Doherty's version. Although Doherty corrected some of the minor errors in Carlile's 1828 edition, many more were introduced; and the paragraph-long passages that Doherty added (see Appendix A.4) contain very casual punctuation and grammar, the kind more characteristic of the spoken than of the written word. Blincoe apparently complained about two incorrect place names that appeared in Carlile's versions of his life (see Appendix A.2), but neither of

those designations seems actually to have been in error (see note on page 119 and note 3 on pages 172-73).

3. The text added in the Doherty edition appears in curly brackets {}, whereas the text replaced from the Carlile edition of the *Memoir* has been reprinted in Appendix A.4.

A Narrative of the Experience and Sufferings of William Dodd, A Factory Cripple. Written By Himself. Giving an Account of the Hardships and Sufferings He Endured in Early Life, under What Difficulties He Acquired His Education, the Effects of Factory Labour on His Mind and Person, the Unsuccessful Efforts Made by Him to Obtain a Livelihood in Some Other Line of Life, the Comparison He Draws between Agricultural and Manufacturing Labourers, and Other Matters Relating to the Working Classes. Second Edition. London: Published by L. & G. Seeley, 169, Fleet Street, and Hatchard & Son, 187, Piccadilly. 1841. Price One Shilling.

The second edition, under the imprint of L. & G. Seeley and Hatchard and Son, is to our knowledge the only one extant. (Dodd may have added "second edition" to give his work an aura of success, or he may have been referring to the earlier account of his life that he mentions in his dedication of his *Narrative* to Lord Ashley.) The Seeley and Hatchard edition is reproduced as it appeared, with no silent emendations of any kind. Dodd, who retold the story of his life in his *The Laboring Classes of England* (1847; see Introduction 49), gave no indication in that work, reported conversation, or extant correspondence that he was anything other than a full partner in the collaborative process of the production of this British edition, even though it may be the book that he repudiated in one of the letters that John Bright introduced as evidence during a parliamentary speech (see Introduction 52).

Chapters in the Life of a Dundee Factory Boy; An Autobiography. Dundee: James Myles. Edinburgh: Adam & Charles Black. London: Simpkin, Marshall, & Co. 1850.

The fictional autobiography of Frank Forrest first appeared in the eight-page weekly newspaper, *The Northern Warder and General Advertiser for the Counties of Fife, Perth, and Forfar* (Forfar being an earlier name for the county now called Angus). The ten individual chapters of *The Dundee Factory Boy* each appeared anonymously on page 4 of the newspaper in the issues between

January 3 and March 7, 1850. The chapters were printed without titles, which were introduced in the appearance of the text as a book published in 1850 by James Myles (1819-51). (The Thomas Cooper Library of the University of South Carolina has another edition published in Dundee in 1850, this one with the subtitle *Written by Himself* and the information that it was "Published by James Myles" for the "New Popular Library Series.") In the newspaper version, the opening chapter is cast in a relatively small font, but the type for the later installments becomes larger, and this type-setting seems to have been used for the 1850 book edition with only infrequent and minor changes and corrections, such as the altering of the phrase "but perhaps" to "though perhaps" at the end of Chapter VII possibly to avoid the use of "but" in two consecutive lines. A note at the end of Chapter VII of this periodical version gives some sense of at least one kind of response to Myles's work: it tells of his having "learned with sincere regret that one of his chapters has given offense to a section of moral reformers whose principles and aims he heartily sympathises with," and he goes on to assert that he has never meant to condemn the temperance movement or "befriend ... drunkenness" (February 14, 1850: 4; see note 1 on page 278). Another note—this one at the end of the last chapter in *The Northern Warder*, describing the attention that Myles's work has received (see the note on page 300)—was replaced in the book edition by the final paragraph that appears in the present volume. According to *Autobiography of the Working Class: An Annotated, Critical Bibliography* (Burnett, Vincent, and Mayall), which gives James Myles as the editor of the *Chapters in the Life of a Dundee Factory Boy*, it also appeared in 1850 in *The Champion* in ten installments between February 9 and April 13, 1850. *The Champion* was a weekly newspaper started by Joseph Rayner Stephens in 1849, for which Richard Oastler wrote frequently, and the organ of the Fielden Society (Association for the Protection of John Fielden's Ten Hours Act), which used the paper to make known the continuing problems involved in factory labor (Driver 491).

Authorship of *Chapters in the Life of a Dundee Factory Boy* has been mistakenly attributed to the fictional character Frank Forrest, but Myles retold this story as its author in his *Rambles in Forfarshire, or Sketches in Town and Country* in 1850, which consisted, "for the most part, of papers which had previously appeared in the *Dundee Courier*" (Norrie 133; see Appendix C.2). A list advertising the books that Myles offered for sale, now that he had been a book seller and printer for "fully seven years," includes the *Dundee Factory Boy* under "BOOKS BY JAMES MYLES" (see Introduction 33), and the catalogue includes a testimonial by George Gilfillan, the well-known literary arbiter in Dundee who also provided an introductory note to Ellen Johnston's 1867 edition of poems (see note 3 on page 314): "Those 'Rambles,' as well as his 'Chapters in the Life of a Factory Boy,' are amusing and singularly graphic sketches of humble life." This information, including the testimonial, is repeated in the issue for January 4, 1851, of the newspaper that Myles published, *Myles' Forfarshire Telegraph, and Monthly Advertiser; A Journal of Politics, Literature, and Social Progress.* (This issue may have been a sample of the paper that Myles had planned to put into circulation just before his death in February of 1851 [see Appendix C.2]). In addition to this evidence of authorship, *Chapters in the Life of a Dundee Factory Boy* was recorded as having been written by Myles in Norrie's 1873 *Dundee Celebrities of the Nineteenth Century.* The few autobiographical similarities between character and creator, such as their sharing an "ambition to be permanently connected with the press" (Norrie 262), are far outweighed by the evidence pointing to the status of the *Chapters* as a fiction (see Whatley; Introduction 33-34). The copytext adopted here argues for his authorship of a carefully written and printed work.

"Autobiography of Ellen Johnston, 'The Factory Girl.'" From *Autobiography, Poems and Songs of Ellen Johnston, The "Factory Girl."* Glasgow: W. Love, 1867. And "Autobiography." From *Autobiography, Poems, and Songs of Ellen Johnston, The "Factory Girl."* Second Edition. Glasgow: W. Love, 1869.

Johnston published her *Autobiography, Poems and Songs* by subscription in 1867 after almost two years of gathering the support of those willing to buy copies of it. Alexander Campbell, editor of the *Penny Post*, in which her poems had appeared, used his newspaper to encourage and promote Johnston's efforts to launch her volume, announcing a "call" for subscribers and asking for aid for the author of the collection when its sales were slow. By 1869 nearly eight hundred copies of the first edition had been sold, and a second edition, also supported by subscription, was printed in that year (Klaus, ch. 8). The 1869 edition carries a reset title page, which changes the punctuation of the title to *Autobiography,*

Poems, and Songs. The selections of poetry are largely those of the 1867 edition, with some deletions, additions, and reorganization; the most significant addition involves the appearance in the appendix of "The Last Lay of the 'Factory Girl.'" More extensive are the revisions to the "Autobiography," from the first version of which material was deleted with its sections reorganized.

In keeping with current textual theory, particularly evident in the controversy involved in the treatment of recent editions of *Hamlet,* both extant versions of Ellen Johnston's autobiography are reprinted here. The clear bowdlerization of the 1869 text cannot be attributed with any certainty to any one collaborator in its production: responsibility for it might rest with any number of individuals alone or in combination—the author, the publisher, or perhaps even Johnston's various sponsors and mentors, including those mentioned at the end of the "Autobiography," the Rev. George Gilfillan and Alexander Campbell (see 314). Students and scholars are therefore invited to compare the two versions and speculate on the origins and effects of their differences.

Works Cited

Burnett, John, David Vincent, and David Mayall, eds. *The Auto-biography of the Working Class: An Annotated, Critical Bibliography.* Vol. 1: 1790-1900. Brighton: Harvester, 1984.

Driver, Cecil. *Tory Radical: The Life of Richard Oastler.* New York: Oxford UP, 1946.

Kirby, R.G., and A.E. Musson. *The Voice of the People: John Doherty, 1798-1854, Trade Unionist, Radical and Factory Reformer.* Manchester: Manchester UP, 1975.

Klaus, H. Gustav. *Factory Girl: Ellen Johnston and Working-Class Poetry in Victorian Scotland.* Frankfurt am Main: Peter Lang, 1998.

McGann, Jerome. *The Textual Condition.* Princeton: Princeton UP, 1991.

Norrie, W. *Dundee Celebrities of the Nineteenth Century.* Dundee: William Norrie, 1873.

A Memoir of Robert Blincoe,
An Orphan Boy (1832)

John Brown

[Robert Blincoe was born about 1792, and he was sent to the St. Pancras workhouse in London around 1796. In 1799 he went with a group of paupers from the St. Pancras workhouse to work at Lowdham Mill near Nottingham, and after that mill closed, he was sent to Litton Mill near Tideswell, where he remained until he completed his apprenticeship more than fourteen years later. He then worked in a series of mills in Derbyshire, Cheshire, and Manchester, and in 1817 he started a business as a cotton-waste dealer in Manchester. He married in 1819, and about 1824 he invested what he had been able to save in cotton-spinning machinery.

The story of Blincoe's mistreatment as a factory child, from which he would bear scars on his head, face, ears and limbs for life, had by this time come to the attention of John Brown, a working-class journalist from Bolton, who then recorded Blincoe's tale. After Brown committed suicide in 1825, Richard Carlile, the publisher who in 1828 had started the radical paper *The Lion,* learned that a manuscript existed detailing Blincoe's story, and on 25 January 1828 the "Memoir of Robert Blincoe, An Orphan Boy" began appearing in *The Lion* in a series of five weekly installments that ran through 22 February of the same year in which it also appeared as a pamphlet. Before that time Blincoe had been confined in the Lancaster Castle debtor's prison, a circumstance arising from the financial setbacks of a fire in 1824 that had destroyed the machinery in which he had invested some of his savings. By 1830 Blincoe had been released from prison and was working as a cotton-waste dealer in Manchester, and by 1832 he also had opened a grocer's shop. That same year, trade-unionist John Doherty decided to republish Blincoe's *Memoir* (under the new title *A Memoir of Robert Blincoe, An Orphan Boy; Sent from the Workhouse of Saint Pancras, London, at Seven Years of Age, to Endure the Horrors of a Cotton-Mill*). Although it had previously been published without its subject's knowledge, on this occasion Doherty enlisted Blincoe's support and made additions and deletions to the manuscript with his assistance. (See Note on the Text; Appendix A.4 records the deletions from Carlile's pamphlet. Doherty's additions are included in the text below in curly brackets.)

Despite his youthful privations, the publication of the *Memoir* made Blincoe's a name that was instantly recognizable to proponents of factory reform, and this measure of fame may have helped him put his troubles behind him. The uneducated boy who had no family was able to send his three children to school and keep them out of the factories (one of his sons would be graduated from Queen's College, Cambridge in 1848, and subsequently become a clergyman in the Church of England). Blincoe apparently continued to work in the cotton business until about 1843. He died of bronchitis in Macclesfield in 1860 at the age of approximately 68.]

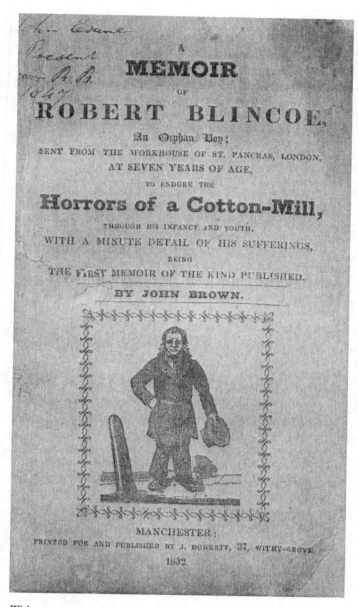

A

MEMOIR

OF

ROBERT BLINCOE,

An Orphan Boy;

SENT FROM THE WORKHOUSE OF ST. PANCRAS, LONDON,

AT SEVEN YEARS OF AGE,

TO ENDURE THE

Horrors of a Cotton-Mill,

THROUGH HIS INFANCY AND YOUTH,

WITH A MINUTE DETAIL OF HIS SUFFERINGS,

BEING

THE FIRST MEMOIR OF THE KIND PUBLISHED.

BY JOHN BROWN.

MANCHESTER:

PRINTED FOR AND PUBLISHED BY J. DOHERTY, 37, WITHY-GROVE.

1832.

Title page courtesy of Rare Books and Manuscript Library,
Butler Library, Columbia University.

Publisher's Preface.[1]

THE various Acts of Parliament, which have been passed, to regulate the treatment of children in the Cotton Spinning Manufactories, betoken the previous existence of some treatment, so glaringly wrong, as to force itself upon the attention of the legislature. This Cotton-slave-trade, like the Negro-slave-trade, did not lack its defenders, and it might have afforded a sort of sorry consolation to the Negro slaves of America, had they been informed, that their condition, in having agriculturally to raise the cotton, was not half so bad, as that of the white infant-slaves, who had to assist in the spinning of it, when brought to this country. The religion and the black humanity of Mr. Wilberforce[2] seem to have been entirely of a foreign nature. Pardon is begged, if an error is about to be wrongfully imputed, but the Publisher has no knowledge, that Mr. Wilberforce's humane advocacy for slaves, was ever of that homely kind, as to embrace the region of the home-cotton-slave-trade. And yet, who shall read the Memoir of Robert Blincoe, and say, that the charity towards slaves should not have begun or ended at home?

The Author of this Memoir is now dead; he fell, about two or three years ago, by his own hand. He united, with a strong feeling for the injuries and sufferings of others, a high sense of injury when it bore on himself, whether real or imaginary; and a despondency when his prospects were not good. Hence his suicide. Had he not possessed a fine fellow-feeling with the child of misfortune, he had never taken such pains to compile the Memoir of Robert Blincoe, and to collect all the wrongs on paper, on which he could gain information, about the various sufferers under the cotton-mill systems. Notes to the Memoir of Robert Blincoe were intended by the author, in illustration of his strong personal assertions. The references were marked in the Memoir; but the Notes were not prepared, or if prepared, have not come to the Publisher's hand. But, on enquiring after Robert

---

1   By Richard Carlile, publisher of *The Lion*. This preface preceded
    Chapter III in the version of *A Memoir* printed in *The Lion*, 1.5 (February 1, 1828), but it was placed as the first section of the text when
    Carlile republished the *Memoir* as a pamphlet (see Note on the Text).
2   William Wilberforce (1759-1833), philanthropist and politician, an
    instrumental figure in bringing about the abolition of slavery in Britain's
    colonies.

Blincoe, in Manchester, and mentioning the Memoir of him written by Mr. Brown, as being in the Publisher's possession, other papers, by the same Author, which had been left on a loan of money in Manchester, were obtained, and these papers seem to have formed the authorities, from which the notes to the Memoirs would have been made. So that, though the Publisher does not presume to make notes for the Author, nor for himself, to this Memoir, he is prepared to confirm much of the statement here made, the personalities of Robert Blincoe excepted, should it be generally challenged.

Robert Blincoe, the subject of the Memoir, is {now about 35 years of age, and resides at No.19, Turner-street, Manchester, where he keeps a small grocer's shop. He is also engaged in manufacturing Sheet Wadding and Cotton Waste-Dealer.} The Publisher having no knowledge of Robert Blincoe, but in common with every reader of this Memoir, can have no personal feelings towards him, other than those of pity for his past sufferings. But such a Memoir as this was much wanted, to hand down to posterity, what was the real character of the complaints about the treatment of children in our cotton mills, about which a legislation has taken place, and so much has been said. An amended treatment of children has been made, the apprenticing system having been abandoned by the masters of the mills; but the employment is in itself bad for children; first, as to their health; and second, as to their manners and acquirements; the employment being in a bad atmosphere; and the education, from example, being bad; the time, that should be devoted to a better education, being devoted to that which is bad. The employment of infant children in the cotton-mills furnishes a bad means to dissolute parents, to live, in idleness and all sorts of vice, upon the produce of infant labour. There is much of this in Lancashire, which a little care and looking after, on the part of the masters of cotton-mills, might easily prevent. But what is to be done? Most of the extensive manufacturers profit by human misery and become callous toward it; both from habit and interest. If a remedy be desired, it must be sought by that part of the working people themselves, who are alive to their progressing degradation. It will never be sought fairly out, by those who have no interest in seeking it. And so long as the majority of the working people squanders its already scanty income in those pest-houses, those intoxicating nurseries, for vice, idleness and misery, the public drinking houses, there is no hope for them of an amended condition.

MEMOIR

OF

ROBERT BLINCOE,

AN ORPHAN BOY.

CHAP. I.

BY the time the observant reader has got through the melancholy recital of the sufferings of Blincoe and his associates in cotton-mill bondage, he will probably incline to an opinion, that rather than rear destitute and deserted children, to be thus distorted by excessive toil, and famished and tortured as those have been, it were incomparably less cruel to put them at once to death—less cruel that they had never been born alive; and far more wise that they had never been conceived. In cases of unauthorized pregnancies, our laws are tender of unconscious life, perhaps to a faulty extreme; whilst our parochial institutions,[1] as these pages will prove, after incurring considerable expense to *preserve* the lives of those forlorn beings, sweep them off by shoals, under the sanction of other legal enactments, and consign them to a fate, far worse than sudden death.

Reared in the most profound ignorance and depravity, these unhappy beings are, from the hour of their birth, to the last of their existence, generally cut off from all that is decent in social life. Their preceptors are the veriest wretches in nature!—their influential examples all of the worst possible kind. The reports of the Cotton Bill Committees[2] abundantly prove, that, by forcing those destitute poor to go into cotton-mills, they have, in very numerous instances, been consigned to a destiny worse than death without torture. Yet appalling as are many of the statements, which,

---

1 our parochial institutions] Under the Elizabethan Poor Laws of 1598 and 1601, which remained in force until the Poor Law Amendment Act of 1834, parishes or "parochial" districts were the units of local government charged with the care of the destitute. A parish's overseers of the poor were elected officials empowered to apprentice orphans or children whose parents could not support them. Masters of such apprentices were often forced to take on their care or willing to do so because they could be used as sources of cheap labor (see Introduction 43-44).

2 Cotton Bill Committees] See Introduction (22-24 and 45-46) for accounts of major nineteenth-century parliamentary committees and royal commissions charged with investigating the conditions of factory labor in Britain's textile industries.

through the reports of the Committees, have found their way before the public, similar acts of delinquencies, of a hue still darker—even repeated acts of murder, have escaped unnoticed. Much of the evidence brought forward by the friends of humanity, was neutralized or frittered away by the timidity of their witnesses, or by the base subserviency of venally unprincipled professional men, who, influenced by rich capitalists, basely prostituted their talent and character as physicians, surgeons, and apothecaries, to deceive the government, to perplex and mislead public opinion, and avert the loud cry raised against the insatiate avarice and relentless cruelty of their greedy and unfeeling suborners.

It was in the spring of 1822, after having devoted a considerable time to the investigating of the effect of the manufacturing system, and factory establishments, on the health and morals of the manufacturing populace, that I first heard of the extraordinary sufferings of R. Blincoe. At the same time, I was told of his earnest wish that those sufferings should, for the protection of the rising generation of parish children, be laid before the world. Thus assured, I went to inquire for him, and was much pleased with his conversation. If this young man had not been consigned to a cotton-factory, he would probably have been strong, healthy, and well grown; instead of which, he is diminutive as to stature, and his knees are grievously distorted. In his manners, he appeared remarkably gentle; in his language, temperate; in his statements, cautious and consistent. If, in any part of the ensuing narrative, there are falsehoods and misrepresentations, the fault rests solely with himself; for, repeatedly and earnestly, I admonished him to beware, lest a too keen remembrance of the injustice he had suffered should lead him to transgress the limits of truth. After I had taken down his communications, I tested them, by reading the same to other persons, with whom Blincoe had not had any intercourse on the subject, and who had partaken of the miseries of the same hard servitude, and by whom they were in every point confirmed.

ROBERT BLINCOE commenced his melancholy narrative, by stating, that he was a parish orphan, and knew not either his father or mother. From the age of four years, he says, "till I had completed my seventh, I was supported in Saint Pancras poorhouse, near London."[1] In very pathetic terms, he frequently cen-

---

1   St. Pancras] a large parish in the north of central London. In Blincoe's time it extended from the south end of Gray's Inn Lane up to Camden Town, Pentonville, and Sommers Town.

sured and regretted the remissness of the parish officers, who, when they received him into the workhouse, had, as he seemed to believe, neglected to make any entry, or, at least, any to which he could obtain access, of his mother's and father's name, occupation, age, or residence. Blincoe argued, and plausibly too, that those officers would not have received him, if his mother had not proved her settlement;[1] and he considered it inhuman in the extreme, either to neglect to record the names of his parents, or, if recorded, to refuse to give him that information, which, after his attaining his freedom, he had requested at their hands. His lamentations, on this head, were truly touching, and evinced a far higher degree of susceptibility of heart, than could have been expected from the extreme and long continued wretchedness he had endured in the den of vice and misery, where he was so long immured. Experience often evinces, that, whilst moderate adversity mollifies and expands the human heart, extreme and long continued wretchedness has a direct and powerful contrary tendency, and renders it impenetrably callous.

In one of our early interviews, tears trickling down his pallid cheeks, and his voice tremulous and faltering, Blincoe said, "I am worse off than a child reared in the Foundling Hospital. Those orphans have a name given them by the heads of that Institution, at the time of baptism, to which they are legally entitled.[2] But I have no name I can call my own." He said he perfectly recollected riding in a coach to the workhouse, accompanied by some female, that he did not however think this female was his mother, for he had not the least consciousness of having felt either sorrow or uneasiness at being separated from her, as he very naturally supposed he should have felt, if that person had been his mother. Blincoe also appeared to think he had not been nursed by his mother, but had passed through many hands before he arrived at

---

1   proved her settlement] She met the requirements necessary to have her son receive parish assistance under the Poor Laws in effect at the time by being a resident of the parish or married to one. One could also prove one's settlement in a parish by being an apprentice there, by paying parish rates, or by serving as a parish officer for a year.

2   the Foundling Hospital] the famous London home for abandoned infants chartered by Captain Thomas Coram in 1739, opened in 1741, and moved to its eighteenth- and nineteenth-century location near Gray's Inn Road Lane in northern London in 1745. The christenings of newly arrived infants in the chapel of the Foundling Hospital were open to the public as a way of attracting donors.

the workhouse; because he had no recollection of ever having experienced a mother's caresses. It seems, young as he was, he often enquired of the nurses, when the parents and relations of other children came to see his young associates, *why no one came to him*, and used to weep, when he was told, that *no one had ever owned him*, after his being placed in that house. Some of the nurses stated, that a female, who called soon after his arrival, inquired for him by the name of "Saint;" and, when he was produced, gave him a penny-piece, and told him his mother was dead. If this report were well founded, his mother's illness was the cause of his being removed and sent to the workhouse. According to his own description, he felt with extreme sensibility the loneliness of his condition, and, at each stage of his future sufferings, during his severe cotton-mill servitude, it pressed on his heart the heaviest of all his sorrows—an impassable barrier, "a wall of brass,"[1] cut him off from all mankind. The sad consciousness, that he stood alone "*a waif on the world's wide common*;" that he had no acknowledged claim of kindred with any human being, rich or poor—that he stood apparently for ever excluded from every social circle, so constantly occupied his thoughts, that, together with his sufferings, they imprinted a pensive character on his features, which probably neither change of fortune, nor time itself, would ever entirely obliterate. When he was six years old, and, as the workhouse children were saying their Catechism, it was his turn to repeat the Fifth Commandment—"Honour thy father and thy mother, &c.,"[2] he recollects having suddenly burst into tears, and felt greatly agitated and distressed—his voice faltering, and his limbs trembling. According to his statement, and his pathetic eloquence, in reciting his misfortunes, strongly corroborated his assertion, he was a very ready scholar, and the source of this sudden burst of grief being inquired into by some of his superiors, he said, "I cry, because *I cannot* obey one of God's commandments, I know not either my father or my mother, I cannot therefore be a good child and honour my parents."

It was rumoured, in the ward where Robert Blincoe was placed, that he owed his existence to the mutual frailties of his mother and a reverend divine, and was called the young *Saint*, in allusion to his priestly descent. This name or appellation he did not long retain,

---

1 "a wall of brass"] a common poetic phrase in the eighteenth century, particularly frequent in the hymns of John Wesley and Charles Wesley.
2 Exodus 20: 12.

for he was afterwards called Parson; often, *the young Parson*; and he recollected hearing it said in his presence, that he was the son of a parson Blincoe. Whether these allusions were founded in truth, or were but the vile effusions of vulgar malice, was not, and is not, in his power to determine, whose bosom they have so painfully agitated. Another remarkable circumstance in his case, was, that when he was sent in August, 1799, with a large number of other children, from Saint Prancras [*sic*] workhouse, to a cotton-mill near Nottingham,[1] he bore amongst his comrades, the name of *Parson*, and retained it afterwards till he had served considerably longer than his Fourteen Years, and then, when his Indentures were at last relinquished,[2] and not till then, the young man found he had been apprenticed by the name of Robert Blincoe. I urged the probability, that his right indenture might, in the change of masters that took place, or the careless indifference of his last master, have been given to another boy, and that to the one given to him, bearing the name of Blincoe, he had no just claim. This reasoning he repelled, by steadily and consistently asserting, he fully recollected having heard it said his real name was Blincoe, whilst he remained at Saint Pancras workhouse. His indentures were dated the 15th August, 1799. If, at this time, he was seven years of age, which is by no means certain, he was born in 1792, and in 1796, was placed in Pancras workhouse. With these remarks, I close this preliminary matter, and happy should I be, if the publication of these facts enables the individual to whom they relate, to remove the veil which has hitherto deprived him of a knowledge of his parentage, a privation which he still appears to feel with undiminished intensity of grief.

---

1 Nottingham] a city on the River Trent, approximately 120 miles from London; site of Richard Arkwright's first horse-powered cotton mill (1769) and still a center for hosiery and lace manufacture.

2 Fourteen Years ... Indentures] The normal period of seven years for an apprenticeship did not apply to workhouse children. Under the Elizabethan Poor Laws children were often apprenticed when as young as three-, four-, and five-years old, with the period of their indenture often lasting until they were twenty-one years old. Indentures constituted the agreement between a parent and a master or, in the case of a parish apprentice, between the overseers of the parish and a master, the contract binding the apprentice to serve the master for a set number of years. The agreement was copied twice on a piece of paper and cut in half with jagged edges (thus, "indentures"), the master's copy to be given to the apprentice when the latter completed the required time of service.

Two years have elapsed, since I first began to take notes of Blincoe's extraordinary narrative. At the close of 1822 and beginning of 1823, I was seized with a serious illness, which wholly prevented my publishing this and other important communications. The testimony of as respectable a surgeon, who attended me, as any in the country, even ocular demonstration of my enfeebled state, failed to convince some of the cotton spinners, that my inability was not feigned, to answer some sinister end; and such atrocious conduct was pursued towards me, as would have fully justified a prosecution for conspiracy. Animated by the most opposite views, the worst of miscreants united to vilify and oppress me; the one wanting to get my papers, in order, by destroying them, to prevent the enormities of the cotton masters being exposed; and another, traducing my character, and menacing my life, under an impression that I had basely sold the declarations and communications received from oppressed workpeople to their masters. By some of those suspicious, misjudging people, Blincoe was led away. He did not, however, at any time, or under any circumstances, retract or deny any part of his communications, and, on the 18th and 19th of March, 1824, of his own free will, he not only confirmed all that he had communicated in the spring of 1822, with many other traits of suffering, not then recollected, but furnished me with them. It has, therefore, stood the test of this hurricane, without its authenticity being in any one part questioned or impaired. The authenticity of this narrative is, therefore, entitled to greater credit, than much of the testimony given by the owners of cotton-factories, or by professional men on their behalf, as will, in the course of this narrative, be fully demonstrated, by evidence wholly incontrovertible. If, therefore, it should be proved, that atrocities to the same extent, exist no longer; still, its publication, as a preventive remedy, is no less essential to the protection of parish paupers and foundlings. If the gentlemen of Manchester and its vicinity, who acted in 1816, &c., in conjunction with the late Mr. Nathaniel Gould,[1] had not made the selection of witnesses too much in the power of incompetent persons, Robert Blincoe

---

1   Nathaniel Gould (d. 1820), Manchester merchant who spent large amounts of his fortune on the cause of factory reform. Gould appeared before the 1816 parliamentary committee and, with his brother, "produced voluminous evidence from Sunday Schools and personal researches on immorality, cruelty, and long hours in local mills" (Ward 22).

would have been selected in 1819, as the most impressive pleader in behalf of destitute and deserted children.

CHAP. II.

OF the few adventures of Robert Blincoe, during his residence in old Saint Pancras workhouse, the principal occurred when he had been there about two years. He acknowledges he was well fed, decently clad, and comfortably lodged, and not at all over-done, as regarded work; yet, with all these blessings in possession, this destitute child grew melancholy. He relished none of the humble comforts he enjoyed. It was liberty he wanted. The busy world lay outside the workhouse gates, and those he was seldom, if ever permitted to pass. He was cooped up in a gloomy, though liberal sort of a prison-house. His buoyant spirits longed to rove at large. He was too young to understand the necessity of the restraint to which he was subjected, and too opiniative to admit it could be intended for his good. Of the world he knew nothing, and the society of a workhouse was not very well calculated to delight the mind of a volatile child. He saw givers, destitute of charity, receivers of insult, instead of gratitude, witnessed little besides sullenness and discontent, and heard little but murmurs or malicious and slanderous whispers. The aged were commonly petulant and miserable—the young demoralized and wholly des-titute of gaiety of heart. From the top to the bottom, the whole of this motley mass was tainted with dissimulation, and he saw the most abhorrent hypocrisy in constant operation. Like a bird newly caged, that flutters from side to side, and foolishly beats its wings against its prison walls, in hope of obtaining its liberty, so young Blincoe, weary of confinement, and resolved, if possible to be free, often watched the outer gates of the house, in the hope, that some favourable opportunity might facilitate his escape. He wistfully measured the height of the wall, and found it too lofty for him to scale, and too well guarded were the gates to admit of his egress unnoticed. His spirits, he says, which were naturally lively and buoyant, sank under this vehement longing after liberty. His appetite declined, and he wholly forsook his usual sports and comrades. It is hard to say how this disease of the mind might have terminated, if an accident had not occurred, which afforded a chance of emerging from the lifeless monotony of a workhouse, and of launching into the busy world, with which he longed to mingle.

Blincoe declares, he was so weary of confinement, he would gladly have exchanged situations with the poorest of the poor children, whom, from the upper windows of the workhouse, he had seen begging from door to door, or, as a subterfuge, offering matches for sale. Even the melancholy note of the sweep-boy, whom, long before day, and in the depths of winter, in frost, in snow, in rain {in} sleet, he heard pacing behind his surly master, had no terrors for him. So far from it, he envied him his fortune, and, in the fulness of discontent, thought his own state incomparably more wretched. The poor child was suffering under a diseased imagination, from which men of mature years and elaborate culture are not always free. It filled his heart with perverted feelings—it rendered the little urchin morose and unthankful, and, as undeserving of, as he was insensible to, the important benefits extended to him by a humane institution, when helpless, destitute and forlorn.

From this state of early misanthropy, young Blincoe was suddenly diverted, by a rumour, that filled many a heart among his comrades with terror, viz. that a day was appointed, when the master-sweeps of the metropolis were to come and select such a number of boys as apprentices, till they attained the age of 21 years, as they might deign to take into their sable fraternity.[1] These tidings, that struck damp to the heart of the other boys, sounded like heavenly music to the ears of young Blincoe:—he anxiously inquired of the nurses if the news were true, and if so, what chance there was of his being one of the elect. The ancient matrons, amazed at the boy's temerity and folly, told him how bitterly he would rue the day that should consign him to that wretched employment, and bade him pray earnestly to God to protect him from such a destiny. The young adventurer heard these opinions with silent contempt. Finding, on farther inquiry, that the rumour was well founded, he applied to several menials in the house, whom he thought likely to promote his suit, entreating them to forward his election with all the interest they could command! Although at this time he was a fine grown boy, being fearful he might be deemed too low in stature, he accustomed

---

1   their sable fraternity] Boys as young as five were employed to climb into chimneys to clean them and, on occasion, to put out fires. Ill-clothed and therefore prone to the diseases caused by soot, chimney-sweeps were also frequently injured and disabled. From 1788 well into the middle of the nineteenth-century, Parliament passed laws that were ineffective in protecting these young workers.

himself to walk in an erect posture, and went almost a tip-toe;— by a ludicrous conceit, he used to hang by the hands to the rafters and balustrades, supposing that an exercise, which could only lengthen his arms, would produce the same effect on his legs and body. In this course of training for the contingent honour of being chosen by the master-sweeps, as one fit for their use,—with a perseverance truly admirable, his tender age considered, young Blincoe continued till the important day arrived. The boys were brought forth, many of them in tears, and all except Blincoe, very sorrowful. Amongst them, by an act unauthorised by his guardians, young Blincoe contrived to intrude his person. His deportment formed a striking contrast to that of all his comrades: his seemed unusually high: he smiled as the grim looking fellows approached him; held his head as high as he could, and, by every little artifice in his power, strove to attract their notice, and obtain the honour of their preference. While this fatherless and motherless child, with an intrepid step, and firm countenance, thus courted the smiles of the sooty tribe, the rest of the boys conducted themselves as if they nothing so much dreaded, as to become the objects of their choice, and shrunk back from their touch as if they had been tainted by the most deadly contagion. Boy after boy was taken, in preference to Blincoe, who was often handled, examined, and rejected. At the close of the show, the number required was elected, and Blincoe was not among them! He declared, that his chagrin was inexpressible, when his failure was apparent.

Some of the sweeps complimented him for his spirit, and, to console him, said, if he made a good use of his time, and contrived to grow a head taller, he might do very well for a fag,[1] at the end of a couple of years. This disappointment gave a severe blow to the aspiring ambition of young Blincoe, whose love of liberty was so ardent, that he cared little about the sufferings by which, if attained, it was likely to be alloyed. The boys that were chosen, were not immediately taken away. Mingling with these, some of them said to our hero, the tears standing in their eyes:— "why, Parson, can you endure the thought of going to be a chimney-sweep? I wish they would take you instead of me." "So do I, with all my heart," said Blincoe, "for I would rather be any where than here." At night, as Blincoe lay tossing about, unable to sleep; because he had been rejected, his unhappy associates were weeping and wailing, because they had been accepted! Yet,

---

1 fag] drudge.

his heart was not so cold as to be unaffected by the wailings of those poor children, who, mournfully anticipating the horrors of their new calling, deplored their misfortune in the most touching terms. They called upon their parents, who, living or dead, were alike unable to hear them, to come and save them! What a difference of feeling amongst children of the same unfortunate class! The confinement that was so wearisome to young Blincoe, must have been equally irksome to some of his young associates; therefore, the love of liberty could not have been its sole cause,—there was another and a stronger reason—all his comrades had friends, parents, or relations: poor Blincoe stood alone! no ties of consanguinity or kindred bound him to any particular portion of society, or to any place—he had no friend to soothe his troubled mind—no domestic circle to which, though excluded for a time, he might hope to be reunited. As he stood thus estranged from the common ties of nature, it is the less to be wondered at, that, propelled by a violent inclination to a rambling life, and loathing the restraint imposed by his then condition, he should indulge so preposterous a notion, as to prefer the wretched state of a sweeping-boy. Speaking on this subject, Blincoe said to me, "If I could penetrate the source of my exemption from the sorrow and consternation so forcibly expressed by my companions, it would probably have been resolved by the peculiarity of my destiny, and the privation of those endearing ties and ligatures which cement family circles. When the friends, relatives, parents of other children came to visit them, the caresses that were sometimes exchanged, the joy that beamed on the faces of those so favoured, went as daggers to my heart; not that I cherished a feeling of envy at their good fortune; but that it taught me more keenly to feel my own forlorn condition. Sensations, thus excited, clouded every festive hour, and, young as I was, the voice of nature, instinct, if you will, forced me to consider myself as a moral outcast, as a scathed and blighted tree, in the midst of a verdant lawn."

I dare not aver, that such were the very words Blincoe used, but they faithfully convey the spirit and tendency of his language and sentiments. Blincoe is by no means deficient in understanding: he can be witty, satirical, and pathetic, by turns, and he never showed himself to such advantage, as when expatiating upon the desolate state to which his utter ignorance of his parentage had reduced him.

During Blincoe's abode at St. Pancras, he was inoculated at

the Small Pox Hospital.[1] He retained a vivid remembrance of the copious doses of salts he had to swallow, and that his heart heaved, and his hand shook as the nauseous potion approached his lips. The old nurse seemed to consider such conduct as being wholly unbecoming a *pauper child*; and chiding young Blincoe, told him, he ought to "lick his lips," and say thank you, for the good and wholesome medicine provided for him at the public expense: at the same time, very coarsely reminding him of the care that was taken to save him from an untimely death by catching the small-pox in the natural way. In the midst of his subsequent afflictions, in Litton Mill, Blincoe declared, he often lamented having, by this inoculation, lost a chance of escaping by an early death, the horrible destiny for which he was preserved.

From the period of Blincoe's disappointment, in being rejected by the sweeps, a sudden calm seems to have succeeded, which lasted till a rumour ran through the house, that a treaty was on foot between the Churchwardens and Overseers of St. Pancras,[2] and the owner of a great cotton factory, in the vicinity of Nottingham, for the disposal of a large number of children, as apprentices, till they became twenty-one years of age.[3] This occurred about a twelvemonth after his chimney-sweep miscarriage. The rumour itself inspired Blincoe with new life and spirits; he was in a manner intoxicated with joy, when he found, it was not only confirmed, but that the number required was so considerable, that it would take off the greater part of the children in the house,—poor infatuated boy! delighted with the hope of obtaining a greater degree of liberty than he was allowed in the workhouse,—he dreamed not of the misery that impended, in the

---

1   Small Pox Hospital] This institution, which was established in 1746 for both the care of smallpox victims and its prevention, was located at Battle Bridge in the parish of St. Pancras. In Blincoe's time, a child would have been inoculated there with a dose of the live virus to induce a mild case of the disease.

2   Churchwardens and Overseers] Like overseers of the poor, churchwardens were elected officials of a parish, though they were principally charged with the upkeep of the parish church.

3   the disposal of ... children] The placing of destitute children as apprentices by parish officials was often considered a "disposal" of them because serving an apprenticeship in another parish relieved the one from which the children had been sent of its financial responsibility for them (see Introduction 44).

midst of which he could look back to Pancras as to an Elysium,[1] and bitterly reproach himself for his ingratitude and folly.

Prior to the show-day of the pauper children to the purveyor or cotton master, the most illusive and artfully contrived falsehoods were spread, to fill the minds of those poor infants with the most absurd and ridiculous errors, as to the real nature of the servitude, to which they were to be consigned. It was gravely stated to them, according to Blincoe's statement, made in the most positive and solemn manner, that they were all, when they arrived at the cotton-mill, to be transformed into ladies and gentlemen: that they would be fed on roast beef and plumpudding— be allowed to ride their masters' horses, and have silver watches, and plenty of cash in their pockets. Nor was it the nurses, or other inferior persons of the workhouse, with whom this vile deception originated; but with the parish officers themselves. From the statement of the victims of cotton-mill bondage, it seems to have been a constant rule, with those who had the disposal of parish children, prior to sending them off to cotton-mills, to fill their minds with the same delusion. Their hopes being thus excited, and their imaginations inflamed, it was next stated, amongst the innocent victims of fraud and deception, that no one could be *compelled* to go, nor any but volunteers accepted.

When it was supposed at St. Pancras, that these excitements had operated sufficiently powerful to induce a ready acquiescence in the proposed migration, all the children, male and female, who were seven years old, or considered to be of that age, were assembled in the committee-room, for the purpose of being publicly examined, touching their health, and capacity, and what is almost incredible, touching their *willingness* to go and serve as apprentices, in the way and manner required! There is something so detestable, in this proceeding, that any one might conclude, that Blincoe had been misled in his recollections of the particulars; but so many other sufferers have corroborated his statement, that I can entertain no doubt of the fact. This exhibition took place in August 1799, and eighty boys and girls as parish apprentices, and till they had respectively acquired the age of twenty-one years, were made over, by the churchwardens and overseers of Saint Pancras parish, to Messrs. Lamberts', cotton-spinners, hosiers and lace-men, of St. Mary's parish, Nottingham, the

---

1 Elysium] a paradise, named for the Elysian Fields; in classical mythology, the equivalent of heaven.

owners of Lowdam Mill.[1] The boys, during the latter part of their time, were to be instructed in the trade of stocking weaving—the girls in lace-making.[2] There was no specification whatever, as to the time their masters were to be allowed to work these poor children, although, at this period, the most abhorrent cruelties were notoriously known to be exercised, by the owners of cotton-mills, upon parish apprentices. According to Blincoe's testimony, so powerfully had the illusions, purposely spread to entrap these poor children, operated, and so completely were their feeble minds excited, by the blandishments held out to them, that they almost lost their wits. They thought and talked of nothing but the scenes of luxury and grandeur, in which they were to move. Nor will the reflecting reader feel surprised at this credulity, however gross, when he considers the poor infants imagined there were no greater personages than the superiors, to whom they were, as paupers, subjected, and that, it was those identical persons, by whom their weak and feeble intellects had thus been imposed upon. Blincoe describes his conduct to have been marked by peculiar extravagance. Such was his impatience, he could scarcely eat or sleep, so anxiously did he wait the hour of emancipation. The poor deluded young creatures were so inflated with pride and vanity, that they strutted about like so many dwarfish and silly kings and queens, in a mock tragedy. "We began" said Blincoe "to treat our old nurses with airs of insolence and disdain—refused to associate with children, who, from sickness, or being under age, had not been accepted; they were commanded to keep their distance; told to know their betters; forbidden to mingle in our exalted circle! Our little coterie was a complete epitome of the effects of prosperity in the great world. No sooner were our hearts cheered by a prospect of good fortune,

---

1   Messrs. Lamberts' ... Lowdham Mill] The three Lambert brothers, along with their partner Robert Almond, opened the cotton mill that Blincoe calls Lowdham (variously spelled in Brown's text as "Lowdham" and "Lowdam") on the Dover Beck in 1784 (Chapman 82-83). Reputedly later called Cliffe Mill and now Gonalston Mill, it is near Lowdham, a village approximately eight miles northeast of Nottingham.

2   stock weaving ... lace-making] The goal of serving a traditional apprenticeship was to learn the skills required by a specific trade. The children at Lowdham Mill were promised instruction in the handicrafts of making hosiery and lace during the later years of their apprenticeships there.

than its influence produced the sad effects recited. The germ of those hateful vices, arrogance, selfishness and ingratitude, began to display themselves even before we had tasted the intoxicating cup. But our illusion soon vanished, and we were suddenly awakened from the flattering dream, which consigned the greater part of us to a fate more severe than that of the West Indian slaves, who have the good fortune to serve humane owners.["] Such were Blincoe's reflections in May 1822.

It appears that the interval was not long, which filled up the space between their examination, acceptance, and departure from St. Pancras workhouse, upon their way to Nottingham; but short as it was, it left room for dissension. The boys could not agree who should have the *first ride* on their masters' horses, and violent disputes arose amongst the girls, on subjects equally ludicrous. It was afterwards whispered at Lowdam Mill, that the elder girls, previous to leaving Pancras, began to feel scruples, whether their dignity would allow them to drop the usual bobcurtsey to the master or matron of the house, or to the governess by whom they had been instructed to read, or work by the needle. Supposing all these follies to have been displayed to the very letter, the poor children were still objects of pity; the guilt rests upon those by whom they had been so wickedly deceived!

Happy, no doubt, in the thought of transferring the burthen of the future support of fourscore young paupers to other parishes, the churchwardens and overseers distinguished the departure of this juvenile colony by acts of munificence. The children were completely new clothed, and each had two suits, one for their working, the other for their holiday dress—a shilling, in money, was given to each—a new pocket handkerchief—and a large piece of gingerbread. As Blincoe had no relative of whom to take leave, all his anxiety was to get outside the door. According to his own account, he was the first at the gate, one of the foremost who mounted the waggon, and the loudest in his cheering. In how far the parents or relatives of the rest of the children consented to this migration; if they were at all consulted, or even apprised of its being in contemplation, formed no part of Blincoe's communications. All he stated was, that the whole of the party seemed to start in very high spirits. As to his own personal conduct, Blincoe asserts, he strutted along dressed in party-coloured parish clothing, on his way to the waggon, no less filled with vanity than with delusion: he imagined he was free, when he was in fact legally converted into a slave: he exulted in the imaginary possession of personal liberty, when he was in reality a prisoner. The whole convoy were well guarded by the parish beadles on their way to the waggons; but those officers, bearing their staves, the children were taught to consider as a guard of *honour*. In addition to the beadles, there was an active young man or two, appointed to look after the passengers of the two large waggons, in their conveyance to Nottingham. Those vehicles, and very properly too, were so secured, that when once the grated doors were locked, no one could escape. Plenty of clean straw was strewed in the beds, and no sooner were the young fry *safely lodged* within, than they began throwing it over one another and seemed delighted with the commencement of their journey. A few hours progress considerably damped this exultation. The inequality of the road, and the heavy jolts of the waggon, occasioned them many a bruise. Although it was the middle of August, the children felt very uncomfortable. The motion of the heavy, clumsy vehicle, and so many children cooped up in so small a space, produced nausea and other results, such as sometimes occur in Margate hoys.[1] Of the country they passed through, the young travellers saw very little.—Blincoe thinks the children were suffered to come out of the waggon to walk through St. Alban's.[2] After having passed one night in the waggon, many of the children began to repent, and express a wish to return. They were told to have patience, till they arrived at Messrs. Lamberts, when, *no doubt*, those gentlemen would pay every attention to their wishes, and send back to St. Pancras, those who might wish to return. Blincoe, as might have been expected, was not one of those *back-sliders*—he remained steady to his purpose, exulting in the thought, that every step he advanced brought him nearer to the desired spot, where so many enviable enjoyments awaited him, and conveyed him farther and farther from the detested workhouse! {Blincoe being so overjoyed with the fine expectations he was to receive at Lowdam Mill, he spent his shilling at Leicester[3] in apples.}

The greater part of the children were much exhausted, and not a few of them seriously indisposed, before they arrived at Nottingham. When the waggons drew up near the dwelling and warehouse of their future master, a crowd collected to see the

---

1 Margate] a popular seaside resort on the southeast coast of England; hoys are barges or boats.
2 St. Albans] a cathedral city in Hertfordshire nineteen miles northwest of London.
3 Leicester] a city on the river Soar eighty-nine miles northeast of London.

live stock that was just imported from the metropolis, who were pitied, admired, and compared to lambs, led by butchers to slaughter! Care was taken that they should not hear or understand much of this sort of discourse. The boys and girls were distributed, some in the kitchen, others in a large ware-room, washed, combed, and supplied with refreshments; but there were no plum-pudding,—no roast beef, no talk of the horses they were to ride, nor of the watches and fine clothing that they had been promised. Many looked very mournful; they had been four days travelling to Nottingham: at a more advanced period of their lives, a travel to the East Indies might not have been estimated as a much more important or hazardous undertaking. After having been well refreshed, the whole of the boys and girls were drawn up in rows, to be *reviewed by their masters*, their friends and neighbours. In Blincoe's estimation, their masters, Messrs. Lamberts', were "stately sort of men." They looked over the children and finding them all right, according to the *invoice*, exhorted them to behave with proper humility and decorum. To pay the most prompt and submissive respect to the orders of those who would be appointed to instruct and superintend them at Lowdam Mill, and to be diligent and careful, each one to execute his or her task, and thereby avoid the punishment and disgrace which awaited idleness, insolence, or disobedience. This harangue, which was delivered in a severe and dictatorial tone, increased their apprehensions, but not one durst open a mouth to complain. The masters and their servants talked of the various sorts of labor to which the children were to apply themselves, and to the consternation and dismay of Blincoe and his associates, not the least allusion was made to the many fine things which had so positively been promised them whilst in London. The conversation which Blincoe heard, seemed to look forward to close, if not to unremitting toil, and the poor boy had been filled with expectations, that he was to work only when it pleased him; to have abundance of money and fine clothes—a watch in his pocket, to feast on roast beef, and plum-pudding, and to ride his masters horses. His hopes, however were, not wholly extinguished, because Nottingham was not Lowdam Mill, but his confidence was greatly reduced, and his tone of exultation much lowered.

The children rested one night at Nottingham in the warehouses of their new masters; the next day they were led out to see the castle, Mortimer-hole and other local curiosities, in the forest of Sherwood,[1] which are so celebrated by bards of ancient times. Many shoes, bonnets, and many other articles of clothing having been lost upon the journey, others were supplied; but withal Blincoe found himself treated as a parish orphan, and he calculated on being received and treated as if he had been a gentleman's son sent on a visit to the house of a friend or relative. By the concurring testimony of other persons who had been entrapped by similar artifices, it appears certain, that the *purveyors* of infant labourers to supply the masters of cotton and silk factories with cheap labourers, adopted this vile, unmanly expedient, in most of their transactions. It will be seen, by the evidence of Sir Robert Peel, Baronet,[2] David Owen, Esq.[3] and other witnesses examined in 1816,[4] that, when children were first wanted to attend machinery in cotton-factories, such was the aversion of parents and guardians to this noxious employment,

---

1   the castle ... Sherwood] Nottingham Castle, originally built by William the Conqueror, was expanded until it was destroyed in the seventeenth century when it was rebuilt as a residence of the Duke of Newcastle. When Blincoe saw it in the late eighteenth century, it was in disrepair, its rooms divided up and rented to tenants and a boarding school. Mortimer's Hole, a passage below the castle, was by legend the means by which Roger de Mortimer reached his lover, Queen Isabella, wife of Edward II. Sherwood Forest was the ancient Crown property between Nottingham and Worksop, popularly associated with the legends of Robin Hood.

2   Sir Robert Peel (1788-1850), a major manufacturer and Tory member of Parliament, whose family made its wealth in cotton manufacture. Peel, later Prime Minister, was responsible for the passage of several early, if ineffective factory acts (see Introduction 44).

3   David Owen is clearly meant here for Robert Owen (1771-1858), Welsh socialist and owner of the Scottish mill at New Lanark, where he put his communitarian principles into practice. In 1815 Owen called a meeting of manufacturers at Glasgow where he proposed limiting the hours of children working in factories. Unsuccessful, he went to London and presented his ideas there, in response to which Peel proposed new factory legislation and asked the House of Commons for a select committee to inquire into the issue.

4   the evidence of Sir Robert Peel ... in 1816] Peel's Select Committee met between April and June of 1816. Though the committee heard forty-seven witnesses, Owen among them, Peel was not able to introduce even a highly modified bill until 1818, which passed into law in 1819 (see Introduction 44-45).

that scarcely any would submit to consign their offspring to those mills, the owners of which, under the specious pretext of diminishing the burthens occasioned by poor-rates, prevailed on churchwardens and overseers, to put their infant paupers into their hands. Since then, by a gradual progress of poverty and depravity, in the county of Lancashire alone, there are some thousand fathers, mothers, and relatives, who live upon the produce of infant labor, though alloyed by the dreadful certainty, that their gain is acquired by the sacrifice of their children's health and morals, and too frequently of their lives, whereby the fable of Saturn devouring his children,[1] seems realised in modern times.

CHAP. III.

LOWDHAM Cotton-Mill, situated near a village of that name, stood ten miles distant from Nottingham, on the Surhill road;[2] thither Robert Blincoe and his associates were conveyed the next day in carts, and it was rather late when they arrived. The mill, a large and lofty edifice, being surmounted by a cupola, Blincoe, at first, mistook for a church, which raised a laugh at his expense and some jeering remarks, that he would soon know what sort of service was performed there. Another said, he did not doubt but the young cocknies would be very *regular* in their *attendance.* When he came in view of the apprentice-house, which was half a mile distant from the mill, and was told that was *to be his home for fourteen years to come,* he was not greatly delighted, so closely did it resemble a workhouse. There was one source of consolation, however, remaining—it was not surrounded by lofty walls, nor secured by strong gates, as was the case at Pancras. When the first cart, in which was young Blincoe, drove up to the door, a number of villagers flocked round, some of whom exclaimed, "God help the poor wretches."— "Eh!" said another, "what a fine collection of children, little do they know to what a life of slavery they are

---

1 Saturn devouring his children] In Roman mythology, Saturn led a revolt of his brothers and sisters against his father Uranus, and as a result Saturn became king of the gods. As Saturn had children of his own, he devoured them at birth in order that they might not one day overthrow him. His son Jupiter did survive and did eventually overthrow his father to usurp his position.
2 Surhill] i.e., Southwell Road in Nottingham.

doomed."—"The Lord have mercy upon them," said a third.—
"They'll find little mercy here," said a fourth. The speakers were
mostly of the female sex, who, shaking their heads, said,— "Ah!
what fine clear complexions!"—"The roses will soon be out of
bloom, in {the} mill." Such were a part of the remarks, which
saluted the ears of these children, as they entered the Lowdham
mill. In common with his comrades, Blincoe was greatly dis-
mayed, by the gloomy prognostications, which their guardians
did all they could to check, or prevent the children from hearing,
hurrying them, as rapidly as they could, inside the house.

The young strangers were conducted into a spacious room,
fitted up in the style of the dinner-room, in Pancras old workhouse, viz.: with long, narrow deal tables, and wooden benches.
Although the rooms seemed tolerably clean, there was a certain
rank, oily, smell, which Blincoe did not very much admire. They
were ordered to sit down at these tables—the boys and girls
apart. The other apprentices had not left work, when this supply
of children arrived. The supper set before them consisted of milk-
porridge, of a very blue complexion! The bread was partly made
of rye—very black, and so soft, they could scarcely swallow it, as
it stuck like bird-lime to their teeth. Poor Blincoe stared, recollecting this was not so good a fare as they had been used to at
Saint Pancras. Where is our roast beef and plum-pudding, he said
to himself. He contrived, with some difficulty, to eat about one
half of his allowance. As the young strangers gazed mournfully at
each other, the governor and governess, as the master and mistress of the apprentices were styled, kept walking round them,
and making very coarse remarks. Just as they had passed Blincoe,
some of the girls began making faces, and one flung a dab of
bread against the wall, where it stuck fast, as if it had been plaister [plaster]. This caught the eye of the governor—a huge raw-
boned man, who had served in the army, and had been a drill ser-
jeant, unexpectedly, he produced a large horse-whip, which he
clanged in such a sonorous manner, that it made the house re-
echo. In a moment, the face-makers and bread throwers were
reduced to solemn silence and abject submission. Even young
Blincoe was daunted—he had been one of the ring-leaders, in
these seditious proceedings; but so powerful was the shock to his
nerves, sustained from the tremendous clang of the horse-whip,
it bereft him of all his gaiety, and he sat as demure as a truant-
scholar, just previous to his flogging. Yet the master of the house
had not uttered a single threat; nor indeed had he occasion; his
carbuncled nose—his stern and forbidding aspect and his terrible

horse-whip, inspired quite as much terror as was requisite. Knowing, that the apprentices from the mill were coming, this formidable being retired, to the great relief of the young strangers; but so deep an impression had he created, they sat erect and formal, scarcely daring to look beyond the nose. Whilst they were in this subdued and neutralised state, their attention was suddenly and powerfully attracted by the loud shouting of many voices, almost instantly the stone room filled, spacious as it was, with a multitude of young persons of both sexes; from young women down to mere children. Their presence was accompanied by a scent of no very agreeable nature, arising from the grease and dirt acquired in the avocation, [sic]

The boys, generally speaking, had nothing on, but a shirt and trowsers. Some few, and but a few, had jackets and hats. Their coarse shirts were entirely open at the neck, and their hair looked, as if a comb had seldom, if ever, been applied! The girls, as well as Blincoe could recollect, were, like the boys, destitute of shoes and stockings. Their locks were pinned up, and they were without caps; very few had on, either jacket or gown; but wore, what, in London, are called, pinafores; in Lancashire, bishops!—that is, long aprons with sleeves, made of coarse linen, that reached from the neck to the heels. Blincoe was no less terrified at the sight of the pale, lean, sallow-looking multitude, than his nostrils were offended by a dense and heavy smell of rank oil or grease, that arose at their appearance! By comparison, the new comers appeared like so many ladies and gentlemen. On their first entrance, some of the old apprentices took a view of the strangers; but the great bulk first looked after their supper, which consisted of new potatoes, distributed at a hatch door, that opened into the common room from the kitchen. At a signal given, the apprentices rushed to this door, and each, as he made way, received his portion, and withdrew to his place at the table. Blincoe was startled, seeing the boys pull out the fore-part of their shirts, and holding it up with both hands, received the hot boiled potatoes allotted for their supper. The girls, less indecently, if not less filthily, held up their dirty greasy bishops or aprons, that were saturated with grease and dirt, and having received their allowance, scampered off as hard as they could, to their respective places, where, with a keen appetite, each apprentice devoured her allowance, and seemed anxiously to look about for more. Next, the hungry crew ran to the tables of the new comers, and voraciously devoured every crust of bread and every drop of porridge they had left, and put or answered interrogatories as occasion required." [sic]

Thus unfavorable were the impressions produced by the scene that presented itself on his first entrance into a cotton-factory. Blincoe was forcibly struck by the absence of that personal cleanliness which had been so rigidly enforced at St. Pancras. The apprentices were required to wash night and morning; but no soap was allowed, and without it, no dirt could be removed. Their tangled locks covered with cotton flue,[1] hung about their persons in long wreaths, floating with every movement. There was no cloth laid on the tables, to which the new comers had been accustomed in the workhouse—no plates, nor knives, nor forks—to be sure the latter utensils were not absolutely necessary with a potato-supper. Instead of salt-cellars, as had been allowed at Pancras, a very stingy allowance of salt was laid on the table, and Blincoe saw no other beverage drunk, by the old hands, than pump water.

The supper being devoured, in the midst of the gossiping that ensued, the bell rang, that gave the signal to go to bed. The grim governor entered to take the charge of the newly arrived boys, and his wife, acting the same part by the girls, appeared every way suitable to so rough and unpolished a mate. She was a large grown, robust woman, remarkable for a rough hoarse voice and ferocious aspect. In a surly, heart-chilling tone, she bade the girls follow her. Tremblingly and despondingly the little creatures obeyed, scarcely daring to cast a look at their fellow travellers, or bid them good night. As Blincoe marked the tear to start in their eyes and silently trickle down their cheeks, his heart responsive sank within him. They separated in mournful silence, scarcely a sigh being heard, nor a word of complaint being uttered.

The room in which Blincoe and several of the boys were deposited, was up two pair of stairs. The bed places were a sort of cribs, built in a double tier, all round the chamber. The apprentices slept two in a bed. The beds were of flock. From the quantity of oil imbibed in the apprentices' clothes, and the impurities that accumulated from the oiled cotton, a most disagreeable odour saluted his nostrils. The governor called the strangers to him and allotted to each his bed-place and bed-fellow, not allowing any two of the newly arrived inmates to sleep together. The boy, with whom Blincoe was to chum, sprang nimbly into his birth [berth], and without saying a prayer, or any thing else, fell asleep before Blincoe could undress himself. So completely was he

---

1 flue] fluff, floating particles of textile fibers.

cowed, he could not restrain his tears. He could not forbear exe-
crating the vile treachery of which he felt himself the victim; but
still he declared, it never struck him, at least, not till long afterwards, that the *superiors* of St. Pancras had deceived him. The
fault, he thought, lay with Messrs. Lamberts, their new masters.
When he crept into bed, the stench of the oily clothes and greasy
hide of his sleeping comrade, almost turned his stomach.—What,
between grief and dismay, and this nauseous smell, it was dawn of
day before Blincoe dropt asleep. Over and over again, the poor
child repeated every prayer he had been taught, and strove, by
unfeigned piety, to recommend himself to the friend of the friendless, and the father of the fatherless. At last, sleep sealed his weary
eye-lids; but short was the repose he was allowed to enjoy; before
five o'clock, he was awakened by his bed-fellow, who springing
upright, at the loud tolling of a bell, told Blincoe to dress with all
speed, or the governor would flog him and deprive him of his
breakfast. Before Blincoe had time to perform this office, the iron
door of the chamber, creaking upon its hinges, was opened, and
in came the terrific governor, with the horse-whip in his hand, and
every boy hastily tumbled out of his crib, and huddled on his
clothes with all possible haste! Blincoe and his fellow travellers
were the slowest, not being rightly awake. Blincoe said "bless me,
have you *church-service* so soon?" "church-service you fool,['] said
one of the larger apprentices, ["]it is to the mill *service* you are
called, and you had better look sharp, or you'll catch it!" saying
this, off he scampered. Blincoe, who was at first amazed at the
trepidation, that appeared in the apprentices, soon understood the
cause. The grim-looking governor, with the carbuncled nose,
bearing the emblem of arbitrary rule, a horse-whip, in his hand,
made his appearance, and stalking round the chamber, looked in
every bed-place: as he passed Blincoe and his young comrades, he
bestowed a withering look upon them, which, fully understanding, they hastened below; arrived there, Blincoe saw some of the
boys washing themselves at a pump, and was directed to do the
same.—The whole mass sat down to breakfast at five o'clock in
the morning. The meal consisted of *black bread* and *blue milk-porridge*. Blincoe and his fellow strangers took their places, mingled
with the rest of the apprentices, who, marking their dislike of the
bread, eagerly seized every opportunity of eating it themselves.
Blincoe and his comrades looked wistfully at each other. Consternation sat deeply imprinted on their features; but every tongue
was silent; young as they were, they had sense enough to perceive
the necessity of submission and the prudence of reserve.

They reached the mill, about half past five. The water was on, from the bottom to the top, in all the floors, in full movement.[1] Blincoe heard the burring sound before he reached the portals and smelt the fumes of the oil with which the axles of twenty thousand wheels and spindles were bathed. The moment he entered the doors, the noise appalled him, and the stench seemed intolerable.

He did not recollect that either of the Messrs. Lamberts' were present at the mill, on his first entrance. The newly arrived were received by Mr. Baker, the head manager, and by the overlookers of the respective rooms. They were mustered in the making-up room; the boys and girls in separate divisions. After being looked at, and laughed at, they were dispersed in the various floors of the mill, and set to various tasks.—Blincoe was assigned to a room, over which a man named *Smith presided*. The task first allotted to him was, to pick up the loose cotton,[2] that fell upon the floor. Apparently, nothing could be easier, and he set to with diligence, although much terrified by the whirling motion and noise of the machinery, and not a little affected by the dust and flue with which he was half suffocated. They span coarse numbers;[3] unused to the stench, he soon felt sick, and by constantly stooping, his back ached. Blincoe, therefore, took the liberty to sit down; but this attitude, he soon found, was strictly forbidden, in cotton mills. His task-master (Smith) gave him to understand, he must keep on his legs. He did so, till twelve o'clock, being six hours and a half, without the least intermission.—Blincoe suffered at once by thirst and hunger; the moment, the bell rang, to announce dinner, all were in motion, to get out as expeditiously as possible. Blincoe ran out amongst the crowd, who were allowed to go; never, in his life, before did he know the value of wholesome air so perfectly. He had been sick almost to fainting, and it revived him instantaneously! The cocknies mingled together, as they made progress towards the apprentice-house! Such as were playsome made to each other! and the melancholy seemed to mingle their tears! When they reached the apprentice-

---

1 water ... in full movement] Lowdham Mill was initially powered by water, one of the first forms of energy used in the early mechanized textile industry (see Introduction 17).

2 pick up loose cotton] Blincoe works as what was called a scavenger, a child who cleaned up the textile fibers that had collected on machines or dropped on the floor beneath them.

3 coarse numbers] common or inferior cotton goods.

room, each of them had a place assigned at the homely board! Blincoe does not remember, of what his dinner consisted; but is perfectly sure, that neither roast beef nor plum-pudding made its appearance; and that the provisions, the cookery, and the mode of serving it out, were all very much below the standard of the ordinary fare of the workhouse, in which he had been reared.

During the space of a week or ten days, that Blincoe was kept picking up cotton, he felt at night very great weariness, pains in his back and ancles; and he heard similar complaints from his associates. They might have suffered less had they been taken to the mill at five o'clock, been worked till eight, and then allowed time to eat their breakfast; but six hours confinement, to close work, no matter of what kind, in an atmosphere as foul as that which circulated in a cotton-mill, is certainly injurious to the health and growth of children of tender years. Even in mills worked by water, and where the temperature of the air is nearly the same within the mill as without, this is the case; but incomparably more so in mills such as are found in Manchester, where, in many, the average heat is from 70 to 90 degrees of Farenheit's scale.[1] After Blincoe had been employed in the way described, he was *promoted* to the more important employment of a roving winder.[2] Being too short of stature, to reach to his work, standing on the floor, he was placed on a block; but this expedient only remedied a part of the evil; for he was not able by any possible exertion, to keep pace with the machinery. In vain, the poor child declared it was not in his power to move quicker. He was beaten by the overlooker, with great severity, and cursed and reviled from morning till night, till his life became a burthen to him, and his body discoloured by bruises. In common, with his fellow apprentices, Blincoe was wholly dependent upon the mercy of the overlookers, whom he found, generally speaking, a set of brutal, ferocious, illiterate ruffians, alike void of understanding, as of humanity! Blincoe complained to Mr. Baker, the manager,

---

1 mills ... in Manchester ... scale] Manchester, located approximately 185 miles north by northwest of London, was the main industrial site in Lancashire in the nineteenth century; it is here identified as the site of textile factories powered by steam-driven engines, which created more heat than water power did.
2 roving winder] Rovings were the soft strands that had been thinned and slightly twisted preparatory to their being made into yarn; a roving winder was therefore involved in the next-to-last stage of cotton production.

and all he said to him was:—"*do your work well, and you'll not be beaten.*" It was but seldom, either of the masters visited the mill, and when they did, Blincoe found it was useless to complain. The overlooker, who had charge of him, had a certain quantity of work to perform in a given time. If every child did not perform his allotted task, the fault was imputed to this overlooker, and he was discharged: on the other hand, a premium was given, if the full quantity of work was done and not otherwise. If, therefore, Messrs. Lamberts had remonstrated, or had reprimanded the task-masters, by whom the children were thus mercilessly treated, those task-masters could, and most probably would, have said, that if the owners insisted upon so much work being extracted from the apprentices, and a greater quantity of yarn produced, than it was possible to effect by fair and moderate labour, *they must allow them* severity of punishment, to keep the children in a state of continual exertion. Blincoe had not, of course, sense to understand this, the principal, if not the sole cause, of the ferocity of the overlookers; but such was, and is the inhuman policy prevailing in cotton-mills, and whilst that cause remains unchanged, the effect inevitably must be the same. Each of the task-masters, to acquire favor and emolument, urged the poor children to the very utmost!—Such is the driving system, which still holds its course, and which leads to the exhaustion and destruction of annual myriads, and to the {utmost} frightful crimes:—and such is the force of avarice, there are plenty of spin-ners, so depraved, as not only to sacrifice other people's children, but even *their own*.[1] Blincoe was not treated with that sanguinary and muderous ferocity, in this mill, which these pages will soon delineate; but from morning till night, he was continually being beaten, pulled by the hair of his head, kicked or cursed!

It was the custom, in Lowdham Mills, as it is in most water-mills, to make the apprentices work up lost time, by working over hours! a custom, that might not be deemed unreasonable, or found oppressive, if the regular hours were of moderate duration. Blincoe did not say, that this custom was abused at Lowdham Mill, in an equal degree, to what it was in others; but when chil-

---

1   plenty of spinners] Here Brown criticizes the need felt by adult male
    workers—in his account, variously called "spinners," "overlookers,"
    "overseers," and "task-masters"—to extract as much work as possible
    from the children they supervised. Whether such workers or their
    masters were responsible for the mistreatment of child laborers was a
    frequent subject of debate.

dren of seven years of age, or, by probability, younger, had to work fourteen hours every day in the week, Sundays excepted, any addition was severely felt, and they had to stop at the mill during dinner time, to clean the frames, every other day. Once, in ten days, or a fortnight, the whole of the finer machinery used to be taken to pieces and cleaned, and then they had to remain at the mill from morning till night, and frequently have been unable to find time to get any food from this early breakfast till night, after they had left off, a term frequently extended from fifteen to sixteen hours incessant labour.

As an inducement to the children to volunteer to work, the whole dinner-hour, a premium of a halfpenny was allowed! Small as was the bribe, it induced many, and Blincoe amongst the number! On such occasions, the dinner was brought up in tin cans, and often has Blincoe's allowance stood till night, whilst he was almost famished with hunger, and he has often carried it back, or rather eaten it on the road, cold, nauseous, and covered with flue.

Being half starved, and cruelly treated by his task-masters; being spotted as a leopard with bruises: and still believing his ill-treatment arose from causes beyond the controul of the parish officers, by whom he had been disposed of to Messrs. Lamberts, Blincoe resolved to attempt an escape,—to beg his way to London,—to lay his case before the overseers and churchwardens of Saint Pancras, and not only claim redress of injuries, but the fulfilment of the grand promises that had been made to him. "I cannot deny," said Blincoe, "that I feel a glow of pride, when I reflect that, at the age of seven years and a half, I had courage to resent and to resist oppression, and generosity to feel for the sufferings of my helpless associates, not one of whom durst venture to share the peril of the enterprise.—On the other hand," said he, "I must give them the credit for sincerity; for, if any one had been unguarded or perfidious, who knew of my *intended* expedition, I should have been put under such restraint, as would have effectually prevented a successful attempt to run away! I considered my situation so deplorable, and my state of thraldom so intolerable, that death appeared as a lesser evil. I was not wholly ignorant of the sufferings I might have had to encounter, nor that I might perish on the way, from want of food or shelter, and yet I persevered in an effort, in which, of forty fellow-sufferers, not one had courage to join, although many had parents or relatives, to whom to flee for succour, and I had none! So far, young as I was, I calculated upon difficulty, danger, and sufferings.—In one thing, only, was I deceived; that error consisted in thinking the evils of {my situation} intolerable! I had no recollection of calamities so severe, and consequently no standard by which to regulate my judgment. I therefore, rashly determined in my own mind, that my condition admitted of no aggravation,—I was indeed, soon undeceived! I lived, within the short space of four years, to look back with regret to the comparative degrees of ease, plenty of food, and of all other good things enjoyed at Lowdham Mill!— This sort of knowledge, is, I believe, commonly taught" said Blincoe, "to all the children of misery, as they sink deeper and deeper in woe! The first stage appears the most intolerable; but as they descend, like me, they sink so profoundly in the depths of wretchedness, that in their melancholy progress, those stages and degrees, which, at first, appeared as intolerable, lose all their terrors, in accumulated misery, and the desponding heart, when it takes a retrospective glance at past sufferings, often arraigns its want of patience and fortitude, for murmurings measured by present calamities. Their former condition appeared comfortable! Such was my condition, at a later period, when, to be released from the greater and heavier misery, which I endured at Lowdham, with all its evils, and in the very worst shape, I should have esteemed it as a positive state of happiness." Such was the philosophical reasoning of Robert Blincoe, in 1822. But, to proceed,—steady to his purpose, he embraced the first favourable opportunity of making the projected attempt to escape! He considered his great danger to lie in being retaken on the road between Lowdham and Nottingham; but he knew no other way, and was afraid to make inquiry! When the manager and over-looker of the room he worked in were busy, Blincoe {set} off, dressed in his working clothes. His progress began in a sort of canter, looking behind him every fifty yards for the first half-mile, when, finding he had not been seen or pursued, he continued his rapid flight till he reached {Burton},[1] and there, as fate decreed, that flight suddenly terminated; for, as he trotted onwards, a long-shanked, slip-shod taylor, who worked for Lowdham Mill,

---

1 {Burton}] Now called Burton Joyce, a village on the Southwell Road, six miles east by northeast from Nottingham. The text of *A Memoir* in both *The Lion* and Carlile's 1828 pamphlet prints "Buxton" here; the document in Appendix A.2 offers a confusing commentary on this problem since "Burton," about which Blincoe supposedly complained, is correct (see note on page 326).

slid nimbly from his shop-board, which, unfortunately for Blincoe, faced the road, and, placing himself full in the way, with a malicious kind of grin upon his long, lank visage, said "Oh! young Parson, where art thou running so fast this way?" saying this, he seized him by the hand, and led him very loath into his cottage, and, giving him a seat in the back part of the room, placed himself between his captive and the door.

Blincoe saw, at one glance, by these precautions, that he was caught. His indignation was so great at first, he would not give any answer; noticing which, his false and artful host said to his wife, "Give the young Parson something to eat and drink,—he is weary, and will be better able to pursue his journey, after he has rested and refreshed himself! The Lord commands us to give food to the hungry, and I dare say," addressing himself to him, "thou art not so full, but thou canst eat a bowl of bread and milk." "I must own, to my shame," said Blincoe, "the carnal man, the man of flesh was caught by the bait! I hungered and I ate, and he gave me so much, and I drank so heartily, that my teeth disabled my legs! To be sure, my fare was not very costly;—it consisted of some oaten bread and butter-milk!"

When this sly fox of a taylor found he could eat no more, still blockading the door, [he began] to question Blincoe as to the object of his journey, which the latter frankly explained,—"Aye, I thought so," said the detestable hypocrite, "young parson, I thought so,—I saw Satan behind thee, jobbing his prong into thy ★★★★!—I saw thee running headlong into h—ll, when I stept forth to save thee!" This avowal aroused all Blincoe's indignation, and he was determined to have a scuffle with his perfidious host; but he had swallowed so large a portion of butter-milk, and eaten so much oaten bread, he felt he had lost half his speed! Disdainful, however, of fraud or denial, he again avowed his intention, and its cause. The tailor then commenced an harangue upon the deadly sin of a breach of covenant,—assured Blincoe he was acting under the influence of Satan! that he was liable to be sent to Bridewell,[1] to be flogged, and, when sent back to his work, to be debarred of all liberty, and led to and from the mill with a halter round his neck! Blincoe was neither convinced by this reasoning, nor intimidated by these denunciations; but alas! his gluttonous appetite had disabled him for flight, and being thus disabled, and thus doubly a captive, he made a merit of necessity, and agreed

---

1 Bridewell] famous house of correction in London; *bridewell* was used more generally to indicate any prison.

to go back, if his host would be his mediator with Mr. Baker, the manager. This was the precise point to which the jesuitical[1] tailor wished to bring him. Without relinquishing his seat, the treacherous knave doffed his paper cap, and skeins of thread that still hung round his long, shaggy neck,—he combed his black, greasy locks, that hung straight as candles round his lanthorn [lantern] jaws,—tied a yellow cotton handkerchief round his neck,—put on a pair of shoes,—took a *crab-tree*[2] stick, full of knots, in his right hand, and grasping Blincoe's very tight in his left, he sallied forth on a *work of charity*, as the loathesome hypocrite called his having entrapped and betrayed a poor oppressed orphan child, fleeing from slavery and oppression. "In my heart," said Blincoe, "I detested the wretch with greater bitterness than my task-master; but he held me so tight, I could not escape and the sight of the bit of crab-tree which he brandished, as he chaunted hymns of thanksgiving, had also no small share of influence in overawing me,—in short, into the counting-house this second Judas led me. After an admonition to beware how again I made an attempt of the kind, the manager gave me a severe but not cruel chastisement." As to the *hospitable* tailor, when he had delivered him up, he slunk away, not waiting to receive Blincoe's thanks. Whether he took the *five shillings,* which Blincoe was afterwards told was the standing reward of those who brought back run-away apprentices, or let it stand till he had five pounds to receive for such services, he cannot ascertain; but he was told, this peeping Tom of {Burton}, had rendered many a poor child the same sort of kindness "In consequence of this scurvy trick," said Blincoe, "I have never been able to conquer the aversion it created against Methodists; although I am bound to believe, the wretch was one of the myriads of *counterfeits,* who flock to their standard from venal and corrupt motives."

After Blincoe had received his punishment, every weal and bruise with which he had started found a fellow. He was handed back to Smith, his task-master, by whom he was laughed at and jeered unmercifully, and worked with an increase of severity. When Blincoe left work, his old associates flocked around him, condoling his misfortune, and offering him half-pence and bits of

---

1 jesuitical] Though a Jesuit is literally a member of a Roman Catholic religious order (the Society of Jesus, founded by Ignatius Loyola in 1534), in this usage the term means a cunning, crafty person, characteristics that were attributed to the Jesuits by their detractors.
2 *crab-tree*] a walking stick made from the branch of a wild apple tree.

bread that they had saved! When they heard how the *godly* had caught him, their indignation swelled to such a height, they declared they would drown him in the mill-dam, if ever they had an opportunity. These condolements were grateful to his wounded pride and disappointed hopes. As he retired to his miserable bed, the governor, grinning horribly, made him a low bow in the military style, and gave him a hearty kick on his *seat of honour* at the same instant. In this manner, was he ushered to his bed, laughed at by that portion of the elder apprentices, who had made similar attempts, and had undergone a similar or a more vindictive punishment. Having abandoned all thoughts of escape, Blincoe submitted sullenly and patiently to his fate;—he worked according to his age and stature, as hard as any one in the mill. When his strength failed, and his limbs refused their office, he endured the strap or the stick, the cuff or the kick, with as much resignation as any of his fellow-sufferers. In the faded complexions, and sallow looks of his associates, he could see, as in a mirror, his own altered condition! Many of his comrades had, by this time, been more or less injured by the machinery. Some had the skin scraped off the knuckles, clean to the bone, by the fliers;[1] others a finger crushed, a joint or two nipped off in the cogs of the spinning-frame wheels!—When his turn to suffer came, the fore-finger of his left hand was caught, and almost before he could cry out, off was the first joint—his lamentations excited no manner of emotion in the spectators, except a coarse joke—he clapped the mangled joint, streaming with blood, to the finger, and ran off to {Burton}, to the surgeon, who, very composedly put the parts together again, and sent him back to the mill. Though the pain was so intense, he could scarcely help crying out every minute, he was not allowed to leave the frame. He said but little to any one; but was almost continually bemoaning in secret the cruelty of his fate. Before he was eight years old, Blincoe declared, that many a time he had been tempted to throw himself out of one of the upper windows of the factory; but when he came to look at the leap he purposed taking, his courage failed him—a propensity, he mentioned not as thinking it evinced any commendable feeling, but as an illustration of the natural and unavoidable consequences of working children too hard, and subjecting them to so many severe privations!

---

1   fliers] the parts of a spinning machine that twist the thread as they conduct it to and wind it upon the bobbin. Spinning is the final stage in the series of processes that turn loose, short fibers into long, relatively thickened yarn ready for weaving.

About the second year of his servitude, when the whole of the eighty children sent from Pancras Workhouse, had lost their plump and fresh appearance, and acquired the pale and sickly hue which distinguished factory children from all others, a most deplorable accident happened in Lowdham Mill, and in Blincoe's presence. A girl, named Mary Richards, who was thought remarkably handsome when she left the workhouse, and who might be nearly or quite ten years of age, attended a drawing frame,[1] below which, and about a foot from the floor, was a horizontal shaft, by which the frames above were turned. It happened, one evening, when most of her comrades had left the mill, and just as she was taking off the weights, her apron was caught by the shaft. In an instant the poor girl was drawn by an irresistible force and dashed on the floor. She uttered the most heart rending shrieks! Blincoe ran towards her, an agonized and helpless beholder of a scene of horror that exceeds the power of my pen to delineate! He saw her whirled round and round with the shaft—he heard the bones of her arms, legs, thighs, &c. successively snap asunder, crushed, seemingly, to atoms, as the machinery whirled her round, and drew tighter and tighter her body within the works, her blood was scattered over the frame and streamed upon the floor, her head appeared dashed to pieces—at last, her mangled body was jammed in so fast, between the shafts and the floor, that the water being low and the wheels off the gear, it stopped the main shaft! When she was extricated, every bone was found broken!—her head dreadfully crushed!—her clothes and mangled flesh were, apparently inextricably mixed together, and she was carried off, as supposed, quite lifeless. "I cannot describe," said Blincoe, "my sensations at this appalling scene. I shouted out aloud for them to stop the wheels! When I saw her blood thrown about like water from a twirled mop, I fainted. But neither the spine of her back was broken, nor were her brains injured, and to the amazement of every one, who beheld her mangled and horrible state, by the skill of the surgeon, and the excellence of her constitution, she was saved!["]—Saved to what end? the philosopher might ask—to be sent back to the same mill, to pursue her labours upon crutches, made a cripple for life, without a shilling indemnity from the parish, or the owners of the mill! Such was the fate of this poor girl, but, dismal

---

1 drawing frame] machine made of rollers that straighten out and equalize fibers produced after the first and second stages of cotton manufacture.

as it was, it will be seen by the succeeding parts of this narrative, that a lot still more horrible awaited many of her fellow-sufferers, whom the parish officers of St. Pancras, pursuant to Acts of Parliament authority, had apprenticed for fourteen years to the masters of Lowdham Cotton Mill. The dreadful spectacle Blincoe had witnessed in the racking of Mary Richards, rendered his employment more odious than ever.

It is already stated, that the food was very ordinary and not very plentiful; the apprentices were so oppressed by hunger, that the oldest and most daring sallied out at night and plundered the fields, and frequent complaints were made, and the apprentices got a very bad name, which belonged rather to the masters, in whose parsimony it originated!

When Blincoe had served about three years of his time, an event happened at Lowdham Mill, arising out of the manner in which apprentices were treated, that wrought a complete revolution there, and led to a new era in Blincoe's biography! Among the girls, who were bound apprentices to Messrs. Lamberts of Nottingham and Lowdham, were two sisters, named Fanny and {Mary} Collier, who had a mother residing in London. These young girls finding their health declining from excess of labour, bad provisions, and want of wholesome air and exercise, found means to write a letter to their mother, full of complaints, upon which, the widow undertook a journey to Lowdham, where she resided a fortnight, during which time, she was a reserved and shrewd observer of the condition of her own and of other children, and then returned to the metropolis. As far as Blincoe remembers these circumstances, Mrs. Collier did not make any complaints to Messrs. Lamberts, or to the manager! She reserved such representations for the parish officers of Saint Pancras, which induced them to send down a parochial committee, to inquire into the state and condition of the apprentices. One day, just as the dinner was being served out in the *usual* slovenly manner, without the least notice of the intended visit having been previously given, the Committee arrived, without asking or waiting for permission, they walked into the common room, and tasting the viands upon the table, they found them such as had been described. Whether *conscience* had any concern in the effort to discover and reform abuses in the mill, said Blincoe, I know not; but this I do know, that, if they had had a spark of shame, pity or remorse, the sallow, and sickly appearance of the eighty victims, saying nothing of Mary Richards, who was for ever rendered a cripple, ought to have filled them with sorrow and shame, on account of the base and cruel imposition, that had been practised in 1799. It is more probable, however, that the atrocious treatment experienced by the thousands and tens of thousands of orphan children, poured forth from our charitable institutions and from parish workhouses, and the dreadful rapidity with which they were consumed in the various cotton-mills, to which they were transported, and the sad spectacle exhibited by most of the survivors, were the real causes, which, in 1802, produced Sir Robert Peel's Bill, for the relief and protection of infant paupers employed in cotton-mills.[1] Hence, the extraordinary liveliness evinced by the overseers and churchwardens of Saint Pancras might have been occasioned by the dreadful scenes of cruelty and oppression developed during the progress of that Bill, which Blincoe never heard of, nor ever saw, till eleven or twelve years after it had passed into a law. It would be difficult to produce a more striking instance of the utter contempt, in which the upstart owners of great establishments treated an act, purposely enacted to restrain their unparalleled cruelty and waste of human life. The act itself declared the masters, owners, or occupiers of every cotton-mill in Great Britain and Wales should have a legible copy of the act, placed in some conspicuous and public part of each mill, and accessible to every one; yet, Blincoe, who was reared in the cotton-mill, never saw or heard of any such law, till eleven or twelve years after it had been enacted! When the committee began their investigation, as to the treatment and condition of the children sent from St. Pancras Workhouse, Blincoe was called up among others and admonished to speak the truth and nothing but the truth! So great however was the terror of the stick and strap, being applied to their persons, after these great dons should be at a great distance, it rendered him, and no doubt the great majority of his fellow-sufferers extremely cautious and timid.[2] It is however, likely,

---

1   Sir Robert Peel's Bill] The 1802 Health and Morals of Apprentices Act regulated the conditions in textile factories in which three or more apprentices or twenty or more other persons were employed, but its main provisions dealt with apprenticed labor, which it limited to twelve hours a day (see Introduction 44). Clauses dealing with proper housing of apprentices, along with measures for their religious and secular education, were also enacted by this almost completely unenforced act.

2   cautious and timid] Under the provisions of the Health and Morals of Apprentice Act (1802), magistrates were required to appoint two inspectors, a clergyman and a justice, to oversee conditions at local factories; but such inspectors often had difficulty collecting information from apprentices intimidated by their employers.

that their looks bespoke their sufferings, and told a tale not to be misunderstood. The visitors saw their food, dress, bedding, and they caused, in conjunction with the local magistrates, very great alterations to be made. A new house was ordered to be erected near the mill, for the use of the apprentices, in which there were fewer beds to a given space. The quantity of good and wholesome animal food to be dressed and distributed in a more decent way, was specified. A much more cleanly and decorous mode of cookery and serving up the dinner and other meals was ordered. The apprentices were divided into six classes, and a new set of tin cans, numbered 1, 2, 3, 4, 5, and 6, were made, to be served up to each individual, according to the class to which he or she may belong, to hold the soup or porridge! The old governor was discharged, who had given them all such a fright on their first arrival, and several of the overlookers were dismissed and new ones introduced;—among the latter description of persons was a man, who seemed wholly destitute of humanity—his name was William Woodward—born, I believe, at {Cromford}, in Derbyshire.[1] The appearance of this ferocious tyrant at Lowdham Mill proved a much heavier curse, scourge and affliction to Blincoe, than all the grievances which had existed, or were removed! As Woodward's amusement, in tormenting these poor apprentices, will occupy a large space in the next chapter, I shall say little of him in this.

It was the ill fortune of Blincoe and his associates, that, shortly after the reforms specified were introduced, and the hours of labour reduced, so that their situation became every way incomparably more eligible, Lowdam Mill stopped working.

At this period, Blincoe had served about four years of his time, and had learnt to wind rovings, and spin at the throstle,[2] and certainly earned as much money for his master in {the} week, as would suffice to keep him a month or longer, in meat, drink and clothes; but he had not been instructed in any part of the stocking-trade, nor had he acquired such a degree of knowl-

---

1 {Cromford}, in Derbyshire] The locations that Blincoe mentions in the midlands county of Derbyshire are all located in the sixty miles of the region still called the Peak District of the Southern Pennines. William Woodward becomes Robert in Chapter V (141), and Doherty's additions further complicate this identification (152). Cromford, the site of Richard Arkwright's first water-powered cotton mill (1771), was a village approximately 15 miles north of Derby.

2 throstle] a machine for spinning warp yarn in which the twisting and winding are simultaneous and continuous.

edge of the cotton-spinning, as might enable him to gain his bread elsewhere.

At this juncture, if justice had been done, the apprentices would have reverted to Saint Pancras parish, and not been abandoned as they were, and turned over to a new master, without any care being taken, that he should, if he took them, abide by the condition specified in their first indentures, and act up to the regulations introduced at Lowdham Mill.

Blincoe said, he believed the Messrs. Lamberts wrote to the parish officers of Saint Pancras, informing them of the situation of the children, in order that their friends might take back whom they pleasd to claim, and if, in this conclusion, Blincoe is right, and these officers neglected to take proper measures for the safety and protection of so large a body of children, as they had sent to Lowdham Mill, all healthy and straight limbed, they are morally responsible for the unparalleled sufferings to which they were afterwards exposed. When the subject shall again come before Parliament, it will be requisite to have the conduct of the parish officers on this occasion thoroughly investigated, not so much from a wish to have their offences visited with any legal penalty, if such were practicable, as to shew the necessity of abrogating the power invested in them by act of parliament, to place children beyond a given distance from the place of their birth or settlement: and secondly, to deprive them altogether of the power of tearing away children from their parents, and sending them into any manufactories whatever, without the knowledge and consent of their parents, or next of kin. If the parish officers think proper to apprentice them to any of the ordinary and established trades, they ought to have that power independently of their parents. In the mill, where Blincoe was next consigned, the *parish children* were considered, treated, and *consumed as a part of the raw materials;* their strength, their marrow, their lives, were consumed and converted into money! and as their live stock consisting of parish apprentices, diminished, new flocks of victims arrived from various quarters, without the cost of purchase to supply their place!

It is within the compass of probability, that there have been, and are yet, instances, wherein the {overseers} of the poor, and more especially the *assistant* overseers, who are mere mercenaries, and serve for pay, have been and are, some of them at least, *bribed* by the owners of mills for spinning silk, cotton or woollen yarn, to visit the habitation of the persons receiving parochial aid, and to compel them, when children are wanting, utterly regardless of education, health, or inclination, to deliver up their off-spring, or by cutting off the parish allowance, leave them to perish {for} want!

When Messrs. Lamberts gave up the cotton-yarn establishment, carried on at Lowdham Mill, they permitted all their apprentices who wished to leave their employment in a cotton-mill, to write to their parents and friends, and some few found redeemers; the great bulk were, unhappily left to their fate! Being a foundling, and knowing no soul on earth to whom he could look up for succour, Robert Blincoe was one of the unhappy wretches, abandoned to as dismal a destiny as ever befel *a parish apprentice.* It was his evil fortune, with a multitude of fellow sufferers, to be turned over *en masse* to Mr. ELLICE NEEDHAM, of Highgate Wall, Derbyshire, the master and owner of Litton Mill, near Tideswell.[1]

Before, however, I close this delineation of the character and conduct of the owners of Lowdham Cotton-Mill—Messrs. William, Charles, and Thomas Lambert[2]—it is due to them, if living, whatever may be their fortune, and to their memory, if deceased, to state, that, with the exception of Mary Richards, who was so dreadfully racked upon a shaft, and her bones mostly broken, not one of the children sent to their mill by St. Pancras parish, were injured as to be made a cripple, nor were they deformed in their knees and ancles. That there were deficiencies as to food and an excess of labour exacted, is clear, by the alterations which were introduced; but still, compared with what they soon afterwards suffered, they were humanely treated.

They were kept decently clad, had a bettermost[3] suit reserved for Sundays and holidays—were occasionally allowed a little time for play, in the open air, and upon *Goose fair-day,*[4] which is, or then was, a great festival at Nottingham–the whole of them were

---

1 Mr. Ellice Needham ... Tideswell] Contemporary records list Ellis Needham as a cotton manufacturer living at Hargate Wall (Chapman 200), a few miles west of Tideswell, a town approximately twenty-seven miles northwest of Derby. Reached by Tideswell Dale, a rugged area of rocks, ferns, and bushes, Litton was a village three-quarters of a mile east of Tideswell.

2 William, Charles, and Thomas Lambert] Contemporary records list these three brothers as William, Charles, and Francis Lambert. They went bankrupt in 1809 (Chapman 240).

3 bettermost] best.

4 *Goose fair-day*] a fair held in certain English towns about Michaelmas, September 29, when geese are in season.

conveyed in carts to that celebrated place, and regaled with furmety,[1] and sixpence in money was allowed to the very youngest! They went pretty regularly to Lowdham Church on Sundays; were not confined within gates and walls, as was the case at most other mills, where parish apprentices were immured! nor were there any iron-bars before the windows! They were *worked hard;* but not so hard as to distort their limbs, nor occasion declines or deaths! Their food latterly was good, and cleanly cooked. Their bedding, though coarse, was clean! When they had meat, they were allowed trenchers, knives, forks and spoons. It will presently be seen, when carried away from Lowdham Mill, into what a den of vice, disease and famine, filth and slavery, they were plunged; by what hellions they were worried, and all in defiance of a positive, and recently made law, on purpose for their protection, and in the face of the VISITING MAGISTRATE whose visits were, according to Blincoe's assertion, too frequently directed to the luxurious table of the master, to admit even a chance of justice to the apprentices. May this exposition of crimes and sufferings inflicted upon the friendless, the orphan, the widow's son, induce honest and upright men, senators and legislators, effectually to curb the barbarous propensities of hard-hearted masters, and rescue their nation from a worse stain, than even the African Slave Trade,[2] horrible as was that odious traffic, ever inflicted.

CHAP. IV.

THE next cotton-mill to which poor Blincoe was consigned, together, with those of his companions in tribulation, who had no friend to redeem them from impending misery, belonged to a Mr. Ellice Needham. Like most of his fraternity, his origin was obscure. He is said to have arisen from an abject state of poverty, and had it been by honourable industry, his prosperous fortune had redounded to his credit. Of his primeval state of poverty, it was his weakness to be ashamed. By the profusion of his table, and the splendor and frequency of his entertainments, he seemed to wish to cover and conceal his mean

---

1   furmety] Frumenty or furmety is wheat boiled in milk.
2   African Slave Trade] Trading in slaves within the British empire was abolished in 1807, as slavery itself was in 1833.

descent.[1] His house, lawns, equipage, and style of living, completely eclipsed the neighbouring gentry; yet, boundless as was his ostentation, he was in his heart sordidly mean and parsimonious. His cruelty, in wringing from poor friendless orphans, the means of supporting his guilty and unbecoming pomp, sufficiently evinces the baseness of his heart! His mansion, in 1803, and years later, was at Highgate Wall, near Buxton in Derbyshire.[2]

To this arrogant and unfeeling master, Messrs. Lambert made over the unexpired term of years for which the greater part of the parish apprentices had been bound by their respective indentures. What premium was paid, or, if any, I know not.[3] As this master was neither a hosier, nor a lace-manufacturer, he had not the power to fulfil the conditions imposed on Messrs. Lamberts, viz. to instruct the girls, during the last {three} year{s} of their time, in lace-knitting, and the boys in stocking-weaving. The consequence was, the poor children lost those important advantages, and those who survived the term of their apprenticeship to Ellice Needham, found themselves without that degree of skill which was requisite to enable them to gain their bread, in almost any other cotton-mill, and could touch none but the very coarsest work.

As Messrs. Lamberts were constrained, by circumstances, to stop their works, it might be, that they had not means to support the apprentices; but were forced to get rid of them with the utmost expedition. There have been instances, where, in case of bankruptcy, parish apprentices bound to cotton-masters, have been put into carts, driven to the verge of the parish, and there turned adrift without money—without a friend or a place to shelter them. According to Blincoe's account, although Messrs. Lamberts, informed the guardians of the poor of St. Pancras parish, of the necessity they were under of giving up their apprentices, or turning them over to other masters, no steps were taken for the protection of the friendless children, an imputation, the

---

1 mean descent] Ellis Needham's father owned land in a number of towns and villages in the Peak District of Derbyshire; his son was referred to as a "farmer" or "gentleman" in contemporary records (Chapman 200).

2 Buxton] a watering place near the head of the River Wye, twenty-four miles southeast of Manchester and thirty-eight miles north by northwest of Derby.

3 premium] the fee customarily paid to a master to cover the costs of an apprentice's training and upkeep (see Introduction).

more extraordinary, when the promptitude and decision with which they had acted in the case recited, is considered. It is, therefore, probable, that their activity might be owing to the horrid tales, that had then burst upon the public, descriptive of the cruelty and misery, of which parish children placed out in cotton-mills were the victims. It was, in 1802, that Sir Robert Peel, of Bury, who had the largest number of parish and foundling children, employed in his cotton-mills, of any cotton-master in Great Britain, brought forward his bill for their protection. According to Blincoe's narrative, the committee from St. Pancras arrived at Lowdham Mill, at this juncture, and the reforms introduced at Lowdham Mill, were, therefore, likely to have been owing to the parliamentary agitation of that question; and nothing can be more highly illustrative of the force of public opinion, than this proof of its potent effect on the officers of St. Pancras parish!—Supposing the conjecture to be well founded, at the time the apprentices were removed from Lowdham Mill, this humane act had passed into a law, and had become all but a dead-letter!—It may also have been a reliance upon the effect of that law which induced the parish officers to leave the children to their fate: what *that* fate was will presently appear!

It seems, that Mr. Ellice Needham, the master of Litton Mill, sent to Lowdham, to inspect the condition of the apprentices, who had improved very materially after the introduction of the new regulations. Nothing could be more kind or condescending than Ellice Needham's deportment at Lowdham. To some, he gave money,—to all, he promised most liberal and kind usage: he promised like a Titus: but he performed like a Caligula.[1]

Blincoe could not recollect, with precision, the number of apprentices, male and female, who were removed in carts from Lowdham to Litton Mill. The first day's progress brought them to Cromford, where they halted for the night. The girls were lodged in dwelling-houses; the boys, on straw, in a barn or stable! The next morning, the whole party were marched on foot through the village, as far as Matlock toll-bar,[2] so proud was

---

1 Titus ... Caligula] Titus Flavius Vespasianus (39-81), Roman Emperor from 79-81, whose reign was marked by benevolence and concern for the welfare of his people; Caligula, originally Gaius Caesar (12-41), Roman Emperor from 37-41, whose reign was marked by his extremely cruel and murderous behavior.
2 Matlock toll-bar] a gate or barrier across a road where a toll is taken; Matlock is a town sixteen miles northwest of Derby.

Woodward (their conductor) of their healthy appearance! Here they again mounted their carts! But this improvement is not imputable to the wholesomeness of cotton-factory employment; but to the effect of the recent modifications introduced at Lowdham Mill, and to their diminished hours of toil.

It was in the gloomy month of November, when this removal took place! On the evening of the second day's journey, the devoted children reached Litton Mill. Its situation, at the bottom of a sequestered glen, and surrounded by rugged rocks, remote from any human habitation, marked a place fitted for the foul crimes of frequent occurrence, which hurried so many of the friendless victims of insatiate avarice, to an untimely grave.

The savage features of the adjacent scenery impressed a general gloom upon the convoy, when Woodward pointed out to them the lonely mill to which they were travelling. As the hands were then at work, all of whom, except the overlookers, were parish children, the conductor of the new comers led them through the mill. The effect of the review filled the mind of Blincoe, and perhaps his unhappy associates, with deep dismay. The pallid, sickly complexions; the meagre, haggard appearance of the Litton Mill apprentices, with their filthy and ragged condition, gave him a sorrowful foretaste of the dismal fate that apparently awaited him. From the mill, they were escorted to the 'prentice-house, where every thing wore a discouraging aspect. Their first meal was water-porridge and oaten cakes: the former thin and ill made—the latter, baked in flat cakes, on iron griddles, about an inch thick; and being piled up in heaps, was liable to heat, ferment and grow mouldy. This was a new and not a very palatable diet. Whilst Blincoe and many of his comrades went supperless to bed, their half-starved comrades, the Litton Mill apprentices, ravenously devoured what the more dainty Lowdham children turned from with loathing, and told them *their stomachs* would come to in a few days, and that they would be glad to pick from a dunghill, the mouldiest pieces, then so disdainfully flung away.

The lodging-room, the bedding, every thing was inferior to what it was at Lowdham; and the smell, from oil and filth, incomparably more offensive. Blincoe passed a restless night, bitterly deploring his hard destiny, and trembling at the thought of greater sufferings! Soon after four in the morning, they were summoned to the work, by the ringing of a bell. Blincoe was put to wind rovings. He soon found an immense difference, in his situation, having much more work to perform, and being treated with a brutal severity, hitherto unknown to him.

Blincoe remarked, that few of the apprentices had either knife, fork, or spoon, to use at table, or hats, shoes, or stockings. At Lowdham, particularly during the latter part of their stay there, the children used to wash at the pump, night and day, and were allowed soap! At Litton mill, they were called out so early, and worked so late, that little or no attention was given to personal cleanliness! On Friday night, the apprentices were washed, combed, and shirted! Blincoe found his companions in a woeful condition: their bodies were literally covered with weals and contusions; their heads full of wounds, and, in many cases, lamentably infested with vermin! The eldest girls had to comb and wash the younger apprentices,—an irksome task, which was carelessly and partially performed. No soap was allowed: a small quantity of meal was given as a substitute; and this from the effects of keen hunger, was generally eaten. The first day's labour {at} Litton Mill, convinced Blincoe, into what a den of vice and misery he was cast. The overlookers were fierce and brutal, beyond any thing he had ever witnessed at Lowdham Mill: to which servitude, terrible as it once appeared, he looked back with regret. In the retrospect of his own conduct, he felt shame and sorrow; for, compared with what he had to perform and to endure, he now considered that he had lived in idleness and luxury at Lowdham. The custom of washing and shifting on Friday night, arose, he said from a notion, that it was more *profitable* to allow those ablutions to be then performed, that the apprentices might be kept to work till *midnight* on Saturday, or even beyond that hour. The apprentices slept about fifty in a room. The governor used to unlock the door of each room when the {first} bell rang:—having unlocked the last room door, he went back to the first, with a switch stick in his hand, and if he found any one in bed, or slowly dressing, he used to lay on without mercy; by which severity, the rooms were soon empty. The apprentices had their breakfast generally of water-porridge, called in this part of Derbyshire "stir-pudding," and oaten cake, which they took in the mill. The breakfast hour was eight o'clock; but the machinery did not stop, and so irregular were their meals, it sometimes did not arrive till ten or eleven o'clock. At other times, the overlookers would not allow the apprentices to eat it, and it stood till it grew cold and covered with flue! Skim-milk, or butter-milk was allowed; but very sparingly, and often in a stinking state, when it was served out. Forty minutes were allowed for dinner; of which time, full one half was absorbed in cleaning the frames. Sometimes the overlookers detained them in the mill the whole dinner-time, on which occasion, a half penny was given, or rather promised. On these occasions, they had to work the whole day through, generally *sixteen hours, without rest or food!* These excessive labours, accompanied by comparative starvation, may appear to my reader, as, at first, it did to me, almost *incredible;* but Blincoe's relation, marvellous as it may appear, was afterwards confirmed by individuals, whose narratives *will be given*, and with whom no sort of acquaintance or intercourse had latterly subsisted.[1] Owing to this shamefully protracted time of labour, to the ferocity with which the children were driven by stripes, cuffs, and kicks, and to the insufficiency of food, no less than its bad and unwholesome quality, Blincoe, in common with his fellow-sufferers has often dropped down at the frames, and been so weary, when, at last, he left work, he has given a stronger boy a halfpenny, or a part of his supper, to allow him to lean upon him on his way back to the 'prentice-house.

Bad as was the food, the cookery was still worse. The most inferior sort of Irish-fed bacon was purchased for the consumption of these children, and this boiled with turnips, put into the water, I cannot say without washing; but certainly without paring!—Such was the *Sunday* fare of the parish children at Litton Mill. When first Blincoe, and the rest of the children arrived from Lowdham, they noticed many of the other apprentices had neither spoon nor knife; but had to eat as they could, meat, thick-porridge, or broth, nor were the new comers long allowed any such implements. On Sunday, bacon-broth and turnips were served out, which they eat with oaten-cake, in dirty wooden bowls. It could not be otherwise, than unpalatable; for the portion of water to be converted into *broth*, was very ample. In this, rusty, half putrid, fish-fed bacon, and unpaired turnips were boiled!—A portion of this broth, with coarse oaten-cake was served out, as the first course of a frequent Sunday's dinner. Next, the rusty bacon was portioned out with the boiled unpared turnips!—There was generally, a large quantity of broth to spare, which often became very fetid before it was cold. Into this stuff, no better than hog-wash, a few pails more of water were poured and some meal stirred in, and the disgusting mess was served out for supper or the next day's breakfast, as circumstances required. Blincoe declared, that the stench of this broth was often so powerful as to turn his stomach, and yet, bad as it was, keen hunger

---

1   whose narratives *will be given*] Carlile printed one and Doherty added another of such confirmations to the *Memoir* (see 177-79).

forced him to eat it. From all these and other sources of sickness and disease, no one will be surprised that contagious fevers arose in the mill; nor that the number of deaths should be such as to require frequent supplies of parish children, to fill up the vacancies. That such numerous draughts made from mills, where there was no increase of building or of machinery, or apparent call for more infant labourers should not have caused parish officers to institute enquiry, as to the fate of their predecessors, goes far toward confirming the worst imputations cast by the surviving sufferers, upon their parochial guardians. The evidence given by Sir Robert Peel and others, before parliamentary committees, will throw still further light on this important subject, and prove how generally the offspring of the poor have been abandoned by their legal guardians, and left at the disposal of greedy and unfeeling sons of traffic. This neglect on the part of parish officers, was the producing cause of many of the avaric[i]ous cotton-masters escaping punishment, for offences which richly merited the gallows. Contagious disease, fatal to the apprentices, and dangerous to society, was the degree of magnitude, at which, the independent rich, more, perhaps, from selfish than social feelings, took alarm, and the public prints exposed a part of the existing abuses in cotton-mills,[1] of which parish children were the victims. So horrid were those recitals, and so general and loud the indignation which they excited, that it reached the inmost recesses of the flinty hearts of the great cotton-masters. Their fears taught them mercy, when no longer able to withstand, nor to silence the accusations brought against them by public-spirited and disinterested opponents. Some of the greatest delinquents yielded, and even became advocates for the interference of the legislative power, between themselves and their servants. A reference to the Appendix will shew,[2] that they were accused by the genuine friends of humanity of aiming, by this concession, to insinuate themselves into the confidence of their opponents, and thereby neutralize and subdue the fine spirit by which they found their grasping, vile, insatiate avarice controlled. Be this as it may, those individuals who took so much pains to obtain the act of 1802, seem to have given themselves no manner of trouble, to see it enforced. Almost before the first year expired, it was considered a dead-letter. Just at this crisis, the cruelties, exercised on appren-

---

1 public prints] newspapers or the press.
2 Appendix] Here Brown refers to a portion of the *Memoir* that does not appear in any extant edition.

tices at Litton Mill, were at their height. Excess of toil, of filth, and of hunger, led to the poor children being visited by contagious fevers. This calamity, which often broke, by {premature death}, the bands of this vile thraldom, prevailed to such an extent, as to stop the works. At last, such was Blincoe's declaration, he had known forty boys sick at once, being a fourth of the whole number employed in the mill. From the combined testimony of many apprentices, none were considered sick, till it was found impossible, by menaces or by corporeal punishment, to keep them to their work. The medical gentleman, who sometimes attended the sick, aware of the cause of the deaths, used to say, and like a sensible man he spoke:—"It is not drugs, but kitchen physic they want:" and his general prescription was plenty of good bread, beef, soup and mutton broth. When I questioned Blincoe and others, why this medical man did not represent the horrid plight they were in to the magistrates, he said, the surgeon and magistrates were friends and guests of the master, and in the frequent habit of feasting with him! Blincoe was among the number of the sick, and remembers pitch, tobacco, &c. being burnt in the chamber, and vinegar sprinkled on their beds and on the floor. Circumstances which sufficiently denote the malignity of the disease, and the serious apprehensions that were entertained. So great has the mortality been, that Mr. Needham felt it advisable to divide the burials, and a part of the dead were buried in {Tadington} church-yard,[1] although the burial fees were double the charge of those at Tideswell. Notwithstanding this extraordinary degree of sickness and mortality, Blincoe declares that the local magistracy took no manner of notice of these occurrences!!!

It might be hazardous to trust so far to the memory, the integrity, or the judgment of Blincoe, or to affirm that the conduct of the local magistrates really was thus culpable; but the imputation is corroborated by the total silence of the magistrates of this part of Derbyshire, as to the character and conduct of the owners of Litton Mill, during the parliamentary investigation of 1816, 17, 18, 19.[2] The concurrent testimony of Blincoe and

1   {Tadington} church-yard] Taddington is a village approximately four miles south of Tideswell in the Peak District of Derbyshire.
2   parliamentary investigation of 1816, 17, 18, 19] The only formal select committee that met to investigate factory conditions during these years was that of 1816; illness delayed Peel's introduction of a factory bill until 1818 (see note 4 on page 109).

several of his fellow-sufferers confirm the fact of contagious fevers having occurred in this mill; of the numerous deaths it occasioned; of the consequent division of the funerals; and of the remarks of the clergyman, by whom the last sad rites were performed; and also, that, *once,* there was a Coroner's inquest held! (there exists some difference of opinion, as to the material fact, whether the body had not been first deposited in the earth, and afterwards taken up.) Not a spark of pity was shown to the sick of either sex: they were worked to the very last moment it was possible for them to work; and when it was no longer possible, if they dropped down, they were put into a wheel-barrow, and wheeled to the 'prentice-house. According to Blincoe's statement, they were left in the common room below, or carried to their birth in the bed-room, and there left to live or die! In this melancholy state, all the change that took place in the diet, was an allowance of some *treacle-tea,* that is, hot water sweetened with treacle. The doctor was seldom called, till the patient was in the agonies of death. Generally speaking, the dying experienced less attention than a sheep or a hog! The owner of Litton Mill was more tender {to} those animals; because they cost money, and the anxiety of a character like Mr. Needham's could alone be excited by the prospect of a loss of capital! This solicitude was proportioned to the extent of that risk; and as parish children and destitute orphans could be had at a less price than sheep or pigs, to supply the place of those that died, it followed, that they were less thought of. I would not willingly exaggerate the atrocities I am depicting. I would not act so unwisely as to overcharge the picture I am drawing; and it is with some degree of diffidence, I state, in consequence of combined and positive testimony, that no nurses or *nursing* was allowed to the sick, further than what one invalid could do for another! That neither candle nor lamp-light was allowed, nor the least sign of sympathy or regret manifested! These facts, I admit, are so repugnant to every feeling of Christian charity, that they wear the aspect of greatly embellished truths, or, what is but little worse, of malignant fabrications. If they are such, the fault is not mine; for repeatedly, and in the most impressive manner in my power, I admonished Blincoe and his fellow-sufferers, to abstain from falsehood, telling him and them, it would be sure to be detected and lead to their disgrace. What I thought might have more influence with such persons, I also urged the triumph, such baseness on their part, would confer on the master cotton spinners, most distinguished by cruelty and tyranny; yet, still Blincoe and the whole of his former comrades perseveringly and consistently adhered to the truth of the horrid imputations, and declared, if they were called upon, they would at any time confirm their statement. I was bound to given them publicity—if they are founded in truth. If their great features are correctly delineated, no lapse of time ought to be allowed to shelter the delinquents. They should be brought to a public trial; for the imputations extend to too many acts of torture and of wilful deliberate murder; and to the indulgence of propensities,[1] as to overpower scepticism. They embrace atrocities exercised upon poor and friendless boys and girls, of a nature no less abominable than the worst of those which apply to that disgrace to womanhood, Elizabeth Brownrig, or more recently, to the unhappy culprit, Governor Wall.[2] There are yet living, perhaps a hundred witnesses who have been partakers of these ferocious inflictions. Many of them, though in the prime of life, are reduced to such a state of decrepitude, as to flash conviction upon the most incredulous, that it could have resulted from nothing but the most unexampled and long continued cruelty. From the continued and relentless exercise of unlimited despotism upon the truly {insulted} and most friendless of human beings, upon those, for whose especial protection, a law had been then recently enacted, which, had it been enforced, would have efficiently prevented the occurrence of these crimes, and if I were to assert, that it would be difficult, if not impossible, from the record of sufferings inflicted upon Negro slaves, to quote instances of greater atrocity, than what I have, or am about to develope, I should not exaggerate, nor should I be guilty of bombast, were I to affirm, that the national character has been, and is seriously dishonoured by that system of boundless commercial avarice, in which these detestable crimes originated. It will continue thus shaded, till a full and fair investigation takes place. There never yet was a crisis, when, in the commercial world, the march of avarice was so

---

1 Between "propensities," and "as" the Carlile text prints: "so truly diabolical, as to stagger belief, and yet so well authenticated." Doherty's compositor seems to have mistakenly omitted this line (see entry for this page in Appendix A.4).

2 Elizabeth Brownrigg (d. 1767) was executed at Tyburn for the murder of her eleven-year-old apprentice, who was beaten and tortured for two years before she died. Joseph Wall (1737-1802) was executed for the murder of one of his troops, several of whom he ordered flogged with eight hundred lashes while he was Governor of Goree (Senegal). Wall's body was buried in St. Pancras Churchyard.

rapid, or its devastations so extensive upon the morals and well being of society, as within the period embraced by this narrative; a march that seems to acquire celerity in proportion to the increasing spread of its malific *influence*, and to derive *impunity* from the prodigious wealth it accumulates in the hands of a few great and unfeeling capitalists, at the expence of the individual happiness, health, and morals of the million. This iniquitous system is the prolific parent of that tremendous flood of vice, which has saturated the manufacturing populace, with the most appalling depravity. This has reduced those many hundred thousand weavers, to a state of destitution so extreme, as to render the condition of the most destitute portion, incomparably worse than that of the field-slave in the West India plantations, who has the good fortune to belong to a humane proprietor.[1] This baleful and wide wasting system throws upon the crown the undeserved odium of being the cause or the abettor of these dreadful evils, by which the poor weaver is oppressed; an impression that has neutralized the loyalty of myriads, and fitted them to become, in the hands of unprincipled demagogues, the source of popular commotions, of foul and iniquitous conspiracies, of deep and radical disloyalty. So indurated, so inveterate, is the loathing and aversion cherished towards the executive government, in all its ramifications, by a large portion of weavers, that it has induced multitudes wholly to renounce, to vilify in every practicable manner, to degrade christianity! I do not, in this declamation, indulge in light, personal, or selfish motives; for whatever I assert, as positive matter of fact, I hold myself morally responsible, and stand publicly pledged to substantiate my assertion, by adducing, if requisite, not alone the authorities on which I make them, but also to *prove* the validity of those authorities.

With this digression, I close the present chapter. In those that follow there will be found a narrative of crimes which cannot fail to excite, in an equal degree, horror and incredulity:—at the recital of acts of wanton, premeditated, gross, and brutal cruelty, scarcely to be equalled in the annals of the Inquisitorial tribunals of Portugal or Spain;[2] yet all those acts of murder and wanton

---

1 weavers ... destitution] For the conditions of nineteenth-century hand-loom weavers, see Introduction 17.

2 Inquisitions were official investigations, usually of a political or religious nature. They were characterized by lack of regard for the individual, sadistic and brutal treatment, and torture. The most famous of these was the Spanish Inquisition, beginning in 1478.

cruelties, have been perpetrated by a solitary master cotton-spinner, who, though perhaps one of the worst of his tribe, did not stand alone; as will be shewn by evidence that cannot be successfully rebutted. Nor was it to be expected that the criminality of that master spinner could fail to produce corresponding depravity amongst the wretched apprentices subjected to his rude and savage dominion. In the eventful life of W——— {Pitt} the depth and extent of that depravity will be strikingly illustrated![1]— It will be seen that acts of felony were committed in the vicinity of Litton Mill, by the parish apprentices, not, if I am rightly informed, from *dishonest intention;* but from a desire to be transported to Botany Bay;[2] deeming even that alternative preferable to the endurance of the horrors of the servitude, to which, as parish apprentices, they had been consigned.

CHAP. V.

Recurring to the description, given to me by Robert Blincoe, of the dreadful state of thraldom, in which, with a multitude of juvenile companions, he was involved at Litton Mill, I am instructed to say, that as excessive toil, the want of proper time for rest, and of nourishing wholesome food, gave rise to contagious diseases, so a liberal supply of good provisions and a cessation from toil, quickly restored many to health; instead of taking warning by the results of these terrible examples, no sooner were the invalids sent back to the mill, than the system of over-toil, of boundless cruelty, starvation and torture, was at once resumed. Let it not however be supposed, that any thing in the shape of dainties had been dispensed to the sick. Wheaten bread, coarse pieces of beef boiled down in soup, or mutton for broth, with good milk or butter-milk, sparingly distributed, formed the extent of those indulgences. This diet, luxurious as it was considered in Litton Mill, did not surpass the ordinary standard of the daily fare, that Blincoe had enjoyed at St. Pancras workhouse, and also, during the latter period of his stay at Lowdham Mill.

I have not yet done more than to mention the cuffs, kicks, or

---

1 W——— Pitt] This reference seems to promise—incorrectly, as it turns out—that the story of a particular apprentice at Litton Mill will be added to the *Memoir.*

2 Botany Bay] penal colony on the eastern coast of New South Wales in southeast Australia.

scourging, to which, in common with many other of his unhappy comrades, Blincoe stood exposed, since, by his account, almost from the first hour in which he entered the Mill, till he arrived at a state of manhood, it was one continued round of cruel and arbitrary punishment. Blincoe declared, he was so frequently and immoderately beaten, it became quite familiar; and if its frequency did not extinguish the sense of feeling, it took away the terror it excited on his first entrance into this den of ignorance and crime. I asked him if he could state an average number of times in which he thought he might in safety say, he had suffered corporeal punishment in a week. His answer invariably was, that his punishments were so various and so frequent, it was impossible to state with any thing approaching to accuracy. If he is to be credited, during his ten years of hard servitude, his body was never free from contusions, and from wounds inflicted by the cruel master whom he served, by his sons, or his brutal and ferocious and merciless overlookers.

It is already stated, that he was put to the back of a stretching-frame, when he was about eleven years of age, and that often, owing to the idleness, or the absence of the stretcher,[1] he had his master's work, as well as his own to perform. The work being very coarse, the motion was rapid, and he could not keep up to the ends. For this, he was sure to be unmercifully punished, although, they who punished him knew the task assigned was beyond what he could perform. There were different stretchers in the mill: but, according to Blincoe's account, they were all of them base and ferocious ruffians. Robert Woodward, who had escorted the apprentices from Lowdham Mill, was considered the worst of those illiterate vulgar tyrants. If he made a kick at Blincoe, so great was his strength, it commonly lifted him off the floor. If he struck him, even a flat-handed blow, it floored him; [*sic*] If, with a stick, it not only bruised him, but cut his flesh. It was not enough to use his feet or his hands, but a stick, a bobby[2] or a rope's-end. He and others used to throw rollers[3] one after another, at the poor boy, aiming at his head, which, of course was

---

1   stretcher] Since Brown earlier states that Blincoe "was put to wind rovings" (126), the adult male worker referred to here is probably running a roving-frame or stretching-mule, a machine that extends or "stretches" the fibers previously produced by a drawing-frame.

2   bobby] short for *bobbin* (?)

3   rollers] removable cylinders of wood on a drawing-frame, often used by overseers as weapons to punish the children working under them.

uncovered while at work, and nothing delighted the savages more, than to see Blincoe stagger, and to see the blood gushing out in a stream! So far were such results from deterring the monsters, that long before one wound had healed, similar acts of cruelty produced others, so that, on many occasions, his head was excoriated and bruised to a degree, that rendered him offensive to himself and others, and so intolerably painful, as to deprive him of rest at night, however weary he might be. In consequence of such wounds, his head was over-run by vermin. Being reduced to this deplorable state, some brute of a quack doctor used to apply a pitch cap,[1] or plaister to his head. After it had been on a given time, and when its adhesion was supposed to be complete, the *terrible doctor* used to lay forcibly hold of one corner and tear the whole scalp from off his head at once! This was the common remedy; I should not exaggerate the agonies it occasioned, were I to affirm, that it must be equal to any thing inflicted by the American savages, on helpless prisoners, with their scalping knives and tomahawks.

This same ruffian, (Robert Woodward) who, by the concurrent testimony of many sufferers, stands depicted, as possessing that innate love of cruelty which marked a Nero, a Caligula, or a Robespierre,[2] used when Blincoe could not, or did not keep pace with the machinery, to tie him up by the wrists to a cross beam and keep him suspended over the machinery till his agony was extreme. To avoid the machinery, he had to draw up his legs every time it came out or returned. If he did not lift them up, he was cruelly beaten over the shins, which were bare; nor was he released, till growing black in the face, and his head falling over his shoulder, the wretch thought his victim was near expiring. Then after some gratuitous knocks and cuffs, he was released and instantly driven to his toil, and forced to commence, with every appearance of strength and vigour, though he were so much crippled, as to be scarcely able to stand. To lift the apprentices up by their ears, shake them violently, and then dash them down upon the floor with the utmost fury, was one of the many inhuman

---

1 pitch cap] a cap lined with a type of plaster containing tar, which was used to remove hair in cases of extreme scalp disease.

2 Nero Claudius Caesar Drusus Germanicus (37-68), Roman Emperor from 54-68, who was responsible for the deaths of many Roman citizens as well as the burning of Rome; Maximilien François Marie Isidore de Robespierre (1758-94), French revolutionist responsible for the Reign of Terror.

sports in Litton Mill, in which the overlookers appeared to take delight. Frequently has Blincoe been thus treated, till he thought his ears were torn from his head, and this for very trivial offences, or omissions. Another of these diabolical amusements consisted in filing the apprentices' teeth! Blincoe was once constrained to open his mouth to receive this punishment, and Robert Woodward applied the file with great vigour! Having punished him as much as he pleased; the brute said with a sneer; "I do this to sharpen thy teeth, that thou may'st eat thy Sunday dinner the better."

Blincoe declared, that he had often been compelled, on a cold winter's day, to work *naked*, except his trowsers, and loaded with two half hundred weights slung behind him, hanging one at each shoulder. Under this cruel torture, he soon sunk; when, to make the sport last the longer, Woodward substituted quarter of hundred weights, and thus loaded, by every painful effort, Blincoe could not lift his arm to the roller. Woodward has forced him to wear these weights for hours together, and still to continue at his work! Sometimes, he has been commanded to pull off his shirt and get into a large square {skip},[1] when, the savage, being sure of his mark, and that, not a blow would be lost, used to beat him till he was tired! At other times, Blincoe has been hoisted upon other boys' shoulders, and beaten with sticks till he has been shockingly discoloured and covered with contusions and wounds.

What spinners call, a *draw off*,[2] at one of those frames at which Blincoe worked, required about forty seconds. Woodward has often insisted upon Blincoe's cleaning all the cotton away under the whole frame, in a single draw, and to go out at the further end, under pain of a severe beating. On one of these occasions, Blincoe had nearly lost his life, being caught between the faller[3] and the head-piece, his head was jammed between them. Both his temples were cut open and the blood poured down each side of his face{, the marks to be seen}! It was considered next to a miracle, that he escaped with his life! So far from feeling the least compassion, Woodward beat him cruelly, because he had not

---

1 {skip}] box or basket; here, a bed.

2 a *draw-off*] apparently the act of removing the processed cotton thread from a spinning machine, but here again Brown may be referring to a roving-machine, which also produced cotton yarn through a process often called *spinning*.

3 faller] wire at the top of the spindles on a spinning machine.

made *more haste!*—Blincoe says, to the best of his recollection, he was twelve years of age, when this accident happened.

It is a fact, too notorious to be denied, that the most brutal and ferocious of the spinners, stretchers, rovers, &c., have been in the habit, from mere wantonness, of inflicting severe punishments upon piecers, scavengers, frame-tenders, winders, and others of the juvenile class, subjected to their power, compelling them to eat dirty pieces of candle, to lick up tobacco spittle, to open their mouths for the filthy wretches to spit into; all which beastialities have been practised upon the apprentices at Litton Mill! Among the rest, Blincoe has often suffered these indignities. What has a tendency to display human nature in its worst state, is, that most of the overlookers, who acted thus cruelly, had arrived in the mill as parish apprentices, and, as such, had undergone all these offensive inflictions!

There was, however, one diversion, which, in all my enquiries as to cotton-mill *amusements*, I never found paralleled. Of this Robert Woodward, if I mistake not, has a claim to the honour of being the *original inventor*. It was thus executed.—A tin can or cylinder, about three feet high, to receive the rovings, and about nine or ten inches in diameter, was placed in the midst of the alley or wheel-house, as the space is called, over which the frames travel at every draw, and pretty close to the race.[1] Upon this can or hollow cylinder, Blincoe had to mount; and there to stand upon one foot, holding a long brush extended in the opposite hand, until the frame came out, about three times in two minutes, invariably knocking the can from under him, both fell to the floor. The villain used to place the can so near the race, that there was considerable danger of Blincoe falling on it, and, if so, it would probably have lamed him for life, if it had not killed him on the spot; and he had, with the utmost possible celerity, to throw himself flat upon the floor, that the frame might pass over him! During this short interval, the amateurs, *i.e.* Robert Woodward, Charnock, Merrick, &c. used to set the can upright again, and it required no small share of ingenuity, in them, to keep time. The frame being returned, poor Blincoe had to leap on his feet, and again to mount nimbly on the hollow column of tin, again to extend his arm, holding the long hair brush, and again sustain a fall, amidst the shouts and yells of these fiends. Thus would the villains continue to persecute and torment him, till they were tired, notwithstanding the *sport* might have been his death. He

---

1 race] the space in which the drums or wheels of a machine revolve.

ran the risk of a broken bone, or the dislocation of a limb, every time he was thus thrown down; and the time the monsters thus wasted, they afterwards made up by additional labour wrung from their wretched victims.

Another of their diversions consisted in tying Blincoe's hands behind him and one of his legs up to his hands. He had then only one leg left free to hop upon, and no use left of his hands to guard him, if he chanced to fall, and if Blincoe did not move with activity, the overlooker would strike a blow with his clenched fist, or cut his head open by flinging rollers. If he fell, he was liable to have his leg or arm broken [or] dislocated. Every one conversant with cotton-spinning machinery knows the danger of such *diversions*, and of their cruelty, every one can judge.

There seemed to exist a spirit of emulation, an infernal spirit, it might with justice be designated, among the overlookers of Litton Mill, of inventing and inflicting the most novel and singular punishments. For the sake of being the better able, and more effectually to torment their victims, the overlookers allowed their thumb and fore-finger nails to grow to an extreme length, in order that, when they *pinched their ears*, they might make their nails meet{, *marks to be seen*}!

Needham himself the owner of the Mill, stands arraigned of having the cruelty to act thus, very frequently, till their blood ran down their necks, and so common was the sport, it was scarcely noticed. As regarded Blincoe, one set of wounds had seldom time to heal, before another set was inflicted; [*sic*] The general remedy that Blincoe applied was, the oil used to keep the machinery in order. The despicable wretches, who thus revelled in acts of lawless oppression, would often, to indulge the whim of a moment, fling a roller at a boy's head, and inflict deep wounds, and this, frequently, without even a shadow of a fault to allege, or even a plausible reason to assign in justification! At another time, if the apprentices stood fair for the infliction of a stripe, with a twig or the whip, the overlookers would apply it, with the utmost vigour, and then, bursting into laughter, call it a———good hit! Blincoe declared he had, times innumerable been thus assailed, and has had his head cut severely, without daring to complain of the cause. Woodward and others of the overlookers used to beat him with pieces of the thick leathern straps made supple by oil, and having an iron buckle at the end, which drew blood almost every time it was applied, or caused severe contusions.

Among Blincoe's comrades in affliction, was an orphan boy, who came from St. Pancras workhouse, whose proper name was

James Nottingham; but better known as "*blackey*," a nick-name that was given to him, on account of his black hair, eyes, and complexion. According to Blincoe's testimony, this poor boy suffered even greater cruelties, than fell to his own share! by an innumerable number of blows, chiefly inflicted on his head!—by wounds and contusions, his head swelled enormously, and he became stupid! To use Blincoe's significant expression, "his head was as soft as a boiled turnip," the scalp on the crown, pitting every where on the least compression. This poor boy, being reduced to this most pitiable condition, by unrestrained cruelty, was exposed to innumerable outrages, and was, at last, incapable of work, and often plundered of his food!—melancholy and weeping, he used to creep into holes and corners, to avoid his tormentors. From mere debility, he was afflicted by incontinency of stools and urine! To punish this infirmity, conformably as Blincoe declared, to the will of Ellice Needham, the master, his allowance of broth, butter-milk, porridge, &c. was withheld! During the summer time, he was mercilessly scourged! In winter, stripped quite naked, and he was slung, with a rope tied {round} his shoulders, into the dam, and dragged to and fro, till he was nearly suffocated. They would then draw him out, and sit him on a stone, under a pump, and pump upon his head, in a copious stream, while some stout fellow was employed to sluice the poor wretch with pails of water, flung with all possible fury into his face. According to the account I received, not alone Blincoe, but several other of the Litton Mill apprentices, when these horrid inflictions had reduced the poor boy to a state of idiotism,—his wrongs and sufferings,—his dismal condition,—far, from exciting sympathy, but increased the mirth of these vulgar tyrants! His wasted and debilitated frame was seldom, if ever, free from wounds and contusions, and his head covered with running sores and swarming with lice, exhibited a loathsome object! In consequence of this miserable state of filth and disease, poor Nottingham has many times had to endure the excruciating torture of the pitch and scalping cap already named!

Having learnt, in 1822, that this forlorn child of misery was then at work in a cotton factory, near Oldfield Lane,[1] I went in search of and found him. At first, he seemed much embarrassed, and when I made enquiries as to his treatment at Litton Mill, to

---

1   Oldfield Lane] Later Oldfield Road, this street was located in the early nineteenth century in southwest central Manchester on the west side of the River Irwell.

my surprise, he told me "he knew nothing whatever about it." I then, related what Blincoe and others had named to me, of the horrid tortures he endured. "I dare say," said he mildly, "he told you truth, but I have no distinct recollection of anything that happened to me during the greater part of the time I was there! I believe," said he, "my sufferings were most dreadful, and that I nearly lost my senses." From his appearance, I guessed he had not been so severely worked as others of the poor crippled children whom I had seen! As well as I can recollect, his knees were not deformed, or if at all, but very little! He is much below the middle size, as to stature. His countenance round, and his small and regular features, bore the character of former sufferings and present tranquillity of mind.

In the course of my enquiries respecting this young man, I was much gratified, by hearing the excellent character given him in the vicinity of his lodging. Several persons spoke of him as being serious and well inclined, and his life and conduct irreproachable.

{["]We frequently had our best dinner in the week on a Sunday, and it was generally broth, meat and turnips, with a little oat-cake, the meat was of as coarse a sort as could be bought. This being our extra dinner, we did not wish to part with it too soon, therefore it was a general practice amongst the 'prentices to save some of it until Monday, in the care of the governor of the 'prentice house, and for each one to know their own. The practice was to cut in their oat-cake, some mark or other, and lay it on their wooden trenchers. It happened one Sunday we had our dinner of bacon broth and turnips with a little oat-cake. This Sunday, one Thomas Linsey, a fellow 'prentice thought he could like a snack, early in the morning, therefore he took a slice of bacon between two pieces of oat-cake to bed with him, and put it under his head[,] I cannot say, under his pillow, because we never was allowed any. The next morning about three or four o'clock, as it was a usual practice in the summer time when short of water, for a part of the hands to begin their work sooner, by this contrivance we was able to work our full time or near. Linsey was found dead in bed, and as soon as some of the 'prentices knew of his death, as they slept about 50 in a room, there was a great scuffle who should have the bacon and oat-cake from under his head, some began to search his pockets for his tin, this tin he used to eat his victuals with; some had pieces of broken pots, as no spoons was allowed. It was reported this Sunday that this pig had died in the Lees, a place so called at the back of the 'prentice-house. There was no coroner's inquest held over Linsey to know the cause of his death.["]¹ I shall leave the reader to judge for himself this distressing sight, at so early an hour in the morning.—This occurred at Litton Mill.}

It might be supposed, that these horrid inflictions had been practised, in this cotton-factory, unknown to the master and proprietor of Litton Mill; but the testimony, not of Blincoe alone, but of many of his former associates, unknown to him, gave similar statements, and like Blincoe, described Ellice Needham the master, as equaling the very worst of his servants in cruelty of heart! So far from having taken any care to stop their career, he used to animate them by his own example to inflict punishment in any and every way they pleased. Mr. Needham stands accused of having been in the habit of knocking down the apprentices with his clenched fists;—kicking them about when down, beating them to excess with sticks, or flogging them with horse-whips; of seizing them by the ears, lifting them from the ground and forcibly dashing them down on the floor, or pinching them till his nails met! Blincoe declares his oppressors used to seize him by the hair of his head and tear it off by a handful at a time, till the crown of his head had become as bald as the back of his hand! John Needham, following the example of his father, and possessing unlimited power over the apprentices, lies under the imputation of crimes of the blackest hue, exercised upon the wretched creatures, from whose laborious toil, the means of supporting the pomp and luxury in which he lived were drawn. To the boys, he was a tyrant and an oppressor! To the girls the same, with the additional odium of treating them with an indecency as disgusting as his cruelty was terrific. Those unhappy creatures were at once the victims of his ferocity and his lust.²

FOR some trivial offence, Robert Woodward once kicked and beat Robert Blincoe, till his body was covered with wheals and bruises. Being tired, or desirous of affording his young master the luxury of amusing himself on the same subject, he took Blincoe to the counting-house, and accused him of wilfully spoiling his work. Without waiting to hear what Blincoe might have to urge in his defence, young Needham eagerly looked about for a stick; not finding one at hand, he sent Woodward to an adjacent coppice, called the Twitchell, to cut a supply, and laughingly bade Blincoe

---

1 Where Blincoe's words end is not clear in this paragraph, which Doherty added in his 1832 edition of *Memoir*.
2 This sentence does not appear in the 1828 version of the *Memoir* published by Carlile in *The Lion*.

strip naked, and prepare himself for a good *flanking!* Blincoe obeyed, but to his agreeable surprise, young Needham abstained from giving him the promised flanking. The fact was, the poor boy's body was so dreadfully discoloured and inflamed by contusions, its appearance terrified the young despot, and he spared him, thinking that mortification and death {might} ensue, if he laid on another "flanking." Hence his unexpected order to Blincoe to put on his things! There was not, at the time, a free spot on which to inflict a blow! His ears were swollen and excoriated; his head, in the most deplorable state imaginable; many of the bruises on his body had suppurated! and so excessive was his soreness, he was forced to sleep on his face, if sleep he could obtain, in so wretched a condition!

Once a week, and generally after sixteen hours of incessant toil, the eldest girls had to comb the boys' heads; an operation, that being alike painful to the sufferer, as disgusting to the girls, was reluctantly endured, and inefficiently performed. Hence arose the frequency of scald-heads,[1] and the terrible scalping remedy! Upon an average, the children were kept to work during a great part, if not all, the time Blincoe was at Litton Mill, sixteen hours in the day. The result of this excessive toil, superadded to hunger and torture, was the death of many of {apprentices}, and the entailment of incurable lameness and disease on many others.

The store pigs and the apprentices used to fare pretty much alike; but when the swine were hungry, they used to squeak and grunt so loud, they obtained the wash first, to quiet them. The apprentices could be intimidated, and made to keep still. The fatting pigs fared luxuriously, compared with the apprentices! They were often regaled with meal-balls made into dough, and given in the shape of dumplings! Blincoe and others, who worked in a part of the mill whence they could see the swine served, used to say to one another—"*The pigs are served; it will be our turn next.*" Blincoe and those who were in the part of the building contiguous to the pigsties, used to keep a sharp eye upon the fatting pigs, and their meal-balls, and, as soon as he saw the swineherd withdraw, he used to slip down stairs, and, stealing slyly towards the trough, plunge his hand in at the loop holes, and steal as many dumplings as he could grasp! The food thus obtained from a pig's trough, and, perhaps, defiled by their filthy chops, was exultingly

---

1 scald-heads] Scald head is a contagious disease caused by ringworm; patches of puss on the scalp form into crusts that can cover the head and face.

conveyed to the privy or the duck-hole, and there devoured with a much keener appetite, than it would have been by the pigs; but the pigs, though generally esteemed the most stupid of animals, soon hit upon an expedient, that baffled the hungry boys; for the instant the meal-balls were put into their troughs, they voraciously seized them, threw them into the dirt, out of the reach of the boys! Not this alone; but, made wise by repeated losses, they kept a sharp look out, and the moment they ascertained the approach of the half-famished apprentices, they set up so loud a chorus of snorts and grunts, it was heard in the kitchen, when out rushed the swine-herd, armed with a whip, from which combined means of protection for the swine, this accidental source of obtaining a *good dinner* was soon lost! Such was the contest carried on for a time at Litton Mill, between the half-famished apprentices, and the well-fed swine.

I observed to Blincoe, it was not very rational, to rob the pigs, when they were destined to bleed to supply them with food, as soon as they grew sufficiently fat! "Oh! you're mistaken," said he, "these pigs were fatted for master's own table, or were sold at Buxton! We were fed upon the very worst and cheapest of Irish-fed bacon." There was, it seems, a small dairy at Litton Mill; but the butter was all sent to his house. The butter-milk alone was dispensed, and but very scantily, to the apprentices. About a table-spoonful of meal was distributed once a week to the apprentices, with which to wash themselves, instead of soap; but in nine cases out of ten, it was greedily devoured, and a piece of clay or sand, or some such thing, substituted: such was the dreadful state of hunger in which these poor children were kept in this mill.

To attempt a specific statement, how often Blincoe has been kept to work from five in the morning till midnight, during his period of servitude, would be hazardous! According to his own testimony, supported by that of many others, it was, at times, of common occurrence, more especially on the Saturday! In most mills, the adult spinners left off on that day at *four* in the afternoon, whilst in these, where parish apprentices were employed, it was often continued, not only till midnight; but till six o'clock on the Sunday morning!

Exertion so incessant could not fail to reduce the majority of apprentices to a state of exhaustion and lassitude, so great as nearly to disqualify them to benefit by such instructions as an illiterate clown could afford, who officiated on Sundays as schoolmaster, or by divine worship, when they were allowed to attend. Nothing could be more cheerless, than the aspect of these juvenile sufferers, these helpless outcasts, nor more piteous than the wailings and lamentations of that portion, chiefly of the tenderest years, whom long familiarity with vice and misery had not rendered wholly callous.

A blacksmith or mechanic, named William Palfry, who resided at Litton, worked in a room under that where Blincoe was employed. He used to be much disturbed by the shrieks and cries of the boys, whom the manager and overlookers were almost continually punishing. According to Blincoe's declaration, and that of others, human blood has often run from an upper to a lower floor, shed by these merciless taskmasters. Unable to hear the shrieks of the children, Palfry used to knock against the floor, so violently, as to force the boards up, and call out "for shame! for shame! are you murdering the children?" He spoke to Mr. Needham, and said, he would not stay in the mill, if such doings were allowed. By this sort of conduct, the humane blacksmith was a check on the cruelty of the brutal overlookers, as long as he continued in his shop; but he went away home at seven o'clock, and as soon as Woodward, Merrick, and Charnock knew that Palfry was gone, they used to pay off the day's score, and to beat and knock the apprentices about without moderation or provocation, giving them black eyes, broken heads; saying, "I'll let you know old Palfry is not here now!" To protract the evil hour, the boys, when they used to go down stairs for rovings, would come back and say—"Palfry and the joiner are going to work all night," and sometimes by this manœuvre, they have escaped punishment.

It happened one day, when Blincoe was about twelve years old, he went to the counting-house with a cop, such being the custom at every doffing.[1] While Blincoe was there, another apprentice, named Isaac Moss, came in on the same errand. Upon the floor stood the tin treacle can, with about 14 pounds of treacle. The sight arrested the attention of Blincoe, who said softly, "Moss, there is the treacle can come from Tideswell!"— "Eh," Moss exclaimed, "so it is." Blincoe said, "I have no spoon." Moss rejoined, "I have two." Putting his hand to his bosom and pulling out the bowl of an iron spoon and another which he kept

---

1   cop ... doffing] Doffing is the act of removing textile fibers from a machine after they have been cleaned and combed; and a cop is a cup, in this case one used as a container to hold the slivers of cotton.

for another person, down they sat on the floor opposite to each other, with the can between them and began operations, lading away as fast as they could! Blincoe had a large sized mouth, and in good condition, but the ruffian, {William} Woodward {the manager, brother to Robert Woodward}, having struck Moss a severe blow on the mouth, with a large stick, it had swollen so much, that the poor lad had the mortification of hardly being able to use it, and Blincoe could stow away at least three spoonsful to Moss's one! While the conscious pair were thus employed, the enemy, unheard and unperceived, stole upon them. It was a dark night; but there was a fire in the counting-house, by the light of which, over some glass above the top of the door, that grim spectre, the terror and the curse of these poor boys, Woodward, saw their diversion! He stood viewing them some time, when suddenly rushing upon them, he seized upon them as a cat pounces upon cheese-eating mice! Blincoe, being most active with his feet, as well as with his spoon, after receiving a few kicks and cuffs, ran off to the factory, leaving Moss in the power, and at the mercy of {William} Woodward.

At ten o'clock, the factory bell rang, and Blincoe went off to the apprentice-house, trembling with apprehension and looking wildly around amongst the apprentices, in hope of seeing his comrade Moss; but Moss was not to be seen! Presently, an order arrived from Woodward, for the master of the apprentices to bring down Blincoe! Richard Milner, the then governor of the apprentices, a corpulent old man, said, "Parson, what hast thou been doing?"—"Nothing," said the parson; his tremulous voice and shaking limbs contradicting his laconic reply; and away they trudged. When they got to the counting-house, they found Moss stuck erect in a corner, looking very poorly, his mouth and cheeks all over treacle. {William} Woodward, in a gruff voice, said, "So you have been helping to eat this treacle?"—"I have only eaten a little, Sir." Upon which, he hit Blincoe one of his flat-handed slaps, fetching fire from his eyes, and presently another, another, and another, till Blincoe began to vociferate for mercy, promising never to eat forbidden treacle any more! Woodward was full six feet high, with long arms, huge raw bones and immense sized hands, and when he had tired himself with beating Blincoe, he exclaimed: "Damn your bloods, you rascals, if you don't lap up the whole can of treacle, I'll murder you on the spot." This denunciation was music to Blincoe's ears, who had never before received such an invitation. To accommodate the young gentlemen, the governor sent to his own kitchen for two long spoons, and then, with renewed execrations, Woodward bade them set to. Moss then crept softly and silently out of his corner, having been cruelly beaten in Blincoe's absence! Looking ruefully at each other, down the culprits knelt a second time, one on each side of the treacle can! Blincoe had still the best of the sport; for poor Moss's mouth remained deprived of half its external dimensions, and being so excessively sore, he could hardly get in a tea-spoon, where Blincoe could shovel in large table-spoonsful! Moss kept fumbling at his lame mouth, and looking rather spitefully at Blincoe, as if he thought he would eat all the treacle. Meanwhile Milner and Woodward sat laughing and chatting by the fire-side, often looking at the treacle-eaters, and anxiously waiting an outcry for quarters! Blincoe ate in a masterly style; but poor Moss could not acquit himself half as well, the treacle trickling down his chin, on both sides of his mouth, seeing which, Woodward suddenly roared out, "Damn you, you villain, if you don't open your mouth wider, I'll open it for you." Poor Moss trembled; but made no reply, and Blincoe being willing to make hay while the sun shone, instead of falling off, seemed, at every mouthful, to acquire fresh vigour! This surprised and mortified Woodward not a little, who, seeing no signs of sickness, hearing no cry for quarter, and being apprehensive of an application for another can, got up to reconnoitre, and, to his amazement, found that the *little Parson*, who was not a vast deal higher than the can, had almost reached the bottom, and displayed no visible loss or diminution of appetite!

Inexpressibly vexed at being thus outwitted before the governor, he roared out in a tremendous voice to Milner, "Why damn their bloods, they'll eat the whole! Halt, you damned rascals, or, I'll kill you on the spot!" In a moment, Blincoe ceased his play, and licked his lips and spoon, to shew how keen his stomach still was! Milner and Woodward then took stock, and found, that, out of fourteen pounds, not three remained; Milner laughed immoderately at Woodward, to think what a luscious mode of punishment he had found out for treacle stealers!—Woodward being extremely exasperated, ordered Samuel {Brickleton}, an overlooker, to fasten Moss and Blincoe together with handcuffs, of which, as well as of *fetters*, there were plenty at Litton Mill, and then forced them to carry the can to the apprentice-house between them. When they arrived at the door, his hand being small, Blincoe contrived to withdraw it from the handcuff, and ran nimbly off into the room amongst the apprentices, leaving the treacle can in Moss's hand. {Brickleton}, unconscious of

Blincoe's escape, arrived in the kitchen, where the Governor and his family resided, looked round, and seeing only one prisoner, cried out, "Eh! where's Parson gone." Moss said, he believed he was gone into the apprentice-house. {Brickleton} examined the handcuffs, and finding they were locked, was much puzzled to think how the parson had contrived to get his hand out. The kind and careful Mrs. Milner, knowing that there was money due to Blincoe, for working his dinner-hour, viz. a farthing a day, proposed to have it stopped, to pay for the treacle which Woodward had compelled him to eat, on pain of putting him instantly to death. Such was the law and equity, which prevailed at Litton Mill! That night, in consequence of his sumptuous supper, Blincoe was forbidden to enter his bed, and he laid all night, in the depth of winter, on the hard cold floor.

This part of the subject requires an explanation, as to the equivalent given by the owner to the apprentices, in lieu of their dinner-hour. This hour consisted, in general, of forty minutes, and not always so many. The master, to induce the apprentices to work all day long, promised each three-pence per week, if they worked the whole of the dinner hour, and they had to eat it, *bite and sup*, at their work, without spoon, knife, or fork, and with their dirty, oily fingers! They were thus kept on their feet, from five o'clock in the morning, till nine, ten, and even eleven o'clock at night, and on Saturdays, sometimes till twelve; because Sunday was a *day of rest!* Frequently, though almost famishing, the apprentices could not find time to eat their food at all; but carried it back with them at night, covered with flue and filth. This liberality did not last long. The halfpenny was reduced to a farthing, and this farthing was withheld till it amounted to several shillings, and then, when the master *pleased*, he would give a shilling or two, and none dare ask for more. Those whom the overlookers pleased to order so to do, had to work their dinner hour for nothing, and their comrades used to fetch their dinners, who, not unfrequently, pilfered a part. The money thus earned, the poor 'prentices used to reserve, to buy wheaten cakes, and red herrings, to them, luxuries of the most delicious kind. Such was the miserable manner in which they were fed, that, when they gave the pence to Palfry (the smith,) to bring the tempting cake of wheaten flour, and the herring, in the morning, they used to say to their comrades "Old Palfry is to bring me a cake and herring in the morning. Oh! how greedily I shall devour them." They commonly dreamt of these anticipated feasts, and talked of their expected luxuries in their sleep. When Palfry arrived, they would, if they dared, have met him on the stairs, or have followed him to the smithy; but, in an eager whisper, enquired "have you brought my cake and herring?" "Aye, lad," said Palfry, holding out the expected provisions. Eagerly they seized the herring and the cake, and the first full bite generally took off head or tail, as it came first to hand, while the cake was thrust inside their bosom; for they worked with their shirt collar open and generally without jackets. The poor souls, who, having no pence, could have no dainties, would try to snatch a piece slyly, if it were possible, and if that failed, they would try to beg a morsel. If the possessor gave a taste, he held the herring so tight, that only a very small portion could be bitten off, without biting off the ends of the owner's fingers, and their whole feast was quickly finished, without greatly diminishing their appetite. It happened, by some extraordinary stroke of good fortune, that Blincoe became possessed of a shilling, and he determined to have what he termed, a proper blow out; he, therefore, requested Palfry to bring him six penny wheaten cakes, and half a pound of butter. Blincoe was then a stretcher, and had, as such, a better opportunity to receive and to eat his dainties unobserved. The cakes he pulled one by one, from his bosom, and laying them upon the frame, spread the butter on them with a piece of flat iron, and giving his two comrades a small part each, he set to and devoured all the rest; but the unusual quantity and quality nearly made him ill. Blincoe had no appetite for his dinner or supper, and, he, therefore, let another comrade eat it, who engaged to give Blincoe his, when he happened to lose his appetite. Such were the prospective and contingent negotiations carried on by these wretched children, relative to their miserable food.

If Blincoe happened to see any fresh cabbage leaves, potato or turnip parings, thrown out upon the dunghill, he has run down with a can full of sweepings, as an excuse, and as he threw that dirt on the dunghill, he would eagerly pick the other up, and carry it in his shirt, or in his can, into the mill, wipe the dirt off as well as he could, and greedily eat them up. At other times, when they had rice puddings boiled in bags for dinner—the rice being very bad and full of large maggots, Blincoe not being able to endure such food, used to go into one of the woods near the factory, and get what the boys called *bread and cheese*, that is, hips and hipleaves, clover or other vegetable, and filling his bosom, run back to the mill, and eat this trash, instead of foul rice, with which neither butter-milk, milk, treacle, nor even a morsel of salt, was allowed.

Amongst the most singular punishments inflicted upon Blincoe, was that of screwing small hand-vices of a pound weight, more or less, to his nose and ears, one to each part; and these have been kept on, as he worked, for hours together! This was principally done by Robert Woodward, Merrick, and Charnock. Of those petty despots, Merrick was the most unpardonable, as he had been a parish apprentice himself, and ought to have had more compassion. This Merrick was a stretcher, and Blincoe when about 11 or 12 years old, used to stretch for him, while he, Merrick, ate his dinner. Out of kindness, or because he could not eat it himself, Merrick used occasionally to leave a small part of his allowance, and tell Blincoe to go and eat it. On Mondays, it was the custom to give the boys bread and treacle, and turnip *broth* made the day before, which generally stunk to such a degree, that most of the poor creatures could only pick out the oat bread, the broth being loathsome. Whenever Merrick left a bit of bread and treacle in the window, Blincoe used to run eagerly at the prize, and devour it voraciously. One Monday, this over-looker, who was a most inhuman taskmaster, sent Blincoe down to the card-room for a basket of rovings, a descent of four or five stories deep, for this burthen of considerable weight. During the time he was gone, Merrick rubbed tar upon the oat cake, and laid it in the window as usual. When Blincoe returned, the brute said, "go and eat what lies in the window." Blincoe, seeing as he supposed, so much treacle upon the bread, was surprised; for Merrick usually licked it clean off, and to his bitter mortification, found, instead of treacle, it was *tar*. Unable to endure the nauseous mouthful, Blincoe spat it out, whilst Merrick, laughing at him, said, "What the devil are you spitting it out for." Poor Blincoe, shaking his head, said, "You know, mon,"[1] and Blincoe left the remainder of the tarred cake in the window, when his comrade, Bill Fletcher, a poor lad since dead, who came from Peak Forest,[2] took up the bread, and scraping off the tar as clean as he could, ate it up, apparently with a good appetite! To such dreadful straights were they driven by hunger, the apprentices have been known to *pick turnips out of the necessary*,[3] which others, who had stolen them, had thrown there to conceal, and

---

1 mon] man (dialect)
2 Peak Forest] a village in northern Derbyshire five miles northeast of Buxton.
3 *the necessary*] a toilet facility or privy.

washing them, have devoured the whole, thinking it too extravagant even to waste the peeling.

Palfry, the Smith, had the task of rivetting irons upon any of the apprentices, whom the masters ordered, and those were much like the irons usually put upon felons! Even young women, if suspected of intending to run {away}, had irons riveted on their ancles, and reaching by long links and rings up to the hips, and in these they were compelled to walk to and from the mill to work and to sleep! Blincoe asserts, he has known many girls served in this manner. A handsome-looking girl about the age of twenty years, who came from the neighbourhood of Cromford, whose name was Phebe Rag, being driven to desperation by ill-treatment, took the opportunity, one dinner-time, when she was alone, and when she supposed no one saw her, to take off her shoes and throw herself into the dam, at the end of the bridge, next the apprentice house. Some one passing along, and seeing a pair of shoes, stopped. The poor girl had sunk once, and just as she rose above the water he seised her by the hair! Blincoe thinks it was Thomas Fox, the governor, who succeeded Milner, who rescued her! She was nearly gone, and it was with some difficulty her life was saved! When Mr. Needham heard of this, and *being afraid the example might be contagious,* he ordered James Durant, a journeyman spinner, who had been apprenticed there, to take her away to her relations at Cromford, and thus she escaped!

When Blincoe's time of servitude was near expiring, he and three others, namely, William Haley, Thomas Gully, and John Emery, the overlooker, took a resolution, to go out of the factory at a fixed hour, meaning not to work so many hours: but, according to Blincoe's account, neither he nor his comrades had ever heard up to that time, of any law which regulated the hours of apprentices working in cotton-mills, nor did they know what an act of parliament meant, so profound was the ignorance in which they had been reared! Blincoe and his mutinous comrades, having left work at the expiration of fourteen hours labour, went off to the apprentice house. Upon this, the manager, William Woodward, sent off an express to the master, (Mr. Needham), at Highgate Wall, a lone and large mansion about four miles distant. Orders came back, to turn all four out of the apprentice-house that night; but not to give them any provisions! Being thus turned out, Blincoe got lodging with Samuel Brickleton! One or two of his comrades slept in the woods, which luckily was hay time.–Brickleton's hospitality did not include provisions, and having had no food since twelve o'clock the day before, Blincoe was sorely hungry in the morning, but still he had nought to eat! About nine o'clock, all four, agreeable to the orders they received the night before, went to the counting-house at the mill. Mr. Needham was there in a terrible ill-humour.—As soon as he saw Blincoe come in, he took from his body, his waistcoat and jacket, and fell upon him with his thick walking-stick, which he quickly broke by the heavy blows laid on poor Blincoe's head and shoulders, and he kept on swearing the while, *"I'll run you out, you damned rascal."* As soon as he could escape, Blincoe ran off to his work, when Haley and Emery, who were apprentices, like Blincoe, caught their share of his fury! At noon, Blincoe went eager enough to the apprentice house, having had no food for twenty-four hours. Having in a few minutes, devoured his portion, he ran off at full speed, without hat, jacket, or waistcoat, his head and body greatly bruised, towards the residence of a magistrate, named Thornelly, who resided at Stanton-Hall, a place about six miles beyond Bakewell, and eleven from Litton-Mill![1] There resided, at this time, at Ashford,[2] about four miles from Litton{-Mill}, a man named Johnny Wild, a stocking-weaver, who had been his (Blincoe's) overlooker, when first he went to Lowdham Mill. Filled with the fond hope of being made at once a gentleman, thither, poor Blincoe, now twenty years of age, directed his course. Johnny Wild was sitting at his frame, weaving stockings, and was surprised to see Blincoe run up to the door like a wild creature, terror in his looks and reeking with perspiration, without hat, coat, or waistcoat. To him, Blincoe told the cruel usage he had met with, and the wounds and bruises he had just received, which were sufficiently visible! Wild and his wife seemed touched with compassion, at the sad plight Blincoe was in, gave him a bowl of bread and milk, lent him a hat, and directed him his way. Thus refreshed, the fugitive set off again, running as fast as he could, looking often behind him. As he passed through Bakewell, Blincoe thought it best to slacken his pace, lest some mercenary wretch, suspecting him to be a Litton Mill apprentice running away, should, in the hope of receiving a reward of a half-crown piece, seize him and send him back to prison! As he passed along, many

---

1 a magistrate, named Thornelly ... Litton-Mill] Stanton is a village south-east of both Tideswell and Bakewell, a market town on the River Wye twelve miles east by southeast of Buxton. An 1817 traveler's guide identifies the owner of Stanton Hall as H.B. Thornhill, Esq., a name that Blincoe could have confused with "Thornelly."

2 Ashford] a village about two miles above Bakewell on the River Wye.

seemed to eye him intently; but no one stopped him. About six o'clock in the evening, being heartily jaded, he arrived at the house of Mr. Thornelly. It happened, that the magistrate was at dinner; but some person, in his employ, understanding that Blincoe came to seek redress for alleged violence, went to the supplicant in the yard, saying, "Who do you want?"—"Mr. Thornelly."—"What for?"—"I am an apprentice at Litton Mill, master has beat me cruelly, do look at my shirt?"—"Never mind, never mind," said this person, "you cannot see Mr. Thornelly to-day; he is at dinner; there will be a bench of justices to-morrow, about eleven in the morning, at the sign of the Bull's Head, facing the church at Heam; you must go there." This place lay {about five} miles from Litton Mill, on the Sheffield road.[1] Finding there was nothing to be done at Stanton-Hall, poor Blincoe began to measure back his weary steps to Litton Mill! He called at Johnny Wild's, as he returned, who allowed him to rest; but, of food, he could not offer any; having a large family, and being but a poor man, he had none to spare! Blincoe gave back his hat, and arrived at the apprentice-house between nine and ten, being then giving-over time![2] William Woodward, the manager, whose heavy hand had inflicted blows and cuffs beyond calculation on poor Blincoe, was about the first person by whom he was accosted! In a tone, about as gentle as that of a baited-bear, and an aspect much more savage, said, "Where have you been?"—"To Mr. Thornelly."—"I'll Thornelly you to-morrow," said he, and turned away. Not knowing what the next day might bring forth, Blincoe applied for his mess of water-porridge, which, after a journey of two and twenty miles, tasted highly {savory}, and then he retired to his bed, praying God to end his life, or mitigate its severity—a prayer that was common at Litton Mill!—Sore as he was, he slept; but it was on his face, his back being too much bruised, to lie in that position, or even on his side! In the morning, he rose and went to his stretching frame. Between seven and eight o'clock, Blincoe saw Woodward going to the apprentice-house, from the window of the factory. Seeing this opportunity, without waiting for breakfast, Blincoe again made a start, still without hat, waistcoat or coat, towards Heam, to state to the magistrates the cruel treatment he had received.—The day was fine. The hay was about, and miserable as was poor Blincoe, he could not but feel delighted with the

---

1   Sheffield road] a main thoroughfare a few miles from Litton Mill.
     Sheffield is a city approximately thirty-seven miles northeast of Derby.
2   giving-over time] quitting time.

sweet air and romantic scenery. Having been thus expeditious, Blincoe was at Heam, an hour and a half too soon. To amuse himself, he went into the Church-yard. As soon as the magistrates arrived, from whose hands he came to supplicate for justice, Blincoe went to the Bull's Head. The officiating clerk was an attorney named Cheek, who resided at Whetstone-Hall, a mansion situated within half a mile of Tideswell. To this person, Blincoe began unbosoming his grief, and in the earnestness of his harrangue, and fearful, lest the attorney did not catch every syllable, the half-naked Blincoe crept nearer and nearer; but Mr. Cheek not relishing the dense, foul scent of oil, grease, and filth, said, "Well, well, I can hear you, you need not come so near; stand back." Poor Blincoe, not a little mortified, obeyed his command, and, by the time Blincoe's piteous tale was ended, the magistrates had mostly arrived, to whom Mr. Cheek, the clerk to the magistrates, read the paper, which Blincoe supposed contained his intended deposition. Blincoe was then sworn. One of the magistrates, Blincoe believes it was a Mr. Middleton, of {Leam} Hall,[1] said, "Where is Mr. Needham?"—Blincoe replied, "He's gone to-day (Tuesday) to Manchester Market." This prevented their sending a man and horse to fetch him. One of the magistrates then said to Blincoe, "Go strait to the mill, to your work."—"Oh! Sir, he'll leather me," meaning, Mr. Needham would beat him again. "Oh, no! he durst na'—he durst na'," said one of the magistrates in reply. Upon this, some one advised, that a letter should be sent to Mr. Needham, in whose much dreaded presence, Blincoe had no inclination to appear! Blincoe cannot recollect who wrote the letter, but thinks it was Mr. Middleton, who said, "If he leathers you, come to me." This gentleman resided at a distance of about eight miles from Litton Mill. Having this powerful talisman in his possession, Blincoe returned direct to the mill, and, advancing boldly to Woodward, the manager, said, "Here's a letter for Mr. John Needham," the son of the old master, who is now resident in Tideswell! Blincoe informed Woodward, he had been at a justice-meeting at Heam, and as a justice had sent this letter, Woodward did not dare to lay violent hands upon him. This day, poor Blincoe had to fast till night, making a complete round of another twenty-four hours of fasting! On Wednesday, John

---

1   Mr. Middleton, of {Leam} Hall] According to a mid-nineteenth-century map, Leam Hall was located about five miles northeast of Litton. An 1817 traveler's guide identifies Leam House as the property of Marmaduke Middleton, Esq.

Needham returned from Manchester market, and appeared, as usual, at Litton Mill.—The letter, from which Blincoe anticipated such beneficial results, was handed to the young Squire, by William Woodward, the manager. He broke the seal, read it through, and ordered Blincoe to be called out of the factory, from his work. Obedient to the summons, and not a little alarmed, he appeared before his young master, whose savage looks shewed, ere he spoke a word, a savage purpose. The first words were, "Take off your shirt, you damned rascal!" Blincoe obeyed, his head and back being still very sore[.] John Needham instantly began flogging him with a heavy horsewhip, striking him with his utmost force, wherever he could get a blow. It was in vain Blincoe cried for quarters: in vain he promised never again to go to a Magistrate, in any case whatever. John Needham kept on flogging, swearing horribly and threatening furiously, resting between while, till he had fully satisfied his sense of justice! He then unlocked the door, and, saying,"You'll go again, will you?" bade Blincoe put on his shirt, and go to his work. Away went Blincoe, scarcely able to stand, and covered with additional bruises from head to foot. Even this horrid flogging did not deprive Blincoe of his appetite, nor of his determination to seek redress of the Magistrates, and accordingly, the next Sunday night, when some of the time-outs were let out of the prison, Blincoe, availing himself of the darkness of the night, watched the opening of the yard door, and crouching almost on his hands and knees, crept out unseen. Shortly after the order was given to set down to supper. Every 'prentice, male and female, knew their own places. In about two minutes, two hundred half-famished creatures were seated. Their names were called over, to see that none were missing, when, little parson could not be found. Governor Thomas Fox, on learning of this event, ordered the door warder to be called, who declared most vehemently, he had not let Blincoe out, and further, he had not passed the door; upon this, a general search was made in all the rooms and offices, high and low; but no where was little parson to be found. Meanwhile, as soon as Blincoe found himself outside the hated walls, he set off again up Slack, a very steep hill close to the mill, and made the best of his way to Litton, and going to the house of one Joseph Robinson, a joiner, who worked in Litton Mill, who had known Blincoe at Lowdham Mill, was well acquainted with the horrid cruelties he had suffered, and heartily compassionating Blincoe's miserable state, gave him a good supper, and let him sleep with his sons. In the morning, Robinson, who was really a humane man, and a friend to the poor children, gave Blincoe some bread and meat, and giving him a strict injunction not to own *where* he had slept, Blincoe set off, about six o'clock in the morning, to Mr. Middleton's house. The morning was showery, and Blincoe had neither hat, coat, or waistcoat, and he had about eight miles to go, in search of justice. He arrived at Mr. Middleton's, long before his hour of appearance. At last, Mr. Middleton got up, and Blincoe approaching, crawling like a spaniel dog, said, "Sir, I have come again, Mr. Needham has been beating me worse than ever, as soon as he read your letter over." Seeing the miserable state Blincoe was in, drenched with the rain and half naked, Mr. Middleton said, "go into the kitchen and rest yourself—you should not have come here first; you should have gone to Mr. Cheek, of Whetstone Hall, and he would have given you a summons;" upon this, poor Blincoe said mournfully, "Eh, Sir, he will do nought for me—he is so thick with my master—they are often drinking together." "Pshaw, pshaw," said the Justice, "he's like to listen to you—he must;" but then, as if recollecting himself, he said. [*sic*] "Stop, I'll write you a letter to Mr. Cheek." In the Justice's kitchen, poor Blincoe got some bread and cheese, which was indeed a luxurious food, though unaccompanied with any beer. Blincoe thus refreshed, again set off to Mr. Cheek, a distance of about eleven or twelve miles, bare headed, and dressed only in trowsers and shoes. The rain continuing pouring in torrents. When Blincoe reached Whetstone Hall, one of the first persons he saw, was a woman of the name of Sally Oldfield, her husband, Thomas Oldfield, then dead, had been governor of the 'prentices of Litton Mill. She was then housekeeper to Messrs. Shore and Cheek, at Whetstone Hall. Those gentlemen were amongst the most intimate friends and visitors of Mr. Needham, and Sally Oldfield, who recollected Blincoe, alias parson, said, "Eh, Parson! what do you want here?" "I have a letter from Mr. Middleton to Mr. Cheek." "Eh!" said little old Sally again, "Are you going against your master?" Blincoe told her he was, and how cruelly he had been treated. Sally could not comprehend any right Blincoe had to complain, and said, "Eh! thou should'st not go against thy master." Saying this, she took him to the kitchen, gave him some bread and cheese, and plenty too, and some good beer, and then said, "Parson, thou mun never go against thy master; what do you have for dinner on Monday?—do you have treacle now?" "No, we have dry bread and broth." "Ah," continued she, "*Treacle is too dear.*" Blincoe could scarce refrain from smiling, recollecting the feast of the treacle can; but he said nothing, and not a soul came near him. There Blincoe sat until night, when he began to think the magistrates were hoaxing him, and he thought there was no utility in waiting for justice, or a possibility of obtaining redress! he would never more complain! seven hours sat Blincoe in Lawyer Cheek's kitchen, and not the least notice being taken of him or his letter, he made his solitary way back to the mill, and arrived there just as the mill had loosed, and going direct to Woodward, told him where he had been, and concealing the conviction he felt, that it was not possible to obtain redress; he assured the tyrant, with tears and lamentations, that if he would intercede to prevent his being flogged again, he would never runaway more. "On these conditions," said Woodward, "I will, if I can," and from that day Blincoe cannot recollect, that he was either flogged or beaten; but, *still* Blincoe had no knowledge, that there was any Act of Parliament for the protection of poor orphans like himself.—He knew of the magistrates coming to the mill; but he has no distinct idea that they came to *redress grievances!* So great was the terror of the poor ignorant apprentices, no one dared complain, and he cannot recollect that they ever gave themselves any other trouble, than merely going over the mill! Every thing was previously prepared and made ready. The worst of the cripples were put out of the way. The magistrates saw them not. The magistrates could never *find out* any thing wrong, nor hear of a single individual who had any complaint to make!—When Blincoe was about twelve or thirteen years of age, he well remembers an apprentice, almost grown up, who lost his life in an attempt to escape. He had tied several blankets or sheets together, to reach the ground from the chamber window, where he slept, which was three or four stories high. The line broke, he fell to the ground, and he was so much hurt at the fall, he died soon after. Blincoe thinks some surgeon or doctor came to him; but he has not the least recollection of any Coroner's inquest being held! In addition to the punishments already stated, Robert Woodward and other overlookers have kicked him down a whole flight of stairs; at other times, he has been seized by the hair of his head and dragged up and down the room, tearing off his hair by handsfull, till he was almost bald! All the punishments he suffered, were inflicted upon others, and, in some cases, even to a worse degree than on himself. He even considers he came off tolerably well, compared with others, many of whom, he believes, in his conscience, lost their lives, and died at the apprentice-house, from the effects of hard usage, bad and scanty food, and excessive labour.

CHAP. VI.

BLINCOE remained in Litton Mill a year after he had received his indentures,[1] not from inclination; but to get a little money to start with. His wages were only four shillings and sixpence weekly, and this was to have been paid monthly; but, month after month elapsed, and, instead of an honest settlement, there was nothing but shuffling! The first money he received was eighteen and sixpence, and being in possession of that sum, he thought himself incalculably rich! He scarcely knew what to do with it! It took away his appetite.—After he was a little composed, he devoted a few shillings to the purchase of some dainties, such as wheaten cakes and herrings! He then worked and lived like others, till his master owed him nearly half a years labour. The pay day came and then he drew nearly thirty shillings, the rest was kept back, so that, Blincoe seeing no prospect before him but perpetual slavery for a merciless master, made up his mind to be off; and on Tideswell May fair, which happens on the fifteenth of May, he put this plan in execution! He knew not where to go; but started the next morning at hazard! When he came to Chapel-a-Frith,[2] he determined to visit a celebrated fortune-teller, called Old Beckka'! She lived in a small back-house, a haggard, black, horrid-looking creature, very old, having a long beard, and dressed like a person who lived in ages past! Her name was very influential all over Derbyshire. So very famous was *old Beckka'*, that people came far and near, and she was reputed to be possessed of land and houses.—She never took a smaller fee than a shilling, even from the very poorest of her votaries. Her name was well known at Litton Mill. If any thing was stolen, Woodward, the manager, or Gully, or some *one* of the overlookers, used to go to Chapel-a-Frith, to consult *old Beckka'*. To this sybil, Blincoe repaired, holding a shilling, between his thumb and finger! Perfectly understanding the object of his visit, she first took the shilling, and then said "Sit down." He felt really frightened, and, if she had bade him stand upon his head, he declared he should have obeyed! He had been told, that she had really enchanted or bewitched persons, who had endeavoured to cheat or deceive her, or by whom she had been offended, causing them to lose their

---

1 indentures] See note 2 on page 97.
2 Chapel-a-Frith] Chapel-en-le-Frith (literally, "Chapel in the Woodlands," but still popularly known as "Capital of the Peak") is a village approximately five miles north of Buxton in the direction of Manchester.

way, and sent ill fortune in many shapes. Our novice was also told, that ladies and gentlemen of high estate had come in their coaches, all the way from London, to learn their destiny, all which circumstances produced, on his uncultivated mind, the sensations described! No sooner was Robert Blincoe seated, than the witch of Chapel-a-Frith, put a common tea-cup in his hand, containing a little tea grounds, "Shake it well," said Beckka. Blincoe obeyed. Then the oracle drained away the water, and twirling the cup round and round, she affected, with the utmost gravity, to read his future fortune, in the figures described in the sediment at the bottom. Assuming a wild stare, and standing erect over him, her eyes apparently ready to leap from their sockets, she exclaimed, in a hollow sepulchral tone of voice, "You came from the outside of London, did you not?" "Yea," said the astonished Blincoe, "I did." "You came down in a waggon, and have been at a place surrounded with high rocks and great waters, and you have been used worse than a stumbling stone." Blincoe's mouth, and eyes, and ears, all seemed to open together, at this oracular speech, as he said, "Yea, yea, it is true." Then she said,—"Your troubles are at an end.—You shall rise above those, who have cast you down so low.—You shall see their downfall, and your head shall be higher than theirs.—Poor lad! terrible have been thy sufferings.—Thou shalt get up in the world! you'll go to another place, where there'll be a big water, and so go thy way in peace, and may God prosper thy steps!" Filled with amazement, mingled with rising hopes of better fortune, Blincoe arose and departed, making a very low reverence to "*old Beckka,*" as he went out, and impressed with the fullest conviction, that she was truly a sorceress; the simpleton, forgetting, that his *costume,* his wild and pallid looks, and the *scent* of his garments, tainted as they were with the perfume of a cotton factory, were more than sufficient to point out to the fortune-teller, the past and present, from which she speedily fabricated the future fortune, for her simple visitor! Blincoe thought he got but a very short story for his shilling! On the other hand, he was very well contented with its *quality,* since it promised him, and in such positive terms, that he should rise above his cruel oppresor and become a great man. Filled with these thoughts, he stepped briskly along, not much encumbered with luggage; for he carried all his wardrobe on his back. When he arrived at a spot called "Orange end," where four ways met, he was perplexed which to take, the oracle of Chapel-a-Frith not having apprised him of this dilemma, nor which road to take! Being quite in an oracular mood, very happy, that he had got so far away from Litton, and fully convinced, that, go where he would, and befall him what would, he could not blunder upon a worse place, nor be oppressed by a more evil fortune, he tossed up a halfpenny in the air, making it spin round its own axis, and waiting its course as it rolled, resolved to follow in that direction. Its course happening to be pointed towards New Mills, Derbyshire,[1] thither he bent his course, but failed in his application for work. Blincoe, therefore, walked on, till he came to Mr. Oldknow's Cotton Factory, at Mellow,[2] and there he crept towards the counting-house, in an humble mood, and said, in a very meek tone of voice, "If you please, Sir, can you give me work?" The manager, Mr. Clayton, a gentleman by no means deficient in self-respect, asked sharply: "Where do you come from?" "From Litton Mill, Sir." "Where are your indentures?" "There they are, Sir," said Blincoe, holding up the papers. There were two or three gentlemen, in the counting-house, and they looked earnestly over the indentures and then at Blincoe, one of them saying, "Did you come from Pancras workhouse?" "Yes, Sir." "Why, we are all come from thence! we brought many children the other day to this Mill." "Indeed, Sir," said Blincoe, pitying, in his heart, the poor creatures, and thinking it would have been merciful to have killed them outright at once, rather than put them to such a place as Litton Mill had proved to him. Looking at the names of the subscribing officers and overseers, one of the Pancras parish officers said to Mr. Clayton: "Some of these officers are dead." Blincoe again exclaimed "Indeed, Sir,"— recollecting the atrocious lies and cruel deceptions, those men had practised upon him, in his infant years, by telling him to believe that, in sending him to a cotton-factory, he was to be made at once a gentleman; to live upon roast beef and plum-pudding; to ride his master's horses; to have a watch in his pocket and plenty of money, and nothing whatever to do! Poor Blincoe could not help thinking to himself:—"Where are the souls of these men gone, who, knowing the utter falsehood of their seductive tales, betrayed me to destiny far more cruel than transportation?" The overseers, looking at the distorted limbs of this victim

---

1   New Mills, Derbyshire] an industrial village approximately eight miles from Buxton in the direction of Manchester.

2   Mr. Oldknow's Cotton Factory, at Mellow] Mellor—spelled variously "Mellow" and "Mellor" in both the Carlile and Doherty versions of the *Memoir*—was a hamlet in Lancashire approximately eight miles north of Chapel-en-le-Frith. Samuel Oldknow (1756-1828) was a major early and relatively benevolent manufacturer of cotton calico and muslin.

of parochial economy, said "Why, how came you so lame? you were not so when you left London, were you?" "No, Sir, I was turned over, with the rest of the unclaimed 'prentices, from Lowdham Mill, to Ellice Needham, of Litton Mill, [sic]" "How did they keep you?—what did you live upon?" "Water porridge—sometimes once, sometimes twice a day—sometimes potatoes and salt for supper: not half enough and very bad food." "How many hours did you work?" "From five, or occasionally six o'clock in the morning, till nine, half-past, ten, and sometimes eleven, and, on Saturday nights, till twelve o'clock." The person wrote these answers down; but made no comment, nor ever noticed the material facts, that Blincoe had not been taught the trade he should have learnt, and that the parish officers of Pancras had utterly neglected him and his miserable comrades, when the Lowdham Mill factory stopped! The Manager then bade a person shew Blincoe where he might get lodgings, and bade him come to work in the morning. Blincoe was too much afraid of giving offence, by asking questions in the counting-house, to venture to enquire as to his parentage; but, as soon as he had got lodgings, he strove to make out where the officers were to lodge that night, at {Mellor}, to enquire further: but hearing they were just then gone, he was deprived of the opportunity! This occurrence, filling his mind with melancholy reflections, he shed many tears in solitude that night! The next morning, he went to his work, and found it was as hard as at Litton Mill; but of more moderate duration; the hours being from six in the morning, till seven in the evening. The 'prentices, whom he saw at work, seemed cheerful and contented; looked healthy and well, compared with those at Litton! They were well fed, with good milk-porridge and wheaten bread for breakfast, and all their meals were good and sufficient! They were kept clean, decently dressed, and every Sunday went twice to Marple Church, with Mr. Clayton, their under-master, at their head! On the whole, it struck Blincoe, that the children were in a Paradise, compared with the unfortunate wretches whom he had left at Litton Mill, and he indulged in the humane hope, that the lot of children just then brought down from London, might escape the dreadful sufferings he had had to endure! Unfortunately, the trade, which Blincoe had been fourteen or fifteen years articled to learn, was by no means so good as husbandry labour. The wages, Mr. Oldknow offered him, were *eleven shillings per week*, at the time that a good husbandry labourer could earn from sixteen shillings to a pound! After having been some months in Mr. Oldknow's factory, Blincoe learnt, that, whilst he did as much work, and as well as any man in the factory, which employed several hundred apprentices, Mr. Clayton had fixed his wages at three or four shillings per week less than any other person's. Blincoe could not impute this to any other cause, than an idea, that he was in so crippled a state, he dared not demand the same as another! Such is the mean and sordid spirit, that sways almost the whole of those establishments. When a poor creature has been crippled at one mill, and applies for work at another, instead of commiserating his condition and giving him the easiest and best work and best pay, it is a common custom, to treat them with the utmost contempt, and though they may be able to do their work as well for their masters, though not with the same ease to themselves, as one who has escaped being crippled, the masters generally make it a rule to screw them down to the very lowest point of depression, and, in many cases, give them only half their wages. On this principle was Blincoe dealt with, at Mellor Factory; but, as the wretched diet on which he had been fed at Litton, enabled him to live upon three shillings per week, he saved money each week. Having an independent spirit and not being willing to work for less than his brethren, he took an opportunity one evening, to go to the counting-house and doffing his hat to Mr. Clayton, said, "Sir, if you please, will you be so good to rise my wages?" Turning sharp round, he said, "Raise your wages! why, I took you in upon *charity only!*" "I am sure it was very good of you, Sir," said Blincoe, who well knew that such hands as himself were scarce, therefore, that his charity began at home.—Hearing Blincoe speak in such humble, yet somewhat ironical terms; for he possessed a rich vein of sarcastic humour, Mr. Clayton said, "Well, go to your work, I'll see." They paid every fortnight at the factory.—The next pay night, Blincoe found himself paid at the rate of thirteen shillings, which was still two shillings under the price of other workmen! This continued a few weeks, when, an old servant, whom they had employed many years, applied for work, and on the Friday night fortnight, Blincoe's wages were sent up to him, with an order *to depart*. This is what is called *getting the bag*. Blincoe being alike surprised and hurt, and knowing he had done his work well and had never lost a minute, set an enquiry on foot, and he was told, from very good authority, it was because he had applied for an advance of wages, and because Mr. Clayton thought it was taking an advantage of him. Curious logic! Mr. Clayton seems totally to forget the advantage he had, in the first instance, taken of poor Blincoe, and feeling very sore, when the young fellow applied for redress, he seized this opportunity, and, in this petty way, to wreak his anger; and as the factory of Mr. Oldknow stood so very high, if compared with that of Ellice Needham of Litton, these blemishes fully prove, how foul and corrupted is the spirit of traffic, since, in its best shape, it could not resist the temptation of taking a mean advantage of the necessities and the misery of a fellow creature.

Although the treatment of parish pauper apprentices was very liberal, compared to what they had endured at Litton Mill, the journeymen were governed by a very tight hand. If they arrived only two or three minutes after the clock had struck, they were locked out; and those, who were within, were all locked in, till dinner time, and not only were the outward doors, below, locked; but every room above, and there was a door-keeper kept, whose duty it was, a few minutes before the respective hours of departure, to unlock the doors, by whom they were again locked, as soon as the work-people arrived! In every door, there was a small aperture. [*sic*] big enough to let a quart can through, so that the food brought by parents and relations could be handed to them within—no one being permitted to go in or out, and, of course, the necessaries, two or three to each room, were within side the room, where the people worked! Such was the rigid order and severe discipline of one of the most *lenient* master cotton-spinners! Mr. Oldknow caused a road to be made from the turnpike to his mill, which saved some length of way, and every stranger, or person not absolutely working in the mill, who used it, had to pay a halfpenny—and, as the road led to New Mills and Mellor, those work-people, in common with all others, had to pay a halfpenny. There was a toll-house erected, and also a toll-bar, and the speculation, if not very neighbourly, is said to have been very profitable.

When Blincoe left this establishment, which seemed to vie with some of the largest factories in Manchester, both in its exterior grandeur, and in magnitude, he had contrived to save the greater part of his wages, and having a few pounds in his pocket, he felt less dismay at this harsh and unexpected treatment, than if he had acted with less prudence and been destitute. He had served faithfully and diligently upwards of half-a-year, and a character[1] from so respectable an employer might be serviceable, he, therefore, made his appearance once more before Mr.

1 character] written evaluation of one's work; letter of recommendation.

Clayton, and doffing his hat, and assuming the most lowly and respectful attitude, said, in his usual slow and plaintive tone:—"Will you please, Sir, give me a character?"—"O no! O no!" replied the manager, "we never give characters here," with an unfriendly aspect! Blincoe thought it was better to be off and seek his fortune elsewhere, than stop and argue. This circumstance strongly marks the oppressive character of these establishments. It is clear, that Mr. Clayton did not chuse to hire Blincoe without a character, or something equivalent, by requiring to see his indentures; and, after the young man had served them diligently and honestly, for six months, he surely should have written to certify, that he had done so, and the denial *might* have prevented his getting another employer. However the law might stand at present, upon this point, in any future legislative measure, a clause should be introduced, to *compel* every master to give a written character, except where some positive act of gross misconduct interposed to neutralise the claim!

From Mellor Mill, Blincoe walked to Bollington, in Cheshire, a village not far from Macclesfield,[1] and about 18 miles distance, having a bundle which, slung upon a stick, he carried upon his shoulder. He passed several road-side houses of entertainment, allaying his thirst from the living fountains,[2] and satisfying his hunger with a penny cake. In this way, he travelled, till he arrived at Bollington, where he obtained work in a factory, situated on the Macclesfield road, belonging to a Mr. Lomax. He was placed in the card-room, which is reckoned the most laborious and unwholesome in the factory, on account of the great quantity of dirt and dust; but Mr. Lomax promised him a stretching frame, at the end of a fortnight. The fortnight having expired, Blincoe saw no signs of being relieved from stripping off the cotton from the cards.[3] He made up his mind to be off, and march on towards

---

1   Bollington ... Macclesfield] Bollington was a village three miles north of Macclesfield and eighteen miles southeast of Manchester.
2   living fountains] fountains of flowing water, much like artesian wells.
3   card-room ... cards] Carding was the second step in the production of cotton, less harmful only than batting, the first stage in which the raw cotton was beaten out of the bales in which it had been packed. A carding machine cleaned and combed out the cotton into its first crude threads. A card was a brush made of wires placed at an angle in leather and mounted on a cylinder; two sets of cards working against each other straightened the cotton fibers.

Staley Bridge,[1] in the hope of bettering his condition! As he was going along some fields, for a short cut, he was met by a couple of suspicious looking fellows, who, stepping boldly up to Blincoe, said in a stern voice, "What have you got in that bundle?" ["]I dunna know, Mester, but if you'll ask the gentleman on horseback, that is coming on the horse road, at the other side of the hedge, he'll tell you." Hearing this, and marking the calm indifference of Blincoe, the interrogators took to their heels, and never once looked behind them, as he could perceive; and thus the poor little wanderer outwitted the marauders, and saved his shirt and stockings, and, by the possibility, the hard-earned treasure he had in his fob. Having thus adroitly got rid of the thieves, Blincoe made the best of his way to the main road, and the best use of his legs, till he got in view of some houses, where he thought himself out of danger. Arrived at Staley Bridge, situate upon a river, which separates Cheshire and Lancashire,[2] and where there are many spinning factories, he applied to a man named William Gamble, who had lived in Yorkshire. This man, twelve or thirteen years before, was one of the overlookers at Lowdham Mill, and very much addicting himself to kicking the apprentices and dragging them about by the hair of the head, up and down the rooms, and then dashing them upon the floor, on account of which propensity, he was reprimanded and removed, when the overseers of Pancras parish arrived. Indeed this man and one Smith, were the terror of the poor children; but Blincoe wanting work and knowing he was an overlooker in Mr. Harrison's factory,[3] which, by way of preeminence, was called *the Bastile*, poor Blincoe had been so many years accustomed to Bastiles,[4] he was not easily daunted. To Gamble he repaired, and who having bestowed so many marks of his *paternal* regard upon Blincoe, he recognized him at once and very kindly got him work at ten

1 Staley Bridge] Now Stalybridge, this industrial town eight miles east of Manchester, was transformed by the coming of cotton manufacture in 1776.
2 a river ... Lancashire] the River Tame.
3 The 1825 trade directory for Stayley Bridge identifies Abel Harrison as a cotton spinner.
4 Bastiles] The Bastille, a famous prison in Paris which housed political prisoners, was stormed and captured by French revolutionaries on 14 July 1789; in its second use here, "bastile" functions as a generic name given to any place of confinement with a particularly negative connotation.

shillings per week, which he drew for the *use* of Blincoe, during a few weeks, to whom he acted as *caterer*, and provided him with a bed, so that Blincoe had nothing whatever to do, but his work, which was tolerably moderate, that is, compared with Litton Mill. Notwithstanding its unseemly appellative, the work-people were not locked up in the rooms, as at Mellor.

The master had another method of restraining his work people from going out, and which saved the pay of a door-keeper, namely, by the counting-house being so placed, the people could not go in or out without being seen! There Blincoe worked some months; but not being perfectly satisfied with the conditions in which the stewardship of William Gamble left him, he took the liberty to remove from his hospitable roof, and the result was, he could live upon and lay up one half of his wages. The wages paid at this mill were very low, and the work very laborious, being the stripping of the top cards! The fixed quantum was six pounds per day, which is a severe task. After this, the master went up to Blincoe and others, as they were at work, and informed them, he would have more weight of cotton stripped off the top cards, or turn them away, and Blincoe not feeling inclined to perform more work for that pay, asked for his wages and left the Bastile!

Hence, Blincoe went to Mr. Leech, the owner of another factory, at Staley Bridge, by whom he was engaged at nine shillings a week; but he found the cotton so foul and dirty, and the work so hard, he staid not long; as the owner paid only once in three weeks, it required some privation, before any wages could be got! After three days toil, Blincoe went to his Master and asked him to lend him as much silver as his work came to, and, having obtained it, he took French leave,[1] to the great offence of his employer. Blincoe still remained at Staley Bridge, though unemployed. He next obtained work at the mill of a Mr. Bailey,[2] whose father had then recently had one of his arms torn off by the blower, and he died in a few hours from the dreadful effects of that accident. Here Blincoe stopped, stripping of cards, for eleven shillings per week, during several months, when, having saved a few pounds, he determined to try his fortune at Manchester,[3]

---

1 took French leave] went away without notice.

2 Mr. Leech ... Mr. Bailey] An 1825 trade directory for Stayley Bridge identifies Leech as John Leech, a cotton spinner, and Bailey as Abel Bailey, also a cotton spinner.

3 According to the document in Appendix A.2, Carlile erred in printing "London" here, but since Manchester, which appears in both the Carlile

which celebrated town was only seven or eight miles distant. Of London, Blincoe retained only a faint recollection, and he thought Manchester the largest and the grandest place in all the world. He took lodgings in St. George's-road,[1] being attracted by the residence of James Cooper, a parish apprentice from the same workhouse with himself, who had been so cruelly flogged at Litton Mill. By this young man, Blincoe was received in a friendly manner, and he lodged in his house near Shudehill.[2] Blincoe arrived at Manchester at a bad time, just at the return of peace,[3] and he had a difficulty of getting work. His first place was in the factory of Mr. Adam Murray. There the engines worked only four days and a half per week; for which he received no more than seven shillings and a penny. Blincoe suffered much from the heat of the factories at Staley; but in this of Mr. Murray's, he found it almost suffocating, and if there had been as great a heat in the factory at Litton, added to the effects of long hours, and bad and scanty food, it is probably [sic] it had cut him off in the first year of his servitude! Blincoe, thinking it was wise to risk the chance of bettering his fortune, left Adam Murray's gigantic factory, at the end of the week, and next went to work in Robinson's factory,* as

editions of the *Memoir*, is "only seven or eight miles distant" from Stalybridge, as the sense of this passage requires, Doherty had no correction to make here (see note on page 326). Manchester had been "celebrated" as the center of cotton manufacture since the end of the eighteenth century.

1 St. George's-road] a street in the nineteenth century extending from the center of Manchester and leading out of the town to the northeast.

2 Shudehill] a major street in the center of early nineteenth-century Manchester.

3 Both the chronology of Blincoe's account and the use of the word "return" here would support a dating of 1815 for his arrival in Manchester, the year in which Napoleon abdicated for a second time after his defeat at Waterloo.

* Whilst Blincoe worked at Robinson's old factory, {Water-street, Manchester,}[1] having, by denying himself even a sufficiency of the cheapest diet, clothed himself more respectably than he had ever been, and having two-pound notes in the pocket, he determined to spend a few shillings, and see the diversions of a horse-race, at {Kersal-Moor};[2] but not being aware that such beings as pick-pockets were in the world, he put his pocket-book in his outside pocket, whence it was stolen by some of the light-fingered gentry, and poor Blincoe had to lament his want of caution. [Brown's note]

[1] Water-street] probably the long street that runs parallel to the River Irwell.

[2] Kersal-Moor] the site of the Manchester Racecourse from 1687 to 1846, as well as a prominent location for public meetings.

it is called, which belongs to Mr. Marriet. There he was engaged to strip cards, at half a guinea per week. He worked at this several months, living in a frugal manner, and never going into public-houses, or associating with idle company; but, when he was engaged, by the rule of the overlookers, he was forced to pay a couple of shillings, by way of footing,[1] and then he went to a public-house in Bridge-street,[2] where this silly and mischievous custom, let Blincoe into the first and last act of drunkenness, in which he was ever concerned, and he felt ill several days after-wards. At the same time, many of his comrades, who worked in the same room, and who contributed each so much money, got drunk also. This was spent contrary to Blincoe's wishes, who grieved that he was obliged to drink the ale. If he had refused, he would have been despised, and might have lost his employ; and if a poor fellow had been ever so low and wanted this money for the most essential purpose, it must not be refused. This is a pernicious custom, and should be abolished. Blincoe continued several months in this factory, living as it were alone in a crowd, and mixing very little with his fellow-work people. From thence Blincoe went to a factory, at Bank Top,[3] called Young's old factory, now occupied by Mr. Ramsbottom, and there, after a time, he was engaged as stoker, or engine man, doing the drudgery for the engineer. Here, he continued three years, sleeping a great part of the time on a flat stone in the fire hole. If it rained in the night he was always drenched! but he had formerly suffered so much by hardships, and the pay was so small, he determined to do his best to save as much money as might suffice to enable him to try to live as a dealer in waste cotton; from which humble state many of the most proud and prosperous of the master cotton-spinners of Manchester have emerged. His employer, liking him, raised his wages to thirteen shillings a week, and, whilst Blincoe was about as black as a chimney-sweeper in full powder, the hope of future independence induced him to bear his sable hue, and his master

---

1 footing] a fee demanded of a person doing something for the first time, such as being admitted to a society or profession; usually among workers, the money was used to treat to drinks one's new fellow employees.
2 Bridge-street] a street leading to what was called from the late eigh-teenth century the New Bailey Bridge.
3 Bank-top] Later London Road, this street in the southeast of Manches-ter was an extension of the major thoroughfares Market Street and Piccadilly.

behaved to him with more humanity, than he had been accustomed to experience. He was however disturbed by some petty artifices of the manager, in the year 1817, and an attempt being made to lower his wages, for which, upon an average, he worked sixteen hours in the day, Blincoe resolved to quit such hard, unremitting and unprofitable servitude, and from that period he commenced dealer and chapman. At the end of the first year, he found his little capital reduced full one-half; but on the other hand, he gained, in experience, more than an equivalent, to what he had lost in money, and, being pretty well initiated into the *mysteries of trade*, and having acquired a competent knowledge of raw or waste cottons, he commenced his second year, in much better style, and, at the end of that year, he had not only regained his lost capital, but added £.5 to it.

Blincoe hired a warehouse and lived in lodgings. In the year 1819, on Sunday, the {27}th of June, he happened to be, with several other persons, at the christening of a neighbour's child, where several females were present. An acquaintance of Mester Blincoe's (no longer poor Blincoe), a jolly butcher, began to jest and jeer him, as to his living single. There was a particular female friend present, whose years, though not approaching old age, outnumbered Blincoe's, and the guests ran their jokes upon her, and some of the company said, Blincoe, get married to-morrow, and then we'll have a good wedding, as well as a christening, to day. Upon which, Blincoe, leering a little sideways at the lady, said, "Well, if Martha will have me, I'll take her and marry her to-morrow." She, demurely, said "Yes." ["]Then,["] said Blincoe, though taken unawares, ["]now, if you'll stick to your word, "I will." She then said, "I'll not run from mine, if you don't." Hearing this, there was a great shout, and when it had subsided, the butcher offered to bet a leg of mutton, that Blincoe would not get married on Monday, the {28}*th of June*, and others betted on the same side, when Blincoe determined to win the bets, and a wife in the bargain. Blincoe said to his comrades, "Well, that I may not be disappointed, I'll even go to see for a licence to night." Two of the party went to see all was fair. When Blincoe had got half way, being fearful of a *hoax* by Martha, he hit on the device of holding back, telling her he could not get the license without her presence, and when she agreed to go, then still more securely to prevent his being laughed at, he said, "I have not money enough in my pocket, will you, Martha, lend me a couple of pounds?" In an instant she produced that sum, giving it to Blincoe, and they proceeded. Blincoe was so bashful he neither took her hand nor saluted her lips; but, accompanied by two of the persons who had laid wagers, went to the house direct, of the very celebrated, though not *very reverend, Joshua Brookes,*[1] lately deceased. The next morning they {went in a coach from his lodgings in Bank-Top, and} were married in the old Church! Blincoe won his bets and his wife? They have lived together with as great a share of conjugal tranquillity, as falls to the lot of many, who are deemed happy couples, and he has ever since kept upon the advance in worldly prosperity. He has lived to see his tyrannical master brought to adverse fortune, to a state of comparative indigence, and, on his family, the visitation of calamities, so awful,[2] that it looked as if the avenging power of retributive justice had laid its iron hand on him and them. In how short a time Blincoe's career will verify the prediction of the old sybil of Chapel-a-Frith remains to be seen; but it is in the compass of probability, that he may, in the meridian of his life, be carried as high, by the wheel of fortune, as in the days of his infancy and youth, he was cast low!!

{In the year 1824, Blincoe had accumulated in business that sum of money he thought would be sufficient to keep his family, with the exception of his cotton-waste business; shortly after he gave up a shop which he had occupied for a few years at No. 108, Bank-Top, Manchester, and took a house at Edge-place, Salford,[3] whilst living there, thought proper to place some of the money he had saved by industry to the purchasing of some machinery for spinning of cotton—and took part of a mill of one Mr. Ormrod, near St. Paul's Church, Tib-street,[4] in this he was engaged six weeks, with the assistance of some mechanics, getting the machinery ready for work—the first day it was at work, an

---

1   Joshua Brookes (1754?-1821), eccentric clergyman of the Church of England. The *Dictionary of National Biography* notes that "as the chaplain of the Manchester collegiate church [in a very large parish] he baptized, married, and buried more people than anyone in the kingdom."

2   calamities, so awful] In 1814 public opinion forced Ellis Needham to leave Litton Mill because too many of his former and now destitute apprentices had become the responsibility of the parish; in the same year, both Ellis Needham and his son John declared bankruptcy (Chapman 203, 240). See also Appendix A.1.

3   Salford] an industrial town adjoining Manchester to its west. In the nineteenth century it suffered some of the worst effects of industrialization.

4   Tib-street] a street parallel to Oldham Street above Piccadilly in central Manchester.

adjoining room of the building caught fire, and burnt Blincoe's machinery to the ground, not being insured, nearly ruined him.—Blincoe declares that he will have nothing to do with the spinning business again—what with the troubles endured when apprentice to it, and the heavy loss sustained by fire, is completely sick of the business altogether.}

END OF THE MEMOIR OF ROBERT BLINCOE.

CONFIRMATION {S} OF ITS VERACITY.

{Ashton-under-Line, Feb. 24, 1828.

DEAR SIR—I have read the narrated sufferings of Robert Blincoe with mingled sorrow and delectation: with sorrow, because I know, from bitter experience, that they have really existed; with delectation, because they have appeared before the public through the medium of the press, and may, peradventure, be the means of mitigating the misery of the unfortunate apprentices, who are serving an unexpired term of apprenticeship in various parts of Lancashire and Derbyshire. In 1806 or 7, I was bound an apprentice, with twelve others, from the work-house of St. James,' Clerkenwell London, to a Mr. J. Oxley, at Arnold-mill,[1] near Nottingham. From thence, after two years and three months' servitude, I was sold to a Mr. Middleton, of Sheffield. The factory being burnt down at this place, I with many others, were sold to Mr. Ellice Needham, of Highgate-wall, the owner and proprietor of Litton Mill! Here I became acquainted with Robert Blincoe, better known at Litton-mill by the name of Parson. The sufferings of the apprentices were exquisite during Blincoe's servitude, both in point of hunger and acts of severity; but, subsequent to Blincoe's departure from that place, the privations we had to endure, in point of hunger, exceeded all our former sufferings (if that were possible), having to subsist principally upon woodland sustenance, or, in other words, on such food as we could extract from the woods. What I now write is to

---

1 St. James ... Arnold-mill] St. James, located in the district of Clerkenwell, north of High Holburn in central London; Arnold, once within the boundaries of Sherwood Forest, a village four miles northeast of Nottingham.

corroborate the statement of Blincoe, having heard him relate during my apprenticeship, all, or nearly all, the particulars that are now narrated in his memoir. I may also add, that I worked under Blincoe, at the same machine, in the capacity that he had done under Woodward, without receiving any harsh treatment from him—nay, so far was Blincoe from ill-treating the apprentices employed under him, that he would frequently give part of his allowance of food to those under his care, out of mere commisseration, and conceal all insignificant omissions without a word of reproach—I cannot close this letter without relating an anecdote that occurred about two years ago. Happening to call at a friend's house one day, he asked if I knew Robert Blincoe. I replied in the affirmative. Because, added, [sic] he, I saw a prospectus of his biography some time past; and related the same to W. Woodward, who was on a visit here, and who immediately said, "HE'LL GIVE IT MA," and became very dejected during the remainder of his visit.

Your humble servant,

JOHN JOSEPH BETTS.}

Samuel Davy, a young man, now employed in the Westminster Gas Works,[1] has called on the Publisher of *Blincoe's Memoir*, and has said, that his own experience is a confirmation of the general statement in the Memoir. Samuel Davy, when a child of seven years of age, with thirteen others, about the year 1805, was sent from the poor-house of the parish of St. George's, in the Borough of Southwark, to Mr. Watson's mill, at Penny Dam, near Preston, in Lancashire;[2] and successively turned over to Mr. Burch's mill, at Backborough,[3] near Castmill, and to Messrs. David and Tho-mas Ainsworth's mill, near Preston. The cruelty towards the

---

1 Westminster Gas Works] The Gas Works in the City of Westminster, London, were located in its south near the Thames.
2 St. George's ... Preston] St. George's was one of a number of parishes in the Borough of Southwark, a large district on the south side of the Thames extending from Lambeth in the southwest to Rotherhide in the east; Preston was a major cotton-manufacturing town in west Lancashire, approximately thirty miles northwest of Manchester.
3 Mr. Burch's mill, at Backborough] Extant vestry records for 1805 confirm that mill owners named Birch and Robinson had been employing parish apprentices in Backborough, Lancashire, since 1785 (see Introduction 21).

children increased at each of those places, and, though not quite so bad as that described by Blincoe, approached very near to it. One Richard Goodall, he describes, as entirely beaten to death! Irons were used, as with felons in gaols, and these were often fastened on young women, in the most indecent manner, from the ancles to the waist! It was common to punish the children, by keeping them nearly in a state of nudity, in the depth of winter, for several days together. Davy says, that he often thought of stealing, from the desire of getting released from such a wretched condition, by imprisonment or transportation; and, at last, at nineteen years of age, though followed by men on horseback and on foot, he successfully ran away and got to London. For ten years, this child and his brother were kept without knowing any thing of their parents, and without the parents knowing where the children were. All applications to the Parish Officers for information were vain. The supposed loss of her children, so preyed upon the mind of Davy's mother, that, with other troubles, it brought on insanity, and she died in a state of madness! No savageness in human nature, that has existed on earth, has been paralleled by that which has been associated with the English Cotton-spinning Mills.

A Narrative of the Experience and Sufferings of William Dodd, A Factory Cripple. Written by Himself (1841)

William Dodd

[When one considers that William Dodd was the most prolific writer of the individuals whose works are contained in this volume—he also wrote *The Factory System Illustrated* (1842) and *The Laboring Classes of England* (1847)—it is surprising that there is so little concrete information available about his life beyond what is contained in his autobiography. He was born in 1804, probably in Kendal, and he started working at the age of five at card making and was a piecer in a woolen mill by age six. After holding a variety of jobs throughout his life, he moved to London in 1839 and found employment as a tailor. As a result of his factory labor, he had a variety of physical problems and was forced to have his right forearm amputated in 1840.

After the publication of *A Narrative of the Experience and Sufferings of William Dodd* in 1841, Dodd had the opportunity to become acquainted with a number of important reformers, including John Fielden, Richard Oastler, and Lord Ashley. It was his relationship with Ashley that would spark the greatest controversy, and the debates between John Bright and Ashley in the House of Commons in 1844 brought Dodd's reliability into question (see Introduction 11-12, 50-53; Appendix B.1). Eventually Dodd emigrated to the United States, and he published in Boston *The Laboring Classes of England*, which went into a second edition during 1848 (see Appendix B.2).]

A

NARRATIVE

OF THE

EXPERIENCE AND SUFFERINGS

OF

WILLIAM DODD,

A FACTORY CRIPPLE.

WRITTEN BY HIMSELF.

GIVING AN ACCOUNT OF THE HARDSHIPS AND SUFFERINGS
HE ENDURED IN EARLY LIFE, UNDER WHAT DIFFICULTIES HE
ACQUIRED HIS EDUCATION, THE EFFECTS OF FACTORY LABOUR
ON HIS MIND AND PERSON, THE UNSUCCESSFUL EFFORTS MADE
BY HIM TO OBTAIN A LIVELIHOOD IN SOME OTHER LINE OF
LIFE, THE COMPARISON HE DRAWS BETWEEN AGRICULTURAL
AND MANUFACTURING LABOURERS, AND OTHER MATTERS
RELATING TO THE WORKING CLASSES.

SECOND EDITION.

LONDON:
PUBLISHED BY L. & G. SEELEY, 169, FLEET STREET,
AND HATCHARD & SON, 187, PICCADILLY.
1841.

PRICE ONE SHILLING.

Price One Shilling.[1]

Title page courtesy of the Beinecke Rare Books and
Manuscript Library, Yale University.

---

1 On the reverse of the title page appears the following information:
"Printed by Vincent Torras & Co., 7, Palace Row, New Road."

TO

LORD ASHLEY, M.P.[1]

My Lord,

The sympathy you were pleased to express for me, after seeing a brief outline of my sufferings, and witnessing the effects of the factory system on my person, and believing that a more extensive circulation of my narrative may, under Providence, be the means of assisting the strenuous exertions your Lordship is making on behalf of that oppressed class of workpeople to which I belong, I have been induced to prepare for the press an enlarged and corrected account, to be issued in a separate form; and beg, as a token of gratitude, to dedicate these, my humble endeavours, to you, who are so thoroughly conversant with the momentous subject to which my remarks refer.

And am,

My Lord,

Your Lordship's

Much obliged,

Humble Servant,

WILLIAM DODD.

23, Little Gray's Inn Lane.[2]
June 18, 1841.

---

1 Lord Ashley, M.P.] Anthony Ashley-Cooper (1801-85), Tory politician, philanthropist, and social reformer; later the Seventh Earl of Shaftesbury. In 1833 he became the unofficial leader in Parliament of the Ten Hours movement (see Introduction 11 and 49-53, 55).
2 Little Gray's Inn Lane] in 1841 a small, winding street off Gray's Inn Lane just north and opposite King's Road.

A NARRATIVE, &c.

DEAR READER,—I wish it to be distinctly and clearly understood, that, in laying before you the following sheets, I am not actuated by any motive of ill-feeling to any party with whom I have formerly been connected; on the contrary, I have a personal respect for some of my former masters, and am convinced that, had they been in any other line of life, they would have shone forth as ornaments to the age in which they lived; but having witnessed the efforts of some writers (who can know nothing of the factories by experience) to mislead the minds of the public upon a subject of so much importance, I feel it to be my duty to give to the world a fair and impartial account of the working of the factory system, as I have found it in twenty-five years' experience.

I cannot, at this distance of time, take upon myself to say what were the predisposing circumstances by which my parents were induced to send their children to the factories, especially as I was very young at the time my eldest sister first went, and cannot be supposed then to have known much of their affairs. I shall, therefore, confine myself, in the following narrative, to such facts as may serve to show the *effects* of the system upon my mind, person, and condition.

Of four children in our family, I was the only boy; and we were all at different periods, as we could meet with employers, sent to work in the factories. My eldest sister was ten years of age before she went; consequently, she was, in a manner, out of harm's way, her bones having become firmer and stronger than ours, and capable of withstanding the hardships to which she was exposed much better than we could: but her services soon became more valuable in another line of industry. My second sister went at the age of seven years, and, like myself, has been made a cripple for life, and doomed to end her days in the factories or workhouse.[1] My youngest sister also went early, but was obliged to be taken away, like many more, the work being too hard for her! although she afterwards stood a very hard service.

I was born on the 18th of June, 1804; and in the latter part of

---

1 According to the Poor Law Amendment Act of 1834, parishes, joined together to form a "union," were required to build a workhouse in which those unable to support themselves were to be kept until they could do so. The conditions in such union workhouses—the separation of members of families, the poor food, and the monotonous make-work—were meant to discourage the poor from seeking relief.

1809, being then turned of five years of age, I was put to work at card-making,[1] and about a year after I was sent, with my sisters, to the factories. I was then a fine, strong, healthy, hardy boy, straight in every limb, and remarkably stout and active. It was predicted by many of our acquaintance, that I should be the very model of my father, who was the picture of robust health and strength, and, in his time, had been the don of the village, and had carried off the prize at almost every manly sport.

A circumstance occurred between my fifth and sixth year, which places the fact of my being strong and active beyond a doubt. I was then about getting my first boy's dress of trousers and jacket, and, being stout, I had long felt ashamed of my petticoats,[2] and was very glad when I heard that a friend had offered to supply my parents with the necessary articles of dress for me, giving them a sufficient length of time for payment. This friend lived at the distance of three-quarters of a mile from our house; and I well remember going with my eldest sister for my clothes. There was a great quantity of ready-made dresses, one of which being selected and tried on, the tailor thought it was rather too little; but I thought it would do very well, especially as it had got a watch-pocket in it; and not liking the idea of losing what I had got, or of having again to wear the petticoats, I ran out of the shop, and did not stop till I had got home, my sister calling after, but not being able to overtake me. I was put into the factories soon after, and have never been able to perform this feat of running three-quarters of a mile since.

From six to fourteen years of age, I went through a series of uninterrupted, unmitigated suffering, such as very rarely falls to the lot of mortals so early in life, except to those situated as I was, and such as I could not have withstood, had I not been strong, and of a good constitution.

My first place in the factories was that of piecer,[3] *worked in a cotton mill* or the lowest situation: but as the term conveys only a vague idea of the duties

---

1 For cards and carding, see note 3 on page 170 and Dodd's explanation in his note on page 197. Dodd suggests here that he began working at home at the age of five.
2 During the early nineteenth century, young boys as well as girls and women wore petticoats or skirts.
3 A piecer, or piecener, was employed in a cotton mill to join together broken pieces of thread so that the spinning could continue uninterrupted. As Dodd goes on to explain, however, a piecer's duties in a woolen mill were more specialized.

to be performed, it will be necessary here to give such explanation as may enable those unacquainted with the business to form a just conception of what those duties are, and to judge of the inadequacy of the remuneration or reward for their performance, and the cruelty of the punishments inflicted for the neglect of those duties. The duties of a piecer in the cotton, worsted, and woollen mills, differ considerably, but their rewards and punishments are very much alike. What I shall have to say in the following pages, must be understood to relate to the woollen mills only, which is, on all hands, allowed to be the best for the piecer. It is in this situation of piecer that the greatest number of cripples are made from over-exertion.

The duties of the piecer will not be clearly understood by the reader, unless he is previously made acquainted with the machine for spinning woollen yarn, called a *Billy*.[1] I must, therefore, crave his patience, till I make this matter as clear as I am able. A billy, then, is a machine somewhat similar in form to the letter H, one side being stationary, and the other moveable, and capable of being pushed close in under the stationary part, almost like the drawer of a side table; the moveable part, or carriage, runs backwards and forwards, by means of six iron wheels, upon three iron rails, as a carriage on a railroad. In this carriage are the spindles, from 70 to 100 in number, all turned by one wheel, which is in the care of the spinner. When the spinner brings the carriage close up under the fixed part of the machine, he is able, by a contrivance for that purpose, to obtain a certain length of carding for each spindle, say 10 or 12 inches, which he draws back, and spins into yarn; this done, he winds the yarn round the spindles, brings the carriage close up as before, and again obtains a fresh supply of cardings. The side of the billy appropriated to the piecers is composed of a number of boards set in a slanting direction the whole length, somewhat like the face of a writing-desk; over these boards are put cloths made of coarse wrapper, in the form of a jack-towel,[2] only not so long, and much wider. These cloths move on two rollers, one at the top, and one at the bottom of the slant-

---

1 *Billy*] Also called a slubbing machine, the billy was often a subject in factory debates. Because it was not steam-driven, it was run at the discretion of the slubber, the adult male worker whom Dodd calls "the spinner" here. Totally dependent on their young assistants' preparation of the wool, slubbers were notorious for their brutal and frequent punishments of slow or ineffective piecers.

2 jack-towel] a towel held on a roller by having its ends sewn together.

ing board: and by this means the cardings, which are laid in parallel lines thereon, are conveyed, as they are wanted, to the points of the spindles. On the top of the cardings, and immediately over the upper roller, runs the billy-roller—the dreaded instrument of punishment for the children. This roller is very easily taken out and put in its place, and is at the full command of the spinner, and, being of great length, it is scarcely possible for the piecer to get out of the way, should the spinner think proper to give him a knock. On these coarse canvas cloths the piecer pieces the ends of the cardings, and prepares them for the spinner.

The cardings are strips of wool 27 inches long, and of equal thickness throughout, (generally about as thick as a lady's finger,) except about 2 inches at each end, which are smaller, in order that when two ends are laid one over the other, and rubbed together with the piecer's flat hand, the piecing may not be thicker than any other part of the carding.

These cardings are taken up by the piecer in his left hand, about 20 at a time. He holds them in nearly the same manner as a joiner would hold a bunch of ornamental shavings for a parlour fire-place, about 4 inches from one end, the other end hanging down; these he takes, with his right hand, one at a time, for the purpose of piecing, and, laying the ends of the cardings about 2 inches over each other, he rubs them together on the canvas cloth with his flat hand. He is obliged to be very expert, in order to keep the spinner well supplied. A good piecer will supply from 30 to 40 spindles with cardings; but this depends, in a great measure, upon the quality of the work to be done, and also whether it is intended for the warp or the weft of the cloth to be made.

The cloths upon which the piecer rubs, or pieces, the ends of the cardings, as above stated, are made of coarse wrappering. The number of cardings a piecer has through his fingers in a day is very great; each piecing requires three or four rubs, over a space of three or four inches; and the continual friction of the hand in rubbing the piecing upon the coarse wrapper wears off the skin, and causes the fingers to bleed. I have had my fingers in this state for weeks together, healing up in the night, and breaking out again in little holes as soon as I commenced work on the following morning.

Another source of pain in the hands of piecers, is their continually swelling from cold in the winter season; and this is an evil which, like the other, cannot altogether be prevented. In a future page, I shall have to describe the process of oiling the wool; at present, it will be enough to say, that the oil gets rubbed into the cloths upon which the cardings are pieced, and, as a matter of course, the cloths get black, greasy, and cold. With continually passing over these comfortless things, the hands get cold, and swell very much; and as there is but little, and in many places no fire allowed, it is next to impossible for them to keep their hands warm; add to this the clothes they have upon their backs, are generally as greasy and comfortless as those upon which they piece, and stick to their arms, legs, and thighs, more like a wet sack than anything intended for warmth and comfort.

The position in which the piecer stands to his work is with his right foot forward, and his right side facing the frame: the motion he makes in going along in front of the frame, for the purpose of piecing, is neither forwards nor backwards, but in a sidling direction, constantly keeping his right side towards the frame. In this position he continues during the day, with his hands, feet, and eyes constantly in motion. It will be easily seen, that the chief weight of his body rests upon his right knee, which is almost always the first joint to give way. The number of cripples with the right knee in, greatly exceed those with the left knee in; a great many have both knees in—such as my own—from this cause.

Another evil resulting from the position in which the piecer stands, is what is termed "splay-foot," which may be explained thus: in a well-formed foot, there is a finely formed arch of bones immediately under the instep and ankle joint. The continual pressure of the body on this arch, before it is sufficiently strong to bear such pressure, (as in the case of boys and girls in the factories,) causes it to give way: the bones fall gradually down, the foot then becomes broad and flat, and the owner drags it after him with the broad side first. A great many factory cripples are in this state; this is very often attended with weak ankle and knee joints. I have a brother-in-law exactly thus, who has tried every thing likely to do him good, but without success.

The spinner and the piecer are intimately connected together: the spinner works by the piece, being paid by the stone[1] for the yarn spun; the piecer is hired by the week, and paid according to his abilities. The piecers are the servants of the spinners, and both are under an overlooker; and liable to be dismissed at a week's notice. Being thus circumstanced, it is clearly the advantage of

---

1   stone] usually a measurement of weight equal to fourteen pounds, although it can vary from eight to twenty-four pounds depending on the item being weighed (see 194).

the spinner to have good able piecers, who ought, in return, to be well paid. At my first starting in the works, I had 1s. per week, and got gradually advanced till I was 14 years old, at which time I had 3s. 6d. per week. The average wages are about 2s. 6d.; and thus, for a sum of money varying from one farthing to one halfpenny per hour, a sum not more than half sufficient to find me in necessaries, I was compelled, under fear of the strap and the billy-roller, (the smart of which I had often been made to feel—with the force of the latter, I have been struck almost motionless on the factory floor!) to keep in active employ, although my hands were frequently swollen, and the blood was dripping from my fingers' ends. I was also compelled to listen to, and be witness of almost every species of immorality, debauchery, and wickedness; and finally, to be deprived of the power of those faculties nature had so bountifully supplied me with.

In order to induce the piecer to do his work quick and well, the spinner has recourse to many expedients, such as offering rewards of a penny or two-pence for a good week's work—inducing them to sing, which, like the music in the army, has a very powerful effect, and keeps them awake and active longer than any other thing; and, as a last resource, when nothing else will do, he takes the strap, or the billy-roller, which are laid on most unmercifully, accompanied by a round volley of oaths; and I pity the poor wretch who has to submit to the infliction of either.

On one occasion, I remember being thrashed with the billy-roller till my back, arms, and legs were covered with ridges as thick as my finger. This was more than I could bear, and, seeing a favourable opportunity, I slipped out, and stole off home, along some by-ways, so as not to be seen. Mother stripped me, and was shocked at my appearance. The spinner, not meeting with any other to suit him, had the assurance to come and beg that mother would let me go again, and promised not to strike me with the billy-roller any more. He kept his promise, but instead of using the roller, he used his fist.

Another ignorant brute of a spinner whom I pieced for, had a great inclination to use his hand as an instrument of punishment. One time, when I was sleepy and tired, and did not keep my ends right, he struck me a blow on the side of the head, which made me reel about, and it was some time before I recovered myself. It was a great mercy I was not taken in by the machinery. For a long time after, I cherished a sort of revenge, and could not look upon the brute without remembering the blow, and used to say within myself, only let me get to be a man, and then I will pay you with interest. I am glad, however, to hear that he has since learned to read, and has become a worthy member of society. Should he see this, he may rest assured he has my forgiveness.

A piecer, it will be seen, is an important person in the factories, inasmuch as it is impossible to do without them. Formerly, boys and girls were sent to work in the factories as piecers, at the early age of five or six years—as in my own case—but now, owing to the introduction of some wise laws for the regulation of factories, they cannot employ any as piecers before they have attained the age of 9 years;[1] at which age their bones are comparatively strong, generally speaking, and more able to endure the hardships to which they will be exposed.

They now enjoy many privileges that we had not, such as attending schools, limited hours of labour, &c.; but still it is far from being a desirable place for a child. Formerly, it was nothing but work till we could work no longer. I have frequently worked at the frame till I could scarcely get home, and in this state have been stopped by people in the streets who noticed me shuffling along, and advised me to work no more in the factories: but I was not my own master. Thus year after year passed away, my afflictions and deformities increasing. I could not associate with any body; on the contrary, I sought every opportunity to rest myself, and to shrink into any corner to screen myself from the prying eye of the curious and scornful! During the day, I frequently counted the clock, and calculated how many hours I had still to remain at work; my evenings were spent in preparing for the following day—in rubbing my knees, ankles, elbows, and wrists with oil, &c., and wrapping them in warm flannel! (for everything was tried to benefit me, except the right one—*that of taking me from the work;*) after which, with a *look at,* rather than *eating* my supper, (the bad smells of the factory having generally taken my appetite away,) I went to bed, to cry myself to sleep, and pray that the Lord would take me to himself before morning.

Even Sunday—that day of rest to the weary and oppressed—shone no Sabbath day for me; for, although I was no longer urged

---

1   9 years] The provisions of the 1833 Factory Act prohibited the employment of children under nine in a wide range of textile factories with the exception of silk mills. It further mandated that no child under eleven—and within thirty months of its passage, under thirteen—would be allowed to work more than nine hours a day or forty-eight hours a week. It also required that the government appoint inspectors and that factory owners provide education for the children working for them.

on and kept in motion by the fear of the strap and the billy-roller, yet the leisure thus afforded to think and refle[ ] situation, only made me the more miserable!—If [ ] as bad, Monday morning was still worse—it was horr[ ] now, it makes me tremble, to think upon the sufferin[ ] mornings! My joints were then like so many rusty hinges, that had laid by for years. I had to get up an hour earlier, and, with the broom under one arm as a crutch, and a stick in my hand, walk over the house till I had got my joints into working order! and then, this day of the week was generally the most painful of the seven.

I frequently pressed my parent to get me something else to do, as I was anxious to leave the factories, and to get some work more tolerable. I got two engagements. At one place, they kept me a week, and the other only about a quarter of an hour. This latter circumstance is still fresh in my memory. I was engaged to be an errand boy to an ironmonger. This engagement was made without him seeing me; and, when he did see me, on account of my deformity, he expressed his fears I should not be able to do his work, but said I might try. On this morning, I had been drilling myself longer than usual on my crutch, and the hopes of getting from the factories had made me tolerably active! So, I set to work, to take down the shop-shutters, as he directed me. There was one step up, from the street into the shop; and, having got one of the shutters down, and on my shoulder, I was about to make this step—but it proved too much for me, and I fell beneath the load! My master seeing this, told me I was of no service to him, gave me three-pence, and dismissed me!

Judge what my feelings must have been at this time; after fancying myself on the point of leaving for ever a place wherein I had suffered so much, and then to see all my hopes dashed to the ground, and I sent back to what appeared to me the most hateful place on earth—the factories!

I have above alluded to the bad smells of the factories, which any one, who has ever been in or near a factory, must have noticed; and I shall here endeavour to explain what is the cause of those smells. If we examine a pile or fibre of wool through a microscope, we find it has a very uneven appearance, being notched or indented along its surface, somewhat similar to the teeth of a saw.[1] It is this unevenness of surface, that causes the

---

1 teeth of a saw] In using this metaphor, Dodd seems to be citing Ure's research on the microscopic composition of textile fibers (*Philosophy of Manufactures* 91-92).

fibres to unite closely and firmly together in the formation of cloths, hats, &c.; but although it is ultimately an advantage, it presents an obstacle to the manufacturer, which he is obliged to overcome in the following manner:—

When the wool is sorted into the different qualities, it is sent in bags of 10 or 12 stones, of 16 lbs. each, to be teased, which may be considered the first process in the manufacture![1] the workman then spreads a layer of wool on the factory floor, and over this wool he sprinkles, by means of a can of a peculiar construction, a quantity of whale oil, (generally in the proportion of one quart per stone,) exactly in the same manner as a gardener watering his plants. Upon this he spreads another layer of wool, oiling it as before, and so on, till the whole is done. This oiling process overcomes in part the ruffness of the fibres, and enables them to slide more easily among each other in carding and spinning. It will be easily seen, that the oil will be pretty equally distributed among the wool, in the act of teasing, where it remains till the wool is formed into cloth: the cloth is then sent to the fulling mill, to have the oil washed and cleaned out by means of urine, fuller's-earth,[2] and water.

Now, as it is imposible for any one to handle a soot bag without getting begrimed with the soot, so it is equally clear, that wool thus all but saturated with oil, will soil not only the hands, face, and clothes of the work-people, but the machines, walls, and floor of the factory, (I have seen it dripping through the floors,) or anything which comes in contact with it, and also emits a very unpleasant odour.

Another source of the offensive smell arises from the quantity of oil used in oiling the machinery. People who are at all acquainted with machinery, well know, that shafts, wheels, and spindles, in short anything, even a common wheel-barrow, that revolves upon its axis, requires to be kept clean and well oiled, in order that it may revolve smoothly and silently, and to prevent the undue friction or wearing of the brass step or collar in which it moves. For spindles and other light machinery oiling is sufficient; but for heavy pieces, such as upright, horizontal, and cylinder shafts, oil alone would not do, unless it was constantly dripping

---

1   first process in the manufacture] After washing, the wool is straightened by machines called teasers or pluckers (see Dodd's notes on 196 and 197).

2   fuller's-earth] an absorbent clay-like substance used for removing grease from fabrics.

upon the part; and as that would be very expensive, the following cheap substitute is applied.

The fat of horses, dogs, pigs, and many other animals, which die a natural death, or are killed with some incurable disease upon them, is sold to the manufacturers, and kept for the purpose of greasing the heavy machinery. It may be imagined what sort of an effluvia will arise from the application of this fat to shafts almost on fire. I have frequently been sent to order this article, and have had to apply it to a shaft very much heated, and as one piece melted away, another was laid on till it got cooled, and all the time the smoke was arising almost sufficient to suffocate me.

One great cause of ill health to the operatives in factories, is the dust and lime which is continually flying about. A large quantity of skin-wool and cow's-hair are used in the manufacture of coarse rugs, carpets, &c. This is obtained from the skins of the animals after they are killed, by means of a strong solution of lime-water. This lime thus gets intermixed with the wool and hair, and in this state it is sold to the manufacturer; it is then put through the teaser, in order to shake out the lime and dust; and, as the teaser goes at an immense speed, the work-people, the machine, and all around, are covered with the lime; and consequently, every inspiration of air in such an atmosphere, must carry with it and lodge upon the lungs a portion of these pernicious ingredients: the result is, difficulty of breathing, asthma, &c.

On finding myself settled for life in the factories, as it was then pretty evident I should not be able to do anything else, I began to think of getting a step higher in the works. It will be necessary to observe, that hitherto I had only been a piecer; so I put myself forward as well as I was able, and master soon noticed me, and gave me a higher place, where the labour was not so very distressing, but the care and responsibility was greater; and although I was a complete cripple, I now began to feel a little more comfortable.

A great many are made cripples by over-exertion. Among those who have been brought up from infancy with me in the factories, and whom death has spared, few have escaped without some injury. My brother-in-law and myself have been crippled by this cause, but in different ways; my sister partly by over-exertion and partly by machinery. On going home to breakfast one morning, I was much surprised at seeing several of the neighbours and two doctors in our house. On inquiring the cause, I found that my second sister had nearly lost her hand in the machinery. She had been working all night, and, fatigued and sleepy, had not been so watchful as she otherwise would have been; and consequently, her right hand became entangled in the machine which she was attending. Four iron teeth of a wheel, three-quarters of an inch broad, and one-quarter of an inch thick, had been forced through her hand, from the back part, among the leaders,[1] &c.; and the fifth iron tooth fell upon the thumb, and crushed it to atoms. It was thought, for some time, that she would lose her hand. But it was saved; and, as you may be sure, it is stiff and contracted, and is but a very feeble apology for a hand. This accident might have been prevented, if the wheels above referred to had been boxed off,[2] which they might have been for a couple of shillings; and the very next week after this accident, a man had two fingers taken off his hand, by the very same wheels—and still they are not boxed off!

The gentlemen she was working for at the time had immense wealth, most of which, I have reason to believe, was got by the factories. They paid the doctor, and gave her ten shillings!—which was about three farthings per day for the time she was off work. To this sum was added seven shillings more, subscribed by the work-people! I need not say, that she has been a cripple ever since, and can do very little towards getting a living.

After the wool has been oiled, as before described, it is then put through the first teaser,* from which it is carried to the

---

1 leaders] the wheels in a machine that move the other wheels or followers; in this case, wheels in a carding machine.

2 Fly-wheels connected to shafts and other mechanical parts were not required to be boxed off or fenced until the Factory Act of 1844. Fencing the wheels and shafts for an entire factory could be extremely expensive, and it also hindered workers' ability to quickly and efficiently clean the machinery. Thus, the boxing or fencing of wheels and shafts was one of the most controversial topics among factory owners, who effectively took advantage of loopholes in the laws—or simply ignored the laws altogether—for many years.

* The first teaser is a machine for breaking up the fleece wool, and consists of a very strong, firmly made cylinder, about 5 feet diameter, and 3 feet broad. Into the surface of this cylinder are firmly screwed a large quantity of iron spikes, about the size of a man's finger, in diagonal lines, about 2 or 3 inches apart from each other: in front of this cylinder are 2 rollers, called feeding rollers, about 8 inches in diameter, also filled with teeth of a different description. These rollers work into each other in such a manner as to hold the fleece of wool firmly between them, and

second teaser,† where it is prepared for the carding-engine. I had once a very narrow escape from death by this machine, when about 16 years of age, in the following manner:—

After finishing one sort of wool, it is usual to clean all the loose wool from the top and sides of the machine, previous to beginning another sort. This I was doing in the usual way, with a broom, and, as use begets habits of carelessness in boys, I had not used that degree of care requisite in such places. The consequence was, that the cylinder of the machine caught hold of the broom, and, if I had not had the presence of mind to let go my hold, I must have been dragged in with it. The broom was torn in a thousand pieces—a great number of the iron teeth were broken out and scattered in all directions—and, by the care of a kind Providence, I came off with a few slight wounds, from these teeth having stuck into me in several places.

The wool is then handed forward from the second teaser to the carding-engine,* where it is prepared for the piecer; it was in this sort of engine my sister had her right hand so dreadfully lacerated.

When about 15 years of age, a circumstance occurred to me

---

as they revolve but slowly, they present the wool gradually to the teeth of the cylinder, which performs 400 or 500 revolutions per minute. The momentum of this cylinder in motion is very great, and the wool or anything which comes in its way is torn in pieces, and thrown out behind. When it is going at full speed, the machine, the floor, and everything around, are in a constant shake. It is called among the work-people the Devil, from its tearing off the arms, &c. of the workmen. I have known 3 arms torn off, and 2 lives lost in consequence, in my time; and I must allow, that I have felt timid, when working at the very same machine that had a little while before been so employed. [Dodd's note]

† The second teaser is a more complicated machine than the first: it consists of a large cylinder and a number of rollers filled with teeth made of iron or steel, of the size and shape of a cock's spur, and thence called "cock-spurs." This teaser opens the wool more equally, and prepares it for the carding-engine: its capabilities of doing mischief to the work-people is nearly equal to that of the first teaser. [Dodd's note]

* The carding-engine may be briefly described as composed of 3 cylinders, from 4 to 5 feet diameter, 3 other cylinders, from 2 to 3 feet diameter, and from 20 to 30 rollers of different dimensions, all covered with cards. The wool is spread very equally upon cloths which carry it to the first cylinder, by which it is taken forward to the second, and so on till it comes out at the other end, in cardings ready for the piecer. [Dodd's note]

which does not often fall to the lot of factory children, and which had a great influence on my future life. I happened one day to find an old board laying useless in a corner of the factory. On this board, with a piece of chalk, I was scrawling out, as well as I was able, the initials of my name, instead of attending to my work, as I ought to have been doing. Having formed the letters W.D., I was laying down the board, and turning to my work, when, judge of my surprise, at perceiving one of my masters looking over my shoulder. Of course, I expected a scolding; but the half smile upon his countenance suddenly dispelled my fears. He kindly asked me several questions about my writing and reading, and, after gently chiding me for taking improper opportunities, he gave me two-pence to purchase paper, pens, and ink—which sum he continued weekly for several years, always inspecting my humble endeavours, and suggesting any improvements which he thought necessary. He also (with the approbation of his brother, the other partner in the firm,) allowed me to leave work an hour earlier than the other work-people every evening for a whole winter, in order that I might improve myself; and thus an opportunity was afforded me, which, with a few presents of books, &c. from both masters, were the means, under Providence, of laying the foundation of what I now consider a tolerable education.

 This kindness on the part of my masters will never be erased from my memory. It is as fresh to me now as if it had occurred but yesterday.

 With this encouragement, and impelled by the activity of my own mind, and an irresistible thirst after knowledge, I set myself earnestly to the acquisition of such branches of education as I thought might better my condition in afterlife; and, although I had still my work to attend, I soon had the happiness to find myself in possession of a tolerable share of mathematics, geography, history, and several branches of natural and experimental philosophy.[1]

So long as I was pursuing these studies, the thoughts of my unhappy condition were in some measure assuaged. But, in proportion as the truths of science were unfolded to my wondering sight, and the mists of ignorance chased from my mind, so the horrors of my situation became daily more and more apparent, and made me, if possible, still more fretful and unhappy! It was evident to me, that I was intended for a nobler purpose than to

---

1 natural and experimental philosophy] science.

be a factory slave! and I longed for an opportunity to burst the trammels by which I was kept in bondage!

Being desirous of turning my newly-acquired learning to some account, I engaged with a tailor, a neighbour of ours, to keep his books, draw out his bills, &c., in the evenings; by which means, I earned part of my clothing, and also got an insight into the trade, which was of service to me afterwards.

I became acquainted with a young man, who was very kind in lending me books, and explaining any difficulty I might be labouring under in my studies. I shall never forget his kindness;— he was to me like a brother. And now that I began to derive pleasure from the perusal of books, (and, in fact, it was the only source of pleasure I had) I did not omit any opportunity of gratifying it, particularly on the Sabbath day. It was customary for me, in the summer months, to take a book, and a crust of bread in my pocket, on a Sunday morning, and go to a very retired and secluded wood, about two miles from the town of Kendal,[1] in which I lived, and there I spent the day alone, on the banks of a rivulet that ran through the wood. I have sat for hours together absorbed in study, unperceived by mortal eye, with nothing to disturb me, but the numerous little songsters that kept up a continual concert, as if to make the place still more enchanting to my imagination. These were seasons of real pleasure to me; they were also attended with some advantages in other respects.

I had for many years enjoyed but a delicate state of health, owing to constant confinement, the smells of the factory, &c.; but these Sunday excursions got me a better appetite for my victuals, and I became more healthy and strong. I also derived considerable pleasure and improvement from the study of nature, in watching the habits of birds, bees, ants, butterflies, and, in short, any natural curiosity that came in my way; and when the evenings began to close in around me, and compelled me to return to the habitations of men, I felt a reluctance to leave my quiet and solitary retreat.

On some occasions, when I have been returning from my retreat in the wood on a Sunday evening, I have stood upon an eminence at a distance, and watched the gaily-attired inhabitants taking their evening walk in the fields and meadows around the

---

1 Kendal] a market and manufacturing town in Westmoreland, approximately 250 miles north of London. On the eastern border of the Lake District, Kendal was known in Dodd's time for its production of coarse woolens for the American market.

town, and could not help contrasting their situation with mine. They were happy in themselves, anxious to see and be seen, and deriving pleasure from mutual friendship and intercourse: I, with the seeds of misery implanted in my nature, surrounded by circumstances calculated to make me truly unhappy,— shrinking from the face of men to a lonely wood, to brood over my sorrows in secret and in silence. They were enjoying the fruits of their industry, but the reward of mine was—misery, wretchedness, and disease.

On one occasion, I was tempted to have recourse to a little of what the world calls policy, in order to gratify my appetite for reading, and which I knew at the time to be wrong. It was usual for us to stop the mill on the Saturday evening at five o'clock; then, after cleaning myself, I had a few hours to call my own, which were generally spent in my favourite occupation. One fine Saturday evening in June, I took a walk to the ruins of an old castle which overlooks the town of Kendal,[1] and which was to me a very agreeable retreat from the noise and bustle of the factory, having previously laid out the only two-pence I had in the loan of a book, which I had got snugly in my pocket, and was calculating on the pleasure it would afford me during the week. It chanced, however, to be one of those thinly printed volumes with large margins; and seating myself on the above-mentioned ruins, I did not rise till I had finished it: when I did, the grey of the evening was fast closing in around me. But I had exhausted my whole week's stock of amusement. What was to be done? I could not think of borrowing two-pence for another volume, because I had no means of paying it back again. At last I hit upon a plan, which, after a little hesitation, I carried into effect. I took the volume back to the librarian, and requested him to change it for another, telling him it did not suit me. He, being a good-natured sort of man, did so, little thinking that I had read it through. I felt ashamed, and for a long time after could scarcely look in the man's face, but I made it up to him in another way, when I had it in my power.

But having completed my second seven years of servitude, (somewhat earlier, indeed, than it is usual for workmen to have finished their first,) I got advanced to 9s. per week, and began to think myself well to do in the world, and could, by following a

---

1 old castle ...] Kendal Castle, probably built in the twelfth century, has been a ruin since the Tudor period; it still commands an impressive view of the town below.

rigid course of economy, spare a shilling or two occasionally for the purchase of such books as I took a fancy to. I kept an account of every item of expenditure, and regularly balanced up once a month; and, though it may surprise many, my expenses for board, lodging, and washing, over a space of three years, averaged exactly 7s. per week; so that I had 2s. a week left for clothes and books; and being a member of the Mechanics' Institute,[1] I became acquainted with the librarian, who engaged me to assist him in giving out books two evenings in the week, which added a little to my resources.

When I came to that period of life when men generally think of taking a partner, and settling in some way in the world, I was again beset by insurmountable obstacles. I saw my more fortunate fellow workmen getting married, and settling around me—I saw them comfortable and happy in their families, and I almost envied them their happiness. But no remedy was at hand: to have married a factory girl, would only have involved both myself and her in greater troubles, I being a cripple; and it would have been something remarkable, if I could have met with one able to make a shirt. How could it be expected from those who had been so wretchedly treated?—who were sent into this world to be the comfort and solace of man, and who, had their faculties been allowed to develope under a more genial sun, might have been the pride and ornament of the age in which they lived. But how different is the sad reality! They have been kept as slaves at one toilsome task, till every fine feeling of their nature is blunted. Ignorant of everything calculated to elevate and raise them to that high station originally intended for them by their Creator, is it to be wondered at, if we find them sunk, degraded, and almost lost to every sense of shame?* and for me to have looked for a partner in another class of society, situated as I then was, would have been ridiculous in the extreme.

---

1 Mechanics' Institute] From the 1820s mechanics' institutes were established to promote education in the sciences for working-class men.
   Ideally, but not always, they had libraries, museums, and laboratories,
   and they offered lectures on a range of subjects. By the time that Dodd
   was writing, they had been largely taken over by men in the lower-
   middle classes such as clerks, although some artisans were still active as
   members.
* I have seen some young women brought to work in the factories, who
   had been nurses in respectable families, and who seemed to be shocked,
   on their introduction, with what they heard and saw; but a very short
   time in such a school made them as bad as the rest. [Dodd's note]

To turn my thoughts from my pitiful situation, I attended lectures on various subjects, repeated the simple experiments at home, made some curious models and drawings of machines, and could thus contrive to pass away my leisure time pleasantly. Besides, one of my sisters dying, left a son; and her husband being unable to provide for him, it was a source of pleasure and gratification for me to attend to his wants and improvement.

Although I was not, at this time, constantly employed within the mills, but had to attend to the packing department in the warehouse, and any other place about the works where I might be required, yet still the effects of former years of factory toil were on me—still my life was one of suffering, although not to so great a degree; and having it now in my power to procure comforts which before were unknown to me, I lived something more like a Christian than I had formerly been enabled to do.

Thinking I might stand in need of assistance at some future period of my life, as I had all along been obliged to prop myself up, and was evidently working above my strength, I joined the Society of Odd Fellows,[1] which is the best of this description that I am acquainted with; but it is not without its faults. In this Society I was soon put into office; and, having an active and persevering mind, I put myself forward, and was elected as the Secretary of the Lodge to which I belonged. On that occasion, I well remember, I had to address, for the first time in my life, a large body of men. I felt rather timid; but having practised in my room for a full hour, I delivered my maiden speech, which still remains fixed on my memory, as follows:

"Mr. Chairman and Gentlemen,—I now stand before you as a candidate for the important office of Secretary—an office which, I am well aware, requires not only talent and abilities, but also great care and attention—(hear, hear); and although I can say nothing in favour of my humble abilities, having received no other education than what I have been able to scrape together after my day's work was done, still I trust that the interest I feel for the good and welfare of this Society, will

---

1 Society of Odd Fellows] one of a number of friendly societies or mutual-aid groups of working men that flourished in the 1830s and 1840s, often developing into national organizations.

stimulate me to use every exertion in my power in the discharge of the several duties of this office, should I be thought worthy of holding it. As I am convinced that you will act in this, as in all other matters, solely for the good of the Society, so I can assure you, that I shall be satisfied with your decision, whether it be for or against me."

There were five candidates for the office; and this was the state of the poll, as taken from the minute-book:—

William Dodd	64
W.S.	4
J.D.	4
J.B.	4
J.M.	4
	80

The other candidates thought I should have the lead, but each expressed a wish to be second. The result proved they were all second. These four members were tradesmen's sons, who had received a good education—I a factory cripple, who had never cost my parents a shilling for my learning. I was elected a second time to this office, and had, in 12 months, about 300*l.* of the Society's money through my fingers. I then received a vote of thanks, and was elected to a higher office. In the year 1835, I was elected to represent the district, a body of 700 men, in the annual meeting of the Society held that year at Derby;[1] and in 1836 I was again thought worthy of a seat in that important meeting held in London. I shall have to speak of this Society again.

An easy clerk's situation being now vacant, I was advised by some friends to avail myself of the opportunity, and thus free myself totally from the factories, especially as I had several influential friends to forward my views. I mentioned the subject to my masters, and, after considering it, they made such advantageous offers, as induced me to remain with them. This step I shall have reason to regret as long as I live.

In 1834, the present law for the regulation of factories was about being put in force. I, being appointed timekeeper for the

---

1 Derby] an industrial town in Midlands England, approximately 130 miles from Kendal.

works, had to take the children before the doctor to be examined, as certificates were required from him,[1] that they were of proper age to be admitted into the factory. I cannot describe my feelings as I went on those occasions, accompanied by about a score of little stunted figures, some of whom had been working in the factories for years, and whose parents had been in vain trying to get them something else to do; but I well remember, that I had great difficulty in convincing the doctor of their being of the age required, although I had no doubt of it myself, as I was well acquainted with their parents at the time of the children's birth; but their appearance was so much against them, that I fancied on some occasions, from certain expressions that the doctor made use of, that he thought I was deceiving him. Had he known my inmost thoughts, he would not for a moment have suspected me.

One of the most trying circumstances that occurred to me in all my factory experience, happened in the winter of 1834-5. I had then a youth, of about 17 years of age, placed under me, for the purpose of learning some of the higher branches of the business. I had been giving him directions what to do one day, and had gone up into the room above, for the purpose of superintending some other part of the works, when suddenly one branch of the machinery stopped, and, on turning round to inquire the cause, I was met by several persons, nearly out of breath, who said to me, "Tom has got into the gig,[2] and is killed." I ran down in haste, but it was too true: he was strangled. A great many bones were broken, and several ghastly wounds were inflicted on various parts of his person!

After his mangled body was extracted from the machinery, by unscrewing and taking the machine in pieces, it was laid in a recess on the ground-floor, the same in which the accident occurred, to await a coroner's inquest, the works being all stopped, and the hands dismissed. One by one they gradually went home, and left me alone for some time. The reader may more easily imagine, than I can describe my feelings on this

---

1   certificates] The Factory Act of 1833 required that children under eleven—and thirty months after its passage, under thirteen—present certificates testifying to their ages. These documents were to be issued by doctors and then countersigned by factory inspectors or magistrates (see Introduction 49).

2   gig] a whirling part of the machine.

occasion, as I paced, with folded arms, the flags of this dreary place. It was a cold, wet night. I had a flickering light burning beside me, just sufficient to cast a sombre and gloomy appearance over the three water-wheels and the heavy machinery by which I was surrounded. Not a sound broke upon my ear, except the wind and rain without, and the water trickling through the wheels within, with the mangled remains of that youth, whom I had carefully instructed in his business, and looked upon almost like a son, laying bleeding beside me.

This boy's death occurred partly through his own carelessness, as he had no business at the place; but the same thing might have happened to people who had business there; and consequently, it shows the necessity of boxing up all parts of machines, and the gearing by which such machines are propelled, where there is the least appearance of danger. Had this precaution been adopted in every mill, such calamities could not have happened: and, in many thousands of cases, limbs and lives which have been lost would have been preserved.

If anything was wanted to make me disgusted with the system, this and other circumstances would have supplied the deficiency: for while I and hundreds of work-people were toiling and sweating day after day for the bare necessaries of life—struggling, as it were, against wind and tide, and still hoping that some favourable turn would afford a resting-place for our wearied and emaciated frames—the manufacturers were amassing immense wealth, and thus converting what ought to have been a national blessing into a national curse—"adding field to field, and house to house,"[1] and rolling about in their carriages, surrounded by every luxury that this world can give, and looking upon us poor factory slaves as if we had been a different race of beings, created only to be worked to death for their gain.

As there is various reports respecting the wages of factory labourers, I here subjoin a table of the money received by me from 1810 to the close of my factory experience:—

---

1 "adding field ..."] Isaiah 5.8: "Woe unto them that join house to house, that lay field to field, till there be no place...."

Age.	Weekly Wages.			Yearly Amount.
	s. d.	s. d.	s. d.	£ s. d.
6 to 7*	1 0	..1 3	..1 6	2 5 0
7 8		1 6	..1 9	4 4 6
8 9			2 3	5 17 0
9 10			2 6	6 10 0
10 11			2 6	6 10 0
11 12			2 8	6 18 8
12 13			2 10	7 7 4
13 14			3 0	7 16 0
14 15			3 6	9 2 0
15 16			4 0	10 8 0
16 17			5 0	13 0 0
17 18			6 0	15 2 0
18 19			7 0	18 4 0
19 20			8 0	20 16 0
20 21			9 0	23 8 0
21 22			10 0	26 0 0
22 23			11 0	28 12 0
23 24			11 0	28 12 0
24 25			12 0	31 4 0
25 26			12 0	31 4 0
26 27			13 6	35 2 0
27 28			13 6	35 2 0
28 29			15 0	39 0 0
29 30			15 0	39 0 0
30 31			17 0	44 4 0
31 32			17 0	44 4 0
Done up				540 2 6
* Part of this year was occupied in card making.	Overtime – –			9 17 6
				550 0 0
	Average about 8 3			

It cannot, with truth or justice, be said that I was an idle workman, or an indifferent hand at my business. I have documents from my master to prove that I was not idle; and the fact of my having been selected from a number of workmen to attend improved and expensive machinery for finishing cloths, with which machinery I was doing as much work as six men by hand, and where I was obliged to lock myself in the room alone,[1] and not allow any one to enter but my master, and sometimes an assistant, (in this manner I have worked for many years,) affords a sufficient proof that I thoroughly understood my business. Besides, the latter part of my time I was a confidential servant, and in this capacity had to receive and pay money, occasionally attending the post office and bank with letters, bills, &c., and have had frequently upwards of 1,000*l.* passing through my hands in a week. At this time I was receiving 3*s.* or 4*s.* a week more than many strong, able-bodied men, which would not have been the case, if I had not been considered worthy of it. This will at once prove that I was receiving as much, or more, than the generality of workmen; and that this table is by no means to be considered an under rate of wages. It is, at least, 70*l.* or 80*l.* more than my brother-in-law has received in the same time.

From the first day I went into the factories, till the time that I left, my lost time, in sickness, holidays, &c., amounted to about four months. This lost time I have worked up at least three times over. When we were busy, I have worked as many as 18 hours per day; and yet all I have received, whether as wages, over-time, perquisites, &c., does not amount, as the preceding table will show, to more than 550*l.*; and for this paltry sum I have sacrificed my health, strength, constitution, nay, almost life itself; while those who have been reaping the benefit of my labours, have been laying by their thousands yearly and every year, and are now wallowing in riches, but nothing awaits me except the workhouse.

Let us see, on the other hand, what would have been the result, had I been brought up to a trade—say a carpenter and joiner, for instance. In that case I should have contracted a considerable debt before I began to receive any benefit—say 50*l.*, for apprentice fee, tools, and clothes, the master finding, as is usual, meat and lodging: then, at 21 years of age, it is reasonable to suppose I should have been a free man,[2] with a good robust form and constitution; and supposing I had earned 1*l.* per week for 20

---

1 in the room alone] Isolating workers who were using technologically advanced machinery was a common way of protecting trade secrets from competitors.

2 Those artisans who had served traditional apprenticeships in a skilled trade were said to have become "free": they were then able to sell their labor as journeymen or set up shops as masters.

years, 15s. per week for 10 years, and 12s. per week for 9 years more, (which, I think, is a reasonable estimate,) this would have brought me to 60 years of age, beyond which no man, in my opinion, ought to work. At this rate, I should have earned, as a journeyman, 1,710l. 16s.; then, deducting 160l. 16s. for the repayment of apprentice fee, tools, and any other incidental expenses, it would leave 1,550l., which is 1,000l. more than I have earned in the factories; and, instead of being subject to daily and excruciating pains, I might have passed through life in comparative comfort, might with confidence have encountered the expenses of a wife and family, enjoyed the evening of my days surrounded by a smiling offspring, and sunk into the grave at peace with myself and all the world. But how different is the picture of my sad fate!

The way in which the bones in the legs become distorted, I mentioned in a former page: I shall here say a few words upon the shapes they assume. The most common is that of in-kneed cripples, generally the right knee, sometimes the left, frequently both, as my own. In this case, when standing in the easiest position, the feet are about 14 inches apart, the knees and thighs are then pressing close together, so that the legs form a sort of arch for the support of the body. On taking a side view of a person standing so, he appears in the act of kneeling, about half way down; the outsides of the feet or abutments of the arch are flat and burst open the shoes, the centre of gravity crossing the thigh and leg bones. Another shape is that furnished by an acquaintance of mine, of the name of Hutton, near Bradford, in Yorkshire,[1] whom I met with in London, a short time ago, and who was put into the factories about the same time as myself, perfectly straight and strong. This man's legs are both turned one way—the right knee in, and the left knee out; so that the legs and thighs are parallel throughout, but forming an angle of about 60 degrees. He is almost frightful to look upon. A brother of his, who was also straight on entering, is still worse. His legs are curved *both outwards*, so that a person may run a wheel-barrow between them. These are some of the most common shapes, but there are others equally bad.

One evil arising from the bending and curving of the legs is the state of the blood-vessels: for if the bones go wrong, the blood-

---

1 Bradford] an industrial town in northern England; in the nineteenth century, it was a major site of woolen and worsted production.

vessels must go wrong also.[1] Nature has provided a beautiful contrivance for propelling the blood to every part of the human frame. This is done, in a well-formed person, with perfect ease, without any appearance of difficulty whatever. But it is not so with us factory cripples. Our blood lodges, as it were, in little pools, in crannies and corners: and the apparatus for forcing it along, instead of being stronger, as in our case required, it is actually weaker, in consequence of our weak state of body. Thus, our very life, (for life depends upon the circulation of the blood,) at best, is only like the half-extinguished flame of a gas-burner, when there is water in the pipes—it jumps and flickers for a little while, and then pops out. But in order to keep it even in this state, we are obliged to have recourse to friction daily, and every day.

One serious evil resulting from this imperfect circulation of the blood, is the drying up of the marrow in the bones. The bones then decay, as in my arm; amputation is resorted to, or life is lost.

A variety of shapes is also visible in the curvature of the spine of factory cripples.

With respect to cripples who have been made so by over-exertion, it is usual for manufacturers to throw the blame entirely upon the parents of such children. How they can divest themselves of all blame, appears to me paradoxical. I cannot look upon them in any other light than as accessaries to the mischief, especially when it is considered that the several cases of distortion of the spine, contraction and other deformities of the limbs, &c., did not take place all in a minute, but that they were coming gradually on for years, and immediately under the eye of the manufacturers, who, by a single word, might have dismissed them from the place, and thus have saved them from utter ruin.

There are a great variety of cripples made by machinery. The most common are those wanting arms and legs, or whose arms and legs have been crushed or torn, and rendered useless.

A fine young girl is now laying under the hands of the doctor, from an accident in the same mill as my sister had her hand torn in. She, poor girl, has had *her leg torn off, both her thigh-bones broken,* and also received several internal and external injuries.

---

1 blood-vessels] Dodd seems here to be describing Raynaud's disease. First labeled in 1862, this ailment involving constriction of the blood vessels, often caused by repetitive motion and vibrating machines, can lead to tissue death, deformity, ulceration, and gangrene.

Accidents by machinery in the North are of weekly, nay, almost daily occerrence.

A list of physicians cases would be too long for me to furnish here.

Looking over, in my mind's eye, those boys and girls who were employed in the factories when I commenced, and who, like me, have been kept close to it from their youth upwards, I find they are generally weak, stunted, and in many cases deformed in person, childish, and ignorant in mind, not having been accustomed to some of the most important duties of life, (their whole faculties have been absorbed in the daily routine of factory labour,) they make, as it is very natural to suppose, but "sorry" heads of families; and their children, as a matter of course, are compelled, by dire necessity, to pass through the same dull, tedious, miserable state of existence.

Spinners suffer considerably. Some of my former masters have died, with every symptom of premature old age upon them, at 45 to 50. The overlooker has no very enviable birth. He has to study the interest of the master, the men, and his own. His own is usually consulted by having a general shop, where the work-people can lay out their money, and by lending small sums, with the understanding to receive interest after the modest rate of 65 per centum per annum, which I have paid. Yet some of them deserve all they get: they are generally ill-paid for their harassing duties. The baneful influence of the system extends even to the manufacturers themselves. As an instance, I may mention the case of the kind master who encouraged me to read and write, and whom, from long service, I looked upon with as much respect and love as if he had been my father. On some occasions when I have been in the counting-house with him, and especially after an unsuccessful journey—when some other manufacturer has been selling goods cheaper than he was—I have fancied I could see the canker-worm, care, corroding and eating into his very existence. The last time I had an opportunity of seeing this gentleman was on the 19th of May, 1840, in St. Martin's-le-Grand.[1] He was with another gentleman, who I took, in the distance, to be his brother. I was on my way to the hospital, with my arm in a sling—that arm I was so soon to lose. He was an exception to the general character of the manufacturers. He died shortly after; and it is my opinion, that had he not been con-

---

1   St. Martin's-le-Grand] a street joining Aldersgate Street and Cheapside in the City of London.

nected with the factories, he might have protracted his existence to a later date.

About two or three years before I left the factories, my mother being then on her death-bed, I thought it was time to look about me for a partner; and being then in comfortable circumstances, on good terms with my master, and everything appearing fair, I almost forgot I was a cripple, and began to look about me for a steady servant girl, on whom I could depend. I had no difficulty in finding one to my mind, and occasionally accompanied her to church and other places. People began to pass remarks; and even my masters spoke of my being about to marry, and were divided in opinion. One said he thought I should not, considering the state I was in—the other said I might do very well. However, the girl was too wise to join her destinies with those of a factory cripple. She left the town, and refused to answer my letters, which was a sufficient reason for my discontinuing to write.

Prejudice against Factory Women

Then I got acquainted with another respectable girl. She also soon left the town, but continued to correspond with me for some time, without signing her name. She soon broke off.

So I thought that I would go to work in another way; and in order to afford a convincing proof that I really did wish to get married, I took a house, and had it well furnished. I then laid siege to a third, and made myself quite sure—there could be no mistake about the matter this time: and as I had heard that after a certain age women would take up with anything, I thought I would try one older than myself. So I paid my addresses to a respectable housekeeper, who had known me for years, and who, apparently, was pleased with my attentions. She would walk with me to church, to a place of amusement, to her relations to take tea, in the fields, or anywhere but to the trap that I had baited for her. So I began to think old birds were not to be caught with chaff. However, I did not like the idea of giving up to be laughed at, so I persevered, and pressed my suit more warmly, but soon found that she was only playing with me, like a cat with a mouse.

One evening, being almost driven to desperation, I went with a determination to have a final answer before we parted. I got half way to her place of residence, and was about to return, in consequence of the moon at that time shining out, and showing my figure before me. However, I went into a public-house, had a glass of ale, and, thus inspired, went on again. When I got there, I was kindly received, as usual; so I made my business known as well as I could, and gave her to understand that I was determined to have an answer. She patiently heard all I had got to say; and I watched every muscle of her countenance, as if my very existence had depended upon her answer. I saw a slight curl of the upper lip—her eyes then began to descend, till they settled the intensity of their gaze upon my knees. At that moment, I wished the earth to open and swallow me up. She, seeing me agitated, took compassion, and told me, what she might have told me at the first, she declined. Thus was I compelled either to return and take a factory girl, (any of whom would have thought themselves highly honoured by the offer,) or live and die a bachelor. I chose the latter as the most preferable.

I have done everything that laid in my power to prevent the evils that have come upon me, and to avert the consequences of those evils I could not prevent, by endeavouring to transplant myself into a more genial soil; but all my exertions have proved fruitless. Wherever I turned for succour, wherever I looked for sympathy or kindly feeling, I was met by repulses, derision, and insult; and this because I was a factory cripple, and aspired to associate with those whom I considered in a more respectable sphere of life. The best feelings of my heart were played with, wounded, crushed, and trampled on; and ultimately, I was driven back, like the daw in the fable,[1] stripped of every feather, to the miserable squad from which I attempted to emigrate, there to encounter the sneers and the buffets of my fellow slaves.

Having now resolved to lead a bachelor's life, for the best of all reasons, not being able to avoid it, I contrived many little helps to make myself as comfortable as I could. I got some self-acting cooking utensils, by means of which I was able to get a warm dinner at the expense of one farthing. So long as the fine warm weather lasted, this Robinson Crusoe sort of life[2] did very well; but when winter came, and I had no fire to go to, and very often wet and cold, it was too much for me to bear. Besides, I had not been able entirely to forget my fair teaser; and giving way under the difficulty, I tried to drown my cares in drink. This only made bad worse, and got me into errors, besides wasting my money; so I resolved to give up my house, sell my furniture,

---

1 the daw] In the Aesop's fable commonly known as "The Vain Jackdaw," the ugly jackdaw disguises himself in the feathers of more beautiful birds so that Jupiter will name him the king of the birds. The other birds subsequently strip him of his borrowed plumes and expose him for what he really is.

2 Robinson Crusoe sort of life] the hero of Daniel Defoe's 1719 novel; surviving a shipwreck, he lives alone for years on a desert island.

and go to lodgings: and thus terminated my fruitless endeavour to get married.

I now turned my attention again to getting totally away from the factories; and getting acquainted with Mr. Hill, schoolmaster of the British and Foreign School in Kendal, and being informed by that gentleman of the advantages held out to young men by the Society in the Borough Road to become teachers, I was inclined to think it might suit me to come and be instructed. This gentleman kindly undertook to apply for me, describing minutely my person. He received for answer, they were sorry to inform him, that in consequence of being a cripple, I could not be admitted. I applied to other schools in the same way, and received the same answer. My masters, partly to encourage me, established a night school for the piecers, and I attended two evenings in the week, and thus drilled myself into teaching. I had a twelve-month's practice in this way. We could scarcely keep the piecers awake, they were so done up. Sometimes they would fall off the form[1] on to the floor, quite overcome with sleep.

Being weary of the factories, and having prepared myself, as well as I was able, I opened a school in the early part of the year 1837, for the instruction of youth in reading, writing, and arithmetic; in hopes by this means to avert the impending danger that had so long threatened me. But I had not been in it long before the school-room was wanted by the proprietor, and, not meeting with another to suit me, I came up to London to the annual meeting of Odd Fellows, as before mentioned.

While in London, I thought I would try to procure a situation as clerk, and was encouraged in this idea by a distant relation, a licensed victualler,[2] who kindly offered to take me into his bar till I succeeded in my wish. I accepted the offer. A few months after, an opportunity presented itself. It being necessary to write to my old masters for a character, I did so, and received the following answer:—

"Kendal, 10 mo., 6th, 1837.

"William Dodd, to whom we direct this, was in our employ for many years, and during that time was a trustworthy servant. We can give him a good character for sobriety and industry.

---

1 form] bench.
2 licensed victualler] a keeper of a public-house, inn, or tavern.

He was in our employ as a warehouseman and packer, with some attention to the books.

"ISAAC AND WILLIAM WILSON."

"P.S.—W.D. left our situation about nine months ago."

The gentleman I was with, as barman, took a liking to me, and wanted to retain me in his service; but it being a line of life unsuitable for me, I was anxious to leave it as soon as possible, but not having any friend in London but him, I did not like to leave contrary to his wish. In his house I remained nearly 12 months, when I was taken ill, and had to go to Gravesend[1] for the benefit of my health; and after five weeks' absence I again returned, and was in his service seven months longer. He then sold off part of his business, and had no more occasion for my services, but kindly allowed me to stay with him a few weeks; and as nobody would give me any work to do, I resolved to go into the west and south of England to seek employment. But very little employment was then to be met with for able-bodied men; as for cripples it was out of the question. Thus I travelled some hundreds of miles, sometimes riding a little, but generally walking: I also crossed over to the Isle of Wight,[2] and visited all the places likely to afford me any employment, and could have got work if I had been a tailor or shoemaker, but not being either, and no chance of anything else turning up, I retraced my steps to London, having paid the last two-pence I had in the world to the boatman at Portsmouth.[3]

While I was in the public line in London,[4] I had to deal with all sorts of people, from the lowest to the highest. I heard all sorts of coarse brutal expressions; but in all that time, I never heard anything more vulgar, brutal, or wicked, than I was accustomed to hear from the master-manufacturers, in my younger days— from men too who had received a liberal education, and who were called to fill the highest office in the town, and who, from their superior station in life, ought to have set an example worthy of imitating. The men eagerly followed the example set them by

---

1 Gravesend] a town on the Thames in Kent, approximately twenty miles east of central London.
2 Isle of Wight] an island located off the southern coast of England.
3 Portsmouth] port city and naval base in Hampshire on the southern coast of England, approximately eighty miles southwest of London.
4 in the public line] working at a tavern or public-house.

the masters, and cursing, swearing, and low language became the order of the day. Respecting the moral conduct of the young, I can say but little; any one may think for himself what will be the result of 100 young people of both sexes working together under such circumstances, going together in the morning, associating with each other through the day, and returning again in the evening with no moral restraint upon their action, no pattern *improperly)* shewn them worthy of imitating; and where acts of gross indecency, low, vulgar, brutal language, singing immoral songs, swearing, &c. are not only tolerated, but in many instances, actually countenanced and encouraged. A person brought up from infancy to maturity in such a school, and who can then retire with clean hands, or a clear conscience, must possess something more in his composition than human nature can boast of—must be such an one as I never yet met with, such an one as I am sure does not exist.*

In my travels through the country in search of employment, I had frequent opportunity of witnessing the condition of the labourers in agricultural districts, I conversed with many who received only 8s. or 9s. per week as wages, who were surrounded by more real comforts than many of my class with several shillings per week more. This may be accounted for by the fact that 8s. in the hands of an agricultural labourer, is at all times equal to 10s. or 11s. in the hands of a manufacturing labourer: and this does not arise from any carelessness or extravagance on the part of the latter. For instance, an agricultural labourer enjoys many privileges and advantages that the other knows nothing of—such as an allowance of potatoes, turnips, and other vegetables, and in many cases wood for the fire; his rent is also considerably lower; he also enjoys the blessings of breathing the pure air. Now, the manufacturing labourer cannot eat his machines or anything he may be making; and in consequence of inhaling the pernicious ingredients from the atmosphere in which he moves, and the nauseous smells by which he is surrounded, he cannot eat his food with a relish, and he is occasionally obliged to have recourse to medicine; and should he have any cripples in the family, (which is generally the case,) he must have a supply of flannel and linen bandages, oils, drugs, &c. constantly by him; and these little things form a considerable item in his expendi-

---

* The scenes which I have witnessed, and it is with sorrow I say have in some instances been participater in, are of such a nature, as to be improper to lay before the public eye. [Dodd's note]

ture. In all my experience, I do not remember ever to have been three months at one time free from bandages; and I have worked for weeks together with three or four of my joints thus secured.

The behaviour of agricultural labourers and their children is much superior to anything we meet with in manufacturing towns; and I have no doubt many of my readers will have noticed this in travelling through the country. This is easily accounted for. They are surrounded by circumstances so totally different, that there is no wonder at it. In the first place, the society around them is more polished and enlightened: in their daily toil they meet with so many instances of the wisdom and power of an all-wise being, that a love for his handiworks is sure to be impressed upon their mind;—the cheering influence of the sun, the refreshing breeze, the singing of birds, &c., all inspire this feeling. The manufacturing labourer knows nothing of these blessings by experience. He is placed in a mill or factory as a machine, for the performance of a quantity of labour—he hears nothing but the rumbling noise of the machinery, or the harsh voice of the over-looker—sees nothing but an endless variety of shafts, drums, straps, and wheels in motion; and though these may, at first, inspire him with a feeling of respect for, and admiration of, the inventive powers of his fellow-creatures, yet this feeling will vanish, when he reflects on their power to destroy or render useless for life that exalted piece of mechanism formed by and after the image of God!

I was forcibly struck with the kind behaviour of the agricultural labourers to me. The manner in which the family generally met together in the evening, brought to my mind the following beautiful description of a cottager's Saturday night, by Burns:—[1]

"At length his lonely cot[2] appears in view,
    Beneath the shelter of an aged tree;
Th' expectant *wee-things*, toddlin, stacher[3] through
    To meet their Dad, wi' flichterin[4] noise and glee.

---

1   beautiful description ... by Burns] a short excerpt from the beginning of "The Cotter's Saturday Night" (1786) by Scottish poet Robert Burns (1759-96).
2   cot] cot-house, cottage.
3   stacher] walk unsteadily.
4   flichterin] fluttering like young birds.

His wee-bit ingle,[1] blinkin bonnilie,
    His clean hearthstane, his thrifty *wifie's* smile,
The lisping infant prattling on his knee,
    Does a' his weary carking cares beguile,
And makes him quite forget his labour and his toil.

"Belyve[2] the elder bairns[3] come drapping in,
    At service out amang the farmers roun';
Some ca'[4] the pleugh, some herd, some tentie[5] rin
    A cannie[6] errand to a neebor town;
Their eldest hope, their *Jenny*, woman grown,
    In youthfu' bloom, love sparklin in her ee,
Comes hame, perhaps, to show a braw[7] new gown,
    Or deposite her sair-won penny fee,[8]
To help her parents dear, if they in hardship be.

"Wi' joy unfeign'd brothers and sisters meet,
    And each for other's weelfare kindly spiers:[9]
The social hours, swift-wing'd, unnotic'd fleet;
    Each tells the uncos[10] that he sees or hears;
The parents, partial, ee their hopefu' years:
    Anticipation forward points the view:
The *Mother*, wi' her needle and her sheers,
    Gars auld claes[11] look amaist as weel's the new;
The *Father* mixes a' wi' admonition due.

"Their master's and their mistress's command
    The younkers[12] a' are warned to obey;
And mind their labours wi' an eydent[13] hand,
    And ne'er, though out o' sight, to jauk[14] or play;

---

1 ingle] fire, fireplace.
2 belyve] by and by.
3 bairns] children.
4 ca'] drive.
5 tentie] heedful.
6 cannie] small.
7 braw] handsome.
8 sair-worn penny fee] sore- or hard-won bit of wages.
9 spiers] asks.
10 uncos] news.
11 Gars auld claes] makes old clothes.
12 younkers] youths.
13 eydent] diligent.
14 jauk] dally, trifle.

'And, O! be sure to fear the LORD alway!
　　And mind your *duty* duly morn and night!
Lest in temptation's path ye gang[1] as[t]ray,
　　Implore his counsel and assisting might:
They never sought in vain that sought the LORD aright.'"

All who have been in a manufacturing town, will recollect the disgusting scenes that are to be witnessed there on a Saturday night.

On Sunday I was much pleased at witnessing the clean, decent, sober, and orderly appearance of the inhabitants of the rural districts, and to see the neighbouring gentry attending the church, preceded or followed by their servants. This was so very different from anything I had been accustomed to before, that it made a lasting impression on my mind.

In a manufacturing town, some, from exhaustion, prefer laying in bed—others are obliged to lay there while the wife washes their clothes; some are strolling about the streets or fields in their working dress, not daring to go to church, for fear of falling asleep; while those who wish to go, and would go if they could, are compelled to labour two or three hours, and getting heated, they must have a glass or two of ale at a public-house to finish with.

The manufacturer and their families attend their place of worship, and wish to be considered patterns of religion and piety; but their pretences and their works are so widely different, that this cloak is easily seen through; for while they are attending meetings for the abolition of slavery, and the propagation of the Scriptures in foreign parts, they are compelling their servants, under fear of losing their situations, to be slaves, and to break the sacred commands of God, at home, even in defiance of the threats of the better sort of the inhabitants, and the public press; and this, too, without fee or reward.

From Portsmouth I came to London. My spirits getting heavier, and my bundle lighter at every stage, and not being able to meet with employment, I suffered considerably from want, visiting any place where I could get a mouthful to eat, and sometimes obliged to walk the streets by night, not being able to pay for a lodging—occasionally resting myself by sitting on the benches in Covent Garden Market, or stretching my weary limbs

---

1　gang] go.

in the recesses of Westminster Bridge.[1] When in this latter place, I was awoke one morning about two o'clock by the policeman on duty, and obliged to move on, cold, tired, and hungry, I dragged myself along, not knowing or caring where I went, with the dark lowering sky above, and the angry foaming billows beneath; and heaven only knows what would have been the consequence at that critical moment, had I not been sustained by that power which had protected me through all my difficulties.

Soon after this, there was a gentleman wanting a man to improve himself as a tailor and draper; and thinking, from the little knowledge I had acquired in the business at Kendal, and the lameness of my knees, that it would be a suitable situation for me, I applied, and was engaged for three years. For the first twelve months I got on very well; and being desirous to gather a connexion of my own against the time I should begin for myself, I took in little jobs on my own account, which privilege my master allowed me. This brought me in a little money, and was paving the way to a business in future; but I did not then consider that I was over-exerting myself, as I had my own work to do, after my day's work for my master was over, and when I ought to have been in bed.

In the spring of 1840, I began to feel some painful symptoms in my right wrist, arising from the general weakness of my joints, brought on in the factories. At first I was not alarmed at it, as I had occasionally felt similar painful sensations in all my joints for years previous to leaving the factories, and which had always gone off, by taking rest for a day or two, rubbing them with liniment, and wrapping them in warm flannel. But, this time, it resisted all my endeavours to restore strength, the swelling and pain increased; and although I had the advice of some of the most eminent medical practitioners, it was all to no purpose; and, having been off work for a length of time, and my resources failing, I was under the necessity of entering St. Thomas's Hospital,[2] where I remained for

---

1   Covent Garden Market ... Westminster Bridge] Covent Garden, located in central London, was the site of the city's principal fruit and vegetable market. The original Westminster Bridge, which was built between 1739 and 1750 and reconstructed in 1836, spanned the Thames. Both were places to which the homeless in London frequently resorted.
2   St. Thomas's Hospital] an ancient institution for the treatment of charity cases. Located until 1871 in the Borough of Southwark, south of the Thames, its architecturally impressive buildings housed approximately five hundred patients when Dodd was there.

upwards of six months; and where every care and attention was paid me, and every expedient tried, that skill and experience could suggest, but with no better success than before. The wrist at this time measured twelve inches round,—and I was worn down to a mere skeleton, not being able to sleep night nor day, except for very short periods, and generally starting up from pain.

It now became pretty evident to all who saw me, that I must, very soon, lose either my hand or my life. A consultation was held by the surgeons of the hospital, who came to the conclusion, that amputation was absolutely necessary; and the result proved their decision to be correct. They gave me a reasonable time to think the matter over—and I decided upon taking their advice.

On the 18th of July, I underwent the operation.[1] The hand being taken off a little below the elbow, in order to clear the affected part of the bone; and thus, another plan to raise myself above want, and keep myself from the workhouse, was frustrated and dashed to the ground! On dissection, the bones of the fore-arm presented a very curious appearance—something similar to an empty honeycomb, the marrow also having totally disappeared; thus accounting at once for the weakness and pain I had occasionally felt in this arm for years, and which, without doubt, may be clearly traced to the same cause as the rest of my sufferings—viz. the factory system.

By the blessing of God, and under the care and attendance of the surgeons and nurses of the hospital, to whom I would ever hope to be thankful, I was restored to tolerable health, and was discharged on the 24th of November, 1840.

It will be necessary here to observe, that in consequence of not being able to meet with employment, I had not paid my contribution-money to the Society of Odd Fellows, and hoping for better days, I did not (as I ought to have done) make my case known; and according to the rules, that I had assisted to make at the annual meeting, I ceased to be a member: however, it is but justice to say, that the members in London behaved very kindly to me.

Having applied to my late master for a certificate of character, I received the following:—

---

1 the operation] This amputation would have been performed as quickly as possible without either anesthetics or antiseptic practices, both of which developed only after Dodd's time.

"The bearer, William Dodd, has been in my employ for twelve months, during which time he conducted himself in a sober, honest, and industrious manner; and I should have taken him again into my service, but for the misfortune of losing his hand, which renders him totally unfit for my business. Given by me this 26th day of November, 1840.

"JOHN KIRBY.

"No. 2, Oldham Place, Bagnige Wells Road, London."

Figure to yourself, dear reader, my deplorable situation at that time—just leaving the hospital, after a residence of six months within its walls, having lost the best part of my right arm!—a cripple in my limbs!—without a home!—without friends!—and with only 8*s.* in money!—in a strange place, and nearly 300 miles from the place to which I belong!—and, in this condition, to brave the horrors of a severe winter! and provide myself a living in an unthinking and unfeeling world! But I put my trust in the Lord, and He has not forsaken me—He has provided me a shelter from the blast, and a crust to satisfy the cravings of nature.

In reading the history of some eastern nations, we find accounts of children having been tied in open baskets to the tops of trees, and there left exposed, an offering to their Gods, till the birds had eaten their flesh from their bones; and of others having been thrown into the Ganges,[1] and there having found a watery grave—and eagerly, in our exalted ideas of civilization, denounce them as barbarians who could be guilty of such cruelties! But how much better would it have been for me, if I had had the good fortune to have been so sacrificed in my infancy, rather than have been put to daily torture for upwards of a quarter of a century, and *with the certainty of my miseries still continuing, till my feeble frame sinks beneath its load!*

Think not, dear reader, that I have here drawn an exaggerated picture of a factory life:—it would be well for me if it could be proved that I am wrong—if, instead of being a miserable cripple, scarcely the shadow of a man, it could be proved that I am straight, strong, and hardy as when I entered the factories. But as I feel convinced that this is not possible, it may be well here to say, that I am prepared to prove myself right; and that I shall not hesitate (if required) to wait upon any individual or party, for the purpose of discussing, explaining, illustrating, or proving any of

---

1 the Ganges] a river, sacred to the Hindus, that flows from the Himalayas into Northern India, and ultimately into the Bay of Bengal.

the preceding statements; and further, that I do not shrink from any investigation, but court inquiry.

I would draw the attention of every person who can feel for the miseries of his fellow creatures, to this important subject; and after convincing him of the reality, and the great extent of country over which these evils prevail, ask the following question:—

Is it consistent with the character of this enlightened, Christian country, which has furnished such a proof of her benevolence and charity, in granting 20 millions of money for the abolition of slavery abroad,[1] that we, who have exerted every means in our power in the production of the wealth of the nation, and have therein sacrificed everything valuable in life, that we, worn-out, cast-off cripples of the manufacturers, should be left to perish and die of want at home?—Forbid it Heaven.

And to you, my fellow sufferers, I would say a word in conclusion. We read in the Scriptures, that God formed man of the dust of the earth, after his own image, breathed into him the breath of life, and endowed him with wonderful powers and faculties; and though these powers and faculties have, in our frames, been injured, rendered nearly useless, and, in many instances, almost destroyed, by our cruel task-masters, yet there still remains that vital principal, over which these earthly tyrants have no power, excepting so far as their evil example extends. It will therefore be our interest to endeavour, by every means in our power, to secure to ourselves this only source of happiness that is left us: and this can only be done by attending to the precepts of the Scriptures. Let us, then, duly appreciate the value of those blessings we do and may enjoy:—let us look abroad and examine the works of our Creator, and we shall soon learn to admire his wisdom, and tremble at his power. We shall learn to despise the riches and pageantry of this perishing scene of things, and fix our hopes on those which are perma[n]ent and worth our care—to tread with patience the rugged paths of virtue, which will at length conduct us to the happy mansions of eternal repose.

23, *Little Gray's Inn Lane*,
   June 18, 1841.

[handwritten: hypocrisy of Christians]

[handwritten: → he still holds onto hope]

---

1   20 millions of money] In 1833 Parliament abolished slavery in the British colonies, passing legislation that compensated slave-owners for the emancipation of their slaves. The cost of the measure, £20 million, exceeded by half the military budget for that year.

Chapters in the Life
of a Dundee Factory Boy (1850)

James Myles

[Though *Chapters in the Life of a Dundee Factory Boy* presents itself as an autobiography of the former factory child Frank Forrest, it was actually the work of James Myles (1819-51), a Scottish artisan turned writer and bookseller. Myles, however, based some of Forrest's experiences on events in his own life (see Note on the Text, Introduction 33-34, and Appendix C.2). As a child Myles was educated at a school in a village near Dundee, and as a young man he worked as a stone mason in Lochee, again close to Dundee. During this time he became interested in Chartism, and because of his eloquence, he was soon a leader and lecturer for the Chartist movement. According to one account, Myles became disenchanted with both Chartism and Owenite socialism, for which he had also been a proponent, and he turned instead to the promotion of evangelical Christianity in the late 1840s (Whatley 73). By this time he had opened a bookshop, and he began to publish his own work, of which *Chapters in the Life of a Dundee Factory Boy* is his best-known contribution. On March 6, 1851, *The Northern Warder*, the newspaper in which Forrest's story first appeared, recorded Myles's early death: "DIED—At his house, Lindsay Street, Dundee, on the 26th ult, Mr James Myles, bookseller, aged 32."]

CHAPTERS

IN THE

LIFE

OF A

DUNDEE FACTORY BOY;

AN

AUTOBIOGRAPHY.

Dundee:
JAMES MYLES.
EDINBURGH: ADAM & CHARLES BLACK.
LONDON: SIMPKIN, MARSHALL, & Co.
AND ALL BOOKSELLERS.

1850.[1]

Title page courtesy of Sterling Memorial Library, Yale University.

---

1 The back of the title page reads "Printed by M'Cosh, Park, and Dewars, Dundee."

To Richard Oastler, Esq. [1]

Respected Sir,

    As you were pleased to express to me your admiration of the following Autobiography, while it was appearing in the columns of the "Northern Warder," and as it bears on a question in which you have, through the course of a long life, taken a deep interest, I respectfully dedicate it to you.

    With the warmest wishes for your welfare, and a sincere declaration of my esteem,

        I am,

            Sir,

               Yours truly,

                  The Author.

---

1   Richard Oastler (1789-1861), Tory Radical and social reformer; leader of the movement for factory reform (see Appendix G.1).

Contents.

LIFE OF A FACTORY BOY.

CHAPTER I.
PLACE OF MY NATIVITY—FAMILY MISFORTUNE—ARRIVAL IN DUNDEE.

A few evenings ago I was "killing time," as the phrase goes, by poring over a frivolous "Autobiography"—a gossiping, flippant, and somewhat coarse picture of fashionable life. The book appeared to me morally aimless, and socially useless, yet it was interesting. I threw it aside, and asked myself the question—Wherein consists the spell of this literary toy? It rests not in the high purpose which ought to belong to such a species of composition, for purpose, in the correct sense of the word, it has none. It dwells not in the intricacy of its plot, nor in the magic circle of successive rounds of romantic details and thrilling incidents, for all of these [sic] it is absolutely barren, yet it is pleasing; and it is so, I concluded, because there is so much individuality about it. The author speaks in the first person. He tells you this own story, and you listen as if in company with a friend who is detailing to you his life and adventures. The secret of its interest, then, can only be ascribed to its style, which is autobiographic. "Well," said I, "after all, every man's life is perhaps worth writing, if he had the ability to do it. Every man's life is an acted drama which deserves perusal, and much may be learned by the different scenes as they are represented to the mind." Such was the conclusion, reader, I arrived at, and need you be astonished when I confess, though the confession may smell of egotism, that I immediately exclaimed—I am sure there are passages in my own career as interesting, and, if properly told, much more useful, than any comprised in the pages of that book, and I will write a few chapters of my life. Though the prolific press of Britain pours forth thousands of books yearly, and millions of broad sheets weekly, yet I am not aware that a single one of the former contains a true picture of the condition, sufferings, and struggles of a Factory Boy, painted by his own pen; and as regards the latter they are, with a few honourable exceptions, compiled by literary scavengers—a mere collection of sickly, nauseous, unhealthy rubbish, that sends a poisonous effluvia through society, and creates an unhealthy mental appetite, by exclusively dealing in romance, rapine, and crime. Abhorring as I do this kind of food, the reader is not to anticipate in these chapters a "thrilling romance" nor "soul-stirring narrative." He is only to be treated with the truthful history of a poor boy, who has drunk pretty deeply of the cup of misery, but who has, by perseverance, industry, and a strong will, surmounted many obstacles, and triumphed over many difficulties.

To begin at the beginning, I may succinctly state that my father was a country shoemaker, and, like the most of his class, somewhat speculative; fond of political and religious disputation, and not altogether devoid of a taste for "the bottle." In addition to carrying on a trade in the locality, which, by the way, was in the vicinity of Glammis,[1] he likewise rented a small "pendicle"[2] of about six acres. Our house was a neat cottage one storey high, and its walls were so white by the frequent lime washings performed by my mother as to be only known by the name of the "White House." It stood on the north bank of the river Dean, a dark sluggish stream that meanders along Strathmore until it falls unto the Isla a short distance from Meigle.[3] A garden tastefully laid out, stretched from its south wall to the edge of the river, and added considerably to the attractions of the spot. One of the most active feelings of our heart is a respect, almost amounting to veneration, for the place which gave us birth. In all our wanderings through life, and however diversified may be our worldly fortunes, our souls instinctively exalt the place of our nativity into the beau ideal of beauty, and long, before they finally quit this sublunary sphere, to feast their outward senses once more with the objects and scenes which charmed us in childhood. This is a deep-rooted feeling in humanity, and all can sympathise with Robert Nicoll when he says:—

> The loch whar first the stream doth rise
> Is bonniest to my e'e;
> And yon auld warld hame o' youth
> Is dearest aye to me.

---

1 Glammis] Glamis, a village about ten miles north of Dundee.
2 pendicle] a small piece of land, usually sublet, which forms a dependent part of an estate.
3 Dean ... Meigle] Dean Water flows near Meigle, a town approximately thirteen miles northwest of Dundee in Strathmore, an old territorial district north of the Sidlow Hills, which extend north of the Tay from Perth to the east beyond Dundee; the River Isla runs near Meigle into the River Tay.

My heart wi' joy may up be heized,[1]
  Or doon wi' sorrow worn,
But, Oh, it never can forget
  The toon where I was born.[2]

Can the reader blame me then, when I affirm that I think the
little cottage where I was born was the sweetest spot on earth.
The tidy garden, the river, the thick plantations, over which
towered the grey turrets of the ancient castle of Glammis,[3] the
soothing solace of an affectionate mother's love, and all the innocent amusements and prattling of youth's warm existence, rush
on my memory, and force me to conclude that I have seen no
place like the place of my childhood. The dim remembrances that
I yet have of these happy days impress me with the belief that my
father and mother lived comfortably, and knew nothing of want
and its grim attendants; but alas, evil days were in store for us,
and the erring footsteps of a parent brought misery on himself,
an innocent wife, and helpless family,—so true is it that the sins
of the father are visited upon the children.[4] Let me briefly detail
the catastrophe alluded to.

In the village of Glammis there is an annual market held,
where a considerable amount of business is done in buying and
selling horses and cows. Like all other country fares, a huge con-
course of young and old are drawn together. Some go for amusement, others to transact business, and too often that business is
managed in "tents," or temporary erections where intoxicating
drinks are sold. One year my father attended this market for the
purpose of selling a young cow which he had fed for the butchers. After disposing of the animal, he entered a tent with a few
friends, and indulged somewhat freely in whisky potations. He

---

1 heized] lifted.
2 Scottish poet Robert Nicoll (1814-37), "The Toon Whar' I Was Born."
   This and all other selections of Nicoll's poetry mentioned herein are
   from *Poems and Lyrics* (1835), the only edition of his work published
   during his lifetime. (See Appendix C.2.)
3 castle of Glammis] A baronial castle associated with Macbeth and therefore, by legend, with the murder of Duncan.
4 Exodus 34:7. To Moses the Lord proclaimed that he keeps "mercy for
   thousands, forgiving iniquity and transgression and sin, and that will by
   no means clear the guilty; visiting the iniquity of the fathers upon the
   children, and upon the children's children, unto the third and to the
   fourth generation."

was naturally quiet and obliging in his every day demeanour, but when unhinged by the whisky demon, he was contradictory and quarrelsome in his disposition, so much so that my mother, who on usual occasions wielded a great influence over his mind, wept with very fear when she saw him coming home intoxicated. On the evening in question he sat long and drank deeply, and while doing so a person belonging to the parish of Kettle, who at one time was guilty of a highly dishonourable action towards him, entered the tent. Both were the worse of drink. Old sores were harshly touched. High words passed, and from words they came to blows, and, alas, my father struck him a dreadful blow on the head with a heavy staff, which felled him to the ground in a state of utter insensibility, and after lingering nearly six hours in unconscious existence, he breathed his last. On the following morning, when my father's drowned reason revived, and the solemn fact was presented to his mind that he was guilty of the death of a fellow creature, he gave way to the deepest and most contrite lamentations. He clung to the neck of my mother, and wept aloud; took me on his knee, kissed me, and sobbed the bitter sobs of grief and repentance. Oh! the house on that day was a house full of mourning and of woe. I was too young to comprehend the dark calamity that had befallen us, and I simply wept because my mother, like Rachel, "would not be comforted."[1] In the afternoon I went to play with my young companions as usual, and while busy at marbles on the turnpike road, two strong burly looking men accosted us by asking where John Forrest lived. Guileless, and destitute of duplicity, I told them he was my father, and offered to take them to the house. They clap't me on the head, gave me a penny, and called me a fine little fellow. In a few minutes I ushered them into the kitchen where my father and mother were sitting, unnerved by sorrow. The strangers said their mission was an unpleasant one, but, as officers of an offended law, they were bound to do their duty, which was, they plainly said, to take my father prisoner on a charge of *murder*. When the tragic and terrific word was pronounced, my mother gave a wild scream and fainted away; I burst into tears, my father moaned,

---

1 Matthew 2:18. "In Rama was there a voice heard, lamentation, and weeping, and great mourning, Rachel weeping for her children, and would not be comforted, because they are not." Rachel and all mothers in Jerusalem (Rama) feared for their children because King Herod ordered that all children two years of age and younger be killed in order that he might find and destroy the newborn baby Jesus.

and the stern officers, accustomed to such scenes, were visibly affected. Why need I dwell on such profoundly melancholy reminiscences, or indulge in describing the agony of my poor mother's soul when she found the object of her youthful love, her mainstay and hope, torn from her; her two children fatherless, and herself all but a widow. On the first night of my father's absence she could scarcely reconcile herself to shut the door. She could not believe that her husband was confined by prison walls and prison bars. The sombre event looked to her like a vision of a troubled spirit. She stood and looked long and wistfully, but not a single footstep sounded on her ear to raise a faint hope to her tender heart. She gazed into the dark boundless sky as if supplicating God for help; shut the door slowly, and in the most hallowed accents of despair, cried, "Oh! John; Oh! John." A few months of weariness and grief rolled by, and my father was brought up for trial at the High Court of Justiciary, Perth.[1] He at once pled guilty to culpable homicide, and the public prosecutor accepted the plea. A numerous and respectable array of testimonials and witnesses to character were produced in court, but the judge dwelt severely on the fact that there was ill-will existing in my father's mind against the deceased at the time the unhappy event occurred; and as intoxication could not, under any circumstances, be admitted as an extenuation for crime, considering his duty to society he could not, he said, sentence him to less punishment than seven years' transportation.[2] It has been remarked that a pebble dropped into the ocean sends out a circle of undulations that terminate only with its boundary. May it not be as justly said that a single false step in a man's life sends forth a train of consequences that are only lost in eternity. "If Cleopatra," said a quaint writer, "had been possessed of a nose a single half inch shorter or a single half inch longer the history of the world would, in all probability, have been different."[3] Who can doubt the truth of the remark, for we every day see trifling incidents the parents of grave and important results? and how often has an evening's debauch or a moment of frenzied passion produced a lifetime of suffering and remorse, and entailed an incalculable amount of

---

1 Perth] an industrial town on the right bank of the River Tay, approximately twenty miles west of Dundee.
2 transportation] the practice in use until the middle of the nineteenth century of sending convicted criminals to the penal colonies of Australia.
3 Blaise Pascal (1623-62), *Thoughts*, Chapter VIII, 29.

pain and misery on innocent relations and friends? My father's case was an illustration of these remarks. When my mother received the intelligence of his sentence, she felt a sorrowful gratitude, as she fearfully anticipated a more terrible doom, and with a fervent faith that all was for good, she gradually reconciled herself to her lot. After my father's conviction she was obliged to sell her cow, to defray some legal expenses incurred, and at the following term, the laird,[1] in conjunction with a few unbending creditors, rouped[2] the whole of her little stock and household furniture, excepting a chest of drawers she had got as a dowry from her father and some other trifles. She was thus left almost destitute, and the crime of my father having raised an ignorant prejudice against her, she determined on leaving the place which had witnessed the disgrace of her husband, and the social degradation of herself and two children. From the general wreck of her worldly fortunes she managed to save a few blankets and sheets, a bedstead, and the chest of drawers spoken of. Though a severe trial to her, she was obliged to sell the latter to a neighbor for L.2, 10s. She then packed up her little property, and consigned it to the carrier who in those days traded between Dundee[3] and Glammis, and with a heavy heart left the spot rendered sacred to her by many endearing associations, and retired to hide her poverty in the busy regions of a great manufacturing town. It was on a warm morning in May, when I had scarcely reached my seventh year, that we set out on foot. I asked my mother if we were going to see my father. She gave me no direct answer, but told me we were going where I would see many strange sights, and where I would require to work in a spinning mill, to help to keep her living. My young heart bounded with pleasure at the prospect of seeing Dundee, a town that I had heard the country people speak of as very large; and by their conversations I had concluded that there was no place equal to it. As a child thinks *his* father is the best and strongest of men, so young people confined to a particular locality, and who know little of geography, think "*the town*" of their district the largest and most important place in the world. I imagined Dundee a vast city, abounding in

---

1 laird] lord of the manor.
2 rouped] auctioned.
3 Dundee] in the mid-nineteenth century the third most populous town in Scotland; located on the north side of the Firth of Tay and also north of Edinburgh, Dundee in the 1820s and 1830s was the site of linen and flax manufacture.

wealth and grandeur, a kind of Elysium where poverty and suffering were not allowed to enter. Such were my boyish conceptions. Alas! they were juvenile castles in the air, that were speedily dissipated by my future experience.[1]

CHAPTER II.
ENTERS A SPINNING MILL—THE LONG-HOUR SYSTEM
CONTRASTED WITH THE SHORT-HOUR SYSTEM.

Those who have spent all their days in the country feel awkward, and even lonely, when they first settle in a large town. They have only been used to live and move amongst a few, whose faces are well known, and whose habits are plain and simple: and when they see the active multitudes pressing and hurrying along the streets of a city, each one bent on his own silent mission, as if regardless of all others, and view the countless shops, warehouses, and public works, the whole appears to them a confused and mysterious social enigma, a complete chaos of houses and crowds. In towns men run a more rapid race for life than in the country, and "as iron sharpeneth iron, so doth the face of a man his friend."[2] Hence the inhabitants of rural districts are deprived of the sharpening process, and they are proportionably blunt and useless when they feel themselves a part of the great whole which makes up a town. On our arrival in Dundee, my mother's wonted perseverance seemed paralyzed. She knew not what to do. Ultimately she spoke to an old woman, who in those days sold vegetables in the Green Market, and she proved to be a good Samaritan, for she kindly offered us a bed, and tendered my mother many useful hints. After lodging a single night in her house, by her instructions my mother left my little brother and me in her care, and went in the direction of the Bonnethill to seek out a house. In less than two hours she returned and announced to us her success; and on the evening of the same day we found our-

---

1 In the version of the *Chapters* published in *The Northern Warder*, there appears the following notice at the end of this chapter: "NOTE.— The writer of these Chapters will endeavour to present one weekly to the reader until they are concluded; but if he should at any time fail in his intentions, no circumstance, he hopes, will oblige him to leap over more than one week at a time."

2 Proverbs 27:17. "Iron sharpeneth iron; so a man sharpeneth the countenance of his friend."

selves the tenants of a small room in an old land near the corner of the Bucklemaker Wynd.[1] The entrance was by the first close[2] on the left hand, and the prospect from our window was circumscribed by a dead wall, distant only the breadth of a narrow passage. My new home was indeed a great change for a romping country boy, such as I then was. I had been accustomed to live in the fresh air of creation, to sport by the river that rolled past our secluded cot,[3] to gaze on the green fields and rustling trees which beautified Strathmore, and to listen to the bleating of sheep, the lowing of cows, or the caroling of the skylark, warbling his matins at the portals of heaven; but now I was shut up in a narrow close where nothing could be seen but old dirty walls of stone and lime; and the music of the morning which fell on my ear was not the sweet songs of birds, but the harsh guttural roars of coal sellers and fish cadgers.

On the second morning of my Dundee life, an incident illustrative of my rural simplicity happened, which I have often laughed heartily at since. My mother, prior to setting out to seek work for me, began preparing porridge for breakfast, and I was dispatched for a halfpenny worth of salt. With a tin can in my hand, I sallied forth in search of this domestic article; but having no idea of town's life, I sauntered down the Wellgate staring at wonders, and ultimately walked into a counting house in Cowgate,[4] where two clerks were busy writing, and gravely asked, "Is't here ye sell saut!" The young men seemed highly amused at my stupidity, but kindly shewed me where I could procure what I wanted. And I assure the reader, in the after years of my life, I never passed the Cowgate without smiling at the idea of me seeking "saut" in a manufacturer's office. My mother now laid down what she conceived a workable programme for our future guidance. She purchased a pirn wheel,[5] and secured the winding of pirns for two handloom weavers. She then applied at several spinning mills for work to me, but did not succeed. This dampened her hopes considerably, and, on the evening of her unsuccessful search, she sat down exhausted, and wept bitterly. To see a strong man "begging a brother of the earth to give him leave to

---

1 Wynd] alley.
2 close] an entry or passage leading from the street to the dwelling, similar to an alley.
3 cot] cottage.
4 Wellgate … Cowgate] two streets in the commercial center of Dundee.
5 pirn wheel] a spinning wheel, the "pirns" being the threads.

toil,"[1] willing to work, unable to want, yet cannot get labour, is, says an eminent writer, "a melancholy sight," but methinks a mother forced to make her child a slave, depending for bread on the use of its bones and sinews, willing to sacrifice these, offering them in the market, and unable to command a purchaser, is a more dismal picture still, and drives the contemplative mind to question the Christianity of civilization, where such pictures can be seen. Our support now depended on my mother's own energies, and, though she rose every morning by five o'clock, and toiled on until nine and ten at night, she could not earn above 6d and 7d per day, or on an average 3s 3d per week. Those accustomed to such labour will make a little more, but it being new to my mother, she could only gain this pittance by fifteen or sixteen hours close application. Every Monday morning she had to pay 11d for rent, which left her with about 2s 4d for our support. On this small sum, and a few shillings that remained of the money which she received for her drawers, we lived four weeks. On the beginning of the fifth week, I got work in a spinning mill at the Dens,[2] which filled our hearts with joy, but so near starvation were we then, that my mother had only 4½d in the world. It was on a Tuesday morning in the month of "Lady June" that I first entered a spinning mill. The whole circumstances were strange to me. The dust, the din, the work, the hissing and roaring of one person to another, the obscene language uttered, even by the youngest, and the imperious commands harshly given by those "dressed in a little brief authority,"[3] struck my young country heart with awe and astonishment. At that time the twelve hours' factory act[4] had

---

1 Robert Burns (1759-96), "Man Was Made to Mourn: A Dirge" (1784). The lines read "Who begs a brother of the earth/To give him leave to toil."

2 the Dens] an industrial district in Dundee.

3 Shakespeare's *Measure for Measure* II.ii.117-22. "But man, proud man,/Drest in a little brief authority,/Most ignorant of what he's most assur'd,/His glassy essence, like an angry ape,/Plays such fantastic tricks before high heaven,/As make the angels weep."

4 twelve hours' factory act] The factory acts passed in 1819, 1825, and 1831 all mandated twelve hours of work for "young persons" under sixteen (1819, 1825) or eighteen (1831), but they pertained only to those working in cotton mills. Since the narrator of the *Chapters* is seven when he enters what is presumably a flax or linen factory in Dundee, he is probably referring to the act of 1833, which legislated twelve hours a day or a sixty-nine-hour week for those between thirteen and eighteen in textile industries, including flax and linen; and like the earlier acts, it did not permit children to work until they were nine years old (see Introduction 46-47).

not come into operation, and spinning mills were in their glory as huge instruments of demoralization and slavery. Mercenary manufacturers, to enable them to beat more upright employers in the markets, kept their machinery and hands active fifteen, and, in many cases, seventeen hours a-day, and, when tender children fell asleep under the prolonged infliction of "work! work! work,"[1] overseers roused them with the rod, or thongs of thick leather burned at the points. The lash of the slave driver was never more unsparingly used in Carolina on the unfortunate slaves than the canes and "whangs"[2] of mill foremen were then used on helpless factory boys. When I went to a spinning mill I was about seven years of age. I had to get out of bed every morning at five o'clock, commence work at half-past five, drop at nine for breakfast, begin again at half-past nine, work until two, which was the dinner hour, start again at half-past two, and continue until half-past seven at night. Such were the nominal hours; but in reality there were no regular hours, masters and managers did with us as they liked. The clocks at the factories were often put forward in the morning and back at night, and instead of being instruments for the measurement of time, they were used as *cloaks* for cheatery and oppression. Though this was known amongst the hands, all were afraid to speak, and a workman then was afraid to carry a watch, as it was no uncommon event to dismiss any one who presumed to know too much about the science of horology. In country mills, a more horrific despotism reigned than in Dundee. There, masters frequently bound the young by a regular contract, which gave them a more complete control over their labour and liberties than taking them from week to week. In one establishment in the vicinity of Dundee, the proprietor, a coarse-minded man, who by accident had vaulted out of his natural element into the position of a "vulgar rich" man, practised the contract system, and had bothies[3] where he lodged all his male and female workers. They were allowed to cook, sleep, and live in any dog and cat manner they pleased, no moral superintendence whatever being exercised

---

1   Though it is possible that "work, work, work" is simply a phrase imitating the factory overseers, given the narrator's penchant for literary allusions, it is more likely a reference to the poem by Thomas Hood (1799-1845) "The Song of the Shirt" (1843), in which the phrase is used repeatedly.
2   "whangs"] beatings.
3   bothies] huts or cottages, much like a barracks, where servants or employees lodged together.

over them. His mill was kept going 17 and frequently 19 hours per day. To accomplish this all meal hours were almost dispensed with, and women were employed to boil potatoes and carry them in baskets to the different flats;[1] and the children had to swallow a potato hastily in the interval of putting up "ends."[2] On dinners cooked and eaten as I have described, they had to subsist till half-past nine, and frequently ten at night. When they returned to their bothies, brose,[3] as it is a dish that can be quickly made, constituted their suppers, for they had no time to wait the preparation of a different meal. They then tumbled into bed; but balmy sleep had scarcely closed their urchin eyelids, and steeped their infant souls in blessed forgetfulness, when the thumping of the watchmen's staff on the door would rouse them from repose, and the words, "Get up; its four o'clock," reminded them they were factory children, the unprotected victims of monotonous slavery. At this mill, and indeed all mills, boys and girls were often found sleeping in stairs and private places, and they have been seen walking about the flats in a deep sleep, with cans of "sliver"[4] in their hands. When found in this state, they were caned or kicked according to the mood of their superiors. One poor boy, who is still alive, and who, by force of mind, great persistency and rectitude, rose to be a mercantile clerk in Dundee, and now fills a responsible situation on one of the principal railways in England, was for some time in this factory. One day he was carrying an armful of bobbins from one flat to another. When ascending the stair, he sat down to rest himself, as his legs were sore and swollen by incessant standing. In a few moments he was fast asleep. Whilst enjoying this stolen repose, the master happened to pass. Without the least warning he gave him a violent slap on the side of the head, which stunned and stupified him. In a half-sleeping state of stupefaction he ran to the roving frame,[5] which he sometimes attended, and five minutes had barely elapsed when his left hand got entangled with the machinery, and two of his fingers were crushed to a jelly, and had to be immediately amputated. His unfeeling taskmaster gave him no recompense,—in fact never asked after him; he was left to starve or die, as Providence might

---

1 flats] floors or storeys of a building.
2 "ends"] fragments of pieces of thread.
3 brose] porridge of milk, oatmeal, butter, and salt.
4 "sliver"] loose untwisted fibers of wool or cotton ready for weaving.
5 roving frame] the machine on which the first spinning process is carried out by turning slivers of a textile into thick threads.

direct. The reader will no doubt imagine that boys working 18 and 19 hours a-day would have nearly double wages to boys at the present time, who only work ten. I can only speak from experience, and what has come under the range of my own knowledge on this point. When I went to the mill, I was paid with 1s 6d per week, and my nominal hours, as already remarked, were 13 hours per day. When the Twelve Hours' Act was in operation, boys had from 3s up to 4s per week; and now since the Ten Hours' Act came into force, their wages vary from 3s 8d up to 4s 3d. In short, as far as I can learn, their wages are as good under the Ten Hours' Act[1] as they were under the Twelve Hours' Act. Of course the Act precludes such young boys as I was from working; yet, considering the hours I was confined, and the wages I was paid with, the contrast is highly favourable to the humanity and wisdom of those good men who procured protection to factory children, and said to competition and capital, "Hitherto shalt thou come but no farther."[2]

My first day's experience as a factory boy damped my ardour, and, on returning home to my mother, I cried bitterly. In the flat in which I was employed there were seventeen girls from nine to twenty-five years of age, and I was the only boy. When the mill was set on, I experienced the most indescribable sensation. I looked strange and even stupid, and when I glanced to any of my companions, as if supplicating sympathy, they returned my kindness by making wry faces and gestures, in ridicule of my country appearance. At the meal hours the other boys of the work gathered round me, as if I had been a natural curiosity imported from some distant clime. They "streaked my buttons," swore, and challenged me to fight; and I soon found I would get no peace to live unless I risked the contingency of a battle. As there is honour among thieves,[3] so I found a modicum of honour amongst mill boys, as one about my own age was selected to be my adversary. Accordingly we adjourned to a park near the Dens, and had a regular "mill,"[4] and in the crowd were animals called men prompting us on. It so happened that I proved the

---

1 Ten Hours' Act] the 1847 Act to Limit the Hours of Labour of Young Persons and Females in Factories (see Introduction 56-58).

2 Job 38:11: here the Lord speaks of his having placed limits on the "proud waves" of the sea.

3 "Honour is sometimes found among thieves." Sir Walter Scott (1771-1832), *Redgauntlet* (1824), Chapter 9.

4 "mill"] a fight.

best pugilist, and ever afterwards I got more peace to attend my work, go and return from my meals, as I then was looked on as a member of the fraternity. About a week after I became a mill boy, I was seized with a strong, heavy sickness, that few escaped on first becoming factory workers. The cause of this sickness, which is known by the name of the "mill fever,"[1] is the pestiferous atmosphere produced by so many breathing in a confined place, together with the heat and the exhalations of grease and oil. All these causes are aggravated in the winter time by the immense destruction of pure air by the gas that is needed to light the e[s]tablishment. This fever does not often lay the patient up. It is slow, dull, and painfully wearisome in its operation. It produces a sallow and debilitated look, destroys rosy cheeks, and unless the constitution be very strong, leaves its pale impress for life. I have already mentioned the wages paid to boys under the Twelve and Ten Hours' Act, and the wages I received myself when there was no act. I may likewise refer to the wages of the female spinners. Those who were employed at the mill I first entered, received fully higher remuneration than what is now paid to the same class; but the reduction cannot by any show of facts or reason be ascribed to factory legislation. In 1824 the spinning trade was very brisk in this locality, and female spinners received 10s per week, for which they attended 36 to 40 spindles during 15 or 16 hours every lawful day. At present a female spinner will attend from 100 to 120 spindles, according to the character of the material, and her wages range from 5s 9d to 6s per week. Though she manages nearly double the quantity of spindles at present as compared with 1824, yet this does not result from extra labour being imposed on her, but from the extensive improvements in machinery since that date. It will thus be seen by the above comparison, which is as unfavourable a one as I could draw for the short-time system, inasmuch as it places in juxtaposition an extra brisk time with the present, which is only moderate, that the wages of female labour is fully 40 per cent. less than in 1824; but the simple cause of this is keener competition in that department of the labour market, which has been greatly aggravated by the immense influx of Irish women during the last twenty years; and though no factory act had been conceived or carried into execution, similar effects would have flowed from the causes indicated.

---

1   "mill fever"] a form of low-grade fever that often affected factory children, probably due to overwork, exhaustion, and poor diet.

If further evidence was needed to demonstrate the justice and correctness of this conclusion, it may be found in the fact, that the wages of spinners in 1832, before factory legislation extended to Dundee, and, when they worked thirteen hours a day, were 6s and 6s 6d per week, being only a mere fraction higher than what they now receive under the beneficent reign of the Ten Hours' Bill.

CHAPTER III.
CAUSES OF THE MORAL DEGRADATION OF FEMALE MILL-SPINNERS—A TERRIBLE ILLUSTRATION.

After the "mill fever" had left me, I had more heart to attend to the instructions given me by the overseer, and better opportunities of listening to the conversations of my new associates. Even at the early age at which I became a factory boy, I was somewhat inquisitive, and naturally fond of observing manners and customs; I therefore embraced all possible chances of storing my mind with facts; and as I have been blessed with a comprehensive memory, I am now, in my mature years, enabled to classify these facts, and speculate largely, and I hope usefully, on them. During our working hours, the doors of the mill were all locked, we were not permitted to go out, excepting at meal hours, and when the works were stopped. Old and young were thus confined promiscuously together for thirteen hours without any governor who cared for aught but manual toil. Indeed, it is almost impossible to wield a healthy control over the conversations and actions of millworkers. The noise caused by the machinery is so great, that the most unhallowed dialogues may be conducted by two persons near to each other, without any one knowing what is going on. This circumstance I found to be the most favourable one for the mutual circulation of anecdotes and ideas which spread and maintain moral contamination amongst young factory workers. The reader will observe that, in those days, and, I suspect, even in our own times, when a female applied at a spinning-mill for work, the question asked her was, what can you do? The equally important one, what are your habits, and can you produce a good character? was not mooted. Mammon suggested the former, and a lax idea of the responsibilities and moral weight of an employer paid no attention to the latter. This is to be deplored, as in no establishment does moral poison circulate so rapidly as in a spinning-mill. I have known a woman of bad character pollute the whole juvenile workers of the flat in which she was employed. She would fill their young minds with wanton and lascivious ideas; teach them to sing obscene songs; gradually introduce them to her own companions; take them to low dancings; lead them to houses of bad fame, and finally accomplish their r[u]in. To a young boy, fresh from the arms of rural innocence, where oaths and ribaldry were, I may safely says [sic] rarely heard, the conversations and manner, of my older fellow-workers surprised and disgusted me; but as the mind of youth can be speedily shaped to any mould, and familiarised with any phase of wickedness, I soon found myself, in spite of the earnest warnings of my mother, able to listen with levity and carelessness to impious imprecations and the worst kind of language. I had not been long in a mill, when a few of the girls, during a temporary absence of the foreman, perched themselves up on a window sill, and beckoned me to come and hear a song. I complied, and heard, for the first time, a vile production called "Sally Kelly," sung with much enthusiasm and glee. This horrible compound of doggerel and obscenity is still popular amongst mill boys and girls, which convinces me that, as a class, they have made little moral progress during the last twenty years. At the conclusion of the song, in my simplicity I asked them where they got that song, and if their mothers had learned them to sing it? They burst into a shrill wild laugh—a laugh that can only be given by mill girls—seized me, pulled me down on the floor, and proceeded to maltreat me in a manner which was neither modest nor merciful. Whilst this scene was enacting, the overseer made his appearance. I was blamed for the whole. He pulled me by the ears, gave me a kick, which made my head come violently in contact with an iron pillar. I protested my innocence, cried severely, but all to no purpose. I was made the butt of the girls' ridicule, and the object on which our foreman spent his ire. I did not remain long in ignorance of where obscene songs were picked up. One day I was oiling the cylinder of a frame, I heard one of the oldest women in the flat busy teaching a little girl a song, so disgusting in its character and even name, that it cannot be mentioned. Young as I was I knew this woman was committing a heinous sin, and I boldly asked her if she did not think shame of herself? With a fierce oath, she vowed she would put the bashfulness out of me. As soon as the overseer was out of sight she sprang on me like a wild beast, tore down my clothes, and lashed me with a belt until I grew sick and vomited. I told the foreman, and all the satisfaction I got was an intimation to mind my own business or he would give me as much again.

Mill-overseers then had, with very few exceptions, their particular female favourites, and the relations that they sustained to each other were not of the best description. Respectable flaxspinners of the present day endeavour to suppress what I am alluding to, but it is to be feared with only partial success. Such instances as I have related above are, I believe, not rare, and they may be set down as one of the causes which foster the lewd and demoral habits that unfortunately belong to the great majority of female millspinners. There are haunts to which the old and hardened lead the young to their ruin. Women thoroughly bankrupt in character make spinning-mills places of refuge when they cannot gain admittance into any other place. I have known them myself living one week in a brothel, working the next in a mill, and so on for a number of months. Such abandoned females mixing with the young, undermine any good principles which they may have inherited from their parents or imbibed at school, and prepare them to recruit the ranks of drunkenness and prostitution. Women of this stamp are cunning and insinuating. They can ply the honied words of Satan and deception in a style that may be justly denominated the eloquence of hell. They know all the haunts of female vice in town, and can guide any blooming girl to houses of assignation, where gentlemen ! can be met with, and the consummation of their fall effected. What are houses of assignation? asks the reader who has not penetrated through the veil th at [sic] hides such mysteries from the public eye. Taverns, I answer, where prostitution is winked at. Places where males and females make appointments, and whoever arrives first, may walk into a private room, tell the landlord, when a person of certain marks comes, to shew him or her, as the case may be, into the same apartment. In Dr Tait's work on Magdalenism,[1] I find it stated that places of this description are common in Edinburgh, and that he has known numbers of decent servant girls drawn into their horrible vortex, and finally ruined. I can scarcely venture an opinion as to what extent the same class in Dundee are influenced by them, but I have a large number of facts at my command which convinces me that they are preparatory schools

---

1 William Tait's *Magdalenism: An Inquiry into the Extent, Causes, and Conse-quences of Prostitution in Edinburgh* (1840). Tate's now dubious statistics claimed that there was one prostitute for every eight adult males in Edinburgh; furthermore, he reported ratios of one to every sixty adult males in London, one to every fifteen adult males in Paris, and one to every six or seven adult males in New York.

for nursing and educating for sin and misery, and in their secret chambers the hope and joy of many a parent's heart have been crushed and blasted for life. On such a subject, reader, it is difficult to preserve purity and boldness; but no false delicacy shall paralyse my pen, or deter me from relating facts drawn from personal knowledge. Prudes and sublimated sentimentalists may croak and cry, Oh! it is a delicate subject to meddle with; but all who regard chastity as the most heavenly adornment of the female character, will admit, that to blink[1] such a question is either a confession of incapacity or moral cowardice. I have indicated the nature of houses of assignation, and hinted at the methods adopted by women of debased character, who gain admittance into spinning-mills, for corrupting the helpless female poor, and preparing them for a life of infamy. I sincerely wish I could exonerate respectable young men, falsely so called, from the dreadful charge of being participators of this worst of all crimes; but several stern facts, which I have noted on the tablet of my memory, tell me that I cannot conscientiously do so. The frightful character of one circumstance obtrudes itself on my mind, and as the whole facts are fraught with sombre interest, and serve to illustrate my remarks, I will give them to the reader.

While I was working in the mill I first went to, a young girl from one of the Protestant counties in Ireland come to the same establishment to learn the spinning. She was tall and proportionately formed. Her bust was one of the best models of feminine symmetry I have ever seen, and her carriage had all the ease and elegance of nature. Her face had not the vulgar contour so common in the most of her countrywomen, but was Grecian in its form, soft and captivating in its expression. Her eyes were large, dark in colour, and surmounted with long black lashes which gave a rich and mellow-tinge to their beauty. Her cheeks were fresh as a new blown rose; in short, the "Irish girl," as she was called, was one of the handsomest of her sex. In addition to her personal attractions, she was artless and cheerful as a laughing child. Born in the country, and reared up by pious, simple-minded parents, she knew nothing of the vices and plots of wicked women, who delight in vitiating the young. She had not been long in Dundee when a young profligate, moving in an affluent circle, fixed his voluptuous and tainted heart on her, and plotted for her ruin. He followed her, spoke to her on the street, and tempted her with brilliant presents if she would consent to

---

1 blink] evade.

make an appointment with him, but she repulsed all his infamous advances, and frequently told him she would call the police if he did not cease his importunities. Foiled by these tactics his corrosive ingenuity, stimulated by the worst passions of pandemonium, planned new plots to entrap the untainted object of his unholy desires, but all failed. At last he employed a factory woman of bad character to aid him in his designs. She worked beside the Irish girl, and was one of the worst of the corrupting class of which I have already spoken. She plied her art with all the cunning and perseverance of a Jesuit.[1] At last, by false representations, she got the unprotected girl to accompany her to a house of assignation in Couttie's Wynd. According to previous arrangement, her persecutor was introduced; and will it be believed, porter strongly drugged was administered to her, and that very night her final ruin was accomplished. Need I tell the consequences which flowed from this villanous crime, black as the darkness of night under which it was perpetrated, or trace the poor girl's subsequent history. No, it is too painful and degraded to be penned; suffice it to say, that she still lives, a bloated piece of physical and moral corruption, one of the most repulsive unfortunates that nightly steal along our public streets. What can I say, or rather what *dare* I say of her heartless seducer? He still lives, and the power of wealth enables him to gloss over his sins, and swim in the same social circle. Society, with its mock morality calls him a respectable man; while it pours out its hatred and indignation on the head of his poor unfriended and unpitied sacrifice. Oh! basest of men, have you no qualms of conscience? Does the spirit of remorse, like a "goblin damn'd,"[2] not torment you by night and by day? Does your haggard victim, like an avenging spectre from another world, never cross your path, and strike an arrow into your guilty soul? Does the vision of a venerable mother, sitting beside the fire in her own humble cottage, bewailing her lost daughter, not haunt you, when trying to bury your vile recollections in the grave of sleep? Do you never see in your troubled dreams an old man, whose hair is grey with grief and age, bending his knee and calling on God to extend the influ-

---

1 a Jesuit] literally a member of a Roman Catholic religious order (the Society of Jesus, founded by Ignatius Loyola in 1534); in this usage the term means a cunning, crafty person, characteristics that were attributed to the Jesuits by their detractors.
2 Shakespeare, *Hamlet* I.iv.40. "Be thou a spirit of health or goblin damn'd."

ence of his mercy, until it embraces within its benign radiance his dear though lost child? You know you ruined that child, and if your mind is not impervious to the biting shafts of scorn, you ought to tremble while there lives *one* who knows you, and is able and bold enough to upbraid you. Time will soon gather the mantle of age around you, and the king of terrors will yet overtake you, God grant that the panoply of thy repentance, and His grace may then be strong enough to afford a balm to thy soul, and that thy spirit may pass the valley of death unclogged with the weighty guilt of destroying one of the fair temples of the Almighty.

Reader, if I had drawn the elements of this sketch from the alembic[1] of my own fancy, and made it subservient to my purpose, I consider I would have been blameable, as on a subject of such delicate and deep importance, it would be neither upright nor honourable to draw on the imagination. I have only described facts which have come under my own cognition, and they point as an index to one of the morally deteriorating causes of female mill-workers. It is surely deplorable that creatures young in years, and full of promise to their fond parents, should be driven by necessity to work in places where those old in vice and even crime gain easy admittance, and are their daily companions. The ancient Spartans taught their children habits of temperance, we are told, by shewing them their drunken and licentious helots,[2] and telling them to avoid such debasing debauchery. I strongly question the applicability of such educational philosophy, and think that Lycurgus[3] has been either misunderstood or not so wise as he has hitherto been represented. What parent would be disposed to teach his children the uselessness and profanity of oaths by keeping them in company with habitual swearers? Or who would think of instilling morality into the young mind by familiarising it with immorality? Example, it is said, is better than precept. Occasional gleams of wickedness may strike the flexible faculties of the young with awe and even disgust, and render them good service in their after journey through life, but to encircle them with evil, to sow thorns and look for grapes[4] is the very

---

1 alembic] a vessel that distills or purifies.
2 helots] In ancient Sparta, Helots were serfs or bondsmen owned by the state.
3 Lycurgus] Ninth-century B.C.E. Spartan lawgiver.
4 Matthew 7:16: "Ye shall know them by their fruits. Do men gather grapes of thorns, or figs of thistles?"

height of folly and ignorance. How beautifully is this doctrine exhibited by Pope in the following four lines;—

> "Vice is a monster of such frightful mein,
> As to be hated needs but to be seen,
> But seen too oft, familiar with her face
> We first endure, then pity, then embrace."[1]

I am satisfied that a rigid scrutiny into the characters of adult factory operatives, would be the greatest moral boon that employers could confer on their young servants. There are many of these gentlemen of kindly dispositions and extensive benevolence, and if they had an experimental knowledge of the amount of evil and suffering, caused by depraved adults mixing indiscriminately with the young, I am sure they would shudder at the appalling picture, and zealously labour to improve the moral and religious characters of those in their employment. The social gulf that divides employer and employed is too wide and deep. The working class have yet much to learn and more to unlearn. Prejudices against wealth and property have to be extinguished, and a more manly independence generated in their minds. Education must be widely diffused, temperance spread abroad, and provident habits fostered, and, finally, they have yet religiously to remember that self-reform is the first, the best and greatest of all reforms. Employers also are too much wrapt up in the cold mantle of ha[u]teur and selfishness. In this age of iron and gold, the dignity of mind has almost been forgotten, and man has been estimated by the mere accident of his social position, and the amount of his wealth. I confess, as a working man, I have often been galled by the coldness and even contempt of men who were placed above me, as I felt conscious that the Deity had stamped them with inferiority in all the attributes which exalt humanity. Employers should cultivate a good understanding with the employed, and shew forth kindness and brotherly love. Kindness is cheap, sweet, and, pleasing, and sheds a halo of felicity over all who move within its holy circumference. Recollect, gentlemen, a becoming humility is the voice of virtue. In the fine language of Chilo, "If you are

---

1 Alexander Pope (1688-1744), *Essay on Man* (1733-34), Epistle ii, lines 217-20.

great be condescending; for it is better to be loved than to be feared.'[1]

CHAPTER IV.

MY FIRST WINTER AT THE MILL—LONG HOURS—SLEEPING ON STAIRS—AN ACCIDENT—FALLS IN WITH THE "LIFE OF SIR WILLIAM WALLACE."

Notwithstanding the many hardships I endured in the course of my first few months at the mill, I got through the summer with ease and comfort compared to the first winter. Though the hours were long, yet the sun I thought rose as soon as I did, and his departing rays lighted my footsteps home at night; and some how or other, the young body can do with less sleep in the summer time than during the long gloomy nights of winter. The constitution of man is finely balanced and adapted to external nature. When the nights are long and dull, he clings more eagerly to the arms of the balmy comforter; but when summer comes, like a virtuous bride clothed in beauty and smiles, he courts her company and delights in her society. Happiness surely depends more on the state of the mind and heart, than on the factitious trappings of worldly circumstances; for, even amidst our misfortunes, wretchedness, and poverty, rays of felicity sometimes penetrated and relieved our minds from the painful monotony of unceasing misery. I know that when under the olive branches of my mother's affections, I often forgot all the ills of my daily life. She too felt so happy when I came home on the Saturday nights, and laid my small wages in her lap, that the tear would sometimes start to her eye. Perhaps it was a tear of gratitude, or sorrow, excited by wanting the protection of a husband, and gaining the premature assistance of a son.

On the approach of winter I began to feel severely the terrible infliction of long hours. As the mill went on at half-past five A.M, I had, as I have already stated, to get out of bed at five, and as trade was very dull at the time, to be behind the hours was not only to lose *double* wages for the lost time, but to run the risk of

---

1 Chilo, or Chilon of Sparta (c. 560 B.C.E.), one of the Greek sages of the seventh and sixth centuries known as "The Seven Wise Men of Greece." In *The Lives and Opinions of Eminent Philosophers* by Diogenes Laertius (c. 200), Chilo advised, "When strong, be merciful, if you would have the respect, not the fear, of your neighbors."

being instantly discharged. At that time mill-masters did not employ men for rousing their hands in the mornings, and each individual had to grope away as he best could. I wish I knew the benevolent person who first conceived and carried into execution the plan of warning them each morning. I certainly would have woven an humble chaplet of literary flowers to have adorned his memory. The plan at once removed a load of anxiety and pain off the minds of the young, as the terror of sleeping in kept them in a nightly state of unhappiness. I know the effect it had on myself, and to use a common expression, it likewise kept my mother on "heckle pins."[1] We had no clock in the house, and my mother used to rise at all hours of the night, and sit until she heard the Cowgate clock strike an hour. Often has she sat from a little past three until five, when she would waken me and return to her bed. I have frequently risen myself, put on my clothes, gone out, and discovered afterwards that it was only about three in the morning; but rather than return to my bed, and run the risk of lying too long, I have gone to a stair in the vicinity of the mill, laid myself down on it, and fallen fast asleep, and on the arrival of the fireman I would creep alongside the boiler to catch a little heat to my cold overworked body. This stair still stands. It is the only outside one opposite the Quarry Lands in the New Roads. A few days ago I visited it, and the sight of it kindled a fire of contending emotions in my breast. I thought on the time when necessity, that iron-hearted slave-driver, backed by the voracious demands of competition, ground the health and strength of children in mills; and I could not help contrasting it with our own time, under the dominion of the Ten Hours' Bill. The contrast was in every way gratifying, as the hours are not only diminished, but corporeal punishment is prohibited, and a more healthy system of usage generally in practice. The recollections I have of sleeping on stairs, and the many severe beatings I got, steal over my mind like something cold and even criminal, and I involuntarily shudder as if I had done an evil deed. If the advocates of the long hours system had all passed through the same severe ordeal, relay systems[2] and opposition to the Ten Hours' Bill never would have

---

1 on "heckle pins"] in a state of painful anxiety.

2 relay systems] When the Factory Act of 1833 limited to nine a day the hours of children, first, under eleven years, and eventually, under thirteen (see note 4 on page 237), one highly criticized way to provide adult workers the assistance with which children provided them involved requiring the latter to work in shifts to cover all the hours when a factory was running.

been heard of. It was during this winter that I got the first unmerciful beating from a mill overseer. I was attending a spinning frame. It got too full in the shifting, and I was unable to keep up the ends. The foreman challenged me. I told him I was doing the best I could. He flew into a furious passion, dragged me into the turning shop, cut a strap off a lathe, and lashed me cruelly. He then seized me by the ears and hung me for a few moments over a window three storeys from the ground. In reading of such a ferocious action as this, methinks I hear the reader exclaim, Surely that is not true; but I beg solemnly to state that it is true to the very letter, and there is one old mill foreman in Dundee who can corroborate all I have said. I know such inexorable tyranny is not and cannot be practised now-a-days, but when I was a boy it was, I regret to say, too common in such places. On the evening of this unlucky day, when I returned home, my eyes were red, and my head sore with weeping, and a second time I gave vent to my pent up feelings under the wings of my mother's sympathy. "Can the fond mother ere forget the infant whom she bore?"[1] No. Cold and callous must be the heart of a mother when it bleeds not for the wrongs and even failings of her children. When I detailed the usage I had got from my foreman, her indignation rose so high that she burst into tears, and vowed vengeance on his head. On the following day she called on Mr H——, the proprietor, and made her complaint. She was told that he never interfered in such matters, and she left without getting any satisfaction. Determined to wreak her wrath on the unfeeling perpetrator of the assault, she proceeded straightway to the mill, and met the foreman at the top of a stair which led down to a malt barn.[2] Made strong by passion, without a moment's warning, she seized him by the neck, and hurled him to the bottom of the stair as if he had been a child. He had scarcely time to think, far less to rise, when she bounded out at the door and vanished from his sight. A few of the workers who witnessed this scene enjoyed it highly, for overbearing masters and foremen receive no sympathy from their workers when an accident happens or the talons of adversity seize on them. Tyranny always earns for a man the hatred and contempt of his fellows. Like debauchery it is generally payable thirty years after date with interest, and its creditors continue an unfailing opposition to the

---

1 Isaiah 49:15. "Can a woman forget her suckling child, that she should not have compassion on the son of her womb?"
2 malt barn] brewery.

end; and even after the hard taskmaster has descended to his narrow house, the detestation of the oppressed follows him there and covers his name and memory with obloquy and shame. The event I have detailed made me more miserable than ever. I knew that my overseer would seize on the first petty fault I might commit, and make it a pretext for dismissing me from my employment. The power that such men have of dismissing servants is a strong weapon in their hands for effecting any purpose they may contemplate. According to my anticipations a fault was soon picked out, and pretext discovered for paying me off. One day, at breakfast time, I had been amusing myself sailing little bits of wood with masts, and paper sails in the mill pond. My cravet, unknown to me, got all wet in the ends while I was bending. On returning to my work it got warped round a shaft that propelled my rove, or elevator. In a moment it was whirled round the shaft, and my head came violently in contact with it; but my cravat providentially nipt in two, or I would have been instantly suffocated. My neck was a little ruffled, and my head sore, and I entered a small room off the flat where yarn was kept, and lay down until I should recover the stun and fright I had received. It was impossible for mill boys then to sit down to rest themselves without falling asleep, and I was of course no exception. In a few minutes I was asleep, and dreaming of falling over precipices, and being worried by wild beasts, which was necessarily caused by the fright I had got. While in this state, a roguish boy of the name of Fleming poured oil on my neck, and painted my face all over with ink and grease. He then went and told the foreman I was lying in the yarn-room sleeping, and for this petty fault—petty when it is considered what happened previous to it—I was instantly discharged. As the spring was approaching, and trade improving, moreover, as I had had some experience as a mill-boy, I was not afraid of getting work. I had heard much of the kindness and generosity of Messrs ———— ———— as employers, and I applied at their establishment and was successful. The reports I had heard of these gentlemen were fully verified by my experience, and, years after I had left their employment, I was pleased, on reading the evidence which was taken before the Committee of the House of Commons on the Factory Question in 1833,[1] to find it stated, by a witness of extensive experience and knowledge, that the Messrs ———— were favourable to a reduction in the hours of

---

1 Committee ... 1833] Apparently a reference to Sadler's Select Committee of 1832 (see Introduction 23).

labour, and were considered the most kind-hearted employers in Dundee. "The deeds of old," says Ossian, "are like paths to our eyes;"[1] and the kind deeds of generous masters and friends are like the frankincense of youth burning in the memory of old age. They are sweet and fragrant, and leave the impress of their divinity for ever in the chambers of the mind[.] When we hear an old and good master praised, our hearts hurriedly respond to the panegyric, and we would willingly swell it into a jubilee. Such is the effect of kindness and love. "Love," says Southey, "is the great instrument and engine of nature, the bud and cement of society, the spring and spirit of the universe."[2] I need scarcely inform the reader that at this early age I had received little or no education. I could read the Testament fluently; but I knew nothing of arithmetic, or the higher branches of learning. To improve the little I had got, my mother made me read a chapter each evening after I returned from my work; but I was so exhausted by the long hours that I very rarely managed to get to the end of it without falling asleep. When Sunday morning came round, I tried always to escape from home and spend the day either on Balgay Hill, or by the banks of Dighty.[3] It was a great relief to me to get out to places similar to the sylvan scenes of my childhood. I breathed more freely, and the joy that I felt was sweeter than the delight of an aspiring monarch on gaining a crown. So intense were my emotions, that I often said to myself, "Surely God has made this a day of rest for the benefit of mill boys." I was so enveloped in happiness, arising from a day of relaxation, that my mind could see no farther than the little world in which I myself moved. None but the poor overworked masses can fully feel the temporal advantages of the Sabbath, or taste the pleasures that spring from a periodical day of complete cessation from labour. On one of these Sunday excursions I happened to wander down the Den

---

1 Ossian (c. third century), or Oisin, was a legendary character in Gaelic literature. Scottish poet James Macpherson (1736-96) published *Poems of Ossian* in 1760-63, claiming that they were translations of Ossian's works. It was later discovered that these poems, although extremely popular, were Macpherson's compositions.

2 Not the work of Robert Southey (1774-1843), English poet and critic, Poet Laureate (1813-43); rather, from a sermon titled "On the Creation of Man in the Image of God" (1662) by Robert South (1634-1716), clergyman in the Church of England.

3 Balgay Hill ... Dighty] a wooded hill west of Dundee, private land until 1869; Dighty Water is a river that runs parallel to the Firth of Tay north of Dundee.

of Mains,[1] and, at the root of a tree, I picked up an old tattered book, which proved to be a copy of the metrical life of Sir William Wallace and King Robert the Bruce.[2] I took it home, and got a severe scolding from my mother, as she thought I had been reading it. However, if I did not that day indulge in a perusal of what she strongly condemned for Sunday reading, I committed the sin on the first Sabbath after this. I had been reading little snatches of it through the week, and was so delighted with the adventures of the Scottish patriot, that I fully determined to give my mother the slip on Sunday, and take Wallace in my pocket. Intent on my design, I supplied myself with one of her bannocks, stole out of the house, and made my escape to the Hill of Balgay. Amidst its arborous solitudes, on a beautiful Sunday morning in June (the better the day the worse the deed)[3] my mind was first awakened to the pleasures of knowledge, and entranced by the martial achievements of our darling hero. I had read for several hours without any interruption excepting the occasional buzzing of a honey bee, which hovered round me as if I had invaded its chosen sanctuary, and had reached the division beginning—

"Now Biggar's plains with armed men are crowned,
And shining lances glitter all around."

I had not got in to the stirring details of the battle of Biggar, but was excited in anticipating the pleasure in store for me, when a familiar voice cried aloud, "Oh Frank, Frank, to haud[4] your mither seekin' you this way on the Sabbath day?" I was certainly astonished, and even afraid when my mother found me under such circumstances. I got a severe lecture for running off on Sunday with Wallace for my companion; but on promising not to

---

1   Den] hollow, small valley.
2   the metrical life ...] The book is Blind Hary's (also known as Henry the Minstrel, c.1440-c.1492) *The Actis and Deidis of the Illustere and Vailyeand Campioun, Schir William Wallace, Knight of Ellerslie* (c.1477), commonly known as *The Book of William Wallace* or *Wallace*. Sir William Wallace (c. 1260-1305) was a Scottish hero who led the resistance against Edward I of England, and who drove English forces from Scotland in 1297; King Robert the Bruce (1274-1329) ultimately defeated Edward II to formally establish independence for Scotland, which was recognized by the English in 1328.
3   Matthew Henry (1662-1714), Presbyterian minister; from his *An Exposition of the Old and New Testament* (1710), Genesis 3:6.
4   haud] hold.

do the like again, I escaped what I expected and perhaps deserved—corporeal punishment. The reading of Wallace opened up a new world to me, and I longed for more mental food to satisfy the cravings of an awakened appetite. There are few books so greedily read by the young as the metrical life of Wallace. The jingling style of its composition, and the fiery patriotism displayed in detailing the exploits of the Scottish chieftian [sic], make it a great favourite with the boys, and secures for Wallace the first and highest place in the affections of our juvenile hero worshippers. I had before read the usual literature of the nursery, such as "Cinderella or the little Glass Slipper," "Whittington and his Cat," "Blue Beard," "Ali Baba," and the renowned "Jack the Giant Killer," some of them, by the bye, being books of a very bad tendency; but blind Harry's Life of Wallace was the first book that stirred my mind, and set me on a career of reading and thinking that will only terminate with my life, or the complete prostration of my faculties. I have, as a natural consequence, a great veneration for the Life of Wallace, and the identical copy, which I found many years ago in the den of Mains, is now in my library, splendidly bound in Morocco, and graced with all the ornamental flourishes of a first-rate bookbinder. This is all the respect I can pay to my old friend who gave the primary impulse to my passion for reading, if I could do more I would with all my heart. Reader, always reverence the first book that excited in you the desire of self-culture, for when this desire is once kindled it ought not and cannot be extinguished. Never forget the useful admonition of Isocrates, "Cultivate your mind as much as you can, for a handsome mind is a noble thing, though it be shut up in a human body."[1]

CHAPTER V.
CAREER OF A MILL BOY—AN ACCIDENT—A DREAM.

In our hours of solitude, when thoughts of bye-gone days arise in the soul, there are no questions we are so apt to ask ourselves as, What have become of all the associates of my youth? Where are they all gone to? Is John This, or Harry That still alive? Has Tom Braine, the clever boy who was always at the top of the class, arrived yet at distinction? Has Peter Simple, the soft stupid lad, descended to the lowest point of the social scale? Have any of my

---

1 Isocrates (436-338 B.C.E.), Greek philosopher; from *To Demonicus* 40.

companions been more fortunate or unfortunate than myself? Such questions often obtrude themselves on the mind; and if we carefully trace the careers of our youthful friends, we will afford ourselves a miniature view of human society in the aggregate. We would find, perhaps, that one careless, daring spirit was busy digging for gold in the El Dorado of the new world; another, perchance, who possessed few primary advantages, risen by perseverance and integrity to an eminent status at home; while a third, who outstripped us at school, and possessed hereditary social advantages, is now far behind us in the race for respectability and comfort; and, it may be, that the clever Tom Braine has been everything and anything, and is now nothing. Such is the way of the world. The careless clever are often last in the worldly race; and the poor now and then supplant the rich, while the plodding and the dull frequently play a better part than the dawning of their manhood promised. I often recur in thought to the days of my boyhood, for

> A pleasant thing it is to mind,
> O' youthfu' thoughts an' things;[1]

and try and trace the history of some of the poor boys who were the companions of my mill days. But alas they are either all dead, or buried in the depths of poverty and obscurity. Only one to my knowledge remains. He was a clever Tom Braine in his way, and by that name, reader, you must know him. I cannot pass him over in silence. He was my chosen counsellor, my every day confidant and friend. He was older, and had received a better education than I, at least a better school training; but his home education was inferior, and some influences wield a greater power over our manhood than all the dry figures and routine of scholastic drilling. "Better to be brought up at a good mother's knee, than at the feet of Gamaliel,"[2] remarks a shrewd observer of human nature, and few will dispute the soundness of the doctrine. Tom Braine and I became acquainted while working at the spinning establishment I alluded to in the last chapter. He was a smart boy, and the son of decent though poor parents, who resided in

---

1 Robert Nicoll, "Youth's Dreams" (see note 2 on page 231).
2 Acts 22:3. Paul explains that he was taught "at the feet of Gamaliel," a rabbi and a Pharisee who warned against interfering with the apostles (Acts 5: 38).

Walker's Close, Seagate.[1] When a mere child death deprived him of maternal protection, and the hiatus in the domestic circle being in a short time afterwards supplied by a stepmother, poor Tom was no longer bound to home by the tender though potent chords of his own mother's love. He began to stop out at night, and frequent low theatres—places that do more harm to the young of both sexes, who are deprived of parental guardians, than any other kind of public exhibitions or haunts I know of. It is easy to prate about the sublimity of dramatic compositions and the monitorial voice of the stage, but the eloquent apologies of theorists cannot subvert the glaring fact that cheap theatres are centres of attractions for the vilest of both sexes, and the numbers they have ruined compared with those they have reformed are, I suspect, fearfully disproportionate. As a natural consequence, Tom conceived a passionate and romantic love for the stage. He learned the trade of shoemaker, and used to entertain his friends, when they were "wetting their inner man," with recitations from the tragic poets; and he was persuaded by his quondam cronies that nature had destined him for a Fuseli or a Kean.[2] Dreaming only of benefits, bumpers, and dramatic renown, he renounced the awls, and essayed to personate the bard of Avon's[3] wonderful creations, with what success the reader may judge when I tell him that the first sight I got of Tom in his theatrical career, he was employed as a prompter to a wandering and poor, half-starved company which belonged to a "character" called Fuzzie Gow, and by this time was the victim of intemperance. Ultimately, he rose in his profession, and performed as a supernumerary in a band of travelling players who were headed by a person of the name of Scott. While in the service of these mountebank masters, he gleaned a large amount of practical experience relative to the baneful influence of intoxicating drinks, read extensively, and improved his capacity of talking. By an adverse blast of fortune he was again driven to cobbling, and a temporary fit of sobriety having seized him, he became a temperance advocate, and earned

---

1   Seagate] one of the four principal streets in the center of Dundee.
2   Probably Edmund Kean (1787?-1833), English actor, though Myles may mean Charles Kean (1811-68), his son, also an actor. Henry Fuseli (1741-1825), painter, writer, critic, and later professor of painting at the Royal Academy; he is perhaps mentioned in this context because he drew many of his subjects from Shakespeare and became known as "Shakespeare's painter."
3   bard of Avon] William Shakespeare.

some local fame as an orator. The habits imbibed whilst a devotee of the drama he found it difficult to cast off, and he frequently forgot in private the solemn asseverations made in public. On one occasion a political agitator, who made high temperance pretensions, and Tom, were invited to Coupar Angus,[1] or some small town in that district, to address the good folks on the abstinence question. The people were moved by their appeals and delighted with their eloquence, and the speakers, on returning the following morning per outside a stage-coach, could not resist mutual congratulations on the success of their mission. The bracing and biting winds, however, that whistled along the muirs of Lundie,[2] were a severe ordeal to their unstable practice and feeble faith. As they approached the toll-bar, they began to smack their lips and cast meaning and sympathetic glances at each other, and make remarks on the coldness of the weather. Finally, Tom, like the dreaming mystic of America, declared that "a foolish consistency was the hobgoblin of little minds,"[3] and boldly broached the questionable doctrine that a man might do good to society by advocating certain principles in public though he did not scrupulously respect them in private. His radical friend jumped at the latitudinarian dogma, and proposed a practical application, as the severity of the season constituted what he called an extreme case. The silent language and obscure hints were now fully understood by both worthies, and they each consumed a drop of the "mountain dew"[4] at Lundie Toll, and, on their arrival at Dundee, they adjourned to a tavern in the Seagate, and when they left it they were only able to hobble home in a rectangular manner, frequently forming with their bodies lines directly parallel with the surface of the street. Such was the finale of Tom's first temperance mission—a striking illustration that a good cause may be injured and disgraced by a bad and unprincipled advocate. As my old friend was not the person to "stick on stepping stones," he

---

1 Coupar Angus] an industrial town approximately twelve miles northwest of Dundee.
2 muirs of Lundie] moors surrounding a village about five miles southeast of Coupar Angus.
3 Ralph Waldo Emerson (1803-82), American essayist, philosopher, and poet. "A foolish consistency is the hobgoblin of little minds, adored by little statesmen and philosophers and divines" is from the essay "Self-Reliance" (*Essays*, 1841).
4 "mountain dew"] any whiskey, but especially illegally made corn whiskey.

applied to a certain association for the Suppression of Drunkenness for a situation, and he was, if I mistake not, appointed one of their missionaries, but was dismissed for a transaction with which I am entirely unacquainted. He then became what is called a "cheap John,"[1] and bade an adieu to temperance; and, as may be expected, he often found himself minus cash, stock, and credit. On the morning of that memorable day when Maberly's bank failed,[2] Tom found himself completely poverty stricken, and he entered an ironmonger's shop near the Cross[3] to solicit a little credit, as he intended to have a sale that evening at the Green Market. While plying the tradesmen with honied words previous to making the grand onslaught, Tom noticed that he had twenty of Maberly's one-pound notes in his possession. By some unknown channel or other he had got a hint of the contemplated catastrophe, and thinking this a good opportunity of ingrafting himself on the ironmonger's confidence, he quietly told him what was anticipated. In the eyes of the ironmonger Tom was at once a person of importance, and he was entrusted with the suspicious paper to get it instantly converted into good hard cash. Elated with the prospect of effecting his contemplated object, he faithfully executed his commission, delivered the twenty pounds of silver into the hands of his confidant, and that very day the bankruptcy of Maberly and Co. was announced, an announcement which fell on Dundee like an avalanche charged with the combustibles of misery, terror, and dismay. Tom chuckled at the turn affairs had taken, and the ironmonger secretly smiled at his good fortune. Ay, but the action was barely honest, and retribution was in store for him. He could not refuse to befriend his sagacious deliverer, and Tom soon got a place in his esteem, but a larger place in his books, and ultimately dropt doing business with him after he stood on the debtor side of his ledger to the tune of nearly double the amount of the Maberly notes he had so smartly put in circulation. The clever "cheap John" again returned to the awls and the bottle; but a second temperance cycle of his life having approached, he got a situation in Dingwall as a clerk, and, in a short time afterwards, he, in company with a surgeon's

---

1   a "cheap John"] or "cheap Jack" was an itinerant tradesman who usually sold cheap metal items, primarily by way of offering a lively "pitch" to passersby on the street.

2   Maberly's bank failed] the 1832 collapse of John Maberley and Co.

3   the Cross] the area in which the four principal streets of Dundee meet, the marketplace called High Street.

apprentice, started an apothecary establishment, and for some time did well, but his partner having separated from him, his abstinence resolution bent before the pressure of circumstances, and he soon melted the whole stock and trade in tumblers of porter and toddy. With no capital, excepting his education and brains, Tom migrated to Paisley,[1] and there opened a small shop in the druggist line. His plausible address and powers of mystifying the vulgar in a short time earned for him a low class popularity, and the Dundee shoemaker was only known as the skillful Dr Braine, who understood all diseases both of mind and body. Tom for some few months warded off the demands of the original demon, but all would not do,—resolutions gave way, and Bacchus[2] triumphed. The shelves of his shop gradually displayed a beggarly account of empty bottles, and last of all the bottles began to move away, and hungry creditors were to be daily seen hunting Dr Braine from one tavern to another until the tormented victim decided on flight. A fortunate event furnished him with funds. A grand soiree was to be held in J—— on the evening of a certain noble lord's birth-day, and Tom knowing that the illustrious personage was highly susceptible of flattery, he composed a sparkling song in his praise. He appeared on the platform and sang it with great effect to the tune of "Scots wha hae wi' Wallace bled."[3] Dr Braine was three times encored, and the notes of his praise reached the halls of the vain nobleman. The happy termination of his poetical panegyric is a high compliment to the keenness of Tom's perception, for on the following morning the noble Lord he eulogised sent him L.20, a fact which enables my old teacher to boast even to this day, I am told, that the only poem he ever wrote fetched him one guinea per line, being equal to the sum paid to Sir Walter Scott for each line of his best and most popular poem.[4] With the fruits of his lyrical genius Tom quietly decamped, leaving his creditors his stock in trade and the good will of his business to "settle scores," as he expressed it, and wended his way to Falkirk,[5] and in one of its suburban streets he

---

1 Paisley] an industrial town seven miles southwest of Glasgow, known in the mid-nineteenth century for its production of fine shawls.
2 Bacchus] in Roman mythology, the god of wine.
3 wha hae wi'] who have with.
4 most popular poem] perhaps a reference to Scott's *The Lady of the Lake* (1810), for which he received two thousand guineas.
5 Falkirk] a town south of the River Forth, twenty-five miles west of Edinburgh.

again attempted to live by selling drugs and pills, but the evil geni of his former days still haunted him, and in a short time he was as destitute and as needful of a lucky "wind fall," as he was on the morning of Maberly's bankruptcy. I cannot follow the footsteps of Tom any further; report sayeth that the mantle of moderation again fell on him, and that he even at times preached to some small quaint and visionary sect, whose dreams, like the responses of the Delphic Oracle,[1] are only comprehended by the chosen few. But, alas! Tom, with all his foibles and eccentricities, now lies buried in Falkirk old churchyard, having fallen victim to the pestilence which lately scourged our country.

Such, reader, is a hasty sketch of my old friend, who was naturally a person of a generous disposition and superior parts, but spoiled by inattention on the part of his parent, as all kinds of evil influences were allowed to play on his young mind; and "the mind of a young creature," as Berkeley truly says, "cannot remain empty; if you do not put into it what is good, it will gather elsewhere what is evil."[2] Though his chequered and foolish life must be strongly reprobated, yet I entertained towards him feelings only of respect and gratitude. His kindness and humanity, too, shewed that he had a good heart, and to have seen this obscure poor boy ever anxious to asists [sic] and oblige, was a sight to impress the mind with the truth that even in the ranks of the youngest and poorest, sparks of the original grandeur and divinity of human nature may often be seen. One day I got my left hand severely bruised, and I turned sick. Tom was the only fellow-worker who manifested an active sympathy for me. He got me on his back and carried me from the mill to my mother's house, and even wept for his little associate. The remembrance of that day will not soon fade from my memory. I found my mother sitting on a little stool beside the fire with her head resting on her hands and weeping bitterly. She had received a long letter from my father, giving a graphic account of the suffering he had endured as a convict, and bewailing in simple, though sincere language, the sad misfortune which had deprived him of the society of his wife and little ones. Its affectionate protestations, harrowing details, and passionate love, stained with the salt tears of a contrite spirit, had plunged my mother into an agony of grief,

---

1 Delphic Oracle] oracle of Apollo at Delphi in Greek mythology, noted for giving ambiguous answers.
2 George Berkeley (1685-1753), Irish Anglican clergyman and philosopher.

and when I was carried in maimed and sick it added greatly to her sorrow. I was put to bed, fell into a deep sleep, but awoke in a confused state of insensibility. I had dreamed such a dream—so vivid and so divine—that I can only compare it to the angelic vision seen by the little and loving daughter of Madame De Pompadour as pathetically described by Lady Bulwer,[1] or to the "sick child's dream," so affectingly painted by our own Robert Nicoll. Can it be that the aspiring and imaginative young soul, when oppressed with grief or pain, flies while its earthly tenement is wrapped in slumber, to the home of the blessed, and bathes itself in those streams of heavenly felicity, which faith can conceive but words cannot describe? I cannot answer; but I know that in that dream I was borne on by a superior being through countless constellations of stars and myriads of suns, each of which shone full of glory, and sung in harmony the praises of their Maker, and I was then laid down in a bed of flowers, the fragrance of which filled me with a burning ecstacy of delight, and I cried aloud "Oh! God," and a strain of music like the "deein' tones o' an anthem far away," burst on my ravished senses, and the far-seeing eye of the soul was opened.

> And I saw the earth that I had left,
> And I saw my mither there,
> And I saw her grieve that she was bereft,
> O! the bairn she thought sae fair.

> And I saw her pine till her spirit fled,
> Like a bird to its young one's nest,
> To that land of love; and my head was laid
> Again on my mither's breast.[2]

But when I awoke, and recovered my senses, the bright vision fled, and I found it was only a dream.

————

1 Jeanne-Antoinette Poisson, Marquise de Pompadour (1721-64), mistress of Louis XV; Rosina Bulwer-Lytton, Lady Lytton (1802-82), British novelist.
2 Robert Nicoll, "The Sick Child's Dream."

CHAPTER VI.

DRINKING HABITS IN MILLS—I LEAVE FOR A COUNTRY FACTORY—
CASE OF A POOR GIRL.

After I recovered from the accident I briefly mentioned in last chapter, I went to work in a mill at the back of the Wards,[1] and continued in it for a considerable time, though I did not like it so well as the establishment in which I was formerly employed. The workers in it were looser and coarser in their habits and conversation than those of any place I had been, and they were also much addicted to intemperance. In our times respectable flaxspinners[2] endeavour to secure the services of foremen of character and sobriety, knowing, as they must do, that a bad and licentious overseer has the power of doing vast mischief; but in the palmy days of physical force and fifteen hours' diurnal toil,[3] little attention was paid to the character even of those in power. Employers, excepting a few high-minded and generous men, wallowed in nought but a sea of selfishness and icy indifference. The common sympathies of humanity were crushed by the raging passion for gold, and the pride of wealth alienated their hearts and understandings so much from the sufferings of the young and moral necessities of the poor who toiled for them, that they surely in the whirlwind of competition and avarice, dreamed they were superior mortals born to trample and tyrannize over those whom necessity had placed at their command. Foremen of inferior character are now the exception. In those days the majority were forced to be cruel, and the position they filled tended to degrade them in their own eyes and in the eyes of all who knew that they had to drive little children by the aid of the lash. It was in this mill I first saw exhibited in a bold light the injurious influence of drunken foremen on the characters of the young of both sex. On the Saturday evenings the females, with a view of courting the favour of the overseers, were in the custom of inviting them to public houses and treating them, and it was no uncommon thing for a poor girl to spend as much in this way as would have purchased for her a comfortable dinner every day during the week; and after she had thus wasted her means on her low-minded superior, she would then be compelled to take for breakfast and

---

1 the Wards] the Ward Lands, a district on the north boundary of Dundee.
2 flaxspinners] owners of flax mills.
3 See note 1 on page 117.

dinner, the following six working days, a few potatoes roasted in the mouth of the furnace. I have even known intemperate over-seers after a debauch beg whisky from females during working hours, and for fear of offending them, they would take a can in their hand, go out as if for water to drink, then proceed to a tavern where they were known, and get credit of whisky until Sat-urday night. The liquid was then put in a small bottle well corked, laid in the can, and carried into the mill amongst the water; and if the fair smuggler was afraid of being detected by the manager, she would fix a long cord round the neck of the bottle, then tie it round her waist under the outside dress, and by this plan elude the suspicions of all parties. This scheme was often adopted in this mill, and, I believe, in too many other establishments of a similar kind: and I am afraid it is even yet practised to some extent, though decent foremen would of course spurn giving the least countenance to such a poltroonish and wicked system. It is the opinion of some men that the inevitable tendency of the mill system is to injure the female character, however well it may be conducted. This can only be partially true now, but when it was left to the individual caprices of men engaged in keen competi-tion with each other, and when the hours extended to fourteen and fifteen daily, its consequences were fearfully bad. The excess of labour, and the stringency and even harshness of the treat-ment, drove many a poor boy and girl to a life of infamy. I am almost afraid to make such statements, and draw such dark pic-tures as I have done, for fear the reader may conclude I am colouring too highly. I know that some have already jumped to that conclusion, but I assure them in all sincerity that I have only dealt in facts; and I fearlessly appeal to the evidence on the factory question, taken before the Committee of the House of Commons in 1833, which demonstrates that I have understated rather than overstated the horrors of long hours' factory slavery. Read the following extract in support of the idea I have broached relative to its influence on females. It is the evidence of a witness still living in Dundee, and his intelligence and experience appear to be extensive.

Was excessive working accompanied with excessive beating?—Yes, very frequently they were beaten. Children were not able to stand the work, and if they had made the least fault, they were beaten excessively.

Did you ever hear of any one attempting to escape from that mill?—Yes, there were two girls that made their escape from the mill through the roof of the house, and left nearly all their clothes behind them.

What became of them?—They were not brought back during the time I was there.

They finally escaped?—Yes.

Do you know any body that escaped and was brought back again?—At the time I was in that mill there was a young woman who had been kept seven months in Dundee jail for deserting, and she was brought back after having been in the jail for seven months, to make up for her lost time and the expenses incurred. One day I was alarmed by the cries of "murder" from the lowest flat, and when I went there she was lying on the floor, and the master had her by the hair of the head, and was kicking her on the face, and the blood was running down.

Was that at Duntroon Mill?—Yes.

How long ago?—About eleven years.

What was the consequence of that?—I understood it would break her engagement, and after the master had retired from the flat I opened the door and let her out, and told her to run; and the master came back, and missing her, began cursing and swearing at me for letting her out, and ordered me to run after her, which I refused to do. I stated that, owing to the ill treatment she had received, I never would be the man that would run after her to bring her back to the torture, and therefore he and I separated.

Was she brought back?—No.

Was she in a situation to get any other employment?—No, she became a prostitute, and was tried at the Circuit of Perth, and transported to Van Diemen's Land[1] for stealing.

Do you think she was very anxious to get a situation if she could have done so without resorting to those courses?—Yes, she had tried to get into service several times; but when they knew she had been at mills they would have nothing to do with her.

Do you think that that severity of treatment has not unfrequently a similar effect in driving females to improper courses?—Undoubtedly.

Thomas Carlyle, in his usual forcible and quaint way, somewhere remarks "that there should one man die ignorant who had

---

1 Van Diemen's Land] later called Tasmania, the island colony south of mainland Australia.

a capacity of knowledge, this I call a tragedy."[1] If so, surely a woman, ignorant, driven by violence and necessity to destruction, is something worse than a tragedy—it is a deliberate and dreadful crime; yet, strange it is, that, in this age of benevolence and extending sympathy for the poor, men may be found who clamour against the Legislature for stretching forth its arm in aid of factory workers, and using its power for the annihilation of a system which could produce such catastrophes! The extract I have given is brief, but it is fraught with mournful interest. The witness, in a few words, gives the elements of a melancholy story. Mark the brevity with which the dark history is told! "She became a prostitute, was tried at the Circuit of Perth, and transported to Van Diemen's Land for stealing." The girl was forced to fly from the violence of her master, and, failing to get employment in another mill, she tried to get a situation as a domestic servant, but respectable families then and even yet instinctively shun employing mill girls as household servants, knowing as they do that the atmosphere of a factory is not the best for nourishing the moral and social qualities of females, and she was thus driven, by the sheer force of circumstances, to earn the wages of sin, and then consummated her career by the commission of a crime; and the law, which did not protect from the harsh power that propelled this girl downwards, stepped forward and punished when it found her at the bottom. Methinks I hear some one whisper, "All very true, but this girl, if she had been desirous of doing well, might have saved herself, even though she was thrown out of employment by the brutality of her master; where there is a will, you know, there is a way." Such an objection is a piece of closet philosophy believed and advocated by those who are well fed and well clothed. I have found from experience that the fortunate can always give very fine advice to the unfortunate, and can tell them how they would have done if they had been placed in the same circumstances, but depend upon it, it is only the few whom God has endowed with innate power to trample down the stumbling-blocks which their condition and events place before them. The great mass of men and women are like corks on the surface of a mountain river, carried hither and thither as the torrent may lead them. Does the reader know experimentally what it is to be out of employment? Has he ever wandered about the streets looking

---

1 Thomas Carlyle (1795-1881), historian, philosopher, essayist, and critic. *Sartor Resartus*, "Helotage," III.iv.

for work and unable to find it? If he has, he must know, as he meets a rebuff here and another there, that his heart sometimes fails him, and he gives way to despair. When he looks around and sees every shop full of goods, and warehouses groaning with wealth from all the regions of the globe, and the machinery of society revolving as well without his labour as with it, he gradually imagines himself an outcast, and he falls even in his own estimation. The prolongation of his idleness increases the intensity of his trial, and through course of time he finds he will almost do anything for food. Need we wonder, then, at the termination of the black story told by the witness—"she could not find work, and she became a prostitute, and was transported to Van Diemen's Land for stealing?" Alas! poor girl, in imagination I see thee an innocent child rocked to sleep by the sweet lullaby of thy fond mother who sits by thy cradle building castles in the air for her youthful darling. In infancy I see thy parents receive the fatal summons from the angel of death, and thou left a poor uneducated orphan to be buffeted about by the cold blasts of a friendless world. Next, I see thee consigned, as was then the custom, to the care of a country mill master, who works and beats thee as if thou hadst no feelings and no soul. Then, when his cruelty comes to a climax, I see thee forced to fly, covered with blood, to seek a more genial home. Again, I see thee begging a "brother of the earth to give thee leave to toil." Thou art unsuccessful, and thou partest with the last spare article of clothing to supply thee with food. Still no helping hand is stretched forth, and despondency takes possession of thy breast. A bleak and desolate prospect opens before thine eyes, and the world appears to thee a vast gloomy vault without a single ray to make the grace of hope apparent to thy vision. Thou retirest to some solitary stair, with hair dishevelled, and heart cast down, and weepest thyself asleep. A watchman rouses thee from the solace of obliviousness, and tells thee to "move on," and thou staggerest along the street drunk with despair, and wishest thou hadst never been born. Thoughts of running "away from this world's ills" cross thy mind, and thou stealest down to the banks of the river, but the reflection of a bright light on its deep dark bosom strikes thee as the eye of Omnipotence watching thee whilst thou art about committing a crime, and thou tremblest at the awful thought of wilfully leaping into eternity. Lastly, I see thee entrapped in the nets of the wicked, and schooled in all the learning of infamy, and now the pure and guileless child has become a criminal, and is transported to Van Diemen's Land. Thy destiny excites our pity; and our condemnation is only the faint whisper which proceeds from charity. When we realise such a history as thine, like Ebenezer Elliot we exclaim "Lord help the poor!"[1]

A boy, with whom I became acquainte d[sic] while working at the back of the Wards, having advised me to run away from my mother to the country, where I could get more liberty, in company with him, I left one Monday morning, but we went no farther north then [sic] Dighty Water, as we both got employment in a small mill situated on the banks of this little river. After getting work, I told the foreman I could not commence till the following morning. I had determined in my own mind to return to Dundee, and confess to my mother what I had done, as my absence at night without her knowledge would have caused her great distress of mind. Contrary to my anticipations, she with little or no reluctance gave me my own way of it, but added that I would soon long to be at home again. I did not tire of my new home so soon as my mother prophesied. I lived there a few months, and enjoyed myself better then ever I had done during my mill life. I visited my mother every Saturday evening, stopped with her over the Sunday, and though I lived in a bothy through the week, yet it was not one of those black dirty places where no attention was paid to the separation of the sexes, which the reader may find described by witnesses before the Committee of the House of Commons, but it was cleanly and orderly kept. An old woman, who was paid by our master, cooked our victuals, made our beds, and took care that the boys and girls did not hold unnecessary intercourse with one each other. And altogether, considering the pleasant rollicking we sometimes had by the banks of the river after working hours, time glided on with less weight and pain than it used to do. Notwithstanding this, personal chastisement was the only current receipt at Dighty for correcting the faults and failings of the young. One day the application of the rod by an overseer produced a bold and ludicrous scene. A boy of the name of Martin, was engaged in oiling the machinery, and for some fault or other the foreman struck him severely with a cane. Martin, smarting under the pain of a harsh stroke on the

---

1   Ebenezer Elliot (1781-1849), poet. Because many of his poems attacked the Corn Laws and described rural poverty, he was known as the "Corn Law Rhymer."

cheek, seized a "sliver" can and hurled it at the head of his assailant. The foreman made a bound at his young adversary, with a view of revenging the insult to his dignity; but Martin wheeled round the end of a frame, and knowing the doors were all locked, he bent his head, stretched forth his arms, and dived right through the window, which was one storey from the ground. The workers in the flat all ran, looked out, and thought the boy was seriously hurt, but their fear was quickly changed to mirth, when they saw Martin running down the north bank of the river with the frame of the window on his back. The fact was, the frame was old and loose, and Martin's head and arms only penetrated through it; the shoulders forced it out of its place, and the boy, more anxious to escape than disentangle himself from the shattered though light encumbrance, ran with it dangling from his neck, while his companions, including his chastiser, sent after him nothing but peals of laughter. The bold Martin afterwards became a sailor, and was washed overboard one stormy day when his ship was entering the Tay. A very remarkable boy once worked in this mill. He was the very impersonation of stubbornness and mischief. Neither father nor foreman could control him, and severity only added fire to his recklessness. He would not work. Six times did he run away, and as often was he brought back, but all attempts to confine him proved ineffectual. At last his father resolved on a barbaric plan, the bare statement of which I am afraid will so shock the general experience of the reader, that he may set it down as a dash of romance. Nevertheless, I assure him what I am to state is strictly true, and there are men living in Dundee who can corroborate the story. The boy's father caused an iron chain to be made the length of the frame he attended. One end of it he caused to be fixed round his leg, and the other attached to a 28lb. weight, and for a number of days the boy worked in chains, as if he had been a ferocious criminal. When he went to his meat he had to shoulder the ponderous tether, and he even had to sleep with it as his companion. Made desperate by this wanton cruelty, he one night left the bothy, dashed his hand through the window of the turning shop, got a file, returned, sat down on his bed, and worked incessantly until freed from his iron tormentor. On the following morning he fled, and as far as I ever could ascertain, he was never again seen or heard of in this locality. This boy was an illegitimate son of Dan. M'Cormack, celebrated as the learned drummer of Dundee.

CHAPTER VII.

ROBINSON CRUSOE—RODERICK RANDOM—PILGRIM'S PROGRESS
—DEATH OF MY MOTHER—I GO ON TRAMP—AN ADVENTURE ON
THE ROAD—BLAIRGOWRIE—SLEEPING ON A BRIDGE.

I cannot suppose that the reader expects, or even wishes me to detail all the passages in my life, for if I were to follow such a course, I fear their prolixity would engulph their interest, and destroy their usefulness. Even in the best managed tales the authors occasionally leave a small hiatus to be filled up as the reader's taste or imagination may direct; and surely, as I am penning a simple story of real life, your generosity, courteous reader, will grant me the same artistic license in the construction of my autobiographical reminiscences. I have already noted for your amusement—may I hope instruction—a collection of the personal and collateral incidents comprised in the first three years of my factory life. I will now pass over other two years in a very cursory manner, as the relation of my mill experience would involve me in something like perfect repetition. While living on the banks of Dighty I employed myself, as far as my opportunities would permit, in self tuition, and made even respectable progress in a knowledge of light literature. An old shoemaker in Trottick lent me Robinson Crusoe and Roderick Random,[1] books which I devoured with as much gusto as I had formerly done the Life of Sir William Wallace. At this time I had no conception of fiction or romance; Robinson and Roderick I believed to be veritable characters, whose adventures and hair-breadth escapes were as true as truth itself; and, I confess, I was grievously disappointed when I afterwards learned that they were both creations of imaginative genius. From the same old book-worm I got a copy of the Pilgrim's Progress.[2] It was on a Saturday night. On the following morning, after partaking of an humble breakfast, I started for Dundee to see my mother, but, on crossing some parks for a near route, I began reading the glorious dream. I gradually walked slower as the exciting scenes were unfolded to my mind, and, on coming to a stone dyke, I mounted it, sat down, and read on. In imagination I traversed the strait and

---

1 *Robinson Crusoe* (1719) by Daniel Defoe (1660-1731) and *The Adventures of Roderick Random* (1748) by Tobias Smollett (1721-71).
2 *The Pilgrim's Progress: From this World to That Which Is to Come* (1678-84), a religious allegory, presented in the form of a dream, by John Bunyan (1628-88), English Nonconformist preacher and writer.

narrow path in company with the pilgrim, trembled at his dangers, rejoiced at his triumphs, and longed for his safe arrival. The wondrous book threw such a spell over my faculties that they forgot everything external to its pages, yea, even the certain march of time, a circumstance that old Zeno[1] would have hailed as a proof that time has no existence excepting in the human soul. The sun was descending from the sky, and the long shadow of myself as it stretched away on the top of my seat told me that sable night was rapidly approaching, and startled me from forgetfulness; and I found, on arriving in town, that I must have travelled with the pilgrim nearly six hours. I could not pass over this little illustration of my early pursuit of knowledge, as it is linked with a book which ever retains a strong hold on the heart, and is connected with the pleasantest associations of childhood. To write a book that young and old read and admire, and the characters of which become familiar as household words, is surely the greatest triumph of literary genius. On arriving at my mother's I found the door locked. At this time the fever was making great havoc in Dundee, and, as usual, the poor and unfortunate inhabitants of lanes and closes were the first objects of its rage, and my mother and brother, a neighbour told me, had both been seized by it, and taken to the Infirmary on the Wednesday previous. With a heavy heart I returned to Dighty, and when I came to a silent place, I acknowledge that I wept aloud. Solitude nourishes melancholy, and I have frequently, when brooding over misfortunes or bereavements, felt, when alone in some solitary spot, a disposition to give vent to my feelings in a flood of tears. When I dropped my work on Tuesday night, I ran off to Dundee to see my mother. I was admitted to the Infirmary, but she was insensible. I looked at her and cried, but not a sign of recognition could be elicited, and I returned with only a faint hope of ever seeing one whose affection was the sunshine of my youth, and who in prosperity and adversity was the faithful guardian and Christian mother. This was a heavy blow to my young heart, and that evening, in midst of my companions at the edge of the bothy fire, I sobbed myself asleep. Two poor orphan boys sympathised with me in my affliction. They lifted me into a bed and covered me with clothes. In my case, I found the truth of Campbell's

---

1 Probably a reference to Zeno of Elea (c. 490-c. 430 B.C.E.), a meta-physician whose famous paradoxes focused on the contradictions of time and space.

remark that "coming events cast their shadows before,"[1] for I tossed about on my bed all night, troubled with strange and even horrific visions of hearses, coffins, and graves, and early on the following morning a little boy, the son of a neighbour, came and told me that my mother and brother were both dead. The one had only lived two hours after the other. This was indeed terrible intelligence for me. I was left alone in the wide world. The event was so overpowering that I could scarcely believe it possible. In my boyish fancy I said, Surely *my* mother cannot be dead; but, alas! I was forced to say, Yes, she is dead, and I shall never see her again in this world; but, if there is truth in those doctrines she has engrafted on my mind, then after this life's "fitful fever"[2] I shall again see and know one who indeed loved me well. My mother was only a poor woman, consequently she was, in a few hours after her death, driven in the Infirmary cart to the grave, without any mourner to bewail her loss, or even any of those poetical trappings of woe which are ancient and external emblems of the feelings of the human heart when death and life are presented to the outward senses. I always feel sorrowful when I see an Infirmary funeral. It strikes me as a severe commentary on our humanity and Christianity, for I cannot but see that the factitious accident of situation, and pride of wealth, follow men as far as the chambers of the grave, and, even when the mould is heard rattling on the coffin, they heed not the monitorial sound, but practically say, "All men are not equal in the sight of God." The funeral of a poor person, too, reads us often a bitter lecture. In a large town they are daily to be seen. A few days ago I was strolling through the New Burying Ground, Constitution Road,[3] for I am fond of ruminating amongst the tombs. I was looking at a huge hole "where all the dead forgotten lie," built above each other, as if they had been hastily huddled together from the gory battlefield, when my attention was attracted by a hearse entering the cemetery followed by one solitary individual. The vehicle of the dead was decorated with the funeral garniture of age, and I felt curious to know whose remains it contained. On coming to the

---

1 Thomas Campbell (1777-1844), Scottish poet. "Tis the sunset of life gives me mystical lore, and coming events cast their shadows before," from the poem "Lochiel's Warning" (1801).

2 Shakespeare, *Macbeth* III.ii.23, "Duncan is in his grave; after life's fitful fever he sleeps well."

3 New Burying Ground, Constitution Road] a cemetery on a street that runs from the north into the center of Dundee.

grave, the single mourner, with the assistance of three sturdy sextons, deposited the coffin in its final resting place. The former gently raised his hat, while the latter, as usual, applied themselves to their duty. No tears were shed; the mourner turned to go away, but anxious to learn something of the being whose death had commanded so little kindly sympathy from neighbours and friends, and whose funeral was only attended by a single person, I accosted him and politely asked who the individual was that he had now interred. "I can tell you very little about her, he replied, her name was Susan; she lived until she was eighty-five years' of age, and resided the greater part of that time in Dundee." Are you not a relative of the deceased, I again asked. "Not I," he answered, "the old woman lived beside me, was very quiet and good, but *very poor*. The neighbours were all invited to the funeral, but when the appointed hour arrived I was the only person present." Such was all the information I could glean, and when my informant left me, I could not help exclaiming, Worthy man, the pride of wealth did not deter you from paying the last tribute of respect to poor though departed worth; but if old Susan had left stores of gold, mourners would have hovered round her death-bed and shed crocodile tears into her tomb, and thou would'st not have had to follow her funeral car alone; but like my mother she was poor, and her body was ushered out of the world, not only void of display, but even destitute of feeling and respect.

After the death of my mother I must admit that I sometimes acted very foolishly, but after all, what could be expected of a boy under twelve years of age. One Saturday night after I got my wages, I left Dighty with the intention of going to Blairgowrie.[1] The lowest class of mill-workers are very migratory in their habits. I had heard them often speak about Blair, as it is commonly called, as a place where work was easily got; and having formed some romantic kind of idea in my mind about seeing the country and ultimately going abroad in search of my father, as my poor mother had told me one Sunday a short time before her death, that he had got his liberty from the Government, and had proceeded to Australia to push his fortune, I started for Blairgowrie with these vague dreams floating through my mind. I proceeded along Strath Dighty, and entered on the Dundee and Coupar Angus turnpike road when about seven miles from the former. It was in the month of October, and by the time I reached

---

1   Blairgowrie] a town approximately fifteen miles northeast of Perth.

the range of the Sidlaws which guard Strathmore on the south, it was pitch dark, and the rain pouring from the clouds in torrents. I never was superstitious, yet some how or other, when alone amidst the rugged and sublime solitudes of nature, I have occasionally felt a slavish fear, like an icy shiver, verberate through my mind, and have even trembled at indistinctly seen physical objects, which my imagination would instantly convert into some mythical being belonging to the pantheon of Scottish superstition. The impressions of youth hold a wonderful sway over the mind, and though reason smiles, yet feeling trembles. When I approached a small bridge, which may be seen as you enter the gorge that penetrates the hills beyond Lundie, I heard a strange and unearthly sound that almost petrified me. I stood and quivered like an aspen leaf, and a cold, clammy perspiration burst out on my body. I listened attentively, indeed was almost afraid to breathe, and still the harsh guttural moaning was wafted on the breeze, and died away in the distance like the hollow grumbling of those ghosts spoken of by the son of Fingal.[1] I moved on a little farther, and the sound became louder and deeper, yet it appeared so unearthly and sorrowful, that I ascribed it to some supernatural agency, and I wonder even to this day how I did not faint. Again I drew nearer its supposed source, and watched for a time its character, still no key of a mundane cast could I discover to unlock its mystery. I began to think that I was only a little boy bent on no wicked mission, and that the evil genii of either the dead or living could have no vials of vengeance to pour out on my head, consequently I boldly leapt the stone dyke, from the opposite side of which the fearful moans and groans proceeded, and there, reader, lay, not a ghost, but an old cart horse in the agonies of death. The poor animal belonged to a farmer, who, unwilling to kill it though suffering from disease, had turned it out into a park to die. This discovery relieved my mind, but I could not altogether efface the influence of the few moments' harrowing suspense in which I was kept. I was therefore happy when I saw a light glimmering in front of me, close to the base of the hill, and on coming to the house I knocked and civilly asked for a drink of water. The matron expressed astonishment at seeing me alone in such a night, and told me to come in. I did so, and found the family all sitting in a circle, with a large potful of potatoes in the centre, which they were eating for supper. The good woman gave me a stool next the fire, and told me she would not allow me to

---

1 Ossian (see note 1 on page 253).

go any farther to-night. I needed no persuasion to comply with her benevolent determination. In a few minutes I was quite at home, while the children and parents were highly interested at my personal history, of which I most frankly gave them a truthful outline; as I described the hardships I had undergone, and the long hours I had been forced to work ever since I was seven years of age, the mother interspersed my story with practical observations, reminding her children of the comforts they enjoyed compared with a boy such as me, and quoted a suitable verse from one of Watts' Hymns,[1] which I have now forgot. I left this amiable cottar's[2] family on the following morning, but I have never forgot their kindness. More than a score of years have become part of the past eternity since I slept in this peasant home, yet the picture of their plain happy fireside is still present to my mind, and it was only about four weeks ago that I visited the place, but found by my inquiries that the father and mother were dead, and the surviving members of the family were scattered over various quarters of the globe.

When I arrived at Blairgowrie on the Sunday, it was almost dark, and I had only one shilling in my pocket. I did not know where to get lodgings, but I met a young woman having the appearance of a millspinner, who took me to a lodging-house kept by an old Highland veteran called Piper Lamond, and I was taken to a garret by his better half, and told that it was her principal bed-room for the boys who boarded with her. After partaking of a little porridge and butter milk, I went to bed, as I was tired and wearied. In the morning when I awoke, I found I had for my two bed fellows, two boys who were then notorious Dundee thieves. They had both fallen into a "snapper,"[3] as they called it, and had gone to the north to screen themselves from justice. In this lodging house there were fourteen boys and girls kept, and their beds, as well as general accommodation, were wretched in the extreme; and the example set them by the heads of the house was the reverse of decent or becoming. Filthy language was their every-day dialect, and Sabbath was uniformly spent in drunkenness and debauchery. The movement now started to provide superior homes for the poor and fatherless operatives employed in factories commends itself to the best

---

1   Isaac Watts (1674-1748), Independent minister and writer, whose *Hymns* (1707) were widely popular.
2   cottar] cottager.
3   "snapper"] blunder, trouble.

wishes and feelings of our nature, and shows that our modern philanthropists are beginning to recognise the old doctrine of Solomon,[1] which commands us by implication to join precept and example in our rearing of the young. I got work at a mill on Monday morning, and continued in Blairgowrie nearly twelve months, my wages being 3s 6d per week. I managed to live on about 2s 9d, and the balance I saved for clothes. One Saturday evening a drunken heckler,—a man nearly forty years of age—advised me into a public house to get pies and porter. After partaking of both, he called for whisky, made me drink a glass of it, and in a short time afterwards I lost all consciousness, and when I awoke from the stupor, I felt benumbed with cold, and my clothes were wet. On recovering myself a little, I found I was sitting on something like a stone dyke, yet a strange rushing noise ascended from beneath; and after carefully examining my position, I was horror-stricken on discovering that I had been sleeping on the parapet of the Bridge of Blair, a situation so dangerous that a movement of ten or twelve inches to one side would have precipitated me into the Erricht[2] amongst rugged stones, where my body would have infallibly been dashed to pieces, then submerged in the icy bosom of this mountain river. My peril had been so great that on its discovery I involuntarily burst into a flood of tears, and, to aggravate my misery, I found on searching my pockets that my week's wages were all gone. "Bought wit is the best of all wit" quoth the old proverb. In my case the truth of the saying was verified, for this incident, when I have been solicited to join for whisky to drink, has ever started up before my eyes, and like a faithful monitor cried to me, "remember the bridge of Blair." Having quarrelled with my overseer's son, I saw that my peace was gone. I accordingly left Blairgowrie on a Sunday morning, intending to come to Dundee, but I got no farther than Lochee.[3] I was so completely exhausted that I went into a public house that was kept by a kindly old man since dead, called Charles Small. I told him my story, and he very cheerfully went out and got lodgings for me. On the following morning, by the advice of my landlord, I applied at the Quarry Mill for work and was successful. I found my landlord a warm-hearted jolly old

---

1 doctrine of Solomon] perhaps a reference to the first seven chapters of Proverbs, which reputedly contain Solomon's advice addressed to "my son."
2 Erricht] The River Ericht runs near the town of Blairgowrie.
3 Lochee] a weaving village a few miles northwest of Dundee.

fellow, with a large share of waggishness in his composition. His wife was a good-natured simple creature, who delighted in ministering to her husband's comforts, and as they had no family, I was treated as if I had been their son. They occupied a snug thatched house, before which was a neat little garden, that constituted their worldly idol. My landlord was by no means troubled with new-fangled notions about liberty and knowledge. The cry for the Reform Bill[1] was by this time beginning to be heard in various parts of the north, but he could not understand this "Bill they were aye speakin' aboot;" he accordingly looked on reformers as a set of fools, who could neither work nor want. His library too was a reflex of his whole character. On the top of the drawers which stood in his room, there lay an old family Bible and a copy of the Proverbs, together with the Crook in the Lot,[2] and the Life of David Haggart.[3] One evening I asked him if he could give me a perusal of something new; he went away and examined a small trunk in which he appeared to keep his cash and papers, and brought forth a copy of Jack the Giant Killer and an old Belfast Almanack, both of which he threw down on the table, triumphantly remarking, "There's something new for you now, laddie." Young as I was, I could not help laughing at this manifestation of his conception of light and useful literature, though perhaps he was not so ignorant as he seemed, but acted on the admonition of Plato, who has said, that "it is better to be wise and not seem so, than

---

1   Reform Bill] Before the passage of the Reform Act of 1832, there was considerable political agitation in northern industrial districts. The act redistributed seats in the House of Commons to conform to recent population growth, adding seats in some areas and abolishing them in others. It also enfranchised many members of the middle classes, raising the ratio of adult males able to vote to one in five. A separate act pertaining to Scotland made the electorate there sixteen times larger than it had been.

2   Thomas Boston (1677-1732), Church of Scotland minister, author of *The Crook in the Lot, or, the Sovereignty and Wisdom of God in the Afflictions of Men.*

3   David Haggart (1801-21), *The Life of David Haggart, alias John Wilson, alias John Morison, alias Barney M'Coul, alias John M'Coulgan, alias Daniel O'Brien, alias the Switcher. Written by Himself, while under the sentence of death* (1821). Haggart was a Scottish petty criminal who was sentenced to death for murder. He wrote his autobiography in prison while awaiting his execution, which was carried out in 1821. Haggart's popular work went into three editions.

to seem wise and not be so, yet men for the most part desire the contrary."[1]

CHAPTER VIII.

I BECOME A SHOEMAKER—A COUNTRY SHOEMAKER'S SHOP—
ISAAC DOBSON, MY MASTER, A METAPHYSICIAN AND
PHRENOLOGIST.

I worked in the Quarry Mill of Lochee nearly eighteen months, lived with the same jolly landlord the whole time, and enjoyed much more comfort than the majority of mill boys who here, as elsewhere, were too often huddled into small crowded lodging-houses kept by people neither cleanly nor temperate. As I had a strong desire to get away from factory life and learn a trade, I solicited the good offices of my landlord to assist me. As he was a weaver himself, he offered to teach me to weave, but when I daily saw how handloom weavers had to toil from six in the morning until ten and eleven o'clock at night, I thought that the transition from the mill to the shuttle was like going "from the deil[2] to the deep sea." I accordingly rebelled against his proposal. On the winter evenings I used to spend most of my spare time in lounging about a shoemaker's garret in the village, where all kinds of political and religious doctrines were discussed; and though I saw that shoemakers worked very late, yet they did not rise early, and the facility they had for gossiping whilst working completely enamoured me with the art of Crispinism.[3] I there-

---

1 Plato (427-347 B.C.E.), *Apology*.
   At the end of this chapter in the version published in *The Northern Warder*, there appears the following notice: "NOTE.— The author of the 'Factory Boy' has learned with sincere regret that one of his chapters has given offence to a section of moral reformers whose principles and aims he hear[t]ily sympathises with. He solemnly assures them that if any passage he has even written can be interpreted into a condemnation of the temperance movement, that such was not his intention; and the testimony of his life is the best refutation to the insinuation of some of its injudicious friends who have charged him, at their meetings, of befriending drunkenness. His object is entirely different from the harsh construction too hastily put on his observations; and to all who cling to the opinion that he has done either systems or individuals wrong, he has only to remind them, 'to err is human, to forgive divine.'"
2 deil] devil.
3 Crispinism] shoemaking, so called for St. Crispin (c. 285), patron saint of shoemakers.

fore settled in my mind that I would adopt the trade of my father. This being decided, the next step was to get a master, who could not be got in Lochee; but my landlord, having seconded my intention with friendly zeal, soon found one for me in a small village on the western confines of Forfarshire.[1] The terms of my agreement were five years apprenticeship, my meat, and £.1 the first year, or a month's absence at the harvest, and £.1 increase of salary each year until its termination. After six months trial, I was to be bound by regular indenture, my landlord generously offering to be one of my securities, at the same time paying for one-half of the expenses of the legal document.[2] These preliminaries arranged and understood, I departed for my new home. The sight of it to me, who had lived nearly six years in towns where the poor "lie buried as in snow-drifts," and who had been confined every working day amidst the dingy atmosphere of spinning-mills, was pleasing and exhilarating. The village was perched on the brow of the elevated ridge which sweeps along the Carse of Gowrie on the north, and commanded a fine view of its fertile plains, together with the prince of Scottish rivers[3] moving on in silent majesty to the sea. An ancient baronial fortalice, in which the titled manor lords of the middle ages lived, feasted, and died, reared its time-worn battlements in the very centre of the village, and gave it an air of antiquity and importance. Close by, yet almost shrouded from the gaze of profane eyes, by the arboreous exuberance of its scenery, stood the parish church, a temple so ancient that the date of its erection is lost in the gloom of a bygone century, and its origin covered with a pious halo of traditional glory. There were likewise the parish school, the smith's shop, the wright's shop, and a grocer's shop, with a small window filled with sweeties, black sugar, and halfpenny picture books; and last of all, there was the shoemaker's shop, my master's, the centre of all kinds of gossip, the evening rendezvous for village politicians, metaphysicians, and rural theologians. I found my master a curious mixture of all sorts of extremes, the determined antipodes of every thing common sense like; in short, he hated to be like other folk. He was somewhat dogged and sullen in his disposition, and as he had a glib tongue, he spoke often, but seldom

---

1 Forfarshire] the county now called Angus.
2 legal document] See indentures, note 2 on page 97.
3 Carse of Gowrie ... prince of Scottish rivers] a wide, flat alluvial plane that extends north of Perth and Dundee between the Tay to the south and the Sidlaw Hills to the northwest.

to much purpose, though he always appeared to consider himself wondrous wise, in truth, as the infallible oracle of the hamlet. It some way or other happens that an illiterate person, who assumes, by force of character, the garb of intelligence, always passes for more than his real worth, yet at times he is doomed to have the barrenness of his mind painfully exposed, and to submit to galling humiliation. So was it with my master. He ruled as mental lord of the village during the winter months, but it so happened that the inhabitants could boast of an embryo clergyman, a young man who had been annually drilled in the classic schools of St. Andrews,[1] and when the stripling academician was rusticating at home, the light of my poor master's genius was completely eclipsed; in one word, Isaac Dobson, that was his name, sung dumb when Mr Elshender appeared. The villagers knew that he had drunk at the Pierean spring[2] of Greek and Roman lore, and they reverentially bowed when he condescended to nod. The two heroes frequently met, as the student, who was somewhat waggish, apparently delighted in tormenting poor Isaac and exposing the shallowness of his cobbled philosophy, which was a simple compound of scratches, barks, and bites, picked up at second hand from the garret retailers of modern Pyhrronism.[3] A cold, useless, barren creed is this; it is like the rotten trunk of a tree, it serves to kindle fires, but does not cheer the heart nor beautify the landscape. Mr Elshender, too, like most young men whose bodies have darkened the walls of a college, was a little proud of his acquirements, and hesitated not to assume the dogmatist when it served his purpose. On one occasion he was endeavouring to convince Isaac that there were no material bodies existing in the universe, that all physical phenomena were nothing more than ideas in the mind. To illustrate his doctrine he took up a piece of leather and proceeded as follows. "Now, Mr Dobson, what do you see?" "Oh, I see a bit of my own leather," replied Isaac. "Not at all," responded his interrogator, "you only see colour, now colour cannot be matter. Now take a hold of it in your hand, what do you feel?" "Feel," answered my master, apparently dumfoundered at this specious piece of Berkleian

---

1 St. Andrews] Scotland's first university, founded in 1412-13, located in the town of St. Andrews on the coast south of Dundee.
2 Pierean spring] a fountain in Pieria, sacred to the Muses and supposedly conferring inspiration or learning on anyone who drank from it.
3 Phyrronism] extreme or absolute skepticism; so called for Pyrrho (c. 365-c.275 B.C.E.), Greek philosopher.

mysticism, "why, I feel a bit o' my ain guid kip[1] hide that I bought in yon leather warehouse, at the tap[2] of the Burial Wynd." "Nonsense, my dear Sir," said the student, "you cannot prove you feel leather, you only feel resistance; now resistance cannot be kip, as you call it. Take any object within your reach, look at it, feel it, smell it, yet you cannot prove to me that any thing exists excepting the idea or sensation in your mind. Subtract the idea from your soul, and what remains to convince you that there is aught in the universe but spirit? The same with space," continued Mr Elshender, "and time. There can be no time external to the soul, or even absolute space. What you call time is only a succession of ideas passing through the mind; in fact, everything exists only in idea, and, beyond the mind, or great Spirit of the universe, there is nothing." This philosophy was beyond poor Dobson's depth. He was smitten with the itch of materialism, could not understand or comprehend any speculation which did not square exactly with this gross business kind of creed, and Mr Elshender meant his little blast of metaphysics as dust to blind the pretender's eyes, and as an instance how reasonable any doctrine may be made to appear if ingeniously stated and cleverly supported. Though the young divine silenced the pugnacious Isaac, yet there was one present earnestly listening to his disquisition who, when he spoke of there being no time, opened his mouth, shrugged his shoulders, and looked at the student's eyes, as if hunting for symptoms of insanity. At length he started to his feet, and exclaimed, "My troth, if you had to trench in a muir[3] ten hours every day, you would ken whether there's time or no. I doubt you would conclude, friend, that the practice was mair a reality than an idea." Such was the reflection of a labourer on the doctrine of idealism. It was the philosophy of common sense, and "common sense," says Guizot, "is the genius of humanity."[4] Tilts similar to the above were quite common in my master's shop, as he industriously picked up any ideas dropped by Mr Elshender, and astonished some of the rustic controversialists by making them the buckler and armour for other displays of his prowess. I must admit that such crude contests excited my curiosity, and

---

1 kip] calf or lamb.
2 tap] top.
3 trench in a muir] dig or cut into rough land or peat.
4 François Pierre Guizot (1787-1874), French historian and politician.
   The quotation is from Johann Wolfgang von Goethe (1749-1832),
   German poet, novelist, and dramatist.

inspired me with a longing to "prove all things, and hold fast that which is good,"[1] and likewise helped to keep alive that passion for reading which had already been generated in my mind. I had now better opportunities for reading than I ever had at my command. In the village there was an excellent library of books in all departments of knowledge, the charge to apprentices being only one shilling per quarter; and though my spare time was scanty, yet during the meal hours, in the summer months, it was my invariable practice to retire to a large park in the vicinity of my master's, stretch myself on the grass, and read until I heard the smith's hammers, which were the signal for me to rise and run. I am afraid, if I were to encourage the reader on the path of self-improvement by telling him the difficulties I had, even as a shoemaker, to encounter, and the number of books I read frequently when I should have been in my bed, that he would scarcely believe me. Let the simple fact suffice, that I read while an apprentice books on nearly all the disputed questions in theology and metaphysics, books on history, belles letters, and science. I even read the celebrated Decline and Fall of the Roman Empire[2] three times from beginning to end. I beg of the reader not to conclude that I am giving these facts in a spirit of pride and ostentation. Such unworthy motives are distant from my mind. I give them as an example of what even a poor working boy may do to improve his faculties, and elevate himself under adverse circumstances, for it is a favourite doctrine of mine that the working classes have better opportunities for self-culture than the middle classes. From the very nature of the circumstances in which they move, their minds are not racked and tortured with so many cares and anxieties as professional and mercantile men. After their day's toil, no ghost of a suspicious bargain haunts them in privacy, and even forbids their eyes to close in slumber, but easy in the conviction that they have fulfilled their diurnal duties, they can quietly explore the pages of the historian, or carefully examine the refined speculations of the philosopher. At the end of the first six months I was bound by indenture according to the terms already mentioned, and I hope diligently attended to my own and master's interest. I have observed boys take a particular delight in getting time dispensed with in an easy and slovenly manner, the ruling idea of their conduct being, that they were

---

1   1 Thessalonians 5:21.
2   *The History of the Decline and Fall of the Roman Empire* (1776-88), by Edward Gibbon (1737-94), English historian.

taking advantage of their masters, whereas they are in reality taking a serious and permanent advantage of themselves; and I have always observed, without even a single exception, that boys who conduct themselves in this way, turn out inferior workmen; and let me tell the young of the working classes that the pride, independence, and even happiness of those who have to work for their daily bread depends on their ability to do work expeditiously and well; hence the importance of industry, anxiety, and care on the part of apprentices.

In our comparatively secluded rural retreat, we were not much troubled with startling novelties either in politics or religion. Occasionally some wandering wight would throw the community into a state of intense excitement by announcing the grand juvenile spectacle of "Punch and Judy,"[1] the whole to conclude with eating fire and swallowing a sword; or perchance the remains of an actor would sometimes appear, post a written placard on the smithy door, and call the inhabitants together to hear him in a barn, mounted on a firlot measure,[2] recite "Hamlet's Soliloquy on Death,"[3] "Number One," or, "My name is Norval on the Grampian hills,"[4] &c. Such exhibitions, though they produced a sensation, only afforded talk to the inhabitants for a few days; but the crowning event in our history was the introduction of Phrenology.[5] It was a perfect epoch in our village, so much so, that the farmers even to this day are often heard say, "It was a guid year that year the Phrenology came here!" It was strange, you may be thinking reader, that the proclamation of the science of brains should have caused such a stir in our clachan,[6] but the real cause lay in the fact, that it almost turned my master's brains, which at the best were only balanced on a pivot. I yet recollect the eventful night, the parish school was the theatre, the lecturer was

---

1 "Punch and Judy"] a slapstick puppet show with the principal characters Punch, a buffoon, and his wife Judy.
2 firlot measure] a container used to measure grain, much like a bushel basket.
3 Shakespeare, *Hamlet* III. i. 56-68: "To be or not to be, that is the question...."
4 "My name is Norval; on the Grampian hills/My father feeds his flocks." John Home (1722-1808), Scottish dramatist, *Douglas* II.i.
5 Phrenology] psychological theory popular during the nineteenth century; based on reading the bumps on a person's skull, in the belief that certain mental faculties and character traits are indicated by those configurations.
6 clachan] village.

a lank bare-boned tailor named M'Glashan, and Dundee was the birth-place of the philosopher of bumps, who essayed to tell fortunes, by scanning protuberances of flesh and bone. When he entered the school-room ladened *cap a pie*[1] with busts and human skulls, he looked as if he had deserted from our ancient graveyard, and the rustics were awe-struck at his presence. His prelection on organs and skulls made us all gape in amazement, and nearly overturned our venerable notions of the dignity of man. After the lecture, the tailor began to manipulate heads and tell fortunes at one shilling per head, and my master's cranium was subjected to a minute inspection. M'Glashan, who I suspect was a bit of a wag, discovered the true character of his customer more from his forward manner than his bumpological development, and made several shrewd guesses highly flattering to his vanity; the consequence was, that Isaac Dobson at once subscribed to the new psychology, in fact, became a phrenological monomaniac. New converts are always enthusiasts; and they can only see the animate and inanimate world through the spectacles of their fresh-born ideas. My master became quite drunk with phrenological enthusiasm—he interpreted all fortunes and misfortunes by the magic of an organ.[2] If I made the slightest mistake, he would seize me by the head and cry out, "You are deficient, man, in the organ of order." If Mrs Dobson ventured to take a quiet cup of tea by herself on an afternoon, he would exclaim, "Your organ of Alimentativeness must be increasing in size, let's feel your head." If a customer entered his shop to get measured for boots or shoes, the first question put to him was, "let's feel your head?" If a stranger solicited credit, he was doomed to be minutely "gribbled" about the region of conscientiousness, and if he was blessed with a good bump in that quarter, his name was fearlessly entered in the ledger; but if the anticipations founded on Isaac's manipulations were afterwards discovered to be deceptive, he would declare, "Well, I forgot to feel his acquisitiveness." Mr Dobson's craniological researches were not confined to the biped creation; though he carried his "size sticks" in his pocket, and when measuring feet he also with the same instrument measured heads, yet he hesitated not to submit all quadrupeds within his reach to the researches of his inquisitive fingers. One day Mrs Dobson called on me to come to breakfast, and on entering the kitchen I found my master seated

---

1   *cap a pie*] from head to foot.
2   an organ] a part of the brain.

at the table, with the cat in his arms, busy investigating the peculiarities of its bumps. Poor puss not sympathising with her master's scientific passion, struggled for some time to escape; at last becoming desperate by the continued fingering at its head, it fixed its claws in Isaac's face and scratched him severely. The phrenologist suddenly let loose the object of his studies, at the same time rather pettishly remarking, "That beast has the organ of destructiveness very fully developed." After my master's craniological mania had subsided, he became a perfect knight errant in anti-ghostism. Wherever he heard of an old woman who believed in the supernatural, he was sure to visit her and proceed to demolish her cherished creed, with what success the reader may safely conclude. In one word, my master was an extraordinary character—a perfect compound of whims, extremes, oddities, and eccentricities. At one time I was a great favourite, a genius who would yet make a noise in the world, at other times I was a dunce, born to live and die without doing any good to society or even myself—at another he would declare my language and ideality were enormous, and that he was sure I would be a great poet or a writer of romance, but never a good shoemaker. Without boldly telling Mr Dobson that he was cracked in the upper tenements, I only laughed at his folly, and longed for an opportunity of breaking through the legal chain which bound me as his servant. By accident I effected my object, and as the plan was as novel as it was effacacious, I must relate it. I must premise that at this early age I had a knack of writing verses and satirical lampoons on the passing events of our locality. These juvenile effusions of my brain are long since consigned to the flames, and it would be fortunate for ninety-nine poetasters out of every hundred if they would dispose of their sickly productions in a similar manner, as it would save them a world of vexation and disappointment. Well, as may be expected, my master was too good a target to shoot at to escape my young shafts. I accordingly penned a rather respectable parody on "Rob Roryson's Bonnet," in which the weak and prominent points of Mr Dobson's character were rather ludicrously and painfully exposed. The song got abroad. The dignity of the philosopher was wounded, and the pride of the master lowered. The author was discovered and ordered to quit the premises of the offended hero of the doggerel *jeu d'esprit*.[1] Accordingly, reader, I packed up my awls, and entered on my career as a journeyman shoemaker. Mr. Dobson

---

1 *jeu d'esprit*] a light literary work showing wit or intelligence.

talked about prosecuting my securities, but found that I occupied the vantage ground, and for aught I know my indenture is still in the hands of the executors of the late David Smith, Esq., writer, Dundee.

CHAPTER IX.
I RETURN TO DUNDEE—AN EPISODE IN LIFE—ROBERT NICOLL, THE POET.

After my summary dismissal from the service of Mr Isaac Dobson, I determined to apply for work as a journeyman. I had been fully two years at the trade, and had a respectable knowledge of all its arts and mysteries. I had little difficulty in achieving my object, and I continued working in the country rather more than three years. I returned to Dundee in the summer of 1835, and found employment as a "woman's man," as the shoemakers call it, that is, an operative who confines himself to the making of women's shoes. During all this time I had heard no word from my father. A friend had written to Australia to try and discover if he still lived; and in the same letter the melancholy news of my mother and brother's death were detailed; but five years had elapsed since this letter was sent off, and no answer had been received. I had almost forgot about him, not having seen him since I was seven years of age. I can barely say that I felt the warm glow of affection which lights up the hearts of the young in presence of their parents. I was now almost twenty years of age, and had even lost all distinct recollection of my father's personal appearance, and when I tried to realize him to my mental eye, he faded from my imagination like a dear friend who has long been dead. When I returned to Dundee, the scene of my former trials and sufferings, I could not help feeling a deep sense of gratitude when I thought on what I was compared with what I had been. True, I was only an operative, but who is more independent and happy than the unmarried, temperate, and good workman. He has less anxiety of mind, and fewer troubles than any class I know of. If he attends to his work, is prudent, and cultivates his mind, he undoubtedly occupies a felicitous position, the sweets of which are only known to those who have tasted of them. If I ever drank of the waters of that holy river called happiness, and whose fountain head is in the "better land," it was when I was a journeyman in Dundee. I easily earned as much as kept me comfortable, and I soon formed a friendly connection with a number of young men of the operative class, whose general intelligence and social deportment would have done honour to any section of society. Their mental aspirations were of a high order, and they freely indulged in discussions on all the various branches of knowledge. An intellectual clergyman, who in those days lived in Dundee, and frequently lectured on science, was the centre around which we circulated; and he delighted in instructing and aiding the studies of his young friends, and the impetus which his conversations and example communicated to their minds materially influenced their after lives. Our little community were all about one age, and the attachment that existed amongst us was reciprocal and sincere. An humble but passionate student of nature, now dead, organised us into a Zoological and Botanical Society, and in his own private museum in the Scouringburn,[1] he weekly drilled us in these interesting sciences. With our tutor as our guide we also had regular floral rambles in the country. In the summer months we rose early, and wandered out in the fields in search of specimens, and often have we climbed the brow of Balgay while the dew drops hung from the tiny grass, and like orient pearls sparkled in the rays of the god of day, as he emerged in full majesty from the bosom of the German Ocean. The specimens gathered were carefully carried to Dundee, and furnished matter for several evening prelections on the flowery science. We had likewise a select debating society, where an original essay was read by each member in succession, and the subject treated of was then fearlessly canvassed by all present. No specific plan was laid down for our guidance, nor any chains imposed on our daring young spirits. We wrote papers on History, Literature, Religion, Theology, and Metaphysics, a branch of study which has been aptly defined as "groping for a science in the dark." It was a custom with a few of us to meet every Monday night in Denham's Hotel, then situated in the Seagate, to enjoy a kind of family supper, and talk over our hopes and aspirations, and even indulge in gentle tilts on our favourite speculative dogmas. I acknowledge our opinions were somewhat extreme, they were the hot and burning scintillations of liberty-loving and imaginative souls, who in the hey-day of youth worship the ideal of beauty and reason, and wonder at all who do not bow before the same idols as they do. The mention of Denham's Hotel recalls an episode to my mind which I will present to the reader.

---

1 Scouringburn] a district in Dundee.

It was on a Sunday evening in the spring of 1836, that four young men, three of whom were barely out of their teens, were sitting in a small though comfortable room, in this establishment. The oldest of the four had only reached his twenty-second year. He was fully above the middle height, slenderly formed, and stooped slightly when he walked. He had a delicate and thoughtful expression of face, which was lighted up with large intellectual eyes of intense blue. His brow was lofty, and shaded by dark brown hair, and his manner of address, as well as general appearance, was winning and pleasing; so much so, that his young friends listened to the sweet flow of his conversation as if he had drunk at the living fountain of inspiration. The other three were then working men, but earnest disciples of literature and science. One of them had a drooping wild flower fixed in the breast of his coat, which he sat quietly examining with apparent interest, as if regardless of the lively conversation of the coterie. At last one of the three snatched the flower from him, and made a careless remark which led to a keen discussion of the doctrine of final causes, and the legitimate province of reason, but the oldest stopped the contest by remarking, "Now you all know, friends, that I have different opinions on many speculative subjects from most of you. You are great admirers of the faculty of reason; so am I. Some of you, however, would discard all beliefs that do not come down or square with your reason. I would not do so. Let me give you a single instance. The universal instincts of humanity yearn after a life to come. The truth of this doctrine is stamped on the heart of man, and is the very foundation of what men in all ages have looked on as their highest and holiest concern. Now, I do not ask my reason if this doctrine is in harmony with its fallible laws. I know that it is true to my feelings, and I reverence what is true to my feelings as much as what is true to my reason. My feelings are as important a part of myself as my reason, and I cannot—dare not—set up the latter as the only touchstone of truth, while the former is perhaps the best guide of the two. In one word, I consider there is a duality in man and a duality in truth, and I am convinced that the truths of the feelings, if I may so express myself, exercise a greater influence on society than the truths of the reason. There has been a fierce battle going on in Europe since the days of Voltaire[1] between these two classes of truths, but the champions of reason make little progress, and

---

1 Voltaire, or François-Marie Arouet (1694-1778), French philosopher, historian, dramatist, and essayist; leading voice of the Enlightenment.

wield no moral power amongst men. The truths of the feelings originate all spiritual and moral force, and stand forth as pre-eminently divine. This is my conscientious opinion on this vexed question, and I have no doubt that more extensive experience and reflection will convince all of you that you are somewhat too fiery in your praise of reason." After these remarks were delivered, silence reigned for a few minutes in the company, which was at last broken by the youngest of the party, who asked if any of them had heard that there was to be supper in Campbell's Hotel, commemorative of the third centenary of the Reformation?[1] Oh yes, answered the former speaker, I am to be present. In fact I am to make a speech. I have likewise been requested to write a hymn suitable for the occasion. "And have you not written it?" was the question simultaneously put by all present. "Yes, I have," was the succinct reply. "Then, do let us hear it," was the united response. "I have no objections," said the young poet, at the same time drawing his manuscript from his pocket, "but I beg of you not to judge it too harshly, as I have written it hurriedly." He then read the following anthem in praise of the Reformation:—

> An offering to the Shrine of Power
>> *Our* hands shall never bring;
> A garland on the car of Pomp
>> *Our* hands shall never fling!
>
> Applauding in the Conqueror's path
>> *Our* voices ne'er shall be;
> But we have hearts to honour those
>> Who bade the world go free!
>
> Stern Ignorance man's Soul had bound
>> In fetters, rusted o'er
> With tears—with scalding human tears—
>> And red with human gore!
>
> But men arose—*the* MEN to whom
>> We bend the freeman's knee,
> Who, God-encouraged, burst the chain,
>> And made our fathers free!

---

1   Campbell's Hotel ... Reformation] For this event, see Appendix C.2 and
    Introduction 34.

Light dwelt where Darkness once had been—
　　The morn of Mind arose—
The dawning of that Day of Love
　　Which never more shall close.
Joy grew more joyful, and more green
　　The valley and the lea—
The glorious Sun from Heaven look'd down
　　And smiled upon the Free!

Truth came and made its home below;
　　And Universal Love
And Brotherhood, and Peace and Joy,
　　Are following from above.

And happy ages on the earth
　　Humanity shall see;
And happy lips shall bless their names
　　Who made our children free.

Praise to the Good—the Pure—the Great—
　　Who made us what we are are!—
Who lit the flame which yet shall glow
　　With radiance brighter far.

Glory to them in coming time,
　　And through Eternity;
They burst the Captive's galling chain,
　　And bade the world go free.[1]

On concluding the reading of this anthem, which was given with modest enthusiasm, the writer received the sincere congratulations of his friends, and the party broke up, but not until they all declared they would be present at the supper to hear the hymn sung. On arriving at the top of the Seagate they separated, and they never again met. Their destinies were very different, yet interesting. The young man, who sat silently examining the wild flower in his breast, was William Jackson, jun., the well-known Dundee naturalist, a sketch of whose life and labours lately

---

1　This poem was published in Robert Nicoll's *Poems and Lyrics* as "The Bursting of the Chain: An Anthem for the Third Centenary of the Reformation."

appeared in *Chambers' Edinburgh Journal*.[1] Mr Jackson, like his gifted father, was for a few years janitor of the Mechanics' Institution,[2] and prosecuted the study of botany with almost unexampled devotion, but sank into a premature grave nearly two years ago. Another of this select band was a mechanic of promise and talent of the name of Robert Forbes. Endowed with a fine flow of animal spirits, and a vast fund of humour, young Forbes was the idol of his friends, and the delight of every circle in which he moved. While little more than a boy he left Dundee for London to push his fortune, and, like numbers of other young men who plunge into that boundless sea of activity and life, he had to pass through many severe vicissitudes, but he never lost the buoyant perseverance of his character and general vivacity of his nature. While out of employment he busied himself corresponding with provincial newspapers, and in the *Dundee Advertiser* for 1840 I find several of young Forbes's communications headed "From London," and signed "Ope." At last he got a lucrative situation as a Government engineer, and was sent to India, where he contracted the seeds of a fatal disease. His sturdy constitution and sprightly spirits battled strongly with the insidious foe, and his superiors, anxious for his recovery, sent him to another clime in the hope that the march of the enemy would be arrested. But, alas! poor Forbes was beyond the reach of human aid. Death had already set its black seal on his young heart. In Aden in Arabia, he breathed his last, and now, far from his native Dundee, he sleeps the sleep of the grave in that genial though distant land. The third and oldest of this little party, as the reader no doubt has anticipated, was the amiable and gifted Robert Nicoll, who has been called by the late Ebenezer Elliot, "Scotland's second Burns." At this time he kept a circulating library in Castle Street,[3] Dundee, but left it at Whitsunday 1836. He went to Edinburgh, and shortly afterwards became Editor of the *Leeds Times*, a paper which he advanced in circulation about 200 every week for a number of weeks after he got the management of it; but the seeds of death too were germinating in Nicoll's constitution, and the excitement of political party strife nourished them and prepared him for an early tomb. He resigned his Editorship and came to Scotland to seek for health amidst the invigorating

---

1   This article, "William Jackson, The Naturalist," appeared in *Chambers Edinburgh Journal* 12 (July-December 1849): 165-66.
2   Mechanics' Institution] See note 1 on page 201.
3   Castle Street] a street near the docks in central Dundee.

breezes of his native mountains. He got no farther than Edin-burgh, where he died, in the house of Mrs Johnstone, and now he lies buried in North Leith churchyard.[1] Robert Nicoll is not yet sufficiently known. True, his genius was not of that dazzling cast, which, like a mighty meteor, astonishes the world, but it was a calm, holy, and radiant light, the beams of which were always charged with pure morality and undefiled religion. Let the reader recollect that he died in his twenty-fourth year. Nicoll had a grand conception of the influence and mission of literary men, and disdained to sully the light which God had kindled in his soul, by the unholy and accursed fumes of vice and immorality. "I fervently hope," he said, writing to a friend, "that the time has for ever gone by when genius was considered an excuse for evil—when the man who could appreciate and express the beautiful and true was supposed to be at liberty to scorn all truth, and all beauty, mental and moral. Our influence on mankind may be small, but it will ever be exerted to purify, and better, and enlighten. The time has come, the day of human improvement is growing to noon, and henceforth men with free and disenthralled souls will strive to make them in very truth 'a temple where a God might dwell.' If the men of mind would but join to intellectual power, more simple-mindedness and purity of heart, if they would but strive to be morally as well as intel-lectually great, there would be fewer complaints against man's proneness to mammon worship. The only legitimate power in sublunary things, *mind*—would, as it ought—aye, and as it will—if men be true to themselves, have its due influence and honour. Literary men, too, now begin to see the power and glory of their own mission, and this is both an omen and an earnest of much good. Oh! for a man like blind old John Milton[2] to lead the way in moral and intellectual improvement, to moral and intellectual light and glory." Such are the lofty and pure aspirations of the warm-hearted and innocent Robert Nicoll. He has stated that he wrote his heart in his poems, and it is worth recording that in these poems there is nothing offen-sive to morality, or what men have universally considered the most sacred of things. I fervently hope that a cheap edition of Nicoll's poems will shortly appear, as I feel certain that he has only to be known to be loved, and that the advance of time will

---

1   See Appendix C. 2.
2   John Milton (1608-74), English poet.

only advance his fame, and add new lustre to his mental and moral greatness. Of the four young men then, reader, who met in Denham's Hotel in the spring of 1836, three are dead, and I have given you a faithful statement of their names, characters, and final ending of this weary pilgrimage, and you may ask me, but what has all this episode to do with your life? Very little, I must admit, but I made the fourth of this little company, *and I alone live*, and gratitude for the memory of my dear friends prompted me to bestow this passing notice of them, especially as I have said so much about myself already, and the incident, methinks, though a transcript from real life, is not altogether devoid of solemn interest and even touching romance.

CHAPTER X.
MY MARRIAGE—I DISCOVER MY FATHER—CONCLUSION.

My story of real life now draws to a close. Those chapters containing the most interest and usefulness have already been told, and few would thank me to describe the common routine of every day life, especially as it was not characterised by any remarkable personal phenomena. Indeed, it was similar to that of other young men of an ardent disposition and ambitious mind. There was one thing I at all times made a religious point of my character, and that was not to spend my hard worked for earnings in animal indulgences. I daily saw the baneful influence of whisky on too many of my fellow-workmen, and instead of imitating their courses, I strived to avoid them, for I could not resist the solemn impression that a momentary phrenzy, produced by intoxicating drinks, had precipitated my own parent from a respectable position, and exiled him from the bosom of his family and country. I had always been studious and anxious to extend the boundaries of my knowledge, and even after I was twenty years of age I attended evening schools, and rarely lost an opportunity of improving the educational materials my teachers furnished me. It is quite possible for a working man whose education has been neglected in youth to educate himself after he arrives at manhood, and even make himself master of those branches which are necessary to enable him to fill situations of trust and respectability. I began when quite a boy, as the reader already knows, to practise composition, such as writing paragraphs, anecdotes, short essays or little stories, and the parody on "Rob Roryson's Bonnet," was not the only time I woo'ed and won the favours of the tuneful nine,[1] for when first smitten by the pawky[2] beams of a maiden's eye, I embalmed her perfections in lengthened poetical stanzas; but bear in mind, reader, I prudently burned them after the days of love and romance had gone by. Sweet, though sentimental, is the remembrance of young love. After all, life would be robbed of much of its felicity and romance if it were not for our early loves. I have often thought that its joys and pleasant foibles are compensation for after troubles, benevolently paid in advance; and their sweet recollections tell us that the world is not such a bad world as the misanthrope believes. A young man who has never been in love is an oddity in creation. I pity him; for life, before it buds and blossoms into manhood, needs the sunshine of love to ripen and prepare it for the rude buffettings of the world. Well and truly has the inspired ploughman said:—

> There's nought but care on every han'
> In every hour that passes O,
> What signifies the life o' man,
> An 'twere na[3] for the lassies O.[4]

There is one event I cannot pass over, as the day on which it happened was perhaps the proudest of my life. Young aspirants for literary laurels will appreciate my motives and sympathise with me in my joy. The following is the circumstance. In my leisure hours I wrote a short story, the elements of which were drawn from my every day experience. It was intitled the "Demon of Crispin." The aim of it was to show that intemperance was the great curse of the poor, and that working men have at their own command the lever to elevate their social condition. It pictured a young man, an excellent workman, who had come from the country, healthy and innocent, but who had become entangled amongst bad associates, was made a drunkard, and finally driven, under the influence of whisky, to commit a crime. As a contrast to this a more cheerful painting was exhibited, in which a poor friendless boy was represented as struggling to educate and keep himself living. He obtained a trade, came to reside in a town, saved money by

---

1 tuneful nine] the muses.
2 pawky] tricky, sly, or cunning.
3 'twere na] were it not.
4 Robert Burns (1759-96), "Green Grow the Rashes" (1784). Burns
   worked as a ploughman on his father's very poor farm.

industry, and ultimately rose to eminence as a merchant. The tale was good in its purpose, though defective in constructive art. With all its imperfections I sent it to the editor of a respectable periodical, and it was inserted. When I received a polite note from the editor thanking me for my contribution, I felt as none can feel but those who have essayed authorship, been unsuccessful, but finally triumph. When Robert Nicoll's first tale appeared in *Johnston's Magazine* he immediately wrote to his brother in the country, and the first words of his letter were, "Dear William, I have great news to tell you," shewing the deep feeling of joy which pervaded the young poet's heart on beholding the first printed emanation of his genius. My joy was as great as Nicoll's, though I had no brother's ear in which to pour the glad tidings. Yet I had a circle of friends to whom I proudly communicated the "great news." It was an exciting and happy morning of my life, when I arose from my bed and found "The Demon of Crispin," in the columns of a periodical. I had certainly some reason to congratulate myself. I was left a poor orphan boy with an education so limited that I could barely read. Now I had, by an indomitable spirit of perseverance, overcome educational barriers and social adversities and was enabled to convey my thoughts in respectable English. Achievements such as these, reader, I am not ashamed to be proud of and I relate them with a lively faith that they will kindle in some poor boy's mind the flame of hope, and spirit of emulation. These sensitive times are gone by. When I seized the pen to trace each successive chapter of my experience, I was neither troubled with hopes nor fears. I freely noted down the current of my thoughts, and scarcely asked myself the question,—is this sufficiently good to appear in print, or will it please the reader? Experience has blunted my love of praise, and almost made me callous to the sneers of hypercritics. Fifteen years ago, if I had heard a whisper of scorn against my dear "Demon of Crispin," I certainly would not have slept for two or three nights, but the progress of time has dissipated such foolish excitability from my mind.

I now ask the imagination of the reader to leap over a period of fully twelve years. I had saved a little money, with which I purchased a small piece of ground in a growing village, not many miles distant from Dundee. Here I built, at a moderate expense, a neat little cottage; surrounded it with a fine flower garden, which had ever been an object of my ambition, since my friend in Dundee had learned me to understand and love flowers. I then started business; and, in a few days, an elegant sign was suspended above my door, which ran thus:—"Frank Forrest, boot and shoemaker." Being unmarried, my trade rapidly extended. I am convinced that young men starting business in my line in the country should never marry until they are thoroughly established. All the young lasses who are not engaged are sure to patronise them. This is a practical hint, derived from my experience, and is worth the attention of those entering on life. I would have been more than mortal if I had long resisted the captivating smiles of so many blooming young country damsels, of whom our village could boast of not a few. There was one whose modesty and good sense I had often admired. She was the daughter of an old man who had long served his country, but was now decrepit, and unable to move without being assisted by his daughter; and the affection and tenderly care she manifested towards her aged parent raised her in my esteem, and finally won my affections. The village, perhaps, contained greater beauties than she was; but then beauty is but "skin deep," and the young man whose affections are rivetted by physical beauty, regardless of the beauty of the mind, will often have to regret that he made the former the sole test of female fitness to be a companion, wife, and mother. Our marriage was arranged and the happy day arrived; and, as a small token of respect and manifestation of gratitude, I invited my old Lochee landlord and his wife, both of whom still live. He was amongst the first guests who arrived, and appeared the happiest and proudest of the company. He cracked jokes, told funny stories, related anecdotes, and kept everybody in as good humour as himself. At last, with great gravity, he asked if I recollected of him giving me an old Belfast Almanac to read. Of course I had not forgotten this, and the details of the circumstance amused the party, and recalled many pleasing reminiscences; and, when I rose and proposed my kind-hearted landlord's health, detailed the disinterested benevolence of his actions, and ascribed to him the whole of my subsequent success in life, a thrill of delight ran through the company. They started simultaneously to their feet, surrounded him in a group, and shook him warmly by the hand. The old man was deeply affected by this unexpected display of sympathy. In returning thanks he was only able to say, "I am much obliged to you all. God bless you." Not content with seeing me married, he came on the following Sunday morning a distance of six miles to see my wife and me "kirkit;"[1] and the affectionate regard he has since shown towards us convinces me that

---

1 "kirkit"] attending church for the first time after marriage.

he looks on us as beings to whom he has some natural right. I cannot but love him, as I respect and labour to live in harmony with the noble sentiment of Confucius, "Love all mankind, but cherish those who are good; forget injuries, but never benefits."[1]

Nearly twenty years had rolled past since I had heard any word of my father. I had concluded that he had died amongst strangers, unnoticed and unknown; yet now and then a thought would steal across my mind that he perhaps still lived, though the hope was nearly groundless, as I was loath to believe that he would allow such a number of years to pass without making an effort to discover if his only son was alive. Yet I thought he might have often written to Dundee after my mother's death enquiring after me; but letters coming to an obscure boy, who had retired into the country, could not, by any possibility, reach their destination,[sic] They would be sent to the Dead Letter Office, read, and consumed. And, as he had no relatives with whom he could communicate, he would write to myself alone, and as letter after letter was sent off and no answer returned, he might give up all hope, and mournfully conclude that he had not a child left on earth. When such thoughts stole in upon my reveries, I often said to myself—Perhaps my father is still alive, and I am blameable in not instituting immediate enquiries; at least before I exhaust all possible attempts to discover something positive, relative to his destiny, I ought not to rest satisfied. Animated with such convictions, I began to ferret out all memorials of him which my mother had left at her death. I ransacked an old chest that I had preserved, as it was the only piece of furniture I procured of my mother's, and in which I kept old newspapers, periodicals, and scraps of half finished tales, &c: and at its bottom I found the last letter that my mother had received. It contained the joyful intelligence of his release from bondage, and an account of his safe arrival at Sydney, New South Wales,[2] and promised, in the event of his being fortunate, in the land of his adoption, to send home for his wife and family. This letter afforded me little clue, as I had no conception whether he had actually settled in Sydney or not. I was about resigning all attempts at discovery, when I happened to mention the subject confidentially to a friend in Dundee. He

---

1   Confucius, fifth-sixth century B.C.E. Chinese philosopher and teacher, famous for many maxims stressing love for humanity, ancestor worship, reverence for parents, and harmony in thought and conduct.
2   Sydney, New South Wales] town and province in southeast Australia.

advised me to write immediately to the chief of the Sydney police, giving him the dtate [*sic*] of my father's arrival, describing his personal appearance, trade and country, but taking care to say nothing to compromise him in the eyes of respectable people, as it was highly probable, if he was alive, that he was in good circumstances. On receiving this prudent advice, I went home, wrote, and posted the following letter:—

Sir,—A stranger, though a brother, claims your sympathy and solicits your aid. About nineteen years ago, a Scotchman and native of Forfarshire, landed in your town. He was about 5 feet 10 inches high, straight and proportionably formed; his hair was jet black, nose aquiline, and face deeply marked with small pox. He was a shoemaker by trade, and spoke with a broad strong accent, which is common in the locality from which he went. It is unnecessary for me to detail the circumstances that induced him to seek a home in the southern hemisphere. Suffice it to say that he, by an unfortunate pressure of events, was forced to leave Scotland, and separate himself from his wife and children. Since then death has carried away all his family excepting one, and that one is myself. When my mother died, Sir, I was only a little boy, and I was destined to a life of poverty; and being ignorant of the whereabouts of my only parent, I have consequently had no communication with him since I was a child; and indeed, Sir, I am not without suspicion that he has gone to his long home. But, notwithstanding this suspicion, the bare possibility that he may be alive, suggests itself to my mind, and has prompted the writing of this letter. Need I tell you, Sir, I burn with eagerness to solve what is to me an exciting problem. I know you will participate in my ardour, and kindly assist me in my search. You can conceive the feelings which agitate my breast, and appreciate my motives. May I beg of you then, my dear Sir, guided by the faint light I have given you, to use your influence and agency in discovering if a person answering to my description, and whose name was John Forrest, still lives. I shall gladly pay any necessary expenses which may be incurred by you in the prosecution of this object. In the hope that you will comply with my request, I am, Sir, yours respectfully,

FRANK FORREST.

After the dispatch of this letter, which was addressed to the Superintendant of Police, Sydney, New South Wales, fully twelve months passed by, and no answer was received. I was beginning to despair of my letter even commanding the slightest attention, but I was too hasty in my conclusions, as an acknowledgment of its receipt reached me in about fifteen months from the date of its being forwarded. In it I was assured in most gentle and brotherly language that every exertion would be used to arrive at a definite knowledge on the subject of my communication. This kindled a new hope in my mind, and I could scarcely describe to the reader the nervous anxiety into which it threw me. Every stranger who opened my little garden gate I fancied was the bearer of further intelligence; every tap that came to my door made me start, for I imagined it was a messenger with a letter for me. This feverish excitement was prolonged for three long months, and every hour seemed a day, and every day a month. At last a huge letter, bearing the Sydney post-mark, came. When I got it I trembled, as if it had contained my death summons. It was a moment of painful suspense, such as few can ever feel or fancy. I opened it, and its contents amply recompensed me for former troubles and anxieties. It was from the chief of the Sydney police, and contained the joyful intelligence that my father still lived and loved me, that he was proprietor of a large farm about thirty miles from Sydney, was married a second time, but had no family. On the following morning I received another letter from the same quarter of the globe. It was from the hand of my own father. It had been sent wrong, through some mistake in the assorting of letters in Dundee, and was a day later in reaching me in consequence. This letter was so long and so affectionate, reader, that I can scarcely give you an epitome of its contents. Suffice it to say that protracted silence and seeming procrastination were clearly and satisfactorily explained. My father, after many inquiries, and the writing of not a few letters, had concluded I had been carried off by fever shortly after the death of my mother and brother, and had long since settled with a conviction that he had no ties to bind him to the old world. He had conducted for a number of years an extensive business in Sydney, made money, and as he was always partial to agricultural life, he had purchased an excellent farm, and was as comfortable as he could desire. Finally, it concluded with a warm, indeed passionate, invitation to come to New South Wales, where a home would be prepared for me, and a father's, and even mother's, welcome given me. Need I continue my narrative farther. I have decided on emigrating to the southern hemisphere. My little property, the fruits of my own industry, will be shortly announced for sale in the public newspapers, and I expect to realise as much from it as will transport and settle my wife and me comfortably in a younger and more buoyant world; and as I have always had an ambition to be permanently connected with the press, I will, if I possibly can, start in Sydney a newspaper on my own account, and out of love to my country I shall name it "The Banner of Scotland," and in its columns I will, to the best of my ability, unfold and defend those great and glorious principles which have made our dear Caledonia "the land of the brave and the free."[1]

My autobiography is now ended. I have concisely, and I hope clearly, traced my own experience as a factory boy, and given an epitome of my subsequent career. My purpose has been, to develope, as far as I could, the evils of the long hours' system, and the necessity there was for Legislative interference in the factory branch of industry. The old system, with all its horrors, is, I hope, for ever blasted with the detestation of the wise and good, and its cruel reign will surely never be imposed on the young females and helpless children of our country. God grant that my anticipations may be fully realised.

FINIS.

---

1 The version of the *Chapters* published in *The Northern Warder* ends with this paragraph. Following it is the notice: "NOTE.— The 'Chapters in the Life of a Factory Boy' having attracted a greater amount of attention than the author anticipated, and having received the warm commendations of not a few eminent men celebrated for their good works, he has decided on issuing them in a handsome little volume, at as low a price as possible. They are in the press, and will be ready in about a fortnight."

"Autobiography of Ellen Johnston, 'The Factory Girl'" (1867) and "Autobiography" (1869)

Ellen Johnston

[The "Autobiography" of Ellen Johnston (1835-73) is important not only because it is one of the few extant autobiographical accounts written by a female factory worker, but also because, as Florence Boos notes, it is "the fullest account that we have ... by a Scottish nineteenth-century working-class poet"(61). Despite its significance, Johnston's "Autobiography" occupies only thirteen pages of her much longer work, *Autobiography, Poems and Songs of Ellen Johnston, the "Factory Girl"* (1867). (For a selection of her poetry, see Appendix D.) In 1867 a reviewer for the *Glasgow Sentinel* criticized the candid revelations in Johnston's narrative: "There are perhaps one or two incidents in her autobiography that it would have been better to have kept back" (qtd. Klaus 73). When Johnston's poems went into a second edition in 1869, her "Autobiography" was revised, perhaps in response to such comments. Both versions are included here so that readers may compare the two quite different ways in which Johnston presented her life story (see Note on the Text).

Unfortunately, little is known of Johnston's life beyond what is written in the following pages, and often that information is shrouded in mystery. Soon after her birth near Glasgow in 1835, her father emigrated to America. After he was erroneously reported to have died, Johnston's mother remarried, and the hints and allusions in both versions of her "Autobiography" suggest that Johnston's stepfather may have molested her. Forced into factory work at the age of ten or eleven, she later had a child out of wedlock. In spite of her hardships, she developed a love for writing poetry, and she became a published poet when a number of local newspapers began to print her poems. With the support of Alexander Campbell, editor of the *Penny Post*, a Glasgow paper, Johnston was able to publish the first edition of her *Autobiography, Poems and Songs* by subscription. Although the book sold neither as well nor as quickly as Johnston had hoped—it apparently did not free her from the fear that she would need to return to factory work— approximately eight hundred copies were sold by 1869, bringing her enough attention the year before to gain her a grant of £50 from the Royal Bounty fund (Klaus 69, 72-74). As Julia Swindells notes, however, Johnston "is unusual in perceiving herself as a successful writer, but there is a revealing discrepancy between how she articulates her literary aspirations ... and the fame she achieves, which is local to her particular area" (176). Despite her promise as a poet and her desire for a better life, Johnston would not live long: a contemporary reported that she died in the Barony or Barnhill Poorhouse near Glasgow in 1873 (Klaus 76-77). If so, she was only thirty-eight years old at the time of her death.]

AUTOBIOGRAPHY

OF

ELLEN JOHNSTON,

'THE FACTORY GIRL.'

Title courtesy of the Division of Rare and Manuscript Collections, Cornell University Library.

GENTLE READER,—On the suggestion of a friend, and the expressed wishes of some subscribers, I now submit the following brief sketch of my eventful life as an introduction to this long expected and patiently waited for volume of my Poems and Songs.

Like every other autobiographer, I can only relate the events connected with my parentage and infancy from the communicated evidence of witnesses of those events, but upon whose veracity I have full reliance.

I beg also to remind my readers that whatever my actions may have been, whether good, bad, or indifferent,—they were the results of instincts derived from the Creator, through the medium of my parents, and the character formed for me by the unavoidable influence of the TIME and COUNTRY of my BIRTH, and also by the varied conditions of life impressing themselves on my highly susceptible and sympathetic natures—physical, intellectual, and moral.

According to the evidence referred to, my father was James Johnston, second oldest son of James Johnston, canvas-weaver, Lochee, Dundee,[1] where he learned the trade of a stone-mason. After which he removed to Glasgow,[2] where he became acquainted with my mother, Mary Bilsland, second daughter of

---

1 Lochee, Dundee] a weaving village a few miles northwest of Dundee.
2 Glasgow] a major industrial city and the most important seaport in Scotland. Located on the River Clyde about forty-five miles west of Edinburgh, Glasgow was also the site of ship building.

James Bilsland, residing in Muslin Street, and then well known as the Bridgeton Dyer.[1]

I do not remember hearing my father's age, but my mother at the time of her marriage was only eighteen years old. I was the first and only child of their union, and was born in the Muir Wynd, Hamilton, in 183—, my father at the time being employed as a mason extending the northern wing of the Duke of Hamilton's Palace.[2]

When the Duke was informed that my father was a poet, he familiarly used to call him Lord Byron,[3] and, as I have been told, his Grace also used to take special notice of me when an infant in my mother's arms, as she almost daily walked around his domain.

When I was about seven months old my father's contract at Hamilton Palace was finished, and being of an active disposition, somewhat ambitious, proud, and independent, with some literary and scientific attainments, with a strong desire to become a teacher and publish a volume of his poetical works, he resolved to emigrate, engaged a passage to America for my mother and himself, and got all things ready for the voyage.

But when all the relatives and friends had assembled at the Broomielaw[4] to give the farewell kiss and shake of the hand before going on board, my mother determined not to proceed, pressed me fondly to her bosom, exclaiming—'I cannot, will not go, my child would die on the way;' and taking an affectionate farewell with my father, he proceeded on the voyage, and my mother fled from the scene and returned to her father's house, where she remained for some years, and supported herself by dressmaking and millinery.

Having given the evidence of others in respect to my parentage and infancy, let me now, gentle reader, state some of my own childhood's recollections, experience, and reflections thereon.

---

1 Bridgeton] a large district near Glasgow, site of many power-loom weaving factories.
2 Hamilton ... Hamilton Palace] Located in a valley near Hamilton, a town surrounded by coal mines and iron works about twelve miles southeast of Glasgow, Hamilton Palace was rebuilt between 1822 and 1838 by Alexander Hamilton, the Tenth Duke of Hamilton. Its renovations were designed by David Hamilton (1768-1845), stone mason turned architect.
3 George Gordon, Lord Byron (1788-1824), British poet.
4 Broomielaw] the first quay built on the Clyde in the center of Glasgow.

In my childhood Bridgeton now incorporated with the city of Glasgow,[1] abounded with green fields and lovely gardens, which have since then been covered over with piles of buildings and tall chimneys. The ground on which the factory of Messrs Scott & Inglis stands was then a lovely garden, where I spent many, many happy hours with 'Black Bess,' my doll, and 'Dainty Davie,' my dog, with whom I climbed many a knowe[2] and forded many a stream, till one day he left my side to follow a band of music, and we never met again; but for whose loss I deeply mourned, and for three successive nights wept myself asleep, for 'Dainty Davie' was the pride of my heart, for I could not live without something to love, and I loved before I knew the name of the nature or feeling which swelled my bosom.

Perhaps there are few who can take a retrospective view of their past lives, and through their mind's eye gaze on so many strange and mysterious incidents. Yes, gentle reader, I have suffered trials and wrongs that have but rarely fallen to the lot of woman. Mine were not the common trials of every day life, but like those strange romantic ordeals attributed to the imaginary heroines of 'Inglewood Forest.'[3]

Like the Wandering Jew,[4] I have mingled with the gay on the shores of France—I have feasted in the merry halls of England— I have danced on the shamrock soil of Erin's green isle—and I have sung the songs of the brave and the free in the woods and glens of dear old Scotland.

I have waited and watched the sun-set hour to meet my lover, and then with him wander by the banks of sweet winding Clutha,[5] when my muse has often been inspired when viewing

---

1 Bridgeton ... Glasgow] In 1846 Bridgeton was annexed by Glasgow.
2 knowe] a small hill, a knoll.
3 Johnston seems here to prepare for the veiled references she makes later in the text to the idea that she was sexually abused. In Elizabeth Helme's Gothic novel *The Farmer of Inglewood Forest* (1796), two of the heroines are threatened with incest: the farmer's daughter Emma, a prostitute, almost sleeps with a customer who is actually her brother Edwin; and Edwin drugs and tries to rape Anna, only to learn later she is his daughter.
4 the Wandering Jew] A well-known later medieval legend told of a Jew who insulted Jesus as he carried the cross to Calvary, and for this the Jew was condemned to wander the earth until judgment day. There are a number of variations to this legend.
5 Clutha] old name for the River Clyde.

the proud waving thistle bending to the breeze, or when the calm twilight hour was casting a halo of glory around the enchanting scene; yet in all these wanderings I never enjoyed true happiness.

Like Rassellas,[1] there was a dark history engraven on the tablet of my heart. Yes, dear reader, a dark shadow, as a pall, enshrouded my soul, shutting out life's gay sunshine from my bosom—a shadow which has haunted me like a vampire, but at least for the present must remain the mystery of my life.

Dear reader, I have wandered far away from my childhood's years. Yes, years that passed like a dream, unclouded and clear. Oh that I could recall them; but, alas! they are gone for ever. Still they linger in memory fresh and green as if they were yesterday. I can look back and see the opening chapters of my life—I can see the forms and faces, and hear their voices ringing in my ears—one sweet voice above the rest echoes like a seraph's song; but I dare not linger longer at present with those joyous hours and beloved forms that were then my guardian angels.

In the course of time my mother received some information of my father's death in America, and again married a power-loom tenter[2] when I was about eight years of age, till which time I may truly say that the only heartfelt sorrow I experienced was the loss of 'Dainty Davie;' but, alas! shortly after my mother's second marriage I was dragged, against my own will and the earnest pleadings and remonstrance of my maternal grandfather, from his then happy home to my stepfather's abode, next land to the Cross Keys Tavern, London Road.[3]

HOW I BECAME THE FACTORY GIRL.

About two months after my mother's marriage, my stepfather having got work in a factory in Bishop Street, Anderston,[4] they removed to North Street, where I spent the two last years of young life's sweet liberty—as it was during that time I found my way to

---

1   *The History of Rasselas, Prince of Abyssinia* (1759), by Samuel Johnson (1709-84), details Rasselas' determination to experience life outside of the perfect world in which he lives as the son of the Abyssinian Emperor. Once in that world, Rasselas' romantic notions prove to be illusory.

2   power-loom tenter] the worker in charge of a water- or steam-driven loom.

3   London Road] a street in central Glasgow.

4   Anderston] a district in western Glasgow.

Kelvin Grove, and there spent many happy hours in innocent mirth and glee—but 'time changes a' things.' My stepfather could not bear to see me longer basking in the sunshine of freedom, and therefore took me into the factory where he worked, to learn power-loom weaving when about eleven years of age, from which time I became a factory girl; but no language can paint the suffering which I afterwards endured from my tormentor.

Before I was thirteen years of age I had read many of Sir Walter Scott's[1] novels, and fancied I was a heroine of the modern style. I was a self-taught scholar, gifted with a considerable amount of natural knowledge for one of my years, for I had only been nine months at school when I could read the English language and Scottish dialect with almost any classic scholar; I had also read 'Wilson's Tales of the Border;'[2] so that by reading so many love adventures my brain was fired with wild imaginations, and therefore resolved to bear with my own fate, and in the end gain a great victory.

I had also heard many say that I ought to have been an actress, as I had a flow of poetic language and a powerful voice, which was enough to inspire my young soul to follow the profession. In fact, I am one of those beings formed by nature for romance and mystery, and as such had many characters to imitate in the course of a day. In the residence of my stepfather I was a weeping willow, in the factory I was pensive and thoughtful, dreaming of the far off future when I would be hailed as a 'great star.' Then, when mixing with a merry company no one could be more cheerful, for I had learned to conceal my own cares and sorrows, knowing well that 'the mirth maker hath no sympathy with the grief weeper.'

By this time my mother had removed from Anderston to a shop in Tradeston,[3] and my stepfather and myself worked in West Street Factory. When one morning early, in the month of June, I

---

1   Sir Walter Scott (1771-1832), Scottish poet and novelist, one of the most important literary figures of the nineteenth century. By using his homeland as a setting for many of his poems, such as *Marmion* (1808) and *The Lady of the Lake* (1810), and novels, such as *Rob Roy* (1817) and *The Black Dwarf* (1825), his work elicited a great deal of respect for the Scottish culture.

2   *Wilson's Historical, Traditionary, and Imaginative Tales of the Borders, and of Scotland*, a series of seventy-three tales published in forty-eight weekly three halfpenny numbers by John Mackay Wilson (1804-35), beginning in 1834. The series was so popular that its circulation reached seventeen thousand a week.

3   Tradeston] a district in southern Glasgow.

absconded from their house as the fox flies from the hunters' hounds, to the Paisley Canal,[1] into which I was about submerging myself to end my sufferings and sorrow, when I thought I heard like the voice of him I had fixed my girlish love upon. I started and paused for a few moments, and the love of young life again prevailed over that of self-destruction, and I fled from the scene as the half-past five morning factory bells were ringing, towards the house of a poor woman in Rose Street, Hutcheson-town,[2] where, after giving her my beautiful earrings to pawn, I was made welcome, and on Monday morning following got work in Brown & M'Nee's factory, Commercial Road. I did not, however, remain long in my new lodgings, for on the Tuesday evening, while threading my way among the crowd at the shows, near the foot of Saltmarket,[3] and busy dreaming of the time when I would be an actress, I was laid hold of by my mother's eldest brother, who, after questioning me as to where I had been, and what I was doing, without receiving any satisfaction to his inter-rogations, compelled me to go with him to my mother, who first questioned me as to the cause of absconding, and then beat me till I felt as if my brain were on fire; but still I kept the secret in my own bosom. But had I only foreseen the wretched misery I was heaping upon my own head—had I heard the dreadful con-structions the world was putting on my movements—had I seen the shroud of shame and sorrow I was weaving around myself, I should then have disclosed the mystery of my life, but I remained silent and kept my mother and friends in ignorance of the cause which first disturbed my peace and made me run away from her house for safety and protection.

However, I consented to stay again with my mother for a time, and resolved to avoid my tormentor as much as possible.

Weeks and months thus passed away, but, alas! the sun never shed the golden dawn of peaceful morn again around my mother's hearth. Apart from my home sorrows I had other trials to encounter. Courted for my conversation and company by the most intelligent of the factory workers, who talked to me about poets and poetry, which the girls around me did not understand,

---

1   Paisley Canal] a shallow canal between Tradeston and Paisley, an indus-trial town approximately ten miles to the west of Glasgow.
2   Hutchestontown] a district in southern Glasgow.
3   Saltmarket] one of the principal streets in central Glasgow; like London Road, it meets four other streets at the medieval intersection called the Cross.

consequently they wondered, became jealous, and told falsehoods of me. Yet I never fell out with them although I was a living martyr, and suffered all their insults. In fact, life had no charm for me but one, and that was my heart's first love. If a sunshine of pleasure ever fell upon me, it was in his company only for a few short moments, for nothing could efface from my memory the deep grief that pressed me to the earth. I often smiled when my heart was weeping—the gilded mask of false merriment made me often appear happy in company when I was only playing the dissembler.

Dear reader, as this is neither the time nor place to give farther details of my young eventful life, I will now bring you to my sixteenth year, when I was in the bloom of fair young maidenhood. Permit me, however, to state that during the three previous years of my life, over a part of which I am drawing a veil, I had run away five times from my tormentor, and during one of those elopements spent about six weeks in Airdrie, wandering often by Carron or Calder's beautiful winding banks.[1] Oh! could I then have seen the glorious gems that have sprung up for me on those banks, and heard the poetic strains that have since been sung in my praise, what a balm they would have been to my bleeding heart, as I wandered around the old Priestrig Pit and listened to its engine thundering the water up from its lowest depth. For days I have wandered the fields between Moodiesburn and Clifton Hill, wooing my sorry muse, then unknown to the world—except to a few, as a child of song—in silence looking forward to the day when the world would know my wrongs and prize my worth; and had it not been for the bright Star of Hope which lingered near me and encouraged me onward, beyond doubt I would have been a suicide. 'Tis, however, strange in all my weary wanderings that I have always met with kind-hearted friends, and there were two who befriended me when I was a homeless wanderer in Airdrie. Fifteen years have passed since I saw their tears roll down the youthful cheeks and heard the heavy sigh that exploded from their sympathising hearts. But the best of friends must part, and I parted with them, perhaps never to meet again in this lovely world of sunshine and sorrow.

Dear reader, should your curiosity have been awakened to ask in what form fate had then so hardly dealt with the hapless 'Factory Girl,' this is my answer:— I was falsely accused by those

---

1   Airdrie ... banks] The Calder is a river that becomes a reservoir five
    miles from Airdrie, a mining and textile-manufacturing town approxi-
    mately ten miles west of Glasgow. Carron Water is a river near Falkirk, a
    town fifteen miles northeast of Glasgow.

who knew me as a fallen woman, while I was as innocent of the charge as the unborn babe. Oh! how hard to be blamed when the heart is spotless and the conscience clear. For years I submitted to this wrong, resolving to hold my false detractors at defiance.

While struggling under those misrepresentations, my first love also deserted me, but another soon after offered me his heart—without the form of legal protection—and in a thoughtless moment I accepted him as my friend and protector, but, to use the words of a departed poet—

'When lovely woman stoops to folly,
And finds too late that men betray,
What can sooth[e] her melancholy,
What can wash her guilt away?

The only art her guilt to cover,
To hide her shame from every eye,
To wring repentance from her lover,
And sting his bosom, is to die.' [1]

I did not, however, feel inclined to die when I could no longer conceal what the world falsely calls a woman's shame. No, on the other hand, I never loved life more dearly and longed for the hour when I would have something to love me—and my wish was realised by becoming the mother of a lovely daughter on the 14th of September, 1852.

No doubt every feeling mother thinks her own child lovely, but mine was surpassing so, and I felt as if I could begin all my past sorrows again if Heaven would only spare me my lovely babe to cheer my bleeding heart, for I never felt bound to earth till then; and as year succeeded year, 'My Mary Achin'[2] grew like the wild daisy—fresh and fair—on the mountain side.

As my circumstances in life changed, I placed my daughter under my mother's care when duty called me forth to turn the poetic gift that nature had given me to a useful and profitable account, for which purpose I commenced with vigorous zeal to write my poetical pieces, and sent them to the weekly newspapers for insertion, until I became extensively known and popular. As an instance, in 1854 the Glasgow Examiner published a song of

---

1   The last two lines here are slightly misquoted from Oliver Goldsmith's *The Vicar of Wakefield* (1766), Chapter XXIV. The character Olivia sings this song when she revisits the setting of her seduction.

2   Achin] perhaps short for Auchinvole (see note 4 on page 312).

mine, entitled 'Lord Raglan's Address to the Allied Armies,'[1] which made my name popular throughout Great Britain and Ireland; but as my fame spread my health began to fail, so that I could not work any longer in a factory.

My stepfather was unable longer to work, and my mother was also rendered a suffering object; my child was then but an infant under three years of age, and I, who had been the only support of the family, was informed by my medical adviser that, unless I took a change of air, I would not live three months.

Under these circumstances, what was to be done? I did not then want to die, although I had wished to do so a thousand times before, to relieve me from unmerited slander and oppression.

Many sleepless nights did I pass, thinking what to try to bring relief to the afflicted household—although I did not consider myself in duty bound to struggle against the stern realities of nature, and sacrifice my own young life for those whose sympathies for me had been long seared and withered. Yet I could not, unmoved, look on the pale face of poverty, for their means were entirely exhausted, without hope to lean upon. Neither could I longer continue in the factory without certain death to myself, and I had never learned anything else.

Under those conflicting conditions and feelings, one night as I lay in bed, almost in despair, I prayed fervently that some idea how to act would be revealed to me, when suddenly I remembered that I had a piece of poetry entitled 'An Address to Napier's Dockyard, Lancefield, Finnieston,' which a young man had written for me in imitation of copperplate engraving, and that piece I addressed to Robert Napier, Esq., Shandon, Garelochhead,[2] who

---

1 Fitzroy James Henry Somerset, Baron Raglan (1788-1855). As one of England's most famous military commanders, Lord Raglan was present at a number of major military actions, from Waterloo to the siege of Sebastopol. He was also the allied commander at Balaclava on October 25, 1854, and therefore partially responsible for the infamous charge of the Light Brigade immortalized in verse by Tennyson that same year. For Johnston's poem, see Appendix D.4.

2 Napier's Dockyard ... Garelochhead] The Napier shipyard in Lancefield on the northern bank of the Clyde was run from 1836 by Robert Napier (1791-1876), reputed to be the chief shipbuilder and engineer in Glasgow. After building the first steamships for Cunard and moving and expanding his shipyards in 1841 and 1850, he retired in 1860. Garelochhead was a large village approximately twenty-five miles northwest of Glasgow at the head of Gare Loch, on the east side of which was located the smaller village of Shandon. For "An Address to Napiers' Dockyard," see Appendix D.3.

was then in Paris, where it was forwarded to him. Having written to my employer for my character, which was satisfactory, Mr Napier sent me a note to call at a certain office in Oswald Street, Glasgow, and draw as much money as would set me up in some small business, to see if my health would revive. According to the good old gentleman's instructions, I went as directed, and sought .10, which was freely given to me; and I believe had I asked double the amount I would have readily received it.

Dear reader, I need not tell you what a godsend those ten pounds were to my distressed family, and kept me out of the factory during five months; after which I resumed work in Messrs Galbraith's Mill, St Rollox, Glasgow,[1] where I continued till July, 1857, when my health again sank; and for a change of air I went to Belfast,[2] where I remained two years, during which time I became so notorious for my poetic exploits that the little boys and girls used to run after me to get a sight of 'the little Scotch girl' their fathers and mothers spoke so much about.

In 1859 I left Belfast and went to Manchester,[3] where I worked three months, and then returned again to my native land, much improved in body and mind.

New scenes and systems made a great change in my natures. I became cheerful, and sought the society of mirthmakers, so that few would have taken me for the former moving monument of melancholy. I had again resumed work at Galbraith's factory, and all went on well. 'My bonnie Mary Auchinvole'[4] was growing prettier every day and I was growing strong; peace and good-will reigned in our household, the past seemed forgiven and forgotten, and the 'Factory Girl' was a topic of the day for her poetical productions in the public press, but the shadow of death was hovering behind all this gladsome sunshine.

My mother had been an invalid for several years, and, to add to her sorrow, a letter had come from her supposed dead husband, my father, in America, after an absence of twenty years, inquiring for his wife and child; on learning their fate he became maddened with remorse, and, according to report, drank a death-

---

1 St. Rollox, Glasgow] a district outside Glasgow's northern gate.
2 Belfast] an industrial city in the north of Ireland; in the mid-nineteenth century, site of cotton manufacture.
3 Manchester] See note 1 on page 116.
4 Auchinvole] a Scottish family name; also the name of a now ruined castle in Kilsyth, a mining town about ten miles north of Airdrie, where Johnston worked for a brief period.

draught from a cup in his own hand; and my mother, after becoming aware of the mystery of my life, closed her weary pilgrimage on earth on 25th May, 1861. Thus I was left without a friend, and disappointed of a future promised home and pleasure which I was not destined to enjoy, I therefore made up my mind to go to Dundee, where my father's sister resided, whose favourite I was when a child.

Dear reader, were I to give details of my trials, disappointments, joys, and sorrows, since I came to 'bonnie Dundee,' they would be, with a little embellishment, a romance of real life, sufficient to fill three ordinary volumes. Suffice here to say, that after myself and child had suffered neglect and destitution for some time, I got work in the Verdant Factory,[1] where the cloth I wove was selected by my master as a sample for others to imitate, until, on the 5th of December, 1863, I was discharged by the foreman without any reason assigned or notice given, in accordance with the rules of the work. Smarting under this treatment, I summoned the foreman into Court for payment of a week's wages for not receiving notice, and I gained the case. But if I was envied by my sister sex in the Verdant Works for my talent before this affair happened, they hated me with a perfect hatred after I had struggled for and gained my rights. In fact, on account of that simple and just law-suit, I was persecuted beyond description—lies of the most vile and disgusting character were told upon me, till even my poor ignorant deluded sister sex went so far as to assault me on the streets, spit in my face, and even several times dragged the skirts from my dress. Anonymous letters were also sent to all the foremen and tenters not to employ me, so that for the period of four months after I wandered through Dundee a famished and persecuted factory exile.

From the foregoing statements some may think that I am rude, forward, and presumptuous, but permit me to say this much for myself, and those who know me best will confirm my statement, that I am naturally of a warm-hearted and affectionate disposition, always willing, to the extent of my power, to serve my fellow-creatures, and would rather endure an insult than retaliate on an enemy. All my wrongs have been suffered in silence and wept over in secret. It is the favour and fame of the

---

1 Verdant Factory] Named for the fields in which it was built in 1833, Verdant Works was near the center of Dundee when Johnston was employed there; in the 1860s it processed jute and had a workforce of about five hundred.

poetic gift bestowed on me by nature's God that has brought on me the envy of the ignorant, for the enlightened classes of both sexes of factory workers love and admire me for my humble poetic effusions, so far as they have been placed before the public, but I merely mention this to clear away any doubt that may possibly arise in the mind of any of my readers.

In conclusion, I am glad to say that the persecution I was doomed to suffer in vindication not only of my own rights, but of the rights of such as might be similarly discharged, passed away, and peace and pleasure restored to my bosom again, by obtaining work at the Chapelshade Factory, at the east end of Dundee, where I have been working for the last three years and a-half to a true friend. I had not been long in my present situation when I fortunately became a reader of the 'Penny Post,'[1] and shortly afterwards contributed some pieces to the 'Poet's Corner,' which seemed to cast a mystic spell over many of its readers whose numerous letters reached me from various districts, highly applauding my contributions, and offering me their sympathy, friendship, and love; while others, inspired by the muses, responded to me through the same popular medium some of whose productions will be found, along with my own in the present volume.[2]

And now, gentle reader, let me conclude by offering my grateful thanks to the Rev. George Gilfillan for his testimony in respect to the merits of my poetic productions,[3] to Mr Alex. Campbell,

---

1 'Penny Post'] Begun in 1855, this Glasgow paper, like the *Glasgow Sentinel*, was edited by Alexander Campbell.

2 present volume] For examples of such verse correspondence by means of a local newspaper, see Appendices D.8 to D.11.

3 Rev. George Gilfillan] Dundee clergyman, literary critic, and patron of working-class writers. The "testimony" referred to here appears in the 1867 edition of the *Autobiography, Poems and Songs*; it is titled "Testimonial from the Rev. George Gilfillan," dated "Dundee, 21st July, 1866," and it reads as follows: "Ellen Johnston, the 'Factory Girl,' has asked me to look over her verses. This I have done with very considerable interest and pleasure. She labours, of course, under great disadvantage, but subtracting all the signs of imperfect education, her rhymes are highly creditable to her heart and head too—are written always with a fluency and often with sweetness, and, I see, have attracted the notice and the warm praise of many of her own class. I hope she will be encouraged by this to cultivate her mind, to read to correct the faults in her style—arising from her limited opportunities—and so doing, she cannot fail to secure still increased respect and warmer patronage." This comment is signed "George Gilfillan."

of the 'Penny Post,' for his services in promoting their publication, as well as to the subscribers[1] who have so long patiently waited for this volume, which I hope may prove a means of social and intellectual enjoyment to many, and also help to relieve from the incessant toils of a factory life.[2]

ELLEN JOHNSTON,
THE FACTORY GIRL.
OCTOBER, 1867.

---

1 subscribers] The "List of Subscribers" in this edition includes approximately sixty names, from the Duke of Buccleuch, who took four copies, to a Mrs. Menzies and a Miss Grant. Their addresses vary from Dundee and Glasgow to Aberdeen, Yorkshire, Oxford, and London.
2 relieve ... life] See page 324 for the 1869 emendation of this phrase.

["Autobiography" (1869)]

AUTOBIOGRAPHY.

GENTLE READER,—On the suggestion of a friend, and the expressed wishes of some subscribers, I now submit the following brief sketch of my eventful life; but, like every other autobiographer, I can only relate the events connected with my parentage and infancy from witnesses, upon whose veracity I have full reliance.

I beg also to remind my readers that whatever my actions may have been, whether good, bad, or indifferent, that they were the results of instincts derived from the Creator, through the medium of my parents, and the character formed for me by the unavoidable influence of the time and country of my birth, and also by the varied conditions of my life impressing themselves on highly susceptible and sympathetic natures—physical, intellectual, and moral.

According to the evidence referred to, my father was James Johnston, second son of James Johnston, canvas-weaver, Lochee, Dundee, where he learned the trade of a stone-mason, after which he removed to Glasgow, where he became acquainted with my mother, Mary Bilsland, second daughter of James Bilsland, residing in Muslin Street, and then well known as the Bridgeton Dyer.

I do not remember of hearing my father's age, but my mother at the time of her marriage was only eighteen years old. I am the first and only child of their union, and was born in the Muir Wynd, Hamilton, my father at the time being employed as a mason extending the northern wing of the Duke of Hamilton's Palace.

When the Duke was informed that my father was a poet, he familiarly used to call him Lord Byron; and, as I have been told, his Grace also used to take special notice of me when an infant in my mother's arms, as she almost daily walked around his domain.

When I was about seven months old, my father's contract at Hamilton Palace was finished, and being of an active disposition, somewhat ambitious, proud, and independent, with some literary and scientific attainments, with a strong desire to become a teacher and publish a volume of his poetical works, he resolved to emigrate, engaged a passage to America for my mother and himself, and got all things ready for the voyage.

But when their relatives and friends had assembled at the Broomielaw to give the farewell kiss and shake of the hand before going on board, my mother, who was a 'strong-minded woman,' at once determined not to proceed further, pressed me fondly to her bosom, exclaiming—'I cannot, will not go, my child would die on the way;' and taking an affectionate farewell with my father, he proceeded on the voyage, and my mother fled from the scene and returned to her father's house in Bridgeton, where she remained for some years, and supported herself by dressmaking and millinery.

Having given the evidence of others in respect to my parentage and infancy, let me now, gentle reader, state some of my own childhood's recollections, experience, and reflections thereon.

In my childhood, Bridgeton, now incorporated with the city of Glasgow, abounded with green fields and lovely gardens, which have since then been covered over with piles of buildings and tall chimneys. The ground on which the factory formerly belonging to Messrs Scott & Inglis, but now occupied by the Messrs Robertson, was then a lovely garden, where I spent many, many happy hours with 'Black Bess,' my doll, and 'Dainty Davie,' my dog, with whom I climbed many a knowe and forded many a stream, till one day he left my side to follow a band of music, and we never met again; but for whose loss I deeply mourned, and for three successive nights wept myself asleep. 'Dainty Davie' was the pride of my heart, for I could not live without something to love me, and I loved before I knew the nature or feeling which swelled my bosom.

In the course of time my mother received some information that my father had died in America, and she married a power-loom tenter when I was about eight years of age, till which time I may truly say that the only heartfelt sorrow I experienced was the loss of 'Dainty Davie;' but, alas! shortly after my mother's second marriage I was dragged, against my own will and the earnest pleadings and remonstrance of my maternal grandfather, from his then happy home to my stepfather's abode, next land to the Cross Keys Tavern, London Road.

HOW I BECAME THE FACTORY GIRL.

About two months after my mother's marriage, my stepfather having got work in a factory in Bishop Street, Anderston, they removed to North Street, where I spent the two last years of young life's sweet liberty—as it was during that time I found my way to

Kelvin Grove, and there spent many happy hours in innocent mirth and glee—but 'time changes a' things.' My stepfather could not bear to see me longer basking in the sunshine of freedom, and therefore took me into the factory where he worked, to learn power-loom weaving, when about ten years of age, from which time I became a factory girl; but no language can paint the suffering which I afterwards endured from my tormentor.

Before I was thirteen years of age I had read many of Sir Walter Scott's novels, and fancied I was a heroine of the modern style. I was a self-taught scholar, gifted with a considerable amount of natural knowledge for one of my years, for I had only been nine months at school when I could read the English language and Scottish dialect with almost any classic scholar; I had also read 'Wilson's Tales of the Borders;' so that, by reading so many love adventures, my brain was fired with wild imaginations, and therefore resolved to bear with my own fate, and in the end gain a great victory.

I had also heard many say that I ought to have been an actress, as I had a flow of poetic language and a powerful voice, which was enough to inspire my young soul to follow the profession. In fact, I am one of those beings formed by Nature for romance and mystery, and as such had many characters to imitate in the course of a day. In the residence of my stepfather I was a weeping willow, in the factory I was pensive and thoughtful, dreaming of the far-off future when I would be hailed as a 'great star.' Then, when mixing with a merry company, no one could be more cheerful, for I had learned to conceal my own cares and sorrows, knowing well that 'the mirth-maker hath no sympathy with the grief-weeper.'

By this time my mother had removed from Anderston to a shop in Tradeston, and my stepfather and myself worked in West Street Factory, when one morning early, in the month of June, I absconded from their house, as the fox flies from the hunter's hounds, to the Paisley Canal, into which I was about submerging myself, to preserve my virtue and end my sufferings and sorrow, when I thought I heard like the voice of him I had fixed my girlish love upon. I started and paused for a few moments, and the love of young life again prevailed over that of self-destruction, so I fled from the spot as the half-past five morning factory bells were ringing, towards the house of a poor woman in Rose Street, Hutchesontown, and on Monday morning following got work in Brown & M'Nee's factory, Commercial Road. I did not, however, remain long in my new lodgings, for on the Tuesday evening, while threading my way among the crowd at the shows, near the foot of Saltmarket, and busy dreaming of the time when I would be an actress, I was laid hold of by my mother's eldest brother, who, after questioning me as to where I had been, and what I was doing, without receiving any satisfaction to his interrogations, he compelled me to go with him to my mother, who first questioned me as to the cause of absconding, and then beat me till I felt as if my brain were on fire; but still I kept the secret in my own bosom. But had I only foreseen the misery I was heaping upon my own head—had I heard the false constructions the world was putting on my movements—had I seen the shroud of shame and sorrow I was weaving around myself, I should then have disclosed the *mystery of my life;* but I remained silent, and kept my mother and friends in ignorance of the cause which first disturbed my peace, and made me run away from her house for safety and protection.

However, I consented to stay again with my mother for a time, and resolved to avoid my tormentor as much as possible.

Weeks and months thus passed away; but, alas! the sun never shed the golden dawn of peaceful morn again around my mother's hearth. Apart from my home sorrows, I had other trials to encounter. Courted for my conversation and company by the most intelligent of the factory workers, who talked to me about poets and poetry, which the girls around me did not understand, consequently they wondered, became jealous, and told falsehoods of me. Yet I never fell out with them, although I was a living martyr, and suffered all their insults. In fact, life had no charm for me but one, and that was my heart's first love. If a sunshine of pleasure ever fell upon me, it was in his company only for a few short moments, for nothing could efface from my memory the deep grief that pressed me to the earth. I often smiled when my heart was weeping—the gilded mask of false merriment made me often appear happy in company when I was only playing the dissembler.

Dear reader, as this is neither the time nor place to give farther details of my young, eventful life, I will now bring you to my sixteenth year, when I was in the bloom of fair, young maidenhood. Permit me, however, to state that during the three previous years, over a part of which I am drawing a veil, I had run away five times from my tormentor, and during one of those elopements spent about six weeks in Airdrie, wandering often by Carron or Calder's beautiful winding banks. Oh! could I then have seen the glorious gems that have sprung up for me on those banks, and heard the poetic strains that have since been sung in my praise, what a balm they would have been to my bleeding heart, as I wandered around the old Priestrig Pit, and listened to its engine thundering the water up from its lowest depth. For days I have wandered the fields between Moodiesburn and Clifton Hill, wooing my sorry muse, then unknown to the world—except to a few, as a child of song—in silence looking forward to the day when the world would know my wrongs and prize my worth; and had it not been for the bright Star of Hope which lingered near me and encouraged me onward, beyond doubt I would have been a suicide. 'Tis, however, strange that in all my weary wanderings I have always met with kind-hearted friends, and there were two who befriended me when I was a homeless wanderer in Airdrie. Fifteen years have passed since I saw the tears roll down their youthful cheeks and heard the heavy sigh that exploded from their sympathising hearts. But the best of friends must part, and I parted with them, perhaps never to meet again in this lovely world of sunshine and sorrow.

As my circumstances in life changed, duty called me forth to turn the poetic gift that Nature had given me to a useful and profitable account, for which purpose I commenced with vigorous zeal to write my poetical pieces, and sent them to the weekly newspapers for insertion, until I became extensively known and popular. As an instance: in 1854 the 'Glasgow Examiner' published a song of mine, entitled 'Lord Raglan's Address to the Allied Armies,' which made my name popular throughout Great Britain and Ireland, and for which I was honoured by receiving a letter from Lord Raglan's secretary, inclosing L.10 from his Lordship; but as my fame spread my health began to fail.

My stepfather was unable longer to work; my mother was also rendered a suffering object; and I, who had been the only support of the family, was informed by my medical adviser that unless I took a change of air, I would not live three months.

Under these circumstances, what was to be done? I did not then want to die, although I had wished to do so a thousand times before, to relieve me from unmerited slander and oppression.

Many sleepless nights did I pass, thinking what to try to bring relief to the afflicted household—although I did not consider myself in duty bound to struggle against the stern realities of nature, and sacrifice my own young life for those whose sympathies for me had been long seared and withered. Yet I could not, unmoved, look on the pale face of poverty, for their means were entirely exhausted, without hope to lean upon. Neither could I longer continue in the factory without certain death to myself, and I had never learned to do anything else.

Under those conflicting conditions and feelings, one night as I lay in bed, almost in despair, I prayed fervently that some idea how to act would be revealed to me, when suddenly I remembered that I had a piece of poetry entitled 'An Address to Napier's Dockyard, Lancefield, Finnieston,' which a young man had written for me in imitation of copperplate engraving, and that piece I addressed to Robert Napier, Esq., Shandon, Garelochhead, who was then in Paris, where it was forwarded to him. Having written to my employer for my character, which was found satisfactory, Mr Napier sent me a note to call at a certain office in Oswald Street, Glasgow, and draw as much money as would set me up in some small business, to see if my health would revive. According to the good old gentleman's instructions, I went as directed, and sought L.10, which was freely given to me; and I believe had I asked double the amount I would have readily received it.

Dear reader, I need not tell you what a godsend those ten pounds were to our distressed family, and kept me out of the factory during five months; after which I resumed work in Messrs Galbraith's Mill, St Rollox, Glasgow, where I continued till July, 1857, when my health again sank; and for a change of air and work I went to Belfast, where I remained two years, during which time I became greatly improved in health, and became so notorious for my poetic exploits, that the little boys and girls used to run after me to get a sight of 'the little Scotch girl' their fathers and mothers spoke so much about.

In 1859 I left Belfast and went to Manchester, where I worked three months, and then returned again to my native land, much improved in body and mind.

New scenes and systems made a great change in my nature. I became cheerful, and sought the society of mirthmakers, so that few would have taken me for the former moving monument of melancholy. I had again resumed work at Galbraith's factory, and all went on well; peace and good-will reigned in our household; the past seemed forgiven and forgotten; and the 'Factory Girl' was a topic of the day for her poetical productions in the public press, but the shadow of death was hovering behind all this gladsome sunshine.

My mother had been an invalid for several years, and, to add to her sorrow, a letter had come from her supposed dead husband, my father, in America, after an absence of twenty years, inquiring for his wife and child; on learning their fate he became maddened with remorse, and, according to report, drank a death-draught from a cup in his own hand, in the village of Cherryfield, State of Maine, North America; and my mother, after becoming aware of the mystery of my life, closed her weary pilgrimage on earth on 25th May, 1861; and disappointed of a promised home and husband, which I was not destined to enjoy, I therefore made up my mind to go to Dundee, where my father's sister resided, whose favourite I was when a child.

Dear reader, were I to give details of my trials, disappointments, joys, and sorrows, since I came to 'bonnie Dundee,' they would be, with a little embellishment, a romance of real life, sufficient to fill three ordinary volumes. Suffice here to say, that after suffering neglect and destitution for some time, I got work in the Verdant Factory, where the cloth I wove was selected by my master as a sample for others to imitate, until, on the 5th of December, 1863, I was discharged by the foreman without any reason assigned or notice given, in accordance with the rules of the work. Smarting under this treatment, I summoned the foreman into Court for payment of a week's wages, and gained the case. For the period of four months after I wandered through Dundee a famished and victimised factory exile.

From the foregoing statements some may think that I am rude, forward, and presumptuous; but permit me to say this much for myself, and those who know me best will confirm my statement, that I am naturally of a warm-hearted and affectionate disposition, always willing, to the extent of my power, to serve my fellow-creatures, and would rather endure an insult than retaliate on an enemy. All my wrongs have been suffered in silence and wept over in secret.

Perhaps there are few who can take a retrospective view of their past lives, and through their mind's eye gaze on so many strange incidents. Yes, gentle reader, I have suffered trials and wrongs that have but rarely fallen to the lot of woman. Mine were not the common trials of every-day life, but like those strange romantic ordeals attributed to the imaginary heroines of 'Inglewood Forest.'

Like the Wandering Jew, I have mingled with the gay on the shores of France—I have feasted in the merry halls of England—I have danced on the shamrock soil of Erin's green isle—and I have sung the songs of the brave and the free in the woods and glens of dear old Scotland.

I have waited and watched the sun-set hour to meet my lover, and then with him wandered by the banks of sweet, winding Clutha, when my muse has often been inspired when viewing the proud-waving thistle bending to the breeze, or when the calm twilight hour was casting a halo of glory around the enchanting scene; yet in all these wanderings I never enjoyed true happiness.

Like Rasselas, there was a dark history engraven on the tablet of my heart. Yes, dear reader, a dark shadow, as a pall, enshrouded my soul, shutting out life's gay sunshine from my bosom—a shadow which has haunted me like a vampire, but at least for the present must remain the mystery of my life.

Dear reader, I have wandered far away from my childhood's years. Yes, years that passed like a dream, unclouded and clear. Oh! that I could recall them; but, alas! they are gone for ever. Still they linger in memory, fresh and green as if they were yesterday. I can look back and see the opening chapters of my life—I can see the forms and faces, and hear their voices ringing in my ears. One sweet voice above the rest echoes like a seraph's song; but I dare not linger longer at present with those joyous hours and beloved forms that were then my guardian angels.

In conclusion, I am glad to say that the persecution I was doomed to suffer in vindication not only of my own rights, but of the rights of such as might be similarly situated, passed away, and peace and pleasure restored to my bosom again, by obtaining work at the Chapelshade Factory, at the east end of Dundee, where I wrought for three years and a-half to a true friend. For nearly two years I studied hard, and sent my poetic productions to the editor of the 'People's Journal,' Dundee,[1] in the hope that something would be done to relieve me from factory labour and pecuniary difficulties. Several of my pieces were published and admired, but otherwise I was sadly disappointed, when I fortunately became a reader of the 'Penny Post,' and shortly afterwards contributed some pieces to the 'Poets' Corner,' which seemed to cast a mystic spell over many of its readers, whose numerous letters reached me from various districts, highly applauding my contributions, and offering me their sympathy, friendship, and love; while others, inspired by the muses, responded to me through the same popular medium, some of whose productions will be found, along with my own, in the present volume.

And now, gentle reader, let me conclude by offering my grateful thanks to the Rev. George Gilfillan for his testimony in respect to the merits of my poetic productions, to Mr Alex. Campbell, of

---

1 'People's Journal,' Dundee] This newspaper, started in 1858, was edited by 1861 by William D. Latto, "an erstwhile handloom weaver and Free Kirk schoolmaster" (Klaus 49).

the 'Penny Post,' for his services in promoting their publication, as well as to the subscribers[1] who have so long patiently waited for this volume, which I hope may prove a means of social and intellectual enjoyment to many, and also help to relieve me from the incessant toil of a factory life.

ELLEN JOHNSTON,
THE FACTORY GIRL.
GLASGOW, *March*, 1869.

---

1 In the 1869 edition, the list of "Patrons and Subscribers" includes almost fifty names, the first of which are "Her Majesty Queen Victoria," "Right Hon. Benjamin Disraeli, M.P.," "Robert Napier, Esq. of Shandon, Gareloch," and "Lord Raglan."

Appendix A: Contemporary Perspectives on A Memoir of Robert Blincoe

[The documents in Appendices A.1 and A.2 appeared in *The Lion* subsequent to the publication of *A Memoir of Robert Blincoe* in 1828. The first item, from the issue for 14 March, is a note confirming some of the information related in the *Memoir*, attributed only as having been reported to *The Lion* by a "correspondent in Derbyshire." The second, which was reported to Carlile by "a friend at Manchester," was published on 28 March and relates Blincoe's opinion of his own story.

In each of these documents, readers were informed about two of the principals in Blincoe's *Memoir* and were able to gain brief insight into their lives in the late 1820s, as first Needham and then Blincoe himself are mentioned. The first document alleges not only that were the children at the Litton Mill physically and mentally mistreated, as the *Memoir* charges, but also that the females were sexually abused as well. When published in *The Lion*, Blincoe's *Memoir* made no such charges, yet when the *Memoir* later appeared in pamphlet form and when it was published by John Doherty, an addition was made to the text that reinforced such charges (see 148)].

1. A Correspondent to *The Lion*, "Confirmation of the Memoir of Robert Blincoe" (14 March 1828)

A CORRESPONDENT in Derbyshire says, that, never in his life did he feel so shocked, as he was on reading the account of the barbarous and inhuman treatment inflicted on the apprentices at Litton Cotton Mill, in that county, as developed, in several of the late numbers of "THE LION." He informs us, that, he knew the then master of the Mill, some of his sons, the magistrates, and their clerk, and most of the principal characters named in the memoir; and, although he has lived the whole of his life (upwards of 50 years), within fifteen miles of the place, yet, he does not recollect, ever before having heard of the cruel treatment, the poor children employed at that Mill, were doomed to suffer. On his first reading the account, he was much inclined to think the statements it contained were greatly exaggerated; and he tells us, that, he has since taken some trouble, in making enquiries, as to their truth; and sorry he is to say, that the unanimous testimony of several persons resident at, or near the place, go to the length of supporting, generally, the statements of Blincoe, with the horrible additions, that the childrens' beds (if the sackcloth stuffed with straw on which they lay deserves the name) frequently, in the summer months, swarmed with maggots!! that the girls were frequently prostituted to the carnal lusts of the young masters, who did not (as occasion required) scruple to make use of the most base means of screening their own infamy. Although these abominations, were carried on under the eye and knowledge of old Needham, yet, he always seemed to sanction, rather than cheque them; and while these poor, miserable, half naked, famished children, were thus used, the masters were rioting in the most voluptuous extravagance. But times (says our correspondent) are now altered with them. Old Needham is a pauper; his wife teaches a few little children their A. B. C., at Hathersage, a few miles distant from Litton, and the sons are vagabonds. So that, old Bekka, of Chapel-en-le-Firth (for so he spells the place) if she was not in reality a witch, she has, at any rate, proved herself a shrewd guesser. The Litton Mill, we understand, is now at work; but, from the generally healthy and decent appearance of the children employed, there is little doubt, that the present master has some humanity about him.

[Source: *The Lion*, 1.11: 14 March 1828. 338-39.]

2. A Friend at Manchester, "Confirmation of Blincoe's Printed Memoir By Himself" (28 March 1828)

Communicated by a friend at Manchester to Mr. Carlile.

Blincoe called on me last week, to ask why you had published an account of his life without his permission, and seemed, at first, inclined to be angry about it. I heard all he had to say, and began a defence for you. Before we parted, he became good-humoured, and acquiesced in the propriety of its being published. I then presented him with a copy in your name, which he promised to read, and to call upon me again with his opinion of the work.

He called the next day and pointed out two errors. The one was *Burton* printed for *Buxton*; and the other, Staley Bridge, seven miles from *London* instead of from *Manchester*. The latter is so glaring an error, that I wonder you did not perceive it.[1]

He said, the whole, with the above exceptions, was true, so far as it went; but that the enormities practised in Litton Mill were much greater than those related in the memoir. He shewed me various scars

---

1 The writer here seems to switch the place names: "Buxton" is the one printed in Carlile's versions (*Memoir,* note on page 119), and "Manchester" appears correctly in all three editions of the *Memoir* (see note 3 on pages 172-73).

on his head and face, which had been inflicted upon him, and the backs of his ears were covered with seams, which had been caused, as he told me, by the pincers and hand-vices, which his merciless taskmasters applied to his ears to punish him, for real or supposed offences. And yet, with all these damning proofs of cruel treatment, he says, that he was not so ill treated as many others were at the same mill.

Note. —The Memoir of Blincoe is now on sale, in a separate pamphlet, and, in addition to all the other confirmations, as to its truth, this of Blincoe himself places the statement beyond all doubt. It is now a standard work, to which future ages may refer, as to a specimen of the christian character of some of the people of England, at the commencement of the nineteenth century. We need not say more about it in this publication.

[Source: *The Lion*, 1.13: 28 March 1828. 401.]

3. Robert Blincoe, Testimony before the 1833 Royal Commission on the Employment of Children in Factories

[In 1833 Robert Blincoe was one of eleven witnesses sworn in and examined by Dr. Bisset Hawkins for the 1833 royal commission on children's factory labor (see Introduction 22-24). Dr. Hawkins prefaced his transcription of this testimony with a "General Report" in which he declared his "deliberate opinion" against employing any children younger than ten years in factory labor and limiting to ten hours the time worked by all those younger than eighteen (D3, 1). Hawkins supported this view with results of a survey of medical opinion and his own statistical investigations in Manchester, commenting at length on the physical debilitation as well as "the intemperance, debauchery, and improvidence" characteristic of factory labor (D3, 4). As if to confirm that Blincoe's testimony about his early experience of factory life was still relevant in 1833, Dr. Hawkins also interviewed two young workers so injured by their labors as to be unemployable: James Hayes, "a Cotton Factory Boy" of fourteen, who had lost all but his "little finger" when his hand was caught in a wheel; and Anne Barnett, "a Cotton Factory Girl" of fourteen, who had been unemployed for the past ten months because her four years of factory labor had given her "swelled" feet and "emaciated" legs. Both reported that their health and, in particular, their appetites had improved since they had become too disabled to work (D3, 12-13).]

ROBERT BLINCOE, a small Manufacturer,
once an Apprentice to a Cotton Mill, sworn,
and examined by Dr. Hawkins, 18th May 1833.

Do you know where you were born?—No; I only know that I came out of St. Pancras parish, London.

Do you know the name of your parents with certainty?—No. I used to be called, when young, Robert Saint; but when I received my indentures I was called in them Robert Blincoe, and I have gone by that name ever since.

What age are you?—Near upon forty, according to my indentures.

Have you no other means of knowing your age but what you find in your indentures?—No; I go by that.

Do you work at a cotton mill?—Not now. I was bound apprentice to a cotton mill for fourteen years from St. Pancras parish; then I got my indentures. I worked five or six years after at different mills, but now I have got a work of my own. I rent power from a mill in Stockport, and have a room to myself; my business is a sheet wadding manufacturer.

Why did you leave off working at the cotton mills?—I got tired of it, the system is so bad; and I had saved a few pounds. I got deformed there; my knees began to bend in when I was fifteen; you see how they are (*showing them*). There are many, many far worse than me at Manchester.

Can you take exercise with ease?—A very little makes me sweat in walking; I have not the strength of those who are straight.

Have you ever been in a hospital, or under doctors, for your knees or legs?—Never in a hospital or under doctors for that, but for illness from over-work I have been; when I was near Nottingham there were about eighty of us together, boys and girls, all 'prenticed out from St. Pancras parish, London, to cotton mills; many of us used to be ill, but the doctors said it was only for want of kitchen physic and of more rest.

Have you had any accidents from machinery?—No, nothing to signify much; I have not myself, but I saw, on the 6th of March last, a man killed by machinery at Stockport; he was smashed, and he died in four or five hours; I saw him while the accident took place; he was joking with me just before; it was in my own room. I employ a poor sore cripple under me, who could not easily get work any where else; a young man came good naturedly from another room to help my cripple, and he was accidentally drawn up by the strap, and was killed. I have known many such accidents take place in the course of my life.

Recollect a few.—I cannot recollect the exact number, but I have known several: one was at Lytton mill in Derbyshire; another was a master of a factory at Staley Bridge, of the name of Bailey. Many more I have known to receive injuries, such as the loss of a limb; there is plenty about Stockport that is going about now with one arm; they cannot work in the mills, but they go about with jackasses and such like. One girl, Mary Richards, was made a cripple, and remains so now, when I was in Lowdham mill near Nottingham; she was lapped up by a shaft underneath the drawing frame. That is now an old-fashioned machinery.

Have you any children?—Three.

Do you send them to factories?—No; I would rather have them transported. In the first place, they are standing upon one leg, lifting up one knee, a great part of the day, keeping the ends up from the spindle; I consider that that employment makes many cripples; then there is the heat and the dust; then there are so many different forms of cruelty used upon them; then they are so liable to have their fingers catched and to suffer other accidents from the machinery; then the hours is so long, that I have seen them tumble down asleep among the straps and machinery, and so get cruelly hurt; then I would not have a child of mine there because there is not good morals; there is such a lot of them together that they learn mischief.

What do you do with your children?—My eldest, of thirteen, has been to school, and can teach me. She now stays at home and helps her mother in the shop. She is as tall as me, and is very heavy; very different from what she would have been if she had worked in a factory. My two youngest go to school, and are both healthy. I send them every day two miles to school. I know from experience the ills of confinement.

What are the forms of cruelty that you spoke of just now as being practised upon children in factories?—I have seen the time when two hand-vices of a pound weight each, more or less, have been screwed to my ears, at Lytton mill in Derbyshire. Here are the scars still remaining behind my ears. Then three or four of us have been hung at once on a cross beam above the machinery, hanging by our hands, without shirts or stockings. Mind, we were apprentices, without father or mother to take care of us; I don't say that they often do that now. Then we used to stand up, in a skip, without our shirts, and be beat with straps or sticks; the skip was to prevent us from running away from the strap.

Do you know that such things are now done in Manchester?—No, not just the same things; but I think the children are still beaten by overlookers; not so much, however, in Manchester, where justice is always at hand, as in country places. Then they used to tie on a twenty-eight pounds weight (one or two at once), according to our size, to hang down on our backs, with no shirts on. I have had them myself. Then they used to tie one leg up to the faller, whilst the hands were tied behind. I have a book written about these things, describing my own life and sufferings. I will send it to you.[1]

---

1 Enclosed for the inspection of the Central Board. It is entitled "A Memoir of Robert Blincoe, &c. Manchester." J. Doherty. 1832. [Original note]

Did the masters know of these things, or were they done only by the overlookers?—The masters have often seen them, and have been assistants in them.

[Source: "Medical Reports by Dr. Hawkins." Second Report of the Central Board of His Majesty's Commissioners Appointed to Collect Information in the Manufacturing Districts, as to the Employment of Children in Factories. *Parliamentary Papers* 21 (1833): D3, 17-18.]

4. Substantive Changes in Doherty's 1832 Edition of the *Memoir*

[In 1832, Brown's *A Memoir of Robert Blincoe* was published for the third time in four years, on that occasion by working-class activist and editor John Doherty. In this instance Blincoe himself apparently contributed information to the earlier versions. In the present edition, for typographical or accidental authority we have used the Carlile pamphlet of 1828, inserting the text that Doherty added in curly brackets "{}" and removing to this appendix the material replaced in the Carlile pamphlet (see Note on the Text).

What follows, therefore, is a comparison of the Carlile and Doherty texts. In each case, the page and line numbers refer to the Broadview edition. Given first is the text in quotation marks as it appeared in Carlile's pamphlet of 1828, followed by the text in Doherty's version of 1832, reprinted within curly brackets. Text in such brackets that does not follow material in quotation marks was added by Doherty to the 1828 edition. In only one instance does it seem that Doherty's compositors mistakenly omitted a line from the Carlile edition (see entry for page 138 below).]

89: 16-17. "London: Printed and Published by Richard Carlile, 62, Fleet Street. Price One Shilling." {Manchester: Printed for and Published by J. Doherty, 37, Withy-Grove. 1832.}

92: 11-14. "still living somewhere in Lancashire. The Publisher was anxious to see him, in the autumn of the last year; but received information, on enquiry, that, having engaged in some kind of shop, he had become insolvent, and was, or had been, confined in Lancaster Castle for debt." {now about 35 years of age, and resides at No. 19, Turner-street, Manchester, where he keeps a small grocer's shop. He is also engaged in manufacturing Sheet Wadding and Cotton Waste-Dealer.}

100: 7. "and" {in}

105: 18. "his own conduct" {his conduct}

107: 29-31. {Blincoe being so overjoyed with the fine expectations he was

to receive at Lowdam Mill, he spent his shilling at Leicester in apples.}
111: 5. "this" {the}
117: 24. "most" {utmost}
119: 2. "my then situation" {my situation}
119: 29. "sat" {set}
119: 33. "Buxton" {Burton}
121: 26. "Buxton" {Burton}
122: 26. "Buxton" {Burton}
124: 19. "———" {Mary}
126: 18. "Crompton Bridge" {Cromford}
126: 30. "one" {the}
127: 38. "overseer" {overseers}
128: 3. "of" {for}
130: 15. "year" {three} year{s}
133: 16. "in" {at}
133: 29. "the bell" {the first bell}
136: 3-4. "a premature death" {premature death}
136: 25. "Toddington" {Tadington}
137: 20. "of" {to}
138: 8. after "propensities,": "so truly diabolical, as to stagger belief, and yet so well authenticated"
138: 20. "insulated" {insulted}
140: 7. "P———" {Pitt}
143: 20. "crib" {skip}
143: 34. {, the marks to be seen}
145: 11. "broken or dislocated" {broken dislocated}
145: 21. {, *marks to be seen*}
146: 19. "under" {round}
147: 18-148: 3. {["]We frequently had our best dinner in the week on a Sunday, and it was generally broth, meat and turnips, with a little oat-cake, the meat was of as coarse a sort as could be bought. This being our extra dinner, we did not wish to part with it too soon, therefore it was a general practice amongst the 'prentices to save some of it until Monday, in the care of the governor of the 'prentice house, and for each one to know their own. The practice was to cut in their oat-cake, some mark or other, and lay it on their wooden trenchers. It happened one Sunday we had our dinner of bacon broth and turnips with a little oat-cake. This Sunday, one Thomas Linsey, a fellow 'prentice thought he could like a snack, early in the morning, therefore he took a slice of bacon between two pieces of oat-cake to bed with him, and put it under his head[,] I cannot say, under his pillow, because we never was allowed any. The next morning about three or four o'clock, as it was a usual practice in the summer time when short of water, for a part of the hands to begin their work sooner, by this contrivance we was able to work our full time or near. Linsey was found dead in bed, and as soon as some of the

'prentices knew of his death, as they slept about 50 in a room, there was a great scuffle who should have the bacon and oat-cake from under his head, some began to search his pockets for his tin, this tin he used to eat his victuals with; some had pieces of broken pots, as no spoons was allowed. It was reported this Sunday that this pig had died in the Lees, a place so called at the back of the 'prentice-house. There was no coroner's inquest held over Linsey to know the cause of his death.["] I shall leave the reader to judge for himself this distressing sight, at so early an hour in the morning.—This occurred at Litton Mill.}

149: 6. "must" {might}

149: 22. "the apprentices" {apprentices}

152: 4. {William}

152: 4-5. {the manager, brother to Robert Woodward}

152: 19 and 31. {William}

153: 36. "Brickman" {Brickleton}

153: 43. "Brickman" {Brickleton}

154: 4. "Brickman" {Brickleton}

157: 6. "run" {run away}

158: 18. "Litton" Litton{-Mill}

159: 12. "a few" {about five}

159: 28. "unsavory" {savory}

160: 18. "———" {Leam}

166: 34. "a destiny" {destiny}

167: 21. "Mellow" {Mellor}

168: 27. "and therefore" {therefore}

173: note *. {Water-street, Manchester,}

173: note *. "Karspool Moor" {Kersal-Moor}

175: 16. "18ᵗʰ" {27ᵗʰ}

175: 32. "19ᵗʰ" {28ᵗʰ}

176: 4-5. {went in a coach from his lodgings in Bank-Top, and}

176: 19-177: 6. {In the year 1824, Blincoe had accumulated in business that sum of money he thought would be sufficient to keep his family, with the exception of his cotton-waste business; shortly after he gave up a shop which he had occupied for a few years at No. 108, Bank-Top, Manchester, and took a house at Edge-place, Salford, whilst living there, thought proper to place some of the money he had saved by industry to the purchasing of some machinery for spinning of cotton—and took part of a mill of one Mr. Ormrod, near St. Paul's Church, Tib-street, in this he was engaged six weeks, with the assistance of some mechanics, getting the machinery ready for work—the first day it was at work, an adjoining room of the building caught fire, and burnt Blincoe's machinery to the ground, not being insured, nearly ruined him.—Blincoe declares that he will have nothing to do with the spinning business again—what with the troubles endured when apprentice to it, and the heavy loss sustained by fire, is completely sick of the business altogether.}

177: 8. "Confirmation" Confirmation{s}

177: 9-178: 19.

{Ashton-under-Line, Feb. 24, 1828.

DEAR SIR—I have read the narrated sufferings of Robert Blincoe with mingled sorrow and delectation: with sorrow, because I know, from bitter experience, that they have really existed; with delectation, because they have appeared before the public through the medium of the press, and may, peradventure, be the means of mitigating the misery of the unfortunate apprentices, who are serving an unexpired term of apprenticeship in various parts of Lancashire and Derbyshire. In 1806 or 7, I was bound an apprentice, with twelve others, from the work-house of St. James,' Clerkenwell London, to a Mr. J. Oxley, at Arnold-mill, near Nottingham. From thence, after two years and three months' servitude, I was sold to a Mr. Middleton, of Sheffield. The factory being burnt down at this place, I with many others, were sold to Mr. Ellice Needham, of Highgate-wall, the owner and proprietor of Litton Mill! Here I became acquainted with Robert Blincoe, better known at Litton-mill by the name of Parson. The sufferings of the apprentices were exquisite during Blincoe's servitude, both in point of hunger and acts of severity; but, subsequent to Blincoe's departure from that place, the privations we had to endure, in point of hunger, exceeded all our former sufferings (if that were possible), having to subsist principally upon woodland sustenance, or, in other words, on such food as we could extract from the woods. What I now write is to corroborate the statement of Blincoe, having heard him relate during my apprenticeship, all, or nearly all, the particulars that are now narrated in his memoir. I may also add, that I worked under Blincoe, at the same machine, in the capacity that he had done under Woodward, without receiving any harsh treatment from him—nay, so far was Blincoe from ill-treating the apprentices employed under him, that he would frequently give part of his allowance of food to those under his care, out of mere commisseration, and conceal all insignificant omissions without a word of reproach—I cannot close this letter without relating an anecdote that occurred about two years ago. Happening to call at a friend's house one day, he asked if I knew Robert Blincoe. I replied in the affirmative. Because, added, [*sic*] he, I saw a prospectus of his biography some time past; and related the same to W. Woodward, who was on a visit here, and who immediately said, "HE'LL GIVE IT MA," and became very dejected during the remainder of his visit.

Your humble servant,
JOHN JOSEPH BETTS.}

179: [22]. "Printed by R. Carlile, 62, Fleet Street."

Appendix B: Contemporary Perspectives on William Dodd's Narrative

1. Lord Ashley and John Bright, from the debate of 15 March 1844, House of Commons

[This selection from the lengthy debate on "Hours of Labour in Factories" highlights not only the contest between Ashley and Bright over the reliability of William Dodd as a witness in the ten-hours cause, but also Ashley's impassioned objections to female factory labor (see Introduction 11-12, 52 and 55, respectively). By moving an amendment defining the word *night* in the proposed "Factories Bill" as "six o'clock in the evening to six o'clock in the following morning," Ashley was asking his colleagues in the House to approve a ten-hour day for women, children, and "young persons under thirteen years of age" since he also proposed that two hours be set aside for meals and rest (1073). As one of the M.P.s who spoke before Bright noted, the effect of Ashley's proposal would have been to legislate a ten-hour day for all operatives since the work of adult men was dependent on that of women and children (1111). As another M.P. further objected, Ashley's account of the effects of industrialized work was "an argument to get rid of the whole system of factory labour" (1120). Throughout his speech, on the length of which Bright twice remarked, Ashley referred repeatedly to his unnamed sources: "I state this on the authority of several practical [practicing?] spinners" (1082) or on that of "a letter from a person who went down to Bolton to make returns [reports] for me" (1083). Bright, as the excerpt below reveals, made the most of the anonymity of Ashley's sources.]

Lord *Ashley:* [...] I do not doubt that several of the statements I have read, will create surprise in the minds of many hon. Members; but if they were to converse with operatives who are acquainted with the practical effects of the system, they would cease to wonder at the facts I have detailed. I might detain the House by enumerating the evils which result from the long working of males and females together in the same room. I could show the many and painful effects to which females are exposed, and the manner in which they lament and shrink from the inconveniences of their situation. I have letters from Stockport and Manchester, from various individuals, dwelling on the mischievous consequences which arise from the practice of modest women working so many hours together with men, and not being able to avail themselves of those opportunities which would suggest themselves to every one's mind without particular mention. Many mills, I readily admit, are admirably regulated, but they are yet in a minority—were all of such a description as several that I have seen, they might not, perhaps, require any enactments. [...]

But listen to another fact, and one deserving of serious attention; that the females not only perform the labour, but occupy the places of men; they are forming various clubs and associations, and gradually acquiring all those privileges which are held to be the proper portion of the male sex. These female clubs are thus described:—Fifty or sixty females, married and single, form themselves into clubs, ostensibly for protection; but, in fact, they meet together, to drink, sing, and smoke; they use, it is stated, the lowest, most brutal, and most disgusting language imaginable." Here is a dialogue which occurred in one of these clubs, from an ear witness:—"A man came into one of these club-rooms, with a child in his arms; 'Come lass,' said he, addressing one of the women, 'come home, for I cannot keep this bairn quiet, and the other I have left crying at home.' 'I won't go home, idle devil,' she replied, 'I have thee to keep, and the bairns too, and if I can't get a pint of ale quietly, it is tiresome. This is the only second [*sic*] pint that Bess and me have had between us; thou may sup if thou likes, and sit thee down, but I won't go home yet[.]'" Whence is it that this singular and unnatural change is taking place? Because that on women are imposed the duty and burthen of supporting their husbands and families, a perversion as it were of nature, which has the inevitable effect of introducing into families disorder, insubordination, and conflict. What is the ground on which the woman says she will pay no attention to her domestic duties, nor give the obedience which is owing to her husband? Because on her devolves the labour which ought to fall to his share, and she throws out the taunt, "If I have the labour, I will also have the amusement." The same mischief is taking place between children and their parents; the insubordination of children is now one of the most frightful evils of the manufacturing districts. "Children and young persons take the same advantage of parents that women do of their husbands, frequently using harsh language, and, if corrected, will turn round and say, '————you, we have you to keep.' One poor woman stated that her husband had chided two of their daughters for going to a public-house; he made it worse, for they would not come home again, stating, 'they had their father to keep, and they would not be dictated to by him.'" This conduct in the children is likewise grounded on the assertion that the parents have no right to interfere and control them, since, without their labour, the parents could not exist; and this is the bearing of children, many of whom are under thirteen or fourteen years of age! Observe carefully, too, the ferocity of character which is exhibited by a great mass of the female population of the manufacturing towns. Recollect the outbreak of 1842, and the share borne in that by the girls and women; and the still more frightful contingencies which may be in store for the future. "I met," says an informant of mine, "with a mother of factory workers, who told me that all the churches and chapels were useless places, and so was all the talk about education, since the young and old were unable to attend, either in consequence of the former being imprisoned in the mills so many hours, and being in want of rest the little time they were at home; and the latter being compelled to live out of the small earnings of their children, and cannot get clothing, so they never think of going to churches or chapels. She added, 'when you get up to London, tell them we'll turn out the next time (meaning the women), and let the soldiers fire upon us if they dare, and depend upon it there will be a break out, and a right one, if that House of Commons don't alter things, for they can alter if they will, by taking mothers and daughters out of the factories, and sending the men and big lads in.'" But further, what says Sir Charles Shaw, for some years the superintendent of the police of Manchester—what is his opinion of the condition of the females of that town, and the effects produced, by the system under which they live, on their conduct and character?—

"Women (says he) by being employed in a factory, lose the station ordained them by Providence, and become similar to the female followers of an army, wearing the garb of women, but actuated by the worst passions of men. The women are the leaders and exciters of the young men to violence in every riot and outbreak in the manufacturing districts, and the language they indulge in is of a horrid description. While they are themselves demoralised, they contaminate all that comes within their reach."

This will conclude the statement that I have to make to the House—and now, Sir, who will assert that these things should be permitted to exist? Who will hesitate to apply the axe to the root of the tree, or, at least, endeavour to lop off some of its deadliest branches? What arguments from general principles will they adduce against my proposition? What, drawn from peculiar circumstances? They cannot urge that particular causes in England give rise to particular results; the same cause prevails in various countries; and wherever it is found, it produces the same effects. I have already stated its operation in France, in Russia, in Switzerland, in Austria, and in Prussia; I may add also in America; for I perceive by the papers of the 1st of February, that a Bill has been proposed in the Legislature of Pennsylvania, to place all persons under the age of sixteen, within the protection of the "ten hours" limit. I never thought that we should have learned justice from the City of Philadelphia. In October last I visited an immense establishment in Austria, which gives employment to several hundred hands; I went over the whole, and conversed with the managers, who detailed to me the same evils and the same fruits as those I have narrated to the House—prolonged labour of sixteen and seventeen hours, intense fatigue, enfeebled frame, frequent consumptive disorders, and early deaths—yet the locality had every advantage; well-built and airy houses in a fine open country, and a rural district; nevertheless, so injurious are the effects, that the manager added, stating at the same time, the testimony of many others who resided in districts where mills are more abundant, that, in ten years from the time at which he spoke, "there would hardly be a man in the whole of those neighbourhoods fit to carry a musket." Let me remind, too, the House, of the mighty change which has taken place among the opponents to this question. When I first brought it forward in 1833, I could scarcely number a dozen masters on my side, I now count them by hundreds. We have had, from the West Riding of Yorkshire, a petition signed by 300 millowners, praying for a limitation of labour to ten hours in the day. Some of the best names in Lancashire openly support me. I have letters from others who secretly wish me well, but hesitate to proclaim their adherence; and even among the members of the Anti-Corn-Law League, I may boast of many firm and efficient friends. Sir, under all the aspects in which it can be viewed, this system of things must be abrogated or restrained—it affects the internal tranquillity of those vast provinces, and all relations between employer and employed—it forms a perpetual grievance and ever comes uppermost among their complaints in all times of difficulty and discontent. It disturbs the order of nature, and the rights of the labouring men, by ejecting the males from the workshop, and filling their places by females, who are thus withdrawn from all their domestic duties, and exposed to insufferable toil at half the wages that would he assigned to males, for the support of their families. It affects—nay, more, it absolutely annihilates, all the arrangements and provisions of domestic economy—thrift and management are altogether impossible; had they twice the amount of their present wages, they would be but slightly benefited—everything runs to waste; the house and children are deserted; the wife can do nothing for her husband and family; she can neither cook, wash, repair clothes, or take charge of the infants; all must be paid for out of her scanty earnings, and, after all, most imperfectly done. Dirt, discomfort, ignorance, recklessness, are the portion of such households; the wife has no time for learning in her youth, and none for practice in her riper age; the females are most unequal to the duties of the men in the factories; and all things go to rack and ruin, because the men can discharge at home no one of the especial duties that Providence has assigned to the females. Why need I detain the House by a specification of these injurious results? They will find them stated at painful length in the Second Report of the Children's Employment Commission. Consider it, too, under its physical aspect! Will the House turn a deaf ear to the complaints of suffering that resound from all quarters? Will it be indifferent to the physical consequences on the rising generation? You have the authority of the Government Commissioner, Dr. Hawkins, a gentleman well skilled in medical statistics—

> "I have never been, (he tells you) in any town in Great Britain or in Europe, in which degeneracy of form and colour from the national standard has been so obvious as in Manchester."

I have, moreover, the authority of one of the most ardent antagonists, himself a mighty millowner, that, if the present system of labour be persevered in, the "county of Lancaster will speedily become a province of pigmies." The toil of the females has hitherto been considered the characteristic of savage life; but we, in the height of our refinement, impose on the wives and daughters of England a burthen from which, at least during pregnancy, they would be exempted even in slave-holding states, and among the Indians of America. But every consideration sinks to nothing compared with that which springs from the contemplation of the moral mischiefs this system engenders and sustains. You are poisoning the very sources of order and happiness and virtue; you are tearing up root and branch, all the relations of families to each other; you are annulling, as it were, the institution of domestic life, decreed by Providence himself, the wisest and kindest of earthly ordinances, the mainstay of social peace and virtue, and therein of national security. There is a time to be born, and a time to die—this we readily concede; but is there not also a time to live, to live to every conjugal and parental duty—this we seem as stiffly to deny; and yet in the very same breath we talk of the value of education, and the necessity of moral and religious training. Sir, it is all in vain, there is no national, no private system, that can supersede the influence of the parental precept and parental example—they are ordained to exercise an unlimited power over the years of childhood; and, amidst all their imperfections, are accompanied with a blessing[.] Whose experience is so confined that it does not extend to a knowledge and an appreciation of the maternal influence over every grade and department of society? It matters not whether it be prince or peasant, all that is best, all that is lasting in the character of a man, he has learnt at his mother's knees. Search the records, examine the opening years of those who have been distinguished for ability and virtue, and you will ascribe, with but few exceptions, the early culture of their minds, and above all, the first discipline of the heart, to the intelligence and affection of the mother, or at least of some pious woman, who with the self-denial and tenderness of her sex, has entered as a substitute, on the sacred office. No, Sir, these sources of mischief must be dried up; every public consideration demands such an issue; the health of the females; the care of their families; their conjugal and parental duties; the comfort of their homes; the decency of their lives; the rights of their husbands; the peace of society; and the laws of God—and, until a vote shall have been given this night, which God avert, I never will believe that there can be found in this House one individual man who will deliberately and conscientiously inflict, on the women of England such a burthen of insufferable toil. Sir, it is very sad, though perhaps inevitable, that such weighty charges and suspicions should lie on the objects of those who call for, and who propose, this remedial measure. I am most unwilling to speak of myself: my personal character is, doubtless, of no consequence to the world at large; but it may be of consequence to those whose interests I represent; because distrust begets delays; and zeal grows cold, when held back in its career by the apprehension that those, whom it would support, are actuated by unworthy motives. Disclaimers, I know, are poor things when uttered by parties whom you listen to with suspicion or dislike; but consider it calmly; are you reasonable to impute to me a settled desire, a single purpose, to exalt the landed, and humiliate the commercial aristocracy? Most solemnly do I deny the accusation; if you think me wicked enough, do you think me fool enough, for such a hateful policy? Can any man in his senses now hesitate to believe that the permanent prosperity of the manufacturing body, in all its several aspects, physical, moral, and commercial, is essential, not only to the welfare, but absolutely to the existence of the British Empire? No, we fear not the increase of your political power, nor envy your stupendous riches; "peace be within your walls, and plenteousness within your palaces!" We ask but a slight relaxation of toil, a time to live, and a time to die; a time for those comforts that sweeten life, and a time for those duties that adorn it; and, therefore, with a fervent prayer to Almighty God that it may please him to turn the hearts of all who hear me to thoughts of justice and of mercy, I now finally commit the issue to the judgment and humanity of Parliament.

[...]

Mr. *Bright* said, it is with unfeigned reluctance that I rise to speak, having so recently addressed the House at some length, but being intimately connected with the branch of industry which is affected by the proposition now under consideration, and having lived all my life among the population most interested in this Bill, and having listened most attentively for more than two hours to the speech of the noble Lord, the Member for Dorsetshire, I think I am entitled to be heard on the question now under discussion. I have listened to that speech without much surprise, because I have heard or read the same speech, or one very like it, on former occasions, and I did not suppose that any material change had taken place in the opinions of the noble Lord. It appears to me, however, that he has taken a one-sided view, a most unjust and unfair view of the question; it may not be intentionally, but still a view which cannot be borne out by facts; a view, moreover, which factory inspectors and their reports will not corroborate, and one which, if it influence the decision of this House, will be most prejudicial to that very class which the noble Lord intends to serve. [...] I am at a loss to discover any grounds on which it can with fairness be asserted that the Bill now in operation has failed in its effect. I know the inspectors affirm that it cannot be fully carried out. Every body who knows any thing of the manufactories of the North, knew when it was passed that it could not be fully carried out; and the proposition now made, is to render this impracticable Act more stringent. In a trade so extensive, employing so many people, carried on under circumstances ever varying, no Act of Parliament interfering with the minute details of its management, can ever be fully carried out. I am not one who will venture to say that the manufacturing districts of this country are a paradise; I believe there are in those districts evils great and serious; but whatever evils do there exist are referable to other causes than to the existence of factories and long chimneys. Most of the statements which the noble Lord has read, would be just as applicable to Birmingham, or to this metropolis, as to the northern districts; and as he read them over, with respect to the ignorance and intemperance of the people, the disobedience of children to their parents, the sufferings of mothers, and the privations which the children endure, I felt that there was scarcely a complaint which has been made against the manufacturing districts of the north of England, which might not be urged with at least as much force against the poorest portion of the population of every large city in Great Britain and Ireland. But among the population of Lancashire and Yorkshire, where towns are so numerous as almost to touch each other, these evils are more observable than in a population less densely crowded together. I can prove, however, and I do not wish to be as one-sided as the noble Lord, I can prove from authorities, which are at least as worthy of attention as his, the very reverse in many respects of what he has stated as the true state of those districts. Now the Committee will bear in mind that a large portion of the documents which the noble Lord has quoted, have neither dates nor names. I can give dates and names, and I feel confident that the authorities I shall cite are worthy of the deepest attention. I must go over the grounds of complaint which the noble Lord has urged, and although I may run the risk of being a little tedious, yet considering that for two hours or more I have listened to the charges which he has made,

I do think that, connected as I am most intimately with the population and the district to which the noble Lord has alluded, I have a right to an audience for the counter-statement which I have to make.

[...]

I do not charge the noble Lord [Ashley] with being actuated by feelings of malice in his conduct towards the manufacturers of this country, but I do believe him to have been, and to be now, grossly imposed upon by the persons upon whose information he relies. I can tell the noble Lord that he will never obtain credit for the statements he makes, unless he can obtain them from more honest characters than those he has hitherto employed. I know that one of these individuals has published many statements respecting the manufactories of the north, some of which are wholly false, and most of which, I believe, are grossly and malignantly exaggerated. I have in my hand two of these publications[:] one is "*The Adventures of William Dodd the Factory Cripple*" and the other is entitled "*The Factory System*," and consists of letters addressed to the noble Lord,—both books have gone forth to the public under the sanction of the noble Lord. I do not wish to go into the particulars of the character of this man, for it is not necessary to my case, but I can demonstrate, that his books and statements are wholly unworthy of credit. Dodd states that from the hardships he endured in a factory, he was "done up" at the age of thirty-two, whereas I can prove that he was treated with uniform kindness, which he repaid by gross immorality of conduct, and for which he was at length discharged from his employment. I have in my possession letters written by this individual, in which he states that the noble Lord and his party had used him as long as they could get any thing out of him. He said also, that the noble Lord had given him dinners at his own house, and that when he applied for a small balance due to him, the noble Lord had written him an angry letter, recounting the dinners he had eaten at his table. He had also stated that the noble Lord had shown him to his visitors as a cripple, as a specimen of what the factories were doing for the population employed in them. I do not wish to dwell upon this point, but I am free to tell the noble Lord, that unless he employs agents more respectable his statements and his professions of benevolence will ever be viewed with suspicion by the manufacturers of the north and I may add, that others who are thus employed, are in no degree more respectable or more creditable than Dodd. I beg the House to remember that Lancashire, the seat of the cotton manufacture contains a larger population than any other county in the United Kingdom. It has a population of 1,600,000, of whom not less than 900,000, or 56 per cent. on the whole, are in employment and in the receipt of wages, and without doubt a larger number are there employed than on any other equal surface in any part of the globe. The labourers employed in the cotton trade are more steadily employed and better paid than in any other trade in this country. I admit this people have suffered severely, but they have struggled manfully with the adversity which has overtaken them, whilst we have been foolish enough to permit the existence of monopolies and injustice, enough to have destroyed for ever the energies and the prosperity of an ordinary people. In addition to these monopolies, we have taxes most oppressive and unequal. The tax on raw cotton alone amounts to 50*l*. to 100*l*. per week on many manufacturing establishments; that with which I am connected being thus burthened to the amount of 75*l*. per week; and as four-fifths of all these manufactures are exported, and compete with foreign manufacturers who pay no such tax, the whole amount of it must come out of the profits and the wages of those engaged in the cotton trade. [...] The people ask for freedom for their industry, for the removal of the shackles on their trade; you deny it to them, and then forbid them to labour, as if working less would give them more food, whilst your monopoly laws make food scarce and dear. Give them liberty to work, give them the market of the world for their produce, give them the power to live comfortably, and increasing means and increasing intelligence will speedily render them independent enough and wise enough to bring the duration of labour to that point at which life shall be passed with less of irksome toil of every kind, and more of recreation and enjoyment. It is because I am convinced this project is now impracticable, and that under our present oppressive Legislation, it would make all past injustice only more intolerable, that I shall vote against the proposition which the noble Lord, the Member for Dorset, has submitted to the House.

Lord *Ashley:* I think the House will feel that in some measure I have a right to make one or two observations on the remarkable speech of the hon. Gentleman: I will thank the hon. Gentleman to explain that charge against me which he has insinuated, and which he said he would not pursue. I will not allow it to pass. I therefore throw myself on the indulgence and on the protection of this House; and I do request all hon. Gentlemen present to exert their influence, as members of this House and as gentlemen, to make the hon. Member for Durham pursue his charge, and state his case.

Mr. *Bright:* What is the charge the noble Lord alludes to? I told the noble Lord, that the instruments he carried on his operations with were not worthy of his cause or of him. I am prepared to maintain that assertion. I make no charge against the noble Lord: I tell him that I think he is much misled by these men. I am prepared to prove that those agents of the noble Lord are of a character, that I would not take their evidence with respect to agricultural matters; and I think it is not fair that it should be taken with respect to manufacturing matters. If the noble Lord wishes to have information respecting manufacturing affairs, nineteen out of twenty, nay, all the respectable manufacturers in Lancashire would be willing to give it him.

Lord *Ashley:* What, no charge? No "unpaid balance," I suppose! No "cripple paraded for exhibition!" Well, if the hon. Member says he has made no charge, and, if before the assembled Commons of England he is prepared to assert that he made no charge against me, I can assure him with satisfaction, that the matter may there rest. But those who heard the hon. Gentleman's statement, can best judge whether a charge were made; and those who hear me can best judge whether the hon. Member had the courage to maintain it. But let me appeal to the House: I ask, did I in the course of a long speech which the House was kind enough to listen to, say anything to provoke personal feeling? Did I utter one single sentence calculated to exasperate a single individual, or throw into the discussion of this great matter sentiments or expressions unbecoming so sacred a subject? If the hon. Gentleman thinks that his course of proceeding is the way in which he can maintain his own case, I must say that I am extremely sorry for it, because I think it is not suited to the dignity of the subject, not suited to the assembly in which we sit, and not suited by any means to that most respectable society of which the hon. Gentleman is a member.

Mr. *Bright;* The noble Lord is entirely mistaken. I say the noble Lord Lord [*sic*] is entirely mistaken if he supposes that I judge of his character by the character of the men in whom I tell him to put no trust. I tell the noble Lord plainly, that I have letters in my hand, which will prove all that I have stated. I will hand them to the noble Lord with pleasure. I will go further, and tell the noble Lord, that the individual who wrote the letters I hold in my hand, offered, for a sum of money, to sell a friend of mine a large number of other letters, which that friend of mine was, as I think, too fastidious to lay hold of. I tell the noble Lord not to trust these men. I have always thought that the noble Lord was honest in his convictions. I have always said so, both in public and in private; but I repeat that the instruments that he has worked with are not worthy of him or his cause. That is all I have to say. [*Cries of* "Read."] Here is the first extract. It is from a letter bearing date
"November 8, 1842."

"As I had strained at a gnat, it was clear to them that I should not do to swallow a camel. In other words, had I allowed their ill-feeling to vent itself, and come before the public under my name, I should have wrote a very different book from that which I produced, and even that I am almost ashamed of."

[An hon. *Member:* "What has that to do with it ?"]

"This is the manner in which I was taken hold of to serve party purposes, the work I was employed on, the hopes and expectations held out to me, the insignificant wages I received, and, now that they have got all out of me that they can, the manner in which I am cast off for ever."

In the same letter there was this passage:—

"In order that you may know what sort of a man he is (a person of the name of Jowett, and connected with Lord Ashley), I will tell you what were the orders I received from him previous to visiting your place last year. He told me—'You must go to Turton and get all the information you can concerning the works of Messrs. Ashworth—they are show mills. The Ashworths are deep, cunning people, and you must take particular care not to come into contact with them or their people.' Thus you see I was to stroll about the vicinity of your mills, and get into the company of your people, and by treating them with beer or by other means, was to get the information I required, and if from one whom you had cast off, so much the better."

In another letter there occurred this passage:—

"In my necessity I wrote to Lord Ashley, stating my circumstances, and asking for a remittance of a small balance due for services rendered."

Here (said the hon. Member) I beg it to be understood that I don't believe a word of this. Why, would I convict the noble Lord upon evidence which I do not credit, and which I would call upon him not to believe if it was used against myself?

"Due for services rendered—and in reply I received a very angry letter saying,"—these words (said the hon. Member) are in inverted commas—'saying that I had no claim on them—that my employment was a mere matter of charity—that I had received so much money,' and he even recounted the dinners I had received at his Lordship's table, and told me of the condition I was in at the time he took notice of me, and other matters equally galling. It is clear that party only used me as a tool, and having made all the use of me they can, send me about my business. If I was clear of the party I could a tale unfold, but, circumstanced as I am, this would be my ruin."

"Now, mind," said the hon. Member, "I bring no charge against the noble Lord of intentionally doing wrong. I say so sincerely. My friends know that in private I have always spoken of the noble Lord with respect, and I can assure him that it was with sorrow I learned that he was employing agents who were not trustworthy. There are other letters from a man named Jowett, which he offered to sell for 35*l.* to a particular friend of mine, but my friend refused to buy them; and I can tell the noble Lord circumstances with respect to other persons, which would lead him, I am sure, to form the same conclusion, that they are not trustworthy. And now I only hope that it is clearly understood that I have not said one word that is derogatory to the character of the noble Lord. I repeat, I have much respect for the noble Lord, but I am as much interested in this question as he can be, and I thought it better for the cause, and fairer to the noble Lord himself, that I should state these things to the world from this place, than that I should write a letter to the newspapers, or publish the statements in a pamphlet. I regret it if in stating these things I have said a word that could be considered derogatory to the character of the noble Lord. I know I am of a warm temperament, but I mean no personal insult; I desire merely to state facts."

Lord *Ashley:* It is high time, I think, that this sort of interlocutory matter should cease. I assure the hon. Gentleman on my part that I willingly accept his explanation. I am ready to believe that he meant nothing that was personally offensive. It is perfectly true that I was acquainted with Dodd, and it is perfectly true also that he called on me in London. I received a letter from him in which he stated, that he had been injured whilst working in a factory. He afterwards called on me, and certainly I never saw a more wretched object. He had lost his hand, and I may say had almost lost his shape. He hardly looked indeed like a human being. I certainly assisted him, and as far as refreshments went he had them, not with me, but I told him that if he chose to come when the servants dined he might have some dinner with them. He afterwards went down into the manufacturing districts, and from there he wrote me some letters; but I assure the hon. Gentleman that I never except once quoted a single fact from any one of his communications. Certain facts regarding him have since come to my knowledge, and I am certainly inclined now to think that he was unworthy my kindness.*

Mr. *Warburton* said, that the matter seem [*sic*] to have taken a new shape. He therefore would move that the Chairman report progress, and ask leave to sit again.

Motion agreed to.

House resumed.—Committee to sit again.

House adjourned at one o'clock.

---

*The following are extracts from the letters referred to by Mr. Bright.

In a letter to Messrs. Ashworth of Bolton, under date September 26, 1842. Dodd writes:—

"You are, Gentlemen, from personal observation, acquainted with my unhappy situation, you are also, I have no doubt, aware that my case has been laid hold of by Lord Ashley and his party in furtherance of their own views and objects; that I have been held up to public view by these philanthropists (?) as an object of charity, and as an instance of the cruelty of the manufacturers, and you will be surprised when I say that after all this fuss, I have been extremely illused by them. I have no blame to attach to Lord Ashley, except being misled, and induced to act contrary to his promises, by a man of the name of Benjamin Jowett, the man of all work for the ten hours' Bill party, and he is also the author of a pamphlet called "The Conspiracy," in which work your name and that of Mr. Greg, of Ashton, is prominently set forth. This man Jowett is not the friend of the working classes, and he deserves to be shewn in his true colours. He has injured me to a great extent. I should most willingly undertake to show the factory operatives and the public, that he and his party are not to be relied on; and was I to state the facts I am in possession of, it would, in my opinion, disperse the junta of which he is the organ; but this exposure would destroy my present source of living, and my future prospects, by setting all my friends against me, and without I was protected by some other parties, it would involve me in inevitable ruin."

"October 1, 1842.
"The manner in which I was taken hold of to serve party purposes, the work I have been employed upon, the insignificant wages I have received, the hopes and expectations which have been held out to me, and now (when they have got all out of me they can) the manner in which I have been cast off, even by Lord Ashley himself, without assigning any reason, and refusing to listen to my claims, all this would form a pamphlet as large as that of Jowett's, which I inclose."
"I could then expose this Jowett, who has taken so much pains, as you will see by the inclosed pamphlet, to cast a stigma on your firm and others. In order that you may know what sort of a man this is, I will tell you the orders I received from him, previous to visiting your place last year. 'You must go to Turton and get all the information you can concerning the works of Messrs. Ashworth, they are show mills. The Ashworths are deep, cunning fellows, and you must take particular care not to come in contact with them, or their people.' Thus you see, I was to stroll about in the immediate vicinity of your mills, and get in the company of any stray person I might

see, and by treating them with beer or by any other means, get all the information I required—if the person was one that you had cast off, so much the better."

"My name having acquired a notoriety in consequence of the manner in which my case has been held up to the public, I have had an offer to write articles on the Factory System, for a low weekly paper; I have already wrote one as a trial, but it is much against my feelings, only it supplies me with a dinner when, otherwise, I might probably be obliged to go without."

"November 2, 1842.
"You will perhaps be surprised to hear, that in my necessity, I wrote to Lord Ashley, stating my circumstances, and requesting the remittance of a small balance due to me for services rendered, and received a very angry letter, saying that I 'no claim upon them,['] that my employment was 'a mere matter of charity,' that I had received so much money, and even recounted the dinners I had received at his Lordship's table, and told me the condition I was in at the time he took notice of me, and other matters equally galling. It is very clear that the party has all along considered me only as a tool, and that having made all the use they can of me, I may now go about my business. I am sorry that I am not in a situation in life as would enable me to speak my mind freely; was I in a good business and entirely independent of the party, I could "a tale unfold,' but this, circumstanced as I now am, would be my ruin."

In addition to the letters from which the foregoing extracts are taken, there were thirteen other letters, placed for a time in the hands of Mr. Henry Ashworth, but afterwards returned to Dodd. The following is a verbatim copy of a letter from Dodd which accompanied them, and from it may be inferred something of their contents, which is all that can now be given of them, as Mr. Ashworth returned them without taking copies or making any extracts from them. This letter is headed

"EXPLANATION.

"Sir,—I have numbered the letters, &c., from one to thirteen, for the purpose of enabling you more easily to comprehend their contents, and hope you will have no difficulty in understanding the whole affair; but lest anything should appear doubtful, I have given the following explanation which will assist you a little. These are but a few of the papers, but they will be sufficient to shew you the nature of the business they wanted me for.

"No. 1.—Card of the gentleman to whom I was engaged.

"No. 2.—Letter I received after Mr. Jowett had waited upon Sir F.W.M——, shewing that it had been asked him to postpone his experiment, till I had done my business for Lord A——.

"No. 3.—Letter from ditto respecting the agreement which I was induced to decline in consequence of the promises and assurances of Mr. Jowett and Lord A——.

"No. 4.—Letter shewing the connection of Lord A——. and Mr. Jowett.

"No. 5.—Letter from Mr. Jowett shewing a little of his instructions to me.

"No. 6.—Letter from ditto on Fielden's mills.

"No. 7.—Two pages of colouring matter on ditto.

"No. 8.—A letter on money matters.

"No. 9.—A letter from the book-binder shewing how he had been reduced in the price of binding from 4 ½ d. per vol. the price I had promised him, to something less than 4d. by the men who are wishing to uphold (?) the wages of the labourer.

"Nos. 10 and 11.—Two letters from Lord A——, commending my dilligence, &c.

"No. 12.—One letter on business.

"No. 13.—A letter I received after I had taken every step I could think of to draw his Lordship's attention to the ill treatment I had experienced from Mr. Jowett. This will shew how his Lordship's mind had been poisoned, and will shew the manner of dismissing those who will not 'go the whole hog' in their service. Had I allowed Mr. Jowett to put forth his statements under my name, I should not have received this letter, neither would I have been cast off without a hearing in the presence of Mr. Jowett, my accuser, as I have been. In this letter there are many erroneous statements, which I could contradict if I had an opportunity."

[Source: *Hansard's Parliamentary Debates*, 3rd series, 73 (1844): columns 1095-1101, 1132-34, 1149-58.]

2. William Dodd, from *The Laboring Classes of England* (1847)

[After Dodd emigrated to the United States, he published an account of British labor in which he contrasted its conditions to those of the "new and ... better system" of New England. Dodd recapitulates much of the material that he offered in his *Narrative* of 1841 and *The Factory System Illustrated* of 1842, telling his own story as that of a man named James Graham (Letter II). Dodd also adds new material, recounting in Letter IX the "History of an Orphan Boy," the story of Robert Blincoe as the life of "Charles Smith," whom Dodd claims to have known personally; included at the end of his book is Caroline Norton's *A Voice from the Factories* (see Appendix G.2), though Dodd does not identify its author. Most significant, perhaps, is the fact that Dodd is no longer a "ten-hours man." Instead of arguing that regulation of factory labor will ameliorate the conditions created by industrialization, he explains to his new audience that the problems faced by British workers can be solved only through the reduction of taxation and an increase in the opportunities for education (142-43), both points that Dodd sees as relevant to the United States, a nation "destined to become the first manufacturing country in the earth" (148). In Letter I, the first and last sections of which are reprinted here, Dodd explains why he is writing *The Laboring Classes of England*—his deformities excite so many questions from Americans who have never seen "cripples ... made by hard labor" that he is moved to "gratify this laudable curiosity"—and he recounts his relation with Lord Ashley, here identified as "a benevolent Nobleman."]

LETTER I.

INTRODUCTION.

In offering the following work to the public, I have been actuated by a desire to diffuse as widely as possible the information it contains; believing it will be interesting and instructive to every well-wisher of the human race.

I have been led to publish the following facts, in consequence of the curiosity manifested by almost every person with whom I have become acquainted in America, to know my history, &c. So great has been the desire to question me upon this subject, that I have felt it, sometimes, to be my duty to refuse to give any information; my own feelings requiring me *to forget, as far as possible*, the injuries of former years. Whenever I feel my heart beat quicker, occasioned by a retrospective view of my sufferings, my peace of mind demands that I should instantly cry, "peace, be still." I believe, that had I fallen from some distant planet in the Solar system, the desire to know my history, and that of my species, could not have been greater. A single glance at my person, as I walk along the street, or stand in the presence of any one, is sufficient to awaken this curiosity in a country like America, where no such cripples are made by hard labor; but in England, where they are to be met in almost every street, it is very different. In order, therefore, to gratify this laudable curiosity, and spare my own feelings, publishing became necessary.

It may be asked how I gained the whole of my information upon this subject. To this I would answer, my situation has been in many respects peculiar. For twenty-five years of my short life, I have been actively engaged as an operative in the English factories. I am not aware that any one else who has published upon the factory system can make a similar assertion. I have not only toiled, but have been a sufferer from protracted mill labor to a painful extent. My experience, therefore, of the factory system has been dear-bought experience. I can speak feelingly, and I trust temperately. I have endeavored to avoid to the uttermost, every unguarded expression, every word which it would not become an humble operative to use; and I can add with truth, that I am not conscious of one unkindly or resentful feeling towards any human being.

In addition to the experience I have had in factories, I was employed in part of the years 1841 and 1842, by a benevolent Nobleman in London to assist him in his laudable endeavors to benefit the laboring classes. It may be interesting to the American reader to know, that my salary under this Nobleman was forty-five shillings per week, (about $11,) and coach hire, while travelling, and twenty shillings per week, ($5,) while stationary in London. Under this engagement I travelled through the West Riding of Yorkshire, Lancashire, Cheshire and Derbyshire; and being well supplied with letters of introduction, I had ample opportunities of conversing with all parties likely to afford me any information on the subject of factory life. In particular, I waited upon Clergymen of various denominations, Manufacturers, Surgeons, Inspectors and Overlookers. I had also opportunities of studying the habits and manners of the operatives, in the mills, cottages, places of amusement, public houses, &c., and of investigating the various causes of decrepitude, mutilation or death;—whether arising from long hours of labor, or accidents by machinery.

The facts contained in this volume have been carefully inquired into on the spot, and in many cases taken from the parties themselves, and corroborated by others not interested in the matter. I have no doubt the reader will be interested in perusing the following letters, which, with many others, I received from this nobleman while in his service.

[No. 1.]

Oct. 12, 1841.

DEAR——. You have discharged your *commission* admirably, and I am much obliged to you for the trouble you take, and the accuracy with which you furnish details.

I trust you will derive from your present duty that real satisfaction, which is the portion of those who labor, in God's name, for the welfare of their fellow creatures. I commit you most heartily to His care, and wish you every happiness in this world, and in that which is to come.

Faithfully yours,

A——.

[No. 2.]

St. G—— House, Nov. 24, 1841.

DEAR——. So far from thinking that you travel beyond your duty, when you write to me your opinions on all matters affecting the moral condition of the working classes, I am exceedingly pleased with your remarks; I altogether concur in them, and request you to continue your observations. I have always been convinced that a reduction in the hours of labor is only a preliminary to the measures we must introduce for the benefit of the working classes; but it is an *indispensable* preliminary. We must first settle this just principle, and then go on, by God's blessing, to draw long advantages from it. Limited as I am *in* Parliament, and *out* of it, I cannot undertake more than one thing at a time; but I think of a great many, and hope to be able hereafter to effect a few of them.

Your labors have been very serviceable. It must be a pleasure to you, to find yourself by God's mercy, in a way to be of use to your fellow sufferers, to make at least an ingenuous effect. I hope that your remaining days may be so assured to you in comfort, that you may have leisure and means to pursue your *plans* for the welfare of the operatives.

Your faithful servant,

A——.

[No. 3.]

March 31, 1842.

——. Pray go to the house of Mrs. Torvey, 41 A——t Street, Regent's Park.

You will there see a poor girl whose arm has been torn off by a wheel in a silk mill. Pray talk to her, and tell me what you think of the case.

You will be able to judge whether I can assist her by giving her a *false hand,* such as you have.

Your humble servant, A——.

My "plans" alluded to in letter No. 2, were chiefly the establishment of a self-acting asylum in the neighborhood of London, for the reception of the thousands of destitute factory cripples, in which they might be provided with the means of spending the remainder of their days in comfort, and in preparing for another and a better world. I had also formed some plans for preventing, as far as human means could prevent, the making of cripples in future. Although I did not succeed in carrying out these desirable objects, it was gratifying for me to know that "I had discharged my *commission* admirably," and that my "labors had been very serviceable."

[...]

In perusing the following pages, it will be necessary that the reader should bear in mind, that the author is a working man, that he never went to school, that he is here describing things which he has witnessed in everyday life, and that his observations are confined to that portion of society in which he has lived and moved.

With these preliminary remarks, I leave the work to the candid reader, and to God's blessing, believing that it does not contain a single sentence which on my deathbed I could wish to erase.

THE AUTHOR.

P.S. Should any lady or gentleman feel desirous of seeing for themselves the horrors of the English factory system, as it is stamped on my person, a letter to my address, post paid, will be attended to.

No. 8 Mount Vernon Avenue.

[Source: (William Dodd). *The Laboring Classes of England, Especially Those Engaged in Agriculture and Manufactures; in a Series of Letters. By an Englishman.* Boston: John Putnam, 1847. 5-9, 12.]

Appendix C: Contemporary Perspectives on Myles's Chapters in the Life of a Dundee Factory Boy

1. James Myles, from *Rambles in Forfarshire; or Sketches in Town and Country* (1850)

[In his *Rambles in Forfarshire*, a collection of essays reprinted from newspaper contributions on Angus "antiquities, churches, church-yards, castles, mansions, noble families, & traditions" (advertisement in 1850 edition of *The Dundee Factory Boy*), Myles tells a "romance in real life" remarkably similar to that offered in Frank Forrest's fictitious autobiography.]

The second flat of the Town House [in Dundee] contains the Guild Hall, where the various Courts of Justice are held, and another finely-finished hall used by the Town Council for their meetings. The upper floors were used as debtors [*sic*] and criminals' prisons up to the year 1836. [...]

About twenty-two years ago, a bold and successful attempt to escape from this jail was made by a convict then lying under sentence of seven years' transportation. As the subsequent career of this unfortunate man, by a curious train of circumstances which excel romance, is only known to his own family and myself, I shall relate his whole story; but the reader will excuse me from giving his real name, as we should under such incidents religiously avoid causing a single pang to a reclaimed fellow-creature, or wounding the feelings of his innocent relations. The names of persons and places then are entirely fictitious; but suffice it to say that the former (excepting the principal actor) as well as the latter exist in the immediate vicinity of Dundee. In the year 1826, a small spinning-mill in the little town of A—— was rented by a man of the name of James Dale. He had formerly been a working mill-wright, and was only known as an ingenious and excellent workman. He was a married man, and his domestic circle was cheered by the presence of an affectionate and industrious wife, whose felicity was cemented to her home and husband by the strong bond of two bloom-ing infant boys. Dale, to use a common phrase, started the world with little or no capital, and in a short time, from the necessary extent of his mercantile transactions, he found himself involved in serious monetary difficulties, which threatened to crush all his dreams of prosperity for life. Thinking, he might "weather the storm," and maintain his credit by a temporary accommodation, he applied to a friend for a loan; but he found to experience the truth of the old proverb, "those who go a borrowing go a sorrowing." He was refused. Driven to despair, he in an evil hour determined on forging a bill on the wealthy relation who had refused to befriend him in his distress. He believed that when it became due he would be prepared to meet it, and thus a knowledge of the fraud would for ever remain unknown. Unfortunately for himself and family his anticipations were blasted—the bill was dishonoured, and the crime discovered. Dale was arrested, tried, convicted, and sentenced to seven years' transportation. After his trial and conviction at the Perth Circuit, he along with the other criminals under a similar sentence was sent back to Dundee Jail preparatory to being forwarded to a penal colony. Dale now suffered the deepest remorse of conscience for the crime which had plunged him into an abyss of infamy, and covered his poor wife and children with shame; and as he of necessity had become the associate of practised villains and thieves, he too readily listened to any of their advices, especially if their adoption was likely to regain him that liberty which he had sacrificed. After the commission of the crime was known to the public, his creditors at once, and without the least mercy, seized the whole of his property, and left his wife and family utterly destitute. They removed from the town in which they had fondly hoped to live long in happiness and comfort, respected and respectable, and came to a small village in the vicinity of Dundee, where the faithful mother and loving wife, like a true heroine of adversity, commenced to work for herself and little children, the oldest of whom was only three years, and she succeeded in gaining a humble though independent living by winding pirns for hand-loom weavers. She was residing in this village, and living by such labour, while her husband was lying in Dundee under sentence, and as a true-hearted comforter, she visited him every day in his gloomy cell, to soothe him with words of tenderness and love, and shed tears of regret on the remembrance of the past. While on one of these diurnal missions of affection, her husband, by the advice of some of his prison companions, persuaded her to introduce, by some bold stratagem or other, a "spring saw," to enable them to escape. The proposition alarmed her, yet the thought of gaining her husband's freedom, and giving him an opportunity of escaping to America, nerved her energy and inspired her ingenuity. On the following day she baked a thick oat cake, came to the jail as usual, broke it in several pieces in presence of the jailor, and gave a piece to each of the prisoners who were confined beside her husband. On the succeeding day she brought two large thick oaten cakes, one of them she divided as formerly, handed the other to her husband, remarking at the same time, "Dinna brake that ane, James, just now; keep it and divide it among you at supper-time." This remark was understood by Dale and his fellow convicts, and he at once replied, "O! yes, I'll lay it in the window sill here or that time." *In this cake was concealed a large and excellent spring saw.* It was speedily used for the purpose intended, and that very night six men under sentence of transportation made their escape from Dundee jail. They were all recaptured except one, but that one was not the unhappy Dale. It was known to the authorities that a saw had been introduced to them, but the benevolent bannock baker was never suspected. The most romantic part of this story has yet to be told. Dale was sent to Ireland Island, Bermuda, and his poor wife was left to struggle as she best could to procure bread for herself and two little boys. Amidst the frowns of cold-hearted friends, and the prejudices of ignorant neighbours, she toiled and suffered in secret, and endured great privations and pain, rather than solicit eleemosynary aid, which shews that she was actuated by that noble virtue of independence that is yet to be found amongst the Scottish mothers of even the poorest class. Her husband regularly wrote from his compulsory home, assuring her of his unceasing solicitude for her welfare; but, poor woman, she could not write a reply, and did not like to ask a stranger to do so; moreover, she never was able to spare as much as pay a letter to that distant island. Once she verbally communicated with him through the medium of a gentleman who visited the island on business. After five years' service Dale was offered his liberty by the Government, and he proceeded to the United States to push his fortune. From the land of his adoption he again wrote his wife, now separated from him fully five long years. She was in bad health and extreme poverty, and found it entirely beyond her power to pay the postage of one in reply. In those days it was much higher than it is now. Another letter came from the anxious husband, and another, and still no answer. We may imagine though we cannot describe the days of anxiety and nights of inquietude passed by both husband and wife. The one pining in a foreign land, and his whole soul filled with dreams of his once happy home, and burning with intense desire to hear of its dear inmates,—the other tossed on a bed of sickness, enveloped in misery, and nursed only by two little boys, the oldest of whom had to "wind the pirns" to keep his mother, his brother, and himself from starving, and her nights and her days rendered more bitter by a wish to let her husband know that she still "lived and loved,"—a pious wish that she could not realize. Could a picture of misery be more complete? The unfortunate husband now concluded that his family were all dead, or had turned against him in consequence of his crime, and he wrote no more.

The reader now must in imagination leap over a period of fifteen years. James Dale was almost forgotten by all excepting *one*, who still carried his image in her heart. His two children were now men, and one of them, by dint of great perseverance and self-education, filled a respectable situation in the country. The story of his father had been often told him by his mother, and often had he heard her pour out her soul to God on the family altar for his religious improvement and social welfare. Now that he had reached manhood, he felt curious to know his father's fate, and the impression haunted his mind that he still lived; but like many other young men brought up in the country, he had little or no idea of the means to effect such a paternal object. He wrote to the Chairman of the London Missionary Society, but got no answer. In his troubles he consulted the writer of these chapters. His mother advised him against taking any steps, as she was convinced his father was dead. I at once asked him for the last letter his father had sent to his mother. The letter was easily got, as the poor woman had kept it like the apple of her eye. On receiving it I wrote a letter, giving as many details as I prudently could, to guide parties in search. This letter I addressed to the "Mayor or highest Civil Functionary of —— State of ——, U.S." The name of the town being the place where the old letter from Dale was dated from, but as it is not a place of much importance, I did not know if it had a Mayor, consequently I addressed it as above. By return of post I received a letter from the Mayor, telling me that he was "happy to inform me that James Dale was living, and was a very respectable citizen, and manager of the —— Canal, and reputed to be worth money;" and the same post brought two letters from the long-lost father to his long-lost wife and children; and on the following morning the Perth and Dundee parcel van delivered to me a splendid dauguerreotype portrait of him to present to his family. It was sent per vessel to Liverpool, and thence by rail. The duty of delivering and reading these letters was a painfully joyous one. Reader, I cannot describe it. You may image it in your mind, but my pen refuses to paint such a peculiar and powerful emotion of the soul. It is a pleasant thing to pull the good fruit from the tree of memory, and it will ever be a gratifying recollection to my mind that I was the agent in diffusing so much happiness amongst a desolate family, and preparing its long separated members for a re-union which I hope will never end. Verily, reader, "truth is stranger than fiction."

[Source: James Myles, *Rambles in Forfarshire, or Sketches in Town and Country*. Dundee: James Myles, 1850. 52-58.]

2. William Norrie, from *Dundee Celebrities of the Nineteenth Century* (1873): James Myles, Robert Nicoll, and William Jackson

[Three of the "four young men" described as meeting on an evening in 1836 in Denham's Hotel in Chapter IX of *Chapters in the Life of a Dundee Factory Boy* appear in Norrie's *Dundee Celebrities of the Nine-*

teenth Century. In 1850, James Myles was, as Frank Forrest says of himself in *The Dundee Factory Boy*, the only survivor of the group. Norrie's brief biographies, including his account of Myles, reveal the intense literary and scientific ambitions of these short-lived sons of farmers and artisans.]

JAMES MYLES

JAMES MYLES was an eminent member of the Dundee Republic of Letters, who passed away before his talents were fully ripened or known. He was born in the parish of Liff in 1819, being one of a numerous family, and was early sent to the village school, where he received the amount of education generally accorded to the children of the working classes. On leaving school, he chose the occupation of a mason, which trade he followed for several years. At this time, the great Chartist agitation was at its height. Lectures were being delivered, and monster open air meetings held throughout the country. Many of these meetings were attended by Myles; and from them, and the various discussions held amongst his fellow workmen, he was led to embrace Chartist principles. Adopting them with all the enthusiasm of his nature, he was soon found addressing various meetings of his fellow working men. This ultimately led him into contact with the leaders of the movement, who were lecturing and agitating throughout the country; and being known to be a forcible speaker, he was urged to take a more prominent part in the movement. The result was, that the mallet and chisel were thrown aside, and Myles became a public lecturer on the people's rights. The movement ultimately fell into the hands of persons who were for driving things to extremes, which induced him, though still retaining his Radical opinions, to withdraw in a great measure from it. Not liking to resume his occupation as a mason, he opened a bookseller's shop in the Overgate, opposite the Long Wynd, and devoted his leisure time chiefly to literary pursuits. His shop soon became a centre for many of the literary characters in the town, among whom religion, poetry, and politics were freely discussed. Various of the poetical productions of these parties coming under his notice, induced him to give them a more permanent form by having them printed, which he did in a small brochure of some sixty pages, under the quaint title of *A Feast of Literary Crumbs, by Foo Foozle and Friends*, interspersing various comical remarks in the shape of letters, notes, &c. He was also in the habit of writing articles to the local press, as well as to *Hogg's Instructor*. He also wrote *Chapters in the Life of a Dundee Factory Boy*, which originally appeared in the *Northern Warder* newspaper; and *Rambles in Forfarshire, or Sketches in Town and*

Country, published in 1850, and which consisted, for the most part, of papers which had previously appeared in the *Dundee Courier*. A month or two before his death, Mr Myles issued the prospectus of a periodical he proposed to publish, entitled *Myles's Forfarshire Telegraph and Monthly Advertiser*, which was intended to be 'a journal of politics, literature, and social progress.' He did not live, however, to carry out this undertaking. He died on Feb. 26, 1851, aged 32.

ROBERT NICOLL.

ROBERT NICOLL, who was spoken of by Ebenezer Elliott, 'the Corn Law Rhymer,'[1] as 'Scotland's second Burns,' was born in the farm house of Little Tulliebeltane, in the parish of Auchtergavin, in Perthshire, on Jan. 7, 1814. His parents were poor, but respectable; and a few years after Robert was born, misfortune drove the family from the homestead at Tulliebeltane, and the future poet was deprived of almost anything like schooling. It was not much needed, however, for the secret spring had been touched, and he speedily became a keen and earnest reader. At seven years of age, he commenced the battle of life as a 'herd laddie;' and he was not companionless, for he carried a book in his plaid, and doubtless in the *beild*[2] of some friendly bush or brae-side, conned it thoroughly. He might well say, in after year—and there are volumes of poetry in the simple lines—

> Laugh on! but there are souls of love
> In laddies herdin' kye.[3]

One sees, moreover, in this early training the germ of much that Nicoll said and did, when he came to make his voice heard in the crowd. From the 'wee wild flowers,' which adorn Orde braes, and the modest gowans,[4]

> Growing in meadows that are ours,
> For any child to pull,

up to the waving corn and the green trees, he would see—faintly at first, but more clearly day by day—the very marrow of that sublime and cheering truth which he afterwards so sweetly sung, that

---

1 See note on page 268.
2 *beild*] shelter.
3 kye] cows.
4 braes ... gowans] sides of hills, field-daisies.

God in love is everywhere.

At a comparatively early age, Nicoll was apprenticed to a wine merchant and grocer in Perth; and while residing there, anxious as ever for the acquisition of knowledge, he rose betimes in the morning, and made the North Inch his study. Before the expiry of his apprenticeship, he had entered in some measure upon his future vocation: he had taken to the composition of poetry, and had written several tales, which appeared in *Johnstone's Magazine*.

The business of a grocer was not much to Nicoll's taste, which had now taken a decidedly literary turn; and accordingly, upon the termination of his apprenticeship, he came to Dundee, and took a small shop in Castle Street, in which he commenced the business of a bookseller, and also kept a circulating library. To establish him in this small way of business, his mother was under the necessity of borrowing the sum of £20—a matter which, it would seem, weighed somewhat heavily upon the poet's rather sensitive mind. In 1835, he published a small volume, entitled *Poems and Lyrics*, which, not without cause, received from the periodicals of the time, a degree of praise seldom bestowed upon the work of so young a man—for he was then only about 22 years of age. An elaborate notice of the volume appeared in *Tait's Magazine*, in which a very high estimate was given of his talents and genius, and the eulogium supported by ample quotations from his poems. In an appreciative notice of the fourth edition of this book, the *Dundee Advertiser* had the following remarks:—

In a volume of about three hundred pages, we may be prepared, as a matter of course, for poems of a varied and unequal character; but throughout the whole, the versification is smooth and flowing, and the style vigorous and correct. The distinguishing characteristic of the book, as it strikes us, is a pervasive rural air—'a fragrance exquisite as new-mown hay;' and coupled with this, and in a manner springing therefrom, are its kindliness, elevation, and purity of sentiment. These, conjoined, form the main elements of the poet's idiosyncracy. Nicoll could not divest himself of this love for nature and humanity, even if he would—it had become part and parcel of the man; and it is the freshness of the combination which proves the hidden charm of his poetry, and causes us to linger, time after time, with unabated delight over his pages. In his loftiest flights, he carries along with him the perfume of the summer's flowers; and in his most homely subjects, we never fail to trace their beauty—reminding us that everywhere there is much of a good and uplifting character, if we would only set ourselves to seek for it.

We have referred to the kindliness or—what will express ourselves better to Scotch ears—the *couthiness* of Nicoll. It is specially prominent in all he writes. Any one who has had the pleasure of hearing Milne, the vocalist, sing his 'Bonnie Bessie Lee'—a perfect little gem of its kind—will find this feature of his muse lurking pawkily in every line; while in the address to Alice, his young wife, the same characteristic rises to the utmost height of refinement. Nicoll literally luxuriates in portraying the pure affection of home and of kindred; he delights to lead us through the gorse and the broom; or along the harvest-field, with toil-worn labourers—man and maid; he drops with us at even-tide into the cottar's dwelling, and tells us the short and simple annals of the poor. He knows right well the feelings and affections—'the lights and the shadows'—the patience and the self-denial—that hallow their lowly dwellings; and we listen until

> The cottage seems a bower of bliss,
>   A covert for protection
> Of tender thoughts that nestle there—
>   The brood of chaste affection.

Considering Nicoll's limited and desultory education, the simplicity and nerve of his style are remarkable. There is no straining after effect; there are no Latinised vulgarisms, the staple of a 'Babylonish dialect,' which learned pedants most effect; all is simple and natural, and consequently touching and impressive, as it should be in piping a 'lay for thinking hearts.' Nicoll has been likened to Burns on a smaller scale, but we cannot see the resemblance. Willian Thom[1]—both in his writings and career, so reckless, and latterly so eclipsed—comes nearer to the Aryshire bard. Robert Nicoll stands by himself—unbroken in integrity by the pressure of circumstances, and undaunted in heart by the touch of mortal disease—the Radical poet and politician.

As a specimen of his easy, pleasant style of versification, the following selection from the volume may here be given:—

MINISTER TAM.

A wee raggit laddie he cam' to our toon,
Wi' his hair for a bannet[2]—his taes[3] through his shoon;[4]
An' aye when we gart[5] him rise up in the morn,

---

1 William Thom (1798?-1848), Scottish weaver and poet.
2 bannet] bonnet.
3 taes] toes.
4 shoon] shoes.
5 gart] forced.

The ne'er-do-weel herdit the kye[1] 'mang the corn:
We sent him to gather the sheep on the hill—
No for wark, but to keep him frae mischief an' ill;—
But he huntit the ewes, an' he rade[2] on the ram!
Sic a hellicat[3] deevil was Minister Tam!

My auld Auntie sent him for sugar an' tea,—
She kent na,[4] douce woman! how toothsome was he:—
As hamewith[5] he cam' wi't he pakit a bairn,
An' harried a nest doon among the lang fern;
Then, while he was restin' within the green shaw,[6]
My auld Auntie's sugar he lickit it a':—
Syne,[7] a drubbin' to miss, he sair sickness did sham:
Sic a sly, tricksey shangie[8] was Minister Tam!

But a Carritch[9] he took, when his ain deevil bade;
An' wi' learnin' the laddie had maistly gaen mad:
Nae apples he pu'ed[10] noo—nae bee-bikes he smored[11]—
The bonnie wee trouties gat rest in the ford—
Wi' the lasses at e'enin' nae mair he wad fight—
He was learnin' and spellin' frae mornin' to night:
He grew mim as a puddock[12] an' quiet as a lamb,—
Gudesakes! sic a change was on Minister Tam!

His breeks[13] they war' torn, an' his coat it was bare;
But he gaed to the schule,[14] an' he took to the lear:[15]
He fought wi' a masterfu' heart up the brae,[16]
Till to see him aye toilin' I maistly was wae:[17]

---

1   herdit the kye] tended the cows.
2   rade] rode.
3   hellicat] wicked person, good-for-nothing.
4   kent na] did not know.
5   hamewith] homeward.
6   shaw] wooded dell.
7   Syne] then.
8   shangie] mischief-maker (?), after *shangie*, a slender stick used to torment a dog.
9   Carritch] catechism.
10 pu'ed] pulled.
11 bee-bikes ... smored] beehives ... smothered with smoke.
12 mim as a puddock] prim or meek as a frog.
13 breeks] breeches.
14 gaed to the schule] went to the shovel (applied himself).
15 lear] learning.
16 brae] steep hill.
17 wae] woe (woeful).

But his work noo is endit,—our Tammie has grown
To a kirk wi' a steeple—a black silken gown,—
Sic a change frae our laddie wha barefooted cam',
Wi' his wig white wi' pouther,[1] is Minister Tam!

Both before and after the publication of this volume, he contributed largely to *Tait's Magazine*, both in prose and verse. While conducting his bookselling business, under the firm of 'Nicoll & Co.,' at 6 Castle Street, he lent the aid of his tongue and pen to forward the cause of Reform and general enlightenment. Some of the finest and most pungent articles which appeared in the *Dundee Advertiser* early in the year 1836 are said to have been from his pen. He had a very extensive knowledge of English literature—which, indeed, was his favourite study; and on the subject of 'Poetry and the Poets,' he delivered four very able lectures in the Thistle Hall, to the members of the Watt Institution. In his poems is a hymn entitled, 'The Bursting of the Chain,' which is inscribed to the Rev. Henry Clark, and was written under the following circumstances:—Mr Clark, a clergyman of superior intelligence and attainments, along with some friends, proposed to hold a social meeting to celebrate the third centenary of the Reformation, and he requested Nicoll to write a suitable hymn to be sung on the occasion. The young poet gladly complied; and, as he was one of the party, he had the pleasure to hear his beautiful verses sung by a band of experienced vocalists. The celebration took place in the Crown Hotel on the evening of Monday, Sept. 7, 1835.

The library and bookselling business, however, proved a failure, and indirectly paved the way for another change. Quitting the shop in Castle Street at Whitsunday 1836, Nicoll removed to Edinburgh, and, through the interest of Mr John Johnstone, of Laverock Bank, Trinity, and Mr William Tait, he obtained the editorship of the *Leeds Times*, then an organ of the advanced Liberal party in that town. The appointment—although, pecuniarily, worth no more than £100 a year—was a suitable one; and the young editor entered upon it with all the enthusiasm for which he was so largely distinguished. He wrote with a zeal and a heart which speedily attracted attention. His calls to the working classes to arouse themselves from moral and mental sloth were stirring in the highest degree; his dragonades against the see-saw policy of Government—that of the Whigs especially—were pointed and unceremonious. He spared no abuse, exist where it might. The immediate consequence was, that, under his management, the circulation of the paper soon greatly increased, and, before he left, it was nearly quadrupled. Love for his work, and high spirits at its success, bore Nicoll on; but the

---

1 pouther] hair powder.

labour he imposed upon himself was too severe and unremitting. Absorbed in thinking of others, he forgot himself; and the sad result was, that an insidious consumption had gained the ascendancy before serious fears were entertained. In spite of failing health, he struggled on until Oct. 1837, when, at the urgent solicitation of Mr Tait and other friends in Scotland, he resigned his situation, and returned to this country, in the fond hope that his native air and cessation from labour might aid in restoring him to health. His mother, on hearing of his illness, went to Leeds to wait upon him; and on being asked how she obtained the money to undertake so long a journey, she replied: 'I shore [reaped] for it.' With a kindness which did him the highest honour, Mr Johnstone placed his house at Nicoll's service, and every means which the best medical skill could suggest was tried for his benefit. But it was too late. Neither change of scene nor medical skill was of the least avail. After lingering for a brief space, becoming gradually weaker and weaker, yet hopeful and earnest to the close, Nicoll breathed his last in Mr Johnstone's house on Thursday, Dec. 7, 1837, in the 24th year of his age, and was buried in North Leith Churchyard.

The parents of Robert Nicoll survived their gifted son for many years. The father died at Tulliebeltane—the birth-place of the poet—on Nov. 30, 1861, at the advanced age of 87. In May 1863, his mother, who was then nearly 80 years of age, sailed for Auckland, New Zealand, with her daughter, Mrs Allan—who was the heroine of the sweet little poem, 'My Sister'—and her husband. Mrs Allan was the last of a family of eight or nine children, all of whom, except her, were boys; and, save her, the aged mother had seen them all pass away.

WILLIAM JACKSON.

WILLIAM JACKSON, Jun., was born on Oct. 10, 1820. His parents were in humble life, his father being a working tailor, but one who devoted a considerable portion of his leisure time to the study of zoology; and from his father he no doubt inherited much of that taste for natural objects which afterwards characterised him. Unlike his father, however, botany was his favourite study, his mind, no doubt, being led to that science by some of his father's associates. When but a boy, he frequently accompanied his father, and the other lovers of nature who were then associated together, in their excursions to various localities in the neighbourhood. At that time, Dundee could boast of several naturalists, who, though moving in the humble ranks of life, had acquired considerable eminence in natural science—William Gardiner, sen., and Douglas Gardiner, the father and uncle of William Gardiner, the author of the *Flora of Forfarshire*, &c.; D. Butchart, a working shoe-maker; W. Lennox, also a working shoemaker, who devoted his spare time to the cultivation of a botanic garden on the west of what is now North Lindsay Street; and others. Jackson's scholastic education was confined to the elementary branches of reading, writing, and arith-metic, with a smattering of English grammar, &c. On leaving school, he adopted his father's employment, spending his leisure hours in the acquisition of knowledge, especially of his favourite study, botany; and when the nature of his employment afforded him an idle day, he spent it in the country. In the neighbourhood of Dundee, he had ample opportunities of following out the bent of his mind. Will's Braes, Den of Mains, Baldovan Woods, and other localities, were frequently visited in his early morning excursions, and seldom without making some addi-tion to his collection. These excursions sometimes extended to the Sidlaw Hills, where many sub-Alpine species of considerable interest were to be found; at others, to the Links of Barry, where, in addition to several rare botanical gems, the neighbouring beach furnished many species of algae and zoophytes thrown up by the waves. Of these he made a considerable collection, and he several times contributed col-lections of the rarer plants he had gathered to the Botanical Society of Edinburgh. This, together with his devotion to the study of plants, rec-ommended him to the attention of some influential members of the society; and on May 14, 1840, he was elected an associate of that body. This had the effect of still further stimulating him to exertion; and having become pretty well acquainted with the plants in the neighbour-hood of the town, he planned an excursion to the Clova Mountains, with his friend William Gardiner. They set out towards the latter end of July 1840, and remained for several weeks, during which they collected and dried large quantities of specimens of the rare Alpine plants which are to be found on these mountains. These afforded subjects for exten-sive study for a long period after his return, and largely extended his knowledge, especially in regard to mosses and lichens.

But while Jackson was thus becoming a first-rate botanist, he was not unmindful of the other departments of natural science, especially ornithology—his father's favourite study. In this, he latterly made con-siderable progress; but, unlike many so-called naturalists, his studies were not confined to cabinet specimens. He studied the birds in their natural haunts, and at different seasons, and took great delight in wan-dering along the sea-beach, even in the cold and stormy weather of mid winter, observing the habits of the interesting tribe of sea-birds visiting the sea-coast at that season. Many of these observations were subse-quently written out, and several of them appeared in a manuscript magazine to which several of the naturalists in the town contributed, and amongst whom it circulated. After Jackson's death, several of the papers which he had written for this manuscript magazine were published in the *North British Agriculturist*.

In the year 1847, Mr Jackson and a number of other ardent naturalists formed an association called the 'Dundee Naturalists' Association,' for the purpose of mutual help in the study of natural science, by the reading of papers, the exhibition of objects of natural history, excursions, &c. Jackson was chosen Treasurer of the Association, and acted in that capacity up till the time of his death. Several papers of considerable interest were communicated by him to the meetings, and, amongst others, a list of the birds of Forfarshire, exhibiting the occurrence of many rare species in the county, and narrating many facts of great interest from his own and his father's observations. He had often been urged to give his various observations in zoology a more permanent form, by preparing them for the press; and this task he commenced, but did not live to accomplish. In the autumn of 1847, he caught a cold, which, settling down on his lungs, terminated his earthly career in March 1848, at the early age of 27, leaving a widow and two young children to mourn his loss.

[Source: W. Norrie, *Dundee Celebrities of the Nineteenth Century*. Dundee: William Norrie, 1873. 132-33, 52-56, 111-13.]

Appendix D: Contemporary Perspectives on Johnston's "Autobiography": Selected Poems from Autobiography, Poems and Songs of Ellen Johnston, The "Factory Girl" (1867, 1869)

[Johnston's 1867 edition of her *Autobiography, Poems and Songs* contains more than one hundred and twenty lyrics and poetic addresses, and the selection reprinted here represents the great range of genres and styles in which she wrote. Many of these poems are patriotic celebrations of British might or Scottish traditions; many more lament betrayed and abandoned love, often focusing on the magic spells cast upon women by male beauty. Prominent as well are poems that express the speaker's pride in her membership in the working classes, such as "The Working Man," and her appreciation for the efforts made for workers by responsible factory masters, such as "Kennedy's Dear Mill," written to memorialize the weaving factory in Belfast where Johnston worked in the late 1850s. In other poems Johnston reveals the material conditions of her working life, as she does in a stanza from a dialect poem, not reproduced here, "O Come Awa', Jamie," which comments on the difficulty of weaving jute, the raw material that was being newly imported from India to replace the Russian flax that had supported the linen-weaving industry in Dundee:

> Tae weave jute in darkness is eerisome toil,
> And far mair than a' that the work we maun spoil;
> The jute roots like heather come into the camb,
> And the yarn fa's awa' like tow [rope] in oor hand. (127)

Now best-known of Johnston's works is another of her relatively few dialect poems, "The Last Sark," a dramatic monologue in which the speaker expresses her outrage over the sufferings of the poor and the indifference of the rich.

Among the most revealing of Johnston's poems are a number of autobiographical works; reprinted here are: "To my Aunt Phemie," in which she bemoans the hardness to her of her father's sister; "Address to Nature on its Cruelty," which offers a physical description of the poet; and "Lines to Mr James Dorward," which recounts the kindness of a factory foreman who released Johnston from the exile that she suffered after leaving Verdant Mill (see "Autobiography" 313). In the most distinctive feature of her collection, the highly autobiographical fifty-page section called "Poetic Addresses & Responses," Johnston includes poems addressed to her by readers of the Glasgow *Penny Post* and her replies. These poems express not only her readers' praise of her gifts—she is, as one of them says, the "fair empress of the gifted Nine" (175)—but also her pride in her fame: as "The Maid of Dundee to her Slumbering Muse" explains,

> Thy nation's heart in homage bows to claim thee,
>> And thousands wait to read thy coming book,
>
> Which thou composed when in the factory toiling,
>> With aching heart and head beset with woes. (227)

One reader named Edith exchanged a number of verse epistles with Johnston, and three of their poems are reprinted below because they convey both Johnston's attitude toward the past, which she also recounts in her "Autobiography," and the difficulty of her current circumstances, the subject of another poem in which she describes the loneliness of her life, writing poems late into the night after a day's work in the factory and cheered only by her "faithful cat" ("Lines to Edith," 183). Remarkably Johnston received a proposal of marriage from one of her unseen admirers, G.D. Russell, who shortly thereafter emigrated to Australia. A poem addressed to him conveys her plaintive offer to release him from his engagement to her, along with a contradictory message in its postscript.

Reprinted here—again for the sake of its autobiographical relevance—is the final poem from the second edition of the *Autobiography, Poems, and Songs* (1869), "The Last Lay of 'The Factory Girl.'" In 1868 Johnston's health seems to have been declining so quickly that she was anticipating the time when "Scotland's minstrels never more shall hear me/Wail forth my woes in page of 'Penny Post.'" The preface to the edition of 1869 includes a note from the *Penny Post* more hopefully explaining, "we understand that Miss Johnston is still likely to wear her justly-earned laurels, as her health is considerably improved, and she is meeting with great encouragement in the sale of her work" (*x*). "The Last Lay," however, seems to have been her final publication (Klaus 74-75).]

1.

The Working Man.

THE spring is come at last, my freens, cheer up, you sons of toil,
Let the seeds of independence be sown in labour's soil,

And tho' the nipping blast of care should blight your wee bit crop,
Oh dinna let your spirits sink, cling closer aye to hope.

If youth and health be on your side, you ha'e a richer boon
Than him that's dressed in royal robes and wears a diamond crown;
Nae widow's curse lies in your cup, you bear nae orphan's blame;
Nae guilty conscience haunts your dreams wi' visions of the slain.

Tho' light your purse, and worn your coat the darkest hour of night,
Is whiles[1] the very ane[2] that is before it dawns daylight;
And tho' your lot looks unco[3] hard, your future prospects drear,
Hope's sun may burst through sorrow's cloud, your sinking soul to
    cheer[.]

The summer's drawing near, my freens, cheer up ye sons of toil,
Let the sun of independence aye greet ye wi' a smile;
His genial beams will light your hearth when it is mirk[4] wi' care,
When ye ha'e little for to spend, and far less for to spare.

Let him that ne'er kent[5] labour's yoke but come to Glasgow toon,
And let him take a cannie[6] walk her bonny buildings roon,
And let him wi' his lady hands, his cheeks sae pale and wan,
Stand face to face, without a blush, before the Working Man.

But the man who wins fair fortune wi' labour's anxious pain,
He is the man who's justly earned her favour and her fame;
And may he aye keep flourishing wherever he may gang,[7]
And ne'er forget the days that gane when but a Working Man.

The harvest soon will be, my freens, cheer up, you sons of toil,
And the fu'some hand of plenty will store your domicile;
Ye are the sons of nature's art, aye forming some new plan,
Oh what would bonny Scotland do without the Working Man?

[Source: Ellen Johnston, *Autobiography, Poems and Songs of Ellen Johnston, The "Factory Girl."* Glasgow: William Love, 1867. 79-80.]

---

1   whiles] sometimes.
2   ane] one.
3   unco] very.
4   mirk] dark.
5   kent] knew.
6   cannie] cautious.
7   gang] go.

2.

Kennedy's Dear Mill.

OH! Kennedy's dear mill!
 To you I'll sing a song
For winter dark and dull;
 For another season's gone.
And summer's bright sunshine
 Thy little shed doth fill.
Prosperity is thine,
 Oh, Kennedy's dear mill!

'Tis not alone o'er thee
 Adversity hath passed,
For all the kingdoms three
 Hath felt its withering blast,
I shared thy better days,
 I also shared thine ill;
Now I hail hope's rays
 In Kennedy's dear mill.

Thou hast a secret spell
 For all as well as me;
Each girl loves thee well
 That ever wrought in thee.
They may leave thy blessed toil;
 But, find work they will,
They return back in a while
 To Kennedy's dear mill.

The girls so neat and fair,
 The boys so frank and free;
I see a charm that's rare
 In them as well as thee.
The sunlight of their smile
 Doth linger near me still,
And cheers me at my toil
 In Kennedy's dear mill.

And freedom's glorious shrine
 Is center'd in thy walls;
No tyrant knave to bind,
 No slavish chain enthrals.
The workers are as free

As the sunshine on the hill;
Thy breath is liberty,
  Oh! Kennedy's dear mill.

We feel no coward fear
  When our dear master comes;
And when he's standing near,
  And gazing on our looms,
He hails us with a smile
  That is a brother's still,
No haughty lord of toil
  Owns Kennedy's dear mill.

Through Erin's vast commerce
  He bears a generous name;
And o'er the universe
  His praise I will proclaim.
When his workers are in grief,
  It is against his will;
He's the first to send relief
  From Kennedy's dear mill.

We will be happy yet,
  And bid all care adieu;
For we shall have a trip
  In another week or two.
And o'er in Bedford Street
  A happy band we will
In unity all meet
  At Kennedy's dear mill.

Now, Kennedy's dear mill,
  The best wish of my heart
Shall linger near you still,
  When from you I depart.
Whate'er my fate may be,
  Let me wander where I will,
Peace and prosperity
  To Kennedy's dear mill.

[Source: Ellen Johnston, *Autobiography, Poems and Songs of Ellen Johnston, The "Factory Girl."* Glasgow: William Love, 1867. 19-21.]

3.

An Address to Napiers' Dockyard,

LANCEFIELD, ANDERSTON.

HAIL! prince of public works—mechanic arts—
For men of genius and for noble hearts;
Honour and fame, peace, power, and merit,
Men well fill'd with philanthropic spirit.
    I cannot speak like scientific men
Whom literature gives colour to their pen,
Who clothe their genius in that golden robe
Wrought by learning, and not by nature's God.
Those gilded abstracts of high inspiration
Quoted out to gain man's admiration.
Give me origin—such I hold at bay
Who steal from authors of a bygone day;
Pampering pages with records unnumber'd
Robb'd from men who hath for centuries slumber'd.
    Nay, nay, dear Work, to thee I'll only speak!
Like what I am—a woman frail and weak.
My self-taught learning may have power to move,
For it is drawn from truth and heartfelt love,
Free from flattery and from language vain,
The sproutings of a love-sick woman's strain
Whose hopes are centered now within thy walls.
One of thy noble sons my heart enthrals!
No marvel then I love to breathe thy name,
It cheers my heart and fans a secret flame;
No marvel then I oft walk round thy dock,
Gazing intently on each secret spot,
Anxious to know when last my love stood there
That o'er it I might breathe a fervent prayer.
    Dear Work, you know not what a gorgeous sight
Thou art to me when wandering forth each night;
Inhaling the breeze of summer's flow'ry scene,
Musing on nature's lovely mantle green;
When all is still and silent as the grave,
When golden moonbeams kiss the silver wave
That rolleth gently o'er sweet Clutha's breast
That gorgeous stream where commerce never rests;
Upon whose banks I've oft distill'd the dews
Of fervent love, and pour'd on thee my muse,
That prince of rivers that joins the mighty sea
That's borne so many brave ships built by thee;
And will, I hope, yet bear a thousand more

With wealth and tidings to our Scottish shore.
Who would not love that stream, old Scotland's Clyde?
Oft have I watch'd its waters gently glide
Like infant angels o'er fair Shandon's beach,
Where thy dear master's princely mansion stretch
Its Gothic towers beneath the sun's bright rays—
The ancient emblem of departed days.
Oft have I wept in its surrounding woods
Where Gareloch gently rolls her silvery floods,
And sweetly echoes back o'er hill and plain
The monarch organ's sweet and deep-toned strain,
That fell like heavenly music on mine ears,
And filled my soul with thought of brighter spheres.
And I have seen that gorgeous window glass
Filled with the heroes of great mount Parnass—
Shakespeare, Milton, honoured Newton, too,
Burns, Scott, and Goldsmith—Britain's authors true—
And many more brave and distinguished men,
Whose works for centuries yet will wear a gem.
Thy master's library contains a store
Num'rous as sands on Shandon's lovely shore.
    And who could dream I've wandered in those halls
Long ere the painters' hands adorned their walls?
That I have knelt and prayed within that place
Long ere the workman set with taste and grace
The rich enamelled China diamonds neat,
Which oft have kissed thy honoured master's feet?
This was my prayer—that he might live to see
His offspring's offspring all reach maturity.
This was my prayer—that his brave sons might be
The emblem of himself, noble and free,
And useful members through life's fleeting dream,
As their dear father many years has been;
That his gay mansion of such stately grace
May shield for centuries his own kindred race.
And thinkest thou this prayer will not avail,
Because 'twas breathed by woman weak and frail?
God listens to the weak as well's the strong,
And he may yet thy master's life prolong
To be a very aged, honoured man,
Whose name and fame hath sailed to every land;
Yet still thy dusty walls give joy to me
More pure than all the treasures of the sea.
Oh! what were all its wealth heaped mountains high
Could I no more thy towering dock descry?

If hills and mountains, oceans dark and blue,
Between us rolled, to hide thee from my view.
    I would not leave thee, dear beloved place,
A crown, a sceptre, or a throne to grace;
To be a queen—the nation's flag unfurl—
A thousand times I'd be a Factory Girl!
To live near thee, and hear thy anvils clink,
And with thy sons that hard-won pleasure drink.
That joy that springs from wealth of daily toil,
Than be a queen sprung forth from royal soil.
Farewell, dear Work, the twilight hour is past,
Dark Luna's curtain o'er thy walls is cast;
Heaven's vaults distil their crystal dews,
Queen Venus waits to hail my midnight muse.
Farewell! Remember my best wish shall be
Thy master's welfare and success in thee.

[Source: Ellen Johnston, *Autobiography, Poems and Songs of Ellen Johnston, the "Factory Girl."* Glasgow: William Love, 1867. 9-12.]

4.

Lord Raglan's Address to the Allied Armies.[1]
Tune—'KATHLEEN MAVOUREEN.'

HARK! my brave soldiers, the trumpet is sounding,
    The banners are borne on the peril of life;
See how the Cossacks like cowards are bounding
    Away from the field of carnage and strife.
Let not the visions of home and friends haunt you,
    To do or to die is the motto we have;
Let not the groans of the dying e'er daunt you,
    Sebastopol's ours—a prize or a grave.
    Then on to the field, ye brave sons of glory,
        On to the field where the banners wave high;
    Your names are enrolled in fame's golden story—
        Fight for Sebastopol, conquer or die.

There's many a brave man has fallen before you—
    His friends and his country he'll never see more;
And if you should fall, your friends will deplore you

---

1   See note 1 on page 311.

When laurels of honour shall spring from your gore.
Love will dream o'er you which cannot defend you,
    Or watch o'er the danger that threatens your life;
Hearts will deplore you that cannot attend you,
    When death lays you low on the red field of strife.
        Then on to the field, ye brave sons of glory, &c.

Onward ! my heroes—a reward doth await you,
    For Raglan shall never let bravery be lost;
Onward ! let nothing but death e'er defeat you—
    Let yours be the honour, the glory, the boast.
Your orphans and widows shall all be provided
        With food and with raiment if you should be slain,
And each faithful sweetheart be guarded and guided
    If her gallant lover returns not again.
        Then on to the field, ye brave sons of glory, &c.

Do you not deem the scene will be galling
    To Menschikoff while he stands gazing around?
There's ten of his men for one of mine falling—
    On, my bold heroes, and slaughter them down.
What though the wounded are dying around you,
    Dead or alive like stars you will shine;
And if by good chance no bullet should wound you,
    A fame that is matchless around you shall twine.
        Then on to the field, ye brave sons of glory, &c.

See Alma's heights and Inkerman's valleys,
    Balaclava, Odessa, where victory doth shine;
Onward ! my armies, my true loyal allies—
    Victory on victory till Sebastopol's thine.
O, shame on the man that would fly from danger,
    And lose the bright honour he'll win in the cause!
O! who would not die a courageous avenger,
    In conquering the despots of Nicholas's laws?
        Then on to the field, ye brave sons of glory,
            On to the field where the balls round you fly;
        Your names are enrolled in fame's golden story,
            Your honour's immortal, and never can die.

[Source: Ellen Johnston, *Autobiography, Poems and Songs of Ellen Johnston, the "Factory Girl."* Glasgow: William Love, 1867. 212-13.]

5.

The Last Sark.

WRITTEN in 1859.

GUDE[1] guide me, are you hame again, an' ha'e ye got nae wark,[2]
We've naething noo[3] tae put awa'[4] unless yer auld blue sark;[5]
My head is rinnin' roon about far lichter[6] than a flee—
What care some gentry if they're weel though a' the puir wad dee![7]

Our merchants an' mill masters they wad never want a meal,
Though a' the banks in Scotland wad for a twelvemonth fail;
For some o' them have far mair goud[8] than ony ane can see—
What care some gentry if they're weel though a' the puir wad dee!

This is a funny warld, John, for it's no divided fair,
And whiles I think some o' the rich have got the puir folk's share,
Tae see us starving here the nicht wi' no ae bless'd bawbee—[9]
What care some gentry if they're weel though a' the puir wad dee!

Oor hoose ance[10] bean an' cosey, John; oor beds ance snug an warm
Feels unco cauld an' dismal noo, an' empty as a barn;
The weans sit greeting[11] in oor face, and we ha'e noucht to gie—
What care some gentry if they're weel though a' the puir wad dee!

It is the puir man's hard-won toil that fills the rich man's purse;
I'm sure his gouden coffers they are het[12] wi' mony a curse;
Were it no for the working men what wad the rich men be?
What care some gentry if they're weel though a' the puir wad dee!

---

 1 Gude] God.
 2 wark] work.
 3 noo] now.
 4 tae put awa'] to pawn.
 5 sark] shirt.
 6 lichter] lighter.
 7 wad dee] would die.
 8 goud] gold.
 9 bawbee] halfpenny.
10 ance] once.
11 greeting] weeping.
12 het] hot.

My head is licht, my heart is weak, my een are growing blin';
The bairn is faen' aff[1] my knee—oh! John, catch haud o' him,
You ken I hinna[2] tasted meat for days far mair than three;
Were it no for my helpless bairns[3] I wadna care to dee.

[Source: Ellen Johnston, *Autobiography, Poems and Songs of Ellen Johnston, The "Factory Girl."* Glasgow: William Love, 1867. 100-01.]

6.
To my Aunt Phemie.

DEAR AUNT, the thoughts of bygone years rush wildly o'er my
    brain—
I strive to stay their swelling tide, but, ah! it is in vain;
Those innocent and gladsome hours that I have spent with thee,
Above all other after-scenes, float still on memory.

And thou wert young and handsome then—a woman in thy prime;
Thy cheeks wore not what they now wear—the dark impress of time.
Whilst o'er my brow my mother shed my hair's bright sunny wave,
Then wouldst thou speak of him that sleeps far in a foreign grave.

Time on his iron pinions fled, and parted thee and me,
Then came the news that thou hadst wed a husband in Dundee.
When flowing plenty cheered thy home, and joy around thee smiled,
One heart was sad within the home where Ellen was beguiled.

Glad nature swelled my soul with song, my brow was wreathed with
    fame,
Our Royal Sovereign read my muse, and praised my gifted name;
But like the leaves which autumn winds do scatter to and fro,
The withering breath of false love came and laid hope's blossoms low.

'Twas well my future fate was veiled from youth's bright golden view;
I had the name of many friends, yet friends I had but few;
For those that measured all my faults, considered not my wrongs—
I've wept in secret solitude whilst others sung my songs.

---

1   faen' aff] fallen off.
2   hinna] have not.
3   bairns] children.

Twelve silvery moons had jewell'd the sky, the stars with diamond ray
Had gemm'd the dew from Heaven's vaults upon my mother's clay;
No parent link to bind to earth, no house nor hearth for me—
An orphan wrapt in mourning weeds I came unto Dundee.

And Heaven alone can only tell my hardships in that land;
Many a time I've passed thy door whilst thou at it did'st stand;
When I was weary wandering, friendless, cold, and weak,
Oh God, I've passed my own aunt by, yet could not, dare not speak.

And seventeen bright summer suns far in the west had set
Since thou and I had parted first, and thus on Tay's banks met;
Till death my tear-dimm'd eyes doth close, I'll ne'er forget the look
Of haughty scorn thou gavest me—thy cold and stern rebuke.

Dear aunt, thy heart is changed now—some spell has thee beguil'd,
Or thou wouldst ne'er have turned thy back upon thy brother's child;
For couldst thou think as I have thought, and feel as I have felt,
Yea, though thy heart was adamant, my name that heart might melt.

[Source: Ellen Johnston, *Autobiography, Poems and Songs of Ellen
Johnston, The "Factory Girl."* Glasgow: William Love, 1867. 45-47.]

7.
                    An Address to Nature on its Cruelty.

                    O NATURE, thou to me was cruel,
                    That made me up so small a jewel;
                    I am so small I cannot shine
                    Amidst the great that read my rhyme.
                    When men of genius pass me by,
                    I am so small they can't descry
                    One little mark or single trace
                    Of Burns' science in my face.
                    Those publications that I sold,
                    Some typed in blue and some on gold,
                    Learned critics who have seen them
                    Says [*sic*] origin dwells within them;
                    But when myself perchance they see,
                    They laugh and say, 'O is it she?
                    Well, I think the little boaster
                    Is nothing but a fair impostor;
                    She looks so poor-like and so small,

She's next unto a nought-at-all;
Such wit and words quite out-furl
The learning of "A Factory Girl."'
At first they do my name exalt,
And with my works find little fault;
But when upon myself they gaze,
They say some other claims the praise.
O Nature, had'st thou taken time
And made me up somewhat sublime,
With handsome form and pretty face,
And eyes of language—smiles of grace;
With snowy brow and ringlets fair,
A beauty quite beyond compare;
Winning the charms of fortune's smile.
Still dressed in grandeur all the while;
Then those who see me would believe
I never tried for to deceive
By bringing out a publication
Of borrowed lines or yet quotation.
But those who see me in this dress,
So small and thin I must confess,
Well may they dare the words to use.
Can such a vase distil Love's muse;
Well may they ask dare I profess
The talent of an authoress?
Oh who could deem to gaze on me,
That e'er I mused on land or sea,
That I have sat in shady bower
Musing on thy fairest flower;
That I have sought the silvery stream
At midnight hour, calm and serene,
When skies of diamond sparkling flame
Shed pearly tears of heartsick shame,
To see me bound in hardship's blight,
Whilst man did rob me of my right,
And critics read my simple rhyme
And dared to say it was not mine?
Imperfect though my lays may be,
Still they belong to none but me.
My blighted breast is their abode,
They were placed there by nature's God;
And though my years are spent in pain,
Still seeking fortune's smiles in vain,
Still sighing youth's sweet years away,

Changing life's light into clay;
Hard toiling for my daily bread
With burning heart and aching head.
A vision of delusion's dream,
Hastening downward death's dark stream;
Yet nature between you and I,
Beneath the universal sky,
Who dares to say I have bereft
Another genius of their gift.

[Source: Ellen Johnston, *Autobiography, Poems and Songs of Ellen Johnston, The "Factory Girl."* Glasgow: William Love, 1867. 141-43.]

8.

Lines

TO MR. JAMES DORWARD, POWER-LOOM FOREMAN, CHAPELSHADE WORKS, DUNDEE,
THE FIRST AND BEST FRIEND TO THE AUTHORESS IN THE DEEPEST
HOURS OF HER TRIALS AND TRIBULATIONS IN DUNDEE.

The summer's come again, Jamie, twa happy years ha'e fled
Since ye gied me a limm,[1] Jamie, in the dear Chapelshade;
And I will ne'er forget that time until the day I dee,
That happy blessed morning when ye gied that limm to me.

O I was sorry then, Jamie, a wand'ring poor exile,
Begging my brothers of the earth to gie me leave to toil;
Pale poverty stood at my door, my hope on earth was fled,
Until I found a resting-place within the Chapelshade.

There was muckle[2] said and dune, Jamie, by mair than ane or twa,
To take frae me my limm, Jamie, and get me turned awa;
But ye were my faithful friend in need, and I will ne'er forget,
Until I'm numbered wi' the dead, how deep I'm in your debt.

And may Heaven bless ye, Jamie, and a' your kith and kin,
For ye ha'e left it in my power the victory for to win;
I've conquered a' my foes, Jamie, that did my ruin plan,
And noo[3] I bid defiance to every perjured man.

---

1   gied me a limm] *limm,* a variant of *lin,* means flax or dressed flax in Scots; this
    phrase therefore suggests by extension "gave me work in a flax mill."
2   muckle] much.
3   noo] now.

While you are on my side, Jamie, I carena a bawbee[1]
For a' the West-end tenters[2] that ever screwed a key;
I'm happy as a queen, Jamie, in the bonny Chapelshade,
And whilst you're pleased to keep me there, wi' you I'll earn my bread.

And wha[3] are they would blame, Jamie, altho' I wish ye weel?
For words can never name, Jamie, the gratitude I feel;
Ye are the first, the truest friend I've met wi' in Dundee,
And whate'er may be my future lot, I'll bless your mem'ry.

May Heaven bless your wife, Jamie, wha aye will share a part
Of the never dying gratitude that lives within my heart;
May God restore her better health, and may she live to see
Her bairns' bairns[4] smiling in manhood's pride and glee.

And may your bonny Maggie be as gude as she is fair,
Likewise your absent Ellen, that's beneath anither's care;
May their lot through life be happy, and God still be their guide—
May they be their father's comfort, their mother's joy and pride.

And may William, George, and Thomas, all grow up useful men,
Ah! gie them lots o' learning—make them masters o' the pen;
The man that's master o' the pen is master o' an art,
That on the tower o' science still hauds the master part.

And may your dear Elizabeth, and Agnes your wee pet,
And your wee rosebud, Davy, ne'er cause ye to regret;
But twine like ivy round your heart wi' love that still endears,
And licht[5] like sunshine in a storm the winter o' your years.

Frae the bottom o' my heart, Jamie, thus I wish for thee—
May you and yours aye be as weel as I wish ye would be:
May health and wealth and joy and love aye round your hearth be
    spread;
Long may ye be my foreman in the bonny Chapelshade.

[Source: Ellen Johnston, *Autobiography, Poems and Songs of Ellen
Johnston, The "Factory Girl."* Glasgow: William Love, 1867. 86-87.]

---

1 bawbee] halfpenny.
2 tenters] workers overseeing machinery.
3 wha] who.
4 bairns] children.
5 licht] light.

9.

Lines by Edith to the Factory Girl.

THEY ask me, girl, what made thee sing
   'Mid din of shuttle and of loom—
'Mid steam and dust and ceaseless ring
   Of cotton wheels in factory room.

What made thee sing? Ask first the thrush
   That haunts the woods 'bove fair Dundee,
And on her hills the breezes hush
   Till bird and breeze explain to me.

Hail, Spirit of the Golden Muse!
   Thou soul of beauty, that dost fill
The earth, and air, and dost diffuse
   On some thy soft revealings still.

That spirit taught thee, girl, to sing;
   She came to thee when early May
Doth first her golden shadow fling
   Upon the broad blue Frith of Tay;

She came what time the summer wood
   Bursts glorious into leaf and bower;
And oft she came in holier mood,
   At moonlit eve, or Sabbath hour.

And came she ne'er in love, first love,
   With whispers soft of some dark eye,
Whose gleam had flashed thy path above,
   Like meteor gem in life's young sky?

Came she not, too, in sorrow's shroud—
   What poet knows her not so dressed?—
Only to point the silver cloud,
   And whisper dreams of days more blest?

Sing on, young heart, of all that's fair
   Upon the banks of winding Tay;
The old grey towers, the blossoms there
   May mingle well in poet's lay.

When gazing on life's boundary hill,
   Thine eye at length doth long for rest,

Sing even then, thy numbers fill
　　With chords more grand, with hopes more blest.

[Source: Ellen Johnston, *Autobiography, Poems and Songs of Ellen Johnston, The "Factory Girl."* Glasgow: William Love, 1867. 156-57.]

10.

The Factory Girl's Reply to 'Lines by Edith.'

THEY ask thee, Edith, why I sing
　　'Mid factory din, its dust and gloom,
And why I soar on fancy's wing
　　'Mid dreamland bowers and summer's bloom.

Tell them the spirit bids me sing
　　That made my soul, when but a child,
Enraptured with the budding spring,
　　When wandering Cathkin's green woods mild.

While yet a child, scarce six years old,
　　Musing on nature's carpet sod,
Among the fields like waving gold,
　　I prized the works of nature's God.

Though little of His laws I knew,
　　Yet still I felt their power supreme,
And loved His wondrous works to view,
　　And chose them for my childish theme.

But time and tide flew on apace,
　　And I was wafted from those scenes,
Borne thither to a sweeter place
　　Near Kelvin's lovely crystal streams.

And still that spirit round me clung,
　　And bound me in its mystic spell,
While fairy songs to it I sung
　　When sitting by the Three-tree Well.

But like the linnet to the linn
    That's caught and caged in prison air,
They forced me midst the factory's din
    To chase my fairy phantoms there.

But still that spirit lingered near,
    And clasped my form so young and weak,
And kissed away the burning tear
    That scorched the rose-bloom on my cheek.

Then first love came with golden smiles—
    Sweet were the vows he did impart,
And with his false bewitching wiles
    He stole away my trusting heart;

Then left me with a look of scorn
    When he the seeds of grief had sown—
Wrecked in the bloom of life's young morn,
    Ere scarce her infant buds were blown.

Yet still I sung, though all in vain,
    While year in sorrow followed year,
When all at once like magic strain
    My harp burst on the world's ear.

Ah, gentle Edith, see me now,
    With hope's bright banner o'er me spread,
Fame's golden wreath around my brow,
    Love's lyric crown upon my head.

Dear Edith, they had hearts like thine
    Who wove that wreath and wrought that crown,
And built for me that glorious shrine
    That rears its tower on high renown.

Edith, farewell; may joy be thine!
    Perchance with thee I yet may meet,
When I shall press thy hand in mine,
    My kindred sister's love to greet.

[Source: Ellen Johnston, *Autobiography, Poems and Songs of Ellen John-ston, The "Factory Girl."* Glasgow: William Love, 1867. 157-59.]

11.

The Factory Girl's Reply to Edith.

HAIL! spirit of the gifted Nine,
    Again I call my humble muse
Her frail power in response to thine
    A weak and charmless song infuse.

Inspiring spirit, thy lofty lays
    A mystic witchery o'er me fling:
'Tis thee, not I, who claims the praise—
    'Tis of thy worth the world should sing.

The language that pervades thy songs
    Pourtrays a noble soul sublime,
And marks that worth to thee belongs
    I ne'er shall own through endless time.

Edith, beloved one, be it so;
    I love those sweet stray leaves of thine,
And feel what poets only know
    When kneeling by fair poesy's shrine.

'Twas on the banks of winding Esk,
    That murmurs by the Pentland Hills,
Thy sire taught thee thy glorious task,
    Whose golden number richly fills

Thy noble soul and nobler heart—
    Ah, Edith, false, false would they be,
Who would to me the palm impart
    That e'er had read thy minstrelsy.

Thy childhood's home stood in a vale,
    Where balmy breath of fragrant flowers,
Borne on the summer evening gale,
    Oft kissed its ivy-woven towers.

And there thou strayed a lonely child,
    Amongst the honey-suckle bowers,
Through foliage of the greenwoods wild,
    As onward flew youth's golden hours.

Then First Love came like angel queen,
    In robes of gold and tinsell'd maze;

Scarce ere thou hadst her beauty seen,
　　She fled from thy enraptured gaze.

Such is too oft the poet's doom—
　　The flower he ever prizeth most,
Long ere his hope hath reached its bloom,
　　He finds his gem for ever lost.

Thy father was a genius too,
　　His brow was draped with silver hair;
Ere Father Time's iron stamp was due,
　　Deep thought had left her impress there.

A father's love I never knew,
　　He left me when an infant child,
And sailed Columbia's shore to view,
　　And chase ambition's fancy wild.

He was a bard—'tis from his veins
　　That my poetic blood doth flow;
His were the wild and mystic strains
　　Such as in Byron's breast did glow.

Eight years on Time's iron wings had fled,
　　When Hope's gold star began to wane;
My mother, dreaming he was dead,
　　Joined in wedlock's band again.

The grief that I have borne since then
　　Is only known unto the Lord:
No power of words nor author's pen
　　My countless wrongs can e'er record.

Another dozen years had fled:
　　One day a startling letter came—
O God! my father was not dead,
　　But living in the State of Maine.

Edith, I scarce dare tell thee more,
　　Save where the Niagara's wave
Swells proudly o'er its pebbly shore,
　　And points a suicide's sad grave.

Conscience wrung with wild remorse
　　To hear his child, far-famed in song,

Wept 'neath a cruel stepfather's curse,
    That he himself had caused the wrong.

Whilst brooding o'er his past neglect,
    He felt no more a wish to live;
To close the sickening 'retrospect,'
    He took the life he could not give.

Such was my sire, and such his end,
    And such an end was nearly mine;
But Heaven its mercy did extend,
    And sent kind friends to save in time.

Edith, my heart's warm love is thine,
    In kindred soul and kindred thought:
Oh may we at our Saviour's shrine
    Obtain that love which faileth not!

[Source: Ellen Johnston, *Autobiography, Poems and Songs of Ellen Johnston, The "Factory Girl."* Glasgow: William Love, 1867. 163-65.]

12.

Lines to Mr G.D. Russell, Queensland,
ACCOMPANIED WITH A CARTE DE VISITE OF
'THE FACTORY GIRL.'

SAY not, dear George, this feeble form
    Did guide thee o'er the perilous deep—
Thy guardian angel through the storm,
    That did love's constant vigil keep.

Say not these tear-dimmed, sunken eyes
    Did cheer thee through the gloom of night—
Like stars refulgent in the skies,
    Did shed o'er thee a heavenly light.

Say not that melancholy smile
    Did soothe thee o'er to placid rest,
And like an angel all the while,
    With golden wings did shield thy breast.

Say not this heart of throbbing dust
    Did prove to thee a solid rock,
Where thou didst firmly place thy trust
    When Death nigh dealt his fatal stroke[.]

Say not thou lov'st me as thy life,
    That death alone shall thee estrange,
That I must be thy living life,
    For gold thou would'st not me exchange.

What though I wear a gifted name,
    Immortalised in history's page,
What though my brow is crowned with fame,
    Death wars within my bosom wage.

Through weary years of care and toil,
    Deep grief and thought have wrecked this form;
A death-shade round this bosom coils,
    That soon may feed the hungry worm.

And it might wreck thy bosom's peace
    To link thy noble heart with mine,
Yet death alone would only cease
    My heart from yearning after thine.

And it might wrap thy soul in gloom,
    And cloud with care thy lofty brow,
And wed thee to a joyless doom,
    Would'st thou perform thy plighted vow.

Go, loving, trusting, faithful one,
    This image from thy soul remove;
O ! strive this shattered heart to shun—
    It is not worthy of thy love.

Why would'st thou woo the blighting wind,
    And build thy castles up in air,
And dream of hope, then wake to find
    Their towers lie scattered in despair?

Why would'st thou pull the autumn rose,
    And wear it next thy loving heart,
And know that in its breast repose
    Death's deep consuming counterpart?

Why would'st thou to this shadow bow,
  To grasp a flower of phantom bloom,
And e'er its fragrance fanned thy brow,
  Behold it withered in the tomb?

'Tis true that we have never met,
  Yet love like ours was seldom known;
And yet that love might bring regret
  When time had made me all thine own.

O ! gaze upon this little carte,
  The emblem of thy promised wife,
And say could'st thou till death regard
  Her as the love-star of thy life.

Is she thy choice? Then take this hand,
  This heart thou prizest more than gold;
By Heaven's decree, by fate's command,
  The Factory Girl to thee is sold.

                              E.J., THE FACTORY GIRL.
CHAPELSHADE FACTORY, DUNDEE.

                    [POSTSCRIPT.]

O, hasten to thy fatherland!
  Thy God, who led thee o'er the main
In safety with his mighty hand,
  May bring thee safely back again.

Then I shall be thy happy bride;
  And when death's dark, all-sev'ring wave
Shall sweep me from thy faithful side,
  Thy tears, dear George, alone I crave.   E.J[.]

[Source: Ellen Johnston, *Autobiography, Poems and Songs of Ellen John-ston, The "Factory Girl."* Glasgow: William Love, 1867. 172-75.]

13.

The Last Lay of 'The Factory Girl.'

(Written under severe bodily and mental affliction
at Glasgow, in January, 1868.)

FAREWELL, my loved one, fare thee well for ever;
 I come, my love, to sing thee my last lay;
King Death, ere long, life's silver links will sever,
 And leave me slumbering in the silent clay.

My heart is fraught with many a secret sorrow—
 With many a care the world may never know;
I sleep to dream of joy, then comes the morrow,
 With hope deferred, wrapped in wreaths of snow.

I cannot longer live to look upon thee;
 Still doubting, I may not hope thy heart to gain;
In sad despair, my love, I hasten from thee—
 We part; oh, Heaven! have I thus loved in vain?

Once I loved thee only as a daughter—
 Ah! thou wert more than father unto me;
But now, the boundless depths of Lethe's water
 Can never quench my boundless love for thee.

Oh! couldst thou know the war that's wildly raging
 Within this heart that longs thine own to press,
Whilst those bright eyes of thine are still engaging
 Every pulse with throbs of heavenly bliss.

'Tis heaven to know that thou didst never doubt me—
 To dream thou think'st it is for thee I sigh;
'Tis worse than hell, alas! to live without thee;
 I go, my loved one, far from thee to die.

No other star shall ever light my heaven—
 No higher heaven ever shall be mine—
Save thy dear self, till life's last links are riven,
 And Death his iron chains around me twine.

Thy name shines like a beacon, ever sparkling
 Radiant beams where mystery sits unveil'd;
Where Truth lights Error through its waters darkling—
 Where Persecution thy great aim assail'd.

I go, my loved one, and I leave behind me
    This gay, green world of splendour, rich and rare;
It hath no other charm but thee to bind me—
    I've lived and loved, thy name alone to bear.

Some pitying angel may descend to cheer thee,
    When thou may'st think I loved thee so to die;
Perchance my spirit still may linger near thee,
    To guard and guide thee whenever danger's nigh.

Ah! Scotland's minstrels never more shall hear me
    Wail forth my woes in page of 'Penny Post';
No more her heartless Mammonites shall fear me,
    Whose gold could never pay the love I' ve lost.

When this frail form is in the earth reposing,
    Live on, still undisturb'd by thoughts of me,
Whilst to the world this requiem is disclosing
    The worth of one who lived and died for thee.

I go, my loved one, but I leave no token,
    As I would have done, had fortune smiled on me;
The sad remembrance of a heart that's broken
    Is all, my loved one, I can leave to thee.

Stay; I will leave my fame's-crown in thy keeping;
    Its gems may cheer thee at some future day.
Adieu, my loved one, when I' m calmly sleeping,
    Sing to the world—'The Factory Girl's Last Lay.'

[Source: Ellen Johnston, *Autobiography, Poems, and Songs of Ellen Johnston, The "Factory Girl."* 2nd. ed. Glasgow: William Love, 1869. 236-38.]

Appendix E: Contemporary Documents: Parliamentary Testimony as Autobiography

1. Charles Aberdeen, Testimony before the 1832 Committee on the Labour of Children in Factories

[Aberdeen's testimony before Sadler's parliamentary committee became notorious when Aberdeen, recalled as a witness for the 1833 royal commission on children's labor in factories, declined to be sworn in (see Introduction 22-24). Aberdeen explained that he was then making his living by selling pamphlets since he had been discharged from his factory position for supporting the ten-hours cause. Aberdeen's 1832 evidence extends over ten pages of closely printed text in the *Parliamentary Papers*. Excerpted here are the autobiographical portions of his testimony, which reveal his inability to date accurately the beginning of his life or of his working career as a parish apprentice and recount his occupation as a card-grinder, as well as the circumstances of his firing. This document demonstrates not only the way in which question-and-answer testimony can be read as autobiography but also the extent to which it is shaped by the examiner's questions (see Introduction 25).]

Sabbati, 7° die Julii, 1832.

———

MICHAEL THOMAS SADLER, ESQUIRE, IN THE CHAIR.

———

Charles Aberdeen, called in; and Examined.

9496. WHERE do you reside?—At Salford, in Manchester.
9497. What age are you?—Fifty-three.
9498. How long have you resided there?—Between eighteen and twenty years.
9499. What business are you?—A card-grinder in a cotton factory.
9500. Have you long known the business of a cotton-mill?—I have ever since 1796; I was an apprentice from St. James's, Westminster, in London.
9501. To where?—To Holywell in Flintshire, North Wales; to Douglas & Co.
9502. A parish apprentice?—Yes.

9503. Was it at 10 years of age?—Between 11 and 12, I think; as nearly as I can recollect, I was between 11 and 12 when I was apprenticed.

9504. What was the nature of your employment there?—I worked in a card-room when first I commenced working in a factory, spreading cotton.

9505. Is it a very dusty apartment of the mill?—Very dusty; but it is superseded by machines; there is no spreading now by boys.

9506. But still there are various apartments of the cotton-mill now where there are many flues and much dust?—Yes, men that are more lusty than myself, I have seen them die daily for want of breath; because they were not allowed to let the fresh air in and let the foul air out.

9507. Why so?—They consider that it damages the work; and that by not admitting so much air in the room, it makes a smaller surface on the flies of cotton; and if they let too much air in, it becomes ouzy.

9508. In those mills where fine work is pursued, is there not a great deal of heat as well as closeness?—Extremely; but the factory in which I worked is not fine work.

9509. It is sometimes said that the hands have a great objection to ventilation; do you believe that to be the case?—By no means.

9510. You are aware that it has been frequently asserted that the work-people in the mill have an objection to work in a tolerably cool and ventilated air?—I never heard an objection stated to let the foul air out and the fresh in; but a cry and craving for it.

9511. Amongst all the work-people you have known?—Yes.

9512. When were you born?—I was born, I think, in 1780.

9513. To the best of your impression, what was your age when you were sent an apprentice to that mill?—I do not think I was above 12.

9514. Then you are not so old as you have stated?—I am 53, I think.

9515. Are you sure it was in 1796 you went apprentice?—As nearly so as possible.

9516. Can you tell whether you were grown up or not when you were an apprentice, or whether you were a boy?—I was a boy.

9517. And to the best of your belief you were 12 years of age?—Yes.

9518. You do not know when you were born?—Not exactly.

9519. You have no record of it?—I have no record of it at all.

9520. What were the hours of labour in that mill?—From 6 to 7; because the spinning went on day and night while I was an apprentice; there was a sufficiency of carding to allow for the work in the day; it was only the spinning that went on in the night.

9521. What time had you for refreshment?—A whole hour for dinner, none for breakfast, or any thing else, excepting a whole hour for dinner; but if I recollect right, they used to encroach much upon that hour; it might be called an hour, but it was not perhaps three quarters of an hour; it was called an hour.

9522. For what purpose did they encroach upon you, for cleaning the machinery, or resuming the operations of the mill sooner than the appointed time?—On purpose for gain, I think.

9523. Do you mean that the moving power was suspended for a less time than an hour?—It was called an hour, but we generally used to say that they rang us in ten minutes too soon.

9524. Had you to clean the machinery then?—In the dinner-hour, I, for one, used to have to clean and oil the machinery, and I could do that in half an hour, and eat my morsel afterwards.

9525. Was it the common practice to employ the children in that interval to clean the machinery?—Not the children, generally; but the scavengers for the mills were obliged to stop, they were the smallest of the children.

[...]

9532. Has your constant employment been in a factory ever since you were put out apprentice by the parish?—It has so, with a very few exceptions; some few weeks, when the cotton factories used to be stopping at the time of the war, I have known when I had to leave my place in the mills, and take a place as pot-boy in London; but I believe only twice, and for five or six weeks at a time; this has been when I had no employment; I have travelled from Manchester to London, without a penny in my pocket, twice.

9533. You state that there was night-work at that mill?—Yes, while I was apprentice.

9534. Did you observe that to those employed, that work was very pernicious?—I never had work in the night, but I observed it to be the case with those that had.

9535. The hands did not work night and day both?—No; but often the other was dragged out of the bed, whether he would or not, or whether she would or not, the one that had worked in the day.

9536. Then they did work night and day?–Yes; if an accident happened, or any sickness, or if they were stopping away for their own amusement, the one that worked in the day was compelled, by main force, to go instead, whether he liked it or not.

9537. That never happened to you?—I did not work in the night; I worked in the day.

9538. Do you think that the people who worked at night were less healthy than those who worked in the day?—I do.

9539. Did you observe considerable disinclination or otherwise to take the night-work?—I have observed a disinclination to take the night-work.

9540. Would the people have preferred to work by day, if they had had their choice?—They would have preferred to work in the day.

9541. You are sure of it?—I am sure of it.

9542. Is that a prevailing opinion among the hands in those mills, which have pursued night-work, as far as your experience and observation has gone?—It is.

9543. And regarding those children, do you think that after having worked through the night, they took the rest in the day-time that they ought to have done?—I do not think they did.

9544. That they were tempted, in point of fact, to play and move about in the day-time, instead of going to bed?—Yes; and in such weather as this to go a black-berrying, and so on.

9545. So that night-work left them without a proper degree of rest, and consequently deprived them of health?—Yes.

9546. Was there any considerable number of hands in that mill occasionally unwell then?—It is a healthy part, and I have not observed so much sickness, only at one time I observed a prevailing sickness; but that was considered as coming over as a plague, with the cotton. The girls lived a mile distant from the boys, and often there have been six at home at each house sick.

9547. What was the whole number of girls and boys employed?—Five or six hundred.

9548. And there were five or six of each sex often ill at home?—Yes.

9549. Are the hours longer or shorter, or pretty much the same as they were when you were apprentice to a cotton-mill?—Much the same, I think; especially at the place from whence I was last discharged. The master that I was last discharged from, had observed the Act of Parliament more so than any master that I ever knew; indeed it was framed, and hung up at the bottom of the factory stairs. It used to be Phillips & Lee, but now it is Messrs. Lambert, Hoole & Jackson.

9550. Is the Hoole, of that firm, Mr. Holland Hoole?—Yes.

9551. Did you remove from the mill at Holywell to Manchester?—No, I did not at first; I left Holywell for London; I stopped in London for a few months, and then I went to Manchester.

9552. To whose employment did you go then?—To Douglas & Co. at Pendleton.

9553. Did they work by night also in that firm?—They did.

9554. Were you a day-worker there?—Yes, I was.

9555. You never have worked in the night?—Never.

9556. Do you think you could have stood it?—I might have stood it in case of necessity as well as others, I think; but I would prefer the day.

9557. Have the night-workers higher wages?—No, not higher.

9558. Do they work as long?—Not quite so long; there is some trifling difference.

9559. Were their wages as high?—They were full as high; I am not quite so positive whether there was not a 6d. or something more, as an inducement, but I cannot speak positively to that; but I rather think there was something as a kind of inducement to it.

9560. Could a hand choose whether he would be a day-worker or a night-worker?—If the hand, a male or female, would not come in the night, they would not give them a place in the day; and it has been rather compulsory to make them go to night-work.

9561. So as to keep up their stock of night-labourers from those who have been employed by day?—Yes; it has been known that they have discharged persons who have refused to go to night-work often.

9562. Into whose employ did you next go, after Douglas's, at Pendleton?—I worked at two or three places for a very short time; I worked at Ellis Hughes's mill, in Factory-lane, near Oldfield-road; that is close in the neighbourhood where I dwell.

9563. Where did you get permanently fixed again in your present business?—In the last place which I have been discharged from.

9564. What is the firm?—Messrs. Lambert, Hoole & Jackson.

9565. You have stated, that the time of labour which is required from the children and young persons in those mills is much the same as when you first entered upon that employment; will you now inform the Committee whether the labour itself has increased, or otherwise?—The labour has increased more than twofold.

9566. Explain in what way; do you merely mean that a double quantity is thrown off by some superiority in the machinery, or that a greater degree of exertion is demanded from the hands, and to the extent you mention?—The one is consequent upon the other; if the machine is speeded, it will turn off a double quantity; and it requires a double exertion and labour from the child, or from any person that is attending it.

9567. Do you think there is double the quantity of labour required from the children that there used to be?—I am confident of it; since I have been working at the firm of Lambert, Hoole & Jackson, I have done twice the quantity of work that I used to do for less wages.

9568. Do you mean that it required a greater degree of vigilance, or that the actual labour was increased to the extent you have stated?—I mean so; the exertion of the body was required to follow up the speed of the machine.

9569. Has it, therefore, latterly become visibly more fatiguing to the hands than it used to be at first?—Remarkably so.

9570. Did you consider that the hours of labour were full long enough when first you knew the business?—Yes, I did consider them quite long enough.

9571. Did you find them, as a child, fatiguing then?—I did, indeed.

9572. Was that the general effect upon the hands, and more especially the young ones, so employed?—It was, indeed.

9573. Then, recollecting that you found that occupation fatiguing when first you entered upon it, what is your impression as to its nature and effects at present, when you say that the exertion has been doubled?—I believe it both injurious to the morals, health and lives of children in particular, by the exertion that is required from them, and that it supersedes the labour of grown up persons; it preys upon the morals, and health, and lives of the children.

9574. First, as to their health, are they greatly fatigued by their labour?—They are, indeed.

9575. Do you observe it particularly towards the latter part of a day's labour of that kind?—Yes, I do.

9576. Has it any visible effect upon their appearance after they enter upon that course of labour?—It has, indeed, a remarkable effect.

9577. In what respects?—A paleness and a wanness; a factory child may be known easily from another child, that does not work in a factory.

9578. Do you think it interferes with their growth, as well as with their health?—I do.

9579. Has it had the effect of shortening their lives, do you suppose?—I do suppose that; and am beyond supposing it.

9580. Are you, then, confident as to that important and distressing fact?—Yes, I am confident of it from what experience I have had; and I think I have had a good deal.

9581. What grounds have you for thinking so?—I have seen many instances, but cannot state particularly; I have seen men and women that have worked in a factory all their lives, like myself, and that get married; and I have seen the race become diminutive and small; I have myself had seven children, not one of which survived six weeks; my wife is an emaciated person, like myself, a little woman, and she worked during her childhood, younger than myself, in a factory.

9582. Is she alive?–Yes; she was an apprentice from Mile-end, New Town, to the same firm.

[...]

9598. Where do you work now?—I am out of employment now, and have been ever since the 20th of April.

9599. How came you to lose your employment, were you discharged?—I was discharged on the 20th of last April.

9600. Do you know on what account?—I do, I can speak to the point.

9601. Did you leave voluntarily?–No, I was discharged.

9602. Will you state the reasons why you were discharged?—Before the 2d of last March, with respect to the Ten Hours' Bill, I was disposed to be neutral. On the 2d of March, it was on a Friday night, one of the masters where I was discharged from, or two or three, sent the manager to all the rooms; the rooms in that factory are alphabetically arranged; I worked in G. room; the manager put this question to us all, and he said that we must come in the morning, which was Saturday morning, to give the answer to a question, and the question was this: "If we were favourable to Mr. Sadler's Ten Hours' Bill, we must come in the morning with an answer to signify so." An intimation was given at the same time, that if we were favourable to Mr. Sadler's Bill, all the hands under 18 would be discharged. And another question was put, which was this: "If we were favourable for the time as we were working now, we must come with an answer to that effect." Here my opinion changed immediately; I did not attempt to bias any of the men's minds that worked with me; but I was determined to support Mr. Sadler's Bill, from what I had seen so far. On the Saturday morning I came to my work with the rest of the men; the manager called us all into a small room, apart from the large one in which we worked, and he began to speak in praise of the time or hours that we are working now, and to speak disrespectfully of the Ten Hours' Bill, and to endeavour to persuade us that the Stockport masters had prevailed upon the persons that they employed, by mild measures, to be favourable to the hours that we are working now. After he had delivered his instructions to the men, by way of hint he seized an over-looker by the shoulders, and put him gently on one side and told him, and hinted to all the rest, that all those who were for the time we were working now would take that side; one person more left the number, and took sides with him; another person was included, but was not present, though he was an overlooker. At this moment I told the manager; I said, "Thomas Leeman, as I now see the matter, I am determined to support Mr. Sadler's Bill with all my power, whatever may be the consequence." He told me there was no compulsion; I did not say whether there was or was not. At this moment a boy came out of the room underneath and pulled me by the coat, and told me that I should support Mr. Sadler's Bill, as they all had done so in the room where they worked (that was in F. room), excepting the overlooker; I told the boy to go down, for fear he would get ill-treated. At that moment I took sides on the left, to give my support to Mr. Sadler's Ten Hours' Bill; eleven more took sides with me; I understood that there was an overwhelming majority in favour of Mr. Sadler's Ten Hours' Bill, or at least there were eleven to one in favour of it; that was the prevailing opinion that I had at the moment, I mean including the whole of the factory. The master had the whole of Saturday (for this to which I am alluding was early on the Saturday morning) and the Sunday to reflect upon this, and it mortified him. But there is one remark that I have left out; the manager, when first he came up to us, told us that the masters had left it wholly and entirely to us, and what we did they would abide by. On the Monday morning following, which was on the 5th of March, Mr. Lambert, the officiating master, he is the person that goes through the factory more than the other two, indeed the other two do not go through; Mr. Lambert came through the factory on the Monday morning, with a paper ready ruled, with a determination, if possible, to make every person sign contrary to the foregoing. I was informed very soon respecting his errand; I was prepared to meet him, but did not attempt to lead any of the men the way that I intended to take. I understood that when a person was called to him, he told him to sign the paper which he had; I also understood that every one did sign till he came to me. When he came to me he said to me, "Sign that paper;" I wished to know from him what was the intent of that paper; he made me no reply; I pressed it further; I wished to know what was the import of that paper; he made me no reply again; I became more imperative, and I wished to know what that paper expressed, otherwise I might sign to my own degradation: this brought forth a reply from him, and the reply was this, "Why, we do not wish Parliament to interfere with our concerns; we think we are able to manage our own affairs ourselves." I then told him that I thought Parliament had a right to step in between suffering humanity and the oppressor. I left him after those words had passed between us. I had gone half a dozen yards from him; he called me back in an insolent manner, and said, "Here, here, here!" in this manner [*doubling his fist*]; I came to him; he made use of some language, and in the language I understood a threat was conveyed, and the language was this, "You will please to recollect that you are the first that has refused to sign this paper." I told him that if every person signed excepting me, I was determined to abide by my word. He said, "You are a pretty gentleman!" I told him whether I were gentle or simple, I was determined to be honest upon this point.

9603. When did you receive your discharge?—On the 20th of April, when I was coming out of the factory at 7 o'clock at night, it was on Friday night; Mr. Lambert met me at the factory door, and beckoned me, and said softly to me, "When people cannot agree, they are best asunder." That was the language that I received from him, and he told the clerk to pay me my wages.

9604. Had you any difference with him between the 5th of March and 20th of April?—I made what I have been relating known in print. I attended a meeting at the Duke of Lancaster in Salford, of the different hands that work in the factory which I was discharged from, and I was chairman; I wished to object to take the chair, because I had something to speak about, but I was forced into the chair; and they said they would allow me to speak, and I made use of some language, perhaps, that I have been stating here; and they told me at Salford, that it was for the language that I made use of at the Duke of Lancaster Inn, that I was discharged.

9605. Was there any thing personally abusive to your employers in your language?—No, by no means.

9606. All that you said was with reference to the system?—Yes.

[...]

9610. How long were you there?—Seven years.

9611. You have no reason to suppose that you had dissatisfied your masters by your inattention to your work, or in any part of your employment, previous to that period?—By no means.

9612. You had no intimation from them, previous to the exercising of your rights in the manner you state, that you would be discharged?—Not at all.

9613. Is that your confident impression and belief, that if you had not so acted you would not have been discharged?—I have not the least doubt of it; it was for acting honestly and taking the part I did, that I was discharged.

9614. The language held to you, and the course adopted with regard to you, has fully justified you in the impression you have now stated?—Yes, it has.

9615. Were the proceedings at the Duke of Lancaster reported in any public papers?—I think they were not particularly so, they were only hinted at.

9616. But there was nothing personally offensive or insulting towards your employers?—Nothing at all.

9617. It was merely an attempt to get a remission of the hours of labour, with a view to serve the interest, and promote the happiness of the working classes, and especially the children?—Yes.

9618. You are perhaps aware that the Petition obtained in the manner you have described, and purporting to be signed by 700 or 800 individuals, was presented to this House, and that it declares the hostility of that establishment to the measure now under the consideration of Parliament?—Yes, I have heard some talk that one Mr. Heywood presented it.

9619. But as to the further facts connected with that Petition you know nothing?—No.

9620. You have stated that that Petition was presented in a peremptory manner, that the purport of it was not at all explained to the hands, and that in the room where you were, you were the first individual that presumed to ask what it was about?—Yes, I believe I was the first; there was another man that did refuse to sign, but he did not do it so determinately as I did; and there was another person that wished to come in for a triumph, but he kept back; he did not come up at all, he fought shy.

9621. You have already stated, that the great mass of the hands employed in that mill are favourable to the measure now before Parliament?—Yes, I believe it firmly.

9622. And still, owing to the conduct and course that you have described, they were in a manner obliged to sign against their own inclination, and, as they believe, their own interest and welfare?—Yes, that is the prevailing opinion in the establishment.

[...]

9674. Have you observed that this particular employment leads, in a great number of instances, to tippling and drinking when the hours of labour are over, the hands being so much exhausted and fatigued, and in a hot temperature?—I have observed too much of it; but for my own part, if I had the means, if I got my own wages, which I did, I dare not take much ale or spirits, for I am afflicted with a palpitation of the heart; my general observation is that there is too much tippling.

9675. Do you attribute that to the ignorance, to the long labour, and to the emaciated health of the persons employed in factories?—I do.

9676. In every point of view, you think that a remission of the hours of labour would be serviceable to the individuals, and beneficial to society?—I do.

[Source: Report from the Committee on the "Bill to Regulate the Labour of Children in the Mills and Factories of the United Kingdom" with the Minutes of Evidence. *Parliamentary Papers* 15 (1831-32): 439-46, 448.]

2. Elizabeth Bentley, Testimony before the 1832 Committee on the Labour of Children in Factories

[This 1857 presentation of testimony originally given before Sadler's 1832 committee, in Samuel Kydd's *The History of the Factory Movement* is noteworthy for two reasons. First, it demonstrates the way in which such testimony functions as autobiography, a quality enhanced in Kydd's version by his practice of putting its questions and answers in "narrative form" (see Introduction 25). Secondly, Sadler gathered evidence from a relatively small number of workers, thirty-five of whom were male (adults and teenagers), and only three female (Gray 30); Bentley's story represents, therefore, an unusual perspective on early factory labor. Ironically, the final point that she makes in her testimony foretells the outcome of Ellen Johnston's factory life (see the headnote to Johnston's "Autobiography"). According to J.T. Ward, Kydd, a Chartist, was originally a shoemaker from Arbroath, then a barrister and journalist; in 1851 he was serving as Richard Oastler's secretary (391; 473, n47).]

Elizabeth Bentley:—

"I am twenty-three years of age, and live at Leeds. I began to work at Mr Busk's flax mill when I was six years old. I was then a little 'doffer.' In that mill we worked from five in the morning till nine at night, when they were 'throng;' when they were not so 'throng,' the usual hours of labour were from six in the morning till seven at night. The time allowed for our meals was forty minutes at noon; not any time was allowed for breakfast or 'drinking:' these we got as we could. When our work was bad, we had hardly any time to eat them at all: we were obliged to leave them or take them home. When we did not take our uneaten food home, the overlooker took it and gave it to his pigs. I consider 'doffing' to be a laborious employment. When the frames are full, the 'doffers' have to stop them, and take the 'flyers' off, and take the full bobbins off, and carry them to the roller, and then put empty ones on, and set the frame going again. I was kept constantly on my feet; there were so many frames, and they run so quick, the labour was excessive, there was not time for anything. When the 'doffers' flagged a little, or were too late, they were strapped. Those who were last in 'doffing' were constantly strapped—girls as well as boys. I have been strapped severely, and have been hurt by the strap excessively. The overlooker I was under was a very severe man. When I and others have been fatigued and worn out, and had not baskets enough to put the bobbins in, we used to put them in the window bottoms, and that broke the panes sometimes; and I broke one one time, and the overlooker strapped me on the arm, and it rose a blister, and I ran home to my mother. I worked at Mr Busk's factory three or four years.

"When I left Mr Busk's, I then went to Benyon's factory; I was about ten years of age and was employed as a weigher in the card-room. At Benyon's factory we worked from half-past five till eight at night, when they were 'throng' until nine. The spinners at that mill were allowed forty minutes at noon for meals; no more time throughout the day was allowed. Those employed in the card-rooms had, in addition to the forty minutes at noon, a quarter of an hour allowed for their breakfast, and a quarter of an hour for their 'drinking.' The carding-room is more oppressive than the spinning department: those at work cannot see each other for dust. The 'cards' get so soon filled up with waste and dirt, they must be stopped or they would take fire: the stoppages are as much for the benefit of the employer as for the working people. The children at Benyon's factory were beat up to their labour with a strap. I have seen the overlooker go to the top end of the room, where the little girls 'hug' the can to the 'backminsters;' he has taken a strap, and a whistle in his mouth, and sometimes he has got a chain and chained them, and strapped them all down the room. This was done to those children who were 'hugging' the cans. It was in the afternoon; the children were excessively fatigued: they were too slow, and the overlooker was angry with them. The girls have many times had black marks upon their skins. Had the parents complained of this excessive ill-usage, the probable consequence would have been the loss of the employment of the child. Of this result the parents were afraid.

"I worked in the card-room; it was so dusty that the dust got upon my lungs, and the work was so hard. I was middling strong when I went there, but the work was so bad; I got so bad in health, that when I pulled the baskets down, I pulled my bones out of their places. The basket I pulled was a very large one; that was full of weights, upheaped, and pulling the basket, pulled my shoulder out of its place, and my ribs have grown over it. That hard work is generally done by women: it is not fit for children. There was no spinning for me, and I therefore did that work. They gave me five shillings a week, the women had six shillings and sixpence. As a spinner, I had got six shillings. The hands were constantly leaving, because of the unhealthy nature of their employment, and the excessive labour they had to endure. The employment made us very thirsty: we drank a deal of water in the room. It was not so very hot as in the summer time. In the winter it was necessary to have the windows open; it made no matter what the weather was, and sometimes we got very severe colds in frost and snow. We were constantly exposed to colds, and were made ill by that cause also. Then I had not much food to eat, and the little I had I could not eat it, my appetite was so poor. My food being covered with dust, it was no use to take it home. I could not eat it, and the overlooker took it, and gave it to his pigs. I am speaking of the breakfast. I could not go home to dinner.

"I lived two miles from the mill. We had no clock. If I had been too late at the mill, I would have been 'quartered.' I mean that if I had been a quarter of an hour too late, a half an hour would have been taken off. I only got a penny an hour, and they would have taken a halfpenny more. I was never beaten myself. I have seen the boys beaten for being too late. I was generally at the factory in time. My mother has been up at two o'clock and at four o'clock in the morning. The colliers used to go to their work about three or four o'clock, and when she heard them stirring, she has got up out of her warm bed, and gone out and asked them the time; and I have sometimes been at Hunslet Car at two o'clock in the morning, when it was streaming down with rain, and we have had to stay till the mill was opened. Had the hours of labour been moderate, I could have awoke regularly. It was a matter of anxiety and difficulty for me to arouse myself early enough for those hours of labour.

"I am considerably deformed in person in consequence of this labour. I was about thirteen years old when my deformity began to come on, and it has got worse since. It is five years since my mother died, and she was never able to get me a pair of good stays to hold me up; and when my mother died I had to do for myself, and got me a pair. Before I worked at a mill I was as straight a little girl as ever went up and down town. I was straight until I was thirteen. I have been attended by a medical gentleman, Mr Hare. He said it was owing to hard labour, and working in the factories. He told me so. I was coming from Leeds, and he asked a good many questions. He asked me if I had a father and mother? I said, no. He said if I had no objection he would take me in hand. I said I was much obliged to him. He told me to come to his house that night; and I went to the mill, and told them I was going to stop away. I stopped at home ten weeks, and my cousins, that

I was living with, had to maintain me, and they told me they were sure he would not do me any good, and they could not find me with support; and Mr Hare told me it would be a year before I should be straight again. I was obliged to return to my work. It was two years ago that Mr Hare saw me; I was then twenty-one. I cannot express the pain I had all the time that the deformity was coming upon me.

"I next began to work at Tatham and Walker's flax-mill. I went into the spinning room. When they were busy, the hours of labour there were from half-past five in the morning to eight and half-past eight. I have seen the children strapped in that mill, the 'doffers' as well as others[.] The children could not be kept up to their work unless they were beaten. The period allotted for refreshment at that mill, and at the time to which I allude, was forty minutes at noon in winter, and half an hour in summer. Since the factory agitation began, time has been allowed for breakfast and 'drinking.' When they were much thronged in winter, the hours of work were from six in the morning to seven or eight at night. The children were occasionally brought in from their meals before the time was up; they were sometimes whipped in out of the mill yard; the overlooker has got a strap, and gone out and strapped them in before their time, that they might come in and get on with their work.

"I have had the misfortune, from being a straight and healthful girl, to become very much otherwise in person. I do not know of any other girls that have become weak and deformed in like manner. I have known others who have been similarly injured in health. I am deformed in the shoulders; it is very common indeed to have weak ankles and crooked knees, that is brought on by stopping the spindle.

"I have had experience in wet spinning—it is very uncomfortable. I have stood before the frames till I have been wet through to my skin; and in winter-time, when myself and others have gone home, our clothes have been frozen, and we have nearly caught our death from cold. We have stopped at home one or two days, just as we were situated in our health; had we stopped away any length of time we should have found it difficult to keep our situations.

"I am now in the poor-house at Hunslet. Not any of my former employers come to see me. When I was at home, Mr Walker made me a present of 1s. or 2s., but since I left my work and have gone to the poor-house, no one has come nigh me. I was very willing to have worked as long as I was able, and to have supported my widowed mother. I am utterly incapable now of any exertion of that sort, and am supported by the parish."

[Source: (Samuel Kydd). "Alfred." *The History of the Factory Movement from the Year 1802, to the Enactment of the Ten Hours' Bill in 1847.* 2 vols. London: Simpkin, Marshall, 1857. 1: 297-302.]

Appendix F: Factory Life: Contemporary Views

1. Harriet Martineau, from *A Manchester Strike* (1832)

[Harriet Martineau (1802-1876) was a prolific English writer and journalist. *A Manchester Strike* is the best known of her *Illustrations of Political Economy* (1832-34), tales told to explain the benefits of free trade and the dangers of legislative meddling in the workings of capitalist institutions. This particular story is meant to prove, as its concluding "summary of principles" outlines, that because wages depend on population, not profits, strikes for increased wages cannot ever succeed. Instead of engaging in such futile "combinations of labourers against capitalists," workers should instead decrease the population by, presumably, having fewer children and therefore increase their portion of the wages available (134-36). As a number of critics point out, *A Manchester Strike* contradicts its own explicit message (Kovačević 119-23; Gallagher 55-61), perhaps nowhere more than in its depiction of the factory girl Martha: her filial piety and devotion to work would seem to argue for having more, not fewer children. In the first parts of both Chapters I and VI, reprinted here, Martha's sufferings and her virtue are equally apparent.]

CHAPTER I.
THE WEEK'S END.

ONE fine Saturday evening in May, 18—, several hundred work-people, men, girls, and boys, poured out from the gates of a factory which stood on the banks of the Medlock, near Manchester. The children dispersed in troops, some to play, but the greater number to reach home with all speed, as if they were afraid of the sunshine that chequered the street and reddened the gables and chimnies.

The men seemed in no such haste; they lingered about the factory, one large group standing before the gates, and smaller knots occupying the street for some distance, while a few proceeded slowly on their way home, chatting with one or another party as they went. One only appeared to have nothing to say to his companions, and to wish to get away quietly, if they would have let him. He was one of the most respectable looking among them, decent in his dress, and intelligent though somewhat melancholy in countenance. He was making his way without speaking to anybody, when first one and then another caught him by the button and detained him in consultation. All seemed anxious to know what Allen had to relate or to advise; and Allen had some difficulty in getting leave to go home, much as he knew he was wanted there. When he had at length escaped, he walked so rapidly as presently to overtake his little daughter, Martha, who had left the factory somewhat earlier. He saw her before him for some distance, and observed how she limped, and how feebly she made her way along the street, (if such it might be called,) which led to their abode. It was far from easy walking to the strongest. There were heaps of rubbish, pools of muddy water, stones and brickbats lying about, and cabbage-leaves on which the unwary might slip, and bones over which pigs were grunting and curs snarling and fighting. Little Martha, a delicate child of eight years old, tried to avoid all these obstacles; but she nearly slipped down several times, and started when the dogs came near her, and shivered every time the mild spring breeze blew in her face.

"Martha, how lame you are to-day!" said Allen, taking her round the waist to help her onward.

"O father, my knees have been aching so all day, I thought I should have dropped every moment."

"And one would think it was Christmas by your looks, child, instead of a bright May day."

"It is very chill after the factory," said the little girl, her teeth still chattering. "Sure the weather must have changed, father."

No; the wind was south, and the sky cloudless. It was only that the thermometer had stood at 75° within the factory.

"I suppose your wages are lowered as well as mine," said Allen; "how much do you bring home this week?"

"Only three shillings, father; and some say it will be less before long. I am afraid mother—"

The weak-spirited child could not say what it was that she feared, being choked by her tears.

"Come, Martha, cheer up," said her father. "Mother knows that you get sometimes more and sometimes less; and, after all, you earn as much as a piecer as some do at the hand-loom. There is Field, our neighbour; he and his wife together do not earn more than seven shillings a week, you know, and think how much older and stronger they are than you! We must make you stronger, Martha. I will go with you to Mr. Dawson, and he will find out what is the matter with your knees."

By this time they had reached the foot of the stairs which led up to their two rooms in the third story of a large dwelling which was occupied by many poor families. Barefooted children were scampering up and down these stairs at play; girls nursing babies sat at various elevations, and seemed in danger of being kicked down as often as a drunken man or an angry woman should want to pass; a thing which frequently happened. Little Martha looked up the steep stairs and sighed. Her father lifted and carried her. The noises would have stunned a stranger, and they seemed louder than usual to accustomed ears.

[...]

CHAPTER VI.
NIGHT AND MORNING.

"How is Martha?" was Allen's first inquiry on meeting his wife at the head of the stairs. Martha had been asleep when he had returned in the middle of the day; for it was now her turn for night-work at the factory, and what rest she had must be taken in the day. Her mother said that her lameness was much the same; that she had seen Mr. Dawson, the apothecary, who pronounced that rest was what her weak limbs most required; and that as perfect rest was out of the question, her mother must bandage the joints while the child was at her work, and keep her laid on her bed at home. Here was the difficulty, her mother said, especially while Hannah[1] was with her, for they were both fond of play when poor Martha was not too tired to stir. She was now gone to her work for the night.

The little girl repaired to the factory, sighing at the thought of the long hours that must pass before she could sit down or breathe the fresh air again. She had been as willing a child at her work as could be till lately: but since she had grown sickly, a sense of hardship had come over her, and she was seldom happy. She was very industrious, and disposed to be silent at her occupation; so that she was liked by her employers, and had nothing more to complain of than the necessary fatigue and disagreeableness of the work. She would not have minded it for a few hours of the day; but to be shut up all day, or else all night, without any time to nurse the baby or play with her companions, was too much for a little girl of eight years old. She had never been so sensible of this as since her renewed acquaintance with Hannah. This night, when the dust from the cotton made her cough, when the smell and the heat brought on sickness and faintness, and the incessant whizzing and whirling of the wheels gave her the feeling of being in a dream, she remembered that a part of Hannah's business was to walk on broad roads or through green fields by her father's side, listening to the stories he amused her with, and to sit on a stile or under a tree to practice a new tune, or get a better dinner than poor Martha often saw. She forgot that Hannah was sometimes wet through, or scorched by the sun, as her complexion, brown as a gipsy's, showed; and that Hannah had no home and no

---

1 Hannah, daughter of a former worker, has been on tramp earning coins as a dancer.

mother, and very hard and unpleasant work to do at fairs, and on particular occasions. About midnight, when Martha remembered that all at home were probably sound asleep, she could not resist the temptation of resting her aching limbs, and sat down, trusting to make up afterwards for lost time, and taking care to be on her feet when the overlooker passed, or when any one else was likely to watch her. It is a dangerous thing, however, to take rest with the intention of rousing oneself from time to time; and so Martha found. She fairly fell asleep after a time, and dreamed that she was attending very diligently to her work; and so many things besides passed through her mind during the two minutes that she slept, that when the overlooker laid his hand upon her shoulder, she started and was afraid she was going to be scolded for a long fit of idleness. But she was not harshly spoken to.

"Come, come, child; how long have you been asleep?"

"I don't know. I thought I was awake all the time." And Martha began to cry.

"Well, don't cry. I was past just now, and you were busy enough; but don't sit down; better not, for fear you should drop asleep again."

Martha thought she had escaped very well; and winking and rubbing her eyes, she began to limp forward and use her trembling hands. The overlooker watched her for a few moments, and told her she was so industrious in general that he should be sorry to be hard upon her; but she knew that if she was seen flagging over her work, the idle ones would make it an excuse to do so too. Martha curtsied, and put new vigour into her work at this praise. Before he went on in his rounds, the overlooker pointed to the window and told her morning was come.

It was a strange scene that the dawn shone upon. As the grey light from the east mingled with the flickering, yellow glare of the lamps, it gave a mottled dirty appearance to everything; to the pale-faced children, to the unshaved overlooker, to the loaded atmosphere, and even to the produce the of [sic] wheels.

When a bright sunbeam shone in through the window, thickened with the condensed breath of the work-people, and showed the oily steam rising through the heated room, the lamps were extinguished, to the great relief of those who found the place growing too like an oven to be much longer tolerable. The sunbeams rested now on the ceiling, and Martha knew that they must travel down to the floor and be turned full on her frame and some way past it, before she could be released; but still it was a comfort that morning was come.

She observed that the overlooker frequently went out and came back again, and that there was a great deal of consultation among her betters as the hours drew on. A breath of fresh air came in now and then from below, and news went round that the gates were already open, two hours earlier than usual. Presently the tramp of heavy feet was heard, like that of the weavers and spinners coming to their daily work. Martha looked up eagerly to the clock, supposing that the time had passed quicker than she had been aware of; but it was only four o'clock. What could bring the people to their work so early? They could scarcely have mistaken the hour from the brightness of the morning, for it had now clouded over, and was raining a soaking shower. More news went round. Those who had arrived had barely escaped being waylaid and punished for coming to work after a strike had been proclaimed. They had been pursued to the gates and very nearly caught, and must now stay where they were till nightfall, as they could not safely appear in broad daylight, going to and returning from their dinners. Many wondered that they had ventured at all, and all prophecied that they must give up to the will of the Union if they wished to be safe. The overlooker, finding much excitement prevailing on the circulation of the news, commanded silence, observing that it was no concern of any of the children present. There was no strike of the children, and they would be permitted to go and come without hinderance. Martha determined to get away the first moment she could, and to meet her father, if possible, that he might not encounter any troublesome people for her sake.

[Source: Harriet Martineau, *A Manchester Strike: A Tale*. London: Charles Fox, 1832. 1-4, 63-68.]

2. Andrew Ure, from *The Philosophy of Manufactures* (1835)

[Andrew Ure (1778-1857) was a Scottish chemist fascinated by the developments in industry that he saw around him. In the preface to this, the most extensive and the best-known of the arguments for the factory system, Ure states that he is writing for the general public so that he can inform them, on the basis of the "most carefully verified" facts, of the advantages of the factory system. As these extracts from the first chapter of Book the First and the first two chapters of Book the Third ("Moral Economy of the Factory System") demonstrate, Ure depends on his own eyewitness testimony to make many of the points in his case for industrialized labor. Ure sees the factory system as an organism: "Manufactures ... have all three principles of action, or three organic systems; the mechanical, the moral, and the commercial, which may not unaptly be compared to the muscular, the nervous, and the sanguiferous systems of an animal." These three systems—"labour, science, and capital"—constitute a "self-governing agency" (55), one that should be protected from the interference of Parliament and the "ignorance and waywardness of workmen" (x). Ure also implies that he thinks that children are the ideal industrial workers—much more suited than men and women for the demands of the factory system—because children's relative physical weaknesses make them easy to discipline.]

In its precise acceptation, the Factory system is of recent origin, and may claim England for its birthplace. The mills for throwing silk, or making organzine, which were mounted centuries ago in several of the Italian states, and furtively transferred to this country by Sir Thomas Lombe in 1718, contained indeed certain elements of a factory, and probably suggested some hints of those grander and more complex combinations of self-acting machines, which were first embodied half a century later in our cotton manufacture by Richard Arkwright, assisted by gentlemen of Derby, well acquainted with its celebrated silk establishment. But the spinning of an entangled flock of fibres into a smooth thread, which constitutes the main operation with cotton, is in silk superfluous; being already performed by the unerring instinct of a worm, which leaves to human art the simple task of doubling and twisting its regular filaments. The apparatus requisite for this purpose is more elementary, and calls for few of those gradations of machinery which are needed in the carding, drawing, roving, and spinning processes of a cotton-mill.

When the first water-frames for spinning cotton were erected at Cromford, in the romantic valley of the Derwent, about sixty years ago, mankind were little aware of the mighty revolution which the new system of labour was destined by Providence to achieve, not only in the structure of British society, but in the fortunes of the world at large. Arkwright alone had the sagacity to discern, and the boldness to predict in glowing language, how vastly productive human industry would become, when no longer proportioned in its results to muscular effort, which is by its nature fitful and capricious, but when made to consist in the task of guiding the work of mechanical fingers and arms, regularly impelled with great velocity by some indefatigable physical power. What his judgment so clearly led him to perceive, his energy of will enabled him to realize with such rapidity and success, as would have done honour to the most influential individuals, but were truly wonderful in that obscure and indigent artisan. The main difficulty did not, to my apprehension, lie so much in the invention of a proper self-acting mechanism for drawing out and twisting cotton into a continuous thread, as in the distribution of the different members of the apparatus into one co-operative body, in impelling each organ with its appropriate delicacy and speed, and above all, in training human beings to renounce their desultory habits of work, and to identify themselves with the unvarying regularity of the complex automaton. To devise and administer a successful code of factory discipline, suited to the necessities of factory diligence, was the Herculean enterprise, the noble achievement of Arkwright. Even at the present day, when the system is perfectly organized, and its labour lightened to the utmost, it is found nearly impossible to convert persons past the age of puberty, whether drawn from rural or from handicraft occupations, into useful factory hands. After struggling for a while to conquer their listless or restive habits, they either renounce the employment spontaneously, or are dismissed by the overlookers on account of inattention.

[...]

It required, in fact, a man of a Napoleon nerve and ambition, to subdue the refractory tempers of work-people accustomed to irregular paroxysms of diligence, and to urge on his multifarious and intricate constructions in the face of prejudice, passion, and envy. Such was Arkwright, who, suffering nothing to stay or turn aside his progress, arrived gloriously at the goal, and has for ever affixed his name to a great era in the annals of mankind, an era which has laid open unbounded prospects of wealth and comfort to the industrious, however much they may have been occasionally clouded by ignorance and folly.

Prior to this period, manufactures were everywhere feeble and fluctuating in their development; shooting forth luxuriantly for a season, and again withering almost to the roots, like annual plants. Their perennial growth now began in England, and attracted capital in copious streams to irrigate the rich domains of industry. When this new career commenced, about the year 1770, the annual consumption of cotton in British manufactures was under four millions of pounds weight, and that of the whole of Christendom was probably not more than ten millions. Last year the consumption in Great Britain and Ireland was about two hundred and seventy millions of pounds, and that of Europe and the United States together four hundred and eighty millions. This prodigious increase is, without doubt, almost entirely due to the factory system founded and upreared by the intrepid native of Preston. If then this system be not merely an inevitable step in the social progression of the world, but the one which gives a commanding station and influence to the people who most resolutely take it, it does not become any man, far less a denizen of this favoured land, to vilify the author of a benefaction, which, wisely administered, may become the best temporal gift of Providence to the poor, a blessing destined to mitigate, and in some measure to repeal, the primeval curse pronounced on the labour of man, "in the sweat of thy face shalt thou eat bread." Arkwright well deserves to live in honoured remembrance among those ancient master-spirits, who persuaded their roaming companions to exchange the precarious toils of the chase, for the settled comforts of agriculture.

In my recent tour, continued during several months, through the manufacturing districts, I have seen tens of thousands of old, young, and middle-aged of both sexes, many of them too feeble to get their daily bread by any of the former modes of industry, earning abundant food, raiment, and domestic accommodation, without perspiring at a single pore, screened meanwhile from the summer's sun and the winter's frost, in apartments more airy and salubrious than those of the metropolis, in which our legislative and fashionable aristocracies assemble. In those spacious halls the benignant power of steam summons around him his myriads of willing menials, and assigns to each the regulated task, substituting for painful muscular effort on their part, the energies of his own gigantic arm, and demanding in return only attention and dexterity to correct such little aberrations as casually occur in his workmanship. The gentle docility of this moving force qualifies it for impelling the tiny bobbins of the lace-machine with a precision and speed inimitable by the most dexterous hands, directed by the sharpest eyes. Hence, under its auspices, and in obedience to Arkwright's polity, magnificent edifices, surpassing far in number, value, usefulness, and ingenuity of construction, the boasted monuments of Asiatic, Egyptian, and Roman despotism, have, within the short period of fifty years, risen up in this kingdom, to show to what extent, capital, industry, and science may augment the resources of a state, while they meliorate the condition of its citizens. Such is the factory system, replete with prodigies in mechanics and political economy, which promises, in its future growth, to become the great minister of civilization to the terraqueous globe, enabling this country, as its heart, to diffuse along with its commerce, the life-blood of science and religion to myriads of people still lying "in the region and shadow of death."

[...]

No master would wish to have any wayward children to work within the walls of his factory, who do not mind their business without beating, and he there[f]ore usually fines or turns away any spinners who are known to maltreat their assistants. Hence, ill-usage of any kind is a very rare occurrence. I have visited many factories, both in Manchester and in the surrounding districts, during a period of several months, entering the spinning rooms, unexpectedly, and often alone, at different times of the day, and I never saw a single instance of corporal chastisement inflicted on a child, nor indeed did I ever see children in ill-humour. They seemed to be always cheerful and alert, taking pleasure in the light play of their muscles,—enjoying the mobility natural to their age. The scene of industry, so far from exciting sad emotions in my mind, was always exhilarating. It was delightful to observe the nimbleness with which they pieced the broken ends, as the mule-carriage began to recede from the fixed roller beam, and to see them at leisure, after a few seconds' exercise of their tiny fingers, to amuse themselves in any attitude they chose, till the stretch and winding-on were once more completed. The work of these lively elves seemed to resemble a sport, in which habit gave them a pleasing dexterity. Conscious of their skill, they were delighted to show it off to any stranger. As to exhaustion by the day's work, they evinced no trace of it on emerging from the mill in the evening; for they immediately began to skip about any neighbouring play-ground, and to commence their little amusements with the same alacrity as boys issuing from a school. It is moreover my firm conviction, that if children are not ill-used by bad parents or guardians, but receive in food and raiment the full benefit of what they earn, they would thrive better when employed in our modern factories, than if left at home in apartments too often ill-aired, damp, and cold. [...]

At Quarry Bank, near Wilmslow, in Cheshire, is situated the oldest of the five establishments belonging to the great firm of Messrs. Greg and Sons, of Manchester, who work up the one-hundredth part of all the cotton consumed in Great Britain. It is driven by an elegant water-wheel, 32 feet in diameter, and 24 feet broad, equivalent in power to 120 horses. The country round is beautiful, and presents a succession of picturesque wooded dells, interspersed with richly cultivated fields. At a little distance from the factory, on a sunny slope, stands a handsome house, two stories high, built for the accommodation of the female apprentices. Here are well fed, clothed, educated, and lodged, under kind superintendence, sixty young girls, who by their deportment at the mill, as well as in Wilmslow Church on Sunday, where I saw them assembled, evince a degree of comfort most creditable to the humane and intelligent proprietors. The Sunday scholars, equally numerous, belonging to the rural population, appeared to great disadvantage alongside of the factory children, the former being worse clad and worselooking than the latter, and worse behaved during divine service.

Messrs. Greg spin about 60,000 lbs. of cotton per week in their five mills, which amount to the prodigious quantity of 3,120,000 lbs. per annum, being the largest concern in the kingdom.* One penny per pound on the price of cotton wool makes a difference to them of 3000*l*. a-year.

The female apprentices at the Quarry Bank mill come partly from its own parish, partly from Chelsea, but chiefly from the Liverpool poor-house. The proprietors have engaged a man and a woman, who take care of them in every way; also a schoolmaster and schoolmistress, and a medical practitioner. The Messrs. Greg are in the habit of looking after the education of the boys, and their sisters superintend that of the girls, who are taught reading, writing, arithmetic, sewing, and other

---

* 308,602,401 lbs. was the import for home consumption in 1834. [Ure's note]

domestic avocations. The health of these apprentices is unequalled by that of any other class of work-people in any occupation. The medical certificate laid before the Factory Commissioners proves that the deaths are only one in 150, being no more than one-third of the average of Lancashire. Their ages vary from ten to twenty-one years. When they grow up, they almost always marry some of the men belonging to the factory, often continue to work, and receive better wages than the other operatives, as they are obliged to take houses for themselves. Only one or two instances have occurred in the course of forty years, since the system was begun by Mr. Greg, sen., of any of them coming on the parish. The apprentices have milk-porridge for breakfast, potatoes and bacon for dinner, and butcher-meat on Sundays. They have bacon every day. About 550 young people of this description have passed through that mill in the course of forty years. Mr. W. R. Greg says, that the general state of education among their mill hands is remarkably superior to that of the agricultural people. He has attended sometimes a sort of little club established near one of their country mills, to which some of the farmers' people came, and he found an astonishing difference between their intelligence and that of the mill-workers. He has observed, that the children are a great deal more fatigued and less willing to go to school after a holiday, than after the business of an ordinary day. They all attend school with regularity.

I paid an unexpected visit to Hyde, in order to view the factories of Thomas Ashton, Esq., uncle to the amiable youth who was shot dead some time ago near his father's door, by assassins who had hired themselves during the ferment of the spinners' strikes, to murder mill-owners at the rate of ten pounds for each. This lamented victim of violence was not a proprietor, was personally unknown to the assassins, and had never given offence to the operatives. It was an unprovoked murder, which impressed every heart with horror, and has cast upon unions a bloody stain which they will never wash away.

Mr. T. Ashton and four of his brothers possess, in their five independent establishments in the township of Hyde, 4000 power-looms, with all the subsidiary spinning machinery, and expend fully 4000*l*. weekly in wages. At the period of my visit, the work-people were paid 1000*l*. per diem in these several factories of Hyde, a district which consisted, not many years ago, of cold clay land, ill-cultivated and thinly peopled. Along with the adjoining small townships of Duckenfield and Stayley-bridge, it contains now upwards of 60,000 inhabitants, all comfortably employed and fed.

Mr. T. Ashton's cotton-works are agreeably grouped together on a gentle declivity, which is traversed by a little tributary stream of the Mersey. This supplies the condensing power to his steam-engines, while their expansive force is furnished from rich coal-measures immediately under the factory lands. This is the motive-element which pervades and animates the region all around. The houses occupied by his work-people lie in streets, are built of stone, and are commodious; consisting each of at least four apartments in two stories, with a small back-yard and a mews lane. The rent for a good lodging, containing an improved kitchen-grate, with boiler and oven, is only 8*l.* per annum, and good fuel may be had for 9*s.* a ton. I looked into several of the houses, and found them more richly furnished than any common work-people's dwellings which I had ever seen before. In one I saw a couple of sofas, with good chairs, an eight-day clock in a handsome mahogany case, several pictures in oil on the walls, freshly painted for the family, a representation of one of the younger daughters like a smart peasant girl carrying a basket on her arm, one of the Virgin and child at Bethlehem, and another of Christ crowned with thorns, all creditable to the travelling artist. In another house I observed a neat wheel barometer, with its attached thermometer, suspended against the snow-white wall. In a third there was a piano, with a little girl learning to play upon it.

My notice was particularly attracted to a handsome house and shop, in one of the streets where Mr. T. Ashton's operatives dwell. On asking who occupied it, I learned it was a spinner, who having saved from his earnings 200*l.*, had embarked this capital in a retail business, now managed by his wife, a tidy-looking person, while the husband continued to pursue his profitable avocations in the mill.

Many of the factory youths of both sexes cultivate their musical tastes. The proprietor having erected a handsome school-house, the workers subscribed spontaneously among themselves 160*l.*, and bought a good organ, now set up in the gallery of the large hall of the school. It is played upon on the Sundays at divine service, and on certain evenings through the week alternately, by certain of the girls employed at the power-looms. One of them, only seventeen years of age, is said to be a tolerable organist. So much nonsense has been uttered about the deformities and diseases of factory children, that I may hardly be credited by some of my readers, when I assert that I have never seen, among a like number of young women of the lower ranks in any country, so many pleasing countenances and handsome figures, as I saw in Mr. Ashton's nine power-weaving galleries. Their light labour and erect posture in tending the looms, and the habit which many of them have of exercising their arms and shoulders, as if with dumb-bells, by resting their hands on the lay or shuttle-bearer, as it oscillates alternately backwards and forwards with the machinery, opens their chest, and gives them generally a graceful carriage. Many of them have adopted tasteful modes of wearing neat handkerchiefs on their heads, and have altogether not a little of the Grecian style of beauty. One of them, whose cheeks had a fine rosy hue, being asked how long she had been at factory work, said nine years, and blushed from bashfulness at being so slightly spoken to.

[Source: Andrew Ure. *The Philosophy of Manufactures: or, An Exposition of the Scientific, Moral, and Commercial Economy of the Factory System of Great Britain*. London: Charles Knight, 1835. 14-19, 300-301, 346-51.]

3. From *The Young Folks of the Factory* (1840)

[This publication from the Religious Tract Society attempts to offer factory children, as its subtitle says, *Friendly Hints on Their Duties and Dangers*. In the first excerpt reprinted here, an introductory letter to the volume, the anonymous writer points out the commercial importance of factory labor and the advantages that it offers young workers. Chapter V deals with "truth and integrity" by presenting a dialogue between a Sunday school teacher and her students, "almost all [of whom are] employed in the manufactories." On weekday evenings, the teacher offers, along with "instruction in common things" such as sewing, writing, and arithmetic (17), lessons in how the students may use their free time wisely, maintain their health, and, in the case of the second excerpt here, avoid forming indolent, uncleanly habits. The publisher of this text, the Religious Tract Society, founded in 1799, was the largest of the many philanthropic organizations that distributed free Bibles, pamphlets, and "improving" books to the poor. By 1861 it was publishing approximately twenty million tracts a year. Writings such as *The Young Folks of the Factory* were, as Richard D. Altick explains, "a ubiquitous part of the social landscape": "Tracts were flung from carriage windows; they were passed out at railway stations; they turned up in ... jails and lodging-houses and hospitals and workhouses; they were distributed in huge quantities at Sunday and day schools, as rewards for punctuality, diligence, decorum, and deloused heads" (100-101, 103). Such publications, however, were often less than popular with the audiences for which they were intended.]

CHAPTER I.
Letter to "The Young Folks of the Factory."

MY YOUNG FRIENDS,
YOURS is a very numerous, interesting, and important class of the community, and one in which all other classes are deeply concerned. It is

calculated that, at the present time, nearly two millions of persons, under twenty years of age, are employed in the manufactories of Great Britain: perhaps not much less than one-fourth of the inhabitants of the districts in which they reside, and nearly one-tenth of the entire population of the country. To this class there are daily additions, as the extending trade and commerce of our country furnish employment for an increased number of hands, and as younger children rise to a capacity for labour; while those who advance from this class form themselves into families, and become the fathers and mothers of another generation. If we could see the whole class assembled on some vast plain, the sight would be more imposing and overwhelming. We could not but feel the liveliest interest in the welfare and happiness of so many young people, and we should anxiously and earnestly desire that they might be directed in the good and right way. As every situation in life has its peculiar advantages, disadvantages, and dangers, we should wish to make them sensible of their advantages, that they might improve them: we should like to point out to them how they might make the best of any undesirable circumstances in their conditions: and we should tenderly and faithfully warn them of their dangers, and suggest the means of avoiding or escaping them; and our hearts would rise in fervent, humble prayer to the Father of mercies on their behalf. Well, though we cannot see this class of young persons all together, we know that such a class exists; and we ought to feel the same anxiety and regard as though we did. Most of us have never seen the people in China or Hindostan, and yet we can think of them as fellow-creatures; and we can feel a benevolent wish, and make active exertions for their welfare and happiness. The young people whose interests are here contemplated, have, at least, equal claims on our regard, and come much more within the reach of our personal observation. A few hours' journey would bring us within sight of a numerous portion of the class, and enable us, from our own observations of their peculiar circumstances, to form a tolerably accurate idea of the circumstances of the whole, and qualify us to address to them a word of friendly counsel and caution. It is thus, dear young readers, that the individual now addressing you has cultivated an acquaintance with you, and desires to employ it to promote your best interests. It is hoped that this little book, which is dictated by sincere good will, will be received and read in a like spirit;— and may the Divine blessing rest upon the humble endeavour, and render it effectual in promoting the temporal and eternal well-being of the young people for whom it is intended!

Well, my young friends, the writer has been among you, and has gathered up, among others, the following observations, on which are grounded the suggestions about to be presented. That you may not suppose that the observations have been made in a morose, censorious spirit, or that the writer delights in finding fault, or wishes to check the innocent cheerfulness of youth, or to make young folks just like old ones, or to give you a gloomy picture of human life, the first observations shall be, that your situation possesses many advantages. It is a great honour and pleasure to be usefully employed. This honour belongs to the young folks in the manufacturing districts. Boys and girls of nine or ten years old are doing that which is beneficial to society—and which can be done even better by their little nimble, delicate fingers, than it could be by grown men and women. When we wear the nice fine calicoes, stuffs, cloths, or silks, that you assist in making, we ought to think, with gratitude and kindness, of the thousands of little hands engaged in winding, or spinning, or weaving the cotton, silk, or wool: so ought the master manufacturers and the merchants, when they make up their large packages of goods to send to all parts of the world, and when they receive rich returns in money, or in the produce of other countries. Yes; the rich gentlemen and ladies who wear or use the goods you make, and the master of the factory, who, most likely, has a fine house and grounds, and carriages, and servants, are each much obliged to the young persons who work in the mill. If they are wise and good people they are quite ready to acknowledge this; and they are intent on thinking what they can do for you in return. Perhaps they have said, "What can we do for these young people, who assist us in carrying on our business, and gaining our money? How can we best teach them the way to be good, and respectable, and happy?" And they have thought that it might be both interesting and useful to give you a book written on purpose for you.

Well, then, in the first place, we congratulate you on being usefully employed—on being of some consequence in society. How much better is it to be working in a factory than to be idling in the streets! I have often seen children thus idly strolling, from day to day, doing no good to any body, and picking up every kind of mischief and wickedness. I once saw a great boy, fifteen or sixteen years old, lying under a plum tree: I inquired if he were ill. His mother said, No; but that he laid there by the hour together, for the plums to drop into his mouth; and that he was as well there as anywhere, for he had nothing in the world to do. Such boys and girls are very much to be pitied. People who are not usefully employed cannot be happy; and

"Satan finds some mischief still,
    For idle hands to do."

It is a great disgrace to be idle and useless. If all the lazy boys and girls were sent out of the country, who would miss them for any good they do? But if all the industrious boys and girls who work in the factories or potteries were sent out of the country, it would be a real loss: all who make, or sell, or use manufactured articles, would be put to great inconvenience; and, most likely, the loss would not be made up till there were as many more boys and girls grown old enough to be trained to the same employments.

Besides being useful to society, it is one of your advantages that you earn something towards your own support—perhaps enough to maintain yourselves altogether. In places where there is no profitable employment for children, both parents and children are very much straitened and distressed; and large families are considered a burden. There are many mouths to feed, and but scanty means of support; and thus they have suffered great hardships. They have been poorly fed and clothed, and have suffered from want and sickness, without the means of getting relief. This is not the case with you young people in the manufacturing districts. At an early age you can contribute something towards the support of the family, and be a help to your parents instead of a burden. This is an honour and advantage which a dutiful and grateful child will highly value. Then, too, you are learning a business, by which you may hope to get your living at a future day. If you should be left orphans, how different will be your lot from that of children of your own age who have never been taught any kind of useful labour! Or, if your parents should be spared, as you advance in skill, knowledge, and ability, what a pleasure may you enjoy, in helping to make their old age comfortable! It is not intended to say that young people in other situations cannot enjoy this pleasure; but perhaps few possess the means to an equal degree with those who, being employed in extensive manufactories—if they are diligent, faithful, and well-behaved—may expect constant work and advancing wages, in proportion to their ability.

You are in a favourable station, too, for rising in life. Of the present master manufacturers, or their parents, a large proportion began life in humble circumstances, and, by their own industry, ingenuity, and perseverance, under the blessing of God, raised themselves to their present favourable condition. Persons engaged in agricultural employments may, by industry and frugality, generally support themselves and their families in decency and comfort; but they very rarely have an opportunity of rising far above their original condition. These opportunities frequently present themselves in the manufacturing districts. It is by no means said that every ingenious and industrious manufacturer rises in life, or that it is essential to respectability or happiness that he should do so; but it is an encouragement to young persons to feel themselves placed in circumstances which present no obstacle to their rising. Many a London apprentice has been encouraged to bear up under toils and hardships by reading the history of the renowned Whittington; and many a young operative has been cheered and stimulated by reading the lives of Arkwright, Dale, Watt, and others, who have risen from humble life to wealth and fame, and, what is far more than either, to extensive usefulness. It is a great honour to have invented or perfected discoveries, from which thousands of our fellow-creatures are every day reaping the advantage. The early advantages of some of these eminent men were by no means superior to your own.

Another advantage attendant on your kind of employment is, that it tends to quicken your faculties of observation, and thus to render your mind accessible to knowledge of every kind. I have rarely met with a stupid boy or girl at work in a manufactory: they are generally quick and intelligent, above the common run of children. Now, as knowledge is the food and treasure of the mind, it is an advantage to be placed in circumstances favourable to cultivating the capacity for receiving it. These and many other advantages might be pointed out in your situation. The writer will endeavour to show how you may best improve them.

But, then, you are exposed to some peculiar evils, or dangers, which, if not confined to your situation, are more prevalent there than in some others. There is the danger of having your attention confined to one object, and of neglecting to acquire other kinds of valuable and necessary knowledge. There is danger connected with your being able early to earn money, lest you should become your own masters before you have acquired wisdom and knowledge enough for your own guidance; lest you should acquire a habit of extravagantly spending that which is easily earned, and of which you may know the want at a future day. You are in danger of a spirit of vanity, emulation, and display; and you are in danger from the snares of bad company, lest from among your numerous workfellows you should be led to form acquaintance with, and copy the practices of those who would do you harm, and not good. It will be my object to point out these dangers to you, and to show you how you may escape them. You will generally be instructed by the example of boys and girls like yourselves, because that mode of instruction has been found most acceptable to young people; and though you will not find in this little book any wonderful stories, it is hoped that you will find enough to interest you, and to show you that, all things considered, the way of duty, the way of obedience to the commandments of God, is not only the right and safe, but the pleasant and happy way; whereas "the way of transgressors is hard," and "the end thereof is death."

Dear young friends, I cannot conclude this introductory letter without reminding you, first, that you are immortal creatures; that your bodies will soon die, and your souls, which cannot die, will enter on a never-ending state; and that whether you spend the few short years of this life in poverty or wealth, in comfort or distress, is a mere trifle compared with the question, whether the eternity that succeeds it will be one of happiness or misery. Next, I must remind you, that you are sinful creatures; you have broken the commands of God; your hearts have rebelled against Him, and you deserve his anger. It is a dreadful thing to live under the anger of God; and to die under his anger, is to enter upon eternal death. These considerations ought to awaken in you the inquiry, "What must I do to be saved?" If this is a matter of concern with you, it is an unspeakable pleasure to be able to assure you, on good grounds, that if you believe on the Lord Jesus Christ, you shall be saved, Acts xvi. 31; for God has set him forth to be the propitiation, or atonement, for sins, Rom. iii. 25; to declare the righteousness of God, who is so righteous and holy, that He will not suffer sin to go unpunished, and yet so merciful and gracious, and has so loved a sinful world, that He gave his own Son, that whosoever believeth on Him should not perish, but have everlasting life, John iii. 15, 16.

May you, dear young reader, be enabled, in deep humility and genuine repentance, to fall down at the footstool of Divine mercy, as a sinner before God, and by faith lay hold on the hope set before you in the gospel, for there is no salvation in any other way, Acts iv. 12. The soul that is not in Christ, is a lost soul; but the soul that is committed to his hands, is safe for time and for eternity. May it be the happiness of the writer and the reader to know whom they have believed, and to be persuaded that He is able to keep that which they have committed unto Him against that day! 2 Tim. i. 12. Such is the fervent prayer of

Your affectionate Friend,
THE AUTHOR.

CHAPTER V.
TRUTH AND INTEGRITY, CONTINUED.

THE next time that the Sunday-school teacher and scholars met together on a week evening, after the regular business had been gone through, the conversation about Truth and Integrity was resumed. One of the young people in the factory (I am glad that it was not one who had joined in the former conversation) had been guilty of falsehood and deceit, for which she had been severely reprimanded by the overseer, and told if ever she was again detected in the like conduct, she would certainly be discharged from her employment. He had said to her, in the presence of her companions, that he considered a liar next of kin to a thief, and that he had not the least dependence on the honesty of a person whose word he could not trust. [...] The girls were talking this over among themselves; some said it was fair, and other said it was not fair; at length the teacher was appealed to. [...]

Teacher. I have already spoken of the importance of cultivating strict integrity in little things [....] It is your duty firmly to reject all participation in the ill-gotten gain, and to persuade your companion to do the same; but if this fails, it will become your duty to inform the injured party. A false dread of being looked upon as a tell-tale, has led many young persons to connive at dishonesty which they have witnessed, till their abhorrence of the crime has been lessened, and they have been gradually led on to practise the same themselves.

This remark particularly applies to the exercise of an honest principle in reference to your employers. You all seem to have been horror-struck at the wickedness of a man who broke into a dwelling house, and robbed the poor people of their clothes and other little valuables, and left them in absolute distress; and for many reasons, it is hardly likely that you should be tempted to that kind of dishonesty, at least for the present. It is more needful to point out to you your own actual and immediate dangers.

Integrity will teach you to respect the rights of your employers in every particular. If any part of their property comes within your power, either by accident, or in the regular course of your business, you will consider it sacred. Employers of every kind lie very much at the mercy of those they employ; whether in domestic life, in trade, or in manufactories, the master's property necessarily comes very much under the power of his servants. If they are faithful and upright, they may do much to promote his interests, and, at the same time, their own. If otherwise, they may materially injure them, perhaps even bring them to ruin. Many a once flourishing tradesman has been brought to ruin by the tricks of unfaithful servants in whom he trusted.

If you wish to obtain and to deserve the character of a good and faithful servant, you must act conscientiously in the disposal of your time. If your employer pays you so much a week for your work, he has a right to expect that you come punctually at the time of beginning, and work diligently to the time of leaving, just as diligently as if you were working for yourselves. Suppose your master gives you six shillings a week, (and I know some of the younger of you earn as much as that,) to work twelve hours a day, and that either through coming too late, or loitering over your work, you do no more than the work of ten hours, it is just the same thing to your master as if you robbed him of a shilling. Perhaps you have never thought, in this serious light, of squandering a few minutes of your master's time. Perhaps you may even think that your master is such a rich gentleman, that if he does lose a shilling a week by you, it will not much hurt him. The great fallacy of this kind of reasoning has already been shown. It is a sin for you to rob a person, whether he is greatly injured by it or not; but now, suppose that two hundred of the young folks of the factory should act in the same dishonest manner, and every week waste a shilling's worth of their master's time, the damage would amount to ten pounds in a week, or five hundred and twenty pounds in a year. That looks a large sum, when you tell it up together; and it would make you shudder to think of your master being robbed to that amount; but, remember, a large sum is made up of small ones, and, if you would be really honest, tremble at the idea of your master being wronged a single shilling or penny by you.

Some of the young people said, they were not under this temptation to injure their employers, for they were not paid for their time, but for the quantity of work they accomplished.

Teacher. Then you must be careful not to injure him another way,— either by wasting your materials, or slighting your work; for waste, as well as indolence, is a species of dishonesty in those who are entrusted with the goods, and employed in the performance of the work, of others. I know that some wicked persons absolutely defraud their employers in these things, taking for their own use, or even offering for sale, materials which have been entrusted to them to make up, or implements employed in their work. Not long ago I was shocked to hear the overseer of a mill say, that he often had to stop some of the boys and girls of the factory, and search them, to see if they were carrying away the bobbins. I hope, my dear young people, that every one of you would look with abhorrence on such practices; that nothing would induce you to appropriate one farthing's worth of stuff that is not your own; and that if one of your companions should tempt you to do so, you would feel it your duty not only to resist the temptation, but also to give information of the dishonest proposal. To screen dishonesty is to share the crime.

[Source: *The Young Folks of the Factory; or, Friendly Hints on Their Duties and Dangers.* London: Religious Tract Society, 1840. 1-10, 108-109, 115, 118-21.]

4. Frances Trollope, from *Michael Armstrong* (1840)

[Frances Trollope (1779-1863), English travel writer and novelist, is now best known for her *Domestic Manners of the Americans* (1832). In *Michael Armstrong*, which first appeared as a serial novel in 1839-40, Trollope attacks the factory system through two interrelated plots, the first of which involves Michael, a poor, nine-year-old boy tricked into signing indentures for an eleven-year apprenticeship in a Derbyshire mill by the wicked master of the cotton factory where he is working at the opening of the novel (see Appendice G.5 for the second plot). The excerpts here include the reader's first view of Brookford Factory, where Michael is employed before being sent north (Chapter 8) and his introduction to Deep Valley Mill (Chapter 17). In the second of these selections, Trollope depends heavily on the material from Brown's *A Memoir of Robert Blincoe* (see Introduction 47).]

Those persons who have, once in their lives, seen a large cotton-factory, need no description of it; for it has features which, once looked upon, can never be forgotten; but, for the information of those who have not, a slight sketch of Sir Matthew Dowling's establishment shall be given.

It consisted of very extensive buildings constructed in the centre of the enclosed court, and forming three sides of a vast square; the fourth being open on the side fronting the principal gates of entrance. When it is stated that the edifice consisted of six stories, and that each side of it presented six lines of windows, containing forty windows in each line, some idea of its magnitude may be conceived.
[...]

The party entered the building, whence—as all know who have done the like—every sight, every sound, every scent that kind nature has fitted to the organs of her children, so as to render the mere unfettered use of them a delight, are banished for ever and for ever. The ceaseless whirring of a million hissing wheels, seizes on the tortured ear; and while threatening to destroy the delicate sense, seems bent on proving first, with a sort of mocking mercy, of how much suffering it can be the cause. The scents that reek around, from oil, tainted water, and human filth, with that last worst nausea, arising from the hot refuse of atmospheric air, left by some hundred pairs of labouring lungs, render the act of breathing a process of difficulty, disgust, and pain. All this is terrible. But what the eye brings home to the heart of those, who look round upon the horrid earthly hell, is enough to make it all forgotten; for who can think of villanous smells, or heed the suffering of the ear-racking sounds, while they look upon hundreds of helpless children, divested of every trace of health, of joyousness, and even of youth! Assuredly there is no exaggeration in this; for except only in their diminutive size, these suffering infants have no trace of it. Lean and distorted limbs—sallow and sunken cheeks—dim hollow eyes, that speak unrest and most unnatural carefulness, give to each tiny, trembling, unelastic form, a look of hideous premature old age.

But in the room they entered, the dirty, ragged, miserable crew, were all in active performance of their various tasks; the overlookers, strap in hand, on the alert; the whirling spindles urging the little slaves who waited on them, to movements as unceasing as their own; and the whole monstrous chamber, redolent of all the various impurities that "by the perfection of our manufacturing system," are converted into "gales of Araby" for the rich, after passing in the shape of certain poison, through the lungs of the poor.

[...] they gradually approached the level of a stream, running through so very narrow a valley, as in many places to afford barely space enough for the road, between the brook and the precipitate heights which shut it in.

On reaching this level, the road, which for the last quarter of a mile had seemed to be leading them into the little river itself, turned abruptly, and by an angle so acute, following the indented curve of the lofty hill, that they speedily appeared to be shut in on all sides by the towering hills that suddenly, and as if by magic reared themselves in every direction round. It is hardly possible to conceive a spot more effectually hidden from the eyes of all men, than this singular valley. Hundreds may pass their lives within a few miles of it, without having the least idea that such a spot exists; for, from the form of the hills it so happens, that it is possible to wander for hours over their summits, without discovering it; one undulation rising beyond another, so as to blend together beneath the eye, leaving no opening by which this strip of water-level in their very centre can be discerned.*

For about another half mile, the narrow cart-road runs beside the stream without encountering any single object, except its lofty barrier and the brook itself, more remarkable than here and there a reed of higher growth than common, or a plant of Foxglove, that by its gay blossom seems to mock the desolate sadness of the spot. Another turn, however, still following the wavy curvings of the mountain's base, for mountain there it seems to be, opens another view, and one that speaks to many senses at once, the difference between the melancholy caused by nature, and that produced by the work of man. A wide spreading cotton-factory here rears its unsightly form, and at one glance makes the happy wanderer whose foot is free to turn which way he will, feel how precious is the power of retracing his steps back again along the beguiling path that has led him to it.

This was a joy for which our little Michael sighed in vain. On jogged the cart, and nearer it came at every jolt to the object which he most hated to look upon. But then came also the cheering thought, that he was no longer a mere factory boy, but about to become an apprentice to a good and profitable trade, in which hereafter he might expect to get money enough for himself, for mother, and Teddy[1] too! Nevertheless, he certainly did wish, at the very bottom of his heart, that the stocking-weaving business was not carried on in a building so very like

---

* The real name of this valley (which most assuredly is no creation of romance) is not given, lest an action for libel should be the consequence. The scenes which have passed there, and which the few following pages will describe, have been stated to the author on authority not to be impeached. [Trollope's note]
1 Michael's brother, Edward.

a cotton-factory! But though Michael saw this hated cotton factory, he as yet saw but a small portion of the horrors which belonged to the spot he had reached. His position in the vehicle made it impossible for him to look round, and perceive how completely all the acts that might be committed in that *Deep Valley*, were hid from the eye of every human being but those engaged in them. Neither could he recognise in the dismal building detached, yet connected both with the manager's house and the factory, the *Prison Prentice-house* which served as HOME to hundreds of little aching hearts, each one endowed by nature with light spirits, merry thoughts, and fond affections; but all of whom rose to their daily toil under circumstances which rendered enjoyment of any kind both morally and physically impossible. [...]

Michael heard the door [of the apprentice house] close, and looked up. The room he was in was so long as almost to appear like a gallery, and from one end to the other of it a narrow deal board stretched out, having room for about two hundred to sit down at once. The whole of this table was now occupied by a portion of the apprentice children, both boys and girls, belonging to Deep Valley Mill, and their appearance might have wrung the heart of any being who looked upon them, however blessedly wide his own destiny might lead him from the melancholy troop. But to Michael, the spectacle was appalling; and, young as he was, he seemed to feel that the filthy, half-starved wretches before him, were so many ghostly representations of what he was himself to be. A sickness like that of death came over him, and he would have given a limb, only for freedom to stretch himself down upon the floor and see no more. But the master of the ceremonies at this feast of misery bore a huge horsewhip in his hand, without which indeed, it is said, he seldom appeared on the premises, and with it an eye that seemed to have the power of quelling with a single glance, the will of every little wretch it looked upon.

The place that Michael was to take at the board was indicated to him, and he sat down. The food placed before him consisted of a small bowl of what was denominated stir-pudding, a sort of miserable water-porridge, and a lump of oaten cake, of a flavour so sour and musty, that the little fellow, though never accustomed till the fatal patronage of Sir Matthew fell upon him, to any viands more dainty than dry bread, could not at this first essay persuade himself to eat it. The wife of the governor of the Prentice-house, a help meet for him in every way, chanced to have her eye upon the stranger child as he pushed the morsel from him, and the smile that relaxed her features might have told him something, had he chanced to see, and understand it, respecting the excellent chance there was of his having a better appetite in future.

A girl nearly of his own age sat on one side, and a boy considerably older on the other; the first who had as much of beauty as it was perhaps, possible for any human being to have after a six month's residence at Deep-Valley Mill, looked up into his face with a pair of large blue eyes that spoke unbounded pity, and he heard a soft little voice whisper, "Poor boy!" While his lanky neighbour on the other side made prize of the rejected food, venturing to say aloud, "Any how, it is too good to be wasted."

The wretched meal did not last long, and for a few minutes after it was ended, the governor and his wife disappeared. During this interval, those who had strength and inclination moved about the room as they listed, but by far the greater number were already dropping to sleep after a day of protracted labour, during which they had followed the ceaseless movements of the machinery, for above fifteen hours. Among the former was the hungry lad who had appropriated the oat-cake of Michael, and no sooner were the eye of the master and mistress removed, than he turned to the new-comer, and in a tone that seemed to hover between good-humour and ridicule, said, "So you could not find a stomach for your supper, my man?"

"I did not want supper," replied Michael, dolefully. "You didn't want it, didn't you? That speaks better for the living as you have left, than I can speak of that as you'll find," returned his new acquaintance. "Don't you say nothing to nobody, and, to-morrow morning, after the lash have sounded through the room to wake us all, just you start up, and jump into your clothes, and when we goes to pump, I'll show you where we gets our tit-bits from."

Michael was in the act of nodding assent to this proposal, when the woman, who five minutes before had left the room, returned to it, and by a very summary process caused the ragged, weary, prayerless, hopeless multitude to crawl and clamber, half sleeping and half waking, to their filthy beds. They were divided by fifties in a room, but notwithstanding the number, and the little space in which they had to stow themselves, the stillness of heavy sleep pervaded every chamber, ere the miserable little inmates had been five minutes enclosed within the walls. Poor Michael lay as motionless as the rest, but he was not sleeping. Disappointment, fearful forebodings, and excessive nausea, all conspired to banish this only blessing that an apprenticed factory child can know.

He had already laboured, poor fellow, for nearly half his little life, and that under most hard and unrelenting masters; but till now, he had never known how very wretched his young thoughts could make him. His mother's fond caresses, and his brother's fervent love, had in spite of toil, and sometimes in spite of hunger, cheered and comforted the last moments of every day. The rude bed also, on which the brothers lay, was too clean, notwithstanding all the difficulty of keeping it so, to be tainted with the loathsome scent of oil, or sundry other abominations which rendered the place he now lay, almost intolerable. Yet to this den, far, far away from the only creatures who loved and cherished him, he was come by his own consent, his own express desire! The thought was almost too bitter to bear, and the bundle of straw that served him for a pillow, received for the first hour of the night a ceaseless flood of tears.

It was, as his young companion had predicted, by the sound of a flourished whip, that he was awakened on the following morning. In an instant he was on his feet, and a minute or two more sufficed to invest him in his clothes; this speed, however, was the effect of terror, for he remembered not the invitation of the preceding evening. But hardly had he finished the operation of dressing, when Charley Ford, the boy who gave it, was by his side, and giving him a silent hint by a wink of the left eye, and a movement of the right elbow that he might follow him, turned away, and ran down stairs.

Michael did so too, and presently found himself with a multitude of others in a small paved court, on one side of which was a pump, to whose spout every child came in succession to perform a very necessary, but, from lack of soap, a very imperfect act of ablution.

Neglecting to watch his turn for this, and not permitting Michael to do so either, Charles Ford made his way to a door that opened upon another part of the premises, and pushing it open, disclosed to the eyes of Michael a loathsome and a fearful spectacle.

Seven or eight boys had already made their way to the sort of rude farm-yard upon which this door opened, one and all of whom were intent upon purloining from a filthy trough just replenished for the morning meal of two stout hogs, a variety of morsels which, as Michael's new acquaintance assured him, were "dainty eating for the starving prentices of Deep Valley mill."

"Make haste, young'un," cried Charles, good-naturedly, "or they won't leave a turnip-paring for us." And on he rushed to the scuffle, leaving Michael gazing with disgust and horror at the contest between the fierce snouts of the angry pigs, and the active fingers of the wretched crew who contested with them for the offal thus cast forth.

Michael Armstrong was a child of deep feeling; and it was, perhaps, lucky for him, that the burning sense of shame and degradation which pervaded every nerve of his little frame, as he looked upon this revolting spectacle, come upon him while yet too young for any notion of resistance to suggest itself. He felt faint, sick, and broken-hearted; but no worm that ever was crushed to atoms by the foot of an elephant, dreamed less of vengeance than did poor Michael, as the horrid thought came over him, that he was going to abide in a place where little boys were treated with less care and tenderness than pigs!

He turned away shuddering, and feeling almost unable to stand—and then the image of his mother seemed to rise before him—he felt her soft gentle kisses on his cheeks, and almost unconsciously pronounced her name. This dear name, lowly as it was murmured, came upon his ear so like the knell of happiness that was never to return, that the hard agony of his little heart melted before it, and sitting down upon a bundle of fagots that were piled up against the wall, he rested his burning head against the bricks, and burst into a passion of tears. At this moment he felt a hand upon his shoulder, and trembling from head to foot, he sprung upon his feet, and suddenly turning round beheld, instead of the savage features of the overlooker which his fancy had conjured up, the meekest, gentlest, loveliest little face, that ever eyes looked upon, within a few feet of him. It was the same little girl who had been placed next him at the miserable supper of the preceding night, and whose low murmur of pity for all the sorrow he was come to share with her, had reached his ears and his heart.

"You'll be strapped dreadful if you bide here," said the child. "Come away—and don't let them see you cry!" But even as she spoke she turned from him, and ran towards the door through which the miserable pilferers of the pig-trough were already hurrying.

Perhaps no other warning-voice would have been so promptly listened to at that moment by poor Michael, for it was something very like the numbing effect of despair that seemed to have seized upon him, and it is likely enough he would have remained in the attitude he had taken, with his head resting against the wall, till the brutal violence of his task-master had dragged him from it, had not this pretty vision of pity appeared to warn him of his danger.

He rose and followed her so quickly, that by the time she had reached the crowd of children who were still thronging round the pump, he was by her side.

"Thank you!" whispered Michael in her ear, "It was very kind of you to call me—and I shouldn't have come if you hadn't—for I shouldn't care very much if they killed me."

"That's very naughty!" said the little girl.

"How *can* I be good?" demanded Michael, while the tears again burst from his eyes. "'Twas mother that made me good before, and I don't think I shall ever see her any more."

"I never can see my mother any more, till I go to Heaven," replied the little girl—"but I always think every day, that she told me before she died, about God's making every thing come right in the end, if we bear all things patiently for love of him."

"But God can't choose I should be taken from mother, and that's why I can't bear it," said Michael.

The little girl shook her head, very evidently disapproving his theology.

"How old are you?" said Michael.

"Eleven years old three months ago, and that was one week after I came here," answered his new acquaintance.

"Then you are more than one whole year older than me?" said Michael; "and I dare say you know better than I do; and I'll try to be good too, if you'll love me, and be kind to me always, like poor Edward. My name is Michael—What's your name?"

"Fanny Fletcher," replied the little girl, "and I *will* love you and be kind to you, if you'll be a good boy and bear it all patiently."

"I would bear it all patiently," said Michael, "if I knew when I was to get away, and when you was to get away too. But perhaps we are to stay here for ever?" And again the tears ran down his cheeks.

"That's nonsense, Michael," said Fanny. "They can't keep us here for ever. When we die, we are sure to get away from them."

Michael opened his large eyes and looked at her with something like reproach. "When we die?" he repeated sadly. "Are we to stay here till we die?—I am never to see mother and Teddy any more then?"

"Don't cry, Michael!" said the little girl, taking his hand—"We shall be sure to get out if God thinks it right. Don't cry so!"

"I wish I was as old as you," said Michael, with an accent expressive of great respect. "I should bear it better then."

As Michael ceased speaking he felt the little girl shudder. "Here he is!" she whispered, withdrawing her hand from him—"we mustn't speak any more now."

"Off with you, vagabonds!" roared the voice of the apprentice-house governor, from behind them. "Don't you see the factory-gates open?"

The miserable little troop waited for no second summons, well knowing that the lash, which was now only idly cutting the air above their heads, would speedily descend upon them if they did; but not even terror could enable the wasting limbs of those who had long inhabited this fearful abode to move quickly. Many among them were dreadfully crippled in the legs, and nearly all exhibited the frightful spectacle of young features pinched by famine.

★ ★ ★ ★ ★

Let none dare to say this picture is exaggerated, till he has taken the trouble to ascertain by his own personal investigation, that it is so. It is a very fearful crime in a country where public opinion has been proved (as in the African Slave Trade), to be omnipotent, for any individual to sit down with a shadow of doubt respecting such statements on his mind. IF they be true, let each in his own little circle, raise his voice against the horrors detailed by them, AND THESE HORRORS WILL BE REMEDIED. But woe to those who supinely sit in contented ignorance of the facts, soothing their spirits and their easy consciences with the cuckoo note, *"exaggeration,"* while thousands of helpless children pine away their unnoted, miserable lives, in labour and destitution, *incomparably more severe*, than any ever produced by negro slavery.

[Source: Frances Trollope, *The Life and Adventures of Michael Armstrong, the Factory Boy*. London: Henry Colburn, 1840. 79-80, 180-86.]

5. Elizabeth Barrett Browning, "The Cry of the Children" (1843)

[Elizabeth Barrett Browning (1806-61), poet and wife of poet Robert Browning. Though she is perhaps better known for her *Sonnets from the Portugese* and *Aurora Leigh*, "The Cry of the Children" is one of the most scathing commentaries on child labor written during the nineteenth century. Through her association with Richard Hengist Horne, who served on a parliamentary commission that investigated child labor in the factories and mines in 1842 and 1843, Barrett Browning learned of and felt compelled to write about the injustices of child labor. The result was "The Cry of the Children," a poem that, as Charles Shaw (in 1843 a child worker in the Tunstall pottery district) wrote in his autobiography *When I Was a Child*, "comes to me like a sort of poetic autobiography, written not with ink, but with bitter tears. Read that poem, and you have the inner history of English children sixty years ago" (15).

The version of the poem that follows is from the August 1843 issue of *Blackwood's Edinburgh Magazine*. This poem differs slightly from the version that Barrett Browning published in the first edition of her *Poems* in 1844, most noticeably in that it does not have the epigraph from Euripedes' *Medea*, which translates as "Alas, alas, why do you gaze at me with your eyes, my children." With or without the epigraph, "The Cry of the Children" represents the best-known example of poetry that addressed the question of child labor in the factories and mines.]

THE CRY OF THE CHILDREN.
BY ELIZABETH B. BARRET.

Do ye hear the children weeping, O my brothers!
    Ere the sorrow comes with years?
They are leaning their young heads against their mothers,
    And *that* cannot stop their tears.

The young lambs are bleating in the meadows,
The young birds are chirping in the nest,
The young fawns are playing with the shadows,
The young flowers are blowing from the west;
But the young young children, O my brothers!
    They are weeping bitterly!
They are weeping in the playtime of the others—
    In the country of the free.

Do you question the young children in the sorrow,
    Why their tears are falling so?
The old man may weep for his to-morrow
    Which is lost in long ago.
The old tree is leafless in the forest—
The old year is ending in the frost;
The old wound, if stricken, is the sorest—
The old hope is hardest to be lost!
But the young young children, O my brothers!
    Do ye ask them why they stand
Weeping sore before the bosoms of their mothers,
    In our happy fatherland?

They look up with their pale and sunken faces,
    And their looks are sad to see;
For the man's grief untimely draws and presses
    Down the cheeks of infancy.
"Your old earth," they say, "is very dreary—
Our young feet," they say, "are very weak!
Few paces have we taken, yet are weary—
Our grave-rest is very far to seek!
Ask the old why they weep, and not the children;
    For the outside earth is cold—
And we young ones stand without, in our bewild'ring,
    And the graves are for the old.

"True," say the young children, "it may happen
    That we die before our time!
Little Alice died last year—the grave is shapen
    Like a snowball, in the rime.
We look'd into the pit prepared to take her—
Was no room for any work in the close clay!
From the sleep wherein she lieth none will wake her,
Crying–'Get up, little Alice, it is day!'
If you listen by that grave in sun and shower,

With your ear down, little Alice never cries;
Could we see her face, be sure we should not know her,
For the new smile which has grown within her eyes.
For merry go her moments, lull'd and still'd in
    The shroud, by the kirk-chime!
It is good when it happens," say the children,
    "That we die before our time!"

Alas, the young children! they are seeking
    Death in life, as best to have!
They are binding up their hearts away from breaking,
    With a cerement from the grave.
Go out, children, from the mine and from the city—
Sing out, children, as the little thrushes do!
Pluck your handfuls of the meadow cowslips pretty—
Laugh aloud to feel your fingers let them through!
But the children say—"Are cowslips of the meadows
    Like the weeds anear the mine?*
Leave us quiet in the dark of our coal-shadows,
    From your pleasures fair and fine.

"For oh!" say the children, "we are weary—
    And we cannot run or leap:
If we cared for any meadows, it were merely
    To drop down in them and sleep.
Our knees tremble sorely in the stooping—
We fall upon our face, trying to go;
And underneath our heavy eyelids drooping,
The reddest flower would look as pale as snow.
For, all day, we drag our burden tiring,
    Through the coal-dark underground—
Or, all day, we drive the wheels of iron
    In the factories, round and round.

"All day long, the wheels are droning, turning—
    Their wind comes in our faces!
Till our hearts turn, and our heads with pulses burning,
    And the walls turn in their places!
Turns the sky in the high window blank and reeling—
Turns the long light that droppeth down the wall—
Turn the black flies that crawl along the ceiling—

---

* A commissioner mentions the fact of weeds being thus confounded with the
  idea of flowers. [Barrett Browning's note]

All are turning all the day, and we with all!
All day long, the iron wheels are droning—
    And sometimes we could pray—
'O ye wheels' (breaking off in a mad moaning)
    Stop! be silent for to-day!'"

Ay! be silent! let them hear each other breathing,
    For a moment, mouth to mouth;
Let them touch each other's hands, in a fresh wreathing
    Of their tender human youth;
Let them feel that this cold metallic motion
Is not all the life God giveth them to use;
Let them prove their inward souls against the notion
That they live in you, or under you, O wheels!
Still, all day, the iron wheels go onward,
    As if Fate in each were stark!
And the children's souls, which God is calling sunward,
    Spin on blindly in the dark.

Now, tell the weary children, O my brothers!
    That they look to Him, and pray
For the blessed One, who blesseth all the others,
    To bless *them* another day.
They answer, "Who is God that he should hear us,
While this rushing of the iron wheels is stirr'd?
When we sob aloud, the human creatures near us
Pass unhearing—at least, answer not a word;
And *we* hear not (for the wheels in their resounding)
    Strangers speaking at the door.
Is it likely God, with angels singing round him,
    Hears our weeping any more?

"Two words, indeed, of praying we remember;
    And, at midnight's hour of harm,
Our Father, looking upward in the chamber,
    We say softly for a charm.*
We say no other words except *our Father!*
And we think that, in some pause of angels' song,
He may pluck them with the silence sweet to gather,
And hold both within his right hand, which is strong.

---

* The report of the commissioners represents instances of children, whose
religious devotion is confined to the repetition of the two first words of the
Lord's Prayer. [Barrett Browning's note]

Our Father! If he heard us, he would surely
   (For they call him good and mild)
Answer—smiling down the steep world very purely—
   'Come and rest with me, my child.'

"But no," say the children, weeping faster;
   "He is silent as a stone,
And they tell us, of his image is the master
   Who commands us to work on.
Go to!" say the children; "up in heaven,
Dark, wheel-like, turning clouds are all we find!
Do not mock us! we are atheists in our grieving—
We look up for HIM—but tears have made us blind."
Do ye hear the children weeping and disproving,
   O my brothers, what ye teach?
For God's possible is taught by his world's loving—
   And the children doubt of each!

And well may the children weep before ye—
   They are weary ere they run!
They have never seen the sunshine, nor the glory
   Which is brighter than the sun!
They know the grief of men, but not the wisdom—
They sink in the despair, with hope at calm—
Are slaves, without the liberty in christdom—
Are martyrs by the pang without the palm!
Are worn as if with age; yet unretrievingly
   No joy of memory keep—
Are orphans of the earthly love and heavenly—
   Let them weep—let them weep!

They look up with their pale and sunken faces,
   And their look is dread to see;
For you think you see their angels in their places,
   With eyes meant for Deity.
"How long," they say, "how long, O cruel nation!
Will you stand, to move the world, on a child's heart,
Trample down with a mail'd heel its palpitation,
And tread onward to your throne amid the mart?
Our blood splashes upward, O our tyrants!
   And your purple shows your path—
But the child's sob curseth deeper in the silence,
   Than the strong man in his wrath!"

[Source: *Blackwood's Edinburgh Magazine* 54 (1843): 260-62.]

6. R. Arthur Arnold, from *The History of the Cotton Famine* (1864)

[R. Arthur Arnold was an administrator of the Public Works Act (1863), which provided jobs for workers during the Cotton Famine, the crisis caused when the U.S. Civil War cut off the supply of cotton from the South and therefore closed down British factories, resulting in widespread unemployment in the early 1860s. In describing the suffering in the cotton districts of England during those years, Arnold also offers a commentary on the social life of "factory girls." Young women who no longer had work in the mills were reluctant to find positions as servants or to emigrate in search of new opportunities, and Arnold explains this reluctance by pointing out that for the factory girl the circumstances of her work become the "romance of her life." The long dialogue that Arnold transcribes from a newspaper article in the *Manchester Examiner* also provides a good example of the dialect spoken by workers in the industrial north; it demonstrates, therefore, the distance between the speech habits of daily life and the more standardized versions of dialogue offered in parliamentary testimony and in the accounts of the factory lives in this volume.]

[...] It must be remembered that a factory girl has more of the "professional" about her than any class of men, excepting perhaps the soldier. The mill is her only possible. If she does not love its oily floors and noisy rooms, she has, at least, but very little idea of any other mode of life. She is introduced to the cotton factory at a very early age; from morning till night she works in it, as girl, woman, and mother, till old age or good fortune interferes. The romance of her life, her friendships and her love, are associated with the tall chimney, with the long rows of windows, and with her busy fellow-workers. She is one of a caste, and the suggestion to her of another mode of life is by no means welcome. To be associated with her well-known companions in a sewing school—to be tended there by well-dressed ladies—to be thus kept from hunger and misery, and yet to live in her old home, all this is tolerable enough; but her idea of household service is, that it is a sort of domestic slavery, and she is not more ready to accept such an invitation than a red Indian would be, if he were asked to be a "help" in some New York household. The cherished independence of these girls, resulting from the demand for their labour, causes them to rely one upon another rather than upon their parents or relatives; and the following sketch, by the correspondent of the 'Manchester Examiner,' is very characteristic:—

"Three young women stopped on the footpath in front of the inn, close to the place where we stood, and began to talk together in a very free, open way, quite careless of being heard. One of them was a stout, handsome young woman, about twenty-three. Her dress was of light printed stuff, clean and good; her round ruddy arms, her clear blonde complexion, and the bright expression of her full open countenance, all indicated health and good-nature. I guessed from her conversation, as well as from her general appearance, that she was a factory operative in full employ, though that is such a rare thing in these parts now; the other two looked very poor and down-hearted. One was a short thick-set girl, seemingly not twenty years of age; her face was sad, and she had very little to say. The other was a thin, dark-haired, cadaverous woman, about thirty years of age, as I supposed; her shrunk visage was the picture of want, and her frank, child-like talk showed great simplicity of character. The weather had been wet for some days previous, and the clothing of the two looked thin and shower-stained. It had evidently been worn a good while, and the colours were faded. Each of them wore a poor, shivery bit of shawl, in which their hands were folded, as if to keep them warm. The handsome lass, who seemed to be in good employ, knew them both; but she showed an especial kindness towards the eldest of them. As these two stood talking to their friend, we did not take much notice of what they were saying, until two other young women came slowly from townwards, looking poor, and tired, and ill, like the first. These last comers instantly recognized two of those who stood talking together in front of the inn, and one of them said to the other, 'Eh, sitho![1] there's Sarah and Martha here!' ... 'Eh, lasses! han yo bin a beggin' too?'—'Aye, lass, we han,' replied the thin dark-complexioned woman. 'Aye, lass, we han. Aw've[2] just bin tellin' Ann here. Aw never did sich a thing i' my life afore—never! But it's th' first time and th' last for me—it is that! Aw'll go whoam,[3] an' aw'll dee[4] theer, afore aw'll go a-beggin' ony moor,—aw will for sure. Mon,[5] it's sich a nasty, dirty job; aw'd as soon clem![6].... See yo, lasses! we set off this mornin'—Martha an' me; we set eawt this mornin' to go to Gorton Tank, becose we yerd that it wur sich a good place. But one doesn't know wheer to go to these times, an' one doesn't like to go a-beggin' among folk as they know. Well, when we coom to Gorton, we geet twopence hawpenny theer, an' that wur o'. Now, there's plenty moor beggin' besides us. Well, at after that twopence hawpenny, we get twopence moor, an' that's o' at we'n getten. But, eh, lasses, when aw

---

1 sitho] look you.
2 Aw've] I have.
3 whoam] home.
4 dee] die.
5 mon] man, sometimes used for a woman.
6 clem] starve.

coom to do it, aw hadn't th' heart to ax for nought', aw hadn't for sure.'
... 'Martha an' me's walked aboon ten mile iv we'n walked a yard; an'
we geet weet through th' first thing, an' aw wur ill when we set off, an'
so wur Martha too; aw know hoo[1] wur, though hoo say's nought mich
abeawt it. Well, we coom back, throught t' teawn, an' we were both on
us fair stagged up.[2] Aw never were so done o'er i' my life w' one thing
an' another. So we co'de[3] a-seein' Ann here, an' hoo made us a rare
good baggin',[4] th' lass did. See yo! aw wur fit to drop o' th' flags afore
aw geet that saup[5] o' warm tay[6] into me—aw wur for sure! Aw'neaw,[7]
hoo's come'd a gate[8] wi' us hitherto, an' hoo would have us to have a
glass o' warm ale a piece at yon heause lower deawn a bit; an' aw dar
say it'll do me good, aw getten sich a cowd;[9] but eh dear, it's made me
as mazy[10] as a tup, an' neaw, hoo wants us to have another afore we
starten off whoam. But, it's no use, we mun' be gooin on. Aw'm noan
used to it, an' aw connot ston[11] it; aw'm as wake as a kittlin'[12] this
minute.'
    "Ann, who had befriended them in this manner, was the handsome
young woman who seemed to be in work; and now, the poor woman
who had been telling the story, laid her hand upon her friend's shoulder, and said, 'Ann, thee's behaved very weel to us o' roads'; an' neaw,
lass, go thi ways whoam an' dunnut fret abeawt us, mon. Aw feel better
neaw. We's be reet[13] enough to-morn, lass. Now, there's awlus some
way shap't.[14] That tay's done me a deeol o' good.... Go thi ways
whoam, Ann, neaw do, or else aw shan't be yezzy[15] abeawt tho'.' But
Ann, who was wiping her eyes with her hand, replied, 'Naw, naw, aw
will not go yet, Sarah!' ... And then she began to cry. 'Eh, lasses, aw
dunnot like to see yo o' this shap—aw dunnot for sure! Besides, yo'n
bin far enough to-day. Come back wi' me. Aw connot find reawm for
both on yo; but the come back wi' me, Sarah. Aw'll find thee a good

---

1   hoo] she.
2   stagged up] exhausted.
3   co'de] called.
4   baggin'] afternoon meal.
5   saup] drop.
6   tay] tea.
7   neaw] now.
8   a gate] on the way
9   cowd] cold.
10 mazy] dizzy.
11 ston] stand.
12 kittlin'] kitten.
13 reet] right.
14 shap't] managed.
15 yezzy] easy.

bed; an' thae'rt welcome to a share o' what there is—as welcome as th' fleawers i' May—thae knows that.... Thae'rt th' owdest o' th' two; an thae'rt noan fit to trawnce up an' deawn o' this shap. Come back to eawr heawse, an Martha 'ill go forrud to Stopput (Stockport),—winnot tho',[1] Martha?.... Thae knows, Martha,' continued she; 'thae knows, Martha, thae munnot think nought at me axin' Sarah, an' noan o' thee. Yo should both on ye go back iv aw'd reawm; but aw hav'n't. Beside, thae'rt younger an strunger than hur is.'—'Eh, God bless the, lass,' replied Martha, 'aw know o' abeawt it. Aw'd rayther Sarah would stop, for hur'll be ill. Aw can go furrud by mysel', weel enough. It's noan so fur, neaw.'

"But here Sarah, the eldest of the three, laid her hand once more on the shoulder of her friend, and said, in an earnest tone, 'Ann, it will not do, my lass. Go aw mun.[2] I never wur away fro whoam o' neet i' my life—never! Aw connot do it, mon! Beside, thae knows, aw've laft yon lad, an' never a wick[3] soul wi' him! He'd fret hissel' to death this neet, mon, if aw didn't go whoam! Aw couldn't sleep a wink for thinkin' abeawt him! Th' child would be fit to start eawt o' th' heawse i' th' deead time o' th' neet a-seechin' mo,[4]—aw know he would! ... Aw mun go, mon: God bless tho, thae knows heaw it is!'"

Such a conversation might have been overheard in any part of the district throughout which the distress was now so sore [....]

[Source: R. Arthur Arnold. *The History of the Cotton Famine, from the Fall of Sumter to the Passing of the Public Works Act*. London: Saunders, Otley, 1864. 300-305.]

1 winnot tho'] will you not.
2 mun] must.
3 wick] alive.
4 a-seechin' mo] looking for me.

Appendix G: Factory Legislation: Contemporary Views

1. Richard Oastler, "The White Slaves of Yorkshire" (1830)

[Richard Oastler (1789-1861) worked as a steward for an absentee landlord, but he made his fame as a Tory radical denouncing the factory system and the New Poor Law Amendment Act of 1834. According to many accounts, Oastler's letter to the *Leeds Mercury* on the conditions in which factory children worked marks the beginning of the movement to regulate such conditions. Samuel Kydd's version of this episode is offered here because he bases his narrative of this well-known conversion story on the autobiographical account that Oastler provided in 1851.]

Though Mr Oastler had lived for many years in the heart of the manufacturing district of Yorkshire, had often visited the poor, had in their own cottages and in the Leeds Infirmary seen many sickly factory children and factory cripples,—the causes of their sickness, deformity, and lameness were unknown to him. Mr Oastler had often expressed his opinion that the working men of the manufacturing districts suffered, physically, from various causes; that it would be consistent with the professions of those who advocated negro emancipation (with whom he in principle cordially agreed, and actively co-operated), to endeavour to discover those causes, and to apply remedial measures; in his own words—"to apply their avowed principles to the wants of their own neighbours." Of the actual facts of the factories he was then ignorant. When he returned from the various towns of the West Riding to his home, and saw the factories lighted up at night, he accepted of "these sights as signs of prosperity."

In 1830 Mr Oastler was on a visit to his friend, Mr John Wood, of Horton Hall (now of Thedden Grange, Hampshire), a very kind-hearted man, and, at the time referred to, an extensive manufacturer in the town of Bradford, Yorkshire. Mr Wood was wealthy and generous; moved by a sense of duty, he had in vain endeavoured by his own private influence to reform the factory system. Mr Wood knew Mr Oastler well; in the course of conversation one evening Mr Wood said: "Mr Oastler, I wonder you have never turned your attention to the factory system." "Why should I? I have nothing to do with factories," was Mr Oastler's reply. "That may be," rejoined Mr Wood, "You are, however, very enthusiastic against slavery in the West Indies; and, I assure you, there are cruelties daily practised in our mills on little children, which, if you knew, I am sure you would strive to prevent." "Cruelties in mills?" exclaimed Mr Oastler, "I do not understand you; tell me." Mr Wood then informed Mr Oastler of much that Mr Wood knew; among other things, that in "his own mill, little children were worked from six o'clock in the morning to seven o'clock in the evening, and that the only break off they had was forty minutes at noon; which break was ten minutes more than any other millowner allowed. While in some mills in the neighbourhood the poor children were worked all that time without one minute of rest." Mr Oastler was astonished, and to his horror discovered "that little children were worked 14, 15, 16, and even 18 hours a day, in some mills, without a single minute having been set apart for meals, and that implements of cruelty were used to goad them on to this excessive labour. Besides all this, in many mills they were cheated out of portions of their scanty wages by fines and other means of fraud. Worse still, they were often subjected to shocking indecencies, and they were brought up in total ignorance of their duties to God and to man." Mr Oastler was deeply impressed with all he had heard. Mr Wood was fully sensible of the horrors and vices of the factory system, and solicited from Mr Oastler a pledge that he would use all his influence in an endeavour to remove from the factory system the cruelties which were regularly practised in the mills. Mr Oastler has, in *The Home* (1851), a periodical of which he was the editor, narrated a circumstance which very clearly indicates the state of his own mind and that of Mr Wood:—"You will, Edwin, remember," wrote Mr Oastler, "that I was on a visit at the house of a dear friend, a millowner, and that he, to my great surprise, had informed me that I lived not far from a town where human beings—little children, boys and girls—were daily sacrificed for gold. I told you how much I was horrified at his recital. With feelings which I will not attempt to describe, I went to bed. I had requested the servant to call me at four in the morning, having occasion to ride some miles to an early appointment. When my friend's valet aroused me, he said—'My master wishes to see you, Sir, before you leave;' he afterwards showed me into his master's bedroom. My friend was in bed, but he was not asleep; he was leaning upon a table beside his bed. On that table were placed two candles, between them was the Holy Bible. On my advancing towards the side of his bed, he turned towards me, reached out his hand, and, in the most impressive and affectionate manner, pressing my hand in his, he said, 'I have had no sleep to-night. I have been reading this book, and in every page I have read my own condemnation. I cannot allow you to leave me without a pledge, that you will use all your influence in endeavouring to remove, from our factory system, the cruelties which are regularly practised in our mills ..... I promised my friend that I would do what I could. I felt, Edwin, that we were, each of us, in the presence of the Highest. I knew that that vow was recorded in Heaven. I have kept it, Edwin, the grace of God having upholden me; I have been faithful. Trusting in the same power, old and feeble as I am, I hope to be faithful even unto death.'"

In the morning of the next day after the conversation with Mr Wood, Mr Oastler adopted the first step towards the fulfilment of his promise; he wrote a letter narrating the results of his experience at Bradford, and addressed the same to the Editors of the *Leeds Mercury*, then, as now, one of the most influential journals in Yorkshire. This letter was after publication subjected to severe and protracted criticism. In a historical sense, this letter is valuable, as being the foundation of what might not improperly be called, "the active Ten Hours' Bill movement;" the first Sir Robert Peel, as has been shown, had, in the vain hope of conciliating opposition, abandoned the Ten Hours' limit as the rule for factory labour, no legal regulation was then applicable to other than cotton factories. When Mr Oastler addressed the Editors of the *Leeds Mercury*, on the condition of children employed in woollen and worsted factories, he was unacquainted with the labours of Gould, Peel, and their coadjutors; he had resolved to light a flame which should be seen throughout England, and the burning of which was subsequently watched with interest throughout Europe and the American Union. Mr Oastler's first letter on the factory question deserves attention for the facts it contains, and the key which it affords to the state of the mind of the writer, when he entered on what has proved, to him and to his country, a momentous labour:—

"YORKSHIRE SLAVERY.
"To the Editors of the Leeds Mercury.

"'It is the pride of Britain that a slave cannot exist on her soil; and if I read the genius of her constitution aright, I find that slavery is most abhorrent to it—that the air which Britons breathe is free—the ground on which they tread is sacred to liberty.—*Rev. R.W. Hamilton's Speech at the Meeting held in the Cloth-hall Yard, Sept. 22nd,* 1830.

"Gentlemen,—No heart responded with truer accents to the sounds of liberty which were heard in the Leeds Cloth-hall yard, on the 22nd instant, than did mine, and from none could more sincere and earnest prayers arise to the throne of Heaven, that hereafter slavery might only be known to Britain in the pages of her history. One shade alone obscured my pleasure, arising not from any difference in principle, but from the want of application of the general principle *to the whole empire.* The pious and able champions of *negro* liberty and *colonial* rights should, if I mistake not, have gone farther than they did; or perhaps, to speak more correctly, before they had travelled so far as the West Indies, should, at least for a few moments, have sojourned in our own immediate neighbourhood, and have directed the attention of the meeting to scenes of misery, acts of oppression, and victims of slavery, even on the threshold of our homes.

"Let truth speak out, appalling as the statement may appear. The fact is true. Thousands of our fellow-creatures and fellow-subjects, both male and female, the miserable inhabitants of a *Yorkshire town*, (Yorkshire now represented in parliament by the giant of anti-slavery principles,) are this very moment existing in a state of slavery, *more horrid* than are the victims of that hellish system—'*colonial slavery.*' These innocent creatures drawl out, unpitied, their short but miserable existence, in a place famed for its profession of religious zeal, whose inhabitants are ever foremost in *professing* 'temperance' and 'reformation,' and are striving to outrun their neighbours in missionary exertions, and would fain send the Bible to the farthest corner of the globe—ay, in the very place where the anti-slavery fever rages most furiously, her *apparent charity*, is not more admired on earth, than her *real cruelty* is abhorred in heaven. The very streets which receive the droppings of an 'Anti-slavery Society' are every morning wet by the tears of innocent victims at the accursed shrine of avarice, who are *compelled* (not by the cart-whip of the negro slave-driver) but by the dread of the equally-appalling thong or strap of the overlooker, to hasten, half-dressed, *but not half-fed*, to those magazines of British infantile slavery—*the worsted mills in the town and neighbourhood of Bradford!!!*

"Would that I had Brougham's eloquence, that I might rouse the hearts of the nation, and make every Briton swear, 'These innocents shall be free!'

"Thousands of little children, both male and female, *but principally female*, from seven to fourteen years of age, are daily *compelled* to *labour* from six o'clock in the morning to seven in the evening, with only— Britons, blush while you read it!—*with only thirty minutes allowed for eating and recreation.* Poor infants! ye are indeed sacrificed at the shrine of avarice, *without even the solace of the negro slave;* ye are no more than he is, *free agents;* ye are compelled to work as long as the *necessity* of your needy parents may require, or the cold-blooded avarice of your worse than barbarian masters *may demand!* Ye live in the boasted land of freedom, and *feel* and mourn that *ye are slaves*, and slaves without the only comfort which the negro has. He knows it is his sordid, mercenary master's interest that he should *live*, be *strong* and *healthy. Not so with you.* Ye are doomed to labour from morning to night for one who cares not how soon your weak and tender frames are stretched to breaking! You are not mercifully valued at so much per head; this would assure you at least (even with the worst and most cruel masters) of the mercy shown to their own labouring beasts. No, no! your soft and delicate limbs are tired and fagged, and jaded, at only *so much per week*, and when your joints can act no longer, your emaciated frames are cast aside, the boards on which you lately toiled and wasted life away, are instantly supplied with other victims, who in this boasted land of liberty are HIRED—not sold—as slaves, and daily forced to *hear* that they are free. Oh! Duncombe! Thou hatest slavery—I know thou dost resolve that 'Yorkshire children shall no more be slaves.' And Morpeth! who justly gloriest in the Christian faith—Oh, Morpeth! listen to the cries and count the tears of these poor babes, and let St Stephen's hear thee swear 'they shall no longer groan in slavery!' And Bethell, too! who swears eternal hatred to the name of slave, whene'er thy manly voice is heard in Britain's senate, assert the rights and liberty of Yorkshire youths. And Brougham! thou who art the chosen champion of liberty in every clime! oh bend thy giant's mind, and listen to the sorrowing accents of these poor Yorkshire little ones, and note their tears; then let thy voice rehearse their woes, and touch the chord thou only holdest— the chord that sounds above the silvery notes in praise of heavenly liberty, and down descending at thy will, groans in the horrid caverns of the deep in muttering sounds of misery accursed to hellish bondage; and as thou sound'st these notes, let Yorkshire hear thee swear, 'Her *children* shall be free!' Yes, all ye four protectors of our rights, chosen by freemen to destroy oppression's rod,

'Vow one by one, vow altogether, vow
With heart and voice, eternal enmity
Against oppression by your brethren's hands;
Till man nor woman under Britain's laws,
Nor son nor daughter born within her empire,
Shall buy, or sell, or HIRE, or BE A SLAVE!'

"The nation is now most resolutely determined that negroes shall be free. Let them, however, not forget that Britons have common rights with Afric's sons.

"The blacks may be fairly compared to beasts of burden, *kept for their master's use;* the whites, to those *which others keep and let for hire.* If I have succeeded in calling the attention of your readers to the horrid and abominable system on which the worsted mills in and near Bradford is conducted, I have done some good. Why should not children working in them be protected by legislative enactments, as well as those who work in cotton mills? Christians should feel and act for those whom Christ so eminently loved, and declared that 'of such is the kingdom of Heaven.'—I remain, yours, &c.,

"RICHARD OASTLER.

"Fixby Hall, near Huddersfield, Sept. 29, 1830."

The reading of Mr Oastler's letter caused much excitement. As originally written, it was signed "A Briton," Mr Oastler was wishful not to be known as the author, but the senior editor of the *Mercury* insisted on having a real name attached, Mr Oastler consequently appended his signature. Many there were filled with astonishment, some denied the existence of the evils complained of, others affirmed that if Mr Oastler's signature had not been appended to the letter in the *Leeds Mercury,* they could not have believed that such things were, the late Mr Baines (senior editor of the *Leeds Mercury*) admitted that the evils stated therein, if true, constituted a real grievance. A keen controversy followed in the Leeds press, chiefly in the columns of the *Leeds Mercury* and *Leeds Intelligencer.* In this warfare, Mr Oastler was completely triumphant; like a strong and practised wrestler, he closed upon his opponents, and cast them from his arms on the ground. Every fact relating to the labour of children in factories, stated in Mr Oastler's first letter, was proved to be correct; the complaints of his opponents were ultimately confined to the tone and manner of the writer; the intense and protracted interest caused by the letter being a very satisfactory reply to such objections.

[Source: (Samuel Kydd). "Alfred." *The History of the Factory Movement from the Year 1802, to the Enactment of the Ten Hours' Bill in 1847.* 2 vols. London: Simpkin, Marshall, 1857. 1: 95-102.]

2. Caroline Norton, *A Voice From the Factories* (1836)

[Born in 1808, Caroline Elizabeth Sarah Sheridan was the granddaughter of playwright Richard Brinsley Sheridan. She married George Chapple Norton in 1827, and from the beginning it was an unhappy marriage because her husband was physically abusive as well as improvident. After her husband left in 1836 and took their children, she became an activist and lobbied to change the laws respecting a mother's rights towards her children. The Infant Custody Bill of 1839, which granted more rights to mothers, was passed in large part due to her ceaseless efforts to change the laws.

Written during the midst of Norton's personal troubles, *A Voice From the Factories* (1836) uses the familiar slavery metaphor, calling the children "factory slaves" on many occasions. At the same time, however, she recognizes and anticipates opposing arguments. The factory owners speak in her poem, saying, "'Theirs is not/ A life of slavery; if they labour,—still/ We *pay* their toil. Free service is their lot;/ And what their labour yields, by us is fairly got'" and "''Tis their parent's choice"; but such statements are rebutted by Norton with "Are they free/ Who toil until the body's strength gives away?" and "Do not your hearts inquire/ Who tempts the parents' penury?" As Norton's poem refutes the common arguments that justify child labor factories, it, above all, urges its readers to pity working children.]

A

VOICE

FROM

THE FACTORIES.

In Serious Verse.

DEDICATED TO

THE RIGHT HONOURABLE

LORD ASHLEY.

The abuses even, of such a business, must be cautiously dealt with ; lest, in eradicating them, we shake or disorder the whole fabric.   We admit, however, that the case of CHILDREN employed in the Cotton Factories is one of those that call fairly for legislative regulation.   M'CULLOCH.

LONDON:

JOHN MURRAY, ALBEMARLE STREET.

MDCCCXXXVI.

TO
THE RIGHT HONOURABLE
LORD ASHLEY.[1]

MY LORD,

AN anonymous Author, whose own name could give no importance to this ephemeral production, ventures to claim the aid of yours; as one not only noble, but intimately connected with the subject of his verse.

To the just-minded, the opinions of *no* individual, however obscure, should be utterly indifferent; since each man undoubtedly represents the opinions of a certain number of his fellow-men. It is the conviction of this, and the belief, that to abstain from giving our views on any point because we fear due attention will not be paid us, savours rather of vanity than humility, which have induced me to intrude at this time on your Lordship and the Public.

For the *mode* in which I have done so, some apology is perhaps necessary; since the application of serious poetry to the passing events of the day has fallen into disuse, and is, if not absolutely contemned, at least much discouraged.

Doubtless there are those to whose tastes and understandings, dry and forcible arguments are more welcome than reasonings dressed in the garb of poetry. Yet as poetry is the language of feeling, it should be the language of the multitude; since all men can feel, while comparatively few can reason acutely, and still fewer reduce their reasoning theories to practicable schemes of improvement.

My Lord, I confess myself anxious to be *heard,* even though unable to convince. It is the misfortune of the time, that subjects of great and pressing interest are so numerous, that many questions which affect the lives and happiness of hundreds, become, as it were, comparatively unimportant; and are thrust aside by others of greater actual moment. Such, as it appears to me, is the present condition of the Factory Question: and although I am conscious that it requires but an inferior understanding to *perceive* an existing evil, while the combined efforts of many superior minds are necessary to its remedy; yet I cannot but think it incumbent on all who feel, as I do, that there *is* an evil which it behoves Christian lawgivers to remove,—to endeavour to obtain such a portion of public attention as may be granted to the expression of their conviction.

My Lord, my ambition extends so far, and no farther. I publish this little Poem with the avowed hope of obtaining that attention; I publish it *anonymously,* because I have no right to expect that my personal opinion would carry more weight with it than that of any other individual. The inspiriting cheer of triumph, and the startling yell of disapprobation, are alike composed of a number of voices, each in itself insignificant, but in their union most powerful. I desire, therefore, only to *join* my voice to that of wiser and better men, in behalf of those who suffer;

---

1 See note 1 on page 185.

and if the matter or the manner of my work be imperfect, allowance will, I trust, be made for its imperfection, since it pretends to so little.

I will only add, that I have in *no* instance overcharged or exaggerated, by poetical fictions, the picture drawn by the Commissioners appointed to inquire into this subject. I have strictly adhered to the printed Reports; to that which I believe to be the melancholy truth; and that which I have, in some instances, myself had an opportunity of witnessing.

I earnestly hope I shall live to see this evil abolished. There will be delay—there will be opposition: such has ever been the case with all questions involving conflicting interests, and more especially where the preponderating interest has been on the side of the existing abuse. Yet, as the noble-hearted and compassionate Howard[1] became immortally connected with the removal of the abuses which for centuries disgraced our prison discipline; as the perseverance of Wilberforce[2] created the dawn of the long-delayed emancipation of the negroes;—so, my Lord, I trust to see *your* name enrolled with the names of these great and good men, as the Liberator and Defender of those helpless beings, on whom are inflicted many of the evils both of slavery and imprisonment, without the odium of either.

I remain, my LORD,
Your Lordship's
Obedient Servant,
THE AUTHOR.

London, October, 1836.

A
VOICE FROM THE FACTORIES.

I.

WHEN fallen man from Paradise was driven
Forth to a world of labour, death, and care;
Still, of his native Eden, bounteous Heaven
Resolved one brief memorial to spare,
And gave his offspring an imperfect share
Of that lost happiness, amid decay;
Making their first *approach* to life seem fair,
And giving, for the Eden past away,
CHILDHOOD, the weary life's long happy holyday.

---

1 John Howard (1726-90), philanthropist, prison reformer, and author of *The State of the Prisons in England and Wales* (1777).
2 See note 2 on page 91.

II.

Sacred to heavenly peace, those years remain!
And when with clouds their dawn is overcast,
Unnatural seem the sorrow and the pain
(Which rosy joy flies forth to banish fast,
Because that season's sadness may not last).
Light is their grief! a word of fondness cheers
The unhaunted heart; the shadow glideth past;
Unknown to them the weight of boding fears,
And soft as dew on flowers their bright, ungrieving tears.

III.

See the Stage-Wonder (taught to earn its bread
By the exertion of an infant skill),
Forsake the wholesome slumbers of its bed,
And mime, obedient to the public will.
Where is the heart so cold that does not thrill
With a vexatious sympathy, to see
That child prepare to play its part, and still
With simulated airs of gaiety
Rise to the dangerous rope, and bend the supple knee?

IV.

Painted and spangled, trembling there it stands,
Glances below for friend or father's face,
Then lifts its small round arms and feeble hands
With the taught movements of an artist's grace:
Leaves its uncertain gilded resting-place—
Springs lightly as the elastic cord gives way—
And runs along with scarce perceptible pace—
Like a bright bird upon a waving spray,
Fluttering and sinking still, whene'er the branches play.

V.

Now watch! a joyless and distorted smile
Its innocent lips assume; (the dancer's leer!)
Conquering its terror for a little while:
Then lets the TRUTH OF INFANCY appear,
And with a stare of numbed and childish fear
Looks sadly towards the audience come to gaze
On the unwonted skill which costs so dear,
While still the applauding crowd, with pleased amaze,
Ring through its dizzy ears unwelcome shouts of praise.

VI.

What is it makes us feel relieved to see
That hapless little dancer reach the ground;
With its whole spirit's elasticity
Thrown into one glad, safe, triumphant bound?
Why are we sad, when, as it gazes round
At that wide sea of paint, and gauze, and plumes,
(Once more awake to sense, and sight, and sound,)
The nature of its age it re-assumes,
And one spontaneous smile at length its face illumes?

VII.

Because we feel, for Childhood's years and strength,
Unnatural and hard the task hath been;—
Because our sickened souls revolt at length,
And ask what infant-innocence may mean,
Thus toiling through the artificial scene;—
Because at that word, CHILDHOOD, start to birth
All dreams of hope and happiness serene—
All thoughts of innocent joy that visit earth—
Prayer—slumber—fondness—smiles—and hours of rosy mirth.

VIII.

And therefore when we hear the shrill faint cries
Which mark the wanderings of the little sweep;
Or when, with glittering teeth and sunny eyes,
The boy-Italian's voice, so soft and deep,
Asks alms for his poor marmoset asleep;
They fill our hearts with pitying regret,
Those little vagrants doomed so soon to weep—
As though a term of joy for all was set,
And that *their* share of Life's long suffering was not yet.

IX.

Ever a toiling *child* doth make us sad:
'T is an unnatural and mournful sight,
Because we feel their smiles should be so glad,
Because we know their eyes should be so bright.
What is it, then, when, tasked beyond their might,
They labour all day long for others' gain,—
Nay, trespass on the still and pleasant night,
While uncompleted hours of toil remain?
Poor little FACTORY SLAVES—for YOU these lines complain!

X.

Beyond all sorrow which the wanderer knows,
Is that these little pent-up wretches feel;
Where the air thick and close and stagnant grows,
And the low whirring of the incessant wheel
Dizzies the head, and makes the senses reel:
There, shut for ever from the gladdening sky,
Vice premature and Care's corroding seal
Stamp on each sallow cheek their hateful die,
Line the smooth open brow, and sink the saddened eye.

XI.

For them the fervid summer only brings
A double curse of stifling withering heat;
For them no flowers spring up, no wild bird sings,
No moss-grown walks refresh their weary feet;—
No river's murmuring sound;—no wood-walk, sweet
With many a flower the learned slight and pass;—
Nor meadow, with pale cowslips thickly set
Amid the soft leaves of its tufted grass,—
Lure *them* a childish stock of treasures to amass.

XII.

Have we forgotten our own infancy,
That joys so simple are to them denied?—
Our boyhood's hopes—our wanderings far and free,
Where yellow gorse-bush left the common wide
And open to the breeze?—The active pride
Which made each obstacle a pleasure seem;
When, rashly glad, all danger we defied,
Dashed through the brook by twilight's fading gleam,
Or scorned the tottering plank, and leapt the narrow stream?

XIII.

In lieu of this,—from short and bitter night,
Sullen and sad the infant labourer creeps;
He joys not in the glow of morning's light,
But with an idle yearning stands and weeps,
Envying the babe that in its cradle sleeps:
And ever as he slowly journeys on,
His listless tongue unbidden silence keeps;
His fellow-labourers (playmates hath he none)
Walk by, as sad as he, nor hail the morning sun.

XIV.

Mark the result. Unnaturally debarred
All nature's fresh and innocent delights,
While yet each germing energy strives hard,
And pristine good with pristine evil fights;
When every passing dream the heart excites,
And makes even *guarded* virtue insecure;
Untaught, unchecked, they yield as vice invites:
With all around them cramped, confined, impure,
Fast spreads the moral plague which nothing new shall cure.

XV.

Yes, this reproach is added; (infamous
In realms which own a Christian monarch's sway!)
Not suffering *only* is their portion, thus
Compelled to toil their youthful lives away:
Excessive labour works the SOUL's decay—
Quenches the intellectual light within—
Crushes with iron weight the mind's free play—
Steals from us LEISURE purer thoughts to win—
And leaves us sunk and lost in dull and native sin.

XVI.

Yet in the British Senate men rise up,
(The freeborn and the fathers of our land!)
And while these drink the dregs of Sorrow's cup,
Deny the sufferings of the pining band.
With nice-drawn calculations at command,
They prove—rebut—explain—and reason long;
Proud of each shallow argument they stand,
And prostitute their utmost powers of tongue
Feebly to justify this great and glaring wrong.

XVII.

So rose, with such a plausible defence
Of the unalienable RIGHT OF GAIN,
Those who against Truth's brightest eloquence
Upheld the cause of torture and of pain:
And fear of Property's Decrease made vain,
For years, the hope of Christian Charity
To lift the curse from SLAVERY's dark domain,
And send across the wide Atlantic sea
The watchword of brave men—the thrilling shout, "BE FREE!"

XVIII.

What is to be a slave? Is't not to spend
A life bowed down beneath a grinding ill?—
To labour on to serve another's end,—
To give up leisure, health, and strength, and skill—
And give up each of these *against your will?*
Hark to the angry answer:—"Theirs is not
A life of slavery; if they labour,—still
We *pay* their toil. Free service is their lot;
And what their labour yields, by us is fairly got."

XIX.

Oh, Men! blaspheme not Freedom! Are they free
Who toil until the body's strength gives way?
Who may not set a term for Liberty,
Who have no time for food, or rest, or play,
But struggle through the long unwelcome day
Without the leisure to be good or glad?
Such is their service—call it what you may.
Poor little creatures, overtasked and sad,
Your Slavery hath no name,—yet is its Curse as bad!

XX.

Again an answer. "'T is their parents' choice.
By *some* employ the poor man's child must earn
Its daily bread; and infants have no voice
In what the allotted task shall be: they learn
What answers best, or suits the parents' turn."
Mournful reply! Do not your hearts inquire
Who tempts the parents' penury? They yearn
Toward their offspring with a strong desire,
But those who starve *will* sell, even what they most require.

XXI.

We grant their class must labour—young and old;
We grant the child the needy parents' tool:
But still our hearts a better plan behold;
No bright Utopia of some dreaming fool,
But rationally just, and good by rule.
Not against TOIL, but TOIL'S EXCESS we pray,
(Else were we nursed in Folly's simplest school);
That so our country's hardy children may
Learn not to loathe, but bless, the well apportioned day.

XXII.

One more reply! The *last* reply—the great
Answer to all that sense or feeling shows,
To which all others are subordinate:—
"The Masters of the Factories must lose
By the abridgment of these infant woes.
Show us the remedy which shall combine
Our equal gain with their increased repose—
Which shall not make our trading class repine,
But to the proffered boon its strong effects confine."

XXIII.

Oh! shall it then be said that TYRANT acts
Are those which cause our country's looms to thrive?
That Merchant England's prosperous trade exacts
This bitter sacrifice, e'er she derive
That profit due, for which the feeble strive?
Is her commercial avarice so keen,
That in her busy multitudinous hive
Hundreds must die like insects, scarcely seen,
While the thick-thronged survivors work where they have been?

XXIV.

Forbid it, Spirit of the glorious Past
Which gained our Isle the surname of 'The Free.'
And made our shores a refuge at the last
To all who would not bend the servile knee,
The vainly-vanquished sons of Liberty!
Here ever came the injured, the opprest,
Compelled from the Oppressor's face to flee—
And found a home of shelter and of rest
In the warm generous heart that beat in England's breast.

XXV.

Here came the Slave, who straightway burst his chain,
And knew that none could ever bind him more;
Here came the melancholy sons of Spain;
And here, more buoyant Gaul's illustrious poor
Waited the same bright day that shone before.
Here rests the Enthusiast Pole! and views afar
With dreaming hope, from this protecting shore,
The trembling rays of Liberty's pale star
Shine forth in vain to light the too-unequal war!

XXVI.

And shall REPROACH cling darkly to the name
Which every memory so much endears?
Shall *we*, too, tyrannise,—and tardy Fame
Revoke the glory of our former years,
And stain Britannia's flag with children's tears?
So shall the mercy of the English throne
Become a by-word in the Nations' ears,
As one who pitying heard the stranger's groan,
But to these nearer woes was cold and deaf as stone.

XXVII.

Are there not changes made which grind the Poor?
Are there not losses every day sustained,—
Deep grievances, which make the spirit sore?
And what the answer, when *these* have complained?
"For crying evils there hath been ordained
The REMEDY OF CHANGE; to obey its call
Some individual loss must be disdained,
And pass as unavoidable and small,
Weighed with the broad result of general good to all."

XXVIII.

Oh! such an evil *now* doth cry aloud!
And CHANGE should be by generous hearts begun,
Though slower gain attend the prosperous crowd,
Lessening the fortunes for their children won.
Why should it grieve a father, that his son
Plain competence must moderately bless?
That he must trade, even as his sire has done,
Not born to independent idleness,
Though honestly above all probable distress?

XXIX.

Rejoice! Thou hast not left enough of gold
From the lined heavy ledger, to entice
His drunken hand, irresolutely bold,
To squander it in haggard haunts of vice:—
The hollow rattling of the uncertain dice
Eats not the portion which thy love bestowed;—
Unable to afford that PLEASURE'S price,
Far off he slumbers in his calm abode,
And leaves the Idle Rich to follow Ruin's road.

XXX.

Happy his lot! For him there shall not be
The cold temptation given by vacant time;
Leaving his young and uncurbed spirit free
To wander thro' the feverish paths of crime!
For *him* the Sabbath bell's returning chime
Not vainly ushers in God's day of rest;
No night of riot clouds the morning's prime:
Alert and glad, not languid and opprest,
He wakes, and with calm soul is the Creator blest.

XXXI.

Ye save for children! Fathers, is there not
A plaintive magic in the name of child,
Which makes you feel compassion for *their* lot
On whom Prosperity hath never smiled?
When with your OWN an hour hath been beguiled
(For whom you hoard the still increasing store),
Surely, against the face of Pity mild,
Heart-hardening Custom vainly bars the door,
For that less favoured race—THE CHILDREN OF THE POOR.

XXXII.

"The happy homes of England!"—they have been
A source of triumph, and a theme for song;
And surely if there be a hope serene
And beautiful, which may to Earth belong,
'T is when (shut out the world's associate throng,
And closed the busy day's fatiguing hum),
Still waited for with expectation strong,
Welcomed with joy, and overjoyed to come,
The good man goes to seek the twilight rest of home.

XXXIII.

There sits his gentle Wife, who with him knelt
Long years ago at God's pure altar-place;
Still beautiful,—though all that she hath felt
Hath calmed the glory of her radiant face,
And given her brow a holier, softer grace.
Mother of SOULS IMMORTAL, she doth feel
A glow from Heaven her earthly love replace;
Prayer to her lip more often now doth steal,
And meditative hope her serious eyes reveal.

XXXIV.

Fondly familiar is the look she gives
As he returns, who forth so lately went,—
For they *together* pass their happy lives;
And many a tranquil evening have they spent
Since, blushing, ignorantly innocent,
She vowed, with downcast eyes and changeful hue,
To love Him only. Love fulfilled, hath lent
Its deep repose; and when he meets her view,
Her soft look only says,—"I trust—and I am true."

XXXV.

Scattered like flowers, the rosy children play—
Or round her chair a busy crowd they press;
But, at the FATHER'S coming, start away,
With playful struggle for his loved caress,
And jealous of the one he first may bless.
To each, a welcoming word is fondly said;
He bends and kisses some; lifts up the less;
Admires the little cheek, so round and red,
Or smooths with tender hand the curled and shining head.

XXXVI.

Oh! let us pause, and gaze upon them now.
Is there not one—beloved and lovely boy!
With Mirth's bright seal upon his open brow,
And sweet fond eyes, brimful of love and joy?
He, whom no measure of delight can cloy,
The daring and the darling of the set;
He who, though pleased with every passing toy,
Thoughtless and buoyant to excess, could yet
Never a gentle word or kindly deed forget?

XXXVII.

And one, more fragile than the rest, for whom—
As for the weak bird in a crowded nest—
Are needed all the fostering care of home
And the soft comfort of the brooding breast:
One, who hath oft the couch of sickness prest!
On whom the Mother looks, as it goes by,
With tenderness intense, and fear supprest,
While the soft patience of her anxious eye
Blends with "God's will be done,"—"God grant thou may'st
    not die!"

XXXVIII.

And is there not the elder of the band?
She with the gentle smile and smooth bright hair,
Waiting, some paces back,—content to stand
Till these of Love's caresses have their share;
Knowing how soon his fond paternal care
Shall seek his violet in her shady nook,—
Patient she stands—demure, and brightly fair—
Copying the meekness of her Mother's look,
And clasping in her hand the favourite story-book.

XXXIX.

Wake, dreamer!—Choose;—to labour Life away,
Which of these little precious ones shall go
(Debarred of summer-light and cheerful play)
To that receptacle for dreary woe,
The Factory Mill?—Shall He, in whom the glow
Of Life shines bright, whose free limbs' vigorous tread
Warns us how much of beauty that we know
Would fade, when *he* became dispirited,
And pined with sickened heart, and bowed his fainting head?

XL.

Or shall the little quiet one, whose voice
So rarely mingles in their sounds of glee,
Whose life can bid no living thing rejoice,
But rather is a long anxiety;—
Shall he go forth to toil? and keep the free
Frank boy, whose merry shouts and restless grace
Would leave all eyes that used his face to see,
Wistfully gazing towards that vacant space
Which makes their fireside seem a lone and dreary place?

XLI.

Or, sparing, these, send Her whose simplest words
Have power to charm,—whose warbled, childish song,
Fluent and clear and bird-like, strikes the chords
Of sympathy among the listening throng,—
Whose spirits light, and steps that dance along,
Instinctive modesty and grace restrain:
The fair young innocent who knows no wrong,—
Whose slender wrists scarce hold the silken skein
Which the glad Mother winds;—shall *She* endure this pain?

XLII.

Away! The thought—the *thought* alone brings tears!
THEY labour—*they*, the darlings of our lives!
The flowers and sunbeams of our fleeting years;
From whom alone our happiness derives
A lasting strength, which every shock survives;
The green young trees beneath whose arching boughs
(When failing Energy no longer strives,)
Our wearied age shall find a cool repose;—
THEY toil in torture!—No—the painful picture close.

XLIII.

Ye shudder,—nor behold the vision more!
Oh, Fathers! is there then one law for these,
And one for the pale children of the Poor,—
That to their agony your hearts can freeze;
Deny their pain, their toil, their slow disease;
And deem with false complaining they encroach
Upon your time and thought? Is yours the Ease
Which misery vainly struggles to approach,
Whirling unthinking by, in Luxury's gilded coach?

XLIV.

Examine and decide. Watch through his day
One of these little ones. The sun hath shone
An hour, and by the ruddy morning's ray,
The last and least, he saunters on alone.
See where, still pausing on the threshold stone,
He stands, as loth to lose the bracing wind;
With wistful wandering glances backward thrown
On all the light and glory left behind,
And sighs to think that HE must darkly be confined!

XLV.

Enter with him. The stranger who surveys
The little natives of that dreary place
(Where squalid suffering meets his shrinking gaze),
Used to the glory of a young child's face,
Its changeful light, its coloured sparkling grace,
(Gleams of Heaven's sunshine on our shadowed earth!)
Starts at each visage wan, and bold, and base,
Whose smiles have neither innocence nor mirth,—
And comprehends the Sin original from birth.

XLVI.

There the pale Orphan, whose unequal strength
Loathes the incessant toil it *must* pursue,
Pines for the cool sweet evening's twilight length,
The sunny play-hour, and the morning's dew:
Worn with its cheerless life's monotonous hue,
Bowed down, and faint, and stupified it stands;
Each half-seen object reeling in its view—
While its hot, trembling, languid little hands
Mechanically heed the Task-master's commands.

XLVII.

There, sounds of wailing grief and painful blows
Offend the ear, and startle it from rest;
(While the lungs gasp what air the place bestows;)
Or misery's joyless vice, the ribald jest,
Breaks the sick silence: staring at the guest
Who comes to view their labour, they beguile
The unwatched moment; whispers half supprest
And mutterings low, their faded lips defile,—
While gleams from face to face a strange and sullen smile.

XLVIII.

These then are his Companions: he, too young
To share their base and saddening merriment,
Sits by: his little head in silence hung;
His limbs cramped up; his body weakly bent;
Toiling obedient, till long hours so spent
Produce Exhaustion's slumber, dull and deep.
The Watcher's stroke,—bold—sudden—violent,—
Urges him from that lethargy of sleep,
And bids him wake to Life,—to labour and to weep!

XLIX.

But the day hath its End. Forth then he hies
With jaded, faltering step, and brow of pain;
Creeps to that shed,—his HOME,—where happy lies
The sleeping babe that cannot toil for Gain;
Where his remorseful Mother tempts in vain
With the best portion of their frugal fare:
Too sick to eat—too weary to complain—
He turns him idly from the untasted share,
Slumbering sinks down unfed, and mocks her useless care.

L.

Weeping she lifts, and lays his heavy head
(With all a woman's grieving tenderness)
On the hard surface of his narrow bed;
Bends down to give a sad unfelt caress,
And turns away;—willing her God to bless,
That, weary as he is, he need not fight
Against that long-enduring bitterness,
  The VOLUNTARY LABOUR of the Night,
But sweetly slumber on till day's returning light.

LI.

Vain hope! Alas! unable to forget
The anxious task's long, heavy agonies, .
In broken sleep the victim labours yet!
Waiting the boding stroke that bids him rise,
He marks in restless fear each hour that flies—
Anticipates the unwelcome morning prime—
And murmuring feebly, with unwakened eyes,
  "Mother! Oh Mother! is it yet THE TIME?"—
Starts at the moon's pale ray—or clock's far distant chime.

LII.

Such is *his* day and night! Now then return
Where your OWN slumber in protected ease;
They whom no blast may pierce, no sun may burn;
The lovely, on whose cheeks the wandering breeze
Hath left the rose's hue. Ah! not like these
Does the pale infant-labourer ask to be:
He craves no tempting food—no toys to please—
  Not Idleness,—but less of agony;
Not Wealth,—but comfort, rest, CONTENTED POVERTY.

LIII.

There is, among all men, in every clime,
A difference instinctive and unschooled:
God made the MIND unequal. From all time
By fierceness conquered, or by cunning fooled,
The World hath had its Rulers and its Ruled:—
Yea—uncompelled—men abdicate free choice,
Fear their own rashness, and, by thinking cooled,
  Follow the counsel of some trusted voice;—
A self-elected sway, wherein their souls rejoice.

LIV.

Thus, for the most part, willing to obey,
Men rarely set Authority at naught:
Albeit a weaker or a worse than they
May hold the rule with such importance fraught:
And thus the peasant, from his cradle taught
That some must *own*, while some must *till* the land,
Rebels not—murmurs not—even in his thought.
Born to his lot, he bows to high command,
And guides the furrowing plow with a contented hand.

LV.

But, if the weight which habit renders light
Is made to gall the Serf who bends below—
The dog that watched and fawned, prepares to bite!
Too rashly strained, the cord snaps from the bow—
Too tightly curbed, the steeds their riders throw—
And so, (at first contented his fair state
Of customary servitude to know,)
Too harshly ruled, the poor man learns to hate
And curse the oppressive law that bids him serve the Great.

LVI.

THEN first he asks his gloomy soul the CAUSE
Of his discomfort; suddenly compares—
Reflects—and with an angry Spirit draws
The envious line between his lot and theirs,
Questioning the JUSTICE of the unequal shares.
And from the gathering of this discontent,
Where there is strength, REVOLT his standard rears;
Where there is weakness, evermore finds vent
The sharp annoying cry of sorrowful complaint.

LVII.

Therefore should Mercy, gentle and serene,
Sit by the Ruler's side, and share his Throne:—
Watch with unerring eye the passing scene,
And bend her ear to mark the feeblest groan;
Lest due Authority be overthrown,
And they that ruled perceive (too late confest!)
Permitted Power might still have been their own,
Had they but watched that none should be opprest—
No just complaint despised—no WRONG left unredrest.

LVIII.

Nor should we, Christians in a Christian land,
Forget who smiled on helpless infancy,
And blest them with divinely gentle hand:—
"Suffer that little children come to me:"[1]
Such were His words to whom we bow the knee!
These to our care the Saviour did commend;
And shall we HIS bequest treat carelessly,
Who yet our full protection would extend
To the lone Orphan child left by an Earthly Friend?

LIX.

No! rather what the Inspired Law imparts
To guide our ways, and make our path more sure;
Blending with Pity (native to our hearts),
Let us to these, who patiently endure
Neglect, and penury, and toil, secure
The innocent hopes that to their age belong:
So, honouring Him, the Merciful and Pure,
Who watches when the Oppressor's arm grows strong,—
And helpeth them to right—the Weak—who suffer wrong!

[Source: (Caroline Norton). *A Voice from the Factories. In Serious Verse.* Dedicated to the Right Honourable Lord Ashley. London: John Murray, 1836.]

3. John Fielden, from *The Curse of the Factory System* (1836)

[John Fielden (1784-1849), the son of a mill owner, became, along with his brothers, one of the partners in a very successful business manufacturing and selling cotton. Elected to Parliament in 1832, he was an ardent reformer, particularly instrumental in influencing factory legislation after Lord Ashley gave up his seat in the House of Commons in 1846. Writing in *The Curse of the Factory System* to explain his refusal to support his fellow factory owners in their petitions to repeal the legislation already passed to limit the hours of work for children, Fielden makes the case for an eight-hour day for both children and adults. As the following excerpts from his pamphlet reveal, Fielden bases that case on the evidence provided by Brown's *A Memoir of Robert Blincoe*, reports issued by the 1833 royal commission and by

---

1   Luke 18:16. As Jesus was bestowing his blessing on individuals, some people
    asked that he bless their infants, and the disciples refused them. Jesus, however,
    said, "Suffer little children to come unto me, and forbid them not: for such is
    the kingdom of God."

factory inspectors, and, finally, on the evidence of his own experience as both a factory child and a factory owner. Fielden begins in his preface by stressing his financial stake in the issue of the legislative regulation of factories, which his fellow owners claim would give their competitors in foreign countries an unfair advantage over them: "I am concerned in a very large business myself, and ... I must be one of the first to be ruined, if foreign competition is to ruin us" (iv). He ends his pamphlet by denouncing the "curse of the factory system"—"no measure has ever passed the Legislature efficient for the purpose of staying this curse, as mighty as the machine which has caused it." Fielden's last sentence famously attacks the political economists who have opposed further legislation as men who "while they would make England the 'workshop of the world' ... would not scruple to make her also the slaughter-house of Mammon" (74).]

In tracing the progress which has been made in the attempts to better the condition of factory children, it may not be amiss to inquire how it came to pass originally, that, in England, always boasting of her humanity, laws were necessary in order to protect little children from the cruelties of the master manufacturer, and even of their own parents.

It is well known that ARKWRIGHT'S (so called, at least) inventions took manufactures out of the cottages and farmhouses of England, where they had been carried on by mothers, or by daughters under the mother's eye, and assembled them in the counties of Derbyshire, Nottinghamshire, and, more particularly, in Lancashire, where the newly-invented machinery was used in large factories built on the sides of streams capable of turning the water-wheel. Thousands of hands were suddenly required in these places, remote from towns; and Lancashire, in particular, being till then but comparatively thinly populated and barren, a population was all she now wanted. The small and nimble fingers of little children being by very far the most in request, the custom instantly sprang up of procuring *apprentices* from the different parish workhouses of London, Birmingham, and elsewhere. Many, many thousands of these little hapless creatures were sent down into the North, being from the age of seven, to the age of thirteen or fourteen years old. The custom was for the master to clothe his apprentices, and to feed and lodge them in an "apprentice house" near the factory; overseers were appointed to see to the works, whose interest it was to work the children to the utmost, because their pay was in proportion to the quantity of work that they could exact. Cruelty was, of course, the consequence; and there is abundant evidence on record, and preserved in the recollections of some who still live, to show, that, in many of the manufacturing districts, but particularly, I am afraid, in the guilty county to which I belong, cruelties the most heart-rending were practised upon the unoffending and friendless creatures who were thus consigned to the charge of master-manufacturers; that they were harassed to the brink of death by excess of labour, that they were flogged, fettered, and tortured in the most exquisite refinement of cruelty; that they were, in many cases, starved to the bone while flogged to their work, and that even in some instances, they were driven to commit suicide to evade the cruelties of a world, in which, though born to it so recently, their happiest moments had been passed in the garb and coercion of a workhouse. The beautiful and romantic valleys of Derbyshire, Nottinghamshire, and Lancashire, secluded from the public eye, became the dismal solitudes of torture, and of many a murder!* [...]

The question, as it now stands, appears to me to be this: Did not the Commissioners, sent down into the north in 1833 by the Government, find that protection to the children was called for on grounds of bare humanity? And, then, have not the Inspectors, sent down by the Government to put in force the Act founded upon the Commissioners' Report, stated that it is impracticable, because of the attempt to legislate for *children* only?[1]

These two questions must be answered by referring to the Reports, *first*, of the Commissioners, and *then* of the Inspectors. The Commissioners have given a short summary in pp. 26 to 28 of their report, of the "Effects of Factory Labour on Children," from which I make the extracts following. It is taken, it appears, from the mouths of the children themselves, their parents, and their overlookers. The account of the child, when questioned, is,—

> Sick-tired, especially in the winter nights; so tired she can do nothing; feels so tired she throws herself down when she gangs home, no caring what she does; often much tired, and feels sore, standing so long on her legs; often so tired she could not eat her supper; night and morning very tired; has two sisters in the mill; has heard them complain to her mother, and she says they must work; whiles I do not know what to do with myself; as tired every morning as I can be.

---

* See "Memoir of Robert Blincoe, an Orphan Boy sent from the Parish of St. Pancras" in 1799 into Nottinghamshire; and I wish every man and woman in England *would see* and read this pamphlet. It is published at Manchester, where the crippled subject of the memoir now lives to testify the truth of all that I have said above. [Fielden's note]

1 All the early factory acts made no provisions regarding the labor of adults. Not until the Factory Act of 1844 (section 32) would the laws begin to regulate the employment of adults, though initially it would be the labor of women only. See Introduction 55-56.

Another speaks in this way:—

Many a time has been so fatigued that she could hardly take off her clothes at night, or put them on in the morning; her mother would be raging at her, because when she sat down she could not get up again through the house; thinks they are in bondage; no much better than the Israelites in Egypt, and life no pleasure to them; so tired that she can't eat her supper, nor wake of herself.

The Commissioners say the evidence of parents is generally this:—

Her children come home so tired and worn out they can hardly eat their supper; has often seen her daughter come home so fatigued that she would go to bed supperless; has seen young workers absolutely oppressed, and unable to sit down or rise up.

They say that the evidence of the overlooker is,—

Children are very often tired and stiff-like; have known children hide themselves in the stove among the wool, so that they should not go home when the work is over; have seen six or eight fetched out of the stove and beat home; beat out of the mill however; they hide because too tired to go home.

Again, an overlooker says:–

Many a one I have had to rouse when the work is very slack from fatigue: the children very much jaded when worked late at night; the children bore the long hours very ill indeed; after working eight or nine, or ten hours, they were nearly ready to faint; some were asleep; some were only kept awake by being spoke to, or by a little chastisement, to make them jump up; I was obliged to chastise them when they were almost fainting, and it hurt my feelings; then they would spring up and work pretty well for another hour; but the last two or three hours was my hardest work, for they then got so exhausted.

Another child says:—

She often falls asleep while sitting, sometimes standing; her little sister falls asleep, and they wake her by a cry; was up at four this morning, which made her fall asleep at one, when the Factory Commissioners came to inspect the mill.

A spinner says:—

I find it difficult to keep my piecers awake the last hours of a winter's evening; have seen them fall asleep, and go on performing their work with their hands while they were asleep, after the billey had stopped, when their work was over; I have stopped and looked at them for two minutes, going through the motions of piecening when they were fast asleep, when there was no work to do, and they were doing nothing; children at night are so fatigued that they are asleep often as soon as they sit down, so that it is impossible to wake them to sense enough to wash themselves, or even to eat a bit of supper, being so stupid in sleep.

In alluding to the cruelty of parents, who suffer their children to be overworked in factories for their own gain, as spoken of in the Report of the Board of Health in Manchester, above-quoted, the Commissioners say that

It is not wholly unknown in the West Riding of Yorkshire, for parents to carry their children to the mills in the morning on their backs, and to carry them back again at night.

And, further, that

It appears in evidence that sometimes the sole consideration by which parents are influenced in making choice of a person under whom to place their children, is the amount of wages, not the mode of treatment, to be secured to them.

If this is not enough to show that there were grounds for the further protection, I will now refer to the same Report of the Commissioners, to show, that from Scotland the details are full as affecting, and even more disgusting. At page 18 (Report) the Commissioners open with these words:—

Had the fact not been established by indubitable evidence, every one must have been slow to credit, that in this age and country the proprietors of extensive factories could have been indifferent to the well-being of their work-people to such a degree as is implied in the following statements:

And then they quote from the evidence:—

Privies situated in view; common to males and females: this, in his (witness's) opinion, has a tendency to destroy shame and conduce to immorality.

And again:

But one water-closet for both sexes, which children, and men, and women, use indiscriminately.

Referring to the evidence myself, I find in A 1, p. 40, in the mill of Messrs. Duncan and Co., Glasgow:—

No water-closets, but tubs, not peculiar to either sex.

In A. 1, p. 39, a workman deposes, that

He has seen the boys, when too late of a morning, dragged naked from their beds by the overseers, and even by the master, with their clothes in their hands, to the mill, where they put them on; that he has seen this done oftener than he can tell; and the boys were strapped naked as they got out of bed.

A female confirms this statement, having worked at the same mill, and she adds, that she

Remembers William Edwards, an overseer, coming to the boothy one morning when one of the girls was too late and in bed, that he turned her round and took her out of bed naked; that he took her out of the boothy in this state, but she prigged sair (pleaded earnestly), and he at last let her come back to put on her claithes before going into the mill.

In page 41 an half-overseer gives this evidence:

Does not like the long hours; he is very tired and hoarse at night; and that some of the young female workers in his, the spinning flat, have so swelled legs, one in particular, from standing so long, about seventeen years old, that she can hardly walk; that various of them have their feet bent in and their legs crooked from the same cause; that he has seen it, *but the young women will not acknowledge it from pride, as it might spoil their market!*

In short, so universal is this complaint of "sair tired," and of swelled legs, ankles, feet, hands, and arms, that it almost seems as if one voice spoke the facts; for if we find them varied, it is only here and there by touches like the above, so true to nature, that one would think they must pierce even the most callous and avaricious man to the very core. In one page we find a little child of eight years old complaining that she is "sair tired" every night, and has no time *for going to play*; here we find young women concealing the deformities which work has brought on their persons, lest by avowing it they should become repulsive in the eyes of men![...]

As I have been personally and from an early age engaged in the operations connected with factory labour; that is to say, for about forty years, a short account of my own experience may not be useless in this place, as it is this experience which teaches me to scoff at the representations of those who speak of the labour of factories as "very light," and "so easy, as to require no muscular exertion." I well remember being set to work in my father's mill when I was little more than ten years old; my associates, too, in the labour and in recreation are fresh in my memory. Only a few of them are now alive; some dying very young, others living to become men and women; but many of those who lived, have died off before they had attained the age of fifty years, having the appearance of being much older, a premature appearance of age which I verily believe was caused by the nature of the employment in which they had been brought up. For several years after I began to work in the mill, the hours of labour at our works did not exceed *ten* in the day, winter and summer, and even with the labour of those hours, I shall never forget the fatigue I often felt before the day ended, and the anxiety of us all to be relieved from the unvarying and irksome toil we had gone through before we could obtain relief by such play and amusements as we resorted to when liberated from our work. I allude to this fact, because it is not uncommon for persons to infer, that, because the children who work in factories are seen to play like other children when they have time to do so, the labour is, therefore, light, and does not fatigue them. The reverse of this conclusion I know to be the truth. I know the effect which ten hours' labour had upon myself; I who had the attention of parents better able than those of my companions to allow me extraordinary occasional indulgence. And he knows very little of human nature who does not know, that, to a child, diversion is so essential, that it will undergo even exhaustion in its amusements. I protest, therefore, against the reasoning, that, because a child is not brought so low in spirit as to be incapable of enjoying the diversions of a child, it is not worked to the utmost that its feeble frame and constitution will bear.

I well know, too, from my own experience, that the labour now undergone in the factories is much greater than it used to be, owing to the greater attention and activity required by the greatly-increased speed which is given to the machinery that the children have to attend to, when we compare it with what it was thirty or forty years ago; and, therefore, I fully agree with the Government Commissioners, that a restriction to ten hours per day, is *not a sufficient protection to children.*

The work at which I was employed in my boyhood, while it was limited to ten hours a day, was similar to the work that children have to do in the woollen mills of Yorkshire at the present time, with this difference, that wool is the manufacture in the Yorkshire mills to which I allude, and the manufacture that I was employed in was cotton, the mode of manufacturing which, has been altogether changed since that period by the improvements made in machinery. These are facts which I mention, because the labour of the child in the woollen *now*, is what its labour in the cotton *was then*, the work being done on what are called "billies" and "jennies;" and I mention them, too, because the woollen manufacturers would have it believed (and Mr. Rickards the Inspector appears to countenance the opinion) that the work of children in woollen mills is lighter still than that in the cotton factories, and that children, much younger than those whose labour is now limited to eight hours a day, may, without injury to their health, be worked sixty-nine hours per week. Indeed, it is on this, that the Yorkshire mill-owners have petitioned the House of Commons to allow them to work children of *eight years of age* as many as *seventy-two hours* in the week, or, *twelve hours in the day!*

Another remarkable fact within my own knowledge I must also state: when my father introduced the machinery that is now used, into his own mill, the hours of labour were increased to *twelve*, for five days in the week, and *eleven* for Saturdays, making seventy-one hours in the week. This he was obliged to do in his own defence, because others who used the same sort of machinery, worked their hands *seventy-seven* hours, and some even so much as *eighty-four* hours a week, a practice which continued until 1819, when the 59th of Geo. 3. was passed, and which limited the time-labour for children under sixteen years of age to seventy-two hours in the week, that is, one hour more than the time of work of both children and adults at the establishment at which I had worked myself, but in which I had now become interested as a partner. These hours I always thought and said were excessive; I thought so from my own practical bodily experience; and, therefore, I have always been an advocate for a reduction by legislative enactment. When that worthy man, the late Mr. NATHANIEL GOULD of Manchester, began his endeavours to obtain protection for the factory workers (and in which he lost many friends and encountered great persecution), he applied to me to assist him. Accordingly, I and my partners, joined by all our hands, petitioned the House of Commons. I sent the petition to Lord MILTON, requesting him to present it; and, I stated to his lordship, that any Factory Bill, to be effective, must restrict the labour, not only of children, but of those older hands with whom they worked; for that the work of both was so connected, that it could not be carried on by the adult hands without the assistance of the younger. But this fact our adversaries always attempt to turn against us. Most of the masters are obliged to admit the excessive hours of labour imposed on children, and the Ministers have done it in the most solemn manner; but they cannot interfere with the labour, the "free labour" of the adult, because that is against sound principle! According to their own showing, it is a choice of evils; but, contrary to reason, contrary to all acknowledged principle and to universal practice, they would choose the greater: they would overwork the child, though nature forbids it, rather than shorten the labour of the adult, who is also overworked. In short, their "principle"; their true and scarcely disguised "principle," is the principle of pelf against nature.

Here, then, is the "curse" of our factory-system: as improvements in machinery have gone on, the "avarice of masters" has prompted many to exact more labour from their hands than they were fitted by nature to perform, and those who have wished for the hours of labour to be less for all ages than the legislature would even yet sanction, have had no alternative but to conform more or less to the prevailing practice, or abandon the trade altogether. This has been the case with regard to myself and my partners. We had never worked more than *seventy-one* hours a week before Sir JOHN HOBHOUSE'S Act was passed. We then came down to *sixty-nine;* and, since Lord Althorp's Act was passed, in 1833, we have reduced the time of adults to *sixty-seven and a half hours* a week, and that of children under thirteen years of age to *forty-eight* hours in the week, though to do this latter, has, I must admit, subjected us to much inconvenience, but the elder hands to more, inasmuch as the relief given to the child is in some measure imposed on the adult. But the overworking does not apply to children only; the adults are also overworked. The increased speed given to machinery within the last thirty years, has, in very many instances, doubled the labour of both. Mr. Longston's evidence before Mr. SADLER'S Committee establishes this fact beyond dispute, and my own knowledge of the subject requires that I should confirm, as I do, the truth of his statement.

[Source: John Fielden. *The Curse of the Factory System; or, A Short Account of the Origin of Factory Cruelties; Of the Attempts to Protect the Children by Law; Of Their Present Sufferings; Our Duty towards Them; Injustice of Mr. Thomson's Bill; The Folly of the Political Economists; A Warning against Sending the Children of the South into the Factories of the North.* London: A. Cobbett, 1836. 5-6, 18-21, 31-35.]

4. Robert Hyde Greg, from *The Factory Question and the "Ten Hours Bill"* (1837)

[Robert Hyde Greg (1795-1875) was a cotton manufacturer active in local affairs in Manchester. His writings on economic questions conveyed his vehement opposition to both the ten-hours movement for factory reform and the Corn Laws. In this anonymous pamphlet, Greg defends the factory system against legislative interference in its workings. In doing so, he demonstrates that the contest between those in favor of such legislation and those opposed to it was a conflict over different methods of proof: Greg specifically denounces basing government action on the evidence of abuses that were provided by individual workers; "all individual cases" need, according to him, to be ignored. In place of such insufficient forms of proof, Greg champions the virtues of statistical analysis, some of which was drawn from the investigations of the 1833 royal commission.]

THERE are few subjects upon which more erroneous sentiments prevail, than as to the proper objects and limits of legislation. The *"trop gouverner,"* is no less common, than mischievous. The propriety of legislation, as the cure of an evil, is, by most people, considered as a mere corollary of the proof of its existence, and they are surprised when you demur at applying, what they conceive to be, the easy and natural remedy.

It is said that, "Experience is a dear school, but that fools learn in no other," and we fear that, until education be sounder and more universal, until the lower classes are taught something more than reading and writing, and the higher classes, something more than the dead languages and mathematics, the school of experience is the only one in which we must continue to learn. By experience is, of course, meant, that of the individual, for a knowledge of the experience of others, and of other times and actions is wisdom: that wisdom, in which, alas! we are so deficient.

In legislation, upon some subjects at least, it seems as if we stumbled upon the highroad of truth, only after having travelled, in vain, every byeway of error, and until we have been driven, by some impassable barrier, to retrace our steps.

Thus, in our attempts to improve, by legislation, the condition of the poor, we have not only multiplied the number, but reduced them to a state of degradation before unknown. By our poor laws and our charities, we have pauperised, and almost ruined the country.

In our commerce and manufactures also, the effects of legislation have been equally mischievous. By our well meant, but injudicious attempt to foster and protect, we have constantly been driving capital from productive into unproductive channels, encouraging the smuggler, checking our commerce, and stunting our manufactures; and our efforts to procure to the operatives a fair remuneration for their labour, has always ended in a reduction of their wages, or in depriving them altogether of employment.

Thus, after repeated failures, we have been, in some degree, schooled into knowledge, and have purchased our experience at the usual price. Modern legislation is indeed improving, though the improvement is rather of a negative nature, and consists not so much in passing *better* laws, as in repealing bad ones. It may be confidently predicted that all further improvement will be of the same kind, and thus, in matters of commerce and manufactures at least, we shall approach continually to a condition of complete and unrestricted freedom.

[...]

NOTWITHSTANDING our admissions for the sake of argument, we have no hesitation in saying that, on a full review of all the evidence, particularly that adduced by the Parliamentary Commission, that the evils of the Factory System have been much exaggerated.

It may not have been free from mischief, and occasional gross abuses, and may still, even under the new law, be open to improvement, but candour cannot refuse to admit, that the same remarks apply to every occupation, in which civilized man can be engaged.

As the general question of the injury resulting to life, health, and morals, from Factory employment, is again to be brought before the public, and be assumed as grounds for farther legislation, it becomes necessary to enter fully upon it. In doing this, we shall avoid, as much as possible, all details, and particular facts, and appeal only to the general conclusions of unprejudiced observers, or to official documents.

Before considering each of these charges seriatim, we cannot help remarking upon the general *unfairness of the phraseology and assumptions* of the enemies of the system. Thus, *all* the workers in mills, are spoken of as being *children*, all children spoken of as "*delicate*," or, as being "*infants of tender years.*" They are represented as working "*fourteen or fifteen hours*," in "*crowded rooms*," "*amidst the continued roar of machinery*," "*effluvia and every thing most noxious to their health;*" and, moreover, "*in a temperature of eighty or ninety degrees.*" All the employment is spoken of as "*severe and unremitting labour*," and as "*protracted toil.*" The mills, which every one quits at pleasure, no necessity existing for giving even a day's, or an hour's notice of quitting, are styled "*Bastiles*," and "*Prisons*," and those seeking employment therein, "*slaves.*" Thus, in a similar spirit, all the unpleasant, or injurious circumstances, incident to different kinds of manufactures, some carried on at Manchester, some at Leeds, some at Dundee, and even then, peculiar only to some special process in each manufacture, are represented, most absurdly, as being all present at one time and on one spot, and operating, *with concentrated malignity,* upon one person, and that person a child, one of tender years and delicate constitution.

[...]

We come now to the fourth and last charge, *that Factory labour is injurious to health, and destructive of life.*†

In the consideration of this, as of the previous charges, we shall avoid, as much as possible, all details, and encounter the charge by

---

† The Quarterly Review describes the whole population pressing forwards "with alacrity to the grave," as they would do to a fair, or a feast; and the "Short Time Committee" makes use of terms quoted from the slaughter at Hugomont, in the Battle of Waterloo:—thus,

wholesale evidence. Individual cases ought not to influence our judgment. To prove that the population of a city is uneducated, something more is required by a reasonable jury than to produce a man who cannot read and write. Yet, much of the evidence against the Factories has been of this imperfect kind. Thus, a cripple was carried to London, and placed before Mr. Sadler's Committee, as a sample of the lamentable effects of Factory labour, although probably 40,000 people were working in the mills. Many medical men were consulted about the effects of employment in mills, who had never seen even the outside of one, and others, who had been in mills, gave, as doctors are in the habit of doing, contradictory opinions. To the opinions of the first of these, little value can be attached; considering the nature of the questions put to them, their replies could scarcely have been different; and, as to the opinions of the latter, they must be left to neutralize each other.

Quitting, therefore, all individual cases, and contradictory opinions, we appeal once more to the *complete and unexceptionable evidence* supplied by the Factory Commission.

[...]

IT is now time to proceed to a consideration of the measure which it is proposed to substitute for the present law; which is one for preventing all the cotton, woollen, worsted, flax, and silk mills of the United Kingdom from working more than *ten hours in any one day*; not, let it be observed, for preventing the *"Poor Factory Children"* from working more than ten hours a day, but for preventing the *Steam-engines*, *Water-wheels*, and *Machinery*, from being in action for a longer period than ten hours, and adults, grown-up men and women, from working longer than ten hours, whatever may be their desires, or their necessities.

As it is proposed, we believe, to retain the short hours of work now prevalent on the *Saturday*, that is, eight hours, the Bill would be one for fifty-eight hours weekly. It would therefore, in fact, though nominally for ten, *be one for only nine and a half hours;* for, six times nine and a half is fifty-seven, and the hour over is fully lost by having to stop machinery, as now rendered necessary by the strictness of the present law, *before the time appointed for stopping, in order to clean it.* It is proposed, then, by the "Short Time Committee," and Lord Ashley and his party, *to limit the productive energy of the aforesaid great staple manufactures, including steam-engines, machinery, and grown-up men,* to NINE HOURS AND A HALF DAILY.

"We have not appealed to the high and unquestionable authorities, which prove the AWFUL HAVOC *which factory labour made, and is still making, with the* LIVES AND LIMBS *of the population.*"—Letter of John Doherty to the Mill-owners. 1837. [Greg's note]

Such is the proposal which, strange to say, is heard without alarm by the Government, the monied interest, and the corn monopolists; with apathy by those whose property is at stake, and with approbation by a great political party, and by a humane but ignorant public.

The *Quarterly Review* assures us in the December Number, (page 442) that, "one thing is certain, the people in the manufacturing districts, old and young, male and female, are determined that they will never be quiet until Parliament grants them a *"Ten Hours Bill."* How long is their cry to be trifled with? During this unhappy agitation we can hope for nothing but suspicion, hostility, and discontent, throughout the manufacturing districts, a total annihilation of all friendliness and confidence between employer and employed; and something, perhaps, far worse, in periods which may soon come, of suspended labour and commercial revulsion. The masters, residing at a distance from the immediate scene of the evil, know but little, either of the condition, or the temper of their men, they should fathom them more deeply than through the meagre experience which is acquired by a visit to the counting-house or a walk through the mill."*

The *"young,"* he says, as well as the old, will never cease their cry for a *"Ten Hours Bill."* The young work now only *eight hours* a day, and the Reviewer is bound to explain why *they* should cry out so earnestly for a "Ten Hours Bill." Indeed, Lord Ashley and the "Short Time Committee" will have some difficulty in explaining to the public, why they are now so anxious to procure for the *"poor Factory children"* a bill, which will compel them to work two hours a day more than they now work. Surely public sympathy will be at fault!

But it is said, *"the people in the manufacturing districts will never be quiet until Parliament grants them a Ten Hours Bill."* It may be inquired, will they be quiet after it has been granted? Are there no farther demands which may be made? It appears that other views have already opened upon the "working classes;" not more *extensive views, in one sense,* but the reverse.

"A meeting was held at Manchester on the 23rd of Nov. 1833, to form a *'Regeneration Society,'* the object of which is to limit the hours of work for all labourers to *eight,* and at the same time to compel the payment of the present wages. The movers in this business *are the same persons who were the chief agitators of the Ten Hours Bill,* and one of the

---

* The ignorance of the Reviewer of the state of things in the manufacturing districts is strongly displayed, when he speaks of the distance at which the Mill-owners reside from what he terms the *Evil,* that is, their mill. The mill-owners, as a body, live much more in their mills than in their houses. "But most mercantile men, have unfortunately, a disposition to have their house and warehouse within a stone's cast from one another."—*Thackrah,* p. 163. [Greg's note citing Charles Turner Thackrah, *The Effects of Arts, Trades, and Professions, and of Civic States and Habits of Living, on Health and Longevity* (1831).]

resolutions passed at the meeting is that Messrs. Oastler, Wood, Bull, Sadler, and others, be earnestly requested to desist from soliciting Parliament for a Ten Hours Bill, and to use their utmost exertions in aid of the measures now adopted to carry into effect on the 1st of March next, *the regulation of Eight hours work, for the present full day's wages.*"— *Factory Commission, Suppl. Rep. D.* II.

The agitation for an "*Eight Hours Bill*," may not be conducted possibly, by the identical "Short Time Committee" which is now working the "Ten Hours Bill," though we by no means think this unlikely, but quite the contrary,* for as its members live by agitation, they will continue to agitate; but if *they* should not, other Committees would be readily found to agitate for so *desirable* an object. If ten hours' labour with twelve hours wages be popular, *eight hours' labour* with *twelve hours' wages* will be more popular still; if ten hours' labour would leave leisure for recreation and study, or attending public meetings, eight hours' labour would leave yet more. Not an argument can be adduced in favour of a "Ten Hours Bill," which would not apply with, at least, equal force to an Eight Hours Bill, and to draw an Act of Parliament for the one, would be as easy as to draw one for the other.

Surely, however, the "*manufacturing districts would be quiet*," and the country be relieved from all danger of further agitation *after an Eight Hours Bill had been passed?* But no! Mr. Owen, once the advocate of the "Ten Hours Bill," has been lecturing in Manchester during the past winter. The subject of his lectures we understand to have been this, that "*if the working man had his right,* TWO HOURS' *labour a day would be sufficient to procure him all the comforts, and reasonable luxuries of life.*" We understand that he has already 3000 disciples, who have three places of assembly, and who meet, some of them once, and some, twice a week. This new doctrine, popular as it may well be, is spreading so fast, that delegates are going, or are already gone, up and down the country to preach against it, on the ground that the "working classes," that is, some of them, thought two hours labour *too little*, and that if our *mills were to work only two hours a day*, there would be *considerable danger of foreign competition.* The writer of this paper was waited upon repeatedly by one of these delegates, and requested to subscribe to these missionaries.

Here then we have an additional proof, were any required, that legislation, if it be admitted at all, must be confined to narrow and intelligible limits, *such as the protection of children, and securing to them a proper education*, but if "quieting the manufacturing districts," and satisfying the demands of the agitators of the "Ten Hours Bill," be the proposed

---

* "On the contrary, they assert but the truth, when they aver that they think *eight hours a day quite enough, even for* ADULTS, to be employed in the impure and wasting atmosphere of a Factory."—*Letter from John Doherty, Chairman of the Central Short Time Committee.* [Greg's note]

end of legislation, it is evident that we are pursuing an ignis fatuus, which will certainly recede from us as we attempt to approach it.

[Source: (Robert Hyde Greg). *The Factory Question, Considered in Relation to its Effects on the Health and Morals of Those Employed in Factories. And the "Ten Hours Bill," in Relation to its Effects upon the Manufactures of England, and Those of Foreign Countries.* London: James Ridgway, 1837. 2-3, 23-24, 36-37, 74-78.]

5. Frances Trollope, from *Michael Armstrong* (1840)

[In the second main plot of *Michael Armstrong* (see headnote to Appendix F.4), Trollope tells the story of the orphaned young lady, Mary Brotherton, whose fortune of £200,000 is the ill-gotten gain of her deceased father's work as a cotton master. Although raised in the industrial north, Mary is completely ignorant of the conditions in which factory workers live, and she sets off to learn why the system that creates so much wealth also produces so much misery. The selection from Chapter 19 reprinted here involves a conversation that she has with the Rev. Mr. Bell, a clergyman devoted to the ten-hours cause.]

"Alas! alas! is it thus my wealth has been accumulated?" exclaimed Miss Brotherton, shuddering. "Is there no power in England, sir, righteous and strong enough to stay this plague?"

"Miss Brotherton!" returned the clergyman, "such power, and such righteousness, MUST be found, or this plague, as you well call it, will poison the very life blood of our political existence; and long ere any serious danger is likely to be dreamed of by our heedless rulers, the bloated wealth with which this pernicious system has enriched a few, will prove a source of utter destruction to the many. Never, my dear young lady, did the avarice of man conceive a system so horribly destructive of every touch of human feeling, as that by which the low-priced agony of labourine infants is made to eke out and supply all that is wanting to enable the giant engines of our factories to out-spin all the world! But you must see it, Miss Brotherton, you must watch it with your own eyes, you must follow the hateful operations of this atrocious system into the thousands of sordid and forgotten huts which cover its miserable victims, ere you can possibly understand its moral mischief. There is no strength, no power in words to paint it."

"Its moral mischief," said Mary, eagerly; "explain that to me, Mr. Bell, for it is the point I find most puzzling—why is it that these poor factory-people, because they labour more unremittingly, as it should seem, than all the world beside, why, for this reason, instead of being honoured for their industry, are they invariably spoken of with contempt and obliquy?"

"Your question, Miss Brotherton, involves by far the most terrible portion of this frightful commercial mystery," he replied; "but, as I have told you, nothing except personal investigation can enable the inquirer to arrive at the whole truth respecting it. Were a patient, accurate, and laborious detail of all the enormities committed, and all the sufferings endured, under the factory system, to be presented to the public, it would be thrown aside by some, as greatly too tedious for examination, and by others as a statement too atrocious to merit belief. Yet, England MUST listen to it, and that soon, or she may mourn her negligence when it is too late to repair it. That marvellous machinery of which we make our boast, Miss Brotherton, is not more perfect in its power of drawing out the delicately attenuated thread which it is our glory to produce, then [*sic*] the system for reducing the human labour necessary for its production to the lowest possible price is, for degrading the moral nature of the helpless slaves engaged in it."

"That the system has such a tendency I cannot doubt, after the repeated assurances which have reached me, that so it is," replied Mary. "Nevertheless, I am still unable to comprehend why it should be so."

"You have only to take advantage of your residence near Ashleigh, Miss Brotherton, the dense population of which subsists almost wholly by factory labour, in order to understand, but too well, why this terrible result is inevitable. You are as yet too young a lady for me to expect that you should have very deeply studied the nature of the human mind, or made yourself fully aware how greatly the habits and character of all human beings depend upon education, and the circumstances in which they are placed. Nevertheless, if you turn your attention to the subject, you will not, young as you are, be long incapable of detecting the dangers which beset the hearts and souls of those whose unhappy destiny have made them factory labourers. The dark little circle in which they move from birth to death, from father to son, from mother to daughter, is so uniform, that almost any average individual case may fairly serve as a specimen of the whole class. Boys and girls, with few exceptions, labour indiscriminately altogether in the factories. While still almost children, they form connexions, and are married. Having worked in the mills, probably from five years old to the hour of their unweighed and thoughtless union, the boy assumes the duties of a husband with little more knowledge of moral or religious responsibility than the brute animal that labours with a thousand times less degradation in the fields; while the childish wife comes to her important task ignorant of every earthly usefulness, save what belongs to the mechanical drudgery in which throughout the whole of her short, sad life, she has been made to follow the uniform and ceaseless movements of machinery. She cannot sew, she cannot cook, she cannot iron, she cannot wash. Her mind is yet more untaught and undisciplined than her hands. She is conscious of no responsibility, she knows no law by which to steer her actions, or regulate her spirit, and becomes a mother as she became a wife, without one single thought of duty mixing itself with her increasing cares. By degrees, both the husband and the wife find employment in the factory less certain. It is for children, children, children, that the unwearied engine calls, and keenly does the hungry father, and the mother too, watch the growth of the little creatures to whom they have given birth, till the slight limbs have firmness enough to stand, and the delicate joints are sufficiently under the command of the frightened will to tie threads together under the potent inspiration of the overlooker's strap. Then comes a state of deeper degradation still. The father is idle, for often he can get no work, and it is to the labour of his little ones that he looks for bread. Nature recoils from the spectacle of their unnatural o'erlaboured aspect as they return from their thirteen, fourteen, fifteen, hours of toil. He has not nerve to look upon it, and creeps to the gin-shops till they are hid in bed. The mother sees it all, and sternly screws her courage to the task of lifting their bruised and weary limbs upon their bed of straw, putting into their mouths the food she has prepared, their weary eyes being already closed in sleep, and preparing herself to wake before the sun on the morrow, that with unrelenting hand she may drag them from their unfinished slumber, and drive them forth again to get her food. This is no varnished tale, Miss Brotherton, but the bare, naked, hideous truth. And can you wonder that beings thus reared and ripened should form a degraded class? Can you wonder that all others should turn from them, as from a race with whom they have nothing in common? If some sad accident, preceding birth, disturbs the beautiful process by which nature prepares the noble being she has made to be lord of all, and an abortive creature comes to life, curtailed of all its fair proportions, both of mind and body, all within reach of the hapless prodigy shudder as they mourn, and the best and wisest among them pray to God that its span of life be short. But believe me when I tell you, Miss Brotherton, that the effect which the factories of this district is producing upon above two hundred thousand of its population, is beyond all calculation more deplorable, and many a child is born amongst them whose destiny, if fairly weighed against that of such a one as I have described, would appear incomparably more terrible."

"Can such things be, and the rulers of the land sit idly by to witness it?" cried Mary shuddering.

"It seems as if the rulers of the land knew little, and cared less about it," replied Mr. Bell. "The profoundly ignorant opinion that there is some connexion between our national prosperity, and the enormous fortunes amassed by some score of North-country manufacturers has, I believe, produced much of the lamentable non-interference of which the disinterested few complain, who are near enough to look upon the frightful game. Some individual voices have been most gloriously raised on this tremendous theme, and if they will be steadfast and enduring, they must and will prevail—for human nature, with all its vices, is not framed to look coldly on such horrors, and permit them. But the remedial process is so slow—it is so difficult to arouse the attention, and awaken the feelings of busy men concerning things at a distance, whose connexion with all that they deem important they are too ignorant of, or too preoccupied to trace, that the keenest observers, and those who would the most deeply deprecate any remedy but a legal one, begin to fear that mercy will be clamoured for with very dangerous rudeness, before the parliament of England shall have roused up its wisdom to the task of affording it.["]

"And in what way, Mr. Bell, is it wished, or hoped, that the legislature should step forward to cure this dreadful evil? Is it proposed to abolish the use of machinery?"

Mr. Bell smiled, and shook his head.

"You perhaps think," said he, "that there is a great disproportion between my strong sense of the vice and suffering produced by the factory system, and the measure for its mitigation to which I now limit almost my wishes. But it would be vain to look back to the time when steam engines were not, and there would indeed be little wisdom in addressing our lamentations to their introduction. It is not the acquisition of any natural power, principle, or faculty, that we should deplore; all such, on the contrary, should be hailed as part and parcel of our magnificent birthright, and each new use we learn to make of the still much-unknown creation around us, ought to be welcomed with a shout of praise, as a fresh fulfilment of the supreme command 'replenish the earth and *subdue* it.' It is not from increased, or increasing science that we have any thing to dread, it is only from a fearfully culpable neglect of the moral power that should rule and regulate its uses, that it can be other than one of God's best gifts."

"But how," demanded Mary, "how, if machinery continues to be used, can any Act of Parliament prevent the necessity of employing children to wait upon its operations, instead of requiring the strength of men, as heretofore, to perform what the steam-engine does in their place?"

"No Act of Parliament can be conceived capable of inducing a manufacturer to employ the weaker, and at the same time the more costly agent, in preference to a more powerful and cheaper one," replied Mr. Bell. "No reasonable man would ask this, no reasonable man would desire it, and assuredly no reasonable man would attempt to enforce such an absurdity by law. No, Miss Brotherton, this mighty power, as surely given for our use as is the innocent air that fans the woodbine yonder, has at length, after some few thousand years of careless over-looking on our part, been revealed to us. But let us not fly in the face of benignant nature, and say like Caliban,

> "You taught me language; and my profit on't
> Is, I know how to curse."[1]

"If used aright the recannot [*sic*] be a doubt that this magnificent power might, in all its agencies, be made the friend of man. It requires no great stretch of ingenuity to conceive that it might be rendered at once a source of still increasing wealth to the capitalist, and of light-ened labour to the not-impoverished operative. But that, as things are at present, this great discovery, and all the admirable ingenuity with which it is applied, acts as a ban instead of a blessing, upon some hundred thousands of miserable victims is most true, while all the benefit that can be shown as a balance to this horror, is the bloated wealth of a small knot of master-manufacturers. But so monstrous is this evil, that its very atrocity inspires hope, from the improbability that when once beyond all reach of contradiction its existence shall be known by all men, it should be permitted to continue."

"Then why is it not known?" demanded Mary, her colour height-ened as she remembered her own entire ignorance upon the subject a few short weeks before, "surely it is the duty of all lookers-on to pro-claim it to the whole world."

"Alas! Miss Brotherton! It is more easy to raise a voice, than to command attention to it. Loud and long must be the cry that shall awaken the indifferent, and rouse the indolent to action. But this loud, long cry, will be uttered, and by the blessing of God it will be listened to at last."

"But tell me Mr. Bell," resumed his deeply interested auditor, "what is this moderate enactment in mitigation of these wretched people's sufferings, which you say would content you?"

"All that we ask for," replied Mr. Bell, "all that the poor creatures ask for themselves, is that by Act of Parliament it should rendered illegal for men, women and children to be kept to the wearying unhealthy labour of the mills for more than ten hours out of every day, leaving their daily wages at the same rate as now."

"And would *that* suffice," demanded Miss Brotherton with aston-ishment, "to effectually relieve the horrors you have been describing to me?"

---

1 Shakespeare, *The Tempest*, I. ii. 363-64.

"Miss Brotherton it would," replied the clergyman. "I would be loath to weary you with details," he continued, "but a few items may suffice to make you see how enormous are the benefits which would follow such an enactment. At present, if a large demand for manufactured goods arises, instead of being, as it ought, a blessing to the industrious hands that must supply it, it comes upon them as a fearful burden, threatening to crush the very springs of life in the little creatures that are chiefly to sustain it, while the golden harvest that it brings is not for them, but for their masters. For the miserable meed of an extra penny, or sometimes three-halfpence a day, the young slaves (who, observe, have no power of choice, for if they, or their parents for them, refuse, they are instantly turned off to literal starvation—no parish assistance being allowed to those who resist the regulations of the manufacturers), for this wretched equivalent for health and joy, are compelled, whenever our boasted trade flows briskly, to stand to their work for just as many hours as the application of the overlooker's strap, or billy-roller, can keep them on their legs. Innumerable instances are on record of children falling from excess of weariness on the machinery, and being called to life by its lacerating their flesh. It continually happens that young creatures under fifteen years of age, are kept from their beds all night. Fifteen, sixteen, seventeen, hours of labour out of the twenty-four, are cases which recur continually, and I need not say with what effect upon these victims of ferocious avarice. Now not only would all this be mended, the positive bodily torture spared, and as far as is consistent with constant in-door occupation, the health of the labourers preserved, were it made unlawful to keep them at positive labour for more than ten hours of every day; not only would all this follow from the enactment, but innumerable other advantages, some of them more important still, would, beyond all question, be its consequence. In the first place, were there no power of executing great and sudden orders by irregular exactions of labour, the recurrence of those fearful intervals when the starving operatives are thrown out of employ by the accidents which cause a deficiency in the demand, would not happen—for in that case the capitalists would find themselves obliged to be beforehand with the demand, even though some portion of their enormous wealth should for a time lie idle. From this would also follow the necessity of often employing adult hands, where now the cheaper labour of children, forced from their very vitals through the day and night, may be had for the sin of demanding it. Then would the unnatural spectacle of a stalwart father idly waiting to snatch the wages from the little feverish hand of his o'er-laboured child be seen no more. Then would there be strength and spirits left in the young to profit by the Sunday-schools now so often ostentatiously opened in vain, because the only way in which a little piecer can keep holiday is by lying throughout the day stretched upon his straw in heavy sleep. Then too, the demoralizing process by which the heart of a mother is rendered hard as the nether mill-stone, by the necessity of goading her infants to their frightful toil, would cease. Boys and girls would no longer have to return to their homes at midnight—there would be time and inclination then, for those comfortable operations of the needle and the shears, which

'Make old clothes look amaist as weel as new.'

Then would not the disheartened ministers of God's church strive in vain to make the reckless, joyless, worthless race listen to his words of faith and hope. Then, Miss Brotherton, they would arise from that state of outcast degradation which has caused your friends to tell you that it would be 'unsafe, improper, and altogether wrong,' for you, and such as you, to make personal acquaintance with them."

"And do you really think all this mighty, this glorious good, would follow from an enactment so moderate, so reasonable, so every way unobjectionable?"

"I have not the slightest shadow of a doubt, Miss Brotherton, that such good would follow it, and more, much more, than I have named— more than any one could believe or comprehend, who has not, like myself, been watching for years the misery, the vice, the degradation, which have resulted from the want of it."

"Then why, Mr. Bell, have not such representations been made to the legislature as must ensure its immediate adoption?"

The good clergyman shook his head. "It is a most natural, question, my dear young friend—allow me so to call you. All are my friends who feel upon this subject as you appear to do. It is a most natural and a most obvious question. Yet would my reply be any thing rather than easy of comprehension were I to attempt to answer it directly. I sincerely hope I shall converse with you again on this subject. Documents are not wanting, my dear Miss Brotherton, to prove that all, or nearly all, that private individuals can do, in the way of petition and remonstrance, has been already tried; nor are we yet without hope that good may come of it. But it must be long, and perhaps the longer the better, ere your young head and innocent heart, can conceive our difficulties. You would hardly believe the ingenious devices to which frightened avarice can have recourse in order to retard, mutilate, and render abortive a measure having for its object a reduction of profits, with no equivalent save the beholding smiles instead of tears, and hearing the sounds of songs and laughter instead of groans!"

"But while you are still waiting and hoping for this aid from our law-givers," said Mary, "is there nothing that can be done in the interval to help all this misery, Mr. Bell?"

"Nothing effectual, my dear young lady," he replied mournfully. "I may, with no dishonest boasting say, that my life is spent in doing all I can to save these unhappy people from utter degradation and despair. But the oppression under which they groan is too overwhelming to be removed, or even lightened, by any agency less powerful than that of the law...."

[Source: Frances Trollope, *The Life and Adventures of Michael Armstrong, the Factory Boy*. London: Henry Colburn, 1840. 202-208.]

6. Charlotte Elizabeth Tonna, from *Helen Fleetwood* (1841)

[Charlotte Elizabeth Tonna (1790-1846), was a Tory writer, editor, and reformer. She wrote Evangelical tracts, published under the name Charlotte Elizabeth, but she contributed more significantly to public debate as the writer of works attacking the factory system. Although *Helen Fleetwood*, her first novel on the subject, is centrally concerned with the sufferings of young factory workers, Tonna also focuses throughout much of the novel on the question of legislative reform. The widow Green is lured into taking her grandchildren and her ward from the agricultural south to a manufacturing town called "M."—presumably, Manchester—because she believes that "the Parliament has been making new laws they say, and all for the benefit of working people" (30). How misplaced that hope is, she soon learns. In the first passage reprinted here from Chapter X, the widow Green is thinking about Phœbe Wright—another of her grandchildren who has been engaged in factory labor long before her country cousins begin such work—and the false rumors that Phœbe has spread about the saintly Helen Fleetwood; and the grandmother's response to both Phœbe's actions and the physical deformities of Phœbe's sister Sarah constitutes an attack on the factory system. In the second selection, the beginning of Chapter XVIII is remarkable in that it portrays workers trying to organize in support of changes in factory legislation. Here Richard, the eldest and the only grandchild left behind in the country, has come on an errand to "M.," where he finds his siblings and Helen ill and impoverished. His errand leads him to attend a meeting of workers, one of whom, a respectable laborer named Hudson, warns Richard against a man named South, the operative with whom he is lodging. Here Tonna demonstrates the indifference of Parliament to the plight of the factory workers, the need for them to remain lawful and passive under suffering, and their dependence on well-known reformers like Lord Ashley. At the end of this passage, Hudson exclaims, "Oh that we had a few of those Christian ladies [interested in educating "heathen" children] to take the hard case of our factory little ones into their kind and zealous hands!" Tonna saw herself as fulfilling such a function, and she establishes the authority of her account on the same kind of claim to sworn testimony that appears in working-class autobiographies: as she explained to the readers of *The Christian Lady's Magazine*, in which *Helen Fleetwood* first appeared as a serial (1839-41), "Let no one suppose we are going to write a fiction, or to conjure up phantoms of a heated imagination…. Nay, we set forth nothing but what has been stated on oath, corroborated on oath, and on oath confirmed beyond the possibility of an evasive question" (qtd. Kestner 60-61).]

[…] The system, the factory system, under which Phœbe Wright had imbibed the peculiar wickedness that now pervaded her character, also fed the evil, guarded it, and armed it with power to wound whatever excited its enmity. The factory system surrounded her with associates, by whom she had been encouraged in the ways of daring sin, and who were in turn encouraged by her to unite against any one whose uprightness of principle should tacitly condemn them. A few there were, whose souls loathed the scenes that hourly vexed them; but what could they do? Silent endurance was their only refuge; and even this was enough to subject them to ill-will, unless they either feigned excess of stupidity, or baffled suspicion by pretending to be like the rest.

Excluded from the free air, and almost from the pure light of day; shut up in an atmosphere polluted by clouds of fetid breath, and all the sickening exhalations of a crowded human mass, whose unwashed, overworked bodies were also in many cases diseased, and by the suffocating dust that rose on every side; relaxed by an intensity of artificial heat which their constitutions were never framed to encounter in the temperate clime where God had placed them; doubly fevered, doubly debilitated, by excessive toil, not measured by human capacity to sustain it, but by the power of machinery obeying an inexhaustible impetus; badly clothed, wretchedly fed, and exposed moreover to fasts of unnatural length even from that miserable fare; who can marvel if, under such a system, the robust adult speedily acquires a sickly habit of body, and a morbid state of feeling, leading at once to most awful perversion of mind and corruption of morals? But it is not of adults we are called to speak, it is of children, young, tender, growing children, who require a double portion of rest, refreshment, liberty for the body, and of watchful diligence to direct and guide the mind. If, "Train up a child in the way he should go," be a precept that God himself has vouchsafed to give, as the preliminary to an upright walk through life, oh who could marvel though the little ones so fearfully forced into every way in which they should not go, became in riper years incarnate fiends! The child's stomach, unfitted for long abstinence, and delicately susceptible of injury, becomes doubly disordered by the privation of food and the impurities that find their way into the system from that noxious atmosphere: it loses all desire of wholesome diet, and craves the exciting draught that shall lend a transient stimulus to the frame unstrung by toil, and chilled by sudden transition from the heated pandemonium of the mill to the raw keen air of night; the poor little victim who reels from exhaustion as it enters the gin-shop, reels thence a drunkard.

Such, with its accompaniments of nameless evils, had been the school into which in early childhood the Wrights were entered: the ill-usage of a savage overlooker had shortened Sarah's term of suffering, and unintentionally interposed between her and the career of vice that Phœbe remained to engage in. On the system, the vile, the cruel, the body and soul-murdering system of factory labour, we cannot charge the innate depravity of the human heart; but we do denounce it as being in itself a foul fruit of that depravity under its hateful form of covetousness, and of being in turn the prolific root of every ill that can unhumanize man, and render an enlightened Christian country the mark of God's most just and holy indignation, provoking him even to blot its place and name from among the nations of the earth.

[...]

WHEN, on the following day, Richard Green repaired to the gentleman on whose business he came, the latter, struck by the dejection of his countenance, inquired whether he was ill. Richard answered, that he was better in body than in mind: and on being kindly encouraged, owned that he had suffered a grievous disappointment in finding that the factory labour, for which his family had given up the healthful employments of the country, was so very different a thing from what they expected to find it. Of pecuniary distress he said nothing; but expatiated on the ruinous severity of the toil, and the demoralizing tendency of their habits. To all this his hearer most feelingly assented, and told him that he was busily engaged in forwarding the objects of those who sought to obtain legislatorial redress for the crying evils so generally felt. This was a joyful surprise to poor Richard, and with eager delight he accepted a ticket that was to admit him to a select meeting of the labourers, about to assemble for the consideration and adoption of future plans. 'So, then,' thought Richard, as he left the house with a lighter heart than he had felt for two days, 'so, then, after all, there is some good stirring. I wonder why South did not tell me of this.'

Full of anxious expectation, he repaired to the place of meeting; and found about twenty men assembled, principally of the appearance of artizans, but with one or two from a higher class in society. An air of seriousness pervaded the assemblage, and the general aspect of the men bespoke the quiet determination that is not soon turned from its purpose. Several bore the marks of bodily injury sustained in the factories, some were much stunted in growth, and there was not one among them who would in the country have been called a healthy-looking person. They were earnest but calm, and the curiosity that Richard's appearance evidently gave rise to was unmixed with rudeness or suspicion.

A well-dressed respectable-looking man, seated at a table, with a pile of papers before him, invited the stranger to approach, and after looking at his ticket, observed "You got this from our good friend Mr. H., and that is sufficient introduction; but perhaps you will be kind enough to tell us what led you to join us; you don't look like one who has been in the mills.'

Richard felt a little abashed, but summoning resolution, replied, 'True, sir, I never wrought in a factory; my labour, through God's mercy, has been in the country; but those that are dearer to me than my life are in the mills, and suffering enough to make me feel it more than if it was myself.'

'Surely,' said one of the men, 'I saw you in the court, taking a great interest in the case of poor little Mary Green.'

'Well I might,' answered Richard, casting down his eyes as the recollection overcame him.

'Are you related to her?'

'I am her brother.'

A dwarfish, but most intelligent-looking man now held out his hand, saying, 'Mr Green, I honour you and every member of your family, for the part you have acted by that precious girl Helen Fleetwood. If ever there was a persecuted Christian enabled by well-doing to put to silence the ignorance of the foolish, and to shame them of the contrary part, she is such a one.'

Richard grasped the friendly hand as though it had been the richest of earth's treasures; but emotion kept him silent.

'Now,' said the president, 'I proceed to read the last letters from our deputation in London, that we may determine what steps to take next.'

The document that he unfolded was long, and very interesting. It stated that the writer had been closely examined before the Committee of the House of Commons; that every important fact had been fairly elicited by the chairman and other friends to the cause, while all possible pains were taken by some on the other side to draw from him a contradiction of some part of his testimony, or to put a different aspect on the truths stated. He had afterwards been present in the gallery to hear a debate on the subject, where, he said, several of their friends spoke out with great force and feeling. They were met by hot and angry speeches on the part of some whom he named; cool denial from others; and one gentleman had ventured upon such a misrepresentation of the whole concern as would not be believed in that or any other factory town to have passed the lips of a person so well acquainted with the case. 'Generally,' he wrote, 'the matter was not taken up by such members as were personally most interested in it, but by others, who seemed to have got a completely wrong notion of the whole thing instilled into them. The worst part of the case was, the very great indifference shewn by the House; many went out as soon as the subject was started; some folded their arms and feel [*sic*] asleep; others kept up conversations, often rising loud enough to drown the voices of the speakers; while pamphlets and newspapers were being handed about, and consultations held on all sorts of subjects. Lord Ashley———'

Here a general murmur of voices, rising at last to a hearty cheer, interrupted the reader: he paused till the burst of feeling had its way, then said, 'God bless him!' 'Amen,' was the unanimous response, and he resumed.

'Lord Ashley, though he seemed grieved and hurt at all this, was neither daunted nor discouraged. He got up and gave them a lesson, both on our claims and their duties that will not soon be forgotten by any honest man who heard it. It did me good to look at him, and to think how much better than all the rank and all the wealth in the world is the blessing that belongs to him, pleading as he does the cause of the poor, and persevering in striving that those who are in need and necessity have right. Ay, striving against such difficulties as nobody can estimate or understand without seeing it. We used to think that what thwarts him is a hot opposition in the House of Commons. No such thing; it is like pleading with the deaf or preaching to the dead. Give him an adversary, and he can grapple with him; but who can grapple with a painted picture of a man that stares out of a frame, without having either senses, or substance, or reality of any sort? This is just what the gentlemen become when our case is brought forward. Mr. O'Connell———.'

Here another interruption took place, of a character remarkably dissimilar from the former. The reader smiled, and resumed,

'Mr. O'Connell took vast pains not to hear what was said. He had a roll of papers in his hand, and untied them for the benefit of some red-whiskered gentleman near him. Whether they were money drafts or instructions I don't know, but I know what I thought of when I looked from Lord Ashley to him, and back again to Lord Ashley.'

The writer went on to state some of the misrepresentations that had been made, requesting to have a person sent up who could, on oath, from his own knowledge, disprove them.

'Here,' said the president, folding the letter, 'is our difficulty; we cannot rouse a manly feeling in the legislature on behalf of the oppressed children of poverty. If the lukewarm, indifferent people were away, and the battle to be fairly fought between those who are in earnest, we should soon see a good result; but this indifference leaves men so open to the arts of interested individuals, who, if they cannot give them a false view of the matter, so as to make them active opponents, easily persuade them it is a thing of no consequence, a mere waste of public time, the whim of a few sentimental dreamers. The liberal party, and more particularly those at the head of affairs, who could carry it at once if they chose, are liberal enough of fair words, but deeds we seek in vain; and the great liberator has sold us, almost in the open market, into a renewed, and for aught he cares, a perpetual period of hopeless bondage. We cannot change the course of this under-current; all we can do is to go on forwarding to our friends such plain, honest facts as can be proved in the face of day, and praying to God to strengthen the hands of our generous advocates.'

They proceeded to discuss the merits of different persons whom it was proposed to send up; and Richard, meanwhile, entered into conversation with his new friend.

'It does not seem as if you had much to expect,' he sorrowfully observed.

'No; but we use the means, and look to God for the blessing that he can give when he sees good. It is an awful proof of the power of Satan, that such statements should be laid, year after year, before upwards of six hundred gentlemen, chosen to represent the whole body of the people, and to watch over the country's interests, and yet no effectual redress be given. I say effectual, because some bills have been passed, and some improvements made; but at the same time clauses in the old acts that afforded great protection have been expunged, and very grievous alterations made. You saw two instances in court. You saw what a mere farce the fine can be reduced to on the most aggravated charges; where formerly ten or twenty pounds was the lowest that could have been imposed on such a conviction; and, moreover, every separate offence was formerly visited with a fine, whereas now only one can be recovered for any particular day. You also saw, what probably you were not aware of, a near relation of the offender sitting to judge the cause.'

'Yes, I was told of it by a friend of mine—one Mr. South.'

The other looked at him for a moment with less cordiality; then said, 'Have you been long intimate with South?'

'No; I sleep at his house, and that's all.'

'Then let me, as a Christian man, caution you of a danger you may not be aware of. South is loud in his complaints of what we all suffer from; but the remedy that he seeks is even worse than the disease, I fear———.'

He paused, and Richard said, 'You may speak freely to me. I'm no tale-bearer; and to tell you the truth I didn't half like South's way of talking.'

'Then be on your guard; for I greatly fear that he is involved in polit-ical plans that would not bear daylight. Some men who long to overturn all right government have come among us and endeavoured to make our grievances a pretext for engaging in rebellious schemes. This we never can do; those of us at least who know right from wrong, who fear God, and desire to be found in the path of duty, however hard, knowing that the way of transgressors is much harder. Still, from the deplorable ignorance of those brought up in the mills, there are multitudes ready to listen eagerly to such suggestions; and it is too probable that the cruel neglect of the British Government as concerns those employed in the manufactories, to which her commercial prosperity is mainly owing, will yet recoil on themselves in some terrible outbreak, aided by those who are made desperate by oppression, and utterly careless as to future con-sequences, because they have been left in ignorance and unbelief.'

'Thank you for putting me on my guard. I confess I sometimes feel as if I could take vengeance on those who have brought my family to such a state, but it is only the sinful thought of a moment. However, it might be taken advantage of by anybody who observed it. I will watch and pray.'

The other took his hand: 'Green, the lesson you have learned in your young years, and which you are now called on to put in practice, will become more valuable to you every day. Evil men and seducers are waxing worse and worse, as the scriptures have foretold; and the knowledge that is so boasted of is only making men more skilful in mis-chief, or puffing them up with the false pride that comes before a fall. I look about and see all this: I look within myself and understand it. In my heart I find the seed of every evil thing, and I know that it is only by the grace of God working in me that I am not constantly following a multitude to do evil. If I ceased to watch, as you say, and to pray, I should directly fall. How then can I wonder to see others, in their dif-ferent ranks and stations, betrayed into bad courses, when they never think of applying to God for help against the devices of their invisible enemy? If the rulers of England and her great men knew the value of what is now being given over to Satan and his tools, they would endeavour to stop the mischief by imparting religious instruction pro-portioned to the great increase of the demand for it. But I fear they regard us only as machines, while making a great shew of raising us in the scale of knowledge; and so they are loading, as it were to the muzzle, a gun that will burst and destroy them.'

'I think,' said Richard, 'that South is such a man: he seems to have a deal of learning for one in his station; but I should be tempted to fear he would better like to revenge himself than to see what is wrong quietly set right.'

'We must not be too ready to judge others,' answered his new acquaintance, 'but it is our duty to observe and to take warning, and to look to our own ways when we see our fellows slide. I always find South and some others ready enough to dwell upon the grievances we suffer; but when I propose the peaceable, legal way of trying to get them redressed, they fall back, with some excuse or other, generally pointing to the small benefit we have yet got by our efforts, and saying the evil is too great to be remedied by means so tame.'

'And you are expecting to see the success of your endeavours?' asked Richard.

'I hope it may please God, before long, to rouse the feelings of our fellow-countrymen on behalf of the poor children employed in these mills. If that was done, we should soon see a change for the better. Now suppose a lady, the mother of a young family, looking upon her own children and thinking what she would feel if they were situated like the wretched little ones in the factories,—or suppose another, employed in teaching or overseeing a nice school of girls, and comparing their comforts and advantages with what our little labourers want, and what they suffer,—don't you think these ladies would use their influence over their own husbands, fathers, brothers and friends, to make it a point with the candidate they vote for, that he should support our cause in the Parliament? You see, it is no party matter at all; whig or tory, conservative or radical, any man may assist our noble champion Lord Ashley, without interfering with his general politics, or offending the party he belongs to. And, alas, Green, men seem to think much more of being consistent in their party support than in doing what is acceptable before God! We see no obstacle to having a large majority with us, if the country would but take up our distressed situation.'

'There is another thing,' said Richard. 'You know a vast number of the voters that send members to Parliame[n]t are men in humble life. In the farming districts, and such places as I come from, it is so: and I suppose in towns the small shop-keepers and trades-people have a good deal to do in turning the poll where there is a contest.'

'Certainly: and what do you infer from it?'

'Why, the gentlefolk have a power of interest among those people, and might use it with such good effect as to make it worth any candidate's while to let it be known he would do his best to help the cause of the poor factory children. And why don't they do it?'

'For want of being rightly informed upon the subject. You see, the facts are brought before Parliament, by having witnesses up to be examined on oath before the committee; these reports, as they are called, are printed, and sold too: but, Green, I don't think one lady in a thousand ever looks into them, to say nothing of other classes: and if they are not read, how can the statements be known? What we chiefly want is to have some public information given about it, such as will be read, and may stir up the hearts of God's servants to succour us. We want neither their gold nor their silver,' he added, with energy, 'we want nothing that would lessen their wealth or encroach on their time. All we want is, that they should secure to us a fair share in the blessings of the English constitution, by making a right use of their own privileges. As we have shewn, they can all, more or less, bring an influence to bear on the House of Commons; and that has the power of righting all that is wrong and oppressive among their poor country-people.'

He paused: his raised voice had attracted the notice of the president, who remarked, 'True, Hudson; and that is one great object of our meetings here. Many good works are going on through the land; and the time may not be far off when a call will be heard for more information respecting the factory children, by those who know how to draw public attention to any cause they wish to promote. It is not long since, that I happened to be at a meeting called by some ladies who wanted to forward the education of children in some very distant heathen land: it was a new thing, and excited curiosity. The room was full: some gentlemen came forward; read descriptions, commented on the miserable state, both bodily and spiritual, of those children, proposed resolutions, established a society, and made a collection for the express purpose of spreading those facts, and extending that appeal through the land. I listened with interest, and cheerfully gave my mite: but a sadness was on my mind as I thought, 'The children of your own people, the little neighbours of your own houses, are in as bad a plight as these distant heathen babes; and would not He whose eye is alike on both equally bless an effort that should do good at home?' I did not desire to see the benefit withheld from the others, God forbid! but I thought of the words, "These ought ye to have done, and not to leave the others undone."'

A murmur of assent ran through the room, and Hudson remarked to Richard, 'Oh that we had a few of those Christian ladies to take the hard case of our factory little ones into their kind and zealous hands!'

'It is no more than one might expect from them,' he returned, 'considering how well it becomes them to care for poor little friendless children.'

The business of the meeting being over, Richard walked homewards, in company with his new acquaintance, to whom he remarked, 'I cannot but say this has been the best thing I have yet met with in M. Still you seem to be getting on but slowly in your good work; and meanwhile what is to become of those belonging to us who are suffering all these miseries?'

Hudson shook his head: 'That is a question which God alone can supply an answer to. I know how anxious you must feel, and how slow the progress must appear which can bring little, if any relief to those you love. But we have no remedy—no help....'

[Source: Charlotte Elizabeth (Browne Phelan Tonna). *Helen Fleetwood*. R.B. Seeley, 1841. 165-67, 332-45.]

Select Bibliography

Working-Class Autobiographies

Burn, James Dawson. *Autobiography of a Beggar Boy*. London: William Tweedie, 1855.

Elson, George. *The Last of the Climbing Boys. An Autobiography*. London: John Long, 1900.

Green, William. *The Life and Adventures of a Cheap Jack, By One of the Fraternity*. Ed. Charles Hindley. London: Chatto and Windus, 1881.

Harding, Arthur. *East End Underworld: Chapters in the Life of Arthur Harding*. London: Routledge and Kegan Paul, 1981.

Layton, Mrs. "Memories of Seventy Years." In *Life As We Have Known It, By Co-operative Working Women*. Ed. Margaret Llewelyn Davies. London: Hogarth Press, 1931. 1-55.

Rushton, Adam. *My Life as a Farmer's Boy, Factory Lad, Teacher and Preacher*. Manchester: S. Clarke, 1909.

Scott, Mrs. J.P. "A Felt Hat Worker." In *Life As We Have Known It, By Co-operative Working Women*. Ed. Margaret Llewelyn Davies. London: Hogarth Press, 1931. 81-101.

Shaw, Charles. *When I Was a Child*. 1903. Rpt. Firle, Sussex: Caliban, 1977.

Vincent, David, ed., *Testaments of Radicalism: Memoirs of Working-Class Politicians 1790-1885*. London: Europa, 1977.

Literary Contexts

Bowles, Caroline. *Tales of the Factories*. London: Blackwell, 1833.

Braddon, Mary Elizabeth. *The Factory Girl; Or, All Is Not Gold That Glitters: A Romance of Real Life*. New York: Dewitt, 1869.

Brontë, Charlotte. *Shirley: A Tale*. London: Smith, Elder, 1849.

Carlyle, Thomas. *Past and Present*. 1843. Ed. Richard D. Altick. Boston: Houghton Mifflin, 1965.

Dickens, Charles. *Hard Times: For These Times*. London: Bradbury and Evans, 1854.

Disraeli, Benjamin. *Sybil; or, the Two Nations*. London: Colburn, 1845.

Gaskell, Elizabeth. *Mary Barton: A Tale of Manchester Life*. London: Chapman and Hall, 1848.

——. *North and South*. London: Chapman and Hall, 1855.

Glyn, Herbert. *The Cotton Lord*. London, 1862.

Godwin, William. *Fleetwood: or, The New Man of Feeling*. London: 1805.

Martineau, Harriet. *Illustrations of Political Economy*. 25 monthly parts. London: Charles Fox, 1832-34.

Montagu, Frederick. *Mary Ashley, The Factory Girl, or Facts Upon the Factory*. London: 1839.

Norton, Caroline. *A Voice From The Factories*. London: 1836.

Stone, Elizabeth. *William Langshawe, the Cotton Lord*. London: Richard Bentley, 1842.

Tonna, Charlotte Elizabeth. *Helen Fleetwood*. London: Seely & W. Burnside, 1841.

Trollope, Frances. *Life and Adventures of Michael Armstrong, the Factory Boy*. London: Colburn, 1840.

Walker, John. *The Factory Lad.* 1832. Michael R. Booth, ed. *English Plays of the Nineteenth-Century.* Oxford: Clarendon, 1969. 1: 201-33.

Social and Intellectual History

Aldred, Guy Alfred. *Richard Carlile, Agitator: His Life and Times.* London: Pioneer, 1923.

Altick, Richard D. *The English Common Reader: A Social History of the Mass Reading Public 1800-1900.* Chicago: U of Chicago P, 1957.

Bairoch, Paul. *The Working Population and Its Structure.* New York: Gordon and Breach, 1968.

Boyson, Rhodes. *The Ashworth Cotton Enterprise: The Rise and Fall of a Family Firm 1818-1880.* Oxford: Clarendon, 1970.

Briggs, Asa. "John Bright and the Creed of Reform." *Victorian People: A Reassessment of Persons and Themes 1851-67.* 1955. New York: Harper, 1963. 197-231.

Chapman, Stanley D. *The Early Factory Masters: The Transition to the Factory System in the Midlands Textile Industry.* Newton Abbot, Devon: David and Charles, 1967.

Clark, Anna. *The Struggle for the Breeches: Gender and the Making of the British Working Class.* Berkeley: U of California P, 1995.

Clarke, Allen. *The Effects of the Factory System.* London: Grant Richards, 1899.

Cobden, John C. *The White Slaves of England.* 1853. Shannon, Ireland: Irish UP, 1971.

Cook, Chris, and Brendan Keith. *British Historical Facts, 1830-1890.* London: Macmillan, 1975.

Cunningham, Hugh. *The Children of the Poor: Representations of Childhood since the Seventeenth Century.* Oxford: Blackwell, 1991.

Dodd, William. *The Factory System Illustrated.* London: John Murray, 1842.

———. *The Laboring Classes of England, Especially Those Concerned in Agriculture and Manufactures; in a Series of Letters. By an Englishman.* Boston: John Putnam, 1847.

Driver, Cecil. *Tory Radical: The Life of Richard Oastler.* New York: Oxford UP, 1946.

Engels, Friedrich. *The Condition of the Working Class in England.* 1845. Ed. Victor Kiernan. London: Penguin, 1987.

Fielden, John. *The Curse of the Factory System.* 1836. Intro. J.T. Ward. Rpt. New York: Augustus M. Kelley, 1969.

Gallagher, Catherine. *The Industrial Reformation of English Fiction: Social Discourse and Narrative Form, 1832-1867.* Chicago: U of Chicago P, 1985.

Gillespie, Frances. *Labor and Politics in England, 1850-1867.* New York: Octagon, 1966.

Gray, Robert. *The Factory Question and Industrial England, 1830-1860.* Cambridge: Cambridge UP, 1996.

Greg, Robert Hyde. *The Factory Question and the "Ten Hours Bill."* London: James Ridgway, 1837.

Henriques, Ursula R.Q. *Before the Welfare State: Social Administration in Early Industrial Britain.* London: Longman, 1979.

Hodder, Edwin. *The Life and Work of the Seventh Earl of Shaftesbury.* 1886. 2 vols. Rpt. Shannon: Irish UP, 1971.

Hopkirk, Mary. *Nobody Wanted Sam: The Story of the Unwelcomed Child, 1530-1948.* London: John Murray, 1949.

Hoppen, K. Theodore. *The Mid-Victorian Generation 1846-1886.* Oxford: Clarendon, 1998.

Hunt, E.H. *British Labour History 1815-1914.* Atlantic Highland, NJ: Humanities Press, 1981.

Hutchins, B.L. and Harrison, A. *A History of Factory Legislation.* London: P.S. King, 1911.

Johnston, Valerie. *Diet in the Workhouses and the Prisons, 1835-1895.* New York: Garland, 1985.

Klaus, H. Gustav. *Factory Girl: Ellen Johnston and Working-Class Poetry in Victorian Scotland.* Frankfurt am Main, 1998.

Knott, John William. *Popular Opposition to the 1834 Poor Law.* London: Croom Helm, 1986.

Kestner, Joseph. *Protest and Reform: The British Social Narrative by Women 1827-1867.* Madison: U Wisconsin P, 1985.

Kirby, R.G., and A.E. Musson. *The Voice of the People: John Doherty, 1798-1854, Trade Unionist, Radical, and Factory Reformer.* Manchester: Manchester UP, 1975.

Kovačević, Ivanka. *Fact Into Fiction: English Literature and the Industrial Scene 1750-1850.* Leicester UP, 1975.

[Kydd, Samuel.] "Alfred." *The History of the Factory Movement from the Year 1802, to the Enactment of the Ten Hours' Bill in 1847.* 2 vols. London: Simpkin, Marshall. 1857.

Maidment, Brian, ed. *The Poorhouse Fugitives: Self-Taught Poets and Poetry in Victorian Britain.* Manchester: Carcanet, 1987.

Malthus, Thomas. *An Essay on the Principle of Population.* 1798. New York: Norton, 1976.

Martineau, Harriet. *The Factory Controversy: A Warning Against Meddling Legislation.* Manchester: Printed by A. Ireland for the National Association of Factory Occupiers, 1855.

Marshall, J.D. *The Old Poor Law, 1795-1834.* London: Macmillan, 1968.

Marx, Karl. *Capital: A Critique of Political Economy.* Vol. 1. 1867. Intro. Ernest Mandel. Trans. Ben Fowkes. London: Penguin, 1976.

Mathias, Peter. *The First Industrial Nation: An Economic History of Britain 1700-1914.* 2nd ed. London: Routledge, 1983.

Mayhew, Henry. *London Labour and the London Poor.* 1861-62. 4 vols. Rpt. New York: Dover, 1968.

Miles, William Augustus. *Poverty, Mendacity, and Crime.* H. Braddon, ed. London: Shaw, 1839.

Murphy, Paul Thomas. *Toward a Working-Class Canon: Literary Criticism in British Working-Class Periodicals, 1816-1858.* Columbus: Ohio State UP, 1994.

Musson, A.E. "Robert Blincoe and the Early Factory System." *Trade Union and Social History.* London: Frank Cass, 1974. 195-206.

Nardinelli, Clark. *Child Labor and the Industrial Revolution.* Bloomington: Indiana UP, 1990.

Rose, Mary. B., ed. *The Lancashire Cotton Industry: A History Since 1700.* Preston: Lancashire County Books, 1996.

Rose, Sonya O. "Protective Labor Legislation in Nineteenth-Century Britain: Gender, Class, and the Liberal State." *Gender and Class in Modern Europe.* Ed. Laura L. Frader and Sonya O. Rose. Ithaca: Cornell UP, 1996. 193-210.

Rule, John. *The Labouring Classes in Early Industrial England, 1750-1850.* London: Longman, 1986.

Thomas, Maurice Walton. *The Early Factory Legislation: A Study in Legislative and Administrative Evolution.* Leigh-on-Sea, Essex: Thames Bank Publishing, 1948.

Thompson, E.P. *The Making of the English Working Class*. 1963. New York: Vintage, 1966.

Thompson, F.M.L. *The Cambridge Social History of Britain, 1790-1950*. 3 vols. Cambridge: Cambridge UP, 1990.

Trevelyan, George Macaulay. *British History in the Nineteenth Century (1782-1901)*. London: Longmans, Green, 1923.

———. *The Life of John Bright*. Boston: Houghton Mifflin, 1914.

Ure, Andrew. *The Philosophy of Manufactures; or, An Exposition of the Scientific, Moral, and Commercial Economy of the Factory System of Great Britain*. London: Charles Knight, 1835.

Von Plener, Ernst. *The English Factory Legislation, From 1802 Till The Present Time*. Trans. Frederick L. Weinmann. Intro. Anthony John Mundella. London: Chapman and Hall, 1873.

Ward, J.T. *The Factory Movement, 1830-1855*. New York: Macmillan, 1962.

Whatley, Christopher A. "Altering Images of the Industrial City: The Case of James Myles, the 'Factory Boy,' and Mid-Victorian Dundee." In *Victorian Dundee: Image and Reality*. Ed. Louise Miskell, Christopher A. Whatley, and Bob Harris. East Linton, East Lothian: Tuckwell, 2000. 70-95.

Wiener, Joel H. *Radicalism and Freethought in Nineteenth-Century Britain: The Life of Richard Carlile*. Westport, Conn.: Greenwood, 1983.

Autobiographical and Literary Background

Andrews, William L. *To Tell a Free Story: The First Century of Afro-American Autobiography, 1760-1865*. Urbana: U of Illinois P, 1988.

Ashley, Kathleen, Leigh Gilmore, and Gerald Peters, eds. *Autobiography and Postmodernism*. Amherst: U of Mass. P, 1994.

Benstock, Shari, ed., *The Private Self: Theory and Practice of Women's Autobiographical Writings*. Chapel Hill: U of North Carolina P, 1988.

Boos, Florence S. "Cauld Engle-Cheek: Working-Class Women Poets in Victorian Scotland." *Victorian Poetry* 33.1 (Spring 1995): 53-73.

Brodzki, Bella, and Celeste Schenck, eds. *Life/Lines: Theorizing Women's Autobiography*. Ithaca: Cornell UP, 1988.

Bruss, Elizabeth W. *Autobiographical Acts: The Changing Situation of a Literary Genre*. Baltimore: Johns Hopkins UP, 1976.

Burnett, John, ed. *Destiny Obscure: Autobiographies of Childhood, Education and Family From the 1820s to the 1920s*. London: Allen Lane, 1982.

———. *Useful Toil: Autobiographies of Working People from the 1820s to the 1920s*. London: Allen Lane, 1974.

Burnett, John, David Vincent, and David Mayall, eds. *The Autobiography of the Working Class: An Annotated, Critical Bibliography*. 2 vols. Sussex: Harvester, 1984.

Corbett, Mary Jean. *Representing Femininity: Middle-Class Subjectivity in Victorian and Edwardian Women's Autobiographies*. New York: Oxford UP, 1992.

Danahay, Martin A. *A Community of One: Masculine Autobiography and Autonomy in Nineteenth-Century Britain*. Albany: State U of New York P, 1993.

de Man, Paul. "Autobiography as De-facement." *MLN* 94 (1979): 920-23.

Eakin, Paul John. *Fictions in Autobiography: Studies in the Art of Self-Invention*. Princeton: Princeton UP, 1985.

———. *Touching the World: Reference in Autobiography*. Princeton: Princeton UP, 1992.

Fleishman, Avrom. *Figures of Autobiography: The Language of Self-Writing in Victorian and Modern England.* Berkeley: U of California P, 1983.

Folkenflik, Robert, ed. *The Culture of Autobiography: Constructions of Self-Representation.* Stanford: Stanford UP, 1993.

Gagnier, Regenia. *Subjectivities: A History of Self-Representation in Britain, 1832-1920.* New York: Oxford UP, 1991.

———. "The Literary Standard, Working-Class Lifewriting, and Gender." *Textual Practice* 3 (Spring 1989): 36-55.

Hackett, Nan. *XIX Century Working-Class Autobiographies: An Annotated Bibliography.* New York: AMS Press, 1985.

Kadar, Marlene, ed. *Essays on Life Writing: From Genre to Critical Practice.* Toronto: U of Toronto P, 1992.

Lejeune, Philipe. *On Autobiography.* Ed. Paul John Eakin. Trans. Katherine Leary. Minneapolis: U of Minnesota P, 1989.

———. *The Autobiographical Pact.* Paris: Éditions du Seuil, 1975.

Loesberg, Jonathan. *Fictions of Consciousness: Mill, Newman, and the Reading of Victorian Prose.* New Brunswick, Rutgers UP, 1986.

Machann, Clinton. *The Genre of Autobiography in Victorian Literature.* Ann Arbor: U of Michigan P, 1994.

Marcus, Laura. *Auto/biographical Discourses: Theory, Criticism, Practice.* Manchester: Manchester UP, 1994.

Mostern, Kenneth. *Autobiography and Black Identity Politics: Racialization in Twentieth-Century America.* Cambridge: Cambridge UP, 1999.

Olney, James, ed. *Autobiography: Essays Theoretical and Critical.* Princeton: Princeton UP, 1980.

———. *Metaphors of Self: The Meaning of Autobiography.* Princeton: Princeton UP, 1972.

Pascal, Roy. *Design and Truth in Autobiography.* Cambridge: Harvard UP, 1960.

Peterson, Linda H. *Traditions of Victorian Women's Autobiography: The Poetics and Politics of Life Writing.* Charlottesville: U of Virginia P, 1999.

———. *Victorian Autobiography: The Tradition of Self-Interpretation.* New Haven: Yale UP, 1986.

Simmons, James R., Jr. "Ellen Johnston." *Victorian Women Poets.* Ed. William B. Thesing. *The Dictionary of Literary Biography.* Detroit: Gale, 1998. 199: 188-93.

Smith, Sidonie, and Julia Watson, eds. *Women, Autobiography, Theory: A Reader.* U Wisconsin P, 1998.

Spengemann, William C. *The Forms of Autobiography: Episodes in the History of a Literary Genre.* New Haven: Yale UP, 1980.

Swindells, Julia. *Victorian Writing and Working Women: The Other Side of Silence.* Cambridge: Minneapolis: U of Minnesota P, 1985.

Vincent, David. *Bread, Knowledge, and Freedom: A Study of Nineteenth-Century Working-Class Autobiography.* London: Europa, 1981.

Weintraub, Karl J. *The Value of the Individual: Self and Circumstance in Autobiography.* Chicago: U of Chicago P, 1978.

Winn, Sharon A., and Lynn M. Alexander, eds. *The Slaughter-house of Mammon: An Anthology of Victorian Social Protest Literature.* West Cornwall, CT: Locust Hill, 1992.

Wong, Hertha Dawn. *Sending My Heart Back Across the Years: Tradition and Innovation in Native American Autobiography.* New York: Oxford UP, 1992.